Bonhoeffer's Intellectual Formation

Bonhoeffer's Intellectual Formation

Theology and Philosophy in His Thought

edited by
Peter Frick

WIPF & STOCK · Eugene, Oregon

Wipf and Stock Publishers
199 W 8th Ave, Suite 3
Eugene, OR 97401

Bonhoeffer's Intellectual Formation
Theology and Philosophy in His Thought
By Frick, Peter
Copyright©2008 Mohr Siebeck
ISBN 13: 978-1-5326-4156-5
Publication date 10/10/2017
Previously published by Mohr Siebeck, 2008

To

Ruth Victoria

in gratitude and celebration
of the wonder of our marriage
for a quarter of a century

Preface

The idea for this book began in the spring 2005. At that time I was interested in studying the influence that Thomas à Kempis had exerted on Bonhoeffer's spiritual formation. To my great surprise, I discovered that there was not a single study that had explored that question with any degree of breadth and depth; consequently, I decided to pursue that task myself. Soon I realized that other studies dedicated to Bonhoeffer's theological and philosophical formation were either rather sporadic and uneven or difficult to access. To remedy this situation for myself I embarked on a more methodical study of the various philosophers and theologians that I deemed crucial to Bonhoeffer's thought. Following Kempis, I studied Nietzsche, Bultmann and Tillich. As this project began to get too large, however, I realized I needed the assistance of more expert Bonhoeffer scholars to complete this task. This book is thus the result of a collaborative effort of many scholars of the International Bonhoeffer Society.

I would like to acknowledge the financial support of Social Sciences and Research Council of Canada for making possible my own contributions to this volume and the task of editorial assistance. Regarding the latter, I am especially grateful for Stephen Jones and his keen eye in all matters editorial. Similarly, I am deeply grateful for David Corriveau's friendship and his help in the collation of the index of names.

Finally, it is my greatest joy and pleasure to dedicate this book to my magnificent wife. Even though I have a deep love for theology and philosophy, I happily admit that there is for me no greater good on earth than the knowledge and experience of our unconditional love for each other.

Peter Frick
Waterloo
September 2007

Contents

Preface VII
Abbreviations XI

Peter Frick
Introduction 1

Barry Harvey
Augustine and Thomas Aquinas
in the Theology of Dietrich Bonhoeffer 11

Peter Frick
The *Imitatio Christi* of Thomas à Kempis
and Dietrich Bonhoeffer 31

Wolf Krötke
Dietrich Bonhoeffer and Martin Luther 53

Wayne Floyd
Encounter with an Other: Immanuel Kant and G.W.F. Hegel
in the Theology of Dietrich Bonhoeffer 83

Christiane Tietz
Friedrich Schleiermacher and Dietrich Bonhoeffer 121

Geffrey Kelly
Kierkegaard as "Antidote" and as Impact on
Dietrich Bonhoeffer's Concept of Christian Discipleship 145

Ralf Wüstenberg
The Influence of Wilhelm Dilthey
on Bonhoeffer's *Letters and Papers from Prison* 167

Peter Frick
Friedrich Nietzsche's Aphorisms and
Dietrich Bonhoeffer's Theology 175

Martin Rumscheidt
The Significance of Adolf von Harnack
and Reinhold Seeberg for Dietrich Bonhoeffer 201

Peter Frick
Rudolf Bultmann, Paul Tillich and Dietrich Bonhoeffer 225

Andreas Pangritz
Dietrich Bonhoeffer: "Within, not Outside
the Barthian Movement" 245

Josiah Young
Dietrich Bonhoeffer and Reinhold Niebuhr:
Their Ethics, Views on Karl Barth
and African-Americans 283

Stephen Plant
"In the Sphere of the Familiar:"
Heidegger and Bonhoeffer 301

List of Contributors 329
Index of Names 333
Index of Subjects 338

Abbreviations

1. Bonhoeffer's Writings

As far as possible, citations and references to Bonhoeffer's writing follow the new critical standard edition. The 17-volume edition is complete in German but still in the process of being published for the English series. These works are abbreviated as follows: *Dietrich Bonhoeffer Werke* (*DBW*) and *Dietrich Bonhoeffer Works English* (*DBWE*). In the text and notes of the essays in this book, these volumes will be cited as *DBW* or *DBWE*, followed by the volume number and page numbers.

DBW 1	*Sanctorum Communio: Eine dogmatische Untersuchung zur Soziologie der Kirche*. Edited by Joachim von Soosten. Munich: Chr. Kaiser, 1986.
DBWE 1	*Sanctorum Communio: A Theological Study of the Sociology of the Church*. Edited by Clifford J. Green. Translated by Reinhard Krauss and Nancy Lukens. Minneapolis: Fortress Press, 1998.
DBW 2	*Akt und Sein: Transzendentalphilosophie und Ontologie in der systematischen Theologie*. Edited by Hans-Richard Reuter. Munich: Chr. Kaiser, 1988.
DBWE 2	*Act and Being: Transcendental Philosophy and Ontology in Systematic Theology*. Edited by Wayne Whitson Floyd Jr. Translated by Martin Rumscheidt. Minneapolis: Fortress Press, 1996.
DBW 3	*Schöpfung und Fall. Theologische Auslegung von Genesis 1–3*. Edited by Martin Rüter and Ilse Tödt. Munich: Chr. Kaiser, 1989.
DBWE 3	*Creation and Fall: A Theological Exposition of Genesis 1–3*. Edited by John W. de Gruchy. Translated by Douglas Stephen Bax. Minneapolis: Fortress Press, 1996.
DBW 4	*Nachfolge*. Edited by Martin Kuske and Ilse Tödt. Munich: Chr. Kaiser, 1989; second edition, Gütersloh: Chr. Kaiser/Gütersloher Verlagshaus, 1994.
DBWE 4	*Discipleship*. Edited by Geffrey B. Kelly and John D. Godsey. Translated by Barbara Green and Reinhard Krauss. Minneapolis: Fortress Press, 2001.
DBW 5	*Gemeinsames Leben. Das Gebetbuch der Bibel*. Edited by Gerhard Ludwig Müller and Albrecht Schönherr. Munich: Chr. Kaiser, 1987.
DBWE 5	*Life Together* and *Prayerbook of the Bible*. Edited by Geffrey B. Kelly. Translated by Daniel W. Bloesch and James H. Burtness. Minneapolis: Fortress Press, 1996.
DBW 6	*Ethik*. Edited by Ilse Tödt, Heinz Eduard Tödt, Ernst Feil, and Clifford Green. Munich: Chr. Kaiser, 1992; Gütersloh: Chr. Kaiser/Gütersloher Verlagshaus, 2d ed. 1998.
DBWE 6	*Ethics*. Edited by Clifford J. Green. Translated by Reinhard Krauss, Charles C. West, and Douglas W. Stott. Minneapolis: Fortress Press, 2005.

DBW 7	*Fragmente aus Tegel.* Edited by Renate Bethge and Ilse Tödt. Gütersloh: Chr. Kaiser/Gütersloher Verlagshaus, 1994.
DBWE 7	*Fiction from Tegel Prison.* Edited by Clifford J. Green. Translated by Nancy Lukens. Minneapolis: Fortress Press, 2000.
DBW 8	*Widerstand und Ergebung.* Edited by Christian Gremmels, Eberhard Bethge, and Renate Bethge, with Ilse Tödt. Gütersloh: Chr. Kaiser/Gütersloher Verlagshaus, 1998.
DBW 9	*Jugend und Studium 1918–1927.* Edited by Hans Pfeifer, with Clifford Green and Carl-Jürgen Kaltenborn. Munich: Chr. Kaiser, 1986.
DBWE 9	*The Young Bonhoeffer: 1918–1927.* Edited by Paul Matheny, Clifford J. Green, and Marshall Johnson. Translated by Mary Nebelsick, with the assistance of Douglas W. Stott. Minneapolis: Fortress Press, 2001.
DBW 10	*Barcelona, Berlin, Amerika 1928–1931* (Barcelona, Berlin, America 1928–1931). Edited by Reinhard Staats and Hans-Christoph von Hase, with Holger Roggelin and Matthias Wünsche. Munich: Chr. Kaiser, 1991.
DBW 11	*Ökumene, Universität, Pfarramt 1931–1932.* Edited by Eberhard Amelung and Christoph Strohm. Gütersloh: Chr. Kaiser/Gütersloher Verlagshaus, 1994.
DBW 12	*Berlin: 1932–1933.* Edited by Carsten Nicolaisen und Ernst-Albert Scharffenorth. Gütersloh: Chr. Kaiser/Gütersloher Verlagshaus, 1997.
DBW 13	*London 1933–1935.* Edited by Hans Goedeking, Martin Heimbucher, and Hans-Walter Schleicher. Gütersloh: Chr. Kaiser/Gütersloher Verlagshaus, 1994.
DBWE 13	*London 1933–1935.* Edited by Keith Clements. Translated by Isabel Best and Douglas W. Stott. Minneapolis: Fortress Press, 2007.
DBW 14	*Illegale Theologenausbildung: Finkenwalde 1935–1937.* Edited by Otto Dudzus und Jürgen Henkys with Sabine Bobert-Stützel, Dirk Schulz, and Ilse Tödt. Gütersloh: Chr. Kaiser/Gütersloher Verlagshaus, 1996.
DBW 15	*Illegale Theologenausbildung: Sammelvikariate 1937–1940.* Edited by Dirk Schulz. Gütersloh: Chr. Kaiser/Gütersloher Verlagshaus, 1998.
DBW 16	*Konspiration und Haft 1940–1945.* Edited by Jørgen Glenthøj, Ulrich Kabitz and Wolf Krötke. Gütersloh: Chr. Kaiser/Gütersloher Verlagshaus, 1996.
DBWE 16	*Conspiracy and Imprisonment 1940–1945.* Edited by Mark Brocker. Translated by Lisa Dahill. Minneapolis: Fortress Press, 2006.
DBW 17	*Register und Ergänzungen.* Edited by Herbert Anzinger and Hans Pfeiffer. Gütersloh: Chr. Kaiser/Gütersloher Verlagshaus, 1999.
CC	*Christ the Center.* Revised translation by Edwin H. Robertson. New York 1978.
LPP	*Letters and Papers from Prison.* The Enlarged Edition. Edited by Eberhard Bethge. New York, 1972.
NRS	*No Rusty Swords, Letters, Lectures and Notes 1928-1936, Collected Works,* volume 1, edited by Edwin H. Robertson. New York 1970.
WCA	*World Come of Age.* Edited by Ronald Gregor Smith. Philadelphia 1967.
WF	*The Way to Freedom: Letters, Lectures and Notes, 1935–1939.* Edited by Edwin H. Robertson, translated by Edwin H. Robertson and John Bowden. London 1972.

2. Other Writings

Bk of Concord	Robert Kolb and Timothy J. Wenger (eds), *The Book of Concord. The Confessions of the Evangelical Lutheran Church*. Minneapolis 2000.
BSLK	*Bekenntnisschriften der evangelisch-lutherischen Kirche.* Göttingen, ninth edition, 1982.
CCDB	*The Cambridge Companion to Dietrich Bonhoeffer.* Edited by John W. de Gruchy. Cambridge 1999.
CFH	*Cambridge Companion to Friedrich Schleiermacher.* Edited by Jacqline Mariña. Cambridge 2005.
CCH	*The Cambridge Companion to Heidegger.* Edited by Charles B. Guigon. Cambridge, second edition, 2006.
CD	Karl Barth, *Church Dogmatics,* 13 volumes, trans. G. W. Bromiley. Edinburgh: T. & T. Clark, 1936–1963.
City of God	Augustine. *The City of God Against the Pagans*, edited by R. W. Dyson. New York 1998.
Bonhoeffer	Eberhard Bethge, *Dietrich Bonhoeffer. Theologian, Christian, Man for His Times. A Biography.* Revised and edited by Victoria J. Barnett. Minneapolis: Fortress Press, 2000.
KD	Karl Barth, *Kirchliche Dogmatik* 14 volumes. Zurich, 1932-1968.
KSA	Friedrich Nietzsche. *Kritische Studienausgabe*, 15 volumes. Edited by Giorgio Colli and Mazzino Montinari, dtv. Munich 1980.
On Religion	Friedrich Schleiermacher, *On Religion. Speeches to its Cultural Despisers.* Introduction, translation and notes by Richard Crouter. Cambridge 1988.
RGG	*Die Religion in Geschichte und Gegenwart*, fourth edition. Tübingen 2000–2005.
Summa Theol.	Thomas Aquinas. *Summa Theologica.* New York 1948.
Christian Faith	Friedrich Schleiermacher. *The Christian Faith*, 2 volumes. Edited by H. R. Mackintosh and J. S. Stewart. New York 1963.
TF	Geffrey Kelly and F. Burton Nelson. *A Testament to Freedom. The Essential Writings of Dietrich Bonhoeffer.* San Francisco, 1990.
TRE	*Theologische Realenzyklopädie.* Berlin/New York 1977–2004.
WA	*Weimar Ausgabe of Luther's Works*
ZThK	*Zeitschrift für Theolgie und Kirche*

Peter Frick

Introduction

Given Dietrich Bonhoeffer's courageous life as a theologian and pastor who resisted National Socialism to the point of death in a concentration camp, it is not surprising that within one hundred years of his birth Bonhoeffer (1906–1945) has become a phenomenon[1] to many people and to some perhaps even an icon. While it is comprehensible that lay readers of his works are fascinated by Bonhoeffer's spiritual classics *Life Together* and *Discipleship* and his last writing *Letters and Papers from Prison*, it must be stressed that such an eclectic manner of reading cannot make intelligible the reasons why Bonhoeffer lived and died the way he did. Scholars, to be sure, have been aware of such a shortcoming and made significant efforts to present Bonhoeffer in an all-inclusive, comprehensive and complete manner. And yet, it is also clear from even a cursory glance at the *International Bibliography on Dietrich Bonhoeffer*[2] that much research during the last half century focused on topics such as religionless Christianity, the world come of age, the concept of religion, secularization, ethics, christology, the church, and of course his life and legacy. The reason for these foci lies, on the one hand, in the fact that Bonhoeffer was unique and novel among German academic theologians both in the way he lived and in many of his theological conceptions. He was a curious phenomenon for the inquisitive researcher. In this sense, Bonhoeffer's thought was seen as congenial in post-war academic circles to make him a spokesman for the God-is-dead-theology, for political theologies, for secular forms of the Christian faith etc. On the other hand, the fact that his written oeuvre was published slowly, in bits and pieces, and concentrated initially on the major and popular works meant that research itself was directed along the path of the published works. The inevitable consequence was that the emerging picture of Bonhoeffer was tinted with a spiritual, theological, ethical or "religionless" colour. Correspondingly, much of the lay and scholarly interest in Bonhoeffer proceeded in a specific manner: since

---

[1] Cf. the recent study by Stephen R. Haynes, *The Bonhoeffer Phenomenon. Portraits of a Protestant Saint* (Minneapolis 2004).
[2] Ernst Feil and Barbara E. Fink (eds.), *International Bibliography on Dietrich Bonhoeffer/Internationale Bibliographie zu Dietrich Bonhoeffer* (Gütersloh 1998).

Bonhoeffer was a man of such strong convictions that he would choose to die at the hands of the Nazis rather than be found compromising these convictions, the question arose what kind of assumptions had been the cause and backbone of this man's life and world view. In other words, the fateful *end* of Bonhoeffer's life prompted the questions of its intellectual and ethical grounding. The main problem here is not the raising of these questions, but the kind of angle and direction they occupied in the overwhelmingly retrospective approach to Bonhoeffer's thought. Clifford Green rightly rejects such an approach as a "teleological bias" or "teleological method,"[3] especially with regard to Bonhoeffer's theology.

In this collection of essays, the approach taken is intentionally the reverse. Rather than looking at Bonhoeffer's end and attempting to trace his intellectual coming of age in a regressive manner, these studies focus on how particular thinkers have shaped Bonhoeffer's thought. Put otherwise, the focal point of these essays is to demonstrate how a particular theologian or philosopher has shaped Bonhoeffer's intellectual formation. The assumption implicit in such a non-teleological approach is that Bonhoeffer's entire life is shaped at the deepest level by convictions that have extensive roots in his intellectual formation. This formation did not merely emerge in Tegel prison as a reaction to his dire circumstances but can often be traced to the very beginning of his theological studies and throughout the various stages of his life. His death is hence only the consequence of his intellectual formation but not the cause. Only because Bonhoeffer had unshaken convictions that were rooted in his fertile intellect was he prepared to meet his death with seemingly unflinching courage. To repeat, the focus of these studies is thus not so much on the heroic end of Bonhoeffer's life, but on the theological and philosophical influences that led him to make certain decisions about his thought and life and, as a final result, the willingness to accept a violent death. How then will these collected essays contribute to a richer and more comprehensive understanding of Bonhoeffer's intellectual formation?

(1) In spite of the plethora of Bonhoeffer studies there is a large lacuna regarding studies that have addressed Bonhoeffer's intellectual grounding in a thorough, comprehensive and methodical manner. Scholarly attention to this important subject matter has indeed been scarce. Green mentions two dissertations that made the first attempts to examine Bonhoeffer's intellectual background: the 1969 Tübingen doctoral dissertation *Bonhoeffers An-*

---

[3] Clifford J. Green, *Bonhoeffer. A Theology of Sociality* (Grand Rapids/Cambridge, revised edition, 1999), 7 and 8. Green notes that "The hermeneutical problem here is acute. To read the early theology ... from the standpoint of the latter is a hermeneutical method which is historically impermissible. It is self-evident that such a method prevents the early works from being read in their own context and in terms of the primary issues to which they were directed ... Such teleological bias must be studiously avoided" (8).

fänge und seine Wurzeln im 19. Jahrhundert by David Wilcox and the 1969 Berlin dissertation *Adolf von Harnack als Lehrer Dietrich Bonhoeffers* by Carl-Jürgen Kaltenborn.[4] The most substantial research on the topic was carried out by the late Jörg Rades at the University of St. Andrews. At the time of his death he was working on a dissertation entitled *The Intellectual Background of Dietrich Bonhoeffer*.[5] Though the work was never finished, he left the following drafts, now housed in the archives of Union Theological Seminary in New York: "Bonhoeffer and Hegel: From *Sanctorum Communio* to the Hegel Seminar with Some Perspectives for the Later Works;" "Kierkegaard and Bonhoeffer;" "Luther and Bonhoeffer;" "Nietzsche and Bonhoeffer."[6] To be sure, there are several other studies that have dealt with Bonhoeffer's intellectual background, such as Walter Lowe's unpublished study "The Critique of Philosophy in Bonhoeffer's *Act and Being*" and Charles Marsh's essays "Bonhoeffer and Heidegger on Togetherness" and "Human Community and Divine Presence: Bonhoeffer's Theological Critique of Hegel."[7]

Although there are a few studies that have dealt with Bonhoeffer's intellectual grounding, the subject at large has not yet been sufficiently investigated. It is telling in this regard what we read in the Preface to the new critical German edition, the *Dietrich Bonhoeffer Werke*. Heinz Eduard Tödt writes on behalf of the editors. "Die Rezeption der Theologie Bonhoeffers scheint mir trotz vieler zum Teil hochqualifizierter Untersuchungen erst in den Anfängen zu stehen."[8] Tödt also suggests that we have "ein volleres Verständnis und ein tieferes Wirken von Bonhoeffers Theologie nicht hinter uns, sondern größtenteils noch vor uns."[9] Although Tödt does not specifically refer in these words to the intellectual grounding of Bonhoeffer's theology, it is apparent from even a fleeting look at the *International Bibliography on Dietrich Bonhoeffer*[10] that there is much room and a great need for investigations that examine Bonhoeffer's theological formation on their own terms. Along the same lines Green proposed explicitly that "it will obviously be fruitful in the future to have more thorough and comprehensive comparisons between Bonhoeffer and his predecessors and contemporaries, especially Luther and Barth, Bultmann and Tillich."[11] Three of the essays examine the influences of these thinkers on Bonhoeffer.

When it comes to the *philosophical* influences on Bonhoeffer's intellectual formation, the scholarly situation is in dire need. Research has made

---

[4] Green, *Bonhoeffer. A Theology of Sociality*, 10, note 13.
[5] Cf. *DBWE* 3, 166, note 78 (*DBW* 3, 155, note 78).
[6] *DBWE* 2, 207.
[7] For bibliographical details see *DBWE* 2, 205.
[8] *DBW* 1, XIV.
[9] *DBW* 1, XIX.
[10] See note 2.
[11] Green, *Bonhoeffer. A Theology of Sociality*, 10.

little inroads into this hardly ploughed field and even those studies that have ventured to go there are the exception. The problem, as Wayne Floyd notes, "is not so much that the philosophical influences on Bonhoeffer's early work have been misrepresented as that they have not yet been reconstructed in anything approaching a comprehensive manner."[12] Charles Marsh similarly writes that "despite the prominence of philosophical concerns in much of Bonhoeffer's writings, precious little scholarly attention has been given to this facet of his thought."[13] The dearth of secondary studies on Bonhoeffer's philosophy is deplorable not only as a lacuna in Bonhoeffer scholarship, but in the fact that such a dearth presents an incomplete and imprecise picture of Bonhoeffer's thought. Marsh says it well: "The problem is more serious than a paucity of critical secondary literature. Bonhoeffer genuinely loved to read philosophy, and the effects of scholarship which write this interest out of the picture through theological revisionism, interpretive legerdemain, or mere omission create distorted presentations of the man himself."[14]

It is crucial in this context to recognize that the young theology student was extremely interested in the field of philosophy. For example, when Bonhoeffer was studying in Tübingen in 1923–1924, Bethge writes, "the only professor whose lectures Bonhoeffer attended during both the summer and winter semesters was the philosopher Karl Groos ... Bonhoeffer was impressed by his lectures on logic four hours every week in the summer semester, and on the history of modern philosophy five hours every week during the winter term. Bonhoeffer also joined Groos's seminar on Kant's *Critique of Pure Reason* and wrote a paper for it."[15] When Bonhoeffer continued his studies in Berlin, beside courses in theology, he also took "epistemological theory and a seminar on 'Freedom and Necessity' from Heinrich Maier, a representative of the school of critical realism. He also took 'History of Logic' from Rieffert."[16] The fact that the curriculum of the theology student includes several courses in philosophy is indicative of Bonhoeffer's more than fleeting interest in the subject. His profound interest in philosophy came to a culmination in his philosophical *Habilitation* thesis, *Act and Being*, and his seminar on Hegel's *Philosophy of Religion* in the summer semester of 1933 at the University of Berlin.[17] Even in later years did his keen interest in philosophy not abate, as the reading list during the

---

[12] *DBWE* 2, 8.

[13] Charles Marsh, *Reclaiming Dietrich Bonhoeffer. The Promise of His Theology* (New York 1994), ix–x.

[14] Marsh, *Reclaiming Dietrich Bonhoeffer*, x.

[15] Eberhard Bethge, *Dietrich Bonhoeffer*, 55.

[16] Bethge, *Dietrich Bonhoeffer*, 72.

[17] Cf. Ilse Tödt (ed.), *Dietrich Bonhoeffers Hegelseminar*. Nach Aufzeichnungen von Ferenc Lehel. Internationales Bonhoeffer Forum. Forschung und Praxis 8 (Munich 1988).

years of his imprisonment indicates (among others, the list includes Kant, Heidegger, Hartmann, Natorp, Dilthey, Ortega y Gasset).[18] Perhaps surprisingly, the very last book that was in his possession was a volume by Plutarch.[19]

(2) The fact that Bonhoeffer was a serious student of both theology and philosophy makes it an inevitable scholarly requirement to examine those theologians and philosophers who shaped him in the most substantial manner. Without an attempt to examine, trace, and weigh these influences in Bonhoeffer's intellectual formation it will be virtually impossible to gain a comprehensive and complete understanding of his thought. And yet, even though such an analysis is necessary for a deeper understanding of Bonhoeffer, it also raises the methodological issue of the relation of philosophy and theology in Bonhoeffer's structure of thought as a whole.

The methodological question of the relation between theology and philosophy is deeply entrenched in Bonhoeffer's writings. Even though the student Bonhoeffer studied theology and philosophy in the customary division of the disciplines within the academy, it is apparent in his *Habilitation* dissertation that the two fields were not only engaged in conversation but also held in tension. Based on a reading of *Act and Being*, it seems that Bonhoeffer himself saw the fields of theology and philosophy as complementary, although in a manner that philosophy was the handmaid to theology. This subordination of philosophy to theology does not imply, however, that Bonhoeffer was an eclectic theologian and dilettante philosopher. To provide but one brief example: Bonhoeffer's rejection of the philosophical premise of the autonomous self's capacity to come to itself – both in its transcendental and ontological attempts – hinges on the epistemological counter-premise that the self cannot come to itself – apart from revelation. This is to say, Bonhoeffer begins with the theological premise of a person's being "in Adam" and the corresponding *cor curvum in se*. A person's sinfulness is such that there is no human possibility or potentiality (a Heideggerian concept that Bonhoeffer rejects) that could bring about a person's knowledge of truth regarding sin or salvation. For if there is such a thing as a person's coming to him/herself apart from revelation, sin ultimately loses its sting. Hence, Bonhoeffer's epistemological skepticism. The way out of this impasse is by means of divine self-disclosure, namely

---

[18] Bethge, *Dietrich Bonhoeffer*, 944.
[19] Cf. Bethge, *Dietrich Bonhoeffer*, 910, 916, 927. After Bonhoeffer was called away from the other prisoners in Schönberg, "he wrote his name and address in large letters with a blunt pencil in the front, back, and middle of his Plutarch. One of Goerdeler's sons took the book and gave it to Bonhoeffer's family years later, as the last existing evidence of his life. It was the same book that he had requested on 17 January and had received in the Reich Central Security Office on 7 February" (927).

revelation.[20] In a nutshell, we can see in this minimally sketched example how Bonhoeffer pursues both the paths of theology and philosophy at the same time, brings them into dialogical tension, but then gives the theological premise of divine revelation the upper hand over the philosophical attempt to arrive at a self-understanding that can bring the self to itself. In other words, philosophy is crucial for Bonhoeffer, but in a way that it serves him to clarify his theological positions.

(3) The complex relation between philosophy and theology in Bonhoeffer's thought is further complicated by the question of how specific philosophers and theologians shaped his intellectual development. For many readers, some of the writers discussed in this collection of studies may be either exclusively or predominantly categorized as philosophers or theologians while others are more difficult to place in one of these categories. Such a pure classification has certain merits, but it also imposes a structure on Bonhoeffer's thought that is not part of his thinking, at least not in an obvious manner. Because of this, the purpose of this collection is not to categorize Bonhoeffer's intellectual forbearers neatly either as theologians or philosophers. The objective is not on listing several thinkers that influenced him and then draw up a balance sheet that weighs the theological against the philosophical influence. The question of theological and philosophical prominence is far too complex and defies an easy answer.

The issue of the relation between philosophy and theology is not unique to Bonhoeffer but starts with the thinkers presented in the essays. For example, in academic circles Kierkegaard is typically considered a philosopher, but for Bonhoeffer, as for Karl Barth before him, the interest in his writings is for theological reasons, such as the notion of cheap grace. Similarly, Aquinas is usually claimed as the theological doctor of the church, but in relation to Bonhoeffer the issue of the nature of being is paramount. Augustine, predominantly a theologian, is himself decisively shaped by Neo-Platonism. In the twentieth century, Bultmann was always classified as a theologian and yet his existential theology was in fact the result of a substantial dialogue with the philosopher Heidegger. Likewise, when one reads Tillich, it is at times notoriously difficult to draw a line between theological and philosophical reasoning. And even when the category of philosopher seems to be as unambiguous as in the case of Kant, Hegel and Nietzsche, it is evident that they, too, address in their philosophical systems matters of prime theological importance.

(4) The difficulty of drawing a straight line between theology and philosophy in the writers discussed in these essays points to three things. First, as the editor of this collection I have decided to present the influ-

---

[20] Cf. Bonhoeffer's succinct summary regarding the epistemological question for both theology and philosophy in *DBWE* 2, 80 (*DBW* 2, 74).

ences on Bonhoeffer's intellectual life from the perspective of certain *persons*. In other words, the thinkers included in this volume are persons who represent very specific ideas, or if we prefer, we can say that they are representative of a specific theology or philosophy. The reason for choosing to present the currents of Bonhoeffer's intellectual formation by studying the ideas of persons has the distinct advantage of having a firm and clearly-focused starting point. Second, by including certain persons in this collection, it follows that I decided against the approach to trace Bonhoeffer's intellectual coming of age by deciding in advance what topics are crucial for him in this regard. For example, notwithstanding the difficulty of being able to demarcate the line between theology and philosophy in our authors, it seemed nonetheless methodologically inappropriate to me to select topics such as ontology, epistemology, grace, sin, revelation, ecclesiology etc. and then find authors who would write on these subjects. Such an approach would be an undue systematization of Bonhoeffer's thought. Third, and most important, although each of these essays is limited to one or two thinkers, the result of the studies lies in demonstrating how specific *ideas* shaped Bonhoeffer's intellectual formation. In other words, the path of intellectual formation begins with *persons* but ends up with *ideas*. More precisely, we can say that a person's intellectual development pivots on specific ideas that other persons have articulated and that we examine, modify, reject or accept for ourselves. In the case of Bonhoeffer, it seems to me that he was not primarily interested in the *person* of Kempis, Nietzsche, Schleiermacher, Hegel and the other authors, but in the manner in which their *thought* would bring greater depth, clarity, and precision to his own thinking.

(5) The comments expressed above lead me to one further, but crucial comment regarding how the essays in this book should be understood and read. On the surface, it seems as if the present studies deal with the thoughts of particular thinkers and hence should be understood as a contribution to a more profound understanding of that person. In that sense, the essays deal with the theology of Kempis, Luther, Niebuhr and the philosophy of Hegel, Nietzsche and so on. However, to read these studies as if they have the function to shed simply more light on these thinkers would be to miss their intention. Given the nature of this project, it is inevitable that there is a certain degree of overlap. Luther and Heidegger, for example, are discussed in several essays and in different contexts. The same is true of some of the more prominent themes. The question of grace, for example, is addressed in the essays on Kempis and Kierkegaard.

It is, therefore, of greatest significance to understand that all essays have *one focal point and common scope*, namely the thought of Dietrich Bonhoeffer. Important and insightful as these studies may be as individual contributions, their relevance must be appreciated in relation to the other studies and the thought of Bonhoeffer. In other words, all of the studies converge on the thought of Bonhoeffer as a whole in such a way as to illuminate the growth and maturation of his own intellect vis-à-vis the philosophical and theological ideas articulated in the thinkers discussed in the essays. Put differently, the objective of the essays is to open up the intellectual window of Bonhoeffer's thought, as it were, and thereby allow more light to fall on the structure and extension of that thought.

(6) Each of the essays in this volume discusses either one or two thinkers in relation to Bonhoeffer's thought. The selection of the thinkers included in this collection was, on the one hand, a methodological pre-decision made by the editor and, on the other hand, determined by the space limits of the published work.[21] Each of the contributors was asked to write on one or two thinkers with the objective to present how specific philosophical or theological ideas of that person found their ways into Bonhoeffer's thinking and what prominence these gained in the overarching structure of his intellectual formation. The manner of presentation was left up to each of the contributors. As the perusal of the essays indicates, most contributors decided to divide their essays into themes or topics and sought to demonstrate how a particular idea shaped Bonhoeffer's thought in a specific manner. My own approach is somewhat different. Even though it is more cumbersome for the reader, I have decided to provide the primary text and context in which Bonhoeffer cites or discusses a specific theologian or philosopher in a first section. In a subsequent section I have then attempted to draw out the themes and significance that can be gained from the texts and contexts presented in the first section. The objective was to let the primary texts speak for themselves as much as possible before commenting on and, necessarily, imposing my own systematic order on Bonhoeffer's thought.

(7) Finally, given the fact of the dearth of studies that address the question of how particular theologians and philosophers shaped Bonhoeffer's intellectual formation, this work must be seen as a contribution that seeks to stimulate further research. Since all essays are written by Bonhoeffer scholars and none by an academic philosopher, it would be a substantial advancement to Bonhoeffer studies if philosophers would become so inclined as to take some of the thinkers that shaped Bonhoeffer and explore those philosophical relations in Bonhoeffer further and in more detail. In this manner, Bonhoeffer research could press forward in widening its interdisciplinary methodology.

At any rate, the collection of essays presented in this volume is meant to make a beginning into the research of the neglected subject matter of Bon-

---

[21] It is possible, and indeed desirable, that other thinkers (for example, Fichte, Grisebach, Schlatter, Troeltsch, Przywara) could have been included in this volume. Possibly, some scholars will be prompted to take up this research.

hoeffer's intellectual background. Rather than providing definitive answers to the often very complex questions raised in this regard, it is the hope of all contributors to have raised and articulated at least some of the decisive questions and issues that will spurn on other researchers to add their own studies.

Barry Harvey

Augustine and Thomas Aquinas in the Theology of Dietrich Bonhoeffer

I. Introduction

In an essay written in the summer of 1933, Dietrich Bonhoeffer takes issue with those who spoke contemptuously of careful theological reflection. He marvels in particular at those who saw it as a good thing to shun the company of sincere theologians, who thought that it was not necessary to have what these important figures in the history of the church held to be immensely important. He singles out four names for special mention: the apostle Paul, Augustine, Thomas Aquinas and Martin Luther.[1]

That Bonhoeffer often keeps company with the likes of Paul, Luther, John Calvin, and Karl Barth has long been recognized and discussed in the scholarly literature. What is not widely acknowledged, however, is his long-standing interest in patristic and medieval theology and in the works of Augustine and Thomas Aquinas in particular. This is unfortunate, for as his work develops he looks for ways to get beyond conventional descriptions and parochial disputes, to find means of engaging the larger ecumenical Christian tradition. At significant points in Bonhoeffer's theology one sees a budding effort at a *ressourcement* of the early theological tradition of the church, and for his Protestant readers in particular this fact should suggest many opportunities for a *rapprochement* with the Roman Catholic and Eastern Orthodox traditions.

In what follows I shall briefly examine Bonhoeffer's interaction with two of the most significant figures in the Western theological tradition: Augustine (354–430) and Thomas Aquinas (1225–1274). It should come as no surprise that the Protestant Bonhoeffer refers to the former far more often than he does to the latter (more than twice as often), and he returns to selected texts at key points during his lifetime. The celebrated bishop of Hippo is a constant interlocutor as Bonhoeffer works through a wide variety of topics. Eberhard Bethge notes, for example, that he repeatedly quotes Augustine's famous line from *Confessions* that the human heart is restless until it finds its rest in God

---

[1] Cf. *DBW* 12, 417.

in his Barcelona sermons.² This famous work, particularly the last three books, also figures centrally in Bonhoeffer's exegesis of the first three chapters of Genesis in *Creation and Fall*.³ It is on questions of ecclesiology and theological anthropology, however, that Bonhoeffer finds Augustine to be an important conversation partner.

II. Augustine

It is worth noting at the outset that as Bonhoeffer was making plans to write his dissertation he participated in a select seminar conducted by Adolf von Harnack in the winter of 1925–1926 on Augustine's *City of God*. Many have observed that there is a close correspondence between Bonhoeffer's argument in *Sanctorum Communio* and Augustine's understanding of the church, a view that he inherited in part from his dissertation advisor, Reinhold Seeberg. Bonhoeffer's basic axiom that *die Kirche ist Christus als Gemeinde existierend*, the church is Christ existing as community, represents in significant ways a recovery and a restatement of Augustine's contention that in the church we encounter the whole Christ, *totus Christus*, consisting of both head and body.⁴ Together with Augustine, Bonhoeffer consistently emphasizes that Christ cannot be abstracted from the church; indeed, he writes, "it is none other than Christ who 'is' the church."⁵

At the heart of Bonhoeffer's understanding of the church is the assertion that "the love of God, in Christ's vicarious representative action, restores the community between God and human beings," the result of which is that "the community of human beings with each other has also become a reality in love once again." He traces this concept to Augustine's assertion that

---

² Eberhard Bethge, *Dietrich Bonhoeffer*, 112.

³ *DBWE* 3, 28, 31, 37–38, 61 (*DBW* 3, 27, 30, 35–36, 57).

⁴ Cf. "First Homily on 1 John 1:1–2:11," *Augustine: Later Works*, edited by John Burnaby (Philadelphia 1955), 261.

⁵ *DBWE* 1, 157 (*DBW* 1, 100). Parenthetically, we see in this comparison between Bonhoeffer and Augustine one of the peculiarities of the development of theological language. The qualitative sense of human relatedness denoting an active unity in Christ that Bonhoeffer seeks to describe with the German *Gemeinde* and *Gemeinschaft*, Augustine seeks to communicate with the Latin *societas*, while in contemporary thought "society" is normally associated with the more general and abstract sense of *Gesellschaft*. As a result, when Augustine asserted that while the church is on a pilgrimage in this world, it calls out citizens from all nations to form a society of aliens speaking all languages, he was gesturing toward the same kind of community that Bonhoeffer attempts to articulate with the notion of *Gemeinde*. Augustine, *The City of God*, XIX.17, edited by R. W. Dyson (New York 1998), 846–47. On the development of "society" see Raymond Williams, *Keywords: A Vocabulary of Culture and Society* (New York, revised edition 1983), 291–295.

caritas, love, is that which binds together the church-community: "It was Augustine's great insight to portray the community of saints, the core of the church, as the community of loving persons who, touched by God's Spirit, radiate love and grace." The unity of the church, therefore, is the product of love acting through faith. Insofar as this unity does not presently exist it must be won, but the weapon for battle is love: "We must not forget Augustine's great notion that caritas [love] is the *bond* of the unity of the church. But this notion presupposes the unity established by God, and human action as meaningful only on this basis."[6]

In characteristic Lutheran fashion, Bonhoeffer connects the Augustinian emphasis on charity as the bond of the church-community with the authority to forgive sins, which he argues comes not from an ecclesiastical office, but from the community of saints. In his view the deepest insight one can have into the miracle of the church-community is that by virtue of her or his membership in the church-community one person can forgive the sins of another with priestly authority: "It was Augustine who maintained that this is possible only in the community of the saints. It alone is given the promise in John 20:23, for it alone has the Spirit. Nobody can forgive sins but the person who takes them upon himself, bears them, and wipes them out. Thus only Christ can do it, which for us means his church as the sanctorum communio." Luther revives Augustine's notion that it is the *sanctorum communio* that bears the sins of its members, though Luther quickly adds that ultimately "it is Christ who bears them."[7]

This is not to say that everything connected with Augustine's understanding of the church meets with Bonhoeffer's approval. He claims that Augustine's doctrine of election, and in particular the concept of the *numerus praedestinatorum*, the number of the predestined, acts as a solvent that tends to dissolve the church-community into the set number of predestined individuals: "It would seem that this idea has a persistent corrosive effect on the concept of the church, for individual persons perceive themselves as ultimate in God's sight; every community seems to be fragmented into the components of individual persons, and the will of God appears to be directed only toward these."[8] At the same time, however, Bonhoeffer rejects the view of Karl Holl, among others, who argues that this doctrine is the sum total of Augustine's concept of the *sanctorum communio*: "Quite the contrary is true. His concept of the sanctorum communio was only dis-

---

[6] *DBWE* 1, 202; cf. 175 (*DBW* 1, 136; cf. 114–115).
[7] *DBWE* 1, 189; cf. 175 (*DBW* 1, 127; cf. 114–115).
[8] *DBWE* 1, 163 (*DBW* 1, 104).

turbed by the notion of predestination; he developed a tremendously rich view of the sanctorum communio that can match that of Luther."[9]

If Bonhoeffer's basic conception of the church-community is similar to that of Augustine, the record is more mixed with respect to questions of theological anthropology, especially the problem of original sin. It is on this topic that he has his most sustained conversations with Augustine over the years. Many different streams of thought converge on the convoluted question of original sin in the history of Christian thought, and it is far beyond the scope of this essay to disentangle them. It is interesting to note, however, that in *Sanctorum Communio* Bonhoeffer reaffirms the position of the early fathers regarding the effect of the fall on human life. They routinely spoke of the effect of sin as the shattering of the image that all human beings shared, for it was the same mysterious participation in God that caused the soul to exist which also constituted the primordial unity of humankind.

In his commentary on Psalm 95 (96), Augustine writes: "Adam therefore hath been scattered over the whole world. He was in one place, and fell, and as in a manner broken small (*quodammodo comminutus*), he filled the whole world."[10] In the East, Maximus the Confessor also speaks of original sin as the breaking up of the natural unity of humankind into a thousand pieces. Humankind, which should constitute a harmonious whole, in which what is mine and what is thine should involve no contradiction, has been transformed into a multitude of individuals, as numerous as the grains of sand on the seashore, full of violence and enmity: "And now we rend each other like the wild beasts."[11] Bonhoeffer in similar fashion contends that the structure of humanity-in-Adam is composed of isolated individuals who nonetheless form one, collective person: "Whereas in the primal state the relation among human beings is one of giving, in the sinful state it is purely demanding. Every person exists in complete, voluntary isolation; everyone lives their own life, rather than all living the same life in God."[12] These isolated individuals nonetheless form one, collective person who is both "*infinitely fragmented*" and united in the "humanity of sin."[13]

---

[9] *DBWE* 1, 164, note 22 (*DBW* 1, 105, note 22); cf. Karl Holl, *Augustins innere Entwicklung* (Berlin 1922), 41ff., reprinted in *Gesammelte Aufsätze zur Kirchengeschichte*, vol. 3 (Tübingen 1928), 54ff.

[10] *St. Augustine on the Psalms*, XCVI.15, Nicene and Post-Nicene Fathers, Series 1 (volume 8, translated by A. Cleveland Coxe) (Peadbody 1994), 474.

[11] Maximus the Confessor, *Questions to Thalassios*, covering letter and q. 64, cited by Henri de Lubac, *Catholicism: Christ and the Common Destiny of Man*, translated by Lancelot C. Sheppard and Elizabeth Englund (San Francisco 1988), 33–34.

[12] *DBWE* 1, 108 (*DBW* 1, 69).

[13] *DBWE* 1, 121 (*DBW* 1, 76).

With Augustine, Bonhoeffer seeks a concept of original sin that will account for the universality of sin. He states that we must conceive of sin as not only individual, but also supra-individual, "simultaneously the deed of the human race and of the individual."[14] The recognition of one's complete solitude and culpability before God is thus connected inextricably with the broadest sense of shared sinfulness. Augustine's doctrine of original sin is an attempt to account for a twofold question: how are we to understand theologically the universality of sin, and how should we conceive of the empirical spread of sin throughout humanity? Though he maintains that the two must be understood together, Bonhoeffer does criticize Augustine for conceiving of the human race in terms of the biological concept of the species, a position that he believes at this early stage of his work weakens the moral concept of culpability, and thus a Christian-ethical concept of the species must be formulated in its stead.

In the published 1930 edition of *Sanctorum Communio* Bonhoeffer does not trace out the history of the doctrine of original sin, stating that it would lead too far astray from the matters at hand. He states in a footnote that a number of concepts would be of interest to social philosophy: all humanity being "in Adam"; Adam, or any individual person, representing the entire human race; imputation; the collective person of the genus *humanum* as the scholastics conceived of it (Aquinas is singled out in this regard), and "a concept that has repeatedly been confounded with it, that of the human species in the biological sense, which in turn is connected to the sociological importance of infant baptism in Roman Catholicism."[15]

In the original dissertation, however, he does offer an extended discussion of this history, which he takes in large part from Seeberg's *Dogmatik*. Beginning with the writings of the apostle Paul, Bonhoeffer affirms what Seeberg calls the "objectively effective principle," that through one human being, sin enters the world and affects the entire human race, which now lives under the divine imposed sentence of death: "No one will act differently from Adam; that is, there is in principle a universality of sin." Since Paul does not discuss what empirical form this principle takes, writes Bonhoeffer, we have only the general idea that God imputes the one sin of Adam to all human beings, which can be inferred from the universal destiny of death. The theological question that is raised but not answered by Paul is thus, "how the one person relates in principle to the entire human race, and, then, how sin is spread empirically."[16]

Bonhoeffer reads Augustine as trying to do justice to these two aspects of humanity's current state. In his estimation, however, Augustine fails to reconcile the personal aspect of original sin, especially the ascription of

---

[14] *DBWE* 1, 108 (*DBW* 1, 70).
[15] *DBWE* 1, 109–110, note 1 (*DBW* 1, 71, note 1).
[16] *DBWE* 1, 110, note 11 (*DBW* 1, 242, note 9).

culpability, with its connections to the bodily nature of human beings, most especially to the connotations of being a natural power or fate before which women and men are helpless. The problem, says Bonhoeffer, is that Augustine seeks to derive personal culpability from the biological unity of the human in Adam, leading to what he regards as an intractable contradiction. The concept of the human species should instead be based on the concept of culpability, which alone would permit the development of an ethical collective concept of the human race and its shared sinfulness.[17]

Bonhoeffer's comments about Augustine's understanding of original sin in *Sanctorum Communio* are not, however, his last words on the subject. In *Act and Being* he alludes briefly to Augustine in a view of original sin that he still finds problematic: "We may historicize, psychologize, and naturalize the doctrine of original sin. Somehow sin clings to human nature as humanly generated. *Non posse non peccare* [not able not to sin] holds true for this tarnished nature. The concept of nature is intended to warrant the continuity and existentiality of sin."[18] As one would expect, Bonhoeffer also takes up this question again in *Creation and Fall*. What does come as a surprise, particularly in light of what he says in his earlier works, is a reconsideration of the biological dimension to original sin. In his exegesis of Genesis 3:7 (then the eyes of them both were opened, and they became aware that they were naked; and they sewed fig leaves together and made themselves an apron) nakedness is identified as the essence of unity, of being for and respecting the other as limit and as a creature. "Nakedness," he writes, "is the essence of being oblivious of the possibility of robbing others of their rights. Nakedness is revelation; nakedness believes in grace."[19]

Covering up one's nakedness, on the other hand, displays the essential character of a world split into *tob* and *ra*, good and evil. The result is a profoundly contradictory state of affairs, in that human beings qua *sicut deus*, who seek to be without limits, unwittingly and unwillingly disclose their limit when they cover themselves up and feel shame. It is in these feelings of shame that human beings acknowledge their limit: "The shame of human beings is an unwilling pointer to revelation, to the limit, to the other, to God ... This is not because shame in itself is something good – that is the moralistic, puritanical, and totally unbiblical interpretation – but because it is compelled to give unwilling witness to the fallen state of the ashamed."[20]

---

[17] *DBWE* 1, 113–114 (*DBW* 1, 71).
[18] *DBWE* 2, 145 (*DBW* 2, 144). Bonhoeffer refers to Augustine's formula in *DBWE* 3, 119 (*DBW* 3, 111) where he states that, "No theory of posse peccare or of non posse peccare is able to comprehend the fact that the deed [of Adam's disobedience] was done."
[19] *DBWE* 3, 124 (*DBW* 3, 116).
[20] *DBWE* 3, 124 (*DBW* 3, 116).

That church dogmatics has on occasion located the essence of original sin in sexuality, Bonhoeffer argues, is not as absurd as many Protestants have claimed it to be: "Knowing about *tob* and *ra* is not to begin with an abstract knowledge of ethical principles; on the contrary it starts out as sexuality, that is, as a perversion of the relation of one human being to another. And as the essence of sexuality consists of creating in the midst of destroying, so the dark secret of the nature of humankind, essentially conditioned by original sin, is preserved from generation to generation in the course of continuing procreation. The protest that appeals to the natural character of sexuality is unaware of the highly ambivalent character of every so-called 'natural' aspect of our world."[21]

We have here a significant and dramatic revision of the comments made by Bonhoeffer in *Sanctorum Communio* in connection with Augustine's views on original sin. Sexuality, and by extension everything about humanity's bodily character, is fully implicated in the effects of the fall and in whatever we wish to signify by the idea of person (a term which is nowhere near as prominent in *Creation and Fall* as it was in *Sanctorum Communio*). The corruption of humankind's creaturely nature by the desire and the effort to be god means that the whole created world is now covered in a veil, "silent and lacking explanation, opaque and enigmatic. The world of human beings who are *sicut deus* is ashamed along with them and hides itself from their view."[22] For its part, sexuality is sanctified only by being restrained by shame, by being veiled, and by the vocation of the community of marriage to be in the church (a topic which he takes up in his discussion of the mandates in *Ethics*).[23]

Bonhoeffer does not spell out the reasons for his change of mind on this question. The fact that it occurs in the course of a sustained engagement with biblical texts surely has something to do with it. He also does not tell us how he would reintegrate this newfound appreciation for the connection between sexuality and original sin with his earlier concerns about the individual's culpability before God. He does say in *Ethics* that a "deep" or "dark shadow" has been cast over marriage, the mandate within which "new persons are created to serve Jesus Christ. But because the first son of the first human beings, Cain, was born far from paradise and became the murderer of his brother, here, too, a dark shadow falls over marriage and family in this our world."[24] He sets a similar statement about the mandate of labor within the framework of Augustine's *City of God*, noting that Cain's first creation was a city that formed the earthly contrast (*Gegenbild*) to the eternal city of God. The fact that it is the

---

[21] *DBWE* 3, 125 (*DBW* 3, 117–118).
[22] *DBWE* 3, 126 (*DBW* 3, 118).
[23] *DBWE* 3, 125–126 (*DBW* 3, 118). Cf. *DBWE* 6, 67–69, 388–408 (*DBW* 6, 53–56).
[24] *DBWE* 6, 71 (*DBW* 6, 58).

descendants of Cain who now fulfill this mandate "casts a deep shadow over all human work."[25]

III. Thomas Aquinas

Though Bonhoeffer interacts with Augustine far more frequently than he does with Aquinas, this does not mean that there are no interesting exchanges with Aquinas and the Thomistic tradition more generally. Two topics in particular are noteworthy. The first occurs in *Act and Being*, where he takes up the long-standing dispute between Protestants and Catholics over the question of the *analogia entis*, the analogy of being. The second area of conversation involves Bonhoeffer's efforts in *Ethics* to recover the concept of the natural for Protestant ethics.

In *Act and Being* Bonhoeffer addresses what he calls the "Thomist principle of the *analogia entis*."[26] He states that the Thomistic conception, "which [Erich] Przywara especially has restored in our time with methodical brilliance to the center of Roman Catholic philosophy of religion and dogmatics," seems to have opened the idea of being to the transcendent. At the heart of this concept is the relation between *esse* and *essentia* in God and in the human being respectively. In human beings the two are separate, but in God they coincide. To be sure, the *essentia* of human beings is related to their existence, their *esse*, but it is always different from it as well, because they are always in "becoming" while God is in "being." God's eternal "is" abides in every "was" and "will be," but is also infinitely beyond these. The ontological relationship of human beings to God consists entirely in "the *essentia-esse* difference of human beings and the *essentia-esse* identity of God."[27]

Bonhoeffer recognizes that Aquinas' conception of the relation between creator and creature (as explicated by Przywara) does not take the form either of pure exclusivity (i.e., pure difference) or of pure identity, that is, of equivocity or univocity. It is predicated instead on analogy, "a relation of 'likeness' to one another, as being is to becoming." As a result, "God is not enclosed in Dasein nor Dasein in God, but just as God is imagined to exist in absolute originality, so human beings are thought of as existing in their relative but authentic reality before God (*causa secundae*)."[28] This last observation is significant, for as David Burrell contends in one of his insightful discussion of Aquinas's work on this topic, a proper conception of the relation between God and the world must "articulate the distinction

---

[25] *DBWE* 6, 71 (*DBW* 6, 58).
[26] *DBWE* 2, 73 (*DBW* 2, 67).
[27] *DBWE* 2, 73 (*DBW* 2, 67).
[28] *DBWE* 2, 73–74 (*DBW* 2, 67–68).

between God and the world in such a way as to respect the reality appropriate to each."[29]

As Bonhoeffer reads Thomas-Przywara,[30] the concept of analogy requires that creator and creature be conceived as two "substances" that both stand over against, and in relative independence from, each other. The predicate "is" thus stands "in-over" becoming, while the latter "comes from the former." In this way, writes Bonhoeffer, "God is not divorced from the creature but is in it to the degree to which God grants it relative but authentic reality."[31] He does not develop this point further, but it is a crucial one, for according to Aquinas human freedom and autonomy are given to us in this relation of dependence on God. "Free-will is the cause of its own movement, because by his free-will man moves himself to act. But it does not of necessity belong to liberty that what is free should be the first cause of itself, as neither for one thing to be the cause of another need it be the first cause. God, therefore, is the first cause, who moves causes both natural and voluntary. And just as by moving natural causes he does not prevent their acts being natural, so by moving voluntary causes he does not deprive their actions of being voluntary: but rather is he the cause of this very thing in them; for he operates in each thing according to its own nature."[32]

Though Bonhoeffer allows that Aquinas successfully construes creaturely being, that is, Dasein, in terms of temporality "without sealing it in itself," he questions whether the doctrine of analogy as the *Angelicus Doctor* formulates it adequately expresses the transcendence of God's "is" as Christians understand it, "or whether a metaphysics of immanence still lurks behind the scene."[33] In his estimation, the ontology of analogy is valid insofar as it relates to the being of human beings *qua* creatures, that is, inasmuch as human being is determined essentially by creatureliness, which presupposes a continuity of the mode of being in *status corruptionis* (in the corrupt state after the fall) and *status gratiae* (in the state of grace):

---

[29] David B. Burrell, *Knowing the Unknowable God: Ibn-Sina, Maimonides, Aquinas* (Notre Dame 1986), 17.

[30] This construction belongs to Bonhoeffer. As Wayne Floyd, the editor of the English edition of *Act and Being*, puts the matter, Bonhoeffer "apparently took Przywara's position to be akin to, and representative of, that of Thomas Aquinas himself, indeed Thomism in general" (*DBWE* 2, 74, note 82).

[31] *DBWE* 2, 74 (*DBW* 2, 68).

[32] Saint Thomas Aquinas, *Summa Theologica*, Ia. 83. 1 ad.3, translated by the Fathers of the English Dominican Province (New York 1948), 418. As McCabe puts it: "I am free in fact, not because God withdraws from me and leaves me my independence – as with a man who frees his slaves, or good parents who let their children come to independence – but just the other way round. I am free because God is in a sense more directly the cause of my actions than he is of the behaviour of unfree beings." Herbert McCabe, *God Matters* (London 1987), 14; cf. Denys Turner, *Faith, Reason, and the Existence of God* (New York 2004), 35–36.

[33] *DBWE* 2, 74 (*DBW* 2, 68).

"With the continuity of their own ontological condition there is also guaranteed to human beings by the *analogia entis* a continuity of the ontological condition of God. Thus their being, whether in the original state of Adam or in Christ, may always be certain of its analogy to God's being."[34]

The problem with the Thomistic concept of *analogia entis*, says Bonhoeffer, is that though it allows one to affirm that God remains "in-over" human beings, such an affirmation, if it is to make concrete theological sense and not remain purely "formalistic-metaphysical," must be able to account for the modes of being "in Adam" and "in Christ" in their own right. He doubts that there is a being of human beings in general that is not already determined in every respect as "being-in-Adam" or "being-in-Christ," as being-guilty or being-pardoned. It is only on the basis of this distinction, says Bonhoeffer, that one could then initiate a genuinely theological inquiry into the being of human beings.[35] But if one moves in this direction, the possibility of a guarantee of the divine continuity of being loses any basis. As a result, the eternal "is" remains a purely speculative notion that is continuously "in-over" becoming, and thus is capable of being extended into an a priori system of the natural insight of reason, but for that reason is inadequate for a theological ontology: "God is not primarily the sheer 'is'. Rather God 'is' the righteous one; God 'is' the holy one; God 'is' love. The ontological foundation for theological concepts of being must remain precisely the realization that this 'is' can in no way be detached from the concrete definition." In the end, Bonhoeffer concludes, the Thomistic attempt to open the concept of being ends up with an illusory transcendence, arriving at a being but not God, unable to go beyond a metaphysics that remains locked in the closed world.[36]

Foremost among Bonhoeffer's concerns about the Thomistic doctrine of the *analogia entis*, with its "formalistic retreat to something 'more general'" behind the kind of specificity that is the Christian concept of God, is that it destroys the Christian idea of revelation. He claims that the contingency of both law and gospel is twisted into a general theory of being with

---

[34] *DBWE* 2, 74 (*DBW* 2, 68).

[35] Bonhoeffer's concern for the distinction between the modes of being "in Adam" and "in Christ" in their own right re-emerges in *Creation and Fall*, where he goes to great lengths to distinguish between humankind-imago-dei, human being in God's image, and humankind-sicut-deus, human being who desires to be god, who has lost his creatureliness: "Imago dei – bound to the world of the Creator and deriving life from the Creator; sicut dues – the creator-human-being who lives on the basis of the divide…between good and evil. Imago dei, sicut deus, agnus dei [Lamb of God] – the human being who is God incarnate, who was sacrificed for humankind sicut deus, in true divinity slaying its false divinity and restoring the imago dei" *DBWE* 3, 113 (*DBW* 3, 104–105).

[36] *DBWE* 2, 74–76 (*DBW* 2, 67–70). Once again Bonhoeffer seems to be relying on the theology of Reinhold Seeberg, referencing his *Lehrbuch der Dogmengeschichte*; cf. *DBWE* 2, 75, note 88 (*DBW* 2, 70, note 88).

its requisite modifications, effectively blocking the path to a genuinely theological concept of sin and grace. Once the two "like-unlike" images of being are fixed in their interrelatedness, neither human nor divine contingent activity – sin and grace – are conceivable: "everything must already patterned, in principle, on the ontological concept of analogy."[37]

Bonhoeffer is also troubled by what he sees as the theological implications in the concept of existence as supposedly articulated by Thomism. He contends that according to Aquinas, human beings, who exist in the tension between *esse* and *essentia*, must already have within themselves, as a possibility of existence, the possibility of contemplating the divine "is," that is the identity of *esse* and *essentia*. It logically follows from this concept of existence that one is authorized to regard as implicitly already at hand the ways that God and human beings are related, and which therefore can only be made explicit within the limits of the *analogia entis*. For Bonhoeffer, this inevitably means that in the end human existence not only is comprehensible through itself, it also has access to God apart from revelation.[38]

Is Bonhoeffer's understanding of Aquinas on the question of analogy in general, and in particular his conception of the relationship between God and the world, accurate? Unfortunately, no. Bonhoeffer's view involves some fundamental misconceptions that reveal him to be a child of his time theologically. Aquinas is frequently either celebrated or reviled for a theory of analogy that lays the groundwork for a systematic metaphysics or general ontology. But on closer inspection, writes Burrell, it turns out that he never had such a theory: "Rather he made do with a few vague remarks and ... grammatical astuteness."[39] Aquinas thus insists that our language is able to *show* what it otherwise cannot *say*. In the hands of his disciples, these remarks and his adept handling of grammatical subtleties became reified theory.[40]

We must ask ourselves: does every formulation of the *analogia entis* invariably seek to analogize God and creatures under the more general (and univocal) category of being, as Bonhoeffer seems to assume? If the answer is yes, then his criticisms are warranted, and his association of this concept with the theological anthropology and natural theology of liberal Protestant thought is justified. There is no question that certain theologians, beginning with Duns Scotus, have used the notion of analogy in precisely this way. It is Scotus who, on the basis of a general theory of being, insists that God "is" in the same way that any creature "is," the only dif-

---

[37] *DBWE* 2, 75 (*DBW* 2, 69).
[38] Cf. *DBWE* 2, 75 (*DBW* 2, 69).
[39] David B. Burrell, *Aquinas: God and Action* (London 1979), 55.
[40] Burrell, *Aquinas*, 6.

ference being that of a greater quantity of eminence.[41] Some such theory is especially necessary if, as Bonhoeffer believes, Aquinas sets about constructing a proportional analogy. A proportional analogy stipulates that God is related to the human being "as being is to becoming," or to put it in mathematical terms, a:b::c:d. If we know three of the terms, *and* know the meaning of the predicates, we can derive the value of the fourth. Aquinas very clearly states, however, that theology cannot meet the first condition, that is, know anything about the nature of God, and thus no knowledge of God can be arrived at by means of proportional analogy.[42]

I would submit, therefore, that Aquinas does not attempt to analogize God and creatures under a general category of being. He seeks instead to analogize the concept of being in the difference between God and creatures, which sets up a very different kind of argument. Far from undermining a properly theological conception of God's transcendence or destroying the Christian concept of revelation, this use of analogy gives us the linguistic resources to name the infinite gap between God and creatures while at the same time affirming that this gap manifests itself in the world in a way that respects the reality appropriate to God, who is infinitely determined and thus *is* the act of distance posited by the analogical interval (thereby satisfying Bonhoeffer's concern that it is God's act that creates finite being), and the human being, who participates in the infinite plenitude that is God.[43] As conceived by Aquinas, the concept of *analogia entis* does not authorize creatures to ascend up a chain of inferences about discrete essences in order to arrive at a cognitive grasp of the nature of God. On the contrary, it undermines any essentialist idea of the relationship between God and the world, and rules out of bounds a naïve natural theology predicated on such a conception.[44]

A crucial shortcoming in Bonhoeffer's critique of Aquinas (or as he puts it, Thomas-Przywara) is his failure to take into account the complex dialectic of the cataphatic and the apophatic that is central to Aquinas' inquiry into the analogical relationship between God and the world. His claim that Aquinas conceives of God and human being as two substances that stand over, and subsist in relative independence from each other, suggests that a real relationship exists for God between creator and creature, a position that Aquinas explicitly denies.[45] Moreover, like many Protestant

---

[41] See John Milbank, *Theology and Social Theory: Beyond Secular Reason* (Cambridge, MA. 1990), 302–303, and David B. Burrell, *Analogy and Philosophical Language* (New Haven, CT. 1973), 95–118.

[42] Turner, *Faith, Reason and the Existence of God*, 203–204.

[43] David Bentley Hart, *The Beauty of the Infinite: The Aesthetics of Christian Truth* (Grand Rapids, MI. 2003), 242.

[44] Hart, *The Beauty of the Infinite*, 242.

[45] *Summa Theologiae*, Ia. 13. 7; cf. Ia. 45. 3. ad. 1.

thinkers before and after him, Bonhoeffer does not acknowledge that Aquinas very carefully distinguishes between demonstrating *that* God is, which he believes is possible, and saying *what* God is, which he does not: "Now, because we cannot know what God is, but rather what He is not (*scire non possumus quid sit*)."[46] Aquinas contends that we can demonstrate that "God exists," and affirm that predicating existence of God has some meaning from having been shown to be true, but at the same time the very success of this argument also demonstrates that, when predicated of God, we do not know what "exists" means in this case. Aquinas' approach to analogy demonstrates not only "the need for, and the inseparably mutual logics of, both affirmative and negative theologies," but he also shows that the structure and dynamic of human reason is implicated in dialectical tension between knowing and unknowing, thus gesturing toward the essential mystery.[47]

Unfortunately, Bonhoeffer joins many over the years who assume that just because Aquinas commandeers certain concepts from classical and post-classical thought, he is reasoning in the manner of a Plato or an Aristotle. On the contrary: in Aquinas' hands the concepts of *esse* (literally the infinitive "to be") and *essentia* belong not to the domain of "a general theory of being," "a systematic metaphysics," or as we are wont to describe it, an ontotheology, but to the Jewish and Christian doctrine of creation.[48] Indeed, there are some who would turn the table on Bonhoeffer, arguing that the wholesale rejection of the analogy of being effectively denies that creation is an act of grace that reveals the divine love, and becomes instead a Hegelian moment of alienation or dialectical negation. In addition, repudiating the *analogia entis* does not protect the transcendence of the triune God, but objectifies the divine as either a sublime absence or a contradiction. As a result, writes David Hart, "one is left with a duality that inevitably makes of God and creation a dialectical opposition, thus subordinating God to being after all."[49]

Finally, these scholars also argue that without the analogy of being, properly conceived, the concept of revelation is rendered null and void, for it is only to the extent that creaturely being is analogous to divine being, and thus capable of becoming participants in the divine nature (2 Pet. 1:4), that God can show himself as God. Without this similarity grounded in creation "there would be no revelation otherwise, only legislation, emanating from an ontic god separated from us by an impossible distance, or

---

[46] *Summa Theologiae*, Ia. 1. 3, 14. For a classic case of failing to take into account the cataphatic-apophatic dialectic in Aquinas see Jürgen Moltmann, *The Trinity and the Kingdom of God*, translated by Margaret Kohl (San Francisco 1981), 12.

[47] Turner, *Faith, Reason and the Existence of God*, 211; cf. 51, 79.

[48] McCabe, *God Matters*, 43.

[49] Hart, *The Beauty of the Infinite*, 242.

perhaps the ghostly call of the gnostic's stranger God."[50] According to Hans Urs von Balthasar, if revelation is centered in Jesus Christ, by definition there is a periphery to this center: "Thus, as we say, the order of the Incarnation presupposes the order of creation, which is not identical with it. And, because the order of creation is oriented to the order of the Incarnation, it is structured in view of the Incarnation: it contains images, analogies, as it were, disposition, which in a true sense are the presuppositions for the Incarnation."[51] Aquinas and his theological heirs can thus account for the distinction between human being "in-Adam" and "in-Christ" without sacrificing the postlapsarian continuity of creatureliness (as Bonhoeffer eventually comes to recognize in *Ethics*).[52]

In spite of its shortcomings, Bonhoeffer's recognition of the importance of this question of analogy, and his efforts in *Act and Being* to reconcile Barth's actualism with an ontology embedded in a theology of being-in-Christ, should be taken as a call for both parties to continue to engage each other on this issue, to seek ways to go on and go further in an age where secular human reason no longer equates its limits with the limits of reality.[53] The desire of Bonhoeffer and Aquinas to secure the preeminent role of revelation in the economy of salvation, and to rightly conceive of divine transcendence, is one possible *point de départ*; Bonhoeffer's proposal for an *analogia relationis* in *Creation and Fall*[54] is another. Barth writes at one point that there is only a hair's breadth between the two positions (though he also states that, due to the similarity, one must then say that they teach very different things).[55] Could it be that as this debate ages the hair is growing thinner and less distinct?

If the question of the status of the *analogia entis* represents in Bonhoeffer's one opportunity for *rapprochement* between Protestants and Catholics on the question of true transcendence, his recovery of the concept of the natural in *Ethics* affords another. Bonhoeffer, in part on the basis of Josef Pieper's re-working of the theology of Thomas Aquinas, decides to reach out to the old and new Catholic wisdom, with a special concentration on

---

[50] Hart, *The Beauty of the Infinite*, 242.

[51] Hans Urs von Balthasar, *The Theology of Karl Barth*, translated by Edward T. Oakes (San Francisco 1992), 163.

[52] *DBWE* 6, 165 (*DBW* 6, 157–158): "We can only know from the Lord, who is coming and has come, what being human and being good are. Because Christ comes, therefore we should be human and be good ... He comes to his creation that, despite the fall, remains his creation. Christ comes not to devils but to human beings, certainly to sinful, lost, and damned humans, but still to human beings. Because Christ comes to them, because Christ redeems them from sin and from the power of the devil, sinful human beings are still human, the fallen creation remains creation."

[53] See von Balthasar, *The Theology of Karl Barth*, 365.

[54] *DBWE* 3, 65 (*DBW* 3, 61).

[55] Karl Barth, *CD* I.1, 239.

the concept of the natural.[56] He reclaims and develops this notion for Protestant theology in connection with the relationship between ultimate and penultimate: "The origin and essence of all Christian life are consummated in the one event that the Reformation has called justification of the sinner by grace alone. It is not what a person is per se, but what a person is in this event, that gives us insight into the Christian life. Here the whole length and breadth of human life is concentrated in one moment, one point."[57] In this event, and as a consequence of it, human beings are free for God and for each other.

Ultimate and penultimate, though distinct, do not exist in isolation from each other. The ultimate or last word stands in a generative relationship with the things before the last, the penultimate. The things before the last, which he defines as being human (*Menschsein*) and being good (*Gutsein*), possess no separate, autonomous existence: "There is no penultimate as such, as if something or other could justify itself as being in itself penultimate; but the penultimate becomes what it is only through the ultimate, that is, in the moment when it has already lost its own self-sufficiency." But it is also the case that the penultimate precedes the ultimate, and so "it is the case that being human precedes being justified, and seen from the perspective of the ultimate must precede it."[58] Any arbitrary destruction of the penultimate – for example, when a human life is denied the goods that are proper to it – does serious harm to the ultimate, and hinders a life of grace and faith.

For Bonhoeffer the natural functions as a mediating concept between ultimate and penultimate, distinct from the created, in order to take into account the falleness of humankind, and also from the sinful, to include in it the created. The natural is that which, after the fall, is directed towards the coming of Christ, while the unnatural is that which has closed itself off against the coming of Christ. He thus uses the mediating categories of natural and unnatural typologically, as anticipations and refusals, respectively, of justification. Bonhoeffer then asserts, in terms that are reminiscent of Aquinas, that, "The natural does not compel the coming of Christ," and hence it is truly unmerited grace, nor does "the unnatural make it impossible; in both cases the real coming is an act of grace,"[59] an act, which as he says elsewhere, *is* the ultimate.[60] For Aquinas, human beings were created

---

[56] "Afterword" to *Ethics* in *DBWE* 6, 419 (*DBW* 6, 424).
[57] *DBWE* 6, 146 (*DBW* 6, 137).
[58] *DBWE* 6, 159–160 (*DBW* 6, 151–152).
[59] *DBWE* 6, 173 (*DBW* 6, 165).
[60] *DBWE* 6, 163 (*DBW* 6, 155–156).

with a natural desire to see and participate in God, but that desire can only be realized by God's gracious initiative.[61]

Given his interest in, and recovery of the concept of the natural, it is not surprising that Bonhoeffer sees reason as fully embedded in its essential characteristics. "The natural," he writes, "is that form of life preserved (*erhalten*) by God for the fallen world that is directed towards justification, salvation and renewal through Christ."[62] Formally the natural is determined by God's intention to preserve the world and direct it towards Christ and hence in this aspect can only be discerned in relation to Christ. Materially the natural is itself the form of preserved life, embracing the whole of humanity. Reason belongs to the material dimension of the natural as the source of knowledge of itself. It is not a divine principle of knowledge and order that can raise human beings above the natural, but is itself a part of creation that has been graciously preserved by God, and thus wholly embedded in the natural. Its function is to take in (*vernehmen*) as a unity that which is whole and universal in reality. The natural and reason are thus correlated with each other, the former as the form of being of the preserved life, the latter as the form of its awareness. Reason is suited to this task because it too is fully implicated in the fall, hence it "perceives only what is given in the fallen world, and, indeed, exclusively according to its content."[63]

The links between Bonhoeffer's concept of the natural, and especially his understanding of reason, to the ideas of Aquinas are complex. Bonhoeffer is once again relying on secondary sources for his understanding of the Thomistic tradition, in this case, Pieper, whose book *Reality and the Good* he had read, and which formed a basis for his reflections on these questions. By all appearances he draws his definition of reason in *Ethics*, "the part of this preserved form of life that is able to make us conscious, i.e., to 'take in' as a unity, the whole and the universal in reality,"[64] almost directly from Pieper: "First of all, we must not overlook the fact that 'reason' here not only includes but means the essential relation to reality. It is nothing else than the power of man to take into himself the truth of real things."[65]

Bonhoeffer's contention that the natural, including reason, is that within the created order which is open to the coming of Christ and the ultimate, resonates with Aquinas' famous axiom about the relationship between na-

---

[61] Saint Thomas Aquinas, *Summa Contra Gentiles*, 3:55–57, translated by Anton C. Pegis (Notre Dame, IN. 1975).
[62] *DBWE* 6, 174 (*DBW* 6, 166).
[63] *DBWE* 6, 175 (*DBW* 6, 167).
[64] *DBWE* 6, 174 (*DBW* 6, 167).
[65] Josef Pieper, *Living the Truth: The Truth of all Things* and *Reality and the Good*, translated by Lothar Krauth and Stella Lange (San Francisco 1989), 116.

ture and grace or supernature: "Since therefore grace does not destroy nature, but perfects it, natural reason should minister to faith as the natural bent of the will ministers to charity."[66] Yet he still sees a fundamental divide between his understanding of reason and that put forward by "Catholic theory." The differences he sees are twofold. First, he contends that the full scope of reason is completely entangled in the fall, whereas in Catholic thought it is said to retain "an essential integrity."[67] Second and related to the first point, he believes that Catholic doctrine teaches that reason is able to grasp not just the material determinations of the natural, but the formal determinations as well. That is to say, God's intention to preserve the world and direct it towards Christ, which according to Bonhoeffer can be discerned only in actual relation to Christ, can be "taken in" by unaided reason.

It is difficult to know how to reconcile these caveats with what Bonhoeffer otherwise says regarding the natural. Surely he believes that reason retains its integrity qua the natural, which according to his own account includes being human, for as he observes, "being human precedes being justified."[68] He also distinguishes what is natural from what is sinful, though the former is not thereby separated from the latter. It is hard to avoid the conclusion that an ambiguity often found in many Protestant conceptions of human nature, but one that he otherwise manages to circumvent, somehow finds its way back into his thinking on this matter. In the typical Protestant account sin does not just impoverish, rob or weaken human nature but destroys its essence. Nature refers to humankind's original creation, but this no longer exists. And at the same time humankind's sinfulness defines its essence. Hence the ambiguity: sin is both unnatural, contrary to nature, but also now, after the fall, the very expression of human nature.[69]

It would seem, then, that in this disagreement over the scope of reason as part of the concept of the natural we have returned to the question we dealt with in connection to the analogy of being, namely, does Aquinas and his theological offspring claim that human beings, in their natural capacity to reason, have access to God's intention to preserve the world and direct it towards Christ apart from revelation? If so, then perhaps they have imprisoned God and human beings within a systematic metaphysics, and Bonhoeffer's critique has merit. On the other hand, if as I have already argued, that Aquinas neither

---

[66] *Summa Theologiae*, la. 1. 6. ad. 2.
[67] *DBWE* 6, 175, note 1 (*DBW* 6, 167, note 1).
[68] *DBWE* 6, 160 (*DBW* 6, 152).
[69] As Emil Brunner observes in his discussion of Calvin. Emil Bruner, "Nature and Grace," in Emil Brunner and Karl Barth, *Natural Theology: Comprising "Nature and Grace" by Professor Dr. Emil Brunner and the Reply "No!" by Dr. Karl Barth*, translated by Peter Fraenkel (London 1946), 38.

makes such a claim nor does his theology allow for it to be made by others, then Bonhoeffer's description of the difference between his understanding of the concept of the natural and that of Aquinas does not stand up to scrutiny. Indeed the genius of Bonhoeffer's reformulation of this concept is that it allows for us to talk about what it means to be a human being while still acknowledging our fallenness.

IV. Conclusion

Bonhoeffer's interest in the early theological tradition of the church is not limited to the works of Augustine and Aquinas. In his later writings in particular he increasingly adopts idioms from patristic and medieval thought. In *Ethics*, for example, he states that the subject matter of a Christian ethic "*is God's reality revealed in Christ become real [Wirklichwerden] among God's creatures.*"[70] This way of putting the ethical question means, among other things, that the question of the good "becomes the question of participating in God's reality revealed in Christ."[71] As the editors of the *Ethics* volume observe, this kind of emphasis on humanity's participation in the reality of the triune God, though standard fare among the Church Fathers up to the time of Aquinas, is exceedingly rare among Protestants, especially in Germany in 1940.[72]

One finds similar expressions at several points in *Letters and Papers from Prison*. In the course of his critique of the religious *a priori* Bonhoeffer asserts that, "It is not the religious act that makes the Christian, but participation in the sufferings of God in the secular life. That is *metanoia*: not in the first place thinking about one's own needs, problems, sins, and fears, but allowing oneself to be caught up into the way of Jesus Christ, into the messianic event."[73] And in his "Outline for a Book" he writes: "Our relation to God is not a 'religious' relationship to the highest, most powerful, and best Being imaginable – that is not authentic transcendence – but our relation to God is a new life in 'existence for others', through participation in the being of Jesus."[74]

Another example of his use of patristic idioms is found in *Ethics*, where Bonhoeffer offers a variation on a key teaching of the patristic period, and of Athanasius and Augustine in particular,[75] asserting that, "Human beings

---

[70] *DBWE* 6, 49 (*DBW* 6, 34).
[71] *DBWE* 6, 50 (*DBW* 6, 34–35).
[72] *DBWE* 6, 96, note 85 (*DBW* 6, 83, note 77).
[73] *LPP*, 361–62 (*DBW* 8, 535–536).
[74] *LPP*, 381 (*DBW* 8, 558).
[75] Athanasius, *On the Incarnation*, §54 (Crestwood, NY. 2000), 93; Augustine, *The City of God*, XXI.16 (Dyson, 1076).

become human because God became human."⁷⁶ Though some contend that this statement represents a reversal of the ancient dictum that God became human so that humans might become divine,⁷⁷ I would argue that this is not the case, appearances to the contrary notwithstanding. To be sure, Bonhoeffer does state that human beings are not transformed into an alien form, the form of God, but into the form that belongs to them as God's human creatures. With this comment, however, he is contending not so much with patristic thought and its notions of *theosis*, deification or divinization, as with those who are not well versed in the theological grammar of the fathers, who would never have ever asserted that human beings are transformed into an alien form, be it that of God or of anything else.⁷⁸

In closing permit me to cite one final example of Bonhoeffer's embrace of patristic expression. In a letter to Eberhard Bethge written on 19 December 1943, Bonhoeffer recalls a few lines in a hymn by Paul Gerhardt, set in the mouth of the Christ-child:

Let pass, dear brothers, every pain;
What you have missed I'll bring again.⁷⁹

Bonhoeffer interprets the phrase, "I'll bring again," in the context of the doctrine of recapitulation adumbrated in Ephesians 1:10 and paradigmatically articulated by Irenaeus. It alludes to the fact that nothing ultimately is lost, that everything is taken up in Christ, where it is transformed, made transparent, and freed from all selfish desire: "Christ restores all this as God originally intended it to be, without the distortion resulting from our sins."⁸⁰ The thought that God seeks what has been driven away is a magnificent concept that is filled with comfort. As he often does, Bonhoeffer here joins his voice with the church catholic in affirming this word of hope.

---

⁷⁶ *DBWE* 6, 96 (*DBW* 6, 83).

⁷⁷ "Editor's Introduction" to *Ethics* in *DBWE* 6, 6. Cf. also *DBWE* 6, 96, note 86.

⁷⁸ John Meyendorff, in his classic survey of Eastern Orthodox theology, puts it this way: "En-hypostasized in the Logos, Christ's humanity, in virtue of the 'communication of idioms', is penetrated with divine 'energy'. It is, therefore, a *deified* humanity, which, however, does not in any way lose its human characteristics. Quite to the contrary. These characteristics become even more real and authentic by contact with the divine model according to which they were created. In this deified humanity of Christ's man is called to participate, and to share in its deification." John Meyendorff, *Byzantine Theology: Historical Trends and Doctrinal Themes* (New York, second edition 1979), 163–164.

⁷⁹ *LPP*, 170 (*DBW* 8, 246). These lines are from the second part of the fifth stanza of Paul Gerhardt's Christmas hymn, "Fröhlich soll mein Herze springen."

⁸⁰ *LPP*, 170 (*DBW* 8, 246).

Peter Frick

The *Imitatio Christi* of Thomas à Kempis and Dietrich Bonhoeffer*

I. Introduction

No other spiritual classic shaped Bonhoeffer's theology of spiritual formation as much as Kempis's *Imitatio Christi*.[1] It is, therefore, a curious fact that in Bonhoeffer research there is no study that examines the influence of the medieval Augustinian monk Thomas à Kempis (1380–1471)[2] on the life and thought of Dietrich Bonhoeffer (1906–1945).[3] In view of this lacuna, the objective of this present study is to examine the thought of Kempis on the basis of his spiritual classic, the *Imitatio Christi*, a work he finished around the year 1427. Our main question is how this work shapes and influences Bonhoeffer's theological development and lifelong convictions on the spiritual life.

As a careful reading of Bonhoeffer's writings will show, the theological and spiritual insights of Kempis became critical for his theological formation as early as his teaching career at the University of Berlin and as late as his imprisonment in Tegel. The first chronological reference to Kempis in

---

* With gratitude I acknowledge the financial support for this research from the Social Sciences and Humanities Research Council of Canada.

[1] Not even the Spiritual Exercises of Saint Ignatius of Loyola, of which he owed a copy (cf. *DBWE* 6, 407, note 63; *DBW* 6, 411, note 63) had such an impact on Bonhoeffer. It is noteworthy to point out that St. Ignatius treasured the *Imitatio Christi* himself very much and used it for his own spiritual exercises. Indeed, "so devoted was Ignatius to this spiritual classic that he read a chapter a day for the rest of his life and had it on a table at his bedside when he died;" cf. *The Spiritual Exercises of St. Ignatius*, translated by Louis J. Puhl, Vintage Spiritual Classic (New York 2000), xv.

[2] For a succinct introduction on the life and thought of Kempis see Ulrich Köpf, "Thomas von Kempen," in *TRE* 33, 480–483, Nikolaus Staubach, "Thomas von Kempen," *RGG* 8, 377 and the older but still excellent article by Vincent Scully, "Thomas à Kempis," in *Catholic Encyclopedia* (New York 1912), volume 15.

[3] I was not able to access the contribution by Zen-emon Morino, "Zur Logik und Ethik der Nachfolge [Thomas a Kempis und Luther, Kierkegaard und Bonhoeffer]," in *Fukujû no Roni to Roni (Evangelium und Welt)* 3 (1965), 26–31. This is the only entry (#605) that specifically names à Kempis in Ernst Feil and Barbara E. Fink (eds.), *International Bibliography on Dietrich Bonhoeffer/Internationale Bibliographie zu Dietrich Bonhoeffer* (Gütersloh 1998).

Bonhoeffer's written oeuvre is in 1932. Bonhoeffer's grandmother, Julie Bonhoeffer, expresses appreciation for her grandson's gift, apparently a copy of the *Imitatio Christi*, on the occasion of her 90th birthday. In a letter she thanks Bonhoeffer and mentions that she was already familiar with this book. Nonetheless, she says, "Du hast mich sehr erfreut mit dem Thomas von Kempen. Ich lese sehr gerne des Morgens ... ein paar Abschnitte; freilich war mir das Büchlein von früher bekannt."[4] At the time of his grandmother's birthday in January 1932, Bonhoeffer was not yet 26 years old. Possibly he had read Kempis even during his teen years, but our sources do not allow us to draw such a conclusion.

The latest chronological datum in Bonhoeffer's life regarding Kempis can be traced to the end of 1943. According to Eberhard Bethge's masterful biography, Bonhoeffer read Kempis – in a Latin edition[5] – in his cell in Tegel prison during November and December of that year.[6] Between these two chronological markers lies the period of the Berlin, London and Finkenwalde years, namely 1932–1938 – the period that stands out as the one in which Bonhoeffer was most deeply influenced by Kempis's classic work. That influence becomes conspicuously transparent in his own spiritual classics, *Discipleship* and *Life Together*.

II. Discipleship

Bonhoeffer lectured on the various theological aspects pertaining to discipleship when he was director of the underground seminary of the Confess-

---

[4] *DBW* 11, 106.

[5] Bonhoeffer's Latin edition was that of M. J. Pohl (ed.), *Thomas à Kempis. Werke*, vol. 2, *Imitatio Christi* (Freiburg 1904). This Latin copy was given by Bonhoeffer's parents to Bishop George Bell on the occasion of his visit to Berlin in October 1945. It contains the following hand-written dedication: "In seinem Testament bittet unser Sohn Dietrich Ihnen, Herr Lordbischof, ein Buch aus seiner Bibliothek zur Erinnerung an ihn zu übersenden. Er hat diesen Thomas a Kempis noch im Gefängnis in Tegel bei sich gehabt. Eltern Bonhoeffer. Oktober 45." Right below these lines there is the following typed remark: "This book was sent from prison by Dietrich Bonhoeffer to be given to his friend George Bell, Bishop of Chichester, and was handed to him by his parents on October 29 1945. It was given to the Deutsche Evangelische Kirche, in memory of them both, by his wife Henrietta Bell. Saturday November 28 1959." The signature of Henrietta Bell follows. The copy is now located at the Bonhoeffer Church in Forest Hill, London. Cf. *DBW* 8, 246–247, note 20.

[6] Eberhard Bethge, *Dietrich Bonhoeffer*, 943, provides a detailed list of all the books Bonhoeffer read during his imprisonment from April 1943 until April 1945; among the 85 works listed is *The Imitation of Christ* by Thomas à Kempis.

ing Church in Finkenwalde from 1935 to 1937.[7] Shortly after the closing of the seminary in October 1937, his book *Discipleship* [*Nachfolge*] was published in November. However, as Bethge asserts, "both the theme and the underlying thesis of *Discipleship* were already fully evolved before 1933, but the book owes its single-minded, exclusive claims to that year."[8] With Hitler's rise to power, the year 1933 foreshadowed what was to happen in Germany politically. Theologically, Bonhoeffer attempted to work out an understanding of the Christian faith that could take account of the changing ecclesiological reality. In this regard, the decade of the 1930s was decisive for shaping his overall theology. We know from the lecture notes of former students that Bonhoeffer was increasingly attentive to Kempis's *Imitatio Christi* during the winter semester 1932–1933 at the University of Berlin. According to the notes of Erich Klapproth, a student who had attended Bonhoeffer's lectures on "Schöpfung und Sünde" (Creation and Sin),[9] Bonhoeffer commented in his introduction on the importance of hearing God's word in the context of doing a spiritual exercise (*exercitium*). The significance of *exercitium* arose again during the final session of the seminar on Theological Psychology, according to Hilde Pfeiffer's notes.[10] Another participant in the seminar and later a seminarian in the fourth course at Finkenwalde, Gerhard Krause, explicitly asserts that Bonhoeffer's exercises in that seminar "reproduced Thomas à Kempis's *Imitation of Christ*."[11] Krause thus establishes the connection between Bonhoeffer's emphasis on spiritual exercises and Kempis's *Imitatio*. Similarly, we are told by Herbert Jehle, a friend of Bonhoeffer's who studied physics at Cambridge when Bonhoeffer was in London, that during their frequent visits in London they discussed the subject of Christian community and agreed that the reading of St. Francis and Thomas à Kempis's *Imitation of Christ* would be important in that regard.[12]

A second major theological theme linking Kempis's *Imitatio Christi* and Bonhoeffer's *Discipleship* is that of *Nachfolge*, "imitation" or "following after" Christ. Chronologically, the first reference to Bonhoeffer's work on what would later become the book *Nachfolge* is found in a letter Bonhoef-

---

[7] For a listing of the lectures and seminars during the five courses at Finkenwalde, cf. *DBW* 14, 1054–1064. For the seminarians' eager anticipation of the publication of *Discipleship*, cf. *DBWE* 4, 28.

[8] Bethge, *Dietrich Bonhoeffer*, 457.

[9] Published in 1933 as *Schöpfung und Fall* (*DBW* 3), *Creation and Fall* (*DBWE* 3).

[10] *DBWE* 3, 155 (*DBW* 3, 146).

[11] Cf. *DBWE* 4, 312 (*DBW* 4, 330) and Gerhard Krause's article, "Dietrich Bonhoeffer (1906–1945)," in TRE 7, 55–66. The friendship between Bonhoeffer and Krause eventually ended, mainly for reasons of divergent theological positions regarding the church struggle. See, for example, Krause's letter to Bonhoeffer in *DBW* 15, 150–154.

[12] Cf. Larry Rasmussen, "Interview mit Herbert Jehle (1. 3. 1968)," in *Bonhoeffer Jahrbuch/Yearbook* 2 (2005–2006), 110–121, here 116.

fer wrote at the end of April 1934 from his London pastorate to his Swiss friend Erwin Sutz, a fellow student whom he met at Union Theological Seminary. In this letter he comments on the significance of the Sermon on the Mount for the German church struggle and then, towards the end, returns to the same theme in more detail. He says: "Please write and tell me sometime how you preach about the Sermon on the Mount. I'm currently trying to do so, to keep it infinitely plain and simple, but it always comes back to *keeping* the commandments and not trying to evade them. *Following* Christi – what that really is, I'd like to know – it is not exhausted by our concept of faith. I am doing some writing that I think of as a 'spiritual exercise' – only as a first step."[13]

Here Bonhoeffer makes the connection between *Nachfolge*, the Sermon on the Mount, and *exercitium* – all subjects that figure prominently in *Discipleship*. His statement "*Nachfolge* Christi – was das ist, möchte ich wissen" sounds like an explicit allusion to Kempis's *Imitatio*. The very fact that he decided to entitle his book *Discipleship* may also point to the influence of Kempis. The editors of *Discipleship* quite correctly point out the analogy in the book titles between "*Discipleship*" and "*Imitatio Christi*."[14] It is noteworthy here that the opening of the *Imitatio* encapsulates the spirit of *Discipleship* in a most succinct manner. The first chapter has the heading "The Imitation of Christ and Contempt for the Vanities of the World." Its initial lines read as follows: "'*Whoever follows Me will not walk in darkness*,' says the Lord. These are Christ's own words by which He exhorts us to imitate His life and His ways."[15]

In the preface to *Discipleship*, the theme of the book is expressed in three crucial questions: "What did Jesus want to say to us? What does he want from us today? How does he help us to be faithful Christians today?"[16] Although Bonhoeffer does not employ the terms "to follow" or "to imitate" Christ in the preface, the substance of the whole work leaves no doubt that what it means to follow Christ is the key point on almost every page. This theme rises to a powerful crescendo on the very last page of the book: "The followers look only to the one whom they follow. But now the final word about those who as disciples bear the image of the incarnate, crucified, and risen Jesus Christ, and who have been transformed into the image of God, is that they are called to be 'imitators of God.' The follower [*Nachfolger*] of Jesus is the imitator [*Nachahmer*] of God. 'Therefore, be

---

[13] *DBWE* 13, 136 (*DBW* 13, 129). In a letter to Reinhold Niebuhr, dated 13 July 1934 (cf. *DBWE* 13, 182–184 (*DBW* 13, 169–171)), Bonhoeffer once again remarks that he is writing on a work that addresses the questions raised in the Sermon on the Mount.

[14] See *DBWE* 4, 288, 303 (*DBW* 4, 304, 321).

[15] *Imitatio Christi* I 1. The English edition used in this study is that of Joseph N. Tylenda, *The Imitation of Christ* (New York 1998).

[16] *DBWE* 4, 37 (*DBW* 4, 21).

imitators of God, as beloved children' (Eph. 5:1)." In a skilful play on words, Bonhoeffer marries "following Jesus" and "imitating God" by weaving together the words *Nachfolger* and *Nachahmer* into the one notion of discipleship.

It is likewise significant that while Bonhoeffer was the director of the seminary in Finkenwalde he also taught a weekly seminar on the theme of *Nachfolge* at the University of Berlin during the winter semester of 1935–1936.[17] At first glance this seems curious. Why did he dare to present a seminar on a topic that most of his colleagues would not accept as even belonging to the discipline of theology? Bonhoeffer's teacher Adolf von Harnack had so shaped the theological faculty at Berlin in the spirit of Protestant liberalism and culture that a seminar on *Nachfolge* would surely seem misplaced, to say the least, in such an academic environment. An easy answer is difficult to come by, but as we shall see below, in a very considerable sense Bonhoeffer saw the question of following Christ to be an essential theological question.[18] Yet, as his letter to Erwin Sutz indicates,[19] he himself characterizes his work on the Sermon on the Mount neither as theological interpretation – as he did with his lecture on creation and sin during the semester at the University of Berlin[20] – nor as exegesis. Oddly, he calls it *exercitium*. Where does this designation come from?

The most plausible source is Kempis's *Imitatio Christi*, where numerous sections specifically correlate the Christian life with spiritual exercises. The heading of I 19 in the *Imitatio* reads, in the Latin, *De exercitiis boni Religiosi* [the exercises of a good religious]. Kempis speaks of the significance of exercises twice more in the same section. "If a prescribed exercise is omitted because of a brother in need," remarks the Augustinian monk, "or because we must perform some other charitable deed, the exercise may be fulfilled at a later time" (I 19, 3). Further on he exhorts, "See to it that you are not negligent in performing community exercises" (I 19, 5). Elsewhere in the *Imitatio* he remarks that the person who walks in the interior light "needs no special place nor definitive time to perform his religious exercises" (II 1, 7). At the beginning of book III Kempis asserts that "by daily prayerful exercises" the blessed understand the secrets of heaven better (III 1, 1). Finally,

---

[17] Cf. *DBW* 14, 1045. Bonhoeffer started this seminar on 12 November 1935 (to my knowledge, there are no written records of this seminar) and possibly finished 14 February 1936, the last day of his teaching career at the University of Berlin. On 5 August 1936 Bonhoeffer's license to teach theology at the University was officially rescinded; cf. *DBW* 14, 213–214.

[18] It is also evident that Bonhoeffer did not think that theological faculties were well equipped to prepare theology students for pastoral ministry. Cf. his letter to Erwin Sutz, 11 September 1934 (cf. *DBWE* 13, 217 (*DBW* 13, 204)), where he declares that he never really believed in the university; instead, new theological schools are needed to teach theology students within Christian community.

[19] Cf. *DBWE* 13, 136 (*DBW* 13, 129).

[20] The subtitle of *Creation and Fall* (*DBWE* 3) is *A Theological Exposition of Genesis 1–3*.

the heading of section IV 6 reads *Interrogatio de exercitio ante communionem* [exercises of examination before communion], and is further explained in IV 2: "Teach me the right way and give me some short exercises suitable for receiving Holy Communion."

How should we evaluate these affinities between Kempis's *Imitatio Christi* and Bonhoeffer? Given the following facts – that Bonhoeffer presented his grandmother with a copy of the *Imitatio Christi*, that he referred to *exercitium* in his teaching at Berlin, that these references can be clearly identified in Kempis, and that one student made the specific connection between these exercises and Kempis – we can sufficiently establish Kempis's influence on him. Moreover, even though Bonhoeffer does not provide any direct quotation from the *Imitatio* in the text of his *Discipleship*, the overlapping foci of both works are unmistakable. In part IV below, we will draw out the significance of these affinities in terms of Bonhoeffer's theological legacy.

III. Life Together

After the closing of Finkenwalde Seminary by the Gestapo in September 1937, Bonhoeffer crafted *Life Together* a year later "in a single stretch of four weeks" while he and Eberhard Bethge lived in Göttingen at the house of the Leibholz family, who had to emigrate to England.[21] Bonhoeffer is thus looking back at his experience of living in a Christian community among young theologians who aspired to become pastors. As director of the underground seminary for two and a half years he was both the key designer of the theological curriculum and the primary professor. However, we should realize that Bonhoeffer attached as much importance to the spiritual formation of the candidates as to their theological training. *Life Together* must be read as representing some of the core aspects that for Bonhoeffer constitute a genuine Christian community. It is instructive that in this regard he refers to and cites the thought of Kempis three times in the body of the main text.

The first explicit naming of Kempis and a reference to the *Imitatio Christi* is found in the third chapter, "The Day Alone," of *Life Together*. Bonhoeffer writes: "The silence of the Christian is listening silence, humble stillness that may be broken at any time for the sake of humility. It is silence in conjunction with the Word. This is what Thomas à Kempis meant when he said: 'No one speaks more confidently than the one who gladly remains silent'."[22]

---

[21] For details, see the introduction to *DBWE* 5, 3–4.
[22] *DBWE* 5, 85 (*DBW* 5, 68).

The second mention of Kempis is in the chapter entitled "Service." Bonhoeffer asserts that those wishing to serve others "must first learn to think little of themselves" and then cites Kempis's words to underscore his point: "The highest and most useful lesson is to truly know yourself and to think humbly of yourself. Making nothing of yourself and always having a good opinion of others is great wisdom and perfection (Thomas à Kempis)."[23] A few paragraphs further on in the same chapter he again insists that service for others entails recognizing that one's own sins are worse than those of others. "How could I possibly serve other persons in unfeigned humility," he asks, "if their sins appear to me to be seriously worse than my own?" To support his view, he enlists Kempis a third time as his spiritual advisor: "Do not believe that you have made any progress in the work of sanctification, if you do not feel deeply that you are less than all others (Thomas à Kempis)."[24]

Besides these three explicit references to Kempis in the main text of *Life Together*, there is at least one more direct citation from the *Imitatio Christi* that Bonhoeffer does not acknowledge. In between the second and third citations of Kempis's book, he says this: "Not considering oneself wise, but associating with the lowly, means considering oneself the worst of sinners."[25] The last phrase, "the worst of sinners," is taken straight from Kempis. In book IV of the *Imitatio*, the disciple makes the confession: "I am the worst of sinners."[26]

In addition to Bonhoeffer's acknowledged citations of the *Imitatio Christi* at several places in *Life Together*, we can discern further affinities between the two works. Even a cursory reading of both works reveals the parallel concerns of the two authors: the emphasis on silence, the Word of God, meditation, service, agapeic love and the need for confession; these topics we will further discuss in part V below. The spirit and substance of Kempis's *Imitatio Christi* is perhaps also visible in Bonhoeffer's structuring of *Life Together*, whose last chapter has as its subject the importance of "Confession and the Lord's Supper." At first glance this seems totally parallel with the *Imitatio*, at least for modern readers of that work. The reason is that most editions of it published since the 1950s place book IV, "On the Blessed Sacrament [of the Lord's Supper]," at the end. However, Bonhoeffer's Latin version reversed the order of books III and IV; that is, the topic of the Lord's Supper was not the last section of the *Imitatio*. Conceivably, Bonhoeffer also knew of a different order of the books in the *Imitatio*, perhaps from the (German?) copy he gave his grandmother as a birthday gift. Whatever the case, most relevant for our purposes is the fact

---

[23] *DBWE* 5, 96 (*DBW* 5, 80) quoting *Imitatio Christi* I 2, 5.

[24] *DBWE* 5, 98 (*DBW* 5, 82) and *Imitatio Christi* II 2, 2.

[25] *DBWE* 5, 97 (*DBW* 5, 81).

[26] *Imitatio Christi* IV 2, 3.

that both the *Imitatio Christi* and *Life Together* discuss the significance of the Lord's Supper towards the end of their respective discourses. Given what Bonhoeffer says about the transforming power of confession and partaking in the Lord's Supper, he evidently places this chapter at the end of his work for theological reasons. What the theological significance is, we will shortly examine.

Following the closing of the Findenwalde Seminary, Bonhoeffer continued the theological education of the pastoral candidates in the form of collective pastorates in Pomerania. One of his lectures was entitled "Thankfulness." The manuscript begins with a citation from Kempis and reads, in Bonhoeffer's German text, as follows: "Sei also dankbar für das Geringste, so wirst du würdig sein, Größeres zu empfangen." While Bonhoeffer indicates that this text is found on page 159 in his edition of the *Imitatio Christi*, the editors of the German edition identified the citation as section III 22, namely the one entitled "Remembering God's Many Benefits to Us."[27] However, after examining this text, it is clear that Bonhoeffer's citation is not from III 22, but from II 10, 5. Here Kempis remarks, "Be grateful, then, for even the least gift and you will be worthy of receiving greater ones."

Following the Finkenwalde years, a period for which we have ample evidence that Bonhoeffer was influenced by Kempis's *Imitatio Christi*, is followed by a second period in which Kempis seems once more a companion and theological encouragement. That period was during Bonhoeffer's imprisonment in the years 1943–1945.

IV. Letters and Papers from Prison

We have already seen that Bonhoeffer read Kempis's *Imitatio Christi* in his Tegel prison cell in November and December 1943. In two letters from that period, he refers to it. On the fourth Sunday of advent, 19 December 1943, he finished a letter to Eberhard Bethge that he had begun the day before. There he shares with his friend that he has discovered for himself, and to his surprise, the hymn "Ich steh an deiner Krippe hier [Beside Thy Cradle Here I Stand]" composed by Paul Gerhardt.[28] Then he says this

---

[27] Cf. *DBW* 15, 365, note 267.

[28] This Christmas hymn, put to music by J. S. Bach in 1736, consists of ten stanzas; however, it is rather speculative to determine whether certain stanzas were more important to Bonhoeffer than others (although he cites the second part of the fifth stanza in a letter to Eberhard Bethge from Tegel prison in 1943; cf. *LLP*, 170 and *DBW* 8, 246). The first stanza reads: "Ich steh and deiner Krippe hier, o Jesu, du mein Leben / ich komme, bring und schenke dir, was du mir hast gegeben / Nimm hin, es ist mein Geist und Sinn, Herz, Seel und Mut / nimm alles hin und laß dir's wohl gefallen."

about it: "I suppose one has to be alone for a long time, and meditate on it, to be able to take it in properly. Every word is remarkably full of meaning and beauty. There's just a slight flavour of the monastery and mysticism, but no more than is justified. After all, it's right to speak of 'I' and 'Christ' as well of 'we', and what that means can hardly be expressed better than it is in this hymn. There are also a few passages in a similar vein in the *Imitation of Christ*, which I'm reading now and then in the Latin (it reads much better in Latin than in German)."[29]

Given that Bonhoeffer composed this letter just before Christmas and that the Gerhard hymn is a traditional German Christmas piece, his discovery was most likely about how it depicts the life of Jesus. For, as he says, every word is "extraordinarily rich and beautiful." Concretely, he asserts, only a few other places in Kempis's *Imitation Christi* can rival the hymn's depth of expressing the relation between the I, we, and Christ. What this may mean for Bonhoeffer we will examine below.

The second – and chronologically last – reference to Kempis in Bonhoeffer's oeuvre occurs in another letter, written just three days after the one mentioned above. On 22 December 1943 Bonhoeffer again wrote to Bethge. He once more refers to the *Imitatio Christi*. At the very end of the letter he notes that "In der 'Imitatio Christi' las ich gerade: Custodi diligenter cellam tuam, et custodiet te! ('halte treu Wacht über deine Zelle und sie wird Wacht halten über dich')."[30]

V. Kempis's Influence on Bonhoeffer's Theology

We have traced the influence of Kempis's *Imitatio Christi* on Bonhoeffer's writings. Now our task is to examine how and why specific theological emphases in Kempis's work found their way into Bonhoeffer's own theology. We will focus on the themes of following Christ, suffering for Christ, negation of the self, spiritual love, spiritual exercises and meditation, and the Lord's Supper.

1. Following Christ

Eberhard Bethge boldly asserts that the most profound idea ever expressed by Bonhoeffer is that of "discipleship as participation in Christ's suffering for others, as communion with the Crucified One."[31] Indeed, in Bonhoef-

---

[29] *LPP*, 170 (*DBW* 8, 246–247).
[30] *LPP*, 175 (*DBW* 8, 254). The Latin text means "diligently guard your cell and your cell will guard you."
[31] Bethge, *Dietrich Bonhoeffer*, 456.

fer's theology it is absolutely inconceivable that faith could exist in any form apart from following Jesus Christ and the cost of suffering that such following may entail. Against the backdrop of the contemporary Lutheran view that following the commandments of Jesus is meant more metaphorically than literally,[32] Bonhoeffer argues otherwise in *Discipleship*. In a most uncomplicated way he insists that discipleship is "commitment to Christ. Because Christ exists, he must be followed. An idea about Christ, a doctrinal system, a general religious recognition of grace or forgiveness of sins does not require discipleship."[33] His words are directed against those who reduced Jesus' commands to an "inner willingness to invest everything for the kingdom of God" and thus fall prey to "the deliberate avoidance of simple, literal obedience."[34]

Why is Bonhoeffer so insistent that following Christ is the authentic hallmark of genuine faith? Why does he declare so unflinchingly that *"only the believers obey*, and *only the obedient believe."*[35] The answer, in brief, is that his conception of the significance of discipleship stems directly from his theological understanding of grace. During the second course in Finkenwalde in 1935–1936, he offered a lecture on "The Visible Church in the New Testament,"[36] in which he makes a crucial distinction between *hearing* the word of grace and *obeying* the word of grace. Those who hear God's word of grace encounter something entirely new in all their existence.[37] The word of grace demands a concrete, obedient response; otherwise it will be one's word of judgement rather than grace. The hearer of the word of grace cannot simply say that everything is fine with grace and life can go on as before. Discipleship is precisely the movement away from the word of salvific grace to obedience. In Bonhoeffer's words: "Where grace is being proclaimed, a person is confronted by the question of doing."[38] The emphasis on "the doing of grace" is also made explicitly in the *Imitatio Christi*. In one instance, Kempis puts these words in Jesus' mouth: "Whoever tries to withdraw himself from obedience at the same time withdraws himself from grace."[39]

---

[32] Cf. *DBWE* 4, 79 (*DBW* 4, 71).

[33] *DBWE* 4, 59 (*DBW* 4, 47).

[34] *DBWE* 4, 79 (*DBW* 4, 71).

[35] *DBWE* 4, 63 (*DBW* 4, 52); emphasis in original.

[36] Cf. *DBW* 14, 422–466.

[37] Bonhoeffer says (*DBW* 14, 428) that a person's "ganze Existenz [wird] vor etwas neues gestellt."

[38] *DBW* 14, 428: "Dort, wo Gnade verkündigt wird, [ist] der Mensch zur Frage nach dem Tun aufgerufen." In his reflections on the "New Life in Paul," Bonhoeffer summarizes his understanding that grace is discipleship in the poignant expression "Gnade *in* Nachfolge;" cf. *DBW* 14, 622.

[39] *Imitatio Christi* III 2, 1.

For both Kempis and Bonhoeffer it seems to go against the very core of being a Christian that one could lay hold of God's grace but fail to follow Jesus' commandments in obedience. Bonhoeffer works this out more fully in the third course at Finkenwalde, in a lecture on the new life of the Christian and discipleship. There he says that the new life in Christ is not merely a new state of being [*Zustand*] but an action [*Wandeln*], taking concrete and responsible steps.[40] In the next section of the lecture he asserts that "Acting in this space [in Christ] = *discipleship* in the Synoptics. Christian life is not a lifestyle but a constant remaining in Christ who has called."[41] Clearly, in all his remarks during the Finkenwalde years Jesus' call to follow required literal obedience. "Faith is only faith in deeds of obedience," Bonhoeffer admonishes, because "faith is possible only in this new state of existence created by obedience."[42] In this respect an earlier reference in one of his letters to Erwin Sutz is crucial: "*Following* Christi – what that really is, I'd like to know – it is not exhausted by our concept of faith."[43]

Bonhoeffer's sees a necessary connection between faith, grace, obedience, and discipleship. This raises the question of why this correlation is so crucial in his theology. Why, concretely, is discipleship [*Nachfolge*] not exhausted in the concept of faith? In *Discipleship* Bonhoeffer provides a succinct answer: it is "obedience within which discipleship can become real;"[44] hence, only faith that is obedient to the call of Christ *can* become real and genuine. Because "Jesus is the Christ, it has to be made clear from the beginning that his word is not a doctrine. Instead, it creates existence anew."[45] But this new existence is not automatic. For a person who has faith in Christ, obedience "puts [that person] into the situation of being able to believe."[46] Elsewhere Bonhoeffer explains that "the external works have to take place; *we have to get into the situation of being able to believe*."[47] Hence, what is absolutely indispensable is "a situation in which faith can begin."[48] This is the crux of every person's Christian life. Apart from a *situation* in which faith can begin, grow and mature – in other words, apart from obedience in a situation that requires obedience – faith

---

[40] *DBW* 14, 616.
[41] *DBW* 14, 618: "Wandeln in diesem Raum [in Christus] = *Nachfolgen* bei den Synoptikern. Christliches Leben ist nicht Lebensstil, sondern ist durchgehendes Bleiben an Christus, der gerufen hat" (emphasis in original).
[42] *DBWE* 4, 64 (*DBW* 4, 52–53).
[43] *DBWE* 13, 136 (*DBW* 13, 129).
[44] *DBWE* 4, 73 (*DBW* 4, 64).
[45] *DBWE* 4, 62 (*DBW* 4, 50).
[46] *DBWE* 4, 62 (*DBW* 4, 50).
[47] *DBWE* 4, 66 (*DBW* 4, 55); emphasis added.
[48] *DBWE* 4, 62 (*DBW* 4, 50).

and discipleship are mere doctrines and hence dead. Discipleship is thus "the road to faith [that] passes through obedience to Christ's call."[49]

It is difficult to decide exactly which chapters in Kempis's *Imitatio Christi* may have provided the impetus for Bonhoeffer to articulate his own theological view of discipleship in a Christian's life. But we may say with certainty that it was Kempis's work – conceivably more than anyone else's – that helped him formulate his own theology of obedient *Nachfolge* and carrying the cross of Christ.

2. Suffering for Christ

Even though Bonhoeffer says that Jesus' call to discipleship is essentially without content,[50] he nonetheless determines the focus of that call to be the cross of Christ. The correlation of the theme of discipleship – in its specific content of suffering and carrying one's cross – in both Kempis and Bonhoeffer can be further established on the basis of another text. As we mentioned above, Bonhoeffer read the section II 10, 5 in the *Imitatio Christi*[51] and cites it in the context of a discussion of the theme of thankfulness in the New Testament. Just a few lines below this very text, Kempis says this: "Jesus today has many lovers of His heavenly kingdom, but few of them carry his cross ... We all want to rejoice with Him, but few of us are willing to suffer anything for His sake ... Many admire His miracles, but few follow in the ignominy of His cross."[52]

Given the proximity of these statements to the text that Bonhoeffer cited, it seems very unlikely that he would not have known and identified with the sentiment expressed in the words just quoted. For here we have evidence that Kempis sees a correlation between following Jesus and carrying one's cross. In his own words, Bonhoeffer provides a clear echo: "Just as Christ is only Christ as one who suffers and is rejected, so a disciple is a disciple only in suffering and being rejected, thereby participating in crucifixion."[53] Moreover, just as Bonhoeffer maintains that faith is only faith in obedience, he similarly holds that "suffering becomes the identifying mark of a follower of Christ."[54] Indeed, the Christian's following of the call of Jesus culminates in a readiness to give even one's life. In Bonhoeffer's own famous and often-cited words, "Whenever Christ calls us, his

---

[49] *DBWE* 4, 63 (*DBW* 4, 51).
[50] Cf. *DBWE* 4, 58–59 and *DBW* 14, 620.
[51] Cited in *DBW* 15, 365.
[52] *Imitatio Christi* II 11:1.
[53] *DBWE* 4, 85 (*DBW* 4, 78).
[54] *DBWE* 4, 89 (*DBW* 4, 82).

call leads us to death."[55] Perhaps no passage is as profound in all of Bonhoeffer's work in expressing the interrelation between Christ, cross, suffering, grace and discipleship. In his reflections on the cross, Bonhoeffer writes: "The cross is neither misfortune nor harsh fate. Instead, it is suffering which comes from our allegiance to Jesus Christ alone. The cross is not random suffering, but necessary suffering. The cross is not suffering that stems from natural existence; it is suffering that comes from being Christian. The essence of the cross is not suffering alone; it is suffering and being rejected. Strictly speaking, it is being rejected for the sake of Jesus Christ, not for the sake of any other attitude or confession. A Christianity that no longer took discipleship seriously remade the gospel into a solace of cheap grace."[56]

In light of Bonhoeffer's uncompromising view of the cross and suffering, it comes as no surprise to read that "bearing [suffering] constitutes *being* a Christian [*Im Tragen besteht das Christsein*]."[57] Here again we have another crux of the Christian life. According to Bonhoeffer, bearing – that is, suffering – *constitutes* being a Christian. Indeed, suffering is the normal characteristic of every Christian. It is not merely a temporary addition in tough circumstances or a test for the more spiritual ones among us. It is rather a defining and ontological element of being a human being – as a Christian. Hence, to venture a comment in our post-modern context, suffering is not the fate of "those less fortunate" Christians in general or of those Christians who once were forced to live under Communist rule and now perhaps live under governments that despise democracy and freedom. Bonhoeffer's implied assertion that a Christian is *essentially a suffering disciple* squarely challenges those who never associate, let alone experience, suffering as Christians. Nonetheless, because "Christ suffers as vicarious representative for the world," his cross is "the triumph over suffering."[58] That is, in Christ's resurrection the ultimate suffering – death itself – died and hence came to an end for every believer.

Like Bonhoeffer but long before him, Kempis had grasped the centrality of suffering in the life of the Christian. In a section in the *Imitatio Christi* entitled "The Royal Road to the Holy Cross,"[59] Kempis repeatedly speaks of the nexus of the cross and suffering. "Why do you then fear to carry the cross?" he asks, but then immediately affirms that "This is the way that leads to the kingdom... In the cross alone do we find the soul's eternal salvation and hope of everlasting life. *Carrying His own cross Jesus* preceded you, and on the cross He died for you ... if you are His companion in suf-

---

[55] *DBWE* 4, 87 (*DBW* 4, 81).
[56] *DBWE* 4, 86 (*DBW* 4, 79–80).
[57] *DBWE* 4, 91 (*DBW* 4, 84); emphasis added.
[58] *DBWE* 4, 90 (*DBW* 4, 83).
[59] *Imitatio Christi* II. 12.

fering you shall likewise be His companion in glory."[60] Since the theme of suffering is so prevalent throughout the *Imitatio,* there can be little doubt it influenced Bonhoeffer's theology. It is telling, for example, that Kempis ended the section with a quotation of Mark 8:34 and thus pointed to another element in the disciple's faithful obedience: the negation of the self.

3. Negation of the Self

The disciple who follows Christ and carries his or her cross necessarily must have a certain self-understanding, namely the willingness to negate the self. Taking Jesus' words "If any want to become my followers, let them deny themselves and take up their cross and follow me"[61] literally, both Kempis and Bonhoeffer stress the act of self-negation. Kempis's *Imitatio Christi* is indeed saturated with remarks on self-negation. Throughout the text we find statements like this: "If I belittle myself, think of myself as nothing, throw off all self-regard and account myself to be dust, as I truly am, then Your grace will come upon me."[62] Elsewhere he commands the reader: "Stop loving yourself,"[63] "acquire genuine self-contempt,"[64] "realize that there is nothing more harmful to you in this world than self-love."[65] However, he also knew that no person naturally seeks to deny the self. "It is not according to man's nature to bear the cross and love it, to chastise the body and bring it into subjection, to avoid honors and be willing to suffer insults. It is not man's nature to despise one's self and to wish to be despised."[66]

We have already referred to several instances where Bonhoeffer cites from Kempis in *Life Together*. In this present context, it suffices to recall two of these. Bonhoeffer agrees with his forebear that "the highest and most useful lesson is to truly know yourself and to think humbly of yourself. Making nothing of yourself and always having a good opinion of others is great wisdom and perfection (Thomas à Kempis)."[67] Similarly, "Do not believe that you have made any progress in the work of sanctification, if you do not feel deeply that you are less than all others (Thomas à Kem-

---

[60] *Imitatio Christi* II. 12. 2.

[61] Mark 8:34, cited in the *Imitatio Christi* in II. 12.15 and by Bonhoeffer in *DBWE* 4, 84 (*DBW* 4, 77).

[62] *Imitatio Christi* III 8, 1. Similarly IV 15, 3: "The more perfectly a man renounces the things of earth and the more quickly he dies to himself by practicing self-contempt, the more quickly does grace come to him."

[63] *Imitatio Christi* III 11, 1.

[64] *Imitatio Christi* III 13, 1.

[65] *Imitatio Christi* III 27, 1.

[66] *Imitatio Christi* II. 12. 9.

[67] *DBWE* 5, 96 (*DBW* 5, 80) quoting *Imitatio Christi* I 2, 5.

pis)."⁶⁸ Certainly Kempis's characteristic stress on the Christian's denial of self greatly influenced Bonhoeffer's theology. But there seems to be a decisive difference in the two theologians' interpretation of what self-denial means. Kempis's many references to the denial, abnegation and even contempt for one's self are not taken over by Bonhoeffer. For the latter, the denial of self was not primarily a psychological but a theological issue.

For Bonhoeffer, the denial of self⁶⁹ must be seen against the backdrop of sin. As he acknowledged, it is an "extreme statement" to "consider oneself the worst of sinners."⁷⁰ To recognize oneself a sinner is not a psychological but a theological insight;⁷¹ more precisely, it is most of all a matter of revelation.⁷² Hence, recognition of being the worst sinner leads into the depth of humility. For how is it possible to serve "other persons in unfeigned humility if their sins appear to me to be seriously worse than my own?"⁷³ In other words, a *proper* self-understanding as a sinner – and not the denial of self – are significant in Bonhoeffer's theology. Two comments are in order here.

First, while markings are rarely seen anywhere in Bonhoeffer's copy of the *Imitatio Christi*,⁷⁴ one clear pencil marking does appear in the margin of a section entitled "The Need to Look at One's Self." The two lines Bonhoeffer marked read: "If you have scurried about meddling in all sorts of things, *what good has all this done you if you have neglected your soul's welfare*? If you wish to enjoy true peace and perfect union with God you must set all things aside and keep your eyes only upon yourself."⁷⁵ The context speaks of not placing "too much trust in ourselves," nor reproaching "others for their petty faults" or making "harsh judgement against another man." It is apparent from the context and Bonhoeffer's marking that

---

⁶⁸ *DBWE* 5, 98 (*DBW* 5, 82) and *Imitatio Christi* II 2, 2.

⁶⁹ Bonhoeffer unambiguously states in *DBWE* 4, 86 (*DBW* 4, 79): "Self-denial can never result in ever so many single acts of self-mortification or ascetic exercises. It does not mean suicide, because even suicide could be an expression of the human person's own will."

⁷⁰ *DBWE* 5, 97 (*DBW* 5, 81).

⁷¹ Cf. Bonhoeffer's affirmation of Luther's remark in the latter's *Lecture on the Letter to the Romans*: "*Sola fide credendum est nos esse peccatores* [by faith alone we know that we are sinners]" in *DBWE* 2, 136 (*DBW* 2, 135).

⁷² Cf. *DBWE* 9, 300 (*DBW* 9, 324). From Bonhoeffer's student days in Berlin we have a short note on Luther's *Lectures on the Letter to the Romans* that clarifies his view of these matters: "Theological logic intends to set itself free from psychologism. It does not speak of sin and revelation as contents of consciousness. Instead, it speaks of them as realities of revelation."

⁷³ *DBWE* 5, 98 (*DBW* 5, 82).

⁷⁴ The author was able to examine the copy that Bonhoeffer read while in Tegel prison (for details see note 4 above) in April 2005.

⁷⁵ *Imitatio Christi* II 5, 2. In his copy, Bonhoeffer made a pencil mark at II, V, line 20–22 (p. 67). Cf. Bethge, *Dietrich Bonhoeffer*, 430, on Bonhoeffer's habit of not marking the books he read.

the focus is not so much on the denial of self but on the *need* to have a proper self. And that proper self comes into being by not neglecting the soul's welfare and by freeing oneself "from all temporal cares."[76]

Second, we have mentioned Bonhoeffer's affirmation in a letter that "it's right to speak of 'I' [*es gibt ein ich*] and 'Christ' as well of 'we'."[77] Toward the end of his time in prison, he reflects on the 'I', 'we' and 'Christ' relation. However, he does not give us an interpretation of that relation other than to say that Gerhardt's hymn and "a few passages in a similar vein in the *Imitation of Christ*"[78] best express its meaning. We are left to speculate as to what Bonhoeffer meant, but we may venture at least a comment. In Gerhardt's hymn, in the first stanza, the Christian's relationship to Jesus is characterized as "you are my life." While a terse expression, it is conceivable that in Bonhoeffer's context of incarceration it meant what the hymn proclaims: the 'I' comes to Jesus and returns the gifts of life (spirit, purpose, heart, soul and courage). All of life is given by Jesus and all things are returned to him. In the exchange of giving, life becomes possible. Just as Jesus gave his life and thus made life possible for others, so analogously Bonhoeffer affirms the sentiment of the hymn in giving his life back to Jesus – and, a few months later, to Hitler's hangmen. The significance in all this is the paradox of receiving life by denying (but not obliterating) one's self. Christian faith that is not denying its own self cannot issue in fruitful discipleship.

4. Spiritual Love

In *Life Together* Bonhoeffer makes the radical differentiation between spiritual and psychological love. In his own words: "It is essential for Christian community that two things become clear right from the beginning. *First, Christian community is not an ideal, but a divine reality; second, Christian community is a spiritual [pneumatische] and not a psychic [psychische] reality.*"[79] Similarly, Bonhoeffer maintains that "because Christian community is founded solely on Jesus Christ, it is a spiritual [*pneumatische*] and not a psychic [*psychische*] reality."[80] For Bonhoeffer, this distinction is of such pertinence that without it a proper understanding and practice of Christian community becomes impossible. Underlying this distinction is Bonhoeffer's observation that it is quite possible to mistake a merely human community for a Christian one and for people to be drawn

---

[76] *Imitatio Christi* II 5. 3.
[77] Cf. *LPP*, 170 (*DBW* 8, 246–247).
[78] *LPP*, 170 (*DBW* 8, 246–247).
[79] *DBWE* 5, 35 (*DBW* 5, 22); emphasis in original.
[80] *DBWE* 5, 38 (*DBW* 5, 26).

together on the basis of some natural affinities rather than the unconditional love of Christ.

Kempis has similar though less developed views in the *Imitatio Christi*. There he declares, in the voice of Jesus, that "some individuals, in accord with their personal piety, are drawn to one or another of the saints, but this is a human affection or preference on their part and does not come from Me."[81] A few paragraphs further in the same section Kempis criticizes those who are drawn to the saints for the wrong reasons. These people, he says, "are insufficiently enlightened from above, rarely know how to love anyone with a perfect spiritual love. Such individuals are drawn to one or another person by natural affection or human friendship."[82]

Admittedly, we have no conclusive evidence that Bonhoeffer's critical distinction between spiritual and emotional love comes from his reading of Kempis's *Imitatio Christi*. It may be the case that Bonhoeffer was shaped in this regard by both Kempis and Kierkegaard.[83] At any rate, the decisive aspect for us is that Bonhoeffer's understanding of Christian community is fundamentally indebted to the fact that only Christ's unconditional agapeic love can be the foundation of Christian community.

5. Spiritual Exercises: Silence and Meditation

As we saw earlier, Gerhard Krause suggests that Bonhoeffer deliberately modeled his seminar at the University of Berlin in the winter of 1932–1933, entitled "Theological Psychology," on Kempis's *Imitatio Christi*. In the course of that seminar, Bonhoeffer made these remarks on Christian character formation: "The habits of a Christian character are distinct from individuality in that they are formed by exercise ... It is an exercise in which the person of habit looks beyond him/herself. Christian character as such is marked by the basic element of neglecting itself. Knowledge of myself as sinner, namely the knowledge of my justification, makes the formation of character into something secondary, penultimate, and yet significant as an *exercise*."[84]

On the one hand, these words once more illuminate Bonhoeffer's view that a Christian's knowledge of sin leads to a neglecting of oneself and re-

---

[81] *Imitatio Christi* III 58, 3.
[82] *Imitatio Christi* III 58, 6.
[83] Cf. the study below on Kierkegaard by Geffrey B. Kelly.
[84] *DBW* 12, 198: "Der Habitus des christlichen Charakters unterscheidet sich von dem der Individualität dadurch, daß er durch Übung erworben ist ... Es ist eine Übung des über sich Hinaussehens des habituellen Menschen. Christlicher Charakter trägt also als ein Grundelement die Vernachlässigung seiner selbst in sich. Die Erkenntnis meiner selbst als Sünder, diese Erkenntnis meiner Rechtfertigung macht die Chrarakterbildung zu etwas Sekundärem, Vorletztem, doch als *Übung* bedeutsam."

lativizes the significance of one's formation as a person. On the other hand, Bonhoeffer encourages personal formation as *spiritual* formation in two distinct but interrelated exercises.

First, he demanded the practice of silence.[85] According to Bethge, during the seminary days in Zingst and Finkenwalde, Bonhoeffer established one basic but strict rule: "never to speak about another ordinand in that person's absence or to tell that person about it afterward when such a thing did happen."[86] Bonhoeffer likely drew on Kempis's admonition (he marked the immediately following sentences of this section in his Tegel copy of the *Imitatio Christi*[87]): "The interior man places his spiritual welfare before everything else, and because he diligently attends to himself he does not gossip about the action of others. You will only arrive at a devout inner life by watching over yourself and by being silent with regard to others."[88] We have now additional evidence, however, that Bonhoeffer's introduction of the rule not to speak of an ordinand in his absence stems also from his encounter with the Bruderhof communities in Germany, where the rule was practiced.[89]

What, then, is the theological significance of silence for Bonhoeffer? On a practical level, "there is a wonderful power in being silent – the power of clarification, purification, and focus on what is essential." Hence, in silence "much that is unnecessary remains unsaid."[90] On a spiritual level, that which is essential is brought about in the practice of silence: "In the end, silence means nothing other than waiting for God's Word and coming from God's Word with a blessing."[91] In that sense, silence must be seen "in its essential relationship to the Word, as the simple act of the individual who falls silent under the Word of God."[92] Silence as such is not a spiritual exercise; it becomes one only by virtue of its focus on the Word of God. This is precisely Bonhoeffer's intent in teaching his seminarians, namely

---

[85] Cf. *DBWE* 5, 83–86 (*DBW* 5, 67–69).

[86] Bethge, *Dietrich Bonhoeffer*, 428. In a Finkenwalde outline for a meditation on Proverbs 3:27ff Bonhoeffer says: "*Nicht über den Bruder* reden! Du kannst dann nicht mehr *mit* ihm reden" (*DBW* 14, 869; emphasis in original).

[87] See note 75 above.

[88] *Imitatio Christi* II 5, 2. Elsewhere Kempis gives straightforward advice "against slanderous tongues:" "It requires much prudence on your part to keep silent when evil is being heaped upon you; turn inwardly to Me and do not be affected by human judgement. Do not have your peace depend on what other men might say about you" (III 28, 1–2). Kempis also notes: "There are many who talk overmuch, and as a result only a few men pay them any attention" (III 36, 1).

[89] Cf. the letters of Hardy Arnold in which he describes his meetings with Bonhoeffer in London and the latter's interest in community in *Bonhoeffer Jahrbuch/Yearbook* 2 (2005–2006), 75–109, on the rule of silence, 86, note 38.

[90] *DBWE* 5, 85 (*DBW* 5, 68).

[91] *DBWE* 5, 85 (*DBW* 5, 68).

[92] *DBWE* 5, 84 (*DBW* 5, 67).

to help them understand that the practice of silence enables genuine speech which, in turn, comes from the hearing of God's word in meditation.

Second, the spiritual exercise of silence bears fruit in meditation on a text of Scripture. The practice of meditation was so important to Bonhoeffer that he drafted an "Introduction to Scriptural Meditation [*Anleitung zur Schriftmeditation*]" in May 1936 as part of the circular letter that he and Bethge regularly sent to the Finkenwalde brothers who were then working in various pastorates.[93] Later these instructions – in an abbreviated form – became part of Bonhoeffer's reflection on Christian community in *Life Together*. Bonhoeffer identifies "three things for which the Christian needs a regular time during the day: *meditation on the Scripture*, *prayer* and *intercession*. All three should find a place in the *daily period of meditation*."[94] In order to preclude any misunderstanding, he makes it abundantly clear not to "expect from silence anything but a simple encounter with the Word of God ... It [meditation] serves no other purpose. Spiritual experiments have no place here."[95] Elsewhere he repeats: "It is not necessary for us to find new ideas in our meditation [and] above all, it is not necessary for us to have any unexpected, extraordinary experiences while meditating."[96] In his "Introduction to Scriptural Meditation," Bonhoeffer offers four reasons why one should meditate: (1) For a Christian, every day without a deeper knowledge of God is a lost day; (2) A preacher of the Word cannot preach that Word unless it speaks to the preacher him/herself; (3) We need a well-established discipline of prayer; and (4) Preachers need help against the impious haste and unrest of daily life.[97]

In practical terms, "in our personal meditation on Scripture we stick to a brief selected text that will possibly remain unchanged for an entire week ... here we are guided into the unfathomable depths of a particular sentence and word."[98] The whole point of the spiritual exercise of scriptural meditation is thus crystal clear: "We are reading the Word of God as God's Word for us. Therefore, we do not ask what this text has to say to other

---

[93] Cf. *DBW* 15, 945–950.

[94] *DBWE* 5, 86 (*DBW* 5, 69); emphasis in original. Cf. Kempis: "Set aside an opportune time for deep personal reflection and think often about God's many benefits to you. Give up all light and frivolous matters, and read what inspires you to repentance of soul and not what just entertains the mind. If you abstain from unnecessary conversation and useless visiting, as well as from listening to idle news and gossip, you will find sufficient and suitable times for your meditation" (I 20, 1. This section in the *Imitatio Christi* is called "The Love of Silence and Solitude." Bonhoeffer cites a later sentence from this section in *DBWE* 5, 85).

[95] *DBWE* 5, 86 (*DBW* 5, 69).

[96] *DBWE* 5, 88 (*DBW* 5, 71). Bonhoeffer then continues: "We must not get stuck in such experiences. Above all, we must not allow them to dissuade us from observing our period of meditation with great patience and fidelity."

[97] Cf. *DBW* 15, 945–946.

[98] *DBWE* 5, 87 (*DBW* 5, 70).

people. For those of us who are preachers that means we will not ask how we should preach or teach on this text, but what it has to say to us personally ... we are rather waiting for God's Word to us."[99] Meditation on Scripture has nothing to do with exegesis, theology or any other academic reflection. It focuses neither on the practice of silence as such nor on reading a biblical passage in a most concentrated manner, but exclusively on the encounter with God.[100]

6. The Lord's Supper

Bonhoeffer's presentation of the nature of Christian community in *Life Together* reaches an unequivocal crescendo in the last chapter, entitled "Confession and the Lord's Supper." As we mentioned above, unlike his version of the *Imitatio Christi* – which discusses "The Blessed Sacrament" in the penultimate chapter – in *Life Together* Bonhoeffer deliberately placed the discussion of the Lord's Supper at the end of the book. The reason is an obvious theological one: only in the confession of one's sins and the forgiveness of those sins in the celebration of the Lord's Supper lies the unyielding anchor of the continuity of the Christian community.

Kempis believed that preparation for the Lord's Supper needed to include "some short exercise."[101] For him, this meant to "meditate on your transgressions."[102] "In general," he says, "be sorry for all your sins, but in particular, you must grieve and bewail those offenses you commit every day."[103] Bonhoeffer likewise places great emphasis on the confession of sins. Indeed, the act of confession is so vital and crucial that without it "the final breakthrough to community"[104] remains illusory. The real test for Christian community lies in accepting one another not as fellow believers but as sinners. Only when "another Christian hears our confession of sin in Christ's place, forgives our sins in Christ's name" can genuine Christian community begin to take shape. The formation of that kind of genuine community is characterized by Bonhoeffer's word "breakthrough" [*Durch*-

---

[99] *DBWE* 5, 87 (*DBW* 5, 70).

[100] For a possible dependence on Kempis, cf. *DBWE* 5, 89, note 14 (*DBW* 5, 72, note 64). At the very beginning of the *Imitatio Christi*, after mentioning the following after and imitating of Jesus, Kempis concludes the first paragraph with these words: "Let it then be our main concern to meditate on the life of Jesus (*Summum igitur studium nostrum, sit in vita Jesu meditari*)" (*Imitatio Christi* I 1). For Kempis, the content of one's meditation is thus clearly staked out: it is the life and teaching of Jesus (cf. *Imitatio Christi* I 25, 6).

[101] *Imitatio Christi* IV 6, 2.

[102] *Imitatio Christi* IV 12, 1.

[103] *Imitatio Christi* IV 7, 1. Cf. I 1, 3: "It is better to experience remorse than to know its definition," a saying Bonhoeffer marked in his edition of the *Imitatio Christi*.

[104] *DBWE* 5, 108 (*DBW* 5, 93).

bruch]. In practicing the confession of sins and the celebration of the Lord's Supper there is a fourfold breakthrough – to community, to the cross, to new life, and to assurance.[105]

Underlying Bonhoeffer's insistence on confessing concrete sins and receiving forgiveness in the celebration of the Lord's Supper is the conviction that within Christian communities confession of sins often amounts to nothing more than a superficial self-forgiveness rather than a contrite confession before God and humanity. Here Bonhoeffer asks the pointed question: "Is not the reason for our innumerable relapses and for the feebleness of our Christian obedience to be found precisely in the fact that we are living from self-forgiveness and not from real forgiveness of our sins? Self-forgiveness can never lead to the break with sin."[106] Since it is the nature of sin "to remain unknown" and shun the light, "sin must be brought into the light."[107] Unless sin is confessed, its power is not broken. For Bonhoeffer, "Sin that has been spoken and confessed has lost all of its power. It has been revealed and judged as sin. It can no longer tear apart the community."[108] That is, since even in the *sanctorum communio* the committing of sins still occurs, it is precisely here where the power of sin must be brought to light and thus be broken. Unconfessed sins in the Christian community eventually tear it apart or else reduce it to a mere superficial gathering of well-meaning people who are bound together not so much by Christ himself as by some other social purpose.

VI. Conclusion

Although we can find only about a dozen direct citations from Thomas à Kempis's *Imitatio Christi* in Bonhoeffer's writings, the influence of Kempis on Bonhoeffer far exceeds that number. The weight of this influence must be measured not so much in terms of the number of citations but of conceptual affinities. Unquestionably, in this respect the *Imitatio Christi* had virtually a lifelong impact on Bonhoeffer's view of the theology and practice of Christian community. This is most evident in the Finkenwalde and imprisonment periods.

The convergence of the main ideas in the *Imitatio Christi* and Bonhoeffer's writings, most notably *Discipleship* and *Life Together*, is so substantial and obvious as to leave no doubt of Bonhoeffer's deep theological appreciation for Kempis's work. The themes of divine and human suffering, following the call and imitating the life of Christ, carrying one's cross, and

---

[105] Cf. *DBWE* 5, 110–113 (*DBW* 5, 95–98).
[106] *DBWE* 5, 113 (*DBW* 5, 97).
[107] *DBWE* 4, 110 (*DBW* 4, 94).
[108] *DBWE* 4, 110 (*DBW* 4, 95).

practicing spiritual exercises such as silence and meditation are fundamental to both. For Bonhoeffer, the paradoxical and kenotic circle of following Christ, self-denial and carrying one's cross leads to the exclamation that "discipleship is joy."[109] Ultimately Bonhoeffer's *theologia crucis* that was so decisively shaped by Kempis may even today inspire the church to become a joyous *ecclesia crucis*.[110]

---

[109] *DBWE* 4, 40 (*DBW* 4, 24).

[110] Cf. Douglas John Hall, "Ecclesia Crucis: The Disciple Community and the Future of the Church in North America," in Wayne Whitson Floyd, Jr. and Charles Marsh (eds.), *Theology and Practice of Responsibility. Essays on Dietrich Bonhoeffer* (Valley Forge, PA. 1994), 70–73.

Wolf Krötke

Dietrich Bonhoeffer and Martin Luther*

I. The Presence of Luther in the Theology of Bonhoeffer

An examination of Dietrich Bonhoeffer's theology in relation to that of Martin Luther (1483–1546) entails an appreciation of all of Bonhoeffer's theology. For Luther is present more than anyone else at every stage of his path and in every dimension of his thought. This is obvious from even a cursory glance at both Bonhoeffer's life and his writings. One of his main objectives during his academic training was an intense study of Luther, a fact that is apparent in his university teaching in Berlin. Typical in this regard is his lecture of 1931–1932 on "The History of Systematic Theology." Bonhoeffer turns the last question – Where do we stand? – into the question Who will show us Luther?[1]

Bonhoeffer's work within the Confessing Church and especially his training of seminarians in Zingst and Finkenwalde can be seen as his own attempt "to show Luther." Often he integrated and utilized in his order of service Luther's "free confession [*freies Bekenntnis*]" of 1528.[2] He also wrote a "Lutheran catechism."[3] Luther's practice of prayer and piety became a valued model for his own spiritual life. Many of Luther's citations and hymns, which Bonhoeffer knew by heart, often found their way quite naturally into his own language. Luther remained a significant point of reference for his thinking, even when he did not have access to Luther's writings, such as while working on his *Ethics* and during his imprisonment.

These and other very strong traces of Luther in Bonhoeffer's work and life bring something very important to the forefront: Bonhoeffer considered this reformer an authority with whom he desires to be in agreement even and especially when he goes beyond him. Polemics against Luther, as found for example in Karl Barth, are absent in Bonhoeffer. His orientation

---

* Translated from the German by Peter Frick.
[1] Cf. *DBW* 11, 213. One manuscript of the lecture notes ends with the challenge of an exclamation mark rather than a question mark.
[2] Cf. Eberhard Bethge, *Dietrich Bonhoeffer,* 187.
[3] Cf. "Glaubst du, so hast du. Versuch eines lutherischen Katechismus von Dietrich Bonhoeffer und Franz Hildebrandt" in *DBW* 11, 228–237; cf. also *DBW* 14, 786–819.

towards Luther's theology evidently constituted for him the objective orientation of the Protestant Church and theology as such.

It is tempting to label Bonhoeffer a Lutheran confessionalist. Support for this view lies in the fact, as we shall see below, that in the major issues regarding matters of confession he always sides with Luther against the Reformed theologians. The very notion of Reformation for him means "Martin Luther." "Read the Bible, read Luther," Bonhoeffer says in his provocative sermon on Reformation Day in 1932.[4] Zwingli and Calvin obviously played a minor role for him, despite the strong influence the Reformed theologian Karl Barth had on him and his uncompromising support for the ecumenical Theological Declaration of Barmen. Yet he did hold the *Book of Concord* and the decidedly anti-Reformed conclusion to the Wittenberg Reformation in high esteem.

Nevertheless, Bonhoeffer does not fit into the category of a confessionalist, at least not in the sense of being a hard-line member of a so-called "Lutheranism." Apart from his critique of the construal of Luther's theology in the metaphysical systems of "Lutheran Orthodoxy," there are mainly two reasons for this.

First, Bonhoeffer's studies of Luther fell into a period characterized by an idiosyncratic view of Luther that was represented by his Berlin professors Karl Holl and Reinhold Seeberg. Holl saw Luther as the founder of a "religion of conscience,"[5] while Seeberg charged that Luther accepted religious experience as a "canon of truth" in addition to the Scriptures.[6] The young Bonhoeffer was not convinced by either position from his own reading of Luther. "To return to the real Luther"[7] was his objective in studying the Reformer and guided his lifelong theological orientation towards him.

Such an orientation became more urgent when the "German Christians" began around 1933 to use Luther for their religious, anti-Semitic, and racist ideology in the name of God's revelation for the German people and ultimately for the destruction of the church in Germany. For Bonhoeffer, keeping and actualizing the foundations of the church was identical with articulating Luther's genuine understanding of the word of God in law and gospel, faith, the church and Christian action. He dedicated himself uncompromisingly to this task and demanded from the Confessing Church that she speak the clear, decisive "language of Luther and not Melanch-

---

[4] Sermon on Revelation 2:4f on Reformation Day, Berlin, 6 November 1932. Cf. *DBW* 12, 428.

[5] Karl Holl, "Was verstand Luther unter Religion?," in *Gesammelte Aufsätze zur Kirchengeschichte*, volume 1, *Luther* (Tübingen 1921), especially 35–84.

[6] Reinhold Seeberg, *Lehrbuch der Dogmengeschichte*, volume 4 (Leipzig, third edition, 1917), 340.

[7] "Was soll der Student der Theologie heute tun?," cf. *DBW* 12, 417.

thon."[8] Because Bonhoeffer was keen to reach his own conclusions on Luther's theology on the basis of Luther's writings, his path in the 1930s often collided – both within and outside the Confessing Church – with what was called Lutheranism or Lutheran.[9] In those circles he was seen rather as a "zealot [*Schwärmer*]" because of his insistence on putting into practice in concrete terms the confession of the Reformation.[10] He does not fit into any of the confessional schemata of that period and was never explicitly associated with them.

Second, Bonhoeffer did not think of Luther as merely a "dead man."[11] Given the situation in which he lived, his reading of Luther moved him deeply. But his being moved was by no means uniform. What he found significant in Luther during his academic career in Berlin and his time in Finkenwalde underwent decisive modifications while he worked on his *Ethics* and especially in his theological reflections in the prison letters. On the one hand, Bonhoeffer was confronted by the challenges of a dramatic and changing period to reflect on the church, theology, and his own position. On the other hand, given his view of Luther, he felt impelled to bring about a new and concrete realization of Luther's basic theological insights. Luther's word concerning believers who may create "new Decalogues"[12] in the freedom of love meant much to Bonhoeffer. An emphasis of this teaching is seen in his seminar essay on "The Holy Spirit in Luther" (1926)[13] and is visible in his *Ethics* fragments (1942).[14] He was greatly encouraged by finding – and daring to act on – ways of responsible Christian living that corresponded much more closely to the nature of faith in God in Jesus Christ than to old traditions.

This kind of searching and daring – with Luther behind him – is not only characteristic of Bonhoeffer's work on ethics. In a letter from prison he

---

[8] Letter Bonhoeffer wrote together with Franz Hildebrandt to Martin Niemöller, 30 November 1933 (cf. *DBWE* 13, 53 (*DBW* 13, 45)). – In response to the criticism launched against his essay on church community (cf. "Zur Frage der Kirchengemeinschaft" in *DBW* 14, 655–680) in the name of Luther, Bonhoeffer comments in a letter to Erwin Sutz: "Es wird noch dahin kommen, daß das Tier, vor dem sich die Götzenanbeter neigen, eine verzerrte Lutherphysiognomie trägt" (cf. *DBW* 14, 257).

[9] Cf. Bonhoeffer's assessment of false teachings in the Confessing Church ("Gutachten über 'Irrlehre' in der Bekennenden Kirche" in *DBW* 14, 700–713). For a characterization of the various types of Lutheranisms of that period, cf. my essay: "Zur Wirkungsgeschichte von Barmen I in der 'lutherischen Theologie'," in Wilhelm Hüffmeier (ed.), *Das eine Wort Gottes – Botschaft für alle.* Volume 1 (Gütersloh 1994), 312–338.

[10] Cf. Bethge, *Dietrich Bonhoeffer,* 569.

[11] Sermon on the Day of Reformation 1932, in *DBW* 12, 424.

[12] Cf. *WA* 39/I, 47, 27f.

[13] "The Holy Spirit according to Luther. Luther's View of the Holy Spirit according to the *Disputationen* of 1535-1545 edited by Drews" (*DBWE* 9, 346 (*DBW* 9, 381)). Cf. also "Grundfragen einer christlichen Ethik," in *DBW* 10, 331.

[14] Cf. "History and the Good [2]," in *DBWE* 6, 288 (*DBW* 6, 288).

writes to his parents on Reformation Day in 1943: "As long as a hundred years ago Kierkegaard said that today Luther would say the opposite of what he said then. I think he was right – with some reservations."[15] He writes these things in view of the consequences of the Reformation – that Luther himself did not want and criticized – in the sphere of the church, society, and politics. But clearly Bonhoeffer knew of his own freedom in the Lutheran sense and thus said many things opposed to what he found in Luther's writings. This explains why many of his thoughts cannot be directly traced back to Luther yet do not constitute a break from him.

There was one fundamental and most crucial aspect in which Bonhoeffer was always in agreement with Luther: taking seriously the *solus Christus*. None of the various stages of Bonhoeffer's life ever departed from a concentration on Christ alone. Even his desire in the middle of the church struggle to become acquainted with Indian religiosity must be seen as a strengthening, not a weakening, of that concentration.[16] Moreover, it is impossible to comprehend his observations on "religionless Christianity"[17] in his prison letters if they are interpreted as turning away from Luther's fundamental insight that Christ alone justifies us by faith alone. In the catechism mentioned above that Bonhoeffer wrote together with Franz Hildebrandt in 1932, the heading is based on Luther's phrase: "If you believe, you have."[18] In it we read the following: "[Christ] is the answer to all the questions of humanity. He is salvation in the midst of all the sufferings in the world. He is the victory over all sins ... 'You are to point to this person and say: this is God' (Luther)."[19] Unfortunately, it is impossible to verify this citation in Luther,[20] even though it appears like a red thread in Bonhoeffer's writings.[21] It is also present even when it is not used literally. "All that we may rightly expect from God, and ask him for," writes Bonhoeffer from prison on 14 August 1944, half a year before his death, "is to be found in Jesus Christ. The God of Jesus Christ has nothing to do with what God, as we imagine him, could do and ought to do."[22]

---

[15] *LLP*, 123 (*DBW* 8, 179–180).

[16] Cf. the letter to Julie Bonhoeffer (1934), in *DBWE* 13, 151–153 (*DBW* 13, 145–146).

[17] Cf. *LLP*, 279–281 (*DBW* 8, 402–404).

[18] *WA* 7, 24, 13f. This citation also appears in Bonhoeffer's "Paper on 'The Catholic Church' for the Thursday Circle," in *DBWE* 9, 527 (*DBW* 9, 582); cf. also Bonhoeffer's notes for a sermon on Romans 6:1–6 of 1935 (*DBW* 14, 350).

[19] Cf. "Katechismusentwurf," *DBW* 11, 234; Lecture on "Christology," *DBW* 12, 299f., Vergegenwärtigung neutestamentlicher Texte, *DBW* 14, 413; Sermon on Psalm 42, *DBW* 14, 854; *DBWE* 4, 225 (*DBW* 4, 241).

[20] Cf. "Katechismusentwurf," *DBW* 11, 234, note 14.

[21] See note 19.

[22] *LLP*, 391 (*DBW* 8, 572).

Of course, Bonhoeffer knew that in response to asking whether God reveals himself also in the law, in nature, and in history, there are "vacillating opinions" not only in Luther but also in Calvin.[23] For all Christian theology based on the Scriptures and Christ, such revelation poses a genuine problem. Bonhoeffer took this issue seriously and did not drop it. But he did not find himself drawn to Luther in the sense of following the path of a *theologia naturalis* and thereby reducing or compromising the *solus Christus*, not even partially or temporarily. For him, the question was how God – who turned toward the world in Jesus Christ, who emptied himself – is relevant to the world and every person in a concrete, life-changing way, even when the world no longer believes in him.

To demonstrate the significance Luther had for Bonhoeffer's path in respect of the origin and treatment of this question in all its details is our next task. We will draw out several lines running through his work. Some are continuous and broken, some lead nowhere, some are clearly visible, and others more hidden. But as a whole they do not present a harmonious "picture of Luther." Bonhoeffer was not interested in that; for him, Luther – who himself rejected such a picture – represented an unparalleled theological, intellectual, and spiritual impulse and source for his own experiences of faith and reality.

II. The Word of God

Bonhoeffer gained his theological framework and categories from Luther's doctrine of justification. The notions (to name but a few) of law and gospel, sin, conscience, God's righteousness, grace, faith, freedom, sanctification and, of course, Jesus Christ appear in such a way that the latter's influence is unmistakable. Bonhoeffer's reading – of, among other works, Luther's commentary on Romans,[24] the early sermons, major works, and above all the Large Catechism of 1531 – and his seminar essay on the Lutheran *disputationen* between 1535 and 1545,[25] allow him to develop, early on, his own criteria for theological thinking. To be sure, there were also other influences such as that of Barth. But even Barth received the major impulse for his theologizing at that period from Luther's doctrine of justification. Bonhoeffer recognized in Barth[26] what he had encountered in Luther, namely that every meaning we can have of the God who justifies

---

[23] Letter to Sabine and Gerhard Leibholz, 7 March 1940 (*DBW* 15, 298).
[24] Cf. Bonhoeffer's note in 1925 on Luther's lecture on Romans in *DBWE* 9, 300 (*DBW* 9,324).
[25] Cf. *DBWE* 9, 325–370 (*DBW* 9, 355–408).
[26] Cf. the remarks of 1927 on Karl Barth's *Christian Dogmatics* in *DBWE* 9, 436–438 (*DBW* 9, 473–475).

us can come only through the Word of God, through Scripture alone. For this reason Bonhoeffer became a "theologian of the Word" for whom, just as for Luther, the Bible became the "ultimate measuring stick and plumbing line."[27]

The problem that arises here – to what extent a canon of scriptures composed by human beings may be the Word of God, and how this Word should be interpreted – Bonhoeffer decided by following Luther. In his paper on "Historical and Pneumatological Interpretation of Scripture" (1925), he explicitly argues that it is the Spirit of God who makes Scripture into the Word of God. Somewhat awkwardly he notes that "*Scripture* is not experienced as revelation, but the matter that it deals with."[28] This "matter" or "Spirit" that is efficacious in Scripture is the justifying Christ himself. Whether our interpretation participates in this Spirit depends – to use Luther's famous formulation in his Preface to the German Bible – on how we discern in the texts "what drives toward Christ,"[29] what proclaims God who justifies in Christ. In this sense Bonhoeffer says that "What the content of revelation does not have is not canonical."[30] Hence, the task of scriptural interpretation is for us to be moved by the Spirit of Scripture. In this way Luther's maxim, *Scriptura sacra est sui ipsius interpres*,[31] applies.

Bonhoeffer consistently used this principle in his interpretation of Scripture, and educated young theological students along the same lines.[32] While he did not reject the historical-critical method, he did limit its importance in bringing to light the human elements of the biblical witnesses, and he employed it in a very restricted manner. This is evident in three of the six books that he published as interpretations of biblical texts: *Creation and Fall*, *Discipleship* and *Prayerbook of the Bible*. In *Creation and Fall* – an interpretation of Genesis 1–3 for which Bonhoeffer consulted Luther's commentary on Genesis[33] and which ends with the fifth stanza of one of the Reformer's Christmas hymns[34] – we find the following statements in

---

[27] *DBWE* 9, 359 (*DBW* 9, 397).

[28] "Paper on the Historical and Pneumatological Interpretation of Scripture. Can One Distinguish between a Historical and Pneumatological Interpretation of Scripture, and How Does Dogmatics Relate to This Question?," in *DBWE* 9, 285–299, here 289 (*DBW* 9, 311).

[29] *DBWE* 9, 297 (*DBW* 9, 320–321); cf. *WA DB* 7, 385, 26.

[30] *DBWE* 9, 297 (*DBW* 9, 321).

[31] "Holy Scripture interprets itself," cf. *DBWE* 9, 290 (*DBW* 9, 311) and *WA* 7, 79, 23.

[32] Cf. the lecture on homiletics, *DBW* 14, 489.

[33] Cf. the Afterword in *Creation and Fall*, *DBWE* 3, 155 (*DBW* 3, 144).

[34] *DBWE* 3, 146 (*DBW* 3, 136). The hymn is called: "Lobt Gott ihr Christen alle gleich." Bonhoeffer used the fifth stanza: "Once more God opens the gate / to fair Paradise today; / no angel now bars the way. / Glory to God, who is great, / and praise and honour, we say.

the Introduction. The church, Bonhoeffer claims, "reads the whole of Holy Scripture as the book of the end, of the new [vom Neuen], of Christ ... Theological exposition ... is a continual returning from the text (as determined by all the methods of philological and historical research) to this presupposition."[35] Here Bonhoeffer takes over Luther's principle that all of Scripture interprets itself. But in his day he was charged, like Luther, that he raped the Old Testament by reading it as a book of Christ.[36]

No less explosive is his view of Scripture in *Discipleship,* where he claims to return "to scripture, to the world and call of Jesus Christ himself."[37] This return means, however, that "simple obedience" to the literal meaning of the commandments in the gospel becomes the condition for the "Protestant scripture principle."[38] This raises the issue of whether such an understanding in fact violates the "scripture principle." Bonhoeffer seems to accept unquestioningly the word of scripture – which he now identifies with Jesus Christ himself – and thus assigns it priority in the act of understanding before the Spirit of Christ. Hence he falls prey to biblicism. We will return to this issue.

Yet there is a reason for Bonhoeffer's interpretation of scripture in the sense that Luther understands scripture. Bonhoeffer takes very seriously the "outward word" of scripture without which God does not give his Spirit.[39] He holds onto the *extra nos* of our "alien righteousness" bestowed on Christians by God and proclaimed to them through human witness.[40] For this reason Bonhoeffer considered *meditation* on biblical texts, which leads to prayer,[41] an essential dimension of biblical exegesis; this kind of meditation is different from the practice of interpretive reflection on texts for the purpose of preparing a sermon. In his use of scripture he largely followed Luther, as is obvious in the many allusions and citations of the latter in his *Life Together* and *Prayerbook of the Bible.*[42]

---

[35] *DBWE* 3, 22 (*DBW* 3, 22).

[36] Cf. the protest of Friedrich Baumgärtel, *Die Kirche ist Eine – die alttestamentlich-jüdische Kirche und die Kirche Jesu Christi? Verwahrung gegen die Preisgabe des Alten Testaments* (Greifswald 1936). This protest was caused, among other reasons, by Bonhoeffer's concrete application of a christological interpretation of the Old Testament in his biblical exegesis of the reconstruction of Jerusalem in Ezra and Nehemiah; cf. "Wiederaufbau Jerusalems nach Esra und Nehemia" (*DBW* 14, 930–944). Cf. also the comments by Bethge, *Bonhoeffer,* 526–529.

[37] *DBWE* 4, 38 (*DBW* 4, 22).

[38] *DBWE* 4, 81-82 (*DBW* 4, 74).

[39] Cf. Martin Luther, *The Book of Concord,* Smalcald Articles, 322, 3–5.

[40] Cf. *DBWE* 5, 31 (*DBW* 5, 19).

[41] Cf. *DBWE* 5, 86 (*DBW* 5, 69), where Bonhoeffer takes up Luther's teaching on the theological existence as practicing *oratio, meditatio* and *tentatio* (cf. WA 50, 659f.) but in reversed order. *Meditatio* is first and leads to *tentatio,* which in turn calls for *oratio* (cf. Vorlesung über Seelsorge, in *DBW* 14, 588f, note 109).

[42] Cf. the indices in *DBWE* 5, 207 (*DBW* 5, 194).

Today, for those interested in understanding Bonhoeffer's principles of scriptural interpretation, the difficulty lies in his apparent blending together of reflective, meditative, and kerygmatic perspectives and modes of speaking. Unfortunately Bonhoeffer was not able to write his planned "Hermeneutic" on scriptural interpretation because of the pressure of his contemporary challenges. Presumably, in such a work he would have laid out the necessary criteria for a controlled exegesis of biblical texts.[43] How he used the scriptures becomes clear in his "academic" works, in his teaching, in his many sermons and meditative reflections, and in his letters from prison. He consistently stressed that the *Prae* of the Word of God comes before all of our judgments about God and human beings. *Doctrina est coelum, vita est terra*[44] is another one of his favorite Luther citations running through his written corpus.[45] According to the Lutheran-Reformed view, *doctrina* is not merely a dogma or theological statement but rather the living voice of Jesus Christ in Scripture which seeks to be proclaimed in a human voice. As a student of Luther, Bonhoeffer desired to make that voice heard.

III. Jesus Christ

Bonhoeffer's main theological interests undoubtedly lay in the doctrines of the church and ethics, but for him both of these were nothing else but applied Christology. How Christ gains form ["Gestalt"] in the church and the world was the driving question of his dissertation and remained so even in his letters from prison. "What is bothering me incessantly is the question of what Christianity really is, or indeed who Christ really is, for us today." These are the first thoughts on a "religionless Christianity."[46] In a way this sentence hovers over all Bonhoeffer's paths. The narrow christological insights in it stem from the systematic analyses in his 1933 lecture on Christology and would become the foundation for later periods. Unfortunately we have only student records of this lecture and these raise several questions. But one thing is clear: in all the important questions that must be decided in the doctrine of Christology, Bonhoeffer took his bearings from Luther.

---

[43] Cf. the letter to Erwin Sutz in *DBW* 14, 257.
[44] "Doctrine is heaven, life is earth," *WA* 57, 13.
[45] Cf. Lecture on "Konfirmandenunterricht," in *DBW* 14, 626; Bonhoeffer's questions for a discussion of his essay, "Zur Frage der Kirchengemeinschaft," in *DBW* 14, 698; Lecture and discussion on "Schlüsselgewalt und Gemeindezucht," in *DBW* 14, 841; *DBWE* 4, 274f., note 20 (*DBW* 4, 291, note 19); *DBWE* 6, 362 (*DBW* 6, 364).
[46] *LPP*, 279 (*DBW* 8, 402).

Most of all, we must consider Bonhoeffer's decision to understand Jesus Christ in the unity of his person and work – and thus only Christ is *pro nobis* (Bonhoeffer says *pro me*)[47] – and avoid all possible abstractions from this matter. Christ is only *pro me* as the one who is present in the word, the sacrament, and the church community. Regrettably, Bonhoeffer again used a carelessly cited dictum of Luther on Christ's ascension to illustrate his point: "When he was on earth, he was far from us. Now that he is far from us, he is close."[48] The manner and means of the exalted one's closeness is his lowliness in the world that finds expression in the "scandal" and "concealment" of his glory in word, sacrament, and church community.[49] For Bonhoeffer, this insight into Luther's theology of the cross was of fundamental significance. This theology constituted the reason for the readiness of both the church and individual believers, who bear witness to Christ, to take on a lowly existence and to bear suffering.

At precisely this point Bonhoeffer saw the importance of the christological decisions of Luther and early Lutheranism, decisions made in response to the dispute on the Lord's Supper between Lutherans and Reformed. To be sure, he criticized the doctrine of the ubiquity (omnipresence) of the humanity of Christ – on account of which he is present in the Lord's Supper – as an "impossible metaphysical hypostasis."[50] But the teaching that Christ's human nature possesses divine, majestic attributes he accepted, on the condition that the God-person Jesus Christ emptied himself in the world and that these attributes remained concealed and "incognito" during Jesus' earthly life.[51] Luther's phrase – that Jesus, who was without sin, became in the world's eyes the "greatest sinner" (*peccator*

---

[47] *DBW* 12, 291ff.

[48] *DBW* 12, 293 (cf. *WA* 12, 562, 24–26); cf. the homiletic exercises for the day of ascension in 1936, in *DBW* 12, 629 and 632. In a reflection on the "ascension of Jesus Christ" in a circular letter of 1940 addressed to the Pomeranian council of brothers – which in a nutshell introduces all of Luther's Christology – we read in a somewhat changed form of that dictum and in differentiation from Reformed Christology: Jesus Christ "like God, he is simultaneously far from the world and close to it" (*DBWE* 16, 479 (*DBW* 16, 478)).

[49] Cf. *DBW* 12, 301f.

[50] *DBW* 12, 304.

[51] Cf. *DBW* 12, 345. Bonhoeffer accepted the Lutheran teaching of the "Stände" of Christ. These are the consequence of the teaching on the *genus maiestaticum*. In the "standing" of lowliness, the God-person Jesus Christ does not use his majestic attributes and conceals them. In the "standing" of exaltation he uses these. This teaching presupposes that in Jesus Christ neither God himself nor the *Logos asarkos* were made low, but only the incarnate God-person. Cf. my analysis of these matters based on the – not always clear – records of the manuscripts: "Der begegnende Gott und der Glaube. Zum theologischen Schwerpunkt der Christologievorlesung D. Bonhoeffers," in Albrecht Schönherr/Wolf Krötke (eds), *Bonhoeffer-Studien. Beiträge zur Theologie und Wirkungsgeschichte Dietrich Bonhoeffers* (Berlin 1985), 25–35.

pessimus)⁵² as he vicariously took on the sin of sinners – was crucial for Bonhoeffer. He maintains this basic insight even in the main theological passages in the prison letters, where he explicates a "religionless interpretation" of Christianity. "God lets himself be pushed out of the world on the cross. He is weak and powerless in the world," says Bonhoeffer – in a manner that is distinct from the Lutheran christological tradition – "and that is precisely the way, the only way, in which he is with us and helps us."⁵³

Against the background of the lectures on Christology, Bonhoeffer does not speak of "God as such" in his glory but of the God who became human, the person of whom Luther said, "He is God." Many of the adventurous (mis)construals of Bonhoeffer's thought about Jesus as the essential "experience of transcendence" and his "being there for others"⁵⁴ could have been avoided had his interpreters been even half as knowledgeable of Luther's Christology as he was. When Bonhoeffer wrote this, he did not reduce Christology to anthropology. But he went beyond what he had learned from Luther's Christmas hymn "Den aller Welt Kreis nie erschloß, der liegt jetzt in Marien Schoß." Bonhoeffer's dictum, "The child in the manger is God,"⁵⁵ was formulated in view of this Lutheran understanding – but on the assumption that such a statement can only be made in faith in the word in which Christ is present with us.

Ecce homo – look at the person Jesus Christ! To emphasize this was Bonhoeffer's aim for Christology as he followed in Luther's footsteps. In his fragment "Ethics as Formation" (1940) he employed Pilate's exclamation (cf. John 19:5) several times as an introductory phrase for his reflections on the three essential dimensions of Christology – incarnation, cross, and resurrection.⁵⁶ As we shall see, in this Bonhoeffer did go his own way. But in all the christological passages in his work there is the undeniable *cantus firmus* of Luther's Christology, the insight that Christ's life and death represents a vicarious entering into the human situation of sin and guilt. Such an understanding of the mandate [*Amt*] of Christ⁵⁷ had already

---

⁵² Cf. *DBW* 12, 344 (cf. *WA* 5, 602, 21–35). In the Finkenwalde lecture "Sterben und Rechtfertigung" Bonhoeffer negated, according to a student's notes of that lecture, that Christ was the "biggest sinner" (cf. *DBW* 14, 610). The context suggests that Bonhoeffer did not make such a negation.

⁵³ *LLP*, 360 (*DBW* 8, 534).

⁵⁴ Cf. *LLP*, 380 (*DBW* 8, 558).

⁵⁵ *DBW* 12, 341.

⁵⁶ Cf. *DBW* 6, 70–79 (*DBWE* 6, 82–92).

⁵⁷ Bonhoeffer knew of course Luther's teaching of the "threefold mandate" of Christ as prophet, high priest and king and referred to it on occasion (cf. *DBW* 14, 346; *DBWE* 16, 480 (*DBW* 16, 479–480)), but he did not tie his explanation of the work of Christ for us to that scheme. Since for him the centre was the vicarious representation of Christ, the "mandate of the high priest" is dominant for him.

played a major role in Bonhoeffer's dissertation. With deliberate recourse to Luther he interpreted Christ's vicarious representation as "vicariously representative strictly with respect to sin and punishment."[58] His argument is this: "God does take human beings seriously in their culpability, and therefore only punishment and the overcoming of sin can remedy the matter."[59] Therefore, "though innocent, Jesus takes the sin of others upon himself ... [so that] vicarious representative love triumphs" for others.[60]

Bonhoeffer brushed aside ethical objections to the notion of Christ's vicarious sacrifice as untheological concerns.[61] For him it was decisive that the "wrath" of God over sin was inescapable and that God himself takes on the punishment for sin and goes into death. Luther's locution, the "death of God," which was also claimed by G.W.F. Hegel,[62] was important for Bonhoeffer. "God kills the Son of God," he says in *Discipleship*, "and with the Son, God kills everything that bears the name of earthly flesh."[63] He is the "death of death."[64] Bonhoeffer liked the stanza "Scripture has proclaimed how one death devoured another death ["Die Schrift hat verkündet das, wie ein Tod den andern fraß"]" from the Lutheran hymn "Christ lag in Todesbanden."[65] This stanza expresses the crux of Christ's vicarious representation even unto death: it is a matter of our freedom from sin and death. Later in prison Bonhoeffer composes these lines: "For Christians, pagans alike he hangs dead, / And both alike forgiving [God "stirbt für Christen und Heiden den Kreuzestod und vergibt ihnen beiden"]."[66] For him, Luther's teaching of Christ's vicarious representation in his death for us always remained an incontestable and central point of reference for his thinking and faith.

---

[58] *DBWE* 1, 155 (*DBW* 1, 99).
[59] *DBWE* 1, 155 (*DBW* 1, 98).
[60] *DBWE* 1, 155–156 (*DBW* 1, 99).
[61] Cf. *DBWE* 1, 156 (*DBW* 1, 99).
[62] Bonhoeffer mentions in *Creation and Fall* (*DBWE* 3, 48 (*DBW* 3, 34)) the second stanza of "the Lutheran hymn" by Johann Rist "O Traurigkeit, o Herzeleid." Hegel referred to this hymn in his *Vorlesungen über die Philosophie der Religion*, edited by Georg Lasson, Band II/2 (Hamburg 1974), 172, regarding his understanding of the death of God: "O große Not! Gott selbst ist tot." This stanza was later revised to a Trinitarian correct view: "O große Not! Gotts Sohn liegt tot" (cf.. *EG* 80, 2). These statements on the "death of God" – Luther came to them via his teaching on the *communicatio idiomatum* of the divine and human nature (cf. for example "Von Konziliis und Kirchen," in *WA* 50, 590, 11-22) – call for a new *Trinitarian* explication. Bonhoeffer – like Luther – paid little theological attention to the doctrine of the Trinity. Hence he did not develop a systematic doctrine of God, one that is based on his Christology. There are, however, a few starting points. Cf. his sermon meditation on John 3:16-21: "Gott der Vater, trennt sich von Gott dem Sohn, und läßt ihn zu unserem Heil leiden und sterben" (*DBW* 15, 573).
[63] *DBWE* 4, 255 (*DBW* 4, 271).
[64] Cf. *DBWE* 3, 136 (*DBW* 3, 127); cf. also *DBWE* 9, 349 (*DBW* 9, 385).
[65] "Reflection on Easter: Resurrection," cf. *DBWE* 16, 474 (*DBW* 16, 472).
[66] Cf. the poem "Christians and Pagans," in *LLP*, 348–349 (*DBW* 8, 515–516).

Vicarious representation had more than christological significance for Bonhoeffer. He took the insight of *Sanctorum Communio* – that the *present* Christ must be understood as "Christ existing as church-community"[67] – to mean that the Christian community must itself have the structure of vicarious representation. He explicated this idea by drawing on Luther's "The Blessed Sacrament of the Holy and True Body of Christ, and the Brotherhoods" (1519).[68] Christian community exists in love "as being-with-each-other through Christ" and "being-for-each-other."[69] This love exists structurally and actually "as a substitute" in "active work for the neighbor; intercessory prayer and finally, the mutual forgiveness of sins."[70] Here one person becomes "a Christ"[71] for the other. He wanted to teach exactly this in his attempt at creating a catechism in 1932 for those maturing in their faith.[72] But it does not merely amount to a basic principle for Christian existence. Rather, to be "a Christ" for others implies, as Bonhoeffer stressed especially during the church struggle, that the individual must be ready "in the power of the body of Christ [to] suffer in a vicariously representative action 'for' the church-community."[73]

Bonhoeffer's own life shows how seriously he took all of this, even though he did not focus merely on his own fate. The importance of Christ's vicarious representation for humanity is powerfully expressed in the *Ethics* fragment "History and the Good" (1942). Because Jesus "the Son of God who became human lived as our vicarious representation," notes Bonhoeffer, "all human life is in its essence vicarious representation."[74] This statement appears in the context of a Christology that sees him going his own way at a distance from Luther.[75]

---

[67] Cf. *DBWE* 1, 190 (*DBW* 1, 127).

[68] Cf. *DBWE* 1, 178–190 (*DBW* 1, 117–127) and *WA* 2, 742–758.

[69] *DBWE* 1, 182 (*DBW* 1, 120).

[70] *DBWE* 1, 184 (*DBW* 1, 121). See also corresponding passages in the student notes of the lecture during the summer semester 1932 on "The Nature of the Church," in *DBW* 11, 289–298. Here as well Bonhoeffer followed Lutheran texts.

[71] *DBWE* 1, 187 (*DBW* 1, 125).

[72] *DBW* 11, 228 (cf. *WA* 7, 35, 34f); cf. the copy of a section in the lecture on "Gottesdienst und Bruderdienst" of 1936: "A Christian risks his/her life for the soul of a brother/sister. In this way, as one carries the cross of Christ vicariously, the body of Christ carries our cross" (*DBW* 14, 466).

[73] *DBWE* 4, 222 (*DBW* 4, 236).

[74] *DBWE* 6, 258 (*DBW* 6, 257).

[75] Bonhoeffer's interpretation of all of reality as "*the one realm of the Christ-reality* [*Christuswirklichkeit*]" (*DBWE* 6, 58 (*DBW* 6, 43)), in which God and humanity are redeemed in a definitive manner, has major affinities with Luther's Christology, in particular the interpretation of the significance of God's incarnation. But the specific profile in Bonhoeffer's thought in the fragments of *Ethics* emerges from his attempt to make such an experience of faith the foundation for human reality as such and human responsible action in particular.

IV. Sin

Magnificare peccatum – to make sin great – was, according to Luther's lecture on Romans of 1515–1516, the sum of this Pauline epistle.[76] Luther's entire doctrine of justification hinges on a person's existential [*existenziell*] experience of himself as a sinner without the possibility of coming to God. As noted before, Luther's doctrine of justification was among Bonhoeffer's basic theological convictions, and thus taking *sin* seriously was a crucial theme for him.

In the Lutheran school tradition, *the proper distinction between law and gospel*, and paying attention to a person's *conscience* were important. Both are just as essential for Bonhoeffer. Regarding one's knowledge of sin, the law of God and not the gospel is the means by which sin may be perceived in its full extent. The function of the law is to *reveal* sin to the sinner who wishes to conceal it. This happens when the law drives the sinner to despair, from which only God's pronouncement of freedom in the gospel can deliver him. The student Bonhoeffer provides a succinct account of the logic of Luther's doctrine of justification in his seminar essay on "The Holy Spirit according to Luther. Luther's View of the Holy Spirit according to the *Disputationen* of 1535–1545." There he says: "Where there is no law, there is no sin. Where there is no sin, there is no forgiveness. Where there is no forgiveness, Christ came into the world and died in vain."[77]

In this seminar essay, Bonhoeffer relied mostly on those Lutheran passages in which Luther emphasized both the uniqueness and *the unity of law and gospel*. The Holy Spirit works both in the law and the gospel and leads "only to the place ... where revelation is, to Christ".[78] Bonhoeffer took Luther's statements – that the so-called *usus elenchticus legis* (the convicting use of the law) may function somewhat independently before or beside the proclamation of the gospel – and pushed them aside. This perspective he consistently held to the end of his theological work. In 1943 he was still criticizing the Lutheran tradition for its teaching of the "uses" of the law in an assessment for the tenth executive council of the Old Prussian Confessing Synod.[79] Their teaching does not sufficiently indicate that only God, who is revealed in Christ, establishes the right relation between law and gospel in their effects on sinners, among whom are the believers in their earthly existence.[80]

---

[76] Martin Luther, *Vorlesung über den Römerbrief 1515/1516*, Lateinisch-deutsche Ausgabe, volume 1 (Weimar 1960), 8–9.
[77] *DBWE* 9, 349 (*DBW* 9, 385).
[78] *DBWE* 9, 340 (*DBW* 9, 374).
[79] Cf. "The Doctrine of the Primus Usus Legis according to the Confessional Writings and their Critique" in *DBWE* 16, 584–601 (*DBW* 16, 600–619).
[80] Cf. *DBWE* 16, 595 (*DBW* 16, 612).

In a discourse in Finkenwalde in 1936 on "Preaching the Law," Gerhard Ebeling articulated very well what was also important for Bonhoeffer: "The law as the Word of God is enclosed in God's revelation in Jesus Christ so that apart from revelation an adequate theological definition of the 'law' becomes impossible. ... Law and gospel are not opposites because Jesus Christ is the one first and last word."[81] "Law and gospel ... are one as the word of God and Christ," says Bonhoeffer in a similar vein.[82] But he also stresses that these two "belong together because of their antithetical character ... [and] are two as the word which we must proclaim."[83] In this sense it remained true for him that "there is no proclamation of the law without the gospel, and no proclamation of the gospel without the law."[84]

Correspondingly, the law that is embedded in the gospel and proclaimed together with it leads to a "Christian knowledge of sin." Apart from the context of the gospel a person can have only a "sinful knowledge of sin,"[85] which Bonhoeffer finds characterized in Luther's view of the activity of the sinner's conscience. A person charges himself or herself in breaking the law. But at the same time the person tries to work at his or her "possibility for improving" by means of a *contritio activa* (active repentance).[86] Bonhoeffer explained this activity in his *Habilitationsschrift* mostly with reference to the young Luther. Conscience – which comes on the scene only in "humanity in Adam" after the "Fall" – is not "primarily [...] God's, but the human being's own voice."[87] "The conscience and repentance of human beings in Adam are their final grasp at themselves, the confirmation and justification of their self-glorifying solitude."[88]

But when people "see their sin in Christ," as Bonhoeffer says in regard to Luther's commentary on Galatians, they have a "Christian knowledge of sin,"[89] a *contritio passiva* (passive repentance).[90] On one hand, one's situa-

---

[81] Theses presented by Gerhard Ebeling, cf. *DBW* 14, 779.

[82] Cf. Bonhoeffer's notes on law, *DBW* 14, 318.

[83] *DBW* 14, 318.

[84] See the fragment of 1941 on "On the Possibility of the Church's Message to the World," in *DBWE* 6, 357 (*DBW* 6, 359).

[85] Cf. Bonhoeffer's dogmatic exercise "Theological Psychology," in *DBW* 12, 196.

[86] *DBW* 12, 196.

[87] Cf. *DBWE* 2, 155 (*DBW* 2, 155). On Bonhoeffer's view of conscience, cf. the very extensive comments by Reinhold Mokrosch, "Das Gewissenverständnis Dietrich Bonhoeffers. Reformatorische Herkunft und politische Funktion," in Christian Gremmels (ed.), *Bonhoeffer und Luther. Zur Sozialgestalt des Luthertums in der Moderne* (Munich 1983), 59–92. Mokrosch examines the use of the term conscience in Bonhoeffer's works and draws the conclusion that he was a "Vertreter und Interpret zwar nicht des lutherischen, aber eines an Luthers Theologie orientierten Gewissensverständnisses im 20. Jhd."

[88] *DBWE* 2, 139 (*DBW* 2, 137).

[89] Cf. *DBW* 12, 196 and *WA* 40/1, 282, 21ff.

[90] *DBWE* 2, 156 (*DBW* 2, 156).

tion becomes much sharper: the sinner must confess his or her "disregard for the grace offered in Christ."[91] On the other, we must say with Luther: "You may, therefore, safely look upon your sin without your conscience (!), as sins are no longer sins there; they are overcome and swallowed up in Christ."[92] Against Luther, Bonhoeffer concluded that Christ may "kill"[93] one's conscience; yet he says with Luther that in faith a Christian has "a joyful conscience."[94] Statements like this, namely that conscience is only "where sin is"[95] and hence not "in Christ," are somewhat strange. They may be explained by Bonhoeffer's increasing tendency – especially during the period of resistance – to minimize a *Christian's* conscience as a criterion for one's concrete acts.[96]

However, sin itself can never be relativized, least of all in the church. Bonhoeffer assumes with Luther that the Christian is always *simul iustus et peccator* and that the church always remains "a community of sinners."[97] For this reason, the unconditional confession of sin and guilt belongs to the identity of the church. Bonhoeffer stressed, especially in *Discipleship*, "that forgiveness can only be preached within the church community of saints, where repentance also is preached; where the gospel is not separated from the proclamation of the law."[98] This insight led him, by heeding Luther's warning in the *Large Catechism*, to have a very high regard for confession,[99] where it comes to light that a person is "a great, unholy sinner." Precisely in naming sin, sin – which always wants to remain hidden – loses its power.[100] Hence Bonhoeffer can say to those confessing their sin, "You are allowed to be a sinner. Thank God for that."[101]

In this vein, Bonhoeffer often follows Luther's advice in a letter to Melanchthon: *pecca fortiter, sed fortius fide et gaude in Christo*.[102] But in *Discipleship* he warns readers not to take this advice in the sense of "cheap

---

[91] *DBWE* 2, 156 (*DBW* 2, 155).
[92] *DBWE* 2, 156 (*DBW* 2, 156); cf. *WA* 2, 690.
[93] *DBWE* 2, 156 (*DBW* 2, 155).
[94] *DBWE* 2, 161 (*DBW* 2, 161); cf. *WA* 30/1 208.
[95] *DBWE* 2, 155 (*DBW* 2, 154).
[96] Cf. Reinhold Mokrosch, "Gewissensverständnis," 81–89.
[97] *DBWE* 1, 153, 212 (*DBW* 1, 97, 143).
[98] *DBWE* 4, 269 (*DBW* 4, 285-286). Cf. *DBWE* 6, 135–136 (*DBW* 6, 126–127). The Church is the place where recognition and confession of guilt takes place in the world.
[99] Cf. *DBWE* 5, 114 (*DBW* 5, 99); cf. *The Book of Concord*, 479, 32–35.
[100] Cf. *DBWE* 5, 108–111 (*DBW* 5, 93–95).
[101] *DBWE* 5, 108 (*DBW* 5, 93).
[102] "Sin boldly, but believe and rejoice still more boldly in Christ" (*WA* Briefwechsel 2, 372, 84f.), cf. *DBWE* 2, 123, 135 (*DBW* 2, 120, 134). Cf. also Bonhoeffer's letter to Walter Dress of 15 November 1928, in which he asks whether it is possible to say that "sin is the will of God for a person" and answers this question in the sense of Luther's "sin boldly" (*DBW* 17, 84–85). See further his seminary essay "The theology of crisis and its attitude toward philosophy and science", in *DBW* 10, 448.

grace" or in a "blasphemous" manner that may be an "invitation to sin deliberately while relying on grace."[103] But "ultimately ... for those who along the path of discipleship have come to know that they cannot become sinless,"[104] this sentence expresses the sinner's utter dependence on "costly grace."[105]

In Bonhoeffer's prison letters, the way sin is "magnified" in Christianity also plays a definite role in his estimation of the unbelieving "non-religious person."[106] There he sees the strength of the people who have "come of age." But such strength should not be "run down"[107] by Christian apologetics in using human weakness "to blackmail [people] religiously"[108] – that is, to "smuggle" God into their lives.[109] This he deems "pointless," "ignoble," and "unchristian."[110] For here the revelation of sin, which God alone can make effective, falls into the clutches of a religious mechanism. In contrast, Bonhoeffer does not want to conceal in any way the "godlessness" of a religionless world. "The world that has come of age is more godless, and perhaps for that very reason nearer to God, than the world before its coming of age."[111] God himself reveals this, the God who "lets himself be pushed out" of the world onto the cross and who is now in and for the world in his powerlessness.[112] God magnifies the sin of the world, as much as possible, by exposing himself to the power of sin. Thus he is there for the world and its peoples. In this lies the possibility that the world may become a world in genuine worldliness, both from God and for God. Here Bonhoeffer thought of the "profound this worldliness" in which Luther lived.[113]

---

[103] *DBWE* 4, 52 (*DBW* 4, 38). Bonhoeffer did not accept the *pecca fortiter* in the sense that it may be used to justify the oath of allegiance to Hitler by the pastors of the Confessing Church; cf. "An den Bruderrat der altpreußischen Union (1938)," in *DBW* 15, 55.

[104] *DBWE* 4, 52 (*DBW* 4, 39).

[105] Cf. Bonhoeffer's notes on "Wandeln, Wachsen und Frucht" in *DBW* 14, 622, where he says: "pecca fortiter nicht Prinzip christlichen Handelns, sondern letzter Trost verzagten Gewissens."

[106] Cf. my detailed study: "Weltlichkeit und Sünde. Zur Auseinandersetzung mit Denkformen Martin Luthers in der Theologie D. Bonhoeffers," in *Die Universalität des offenbaren Gottes. Gesammelte Aufsätze*, Beiträge zur Evangelischen Theologie 94 (Munich 1985), 152–194. In that study I focussed too much on the last phase of Bonhoeffer's theology and made the one-sided claim that *usus elenchticus legis* played "no recognisable role" (156) for Bonhoeffer. What I have said here stands now as a correction to this earlier view.

[107] *LPP*, 346 (*DBW* 8, 511).

[108] *LPP*, 344 (*DBW* 8, 510).

[109] *LPP*, 346 (*DBW* 8, 511).

[110] *LPP*, 327 (*DBW* 8, 478–479).

[111] *LPP*, 362 (*DBW* 8, 537).

[112] *LPP*, 360 (*DBW* 8, 534).

[113] *LPP*, 369 (*DBW* 8, 541).

Unfortunately, Bonhoeffer had no opportunity to bring sufficient clarity to these thoughts. It is questionable whether the distinction between "strong" and "weak" sins is a helpful starting point for the theological claim that "religionless" persons may be for Christ.[114] If so, this suggests that the significance of the term "sin" to describe the relation to God of either a religionless or religious person is based on a dissimilar weighing of a person's actual sins. Bonhoeffer underscores Luther's teaching that sin is the state of the whole human being. Sin is the sin of a person's personhood and thus characterizes the "collective act" of all humanity in Adam.[115] In this sense Bonhoeffer stresses in the prison letters that human sin refers to "the whole person in relation to God"[116] and not just certain parts of human existence. Similarly, he also sees a person's practice of religionlessness as godlessness, sin in the fullest sense of the word. When this religionlessness is claimed by Christ, it is based on the distinction made possible by Christ between the fact that religionlessness is embedded in sin and that in this embeddedness lies the unfolding of the good intention of creation, namely the world's "coming age" even though marred by sin.

In his prison letters Bonhoeffer was not concerned to revise Luther's teaching on the indispensability of revealing sin. Sin is rather a matter of transformation given that people in modernity live at a far distance from God and that their particular kind of godlessness may nonetheless be judged as "promising."[117] As sin, all "godlessness" is strong in that everyone under its power seeks to put him or herself in the place of God. In the *Disputatio contra scholasticam theologiam* Luther said: *Non potest homo naturaliter velle deum esse deum. Immo vellet se esse deum, et deum non esse deum.*[118] When Bonhoeffer speaks of sin he has in view the prideful, arrogant and "usurped equality with God."[119] In his *Creation and Fall* (1933), he accurately described "humankind's *sicut deus*" in which people

---

[114] On occasion Luther did speak like that. Bonhoeffer once notes, for example, his remark about the "Puppensünden" [sins of dolls], for which Christ did not suffer (cf. Bonhoeffer's exegesis on temptation in 1938, in *DBW* 15, 403). Evidently, such speech regarding sin is untypical in that it suggests that these "sins" are in reality no sins.

[115] Cf. *DBWE* 1, 108–118 (*DBW* 1, 70–73). Bonhoeffer understood the theological substance of the notion of "hereditary sin" in this sense while he rejected the propagation of sin as a biological act of procreation (cf. his lecture on the nature of the church in *DBW* 11, 264, note 165). When he speaks in *Ethics* of the "universal contamination of all human action by original sin" of a person (*DBWE* 6, 235; cf. 279 (*DBW* 6, 234; cf. 279)), he means a person's complete entanglement in the deeds of "Adam."

[116] *LPP*, 346 (*DBW* 8, 511).

[117] Cf. the fragment "Heritage and Decay" in *DBWE* 6, 124 (*DBW* 6, 115).

[118] Cf. *WA* 1, 225,17f: "The natural person cannot will that God is God. Rather s/he wishes her/himself to be God and that God not be God."

[119] "God's Love and the Disintegration of the World" in *DBWE* 6, 301 (*DBW* 6, 302).

want to be their own creators.¹²⁰ He returned to this portrayal in the *Ethics* fragment, "God's Love and the Disintegration of the World," in 1942.¹²¹ Those who want to separate from their origin, from their Creator, "have permanently cut themselves off from life."¹²² They are unable to reverse the situation into which they have brought themselves.

Bonhoeffer repeatedly uses Luther's locution of the *cor curvum in se*,¹²³ the heart turned upon itself, to illustrate the sinner's futile rotating around him or herself. This imprisonment of the person in him/herself, not a person's works as such, is the sinfulness of sin.¹²⁴ The imprisonment is also characteristic of modern philosophy inasmuch "as thinking that is trapped in itself ... is the expression of the person that seeks him/herself in the *status corruptionis*."¹²⁵ Such thinking does not belong to Christian theology¹²⁶ because it would forfeit its grounding in reality, the only foundation on which theology must proceed.¹²⁷

In every phase of his theological thinking Bonhoeffer assumed that it is the reality "in Christ" by which God and human beings are united and redeemed.¹²⁸ This reality is a gift of grace and faith alone.¹²⁹ It alone sets one free "of the imprisonment in one's own ego."¹³⁰ The path of self-justification thus comes to a "complete break."¹³¹ When he speaks of sin it is always, as in Luther, a matter of underscoring that there is no way out of sin that leads to God. Even when Bonhoeffer stresses his view of the sinner's justification through God in Christ differently from Luther, he does so without trivializing the ubiquity of sin.

---

[120] *DBWE* 3, 116 (*DBW* 3, 108); cf. *DBWE* 3, 115–120 (*DBW* 3, 107–113).

[121] Cf. *DBWE* 6, 299–338 (*DBW* 6, 301–341).

[122] *DBWE* 6, 302 (*DBW* 6, 304).

[123] *WA* 56, 137; cf. 304, 30 – 305, 6.

[124] Cf. "Theological Psychology" in *DBW* 12, 196.

[125] Cf. Bonhoeffer's inaugural lecture: "The Question of the human being in Contemporary Philosophy and Theology" in *DBW* 10, 369. See also his seminar paper, "The Theology of Crisis and its Attitude toward Philosophy and Science" in *DBW* 10, 446 and *DBWE* 2, 41, 46, 58, 80, 89, 137 (*DBW* 2, 34, 39, 52, 74, 83, 136) on *ratio in se ipsam incurva*.

[126] Cf. his lecture on Christology in *DBW* 12, 283: The "how-question" in Christology entails the "enslavement to our own authority" [Fesselung an unsere eigene Autorität]. It is the cor curvum in se."

[127] Cf. *DBWE* 2, 88–90 (*DBW* 2, 83–84).

[128] Cf. *DBWE* 2, 150–155 (*DBW* 2, 149–154). Cf. also "Ethics as Formation" in *DBWE* 6, 82–83 (*DBW* 6, 69–70).

[129] Cf. "Ultimate and Penultimate Things" in *DBWE* 6, 146–149 (*DBW* 6, 137–139).

[130] Cf. *DBWE* 6, 148 (*DBW* 6, 138).

[131] Cf. *DBWE* 6, 149 (*DBW* 6, 140).

V. Justification and Sanctification

The "magnifying" of sin allows Luther to magnify the grace of God in Christ, the grace that alone justifies a person. Grace changes the situation of the sinner before God in a fundamental way. The sinner actually encounters grace in the word of proclamation that brings about faith and thus effectively becomes a new person. Justification must thus be seen as "a making of justification" [*Rechtfertig*machung] – as Bonhoeffer puts it in a word-play in 1931.[132] In this regard, his view is clearly distinct from Melanchthon's version of justification. According to Luther, God does not only look at us as if we were righteous. By God's making us righteous "from outside ourselves (*extra nos*),"[133] we are placed in our true reality as God's creatures in comparison to our existence in sin. As Bonhoeffer said in *Act and Being*, taking up an Augustinian formulation via Luther,[134] God is "closer ... than is my existence."[135] When God calls, the righteous person becomes an "essential person" [*wesenhaft Mensch*].[136] Such a person is constantly addressed anew by the proclaimed word of God and delivered in faith "from being turned inward upon oneself" and oriented toward "the outward of one's existence as such [*schlechthinnige Außen der Existenz*]."[137]

A sinful person's justification cannot be viewed theologically as the *possibility* of a person struggling with his or her conscience, but only as a *reality*.[138] Even during the Reformation it became contentious as to how this new reality of a person before God and in faith correlates with the ongoing sinful reality of the person's life. For Bonhoeffer, this issue was of eminent theological and existential significance. We could view his theological intention over the course of his entire life as an attempt to make transparent the new reality, created in Christ, in the life of the church, in

---

[132] Cf. "Charakter und ethische Konsequenzen des religiösen Determinismus," in *DBW* 10, 414 (emphasis added). This terminology, also found in Luther (cf. for example *WA* 7, 30), is used by Bonhoeffer in his sermon on Reformation Day 1934 (*DBWE* 13, 395 (*DBW* 13, 403)) and in *Discipleship* (*DBWE* 4, 256 (*DBW* 4, 272)): "For as human beings we cannot be made right and ready before God except in recognizing that God alone is righteous and we are sinners throughout."

[133] Cf. *DBWE* 5, 62 (*DBW* 5, 47).

[134] Cf. Luther's Writing: "Daß diese Worte 'das ist mein Leib' noch fest stehen," in *WA* 23, 135.

[135] *DBWE* 2, 95 (*DBW* 2, 90).

[136] Cf. Bonhoeffer's inaugural lecture: "Die Frage nach dem Menschen in der gegenwärtigen Philosophie und Theologie" in *DBW* 10, 371.

[137] *DBW* 10, 369.

[138] Corresponding to his thinking in *Sanctorum Communio*, this reality *as community* – which the present Christ carries by his word – has the character of being [Seinscharakter]. Hence: "Nur als Denken der Kirche bleibt letztlich theologisches Denken das einzige Denken, das nicht die Wirklichkeit durch die Kategorie der Möglichkeit rationalisiert" (*DBW* 10, 378).

Christians, and even in the world. "Invisibility destroys us," he writes to his friend Helmut Rößler in October 1931. "No person can stand any longer this constant, ridiculous being thrown back on to this invisible God." [139] Against this background we can understand his effort in *Sanctorum Communio* to answer the question of what social form a person's being in faith and "in Christ" should take. The struggle for a visible, concrete form of the life in faith is even more evident in the theology of *Discipleship*, where "to flee into invisibility is to deny the call" of Christ.[140]

Bonhoeffer charged that this fleeing is the result of misusing Luther's doctrine of the "Freedom of a Christian" in the Protestant church. Given the justified person's freedom from sin, the grace of God is made into a presupposition[141] and thus renders superfluous a Christian's struggle for a life of sanctification and against sin. The sinner's justification on the basis of "cheap grace" implies the "justification of sin and the world"[142] and thus leads to the secularization of the church. Bonhoeffer fervently stressed that this was not Luther's intention, although he does not precisely refer to Luther's view of the sanctified life.

According to Luther, the person who has faith deliberately does what God's commandments require. "Good works" hence grow as the fruit on a "good tree."[143] For this reason, unlike Melanchthon, Luther did not teach the *tertius usus legis* (the third use of the law), namely that the acts of believers are "pre-illuminated"[144] by the law of God.[145] Bonhoeffer, however, emphasizes the law and the commandments of Christ so that God's grace does not become cheap in the Christian's life. He does so in a unique manner. Grace can only remain "costly grace"[146] when the believer obeys in his or her acts and lives out Christ's commandments as found in the Sermon on the Mount. Faith without such obedience makes a life of following Christ impossible. In this sense, it is true that "only the believers obey and only the obedient believe."[147]

---

[139] Letter to Helmut Rößler, 18 October 1931, in *DBW* 11, 33.
[140] *DBWE* 4, 113 (*DBW* 4, 113).
[141] Cf. *DBWE* 4, 43–56 (*DBW* 4, 29–43).
[142] Cf. *DBWE* 4, 50 (*DBW* 4, 36).
[143] Cf. Martin Luther, *Von der Freiheit eines Christenmenschen*, WA 7, 32.
[144] Cf. Epitome 6 in *The Book of Concord*, 502 § 3.
[145] Werner Elert has demonstrated that the only place where Luther employs the expression *tertius usus legis*, namely at the end of the second Antinomian disputation (*WA* 39/1, 485, 16ff), is a falsification (cf. *Das christliche Ethos. Grundlinien der lutherischen Ethik* (Hamburg, second edition 1961), 388–389).
[146] Cf. *DBWE* 4, 43 (*DBW* 4, 29).
[147] *DBWE* 4, 63 (*DBW* 4, 52).

The second half of this sentence was especially provocative to Protestant ears.[148] Bonhoeffer pointedly couched this provocation by characterizing the justifying grace of God with a citation from Kierkegaard. Grace is the "conclusion" of the life that actively participates in discipleship.[149] What Kierkegaard meant was not the result in terms of human accomplishments in obedient living but a "divine conclusion."[150] Bonhoeffer seems to speak especially against a legalistic view of the Christian life, something that Luther also repeatedly warned against. Apart from a person's obedience to Christ's commandment as expressed in the Sermon on the Mount, it is impossible to reach such a conclusion.

Bonhoeffer explained the indissoluble relation between faith and obedience in *Discipleship* as being based on the present "incarnate God's" calling people into discipleship by carrying the cross of Christ[151] and the experience of the presence of the "exalted Christ" in word and sacrament.[152] The *whole* Christ, who brings about faith, is not present for us apart from his call to obedience; we may say that Paul cannot be heard apart from Jesus.[153] It should not be overlooked that Jesus' calling – as found in his interpretation of the law in the Sermon on the Mount – gained a certain independence in Bonhoeffer's life already before 1937. As has been correctly pointed out, the only change in his life as Christian and theologian, on which he commented retrospectively, is in connection with the things mentioned above. The "turning away from the phraseological to the real,"[154] a turn that occurred in 1932, focuses largely on his attempt to follow Jesus' commandments in the Sermon on the Mount.[155] Its most exemplary expression lies in his call for "a large ecumenical council of the holy church of Jesus Christ" that should forbid the waging of war in obedience to Christ's commandment. Such was Bonhoeffer's demand in a speech to the meeting of the World Alliance for Promoting International Friendship through the Churches in 1934 on the Danish island of Fanø in the North Sea.[156]

---

[148] However, Luther could also say: Whoever does not do good "works is a person without faith." This is cited as Lutheran doctrine in the *Solida Declaratio* (cf. *BSLK*, 941,24ff).

[149] *DBWE* 4, 50 (*DBW* 4, 37).

[150] *DBWE* 4, 50 (*DBW* 4, 37).

[151] Cf. *DBWE* 4, 84–91 (*DBW* 4, 77–85).

[152] Cf. *DBWE* 4, 201–204 (*DBW* 4, 215–218).

[153] "The synoptic Christ is neither more nor less distant from us than the Christ of Paul. The Christ who is present with us is the Christ to whom the whole of scripture testifies" (*DBWE* 4, 50 (*DBW* 4, 220)).

[154] *LPP*, 275 (*DBW* 8, 397).

[155] Cf. the letter to Elisabeth Zinn, dated 27 January 1936, in *DBW* 14, 113.

[156] Cf. the lecture at the Conference in Fanø: "The Church and the Peoples of the World" in *DBWE* 13, 307–310 (*DBW* 13, 298–301). To support this claim Bonhoeffer even cited Luther's hymn "Ein feste Burg ist unser Gott." Christians receive an aggressor "bewaffnet mit der allein guten Wehr und Waffen" of prayer (*DBWE* 13, 309 (*DBW* 13, 300)). For an analysis of Bonhoeffer's pacifism, see my essay "Nur das ganze Wort ist mutig. Ökumene als

Luther would likely have mocked Bonhoeffer as an "enthusiast" for his lack of understanding of God's external orders. For the orders are necessary for the preservation of the sinful world and thus Christians must submit to them as well. We will see below how Bonhoeffer dealt with this issue. In *Discipleship* he expressly refers to Luther to highlight the inevitability of "simple obedience" in view of Christ's commandment to live a life of following after him. There Bonhoeffer's point of reference is not Luther's teaching but Luther's life. Luther entered the cloister "because he knew that only those who are obedient can believe" and that faith meant he "invested his whole life."[157] But he saw the monk's "escape from the world" as "a final spiritual self-affirmation" and a "subtle love for the world."[158] Therefore he returned to the world. In Bonhoeffer's estimation, this return was "the sharpest attack that had been launched at the world since early Christianity ... Following Jesus now had to be lived out in the midst of the world."[159]

However, Bonhoeffer's reliance on Luther is somewhat distorted. He overemphasizes Luther's view of "secular vocation." For the Reformer, that vocation[160] did not imply following after Christ and obeying his commandments as expressed in the Sermon on the Mount. Rather it had to do with keeping the commandments of the second tablet of the Decalogue and living a life obedient to the *usus civilis legis* (the civil use of the law). Bonhoeffer's chief concern was what is "unworldly in the true sense [*rechte Weltfremdheit*]"[161] and what for the visible church community is living "its own life" in the world.[162] Community is a community of saints because every follower looks "only to the one ... whom they follow" and not to themselves.[163]

Ernstfall theologischer Existenz. Das Beispiel Dietrich Bonhoeffers," in *Dietrich Bonhoeffer Jahrbuch/Yearbook* 2 (2005–2006), 125–145.

[157] *DBWE* 4, 47 (*DBW* 4, 33).

[158] *DBWE* 4, 48 (*DBW* 4, 34). Cf. also *DBWE* 4, 245 (*DBW* 4, 261). In the cloister, "unworldliness" turned into a "new spiritual conformity to this world."

[159] *DBWE* 4, 48 (*DBW* 4, 34–35). Bonhoeffer learnt about Luther's way in the cloister as a theological paradigm from Karl Holl (cf. Karl Holl, *Religion*, 13–30).

[160] Cf. *DBWE* 4, 47–48 (*DBW* 4, 35). Regarding Luther's understanding of secular profession, cf. his interpretation of the second tablet of the Decalogue in the *Large Catechism* (*The Book of Concord*, 400-431). Everyone in a "profession and stand" should do "right and golden works" (*The Book of Concord*, 406, 148). Thus we read in relation to the fourth commandment: "The Carthusians, both monks and nuns ... will blush with shame before a little child who has lived according to this commandment and will confess that with their entire lives they are not worthy to offer that child a drink of water" (*The Book of Concord*, 402–403).

[161] Cf. *DBWE* 4, 245 (*DBW* 4, 261).

[162] *DBWE* 4, 250 (*DBW* 4, 266).

[163] *DBWE* 4, 288 (*DBW* 4, 304).

Clifford Green has suggested in his biographical and psychological interpretation of the theology in *Discipleship* that Bonhoeffer tried to let go of his "personal autonomy" and to subvert "his own strengths."[164] He juxtaposes this view with the concept of the Christian who has come of age, is "strong" and free for others in responsible action, a view that emerges in the letters from prison.[165] Indeed, the theology in *Discipleship* does not lead to an "ethic of responsibility."[166] Bonhoeffer's theology there does not aim at an "ethical program," not even one of obedience.[167] Rather, the issue is life in relation to a person who frees the believer from the world's obligations and attachments.

Obedience to the trustworthiness of the person of Christ comes with the experience of freedom. It is the experience of "the freedom of God's children,"[168] who, even though they are in the world and "make use of the world,"[169] are not bound by it. This view is congruent with Luther's view of the "Freedom of a Christian Person," which Bonhoeffer did not wish to negate in *Discipleship*. There is no doubt, though, that the strong emphasis on the "unworldliness [*Weltfremdheit*]" of the freedom of the saints leads to downplaying their responsibility for the world. It may be that, beside the legalism of a "holy" life, Bonhoeffer also saw the neglect of responsibility as one of the dangers of the concept of discipleship.[170] But he does mention, in the same breath and in the midst of his reflection on the "nonreligious interpretation of biblical concepts," that what he said in *Discipleship* still stands.[171] He could not imagine a Christian person or a Christian church that was severed from the obligation to live a concrete life.

---

[164] Cf. Clifford J. Green, "Soteriologie und Sozialethik bei Bonhoeffer und Luther," in C. Gremmels (ed.), *Bonhoeffer und Luther. Zur Sozialgestalt des Luthertums in der Mo-derne* (Munich 1983), 111. Green interprets submission to the absolute authority of the commandments of Christ as Bonhoeffer's attempt to free himself from his own narcissism and egocentrism.

[165] Not the "überwältigende Christus der 'Nachfolge'," but "der gekreuzigte Jesus, der menschliche Stärken in dem freien, verantwortlichen Dienst an anderen in Anspruch nimmt," constitutes according to Green the main purpose of a "Theology of Sociality," which was so important to Bonhoeffer from the beginning (Green, "Soteriologie" 116, 123). On the legitimacy and limits of such a Bonhoeffer interpretation, see my review of Clifford J. Green's monograph *Bonhoeffer. A Theology of Sociality* (Grand Rapids/Cambridge, revised edition, 1999) in *Theologische Literaturzeitung* 126 (2001), 1180–1182.

[166] *DBWE* 4, 94 (*DBW* 4, 89).

[167] *DBWE* 4, 136 (*DBW* 4, 138).

[168] *DBWE* 4, 165 (*DBW* 4, 172).

[169] *DBWE* 4, 248 (*DBW* 4, 264). Here Bonhoeffer understands Christian freedom in the sense of 1 Cor. 7:29–32.

[170] *LPP*, 369 (*DBW* 8, 542).

[171] *LPP*, 369 (*DBW* 8, 542).

VI. The Divine Mandates and Free Responsibility

Bonhoeffer's emphasis on the autonomous purpose of the holy life of Christians within the church changes in the fragments of *Ethics*. He continues to orient himself by Luther's path into and out of the cloister. On one hand, this orientation allows him to develop a position on the relationship between "ultimate" and "penultimate." On the other, it prepares the way for a more balanced view of secular vocation in Luther.

Regarding the first, Bonhoeffer defines the sinner's justification by grace alone through faith as the "ultimate" that contains a "complete break with everything penultimate, with all that has gone before" as it happened in the "way of Luther."[172] Nevertheless, "Luther [had to go] through the monastery" and out of it,[173] for the people of this world must "travel a road" even if it does not lead to the ultimate.[174] Based on this paradigm, Bonhoeffer develops his view of the penultimate. In it he deals with the "preparation of the way" for Christ's coming.[175] He includes not only "spiritual preparation of the way"[176] but "creative activity" in the world.[177] He sees such a preparation as a "commission of immeasurable responsibility given to all who know about the coming of Jesus Christ."[178] Thus the paradigm of Luther's way opens a vista onto Christianity's free responsibility for the world.

This is affirmed elsewhere in the fragments of *Ethics* where Bonhoeffer returns to the paradigm and repeats almost verbatim what he had said in *Discipleship*. "Luther's return from the monastery [is] the fiercest attack that has been launched and the hardest blow that has been struck against the world since the time of earliest Christianity."[179] The point of this remark differs from that in *Discipleship*, where Bonhoeffer takes "secular vocation" as being properly comprehended only as the call of Christ. Now this call must be seen as a setting free for "genuine responsibility."[180]

Regrettably, at this stage Bonhoeffer could not explicate his view of responsibility any further while touching on an issue stemming from his ori-

---

[172] "Ultimate and Penultimate Things" in *DBWE* 6, 149–150 (*DBW* 6, 140–141).

[173] *DBWE* 6, 151 (*DBW* 6, 142).

[174] *DBWE* 6, 151 (*DBW* 6, 142).

[175] *DBWE* 6, 160–170 (*DBW* 6, 152–162).

[176] *DBWE* 6, 164 (*DBW* 6, 157).

[177] *DBWE* 6, 164 (*DBW* 6, 157).

[178] *DBWE* 6, 161 (*DBW* 6, 153).

[179] "History and Good [1]," in *DBWE* 6, 163 (*DBW* 6, 155).

[180] *DBWE* 6, 294 (*DBW* 6, 295). It is not correct to maintain that this responsibility came to Bonhoeffer only by way of the *theologia crucis* in the letters from prison (against Green, Soteriologie, 116). In the first work on the version on "History and Good" Bonhoeffer found the notion of "free responsibility" directly from the Sermon on the Mount which confronts a person with "responsibility for others," (*DBWE* 6, 242 (*DBW* 6, 242)).

entation to Luther. Bonhoeffer had to ask himself how "responsible action" stood *vis-à-vis* "the law of God as revealed in the Decalogue." How can a responsible act not in effect be limited by the "divine mandates of marriage, work, and government?"[181] For Luther, a Christian is obedient by his or her own free will to the law of God as expressed in the "orders" for this world. If obedience is impossible – for example, because of the misuse of an authority's power – then the only option is to suffer. But Bonhoeffer considers that "a deed that arises from freedom" may lead to "guilt [that] one incurs by breaking the law," and precisely in this way may the law be sanctified.[182] No doubt he is thinking of resistance against the National Socialists' usurped "authority."[183] Yet he was far from granting either a people or an individual the right of revolution and in effect he explicitly rejected that option.[184] Disobedience to authorities "can only be a concrete decision in each individual case"[185] and always remains "a venture of one's own responsibility."[186]

Such a daring act is fragile because on the basis of faith in Christ it turns against Christ, who himself established the mandate and hence the "task" of the authorities. Bonhoeffer thus replaces Luther's term "order," which puts too much emphasis "on the static element" and encourages a "romantic conservatism,"[187] with the term "mandate." Even in the early 1930s he had argued against the view that God's orders should be seen as "orders of creation." In *Creation and Fall* he says that "All orders of our fallen world are God's orders of preservation that uphold and preserve us for Christ ... [They have] no value in themselves; instead they find their end and meaning only through Christ."[188] In the fragment "Christ, Reality and Good" in *Ethics*, he interprets this view of the orders even more christologically. It is characteristic of "pseudo-Lutheranism," he says, to separate the orders from the realm of Christ and pronounce their autonomy in the world.[189]

---

[181] "History and Good [2]," in *DBWE* 6, 296 (*DBW* 6, 297).

[182] *DBWE* 6, 297 (*DBW* 6, 299); cf. also *DBWE* 6, 275 (*DBW* 6, 275). The "structure of responsible action" includes the *"willingness to become guilty."*

[183] In his review of the past decade at the turn of the year 1943 Bonhoeffer complains in "After Ten Years" that the German lacks the insight into "the need for free and responsible action, even in opposition to his task and his calling" (*LPP*, 6 (*DBW* 8, 24)).

[184] Cf. his theological assessment "State and Church" in *DBWE* 16, 525 (*DBW* 16, 532).

[185] *DBWE* 16, 517 (*DBW* 16, 522).

[186] *DBWE* 16, 518 (*DBW* 16, 523).

[187] "The Concrete Commandments and the Divine Mandates" in *DBWE* 6, 389 (*DBW* 6, 393).

[188] *DBWE* 3, 140 (*DBW* 3, 129–130). Cf. also "Zur theologischen Begründung der Weltbundarbeit," in *DBW* 11, 337f. Here Bonhoeffer even says: *"Jede Ordnung – und sei es die älteste und heiligste – kann zerbrochen werden und muß es, wenn sie sich in sich selbst verschließt, verhärtet und die Verkündigung der Offenbarung nicht mehr zuläßt."*

[189] "Christ, Reality and Good," in *DBWE* 6, 56 (*DBW* 6, 41). Cf. Bonhoeffer's view of the genesis of this "Pseudolutheranism" in *DBWE* 6, 114 (*DBW* 6, 110).

When "Luther's doctrine of the two kingdoms [is] used ... [in] "its original meaning," it must be in the polemical sense that "the worldly" battles "against the sacralizing trend" of the world and the "sacred" (Christ) against the world's claim to autonomy.[190] One principle alone is valid: there is only "the one realm of the Christ-reality in which the reality of God and the reality of the world are united."[191]

For the formation of this one reality God provides humanity with certain mandates, which at their core are identical with those that Luther taught: authority, marriage, and church.[192] These mandates were based on the medieval social order [*Stände*] and accepted as God's order for the world. To these Bonhoeffer further adds the mandates of work[193] and culture.[194] The reason for these additions is probably found in his experience of the modern world. However, he did not pursue the possibility of considering that even though these mandates originate in human experience they may still lead to humanly responsible and historically adaptable institutions before God. Rather, Bonhoeffer concretizes some of Luther's ideas, particularly that some people are God's "commissioners, vicarious representatives, and stand-ins."[195] They represent "within an earthly relationship of authority" God's authorization and thus designate "an irrevocable above and below."[196] State, marriage and family, economics, culture, and church are not established "from below" but "from above."[197]

This authoritarian conception of the mandates may be prompted by the trauma that the Germans voted Hitler into power on the basis of a form of government "from below," namely democracy. But this does not excuse Bonhoeffer *theologically* for a development in his thought that uses Luther but sets aside a crucial insight of his Christology. As we have seen, the latter holds to a Christology of vicarious representation, stressing Christ's solidarity with those who are "below." But here Bonhoeffer puts claims on Christ in order to legitimatize authoritarian power as "God's representative" in the world. Regarding the church's mandate, even the teaching of the Reformation on the priesthood of all believers is called into question.[198]

---

[190] Cf. *DBWE* 6, 59–60 (*DBW* 6, 45).

[191] *DBWE* 6, 58 (*DBW* 6, 43–44).

[192] On this point, see his deduction of these orders from Luther's interpretation of the fourth commandment in the *Large Catechism* (*The Book of Concord*, 400–410).

[193] Cf. *DBWE* 6, 67–68 (*DBW* 6, 54).

[194] Cf. *DBWE* 6, 366–389 (*DBW* 6, 392). The way in which Bonhoeffer speaks of the mandates, for example the inconsistency in listing them, indicates how tentative his own perspective on these matters were.

[195] *DBWE* 6, 391 (*DBW* 6, 394).

[196] *DBWE* 6, 390–391 (*DBW* 6, 394–395).

[197] Cf. *DBWE* 6, 392 (*DBW* 6, 396).

[198] Cf. DBWE 6, 396–397 (*DBW* 6, 400–401): "The preacher is not the mouthpiece of the congregation ... the mouthpiece of God vis-à-vis the congregation ... The preaching office's

Given such thinking, his teaching on the state is transformed into an outdated conception of "a properly understood divine right of government [*recht verstandene[s] Gottesgnadentums der Obrigkeit*]."[199]

The way Bonhoeffer employed Luther for this conception of political ethics is difficult for us today. His appropriation of Luther is not in accord with the theological presuppositions he had gained from studying Luther, and it goes against the grain of modern conceptions of ethical and political institutions. Perhaps Bonhoeffer could have reconceived his perspectives on God's "mandates" if he could have written his proposed work on the "Church for Others" while in prison. For the prospect arising here is to see social institutions from the viewpoint of God's commandments as a matter of free responsibility.

VII. Temptation and Guidance

Given what we have noted so far, Luther had a persuasive influence on Bonhoeffer in matters of theological formation. It is impossible to fully comprehend how Bonhoeffer thought about God's word, Jesus Christ, and all the other themes central to Protestant theology apart from Luther's insights, whether these played a direct or indirect role. But Luther was even more than a theologian whose insights into the truth of the gospel became paramount for Bonhoeffer's own reflections. The Wittenberg Reformer also demonstrated by his life what it meant to be a Christian and a theologian in a world marred by sin. For Bonhoeffer, theological insights always posed the challenge to live according to them. Luther's theological and spiritual existence became a constant source of encouragement for his own experiences.

Most significant here is "temptation" in Luther's thought. What Bonhoeffer understood by temptation he had clarified in his 1925 seminar essay on "Luther's Feeling about His Work."[200] Luther lost the certitude both that God in his grace is there for a person and that he was properly teaching the gospel. God himself questioned Luther, who is engulfed by *acedia*, a deep sadness.[201] Bonhoeffer frequently refers to Luther's experience.[202]

---

being above is protected ... by a genuine being below of the congregation." Only the person in this office may exegete scripture, a book which is in essence "not a devotional book of the congregation."

[199] "State and Church," in *DBWE* 16, 527 (*DBW* 16, 534–535). Bonhoeffer says that this report should not really be called "State and Church," because "state" implies for him a category of thinking "from below." The title would be better called "Authority and Church."

[200] "Luther's Feelings about His Work as Expressed in the Final Years of His Life Based on His Correspondence of 1540–1546," in *DBWE* 9, 265–267; 296–297 (*DBW* 9, 282–284; 296–297).

[201] Cf. *DBWE* 9, 280–281 (*DBW* 9, 300).

From prison he writes, "I never realized as clearly as I do here what the Bible and Luther mean by 'temptation.' Quite suddenly, and for no apparent physical or psychological reason, the peace and composure that were supporting one are jarred."[203] His petition before God to be spared such temptation was hence vital to him.[204]

He also knew from Luther that temptations could not be arbitrarily circumvented. It is impossible to be a Christian and theologian in a self-confident fashion.[205] As for Luther's "self-knowledge," Bonhoeffer recorded that "To have no temptation is the most severe temptation."[206] "No one should be ashamed when he is profoundly crushed by temptation," he writes in 1936 to participants in the first and second course at Finkenwalde.[207] The reasons are given mainly in his sermons, for example in one on Matthew 8:23–27 in 1933, where he assumes that God shares in our experience of God's distance in the cross of Christ. Whenever God allows us to falter on our path, "in destiny and guilt ... he throws us back on to himself, onto God, because he wants to show us: there, where you let go of everything, where you lose all of your security or must forfeit it, there you are utterly free for God and you are wholly shielded by him."[208]

Luther's experience of temptation became an insight for Bonhoeffer in two ways: it shaped both his theological thinking and the practice of his own piety. This is particularly true for his time in prison. Seen against the backdrop of how he dealt with the temptation of concluding that God is powerless in the world and in the life of a Christian, it is nonetheless false to posit a gap between his theological reflections and his personal faith during that time. With respect to his theology, with the knowledge that

---

[202] In this respect, cf. his impressive biblical interpretation on temptation from the year 1938 in *DBW* 15, 401f. Here Bonhoeffer unfortunately deleted Luther's word *tentatio facit theologum* (temptation makes the theologian) from the manuscript – most likely because the topic for the biblical interpretation was that of "temptation."

[203] *LLP*, 39 (*DBW* 8, 70). Cf. also Bonhoeffer's comments on *acedia* and *tristitia* which often afflicted him (*DBW* 8, 187; cf. 399 (*LPP*, 129; cf. 276)).

[204] Cf. Bonhoeffer's evening prayer in *LPP*, 141–142 (*DBW* 8, 207). That prayer can overcome temptation was also a profound experience of Luther (cf. *DBWE* 9, 266–268 (*DBW* 9, 284–285)).

[205] Cf. *DBWE* 9, 266–267 (*DBW* 9, 284).

[206] "Psychologie," in *DBW* 12, 181. Cf. also the citation of Luther: "Keine Anfechtung haben ist die schwerste Anfechtung [to have no temptation is the most severe temptation]" (*WA* 3, 420), which is also mentioned in the lecture on pastoral counselling in 1936 in *DBW* 14, 584. Bonhoeffer described the lack of temptations in this manner: "Immer größere Gleichgültigkeit gegen Gott und sein Wort, (der Mensch) kann nicht mehr *recht* beten, Gott rückt ihm fern, er empfindet seine Sünde nicht mehr, kennt keine Reue mehr, keine Zuflucht zur Gnade."

[207] Circular letter to the brothers who attended the first and second course in Finkenwalde, in *DBW* 14, 200.

[208] Sermon on Matt. 8:23–27, in *DBW* 12, 445.

God is near his creatures even in the seemingly unbridgeable distance of the cross of Christ, he claimed for Christ the world's "religionlessness" apart from the usual securities of "religion." And with respect to his own life under the threat of death, he accepted it as a "station on the road"[209] on which God was guiding him.[210] In a letter to Eberhard Bethge, Bonhoeffer wrote that "I am so sure of God's guiding hand that I hope I shall always be kept in that certainty. You must never doubt that I'm travelling with gratitude and cheerfulness along the road where I'm being led."[211]

Bonhoeffer scholarship hardly recognizes that Bonhoeffer's emphasis on his certitude in prison belongs to the context of his perception of Luther's existential temptations.[212] In the seminar essay on "Luther's Feelings," Bonhoeffer contended that Luther saw his path to be under "divine guidance."[213] On his own he lacked the strength and insight to go down that path.[214] This was so because, according to Luther, the omnipotent God brings about both good and evil, and thus the resulting temptation must always be overcome anew in *prayer*. Bonhoeffer shared Luther's belief that no one who lives a life in God's presence can escape the experience of a God who is concealed in his acts. But it was essential "that the God who guides can only be known as the God who justifies."[215] This certitude carried him through his imprisonment. Even when God, as Luther put it, becomes disguised in the "It" and meets us in "fate," it is important how we "find the 'Thou' in this 'It'" and learn how fate really becomes guidance.[216] We can find this Thou only in Christ.[217] Guiding is only possible for the God who has already guided us from the state of sin into the state of faith. The darkness and obscurity of the paths on which God leads us are now no longer darkness and obscurity unto death; they are embedded in

---

[209] Cf. the poem "Stations on the Road to Freedom," in *LPP*, 370 (*DBW* 8, 570–572).

[210] *LPP*, 370 (*DBW* 8, 570–572).

[211] *LPP*, 393 (*DBW* 8, 576).

[212] I did not sufficiently emphasize the significance of "guidance" for Bonhoeffer's theology and life in my essay "Gottes Hand und Führung. Zu einem unübersehbaren Merkmal der Rede Dietrich Bonhoeffers von Gott in der Zeit des Widerstandes," in *Bonhoeffer-Rundbriefe*. Mitteilungen der Internationalen Bonhoeffer-Gesellschaft Sektion Bundesrepublik Deutschland, 70 (2003), 22–41.

[213] Cf. "Luther's Feelings about His Work," in *DBWE* 9, 259–261; 265–266 (*DBW* 9, 275–277; 282).

[214] We find a telling similar confession in Bonhoeffer from prison: "I must be able to know for certain that I am in God's hands, not in men's. Then everything becomes easy, even the severest privation" (*LPP*, 174 (*DBW* 8, 252)).

[215] "Determinismus," in *DBW* 10, 415.

[216] *LPP*, 217 (*DBW* 8, 333–334). Cf. also Luther's understanding of the "Disguised" God in *WA* 40/I 174, 13–15.

[217] In a sense, Luther's expression of the "Thou" corresponds to his expression of the concealed and revealed God; cf. *De servo arbitrio*, *WA* 18, 689, 22–25.

the certitude that our lives "have now been placed wholly in better and stronger hands."[218]

We must come to the end, though much more could be said about the relationship of Bonhoeffer and Luther on specific theological and existential questions. Nonetheless, it should now be evident that in this Christian, theologian, and pastor, whose theological clarity and faith-full courage impress Christians everywhere – we often encounter Luther. In Bonhoeffer's theology and life we encounter – far from any Luther cult or Lutheran confessionalism – the heartbeat of one who has a living, Reformed faith in the midst of difficult circumstances. It would be an encouraging sign if those who honour Bonhoeffer today as a martyr would find their own hearts similarly ignited given the conditions of their own time.

---

[218] *LPP*, 190 (*DBW* 8, 287).

Wayne Whitson Floyd

Encounter with an Other: Immanuel Kant and G.W.F. Hegel in the Theology of Dietrich Bonhoeffer

Immanuel Kant (1724–1804) and Georg Wilhelm Friedrich Hegel (1770–1831) were not, for Dietrich Bonhoeffer, distant figures from the eighteenth and nineteenth century. They were thinkers of contemporary significance who still shaped the European and American intellectual landscape within which Bonhoeffer's university education took place, his theology was written, and his life in the resistance movement against Nazism was carried out.

Living in "the west" in a self-consciously "post-modern" age, it is all too easy for twenty-first century interpreters of Bonhoeffer to forget the radicality, at the *terminus a quo* of the Enlightenment, of Kant's original "modern" dare to use one's own reason, rather than submitting to the authority of tradition. And when the intellectual universe of western culture has for a generation now felt rocked by the critique and deconstruction of all the authorities of modernity – intellectual, spiritual, cultural – it can go unnoticed that many of the basic tenets of postmodernism themselves are the *terminus ad quem* of a long run of dialectical strategies for critical inquiry stretching back at least to Hegel and philosophical idealism. Kant and Hegel, for us as for Bonhoeffer, serve as important benchmarks for understanding our own place in the evolution of western thought and culture.

A full and fair reading of Bonhoeffer's theology – particularly the years of its genesis and original development – demands from his interpreters far more attention to the early and ongoing impact of the transcendental-idealist philosophical tradition from Kant to Hegel than has for the most part been given until now. For Bonhoeffer, the legacy of Kant and Hegel was never merely an academic matter, any more than it could be reduced to a topic of historical interest; rather, it not only framed many of his views on the modern world, but also the parameters for theology as a meaningful contemporary undertaking. If in our imaginations we can allow these two modern philosophical giants to linger, figuratively peering over our shoulders – wondering and murmuring at our reading of Bonhoeffer's theology – we may arrive at different conclusions not only about his own theology, but its ongoing significance for a renewal of stratagems for publicly intelligible God-talk in our own place and time as well.

I. Kant: The Copernican Revolution – Modernity

Kant's impact on western intellectual life in the eighteenth century has been likened to the Copernican revolution in cosmology more than two centuries before. Copernicus, in postulating that the earth revolved around the sun and not vice versa, did not just de-center the earth as the privileged central viewing platform for the remainder of reality, but also in the process affirmed the power of human reason itself to make this imaginative leap in perspective. On both fronts the result was the relativizing of the authority of religious – indeed all metaphysical – claims about the nature of reality.

Kant argued that everything we know is perspectival – the objects of our knowledge are known in exactly the way that they are because our minds are built in exactly the way they are. This is what Kant calls "transcendental apperception." The human mind does not passively record the impress of external reality, but actively "imposes upon the material of experience its own forms of cognition, determined by the very structure of the human understanding"[1] – for example, space, time, quantity, quality, relation, etc.

We can know the objects of our knowledge only because the human mind provides the conditions of the possibility of that knowledge. In each and every case, the knowing "subject" makes *a priori* contributions to the "objects" of knowledge. Everything that we experience as "an other" has the inevitable subjective imprint of transcendental apperception. As David Kelsey has explained it, the subject as knower "has a kind of autonomy in that it is not dictated to by a world of already determinate 'objects' that is over against it and simply given to it. [According to Kant] the 'objectivity' of the objects we know is not a given. Rather it is largely constituted by the knowing consciousness ... It is consciousness that organizes experience into an intelligible field of individual objects. So there is a way in which the subject as consciousness is 'behind' or 'outside' the world as a field of knowable objects. It is not an item in the world ... Neither the

---

[1] James C. Livingstone, *Modern Christian Thought: from the Enlightenment to Vatican II* (New York 1971), 65.

knowing subject (or 'transcendental ego') itself nor any other transempirical substance can be a possible object of knowledge."[2]

If this is so, then along with the inevitability of the knower's participation in what is known comes a necessary agnosticism about claiming to know reality "as it really is." Human reason does not provide us with "theoretical knowledge about reality as a whole" – what Kant called "metaphysics." Rather human knowledge must be thought of in a much more modest context. In James C. Livingstone's words, "Kant came to recognize that the human mind finds itself in the peculiar situation of being burdened by certain metaphysical questions which it is unable to ignore but which also appear to transcend the mind's power to answer."[3] That is to say, just because human understanding feels *compelled to ask* foundational questions does not mean that it is *capable of answering* them, however integral the knowing subject remains to all that we can claim to know.

This *a priori* role of the subject in all objects of knowledge clearly called into question the metaphysical underpinnings of previous theology. "The coherence of reality could not any longer be based upon transcendent metaphysical foundations, but must at all times take critically into account the ... activity of the knowing subject,"[4] which was universal and unavoidable in all claims to knowledge.

The metaphysical reserve, or even scepticism, in Kant's position – *vis-à-vis* any renewed metaphysical pretensions of the subject simply to constitute knowledge – came in the form of what Kant called the *Ding-an-sich*, or thing-in-itself, which understanding can neither affirm nor definitively deny, unknowable as it is in any pure, non-interpreted form. As George Stroup puts it, "Human reason cannot claim to know things as they are in themselves, only as they appear to reason."[5] The mystery of finite reality for Kant was irreducible, however thorough our comprehension of the mechanism by which we come to knowledge of it. The mind, prodigious though it was, had limits; as Bonhoeffer will put it, knowledge is always "suspended" between the two boundaries of transcendental apperception and the thing-in-itself.[6] Our understanding does not exhaust reality, but it does say about "the real" everything that we are capable of saying.

---

[2] David H. Kelsey, "Human Being" in Peter Hodgson and Robert King (eds) *Christian Theology: An Introduction to Its Traditions and Tasks* (Minneapolis, newly updated edition, 1994), 178–179.

[3] Livingstone, *Modern Christian Thought*, 63.

[4] Wayne Whitson Floyd, *Theology and the Dialectics of Otherness: On Reading Bonhoeffer and Adorno* (Lanham, Maryland, 1988), 1.

[5] George Stroup, "Revelation" in *Christian Theology*, 125.

[6] Cf. Bonhoeffer, "The Theology of Crisis and its Attitude Toward Philosophy and Science," *DBW* 10, 444–445 on Kant's transcendental attempt to resist the limitlessness of idealism through the *Ding an sich*. Cf. also *DBW* 12, 180: "Das Ich läuft zwischen zwei Grenzen der transzendentalen Apperzeption und dem Ding an sich."

Stroup's conclusion is in the form of understatement: "The consequences of Kant's philosophical program for classical theology and for the natural religion of the Enlightenment were nothing less than revolutionary."[7]

II. Hegel: Dialectical Method – Idealism

If Kant himself is rightly remembered for his role in the modern "turn towards the subject" as well as for the "resistance to subjectivity *par excellence*" – the infamous thing-in-itself – most post-Kantians have been far less hesitant, given the preponderance of *subjective activity* in their dialectical forms of thought, to draw metaphysical conclusions concerning *otherness*. The unstoppable march of the modern "triumph of subjectivity"[8] – whose exemplar for Bonhoeffer was idealism – increasingly came to obscure the function of the ambivalent recalcitrance of the thing-in-itself. Kant's tactical duality of the unity of transcendental apperception and the thing-in-itself, denounced for its supposedly incipient dualism, fell prey to the strategic power of dialectic. The heterogeneity of the object, vilified as mere heteronomy, increasingly came to lose its ability to sustain the resistance, much less any form of priority, of "an other." The thing-in-itself came to be excoriated as pre-critical, a lapse back behind Kant's own Copernican turn. Genuinely critical philosophy was understood to be incompatible with even the postulate of the thing-in-itself.

The transcendental tradition's response to the legacy of Kant is epitomized for Bonhoeffer by Hegel, whom he thought had responded to the Kantian duality – the "unity of transcendental apperception" which pointed to, but could never overcome, the ontological resistance of the "thing-in-itself" – by attempting to collapse it, to conflate act and being. The paradigmatic expression of this was Hegel's *Phenomenology*, which sought to demonstrate that anything *an sich*, in-itself, in the very event of being known "becomes something that is the in-itself only for consciousness."[9] Thus the movement of consciousness "itself becomes the object" of thought.[10] There is nothing which "is" beyond appearance. Knowing may have "limits," but for Hegel they are limits set by reason itself.[11] To know the limits of thought is to have transcended them already.

---

[7] Stroup, "Revelation," in *Christian Theology*, 125.

[8] To borrow from the title of Quentin Lauer's book *The Triumph of Subjectivity: An Introduction to Transcendental Phenomenology* (Fordham 1979) of the same name.

[9] Hegel, *Phenomenology of Spirit*, translated by A. V. Miller (Oxford 1979), 55 (§86).

[10] Hegel, *Phenomenology of Spirit*, 37 (§60).

[11] Bonhoeffer, "The Theology of Crisis," in *DBW* 10, 445: "Kant had tried to limit human thinking, in order to establish it anew. But Hegel saw that limits only can be set from beyond these limits. That means applied to Kant, that his attempt to limit reason by reason presupposes that reason must have already passed beyond the limits before it sets them... The fact is

If Hegel's philosophy can be rightly described as having endeavoured precisely to do away with the thing-in-itself, yet still his critical idealism gives evidence that Hegel knew that the question of anything "beyond" the constitutive power of reason had to be addressed, not ignored, by any philosophy that would ultimately be adequate to the challenges Kant's transcendental philosophy had posed. The result was the nuanced complexity of Hegel's dialectical method of thesis, antithesis, and synthesis – capable in the end of making sense of otherness itself as but a moment in the subject's emerging self-understanding. As we shall see below, the crucial word here for Bonhoeffer is "moment."

III. The Post-Hegelian Terrain

Nineteenth century European philosophy was a drama of competing camps. The one – the so-called left-wing-Hegelians (Feuerbach, Nietzsche and Marx) – emphasized Hegel's critical, "de-constructive" dialectical methodology. The other – the so-called right-wing-Hegelians and their progeny – granted priority to Hegel's own rather dogmatic "constructive" ontological judgment that a rational totality can be a historical achievement, resulting ironically in a philosophical tendency to subordinate the power and freedom of critical reason to the authority of established facts.

The former group understood the legacy of Hegel to imply a dynamic, dialectical approach to society. The latter understood the task of post-Hegelian philosophy to be the systematic explication of static, given forms. As Nietzsche had observed of post-Hegelian culture in his own country, "the whole tendency of the Germans ran counter to the Enlightenment, and to the revolution of society which by a crude misunderstanding, was considered its result: piety toward everything still in existence sought to transform itself into piety toward everything that had ever existed, only to make heart and spirit full once again and to leave no room for future goals and innovations. The cult of feeling was erected in place of the cult of reason."[12] This was to give support to increasingly romantic and even conformist views of society rooted in blood and soil, which prepared in part the ground for National Socialism.

Over against these tendencies there arose in the 1860s a renewed post-Hegelian interest in transcendental philosophy that took form in a "back to

---

that thinking can never limit itself; in limiting itself it establishes itself." Cf. Bonhoeffer, *DBWE* 2, 44–45 (*DBW* 2, 37–39).

[12] Quoted in Fritz Stern, *The Politics of Cultural Despair. A Study in the Rise of the Germanic Ideology* (Berkeley, CA. 1961), 277.

Kant" movement known as neo-Kantianism.[13] The label "neo-Kantian" is, however, misleading, having been used to designate both of the competing Marburg and Heidelberg (or Baden or Southwestern) approaches to a return to Kant. The Marburg School, including Hermann Cohen, Paul Natorp, Nicolai Hartmann (in dialogue with whose positions several crucial sections of Bonhoeffer's *Act and Being* were to be written) and later, Ernst Cassirer, "can be said to have concentrated principally on logical, epistemological and methodological themes," particularly relating to the natural sciences. The Baden School, including Wilhelm Windelband and Heinrich Rickert, alternatively "emphasized the philosophy of values and reflection on the cultural sciences." In addition, "neo-Kantian" also has been used to speak of such diverse thinkers as Rudolf Otto, Max Weber, Eduard Spranger, Karl Mannheim, Georg Simmel and Wilhelm Dilthey.[14]

There were, however, at least five assumptions shared by those who saw themselves beneath the broadly neo-Kantian umbrella: (1) the use of a "transcendental method" to ascertain the conditions of the possibility of knowledge, value and action; (2) the "critical" rejection of "knowledge of contents or essence" beyond experience, resulting in a shared metaphysical agnosticism; (3) the continued inquiry into the broad tradition of idealist epistemology; (4) the rejection of Kant's thing-in-itself; and (5) the assertion of the primacy of practical reason.[15] These five assumptions in large measure shaped the immediate intellectual environment in which Bonhoeffer developed his theology, which affirmed the first three of neo-Kantianism's assumptions, while differing markedly with neo-Kantianism about the thing-in-itself, as well as the primacy, if not sole intelligibility, of practical reason. On the one hand, he was indebted to neo-Kantian philosophy and the protestant liberalism it had inspired through Hermann Lotze to Albrecht Ritschl and Adolf von Harnack (Bonhoeffer's teacher at Berlin), for having reinvigorated the Kantian transcendental approach. But it had waged its consistent battle for metaphysical agnosticism and the primacy of practical reason only at the price of losing the critical, de-ontologizing, de-totalizing function of Kant's retention of the thing-in-itself.

On the other hand, the Schleiermachian-romanticist and the Hegelian-monistic strategies, which had originally arisen, we should remember, as supposedly superior alternatives to the "abstractness" of Kantian "criticism", were both all too easily co-opted by the "antirepublican, chauvinist,

---

[13] See Lewis W. Beck, "Neo-Kantianism," in *The Encyclopedia of Philosophy* (New York 1967), vol. 5, 468–473. The following description of neo-Kantianism was previously published in similar form in Floyd, *Theology and the Dialectics of Otherness*, 42–43.

[14] Beck, "Neo-Kantianism," 472–473.

[15] Thomas Willey, *Back to Kant. The Revival of Kantianism in German Social and Historical Thought, 1860–1914* (Detroit 1978), 37.

Pan-German, and *völkisch* sentiments"[16] of totality, wholeness, identity. The loss of the ongoing significance of critique – critical reason – was significant in the generation leading up to Bonhoeffer, for whom, as Herbert Marcuse has noted, "this demotion of reason made it possible to exalt certain particularities (such as race or the folk) to the rank of the highest value."[17] As the intellectual historian Martin Jay has pointed out, it was this line of "Hegelianism" which nourished "the *völkisch* ideology of the national *Gemeinschaft* transcending social contradictions."[18]

Thus by the 1930s the dialectical-method, and the critique of the given state of affairs that had characterized both Kant's transcendentalism and Hegel's philosophy was, according to Marcuse, "an integral part of the culture which authoritarianism had to overcome." Kant's dare to use one's own reason, as well as Hegel's dynamic conception of society, always standing under the critical gaze of *theoria*, stood in stark contrast with Nazi ideology's conception of the *Volk* as "a natural reality bound together by 'blood and soil' and subject to no rational norms or values." Carl Schmitt, whom Marcuse called "the one serious political theorist of National Socialism," ironically proclaimed that on the day of Hitler's ascent to power: "Hegel, so to speak, died."[19] In Bonhoeffer's time, as in ours, the legacy of Kant and Hegel was never merely an academic matter.

IV. Kant and Hegel in Bonhoeffer's Theological Education

While Adolf Hitler was writing *Mein Kampf* from prison, Dietrich Bonhoeffer was still a seventeen year old teenager immersed in a first reading of Kant's *Critique of Pure Reason*. A letter of 3 November 1923 from Tübingen (where he was a student for a year before entering the Friedrich-Wilhelm University in Berlin) glowingly reported to his family: "A seminar class given by Groos on the *Kritik der reinen Vernunft* began today. I liked it a lot."[20] As a seventeen and eighteen year old student at Tübingen, Bonhoeffer was taking seminars from Karl Groos in logic, history of modern philosophy, and Kant's *Critique of Pure Reason*.

Then at the University of Berlin from 1924–1927 Bonhoeffer studied church history in a seminar with Adolf von Harnack and theology with Reinhold Seeberg. He encountered the work of Luther scholars such as

---

[16] Fritz K. Ringer, *The Decline of the German Mandarins. The German Academic Community 1890–1933* (Cambridge, MA. 1969), 250.

[17] Herbert Marcuse, *Reason and Revolution. Hegel and the Rise of Social Theory* (Boston 1960), 267.

[18] Martin Jay, "Metapolitics of Utopianism," in *Dissent* (1970), 347.

[19] Quoted in Marcuse, *Reason and Revolution*, 419.

[20] *DBWE* 9, 66 (*DBW* 9, 63).

Karl Holl and that of young "radical" theologians such as Karl Barth and Rudolf Bultmann. He read Max Weber, Ernst Troeltsch, and Friedrich Schleiermacher.

Berlin and its great University, however, also had been the home of renowned faculty in philosophy such as J. G. Fichte and Hegel himself (1818–1831). Students at Berlin had included Karl Marx, who attended there in the 19th century, as did in the early twentieth century Walter Benjamin, Gerschom Scholem, and Martin Buber. So it should not surprise us that Bonhoeffer the theology student was in the summer of 1924 also studying epistemology with Heinrich Maier, and later in the winter of 1924–1925, history of ideas of logic from University Instructor Rieffert. Bonhoeffer was to return to the University of Berlin in 1929, at the age of twenty-three, to serve as *Voluntärassistent* in Systematic Theology to Wilhelm Lütgert, a specialist in German Idealism who was the successor to Seeberg, and the author of *Die Religion des deutschen Idealismus und ihr Ende*.

V. Kant and Hegel in Bonhoeffer Interpretation

In the first phases of Bonhoeffer studies in the 1950s and 1960s, the impact on Bonhoeffer's theology of Kant and Hegel – indeed of philosophy and philosophical theology in general – was minimized, if not totally neglected. Even now a bibliographical search of secondary literature turns up barely a dozen citations specifically on Bonhoeffer and either Kant or Hegel, and more than half of these are from the past decade. During the 1970s and 1980s, prior to the rediscovery of the philosophical influences on Bonhoeffer in the writings of Wayne Floyd and Charles Marsh, and later, Laurie Brandt Hale, there were, in fact, only three published articles on Bonhoeffer and Kant and four published articles on Bonhoeffer and Hegel.[21]

---

[21] Hiroshi Obayashi, "Bonhoeffer's Kantianism" at Union Theological Seminary, Archives and "Implicit Kantianism in Bonhoeffer's Conception of Religionless Christianity," in *Northeast Asian Journal of Theology* 5-6 (1971), 107–126 ; Stuart Picken, "Kant and Man's Coming of Age," in *Scottish Journal of Theology* 26 (1973), 63-70; Richard Comstock "Young Hegelians and Radical Theologians Revisited," in *Religion in Life* 46 (1977); William J. Peck, "Preliminary Considerations on Bonhoeffer's Relation to Hegel," in Fourth International Bonhoeffer Congress, Hirschluch, Bonhoeffer Secondary Papers; Rolf Ahlers, "Hegel and Bonhoeffer: Community and Return," in *The Community of Freedom: Barth and Presuppositionless Theology*, Theology and Religion 40, American University Studies, Series 7 (New York 1989), 148-88; Maruo Bozzetti, *Bonhoeffer ed Hegel. A proposito del seminario su Hegel tenuto nel 1933 dal Privatdozent Dietrich Bonhoeffer*," in *Hermeneutica, Annuario di filosofia e teologia*. Nuova Serie 1996: Rileggere Bonhoeffer (Brescia 1996). On the Bonhoeffer interpretations of Floyd, Marsh, and Hale, see below.

Eberhard Bethge's *Dietrich Bonhoeffer: A Biography* gave scholars their first tool for surveying the presence of philosophical interlocutors throughout Bonhoeffer's writings, but it tended to segment out the philosophical conversations rather than seeing them as essential to the very world of thought that Bonhoeffer inhabited as a scholar, theologian and participant in the life of his church and nation. "In *Act and Being*," Bethge wrote, "Bonhoeffer was essentially addressing philosophers, whom he found guilty of the original sin of idealism, namely, confinement in the self."[22] Unfortunately this had the result of making the early philosophical-theological explorations of Bonhoeffer seem propadeutic at best, if not actually unnecessary in order to understand Bonhoeffer's emerging theological voice. In the United States, Bonhoeffer's comment in *Letters and Papers from Prison* about turning from "phraseology to reality"[23] became an oft-quoted excuse to view Bonhoeffer as a practically-minded ethicist and ecumenist who had turned aside from his youthful intellectual philosophical-theological indiscretions.

Even the more intellectually sophisticated scholarly treatments of Bonhoeffer's early theology were not immune to misleading their readers about Bonhoeffer's approach to philosophy and theology. Two of the most influential, Ernst Feil's *The Theology of Dietrich Bonhoeffer* and Clifford Green's *Bonhoeffer. A Theology of Sociality*, were the first major interpretations of Bonhoeffer to inquire systematically into the significance of Kant and Hegel among the myriad philosophers who had influenced Bonhoeffer's theological project. Feil, however, does not differentiate between Kant and Hegel as what he thinks of as subject-object thinkers,[24] and he reduces Bonhoeffer's distinction between the *actus directus* of pure-intentionality and the *actus reflectus* of totalizing thinking to "the distinction between faith and theology."[25] And Green, although the first to explore with any thoroughness the intellectual resources upon which Bonhoeffer drew in his "theological development,"[26] still in *Bonhoeffer. A Theology of Sociality* tends to misplace too much emphasis on anthropology as Bonhoeffer's guiding concern.[27] Bonhoeffer's own personal psychology, particularly struggles with his own ego, also is misrepresented as

---

[22] Bethge, *Dietrich Bonhoeffer*, 133, note 24; cf. 135: "*Act and Being* was criticized correctly for its one-sidedness and conceptual oversimplifications."

[23] *LPP*, 275 (*DBW* 8, 397).

[24] Feil, *The Theology of Dietrich Bonhoeffer*, 7.

[25] Feil, *The Theology of Dietrich Bonhoeffer*, 28.

[26] Clifford Green, *Bonhoeffer. A Theology of Sociality* (Grand Rapids/Cambridge, revised edition, 1999), 68.

[27] Green, *Bonhoeffer. A Theology of Sociality*, 70: "His actual preoccupation in *Act and Being* is unmistakable... He now concentrates on *theological anthropology*." Cf. 74: "*Act and Being* begins with a critique of philosophical anthropology, proceeds to interpret revelation... and concludes by building ... a more concrete Christian anthropology."

"largely responsible" for Bonhoeffer's schematic portrayal of idealism as the central philosophical danger to be avoided by theology.[28] Green then subverts much of his own nuanced work on Bonhoeffer's formative projects when he states that in the early dissertations Bonhoeffer "attacks all philosophy ... by tending to reduce it to the form he found most problematic, namely, an absolute idealism."[29]

Beginning in the mid-1980s a series of dissertations began to emerge, primarily in the United States, that signalled a sea-change in reading Bonhoeffer's early theology in dialogue not only with the philosophy of his own time but with philosophers who after Bonhoeffer's death continued to work on themes that had preoccupied him. These inquiries into Bonhoeffer's theology were unique in that they saw the philosophical issues he explored as expressions of the very architectonic of his thought – essential to the substance, not just the style or historical circumstances of his theology.

My own dissertation, "Theology and the Dialectics of Otherness: Epistemology, Sociality and Ethics in Bonhoeffer's *Act and Being* and Adorno's *Negative Dialectics*" (Emory University, 1986), subsequently published as *Theology and the Dialectics of Otherness*, brought Bonhoeffer's reading of the idealistic and dialectical philosophical traditions of the west into conversation with the uncannily similar proposals made by Bonhoeffer's contemporary, the formative critical theorist, Theodor Adorno. Bonhoeffer and Adorno never met, or so far as I can tell ever were aware of the other's existence, but Adorno lived in both Berlin and London during times when Bonhoeffer did as well, and from a secular Jewish left-Hegelian perspective asked the same questions, and at times replied in ways strikingly parallel to Bonhoeffer's relatively bourgeois Protestant Christian point of view. The published version of *Theology and the Dialectics of Otherness* was preceded in print by what was actually a synopsis of the dissertation, "Christ, Concreteness and Creation in the Early Bonhoeffer," and then was followed by a more constructive interpretive essay, "Style and the Critique of Metaphysics" in a volume co-edited with Charles Marsh, *Theology and the Practice of Responsibility*. These three pieces remain central to understanding why in my own work the Bonhoeffer-Adorno conversation has proved so fruitful, despite my subsequent growing appreciation of the not insignificant distance between them in social location and intellectual phylogeny.

---

[28] Green, *Bonhoeffer. A Theology of Sociality*, 78, note 35: Green observes that "the philosophers who reviewed the book were very critical, especially of Bonhoeffer's oversimplification in consistently forcing the epistemological problem back to idealism ... Bonhoeffer's own almost subterranean personal involvement in the anthropological problem of the book is largely responsible for this distortion," although later Green says "I oppose the use of this insight in any form of psychological reductionism."

[29] Green, *Bonhoeffer. A Theology of Sociality*, 70.

Charles Marsh's dissertation, "Philosophy and Community in the Early Theology of Dietrich Bonhoeffer" (University of Virginia, 1989) was followed by two articles on Hegel and idealism, "Human Community and Divine Presence: Bonhoeffer's Theological Critique of Hegel" and "The Overabundant Self and the Transcendental Tradition: Bonhoeffer and Luther Against the Self-Reflective Subject." His excellent book, *Reclaiming Dietrich Bonhoeffer: The Promise of His Theology*, has done much to deepen our understanding both of Bonhoeffer's reading of Hegel and his fascination with the dialogical-personalist tradition.

More recently another University of Virginia doctoral student, Lori Brandt Hale, completed a theologically perceptive and philosophically sophisticated study of Bonhoeffer, "Love Your Enemies? Dietrich Bonhoeffer and the Question of the Other" (University of Virginia, 2004). Such conceptually-astute readings of Bonhoeffer also can be seen in Walter J. Lowe, "Bonhoeffer and Deconstruction: Toward a Theology of the Crucified Logos" and Robert P. Scharlemann, "Authenticity and Encounter: Bonhoeffer's Appropriation of Ontology." I also must mention the quite promising proposals of the late Jörg Rades, whose enticing dissertation chapter drafts, one entitled "Bonhoeffer and Hegel: From *Sanctorum Communio* to the Hegel Seminar, With some Perspectives for the Later Works," remained unfinished and unpublished with his untimely death while pursuing his graduate degree at the University of St. Andrews.[30]

VI. Bonhoeffer's Doctoral Dissertation: Sanctorum Communio

One of the reasons that there have been only sporadic attempts to unravel the tangle of philosophical influences on Dietrich Bonhoeffer is that his own two main attempts to locate himself within a broader intellectual context were his densely argued doctoral dissertations: *Sanctorum Communio* and *Act and Being*. These two books bear many of the same recognizable marks of intellectual virtuosity combined with unfocused youthful precociousness that can be seen in most doctoral dissertations. Each was heavily influenced by the subjects and sources his mentors themselves had encouraged; and each draws heavily on secondary sources, leaving it unclear at times just how much of the primary corpus Bonhoeffer had at that point managed to tackle. And yet each of these works stands on its own today as remarkable expressions of a unique new theological voice, as comfortable with Nietzsche as with Barth.

---

[30] The sections that follow below concerning *Sanctorum Communio* and *Act and Being* could not have been written in the form they take were it not for my ongoing conversations with Marsh and Hale, especially given the clarity they each have brought about the implications of the Kant-Hegel debate for contemporary theology.

Sanctorum Communio, his doctoral dissertation, bears striking thematic and terminological similarities to the seminal writings of several existentialist and dialogical-personalist thinkers who were his contemporaries, including Martin Buber, *Ich und Du* (1920) and Eugen Rosenstock-Huessy, *Angewandte Seelenkunde* (1924).[31] Indeed, the general question of the relationship between the "I" and "An Other" (You or Thou) was drawing thematic attention during the 1920s in numerous other quarters as well, as manifested in Hans Ehrenberg's *Disputation: Drei Bücher vom Deutschen Idealismus* (1923–1925), Ferdinand Ebner's *Das Wort und die geistigen Realitäten: Pneumatologische Fragmente* (1921), and Franz Rosenzweig's *Der Stern der Erlösung* (1921). Otherness was in the air, and Bonhoeffer was not the only one to catch on to the significance this theme had far beyond the usual confines of his academic discipline.

So it is not surprising that the I-You relationship of personalism provided the initial frame for Bonhoeffer's thinking – and for his initial counter-readings of Kant and Hegel. The immediate impetus for this is Max Scheler (*Formalism in Ethics and Non-formal Ethics of Values*) and Theodor Litt (*Individuum und Gemeinschaft*) as well as Eberhard Grisebach, whom Bonhoeffer had discovered from his reading of Friedrich Gogarten,[32] and Emmanuel Hirsch. As Joachim von Soosten has commented: "In contrast to the epistemological inquiry that had dominated modern philosophy, Bonhoeffer finds himself attracted to the 'phenomenological method' which no longer has the cognitive self as its center. The other who confronts the self as a You guarantees that reality cannot be deduced from the cognitive self ... the I-You-relation serves as a countermodel to modernity's subject-object scheme."[33]

Without a doubt, the thing that struck Bonhoeffer about philosophical personalism was that from this perspective the resistance to the power of the subject is, in the words of Charles Marsh, part of "a social, ethical dynamic." For "when I am encountered by the dialogical other in ethical action, I am arrested in my own attempts to master the world; for in responding to the call of the Thou, I am taken out of myself and repositioned in relation to the other. I no longer control the other, nor does the other con-

---

[31] Jürgen Moltmann in 1959 was the first to notice the roots of Bonhoeffer's personalism in "Dilthey, Buber, Grisebach, Gogarten, Rosenstock-Huessey, and others;" see "The Lordship of Christ and Human Society," in *Two Studies in the Theology of Bonhoeffer*, edited by Jürgen Moltmann and Jürgen Weissbach, translated by Reginald and Ilse Fuller (New York 1967).

[32] Eberhard Grisebach's *Die Grenzen des Erziehers und seine Verantwortung*, was published in Halle, 1924. There is no evidence that Bonhoeffer was acquainted with the works of either Ebner or Rosenzweig at that time; see Bethge 83. See also Joachim von Soosten, "Editor's Afterword" to *Sanctorum Communio*, *DBW* 1, 298.

[33] Joachim von Soosten, "Editor's Afterword to the German Edition," *DBWE* 1, 297 (*DBW* 1, 315).

trol me, but we both discover our individual and social identities in the place of our difference," namely "in the space of the relational between."[34]

Indeed, Kant comes into Bonhoeffer's argument for the first time when he speaks of "Kant's development of the epistemological concept of person" that had come on the heels of Descartes' "transformation of the metaphysical question into an epistemological one."[35] As the young scholar summarizes Kant at this point, "the knowing I becomes the starting point of all philosophy. Because the synthesis of transcendental apperception resolves the opposition of subject and object as well as the I-You-relation in the higher unity of spirit, of intellectual intuition, a new philosophical approach is created for solving the problem of the social basic-relation as well."[36] Bonhoeffer's complaint is that as Kant's philosophy "resolves the opposition of subject and object in the unity of mind ... it does not distinguish at all between a subject-object-relation and an I-You-relation; rather, the latter is subsumed under the former."[37]

I and You – the very relationships that are the basis of human community – are for Bonhoeffer always to be understood as providing an ethical boundary, not merely a conceptual challenge, for one another. The other person is indeed to be encountered as a limit beyond which responsible behaviour cannot transgress. "I enter [the social sphere]," Bonhoeffer says, *"only when my intellect is confronted by some fundamental barrier [Schranke]."*[38] Although Kant had posed the *Ding an sich* as a limit to the pretensions of reason, "to the extent that the *Ding an sich* is posed as barrier ... thinking has surpassed any limit. In conceiving the barrier of thought, thought has already gone beyond it."[39] Only when we define the You as "the other who places me before an ethical decision" do we move, according to Bonhoeffer, "beyond the epistemological subject-object-relation."[40]

Much of Bonhoeffer's early intellectual journey must be understood as a journey to discover an adequate barrier or resistance to the power of the

---

[34] Marsh, *Reclaiming Dietrich Bonhoeffer*, 69, speaking about the argument of *Sanctorum Communio*.

[35] *DBWE* 1, 40 (*DBW* 1, 22).

[36] *DBWE* 1, 40 (*DBW* 1, 22).

[37] At this point Bonhoeffer inserted a footnote in *DBWE* 1, 42, note 5 (*DBW* 1, 23, note 5) saying that "one may perhaps object to finding Kant mentioned here, without qualification, among the Idealists." Yet at this point in his intellectual development, as well as his argument in *Sanctorum Communio*, it is clear that Bonhoeffer – under the influence of Scheler and Hirsch – thinks of Kant as "the first of a line that progresses up to Hegel;" cf. *DBWE* 1, 43, note 26. Later in *Act and Being*, Bonhoeffer distinguishes Kant's "genuine transcendental philosophy" from post-Kantian idealism; cf. *DBWE* 2, 33–35 (*DBW* 2, 27–29).

[38] *DBWE* 1, 45–46 (*DBW* 1, 26); emphasis in original.

[39] Marsh, *Reclaiming Dietrich Bonhoeffer*, 70.

[40] *DBWE* 1, 52 (*DBW* 1, 32).

intellect to try to comprehend all of reality – sometimes sought in will, sometimes in ethical demand, sometimes through embodiment, and ultimately in community. Thus his ultimate judgment on Kant is that, beginning as he does with an understanding of person as epistemological object, we should not be surprised that in the end Kant in Bonhoeffer's judgment "does not grasp the idea of concrete community."[41]

Throughout *Sanctorum Communio*, the personalist argument drives Bonhoeffer's initial reading of Hegel, just as had been the case with his reading of Kant, although the tragic thing about idealism was its inability to break through to personal spirit. Bonhoeffer had sought through the language of personalism to state the contours of an ontological diversity beyond the I: "For the individual to exist, 'others' must necessarily be there. But what is the 'other'?"[42] – Bonhoeffer asks. "The You sets the limit for the subject."[43]

The crucial question arises at this point whether we can "simply exchange dialogicalism for transcendentalism and claim that we have gotten beyond the synthetic grasp of the Kantian subject."[44] Marsh is among the few who have seen the difficulty that faced a thinker such as Bonhoeffer, who wanted to escape the vicious circularity of the epistemological subject-object paradigm: "As a rejection of the philosophy of the universal subject and a turning toward the factual human I, the philosophy of dialogue belongs entire to the same movement of thought as transcendental inquiry ... If the place of the person's encounter with the absolute is taken by his encounter with the Thou of his neighbor, and if the I's claim to be absolute is transferred willy-nilly to the encounter by the other in the between, then what occurs is not the overcoming of the absolute claim per se to master the world but the inversion of the absolute claim from the I to the encountering other."[45]

Later in *Act and Being* Bonhoeffer will come to exactly this conclusion, that in the dialogical approach, "in the attempt to avoid all absolutizing, it is the You which is absolutized."[46] Thus, personalism fails to provide Bonhoeffer what he sought, "a conception in which the difference of the I and other remains in every case uncompromised."[47] As Bonhoeffer later wrote

---

[41] *DBWE* 1, 197, note 210 (*DBW* 1, 132, note 68). Even here, though, Bonhoeffer already is struck by something distinctive in Kant among the idealists, continuing on to say "And yet it is Kant who came closest to the Christian concept of community." See also, *DBWE* 1, 210, note 79 (*DBW* 1, 142, note 79), where Bonhoeffer refers to *Religion Within the Limits of Reason Alone*, concerning Kant's "commonwealth" and the church.
[42] *DBWE* 1, 51 (*DBW* 1, 30).
[43] *DBWE* 1, 51 (*DBW* 1, 31).
[44] Marsh, *Reclaiming Dietrich Bonhoeffer*, 77.
[45] Marsh, *Reclaiming Dietrich Bonhoeffer*, 79.
[46] *DBWE* 2, 88 (*DBW* 2, 82).
[47] Marsh, *Reclaiming Dietrich Bonhoeffer*, 71.

in his inaugural lecture at Berlin, "Grisebach succeeds ... by making the Thou absolute in place of the I and by giving it a position which can only be God's ... Grisebach's intentions certainly deserve serious consideration, but he is unable to carry them through with his own means."[48]

In *Sanctorum Communio* Bonhoeffer took two large steps towards fulfilling his own requirements for a philosophical theology that can sustain the difference between I and other, resisting the pretensions of idealism, and yet at the same time can account for the essential sociality of human beings and the essential bonds between human beings in community. First, he turned from the individualism of the subject-object relationship – even when transmuted into a relationship of I and You – towards a more communitarian understanding of "person" within the framework of the church-community, the *Gemeinde*. Second, in the way he portrayed the distinctiveness of the church-community, he turned in a decidedly christological direction, with an emphasis on the concreteness of incarnation as that alone which can sustain the self-other distinctiveness, arguing that the church itself should be understood as "Christ existing as church-community." Therefore, it is the community-as-incarnate-existence to which Bonhoeffer will repeatedly turn as a way of sustaining the mutuality of relatedness and otherness in human interactions.

As Charles Marsh has put it, if "the relation of I and other cannot be reduced to the identity of I and other, but is animated by the ethical demand of the Thou, then the pivotal question must be addressed of how I and other can be thought together in community ... Bonhoeffer's sustained response in the dissertation to the quandary of the separateness of persons and their life together in inseparable community is Christological in character"[49] – Christ existing as church-community. "If a connection cannot be made between the difference of I and other and the unity of their life together, then we must concede that Bonhoeffer fails to carry through on his promise that 'Christ existing as community' ... avoids many of the pitfalls of the transcendental tradition."[50]

It was Hegel, not surprisingly, who provided Bonhoeffer the language to connect his concern with community with this developing incarnational-christological focus. In the first case, his concern with inseparable com-

---

[48] "Man in Contemporary Philosophy and Theology," *NRS*, 55 (*DBW* 10, 367–368).

[49] Marsh, *Reclaiming Dietrich Bonhoeffer*, 72–73.

[50] Marsh, *Reclaiming Dietrich Bonhoeffer*, 72. With this philosophical-theological quandary in mind, Bonhoeffer's chapters in *Life Together* on "Community," "The Day Together," and "The Day Alone" read quite differently than they originally did for English speaking readers with the first paperback edition of *Life Together* with the idyllic church camp fireside gathering on the cover. When we also remember that *Life Together* was itself written in four weeks in the fall of 1938 just preceding *Kristallnacht*, we are reminded that what has often been dismissed as an abstruse philosophical conundrum actually continued to shape and drive Bonhoeffer's thinking right up into the time of the outbreak of war.

munity, Bonhoeffer borrows Hegel's concept of "objective spirit."[51] By this Bonhoeffer means "social spirit as opposed to subjective spirit"[52] – "an objective spirit, the spirit of sociality, which is distinct in itself from all individual spirit."[53] Later he goes on to say that "where wills unite, a 'structure' is created – that is, a third entity, previously unknown, independent of being willed or not willed by the persons who are uniting."[54] Thus, Bonhoeffer concludes, "in the dialectical movement through which alone persons originate, individual collective persons come into being as well."[55] This is important for Bonhoeffer because he wants to argue that it is not the "object" or the "You" but the collective person of the church-community that alone is capable of providing the boundary, the limit, adequate to assert itself against the pretensions of the knowing subject.

It is quite suggestive that "Christ existing as church-community" is used by Bonhoeffer not just to describe the "being" of the church, but a paradigmatic "act" of that community in which "each one bears the other's burden," for example in intercessory prayer.[56] Here the need of the other impinges upon me from outside and completely beyond my control, and I can either respond to the challenge of the other's need or not, but the need remains, not of my doing. As Bonhoeffer himself put it: "Thus, when one person intercedes in the name of Christ on behalf of the other, the whole church-community – which actually means 'Christ existing as church-community', to use a modification of the Hegelian concept – participates in that person's prayer."[57]

The epitome of this act is what Bonhoeffer calls *Stellvertretung*, or vicarious representative action,[58] in which one person intercedes not just on

---

[51] Hegel, "The Philosophy of Spirit," 483ff. Bonhoeffer draws here on his teacher Seeberg, *Dogmatik*, volume 1, 505ff. Bonhoeffer acquired much of his initial Hegelian conceptuality from Seeberg and Lütgert.

[52] *DBWE* 1, 98 (*DBW* 1, 62).

[53] *DBWE* 1, 74 (*DBW* 1, 46). See Hegel, *Encyclopedia of the Philosophical Sciences in Outline*, edited by Ernst Behler (New York 1990) in which Part C, "The Philosophy of Spirit," section 2, deals with "The Objective Spirit."

[54] *DBWE* 1, 98 (*DBW* 1, 62).

[55] *DBWE* 1, 103 (*DBW* 1, 66).

[56] *DBWE* 1, 188 (*DBW* 1, 126). Again, we can see the practical consequences of this in unexpected places like the chapter on "Service" in *Life Together*, *DBWE* 5, 100 (*DBW* 5, 85), where Bonhoeffer writes: "The other person is a burden to the Christian, in fact for the Christian most of all... Only as a burden is the other really a brother or sister and not just an object to be controlled."

[57] *DBWE* 1, 189 (*DBW* 1, 126); Hegel's phrase was "God existing as church-community" which Bonhoeffer probably got from Seeberg's *Dogmatik*, volume 2, 298ff.

[58] *DBWE* 1, 79, 120, 146, 148, 155ff., 178, 184, 191. Many readers encounter *Stellvertretung* first in Bonhoeffers *Ethics* (cf. *DBWE* 6, 231, 235, 257-258, 288, 404) and assume it to be an expression of his later, rather than his early, theology.

behalf of, but in the place of another,[59] even to the point of being willing to accept as one's own the fate or the punishment deserved by the other. This dynamic describes both an individual person and the collective person of a community such as the church-community. In doing so, Bonhoeffer says, "the church-community as a whole is in Christ, is the 'body of Christ'; it is 'Christ existing as church-community'."[60] One must not miss the counter-idealist thrust of this claim that the church-community, which later from prison he will describe as defined by the fact that it "exists for others,"[61] holds open the space for the encounter with "an other." Such an encounter comes not from my own willingness to allow an other to exist, but through the claim of the other person on me, the burden of their freedom to be who they are.

It is important to notice at this point that even Bonhoeffer's attempt to see the collective person of communities as "an other" capable of resisting the pretensions of the "I" had itself already been anticipated in Hegel, for whom "the church or 'community of Spirit' originates with the transition from the sensible presence of God in Christ to God's spiritual presence in the community of faith. The essence of this community is a unique, transfigured intersubjectivity, distinguishable from all other forms of human love and friendship."[62] The claim of the other on the "I"-who-am-placed in a posture of obligation is for Hegel just the antithesis of the claim of the subject's constitutive power. And in the end, the dialectical synthesis will sublate even this other, overcoming its perceived resistance and raising it to a higher level of subjective fulfillment.

At this point Bonhoeffer appears to have mostly an intuitive sense both of how difficult it will be to think in a dialectical fashion more clever than Hegel's and of the way he will come to his own alternative approach. Already, however, he is turning to the significance of the theological concept of "revelation" and in particular the incarnation as the expression of God's chosen way of being "an other" to human beings. This comes not as moral demand, or ethical obligation, but as pure gift of grace – "God's own love in Christ ... no longer approaching us in demand and summons, purely as You, but instead by *giving God's own self as an I, opening God's own heart. The church is founded on the revelation of God's heart.*"[63]

---

[59] Cf. *DBWE* 1, 118–121 (*DBW* 1, 74–76) on ethical collective persons; one then hears the deeper significance of Bonhoeffer's asking his seminarians at Finkenwalde to do what was for them the very un-Lutheran thing of learning to make and hear private confessions with one another (see *DBWE* 5, 108–118 (*DBW* 5, 93–102)).

[60] *DBWE* 1, 190; cf. 121, 130, 136, 139, 141, 189ff., 199f., 207, 211, 214, 216, 231, 260, 275, 280, 288. Also see *DBW* 11, 269, 271f.

[61] *LPP*, 382 (*DBW* 8, 560).

[62] Peter Hodgson and Robert C. Williams, "The Church," in *Christian Theology*, 259–260.

[63] *DBWE* 1, 145 (*DBW* 1, 91); emphasis in original. It is instructive to compare at this point Bonhoeffer's response to idealism with that of Karl Barth, both on the theme of revela-

If so, then for "the person living in the community of the I-You-relationship ... the other member of the church-community is essentially no longer claim but gift, revelation of God's love and heart. Thus the You is to the I no longer law but gospel, and hence an object of love." Bonhoeffer concludes: "each may and ought to become a Christ to the other."[64]

VII. Bonhoeffer's Habilitationsschrift: Act and Being

When Bonhoeffer continued in *Act and Being* his conversation and dispute with the transcendental tradition, he recapitulated at the start his position *vis-à-vis* the dialogical personalism of Gogarten and Grisebach. He would reaffirm his conclusion that the concept of person in itself did not provide the barrier to the pretensions of the ego to define reality, indeed that personalism "remains within the hegemony of the transcendental tradition," itself "unable to secure the continuity of human togetherness"[65] beyond one-on-one encounters. This is familiar ground already for the reader of Bonhoeffer's *Sanctorum Communio*.

Had Bonhoeffer there been intent on simply rejecting philosophy's error, one might be surprised to find him in *Act and Being* returning to a deepening conversation with the very epistemological tradition against which he had turned seemingly in favour of personalism. In his *Habilitationschrift* Bonhoeffer makes clear the importance of understanding the dynamic relationship between Kant's transcendentalism and Hegel's idealism. Bonhoeffer understood, as a later interpreter would put it, that Kant's "unfinished business" with the thing-in-itself had been the occasion for Hegel to charge that despite Kant's "concentrated attention upon the fundamental capacities of the human subject," in the end "he had not taken with full seriousness the character of human subjectivity as all-determinative and self-transcending."[66] The reason he retraces his contention against idealism, only now with growing subtlety, is that Bonhoeffer saw an as yet unexamined ethical issue hidden within Hegelian epistemo-

---

tion. As Charles Marsh has shown in *Reclaiming Dietrich Bonhoeffer*, 10, Barth, in "the delineation of God as the one who is always subject... reverses Kant's skepticism about the presence of God in experience by the ironic means of beating him at his own game." Bonhoeffer to the contrary, realizing that Barth has overcome Kant's scepticism about the presence of God in experience only at the cost of being able to speak meaningfully of "the continuity of God's relation to the world" (11), counters by insisting that "the divine subject act is the being of revelation in community. 'Christ existing as community' is the concretization of God's knowing act in time and history" (12). In Bonhoeffer's words from *Act and Being*, *DBWE* 2, 112 (*DBW* 2, 108): "the community of faith is God's final revelation."

[64] *DBWE* 1, 183 (*DBW* 1, 121).
[65] Marsh, *Reclaiming Dietrich Bonhoeffer*, 68.
[66] Walter Lowe, "Christ and Salvation," in *Christian Theology*, 234–236.

logy's responses to the unfinished work of Kant: the morality of the process of the subject's exertion of power and control over the possibility of any authentic otherness.

We must remember that Kant crafted his "critical philosophy" vis-à-vis both the "dogmatism" of metaphysics, "the presumption that it is possible to make progress with pure knowledge, according to principles, from concepts alone," and any easy "scepticism" that "makes short work with all metaphysics." Kant proposed his critical philosophy, to the contrary, as "the necessary preparation for a thoroughly grounded metaphysics."[67]

Hegel, in turn, defined "dogmatism" not over against licentious progress in knowledge, but rather opposing "the opinion that the True consists in a proposition which is a fixed result, or which is immediately known," rather than emerging in a dialectical process.[68] The result was that in Hegel's hands Kant's search for the transcendental conditions of the possibility of knowledge turned into the idealistic proposal that knowing is a process, not fixed, in which the knower mediates all that is known. Finally, according to Johann Gottlieb Fichte, a full-blown idealism does away with any enduring "otherness" to the knowing-I whatsoever, for any philosophy "which equates the I in itself with something else and sets something else in opposition to it" is "dogmatic".[69]

Bonhoeffer's return to the epistemological paradigm in *Act and Being*, on the heels of his quasi-personalist dismissiveness of subject-object conceptuality in *Sanctorum Communio*, betrays his growing understanding of both the complexities of the transcendental tradition itself, and the difficulties in easily escaping its philosophical grasp. His return to the Kantian definition of the limits of philosophy – and Hegelian and Fichtean idealism's constant abuse of power in transgressing the limits of genuine Otherness through the pretensions of reason – led Bonhoeffer also into conversation with the problem of intersubjectivity in the philosophies of Edmund Husserl and Martin Heidegger, whose *Being and Time* had been published in 1927, just after Bonhoeffer's work on *Sanctorum Communio* was complete.[70]

---

[67] Kant, *Critique of Pure Reason*, translated by Norman Kemp Smith (New York 1965), B, xxxv-xxxvi, 32.

[68] Hegel, *Phenomenology of Spirit*, 23 (§ 40).

[69] J. G. Fichte, *Grundlage der gesamten Wissenschaftslehre als Handschrift für seine Zuhörer* (Leipzig [1794] 1911); see Bonhoeffer, *DBWE* 2, 37, note 10. See Marsh, *Reclaiming Dietrich Bonhoeffer*, 57, who says that although Bonhoeffer attributes the modern origin of the "totalizing claims" of philosophy to Kant and Hegel, his definition of "idealism" is actually far closer to Fichte's *Wissenschaftslehre*.

[70] Hans-Richard Reuter, "Afterword" to *Act and Being*, *DBWE* 2, 165 (*DBW* 2, 166): "It would appear that Bonhoeffer, at least at the time of writing *Act and Being*, had gained his understanding of the basic conceptual constellations of the European tradition from secondary sources ... The philosopher Hinrich Knittermeyer, on whose interpretation of Kant Bonhoef-

Throughout *Act and Being*, Bonhoeffer is arguing that what is needed is a form of theological thinking that takes seriously both philosophy's own repeated attempts to desist from its own intrinsic tendency toward system, toward totality, and the reasons they must be judged a failure. To do so Bonhoeffer picked what can only be seen as the most difficult test case both for anti-metaphysical Kantians or totalistic-leaning Hegelians: the theological category of revelation. Is there a way to speak meaningfully in a modern context of any unveiling or disclosing of ultimate truth that honours both the Kantian retention of the thing-in-itself and the Hegelian dialectical reason that Fichte had thought he had merely taken to its logical conclusion? That, Bonhoeffer said, was the question that Kant and idealism have posed for theology.

Here we see why it has been so important for Bonhoeffer to be more and more careful to distinguish Kant's transcendentalism from post-Hegelian idealism, but also to distinguish Hegel's dialectical method from the metaphysical claims made on its behalf by those like Fichte who wished to say that thought was capable of exhausting reality. "Bonhoeffer is inquiring here about the totalizing urge of reason, *Vernunft*, to overcome 'the being between' that is human existence. Thinking, according to Bonhoeffer either will be *genuinely* transcendental and ontological, or it will be *systematic* and totalizing. The latter option" – which Bonhoeffer described with the word "idealism" – "recognizes *neither* the true act of thinking-within-limits (the goal of genuine transcendental philosophy) nor the nature of the being of what-is-thought, yet remains beyond-thought, as something transcendent (the goal of genuine ontology)."[71]

Bonhoeffer is attempting in *Act and Being* to state the shape of a "genuine transcendentalism" and its corollary "a genuine ontology"; and he does so with constant reference to Kant's distinction between thought's unifying function (the unity of transcendental apperception) and that which resists being brought completely under the sway of reason (the thing-in-itself). A genuinely dialectical form of thinking is possible only to the extent that it sustains both thought – understood to be always "in reference to" but not totally able to grasp reality in its entirety – and the ontological resistance of authentic otherness itself[72] – both act and being. In Bonhoeffer's typology, the prospects for either a genuine transcendental philosophy or a

---

fer had built his case in *Act and Being* against Neo-Kantianism and idealism, immediately referred to this critically in his review of Bonhoeffer's book." Bethge also quotes a letter he received in 1964 which said: "At the time of *Sanctorum Communio* Bonhoeffer had absorbed the bourgeois Hegelian renaissance but hardly Hegel himself" (Bethge, *Dietrich Bonhoeffer*, 82, note 110). Bonhoeffer benefited from the appearance during this time of the new edition of Hegel edited by Georg Lasson, as well as Lasson's own commentary, *Einführung in Hegels Religionsphilosophie* (Leipzig 1930).

[71] Floyd, "Editor's Introduction," *DBWE* 2, 12.
[72] Cf. *DBWE* 2, 10.

genuine ontology are dependent on philosophy's capacity to maintain the relationship between both the activity of thinking and something transcendent, *ein Tranzendentes*, to thought – ontologically distinct from the thinking subject –neither of which "swallows up" the other. This is why in *Act and Being* Bonhoeffer had boldly stated that "We need to ask whether Kant did not proceed to place reason within it rights precisely by defining its limits and whether, for that reason, he is not to be given from the outset the title of the epistemologist par excellence of Protestantism."[73]

Bonhoeffer's dialectical claim that "'being between' that which is transcendent is 'Dasein'"[74] brings to mind the dialogical philosophy of Martin Buber, whose work Bonhoeffer seems not to have known in any detail, and the whole personalist school of thought, particularly the philosophy of Eberhard Grisebach, whose influence on *Act and Being* was profound. If "metaphysics" names the pretensions of reason to be comprehensible through itself, Bonhoeffer asks, to acquire an illusory "access to God,"[75] then what would be the outlines of a post-metaphysical doctrine of revelation?

Bonhoeffer in *Act and Being* was concerned, therefore, with the question of whether Kant's restraint, his refusal to conclude that thought was capable of exhausting reality, could be sustained by critical thinking itself in what Bonhoeffer called a "purely transcendental understanding of Dasein,"[76] or human existence. For such genuine transcendentalism, Bonhoeffer writes in *Act and Being*, "there is no knowledge capable of going beyond the proposition that phenomena, the external world, are 'in reference to' the I and are, consequently, knowable only via the I. It does not lie within the competence of a purely transcendental thinking to draw from this a subsequent judgment about being, negative or positive."[77] There is in genuine transcendentalism an openness to being that is sustained by its refusal to replace "the transcendental reference with the ontological judgment concerning the creative power of the I,"[78] which for Bonhoeffer would amount to letting "the I and God the creator exchange roles."[79]

This is why for Bonhoeffer the concept of revelation is so important, for it names that situation of openness, where reality is always and only to be understood "in reference to" the thinking subject, whose process of thought is ontologically "suspended" in being that it has not created.

---

[73] *DBWE* 2, 34 (*DBW* 2, 28–29). See also *DBWE* 2, 34, note 5, which points out an important mistranslation of this passage in the earlier English edition of *Act and Being*.
[74] *DBWE* 2, 35 (*DBW* 2, 29).
[75] *DBWE* 2, 75 (*DBW* 2, 70).
[76] *DBWE* 2, 43 (*DBW* 2, 36).
[77] *DBWE* 2, 43 (*DBW* 2, 36).
[78] *DBWE* 2, 43 (*DBW* 2, 36).
[79] *DBWE* 2, 44 (*DBW* 2, 37).

"Revelation stands against the system."[80] The notion of thought-as-spontaneity of genuine transcendentalism thought must "for the sake of the freedom of being ... become receptivity – that is, creative thinking must become a viewing."[81] This can only be accomplished by leaving being 'fully independent of thinking'."[82]

In *Act and Being* Bonhoeffer is arguing that this "'in reference to' [*in Bezug auf*] and the 'suspension' [*Aufgehobensein*] of the act in being are basically amenable to a theological interpretation and, therefore, of help in the understanding of the concept of revelation."[83] To speak of revelation invites a form of thinking in which thought "really surrenders its claim" and acknowledges the claim of "an other." The question that revelation thus poses to the philosopher is whether reason itself "can possibly carry this out."[84]

Immediately following the completion of *Act and Being* Bonhoefer on three occasions interpreted his densely argued *Habilitationschrift* for a variety of audiences. The first occasion was his inaugural lecture at Berlin on July 31, 1930, "Die Frage nach dem Menschen in der gegenwärtigen Philosophie und Theologie."[85] The second was a lecture prepared in English at Union Theological Seminary in 1931, "The Theology of Crisis and its Attitude toward Philosophy and Science," in which Bonhoeffer presents his own ideas in close concert with the early dialectical theology of Karl Barth.[86] The third, also written in English in 1931 is "Concerning the Christian Idea of God."[87]

The premise shared by all three is that "In the very moment when the idealists pushed away the *Ding an sich*, Kant's critical philosophy was destroyed; a fact, which Hegel clearly recognized."[88] What remains to be said is what effect this has on the very possibility of theological language to resist merely doing likewise, reducing the mystery of revelation to the intelligibility of reason and in the process destroying theology's ability to remain in "the between" of revelation, suspended between act and being – that is to say, to continue to affirm both the subject's role in constituting the phenomena of experience and the resistance of reality to being grasped in its totality.

---

[80] *DBWE* 2, 94 (*DBW* 2, 89).
[81] *DBWE* 2, 61 (*DBW* 2, 54).
[82] *DBWE* 2, 60 (*DBW* 2, 54).
[83] *DBWE* 2, 79 (*DBW* 2, 73).
[84] *DBWE* 2, 60 (*DBW* 2, 54).
[85] Cf. "Man in Contemporary Philosophy and Theology" in *NRS*, 46–65 (*DBW* 10, 357–378).
[86] *DBW* 10, 434–449.
[87] *DBW* 10, 423–433.
[88] "The Theology of Crisis," in *DBW* 10, 445.

In the inaugural lecture, the two possibilities for understanding humanity are either to recognize the limits on understanding that have been proscribed by Kant's notion of an "I" that is essential to all knowledge yet cannot itself become an object of knowledge, remaining rather its presupposition, or to "take possession of one's own I, to see the central occurrence of intellectual happening in the coming-to-itself of the I"[89]– the "closing of the circle" that happens when the "I" snatches at transcendence and draws it into itself.[90] In the latter case, Bonhoeffer concludes, "We notice that we are thrown back firmly on Hegel."[91]

Although one may argue against the wisdom of Bonhoeffer's use of the shorthand, one-size-fits-all reduction of all "thinking" to "Hegel" or "idealism," it reinforces Bonhoeffer's ongoing and unwavering suspicion that distinctions among various forms of idealism are but different stages in the evolution of a single philosophical motive. Once one sets out on the path of "system", its totalizing pull knows no limits. As he concludes in "The Theology of Crisis": "its power and its claim are boundless; it is its own standard. Here all transcendence is pulled into the circle of the creative ego."[92]

The essay, "The Theology of Crisis," written during Bonhoeffer's time at Union Theological Seminary, provides an interesting example of the young Bonhoeffer – in many ways swept off his feet by the dialectical theological approach of Karl Barth – distinguishing himself from Barth on this critical issue of how theology is to understand its own role given the seemingly inherent tendency towards "system" in the nature of thought itself. In the "essential boundlessness of thinking, in its claim to be a closed system, in its egocentricity," Bonhoeffer writes, Barth himself sees "a philosophical affirmation of the theological insight of the Reformers, which they expressed in terms of the *cor curvum in se, corruptio mentis*. Human beings in *statu corruptionis* are indeed alone, they are their own creator and lord, they are indeed the center of their world of sin. They have made themselves God and God their creature."[93] Bonhoeffer's understanding of Barth's appeal to Luther's theological insight that sin is about our hearts being turned in on themselves, rather than being open to God, seems to go hand in glove with Bonhoeffer's own insight that philosophical idealism fails because it is the product of a humanity that "refers everything to itself, puts itself in the center of the world, does violence to reality, makes itself God, and God and the other person its creatures."[94] As he put it in the

---

[89] *NRS*, 51 (*DBW* 10, 358).
[90] *NRS*, 52 (*DBW* 10, 359).
[91] *NRS*, 57 (*DBW* 10, 365).
[92] *DBW* 10, 443.
[93] *DBW* 10, 446.
[94] *DBW* 10, 425; translation altered.

inaugural lecture, "The I really remains in itself and that is not its credit, but its guilt."[95]

If his audience was expecting Bonhoeffer, therefore, simply to join Barth in appealing to the Christian revelation of Christ as the "from outside"[96] that thinking cannot provide itself – and thus to join the "Barthians" in concluding that "there is no Christian philosophy"[97] – Bonhoeffer's alternative approach must have come as a surprise.

He approaches the issue with the wariness of the student about to criticize his teacher, asking seemingly rhetorically: "What ought to be according to Barth and his friends the task of philosophy"? Bonhoeffer continues: "Barth himself has not answered this question sufficiently, but his friends have thought a great deal about this problem: Philosophy remains profane science, there is no Christian philosophy."[98] Bonhoeffer agrees that "philosophy has to be critical philosophy, not systematic." But instead of rejecting all philosophy outright, he concludes that "since even critical philosophy is bound to be systematic ... philosophy must work in sight of this fate."[99]

Bonhoeffer rather concluded that theology is not itself an impossible discipline, nor is philosophy *per se*, so long as each "gives as far as it can room to God's revelation, which indeed makes room for itself by itself."[100] Theology brings to the table the fact that, although philosophy "essentially remains in reflection" – *actus reflexus* – "theology at least knows of an act of God, which tears man out of this reflection into an *actus directus* toward God."[101] As Bonhoeffer continues this line of thought in "The Christian Idea of God," what is needed is "a genuine theological epistemology"[102] that, "as thinking per se ... is not excepted from the pretension and boundlessness of all thinking," but which "knows its own insufficiency and its limitations" and thereby can "leave room for the reality of God," even in theological thought.[103]

Such a theology cannot be achieved merely by willing to turn aside from the systems of idealistic thinking. "The will to refrain from a system," Bonhoeffer had written in *Act and Being*, perhaps thinking of his own earlier susceptibility in *Sanctorum Communio* to the temptations of dialogical-personalism, "as a deliberate act of ethical modesty toward the other, is no more a basis for the understanding of revelation than are good

---

[95] *NRS*, 60 (*DBW* 10, 365).
[96] *DBW* 10, 440.
[97] *DBW* 10, 447.
[98] *DBW* 10, 440.
[99] *DBW* 10, 440.
[100] *DBW* 10, 448.
[101] *DBW* 10, 448.
[102] *DBW* 10, 425.
[103] *DBW* 10, 426.

works."[104] Rather, what is needed is a form of theological thinking that can affirm the finitude of God's "revelation in history,"[105] – "the foolishness of the Christian idea of God, which has been witnessed to by all genuine Christian thinking from Paul, Augustine, Luther, to Kierkegaard and Barth" that "God himself dies and reveals [the divine self] in the death of a man, who is condemned as a sinner."[106] And yet such thinking must be able to distinguish between God's finite, historical "revelation in hiddenness," and humanity's sinful desire for "revelation in openness,"[107] the ironic "openness" of "the captivity of human thinking within itself"[108] that is itself the truest sign of human brokenness.[109] Revelation needs a form of thinking that both attends to the "immediacy" of that historical particularity of revelation – which can "take seriously the ontological category in history"[110] – and yet continues to distinguish itself, as thought, from the reality whose presence it mediates.

Bonhoeffer had already been well aware in *Act and Being* that the challenge for theology is not somehow to escape the act-being framework of western metaphysics. There Bonhoeffer had chastised his potential critics by saying that "the objection that categories of a general metaphysical kind also have been employed in these proceedings overlooks the necessity of a certain formal 'preunderstanding', on the basis of which alone questions – even wrong ones – can be raised, whose answer is then surrendered by revelation, together with a fundamental correction of the question."[111] The problem for theology, as *Act and Being* understood it, is not to step outside metaphysics; it is that of adequately interpreting the idea of revelation from the standpoint of the act-being problem. "The concept of revelation must therefore yield an epistemology of its own."[112]

In summary, the attempts of genuine transcendental philosophy (Kant) to resist becoming idealism (Hegel) and the attempts of critical ontology (Heidegger and Grisebach) to overcome the temptations of systematic ontology (Scheler and Fichte) are not statements of the polar extremes of the argument of *Act and Being*; rather, for Bonhoeffer, they are to be understood as successive attempts to maintain the contrast of act and being, to give expression to the necessary discontinuity of concrete existence – all of them unsuccessful.

---

[104] *DBWE* 2, 89 (*DBW* 2, 83).

[105] *DBW* 10, 429–430.

[106] *DBW* 10, 432; translation altered.

[107] *DBW* 10, 429.

[108] *DBW* 10, 425.

[109] Cf. *DBW* 10, 437: "God's revelation in Christ is revelation in concealment, secrecy. All other so-called revelation is revelation in openness."

[110] *DBW* 10, 429.

[111] *DBWE* 2, 153 (*DBW* 2, 152).

[112] *DBWE* 2, 31 (*DBW* 2, 26).

VIII. Traces of Kant and Hegel in Bonhoeffer's Later Theology

Even looking just at these early university writings, it should be clear that Bonhoeffer's readings of Kant and Hegel did not by any means remain static. Kant's transcendentalism needed to be distinguished from Hegel's idealism; Hegel's dialectic needed to be distinguished from Fichte's absolute idealism. And following the completion of *Act and Being* – as Marsh and Rades and Hale all have in one manner or another observed – "Bonhoeffer's approach toward Hegel matures strikingly. His writings become more attentive to the richness and polyvalence of Hegel's thought. He is less concerned with overcoming Hegel than in thinking along with the philosopher on the meaning of God's presence in the complex drama of divine worldliness."[113]

One of the best indications of Bonhoeffer's growing appreciation for the nuances of Hegel's dialectic unfortunately did not survive – the text of his final seminar lectures at Berlin from the summer of 1933, "Dogmatics: Hegel's *Philosophy of Religion*." The set of student notes that did manage to make it through the war and into print unsurprisingly show more about what Bonhoeffer's students didn't understand than what their professor was attempting to say! Yet as Marsh has said, they "give us a clear sense of Bonhoeffer's openness to and interest in the theological dimensions of *The Phenomenology of Spirit* and *Lectures on the Philosophy of Religion*."[114]

The broader import of Bonhoeffer's Kantian-Hegelian explorations of revelation was first seen in his theological interpretation of Genesis, published as *Creation and Fall*. One cannot help but hear Bonhoeffer's meditations on this text as a parable of the promise and failure of idealism to sustain the ethical challenge of "an other" to escape the power and domination and control of "the I." According to *Creation and Fall*, God comes in the middle of time and the world,[115] creating humanity in its creaturely freedom,[116] the freedom of one creature to be in relation both with another and with God.[117] The *imago dei*, the image of God in which Genesis says human beings were created, "is" this relationality – this sociality of creatureliness. The analogy to be drawn between humanity and God is not an *analogia entis*, an analogy of being; it is an *analogia relationis*, an analogy of relationship.[118] As God is freely in relationship with God's creation, so

---

[113] Marsh, *Reclaiming Dietrich Bonhoeffer*, 91.
[114] Marsh, *Reclaiming Dietrich Bonhoeffer*, 91.
[115] *DBWE* 3, 31 (*DBW* 3, 30).
[116] *DBWE* 3, 62–64 (*DBW* 3, 58–60).
[117] *DBWE* 3, 64 (*DBW* 3, 60).
[118] *DBWE* 3, 65–66 (*DBW* 3, 61).

is the creature created to be free-for the other.[119] This is the basis of all authentic community; it is the basis of the church itself.[120] To stay centered in relationship is to have life;[121] to transgress the limits of relationship – to transgress the other as a limit or boundary to one's own pretensions of power – is to desire to be *sicut deus*, like God, not a creature.[122] It is in fact a desire to be even more in love with power than God, whose power is shown in God's creating humanity in our freedom not from, but for, others.

Already in *Sanctorum Communio* Bonhoeffer had drawn the ethical inference that idealist epistemology "overcomes in principle the limit of the individual person."[123] Now "the fall" is portrayed by Bonhoeffer as the Promethean attempt to take the place of God – at least God as the serpent has tempted the first human beings to see God – and to become limitless, all-powerful, one whose very existence comes to be defined by the violent transgression of the limit of the Other. The result is that for Bonhoeffer the theological category of sin is understood to be not so much a basic as a derived theological category – sin is the breaking of the very relationships with God and one another that constitute who we are. Sin is the violation of a limit, the transgression of a boundary, the denial of the freedom of "an other" person to "be" who they are so that we might enter into relationship with them, the desire to make the "other" into but an image of myself.[124]

Thus, in *Creation and Fall* Bonhoeffer restores the Cain and Abel story as the conclusion of the whole creation-fall narrative in Genesis – seeing fratricide as the ultimate outcome of a humanity living *sicut deus*, in the serpent's misrepresented image of God rather than in the image of God in which humanity actually was made, as essentially sociality. For to transgress the limits of relationship – to transgress the other as a limit or boundary to one's own pretensions of power – is to desire to be God, not a creature.[125] The failure of the moral claim of Abel to call to a halt the totalizing power of the I of Cain, was of course the failure of transcendental philosophy up to and including philosophical personalism, a failure Bonhoeffer was to address by invoking the "second Adam," Christ, who restores the *imago dei* and makes possible the recognition of the limits within which humanity was created to live.

The lectures on christology, which preceded those on creation and sin by just a semester, had already in fact proposed that Jesus is the Other –

---

[119] *DBWE* 3, 66 (*DBW* 3, 61).
[120] *DBWE* 3, 99 (*DBW* 3, 92).
[121] *DBWE* 3, 83 (*DBW* 3, 78).
[122] *DBWE* 3, 112 (*DBW* 3, 104).
[123] *DBWE* 1, 42 (*DBW* 1, 23).
[124] See *Sanctorum Communio*, chapter 4, "Sin and Broken Community," *DBWE* 1, 107–121 (*DBW* 1, 69–76).
[125] *DBWE* 3, 113 (*DBW* 3, 104–105).

par excellence, the sought-for limit to human pretensions, the center of human existence, history, and nature precisely because the concreteness of revelation in Christ – the new Adam – provides the creative limit that allows humanity to be authentically human, rather than a demonic usurper of divine power. Bonhoeffer returned to this theme of the limits of creatureliness and their role in human responsible action in *Discipleship* and his *Ethics*, saying "The life of a brother or sister is a boundary for Jesus' followers which may not be crossed."[126] It is at the conceptual heart of all his writing about peace and the love of even one's enemies. This enduring theme of the transgression of the other, the refusal to know any limits, is what Bonhoeffer in *Act and Being* had warned theology against – its perpetual temptation to let "the I ... [become] the point of departure instead of the limit-point."[127] And to be limitless is to be incapable of being encountered by the revelation of Christ and the gift of "an other" in the church-community as well. This is what Bonhoeffer meant in *Act and Being* when he wrote that "Thinking, including theological thinking, will always be 'systematic' by nature and can, therefore, never grasp the living person of Christ into itself. Yet there is obedient and disobedient thinking (2 Cor. 10:5). It is obedient when it does not detach itself from the church, which alone can 'upset' it as 'systematic' thinking, and in which alone thinking has meaning."[128]

IX. Bonhoeffer's "Kantian" Fragmentariness – The Letter and Essay as Style

"When we look at Kant's philosophical theology as a whole and form the vantage point of the mid-twentieth century, it is true to say that Kant's contribution to modern theology lies primarily in the far-reaching influence and use of his ideas rather than in the intrinsic worth of his own theological doctrine ... Kant's importance, then, lies in the wealth and suggestiveness of his ideas."[129] Livingston's words about Kant might well have been said about Bonhoeffer, for the details of his early theological work have been as little known by most of his interpreters as Kant's *Critique of Pure Reason*. And yet the reach and influence of Bonhoeffer's struggles with Kant and Hegel extends far beyond their technical arguments about transcendental philosophy and idealism.

Hanfried Müller wrote what I still think are important words of advice for all those who try to put Bonhoeffer's youthful theological house in or-

---

[126] *DBWE* 4, 122 (*DBW* 4, 123); cf. *DBWE* 6, 189–190 (*DBW* 6, 183–184).
[127] *DBWE* 2, 39 (*DBW* 2, 32).
[128] *DBWE* 2, 132 (*DBW* 2, 130–131).
[129] Livingston, *Modern Christian Thought*, 75–76.

der: "I think that [an] understanding of the whole Bonhoeffer will come about not by systematizing everything he thought as though it were all on the same level, and thus relativizing it, but rather by taking up the movement of his thought in its entirety as the thing which can lead us further."[130] In trying to take up the movement of his thought, interpreters of Bonhoeffer, from Karl Barth forward, have lamented the fragmentariness of his thought, while seldom taking into account the fact that his 'mature thought' may never even have begun to emerge. Especially as we look for the enduring impact of Kant and Hegel on Bonhoeffer's emerging theology, we need to keep in mind that Bonhoeffer completed and published both his doctoral dissertation, *Sanctorum Communio*, and his second or *Habilitation* dissertation, *Act and Being* (which allowed him to teach at the university), and then had presented his inaugural lecture at Berlin, all by the ripe age of twenty five. When we compare this to Kant's having written the *Critique of Pure Reason* at the age of forty-eight – and Hegel's having only begun by the age of fifty-seven virtually all of the works for which he is remembered – it should be sufficient reminder that Bonhoeffer was, for his entire "adult" life quite a "young" theologian, though intellectually precocious beyond his chronological age, and wizened far beyond his years by the struggles and demands of life in the midst of the cultural crisis in Europe between the world wars and throughout the dozen years of Nazism.

Inspirational as he may have been, the fact that he produced no "systematic" theological opus has allowed him to be disregarded as a thinker to reckon with. The obvious danger in this is that, lacking Bonhoeffer's mature systematization of his own theological position, we are in danger of seeing ourselves as left with but a pastiche of "eminently quotable but egregiously misconstruable" aphorisms from a heroic and tragic figure from our past.[131]

Our reading of Kant and Hegel in Bonhoeffer's theology suggests, however, a quite different reading of the fragmentariness of Bonhoeffer's theological corpus – that Bonhoeffer's non-systematic style is not so much a symptom of its incompleteness as it is an affirmation of incompletion in theological method, the open-endedness of any theology that would claim to be heir of the transcendental and dialectical approaches of Kant and Hegel. If so, then one of the main lessons to learn from reading Kant and Hegel alongside Bonhoeffer is that a systematic, exhaustive accounting of his theology is not to be had – not because he did not live long enough – or have adequately systematic a mind – to bring together a theological com-

---

[130] "Concerning the Reception and Interpretation of Dietrich Bonhoeffer," in *World Come of Age*, 183–184.
[131] Gillian Rose, *The Melancholy Science. An Introduction to the Thought of Theodor W. Adorno* (New York 1978), ix-x.

pendium, but because his anti-systematic or anti-metaphysical style of thinking points towards what he himself from prison dubbed a polyphonic form of theological practice, best enacted through the interventions and interruptions of the literary forms of letter and essay, sermon and poem, novel fragment and lecture. These are the forms of a theology in the "between" – where in Bonhoeffer's theology God has chosen to dwell and make God known.

The fragmentariness of expression of Bonhoeffer's theology may be the result of the fact that his own words are themselves always and only "*in bezug auf*" – with reference to, pointing toward something. And his theology may be one of those forms of performative thinking that itself must be "suspended" within the communities of those who have been called together by the revelation of what they are not, by the prerogative and gift of the Other. In this way, the particularity and continuity, the fragmentariness and urge towards wholeness, that defines us as human being will remain in the productive tension that defined for Bonhoeffer the church-community; in Hegel's terms they will continue to mediate one another. Such is the nature of theology done in finitude.

X. Bonhoeffer's "Hegelian" Critique of Idealism – Music, History and Time

Jacques Derrida once wrote that "We will never be finished with the reading or rereading of Hegel."[132] I understand him to mean at the least that anyone who writes about Hegel when they are young discovers in later life just how lacking in subtlety and cleverness they really were. I still remember as a graduate student proudly bringing home my new copy of Karl Barth's *Protestant Theology in the Nineteenth Century*, which I had bought just so I could read the section on Hegel, only to find Barth himself warning against facile attempts to reject Hegel's dialectic, "because we might find that everything we are tempted to say in contradiction to it has already been said within it."[133] As his own wrestling with Hegel continued to grow in sophistication, Bonhoeffer found himself less frequently tempted "to reject Hegel's dialectic" and rather to seek in dialogue and dispute with Hegel a form of thinking and speaking adequate to Christian theological claims about revelation and incarnation. Ironically, Bonhoeffer found, it was Hegel who had provided the most-nearly-successful attempt.

In this Bonhoeffer joined Barth, who too had discovered that in Hegel's dialectical posture all truth is discovered in the "ceaseless completion of

---

[132] Quoted in Mark C. Taylor, "Introduction," in *Deconstruction in Context: Literature and Philosophy* (Chicago 1986), 1.

[133] Barth, *Protestant Theology in the Nineteenth Century* (Valley Forge 1976), 396.

the circle, all error is contained in stopping and staying at one of the moments of the concept, which are necessary as stages, but are thought of not as points to be stopped at but as points to be passed through." Hegel's dialectic is at best a captivating, widening gyre, whose fascination has caused some to lament "the sorcery of Hegel."[134] At its worst, to use Theodor Adorno's graphic image, it is all-consuming "belly turned mind, and rage is the mark of each and every idealism."[135] One can see why Barth wound up with the summary judgment of Hegel: "a great problem and a great disappointment, but perhaps also a great promise."[136]

Bonhoeffer himself clearly remained under the spell of "the legacy from Kant and Hegel," who continued to shape his approach to theology long after they themselves ceased to be the focus of his inquiry. Indeed, such was the influence of the latter on Bonhoeffer's understanding of the theological task that, as Charles Marsh has put the matter, "Whether Bonhoeffer turns out to be a Hegelian by default is a question that must not be ignored."[137]

Yet the difficulty in asking this question in the later writings of Bonhoeffer is that to a significant extent he ceases to talk about Kant or Hegel *per se*, despite the fact that their names continue to appear sporadically throughout his corpus – not because he has lost interest or changed his mind, but because, like grammar in a sentence, they have disappeared as topics of conversation because they have become part of the very structure ordering all topics of conversation that do get discussed. Marsh is right that in his later writings, Bonhoeffer continues to "position his conversation ... in the Hegelian problematic of identity and universal subjectivity," although "most of his later conversations with Hegel are subtextual."[138] Marsh also aptly understates the necessary caution that "whether, in the end, Bonhoeffer's own description of reconciliation and life with God succeeds in illustrating a different theological conception than Hegel's is a complicated question," despite the fact that Bonhoeffer's own particular "appropriation of Hegelian themes is always one of creative and critical redescription in light of his Christological axiom."[139] It is a safe wager that Bonhoeffer, however, already in his short life had come to appreciate Derrida's statement from a half-century later, that "Misconstrued, treated lightly, Hegelianism only extends its historical domination."[140]

---

[134] The phrase if Eric Voegelin's.
[135] Adorno, *Negative Dialectics*, translated by E. B. Ashton (New York 1973), 23.
[136] Barth, *Protestant Theology in the Nineteenth Century*, 421.
[137] Marsh, *Reclaiming Dietrich Bonhoeffer*, 80.
[138] Marsh, *Reclaiming Dietrich Bonhoeffer*, 83.
[139] Marsh, *Reclaiming Dietrich Bonhoeffer*, 91.
[140] Derrida, *Writing and Difference* (Chicago 1978), 251. It is instructive to note that late in the Nazi period Bonhoeffer is still making up for lost time with primary sources, for example in his letter to Eberhard Bethge on 28 November 1940 he asked for Kant's *Sämtliche*

It is clear that the 'sorcery of Hegel' worked on him until the end, the lure of the desire to be able to resolve the alienation of antithesis into a final synthesis of Spirit.[141] It is with this in mind that we should read the remarkable letter that Bonhoeffer wrote from prison, saying "the important thing today is that we should be able to discern from the fragment of our life how the whole was arranged and planned, and what material it consists of. For really, there are some fragments that are only worth throwing in the dustbin ... and others whose ... completion can only be a matter for God ... If our life is but the remotest reflection of such a fragment, if we accumulate, at least for a short time, a wealth of themes and weld them into a harmony in which the great counterpoint is maintained from start to finish ... we will not bemoan the fragmentariness of our life, but rather rejoice in it."[142]

In my own work I have previously asked whether "this appeal to 'wholeness' *vis-à-vis* the fragmentation of his life simply represents Bonhoeffer's own final longing for a metaphysical-theological system? Or does the musical imagery of 'harmony' and 'counterpoint' lead us to the brink of a genuinely non-metaphysical style of theological thinking?"[143] From prison he celebrated the fact that "life isn't pushed back into a single-dimension, but is kept multi-dimensional and polyphonous. What a deliverance it is to be able to think, and thereby remain multidimensional."[144] Was the musical metaphor of "life's polyphony" merely a felicitous figure of speech, or was it an intuitive extension of a whole manner of thought that had informed his life to that point, the legacy of Kant and Hegel?

Among late-modern philosophers, both Theodor Adorno and Franz Rosenzweig would later also appeal, as had Bonhoeffer, to metaphors of multi-voiced, contrapuntal strands being woven together into harmonic diversity in order to try to subvert the pretensions of the system, to keep open space for what Bonhoeffer had called "the concept of contingency, as

---

Werke in six volumes, and in Tegel prison in May 1943 he got a copy of Kant's *Anthropologie* (see Bethge, *Dietrich Bonhoeffer*, 943 and *DBW* 17, 101). From Bethge's biography onward, interpreters of the phrase from the *Letters and Papers from Prison*, "world come of age," have assumed that Bonhoeffer was borrowing this phrase from Kant's *What is Enlightenment?* (see Bethge, *Dietrich Bonhoeffer*, 867), whereas Feil and then Green have definitively demonstrated that the phrase came from Bonhoeffer's reading of Wilhelm Dilthey; cf. Green, "Bonhoeffer, Modernity and Liberation Theology," in *Theology and the Practice of Responsibility: Essays on Dietrich Bonhoeffer*, edited by Wayne Whitson Floyd Jr. and Charles Marsh (Valley Forge 1994), 122.

[141] Robert H. King, "Introduction to the Task of Theology," in *Christian Theology*, 16: "Our alienation from God is overcome by God's identification with us; through incarnation comes reconciliation."

[142] *LPP*, 219 (*DBW* 8, 336); cf. also *LPP*, 297 (*DBW* 8, 432).

[143] Floyd, "Style and the Critique of Metaphysics: The Letter as Form in Bonhoeffer and Adorno," in *Theology and the Practice of Responsibility*, 247.

[144] *LPP*, 311 (*DBW* 8, 444); cf. also *LPP*, 305 (*DBW* 8, 453).

the occurrence that comes to us from outside,"[145] and which the Christian theologian calls "revelation." Perhaps the common musical metaphor was but another moment of synchronicity, like Bonhoeffer's fascination with "otherness" – something that was just "in the air," so to speak, in German culture as a common artifact of modernity's unraveling demise. The historian Fritz Ringer speaks of the persistence of the symphonic analogy in German academic thought in the late-nineteenth and early twentieth centuries: "The symphonic analogy, like the concept of wholeness, certainly did not originate in the 1920s. One might almost say that it was always implied in the German intellectual tradition. But it acquired a new popularity – and the status of a habit – during the crisis of learning. It almost always came into play when a German academic of this period discussed the relationship between an individual and the group to which he belonged."[146]

In Bonhoeffer's case one suspects it is at least this and something more – a groping towards revelation's own epistemology, a way of speaking what the human spirit longs toward and yet is unable to take within the grasp of any of the systems of human power and control. In this sense we might think of Bohoeffer's whole theological project as built on the architectonic of a sort of post-Hegelian Kantianism, or a Hegelianism for modernity in its declining years.

As Langdon Gilkey has written, "There is hardly a conception of God from Hegel onward that is not dynamic, changing, and in some manner intrinsically related to the world of change."[147] And Bonhoeffer is no exception, for he indeed does not conceive the "beyond" transcending the system with a spatial analogy, but a temporal one, caught up in the world of change. As Bonhoeffer expressed this already in *Act and Being*, whereas "in the system the present is determined by the past," by means of the reflection of the subject on what already exists, to the contrary "in the concept of contingency, as the occurrence which comes to us from outside, the present is determined by the future."[148] The question always to be placed to Bonhoeffer is whether such proposals yet are entangled in 'the sorcery of Hegel' or whether Bonhoeffer has at least had a glimpse of a genuinely post-Hegelian theological strategy.

Even in *Act and Being*, Bonhoeffer clearly thought that this turn to temporality – and God's gifting time with God's incarnate self – was the closest that theology came to providing the category of revelation with "an epistemology of its own." There he wrote: "Future means: the definition of being by something outside 'yet to come'; there is a genuine future only through Christ and the reality, created anew by him, of the neighbor and

---

[145] *DBWE* 2, 111 (*DBW* 2, 107).
[146] *The Decline of the German Mandarins*, 397.
[147] Langdon Gilkey, "God," in *Christian Theology*, 105.
[148] *DBWE* 2, 111 (*DBW* 2, 107).

creation.[149] Estranged from Christ, the world is enclosed in the I, which is to say, already the past. In it life is reflection. What is 'yet to come' demands immediate acceptance or rejection, and reflection signifies refusal. As the one absolutely yet to come, Christ demands faith directed towards him without reflection."[150] Bonhoeffer does not say faith without thinking, but faith that can be conceived as shattering the closed system of metaphysical thinking – a rapprochement of dialectic and *Ding-an-sich*, revelation's own epistemology.

"To let oneself be defined by means of the future is the eschatological possibility of the child," Bonhoeffer wrote at the end of *Act and Being*. "The child (full of anxiety and bliss) sees itself in the power of what 'future things' will bring, and for that reason alone, it can live in the present. However, they who are mature, who desire to be defined by the present, fall subject to the past, to themselves, death and guilt. It is only out of the future that the present can be lived."[151] It is this "outside" – beyond our present preoccupation with the guilt of the past – that opens the "childlike" possibility for the future to break into the present, freeing us to be for others. Bonhoeffer is seeking a form of *logos* about *theos* – a new theology – that can be interrupted by the transcendent, the encounter-from-"beyond," and yet which can make that encounter intelligible, and thus be "of some help for the church's future."[152]

XI. Postmodernism - A Postscript

What does it mean from within the context of postmodernity to retrace with Bonhoeffer the path from modernity's rise, through its height in idealistic thought, and then into its late-modern decline? The face of the other seems ubiquitous on newscast and website and podcast and blog – we define our situatedness in time by the momentary technologies we employ to allow the other closer, while keeping at least a screen between "us" and "them," the illusion of safety from harm in a world where violence too often threatens to become ubiquitous as well.

Bonhoeffer's wrestling with Kant's *Ding an sich*, and the constant threat of the Hegelian dialectic to close off all interplay between self and anything genuinely "other," needs to be heard as a sort of proto-postmodern plea for a philosophy and theology of radical hospitality – the sort of welcome one gives not just to those who have been intentionally invited, but

---

[149] Cf. Jürgen Moltmann, "The Future as a New Paradigm of Transcendence," in *The Future of Creation* (Minneapolis 1979), 1–17.
[150] *DBWE* 2, 157 (*DBW* 2, 157).
[151] *DBWE* 2, 159 (*DBW* 2, 159).
[152] "Outline for a Book," in *LPP*, 383 (*DBW* 8, 561).

to those who show up and make a claim on who we are, and still may become, whether or not their presence was desired. This was what made the images of encounter from personalism so compelling for Bonhoeffer, the mutual constitution of selves in dialogue not despite but because of the fact that each is utterly foreign, and thus unique, one to an other. Bonhoeffer's theology of revelation was a plea, I believe, to keep alive the theological categories of wonder and awe – of that from "outside" the world we normally inhabit, beyond our control even to name the other definitively as neighbour or enemy.

The threat of the system of dialectical meaning-making lies behind not just the early "academic" writings of Bonhoeffer but even more importantly behind letters such as that from Bonhoeffer to his brother Karl-Friedrich, describing the pathos of the visits to him of the first German immigrant arriving in London after Bonhoeffer's own arrival there in 1935: "most of them Jews, who know me from somewhere and want something from me."[153] Was it these same faces Bonhoeffer had in mind when, after six months of interrogation in Tegel prison, Bonhoeffer reflects on the knock at the door that was to be heard by so many across Europe in the following decade, each person confronted with the insufficiency of a Kantian principled ethic of telling the truth. "What does it mean to 'tell the truth'?" when the answer one gives can cost another their life, just for being an "other"?[154]

One need not hear the technical language of Kant or Hegel in order to recognize the desire to escape the dilemma of idealism in many of Bonhoeffer's words to his students at Finkenwalde. "To learn not merely to tolerate, but to delight in, the freedom of the other," Bonhoeffer wrote in *Life Together*, "is not the maximal requirement for the Christian. It is a minimal description of our utter faith in God's ways ... It means the recognition, indeed our delight, that God did not make others as I would have made them. God did not give them to me so that I could dominate and control them, but so that I might find the Creator by means of them ... God does not want me to mold others into the image that seems good to me, that is, into my own image. Instead, in their freedom from me God made other people in God's own image."[155]

Today we share the pathos of Bonhoeffer's plea to the church itself when he said to his colleagues in the ecumenical movement, "The hour is late. The world is choked with weapons, and dreadful is the distrust which

---

[153] *DBWE* 13, 81 (*DBW* 13, 75).

[154] *DBWE* 16, 601–608 (*DBW* 16, 619–629) "What Does it Mean to Tell the Truth?;" cf. Kant, "On a Supposed Right to Lie from Altruistic Motives," *Critique of Practical Reason and Other Writings in Moral Philosophy*, 346–350. Bonhoeffer refers to this writing in *DBWE* 6, 279–280 (*DBW* 6, 280).

[155] *DBWE* 5, 95 (*DBW* 5, 79).

looks out of all men's eyes. The trumpets of war may blow tomorrow. For what are we waiting?"[156] Even when the encounter between I-and-You goes badly, even when the other is our enemy, even there we are constituted by that encounter. In *Discipleship* Bonhoeffer made a most remarkable case for claiming that the thing that makes Christians distinct, indeed what is extraordinary about being a Christian at all, is Christ's costly command to love our enemies. Loving one's enemies is what distinguishes not just the most saintly of the followers of Christ, but any Christian precisely as a Christian. Without it, for Bonhoeffer, we are no different from the unbelievers, who also love their family and friends, while "loving enemies makes unmistakably clear what Jesus intends."[157]

Bonhoeffer has endeavoured not just to explain, but to understand the significance of the fact that "revelation as community surpasses any analytical reduction to idealist-transcendental epistemologies and their various architectures as well as to existential-phenomenological possibilities of existence. He holds that neither Kantian nor Hegelian systems are adequate to encompass the christological description of community."[158] Bonhoeffer to the end of his life saw the theological task as defined by the Copernican revolution of Kant and tempted by the dialectical approach of Hegel and idealism. What distinguishes Bonhoeffer's approach from Kant's is the thoroughly historical and concretely embodied understanding of personhood as constituted in community. And in speaking of Christ existing as church-community "what distinguishes Bonhoeffer's description form Hegel's [notion of God existing as community] is not so much the emphasis on divine embodiment but his sweeping, uncompromising christocentrism."[159]

Reading Bonhoeffer in conversation with Kant and Hegel make us listen for resonances in his thought and vocabulary that we otherwise might not have noticed, or as fully understood, especially enigmatic words such as these: "It always seems to me that we are trying anxiously ... to reserve some space for God; I should like to speak of God not on the boundaries but at the center, not in weakness but in strength; and therefore not in death and guilt but in man's life and goodness ... Belief in the resurrection is not the 'solution' of the problem of death. God's 'beyond' is not the beyond of our cognitive faculties ... God is beyond in the midst of our life. The church stands, not at the boundaries where human powers give out, but in the middle of the village."[160]

---

[156] *DBWE* 13, 309 (*DBW* 13, 304).
[157] *DBWE* 4, 137 (*DBW* 4, 140).
[158] Marsh, *Reclaiming Dietrich Bonhoeffer*, 99.
[159] Marsh, *Reclaiming Dietrich Bonhoeffer*, 103.
[160] *LPP*, 282 (*DBW* 8, 407–408).

After reading Hegel and Kant we should never again be capable of listening to Kant's arguments for the thing-in-self in *The Critique of Pure Reason* or Hegel's descriptions of the dynamic of dialectics in *The Phenomenology of Spirit* without hearing the echoes of the words from Bonhoeffer's *Ethics* on the heels of a decade of National Socialism: "The church confesses its timidity ... its dangerous concessions ... It has often withheld the compassion that it owes to the despised and rejected. The church was mute when it should have cried out, because the blood of the innocent cried out to heaven."[161]

Having watched him wrestle to overcome philosophy's and theology's perpetual addiction to the power of the system, I imagine that Bonhoeffer in his more mature years might have smiled in amusement and recognition at Jacques Derrida's later observation that "the step 'outside philosophy' is much more difficult to conceive than is generally imagined by those who think they made it long ago with cavalier ease, and who in general are swallowed up in metaphysics in the entire body of discourse which they claim to have disengaged from it ... What I want to emphasize is simply that the passage beyond philosophy does not consist in turning the page of philosophy (which usually amounts to philosophizing badly), but in continuing to read philosophers in a certain way."[162] For rather than "turning the page" on the idealistic tradition, Bonhoeffer had sought to read Kant and Hegel "in a certain way" that would allow him to clarify the extent to which transcendental epistemology's subject-object paradigm can contribute to a form of theological thinking capable of rendering the "encounter with an other" which "idealism" could not – whether God, neighbour or enemy. And I suspect that Bonhoeffer might find amusement, as well as a certain satisfaction, at our continuing to read him along with Kant and Hegel – "in a certain way" that leads us faithfully towards finding for the revelation of God's-heart-in-Christ "an epistemology of its own."

---

[161] *DBWE* 6, 138 (*DBW* 6, 129).
[162] Derrida, *Writing and Difference*, 284 and 288.

Christiane Tietz

Friedrich Schleiermacher and Dietrich Bonhoeffer

While Karl Barth's influence on the theology of Dietrich Bonhoeffer is obvious,[1] the impact of Friedrich Schleiermacher (1768–1834), the other great figure in modern Protestantism, is far more inconspicuous. Nevertheless, Schleiermacher, the church father of the nineteenth century,[2] was of no little importance for Bonhoeffer's early ecclesiology (I). And Schleiermacher's idea of religion was part of the background against which Bonhoeffer developed his own understanding of religion and faith (II). When discussing both subjects in the following I will not so much ask if Bonhoeffer understood Schleiermacher correctly but show how what Bonhoeffer understood *as* Schleiermacher's point of view became important for his own theology.

I. Ecclesiology

It is quite astonishing how many aspects of Bonhoeffer's early ecclesiology were influenced by Schleiermacher, always in both appreciation and criticism. Bonhoeffer appreciates that Schleiermacher focuses on the church[3] and correspondingly has a strong interest in the idea of social community.[4] But Bonhoeffer criticizes the way this community is con-

---

[1] See Andreas Pangritz's article on Barth in this volume.

[2] Friedrich Daniel Ernst Schleiermacher was born in 1768 in Breslau and educated in Moravian spirituality. He studied Protestant theology in Halle/Saale. As a pastor he became a member of the early romanticism movement in Berlin. 1804 he became professor at the University of Halle, 1810 at the newly-founded University of Berlin. He was one of the most influential intellectuals at the time. Schleiermacher died in 1834 in Berlin. Cf. K. Nowak, *Schleiermacher. Leben, Werk und Wirkung* (Göttingen 2001). Bonhoeffer studied Schleiermacher's *Speeches on Religion* already as a pupil (cf. Eberhard Bethge, *Dietrich Bonhoeffer,* 42).

[3] Cf. "Das Wesen der Kirche," (1932) in *DBW* 11, 253: "For him [Schleiermacher] a new appreciation of the church. [His] ... central thought is the 'church'."

[4] Cf. "Church and Eschatology," (1926), in *DBWE* 9, 319 (*DBW* 9, 347): "The fact that idealism understood the concept of the church so poorly also derives from the fact that, although the concept of the spiritual [*geistig*] personality was clearly understood,

ceived. In Bonhoeffer's eyes, the concept of community is the crucial point of salvation history: the primal state (1) is the "idea of unbroken community;"[5] sin (2) is the breaking of this unbroken community; the church (3) and (4) finally is the reconciled community with God and with human being.

1. Social Community in the Primal State

Bonhoeffer pays tribute to Schleiermacher as "the first to speak of relationships in community in the primal state."[6] Schleiermacher recognized that the *primal state* not only means community with God (which in Bonhoeffer's eyes "has always been recognized") but also social community of human beings. Thus, Schleiermacher understood that "community [with God] and social community belong together."[7] He comprehended that "apart from [social] community 'there is no living and vigorous piety'."[8] For Bonhoeffer, the insight "that human beings, as spirit, are necessarily created in a community – that human spirit in general is woven into the web of sociality"[9] is of great importance. It is nothing less than the characteristic of creaturely existence: "The creatureliness of human beings ... can be defined in simply no other way than in terms of the existence of human beings over-against-one-another, with-one-another, and in-dependence-upon-one-another."[10] Being a creature means being created in social community.

While appreciating Schleiermacher's emphasis on this primal social community, Bonhoeffer complains how Schleiermacher understands this community. Schleiermacher names as reason for the human community "the inner union of species-consciousness [*Gattungsbewußtsein*]" and "personal self-consciousness."[11] For Schleiermacher, this union has a twofold function: On the one hand, it is "the general source of all recognition

---

the concept of the community remained completely ignored and had to be reintroduced in the romantic era in the theology of Schleiermacher."

[5] *DBWE* 1, 62 (*DBW* 1, 37).

[6] *DBWE* 1, 64, note 1 (*DBW* 1, 38, note 1).

[7] *DBWE* 1, 64, note 1 (*DBW* 1, 64, note 1). Cf. *DBW* 11, 276: "[Der] Begriff des *Individualismus* [ist] bei Schleiermacher noch bereichert!" and note 255: "Schleiermacher bereichert das durch soziale Bezogenheit."

[8] *DBWE* 1, 64, note 1 (*DBW* 1, 64, note 1). The Schleiermacher citation is from *The Christian Faith*, 2 volumes (second edition of 1830–1831). Edited by H. R. MacKintosh and J. S. Stewart (New York 1963); here 1, 246 (§ 60.1).

[9] *DBWE* 1, 65 (*DBW* 1, 39).

[10] *DBWE* 3, 64 (*DBW* 3, 60).

[11] *The Christian Faith*, 1, 246 (§ 60.1); Bonhoeffer's citation in *DBWE* 1, 64, note 1 (*DBW* 1, 38, note 1) is not very precise.

of others as being of *like nature with ourselves.*"[12] On the other hand, it is "the only source of the presupposition and the ground of the fact that the 'inner' is known and grasped along with and by means of the 'outer'."[13] "This inclusion of the species-consciousness [*Gattungsbewußtsein*] in the personal self-consciousness and the communicability of the 'inner' through the 'outer,' which is connected with it, is the fundamental condition or basis of social life, for all human fellowship rests solely upon it."[14] Through the unity of species-consciousness and self-consciousness a person is connected with all the other persons by "a common bond of consciousness."[15] Bonhoeffer can summarize: "only in species consciousness does one human being encounter another."[16] It might not be precise to say that human beings encounter each other *in* species consciousness. However, the latter is the reason for their encounter.[17]

Bonhoeffer's own understanding of human encounter is quite different. Certainly, Bonhoeffer as well discusses the general character of the human spirit. Like Schleiermacher, he is convinced that people "*understand, express themselves, and are understood.*"[18] But Bonhoeffer distinguishes this general characteristic of the human spirit from the ethical I-You-relation, which is the place where people truly encounter each other.[19] What is the character of such an encounter?

For Bonhoeffer, human beings truly encounter each other only in the ethical sphere of claim and responsibility. Here human beings "constitute limits, boundaries, or 'barriers' [*Schranke, Grenze*] for each other."[20] In the encounter with the other his or her claim is a barrier for me which forces me to decide if I want to answer this claim or not. The situation of

---

[12] *The Christian Faith*, 1, 246 (§ 60.2); emphasis added.
[13] *The Christian Faith*, 1, 246 (§ 60.2). Cf. *DBWE* 1, 64 note 1 (*DBW* 1, 38, note 1): This union "is intended to ensure the possibility of mutual communication, of religious relationship in community ... If this were not present, people could never enter into relationship in community."
[14] *The Christian Faith*, 1, 246 (§ 60.2).
[15] Friedrich Schleiermacher, *On Religion*, 80. Cf. E. Herms, "Schleiermachers Erbe," in idem, *Menschsein im Werden. Studien zu Schleiermacher* (Tübingen 2003), 200–227, here 204, and D. Schlenke, *Geist und Gemeinschaft. Die systematische Bedeutung der Pneumatologie für Friedrich Schleiermachers Theorie der christlichen Frömmigkeit* (Berlin/New York 1999), 102: The individual is "qua Gattungsbewußtsein ... gleichursprünglich auf andere Individuen bezogen."
[16] *DBWE* 1, 64, note 1 (*DBW* 1, 38, note 1).
[17] Species-consciousness makes possible a "geistige[n] Akt der Identifikation mit einem anderen Menschen als einem Wesen gleicher Natur ... An diesen geistigen Akt ... schließt sich dann unmittelbar ein Mitempfinden des spezifischen Lebenszustandes des anderen Menschen an" (D. Schlenke, "Geist und Gemeinschaft," 43).
[18] *DBWE* 1, 68 (*DBW* 1, 41).
[19] Cf. *DBWE* 1, 66 (*DBW* 1, 40).
[20] Clifford J. Green, *Bonhoeffer. A Theology of Sociality* (Grand Rapids/Cambridge 1999, revised edition), 31.

responding to the other's claim is basic for human community; here responsibility and personhood take place: "It is a Christian insight that the person as conscious being is created ... in the situation of responsibility, passionate ethical struggle, confrontation by an overwhelming claim; thus the real person grows out of the concrete situation."[21] Thus, the true encounter between two human beings takes place when "the other ... places me before an ethical decision."[22] So, acknowledgement of the other is not possible through recognition of "others as being of *like nature with ourselves*" in the species-consciousness but only in the ethical situation. If I am truly acknowledging his or her ethical claim, then I am acknowledging the other – as a You. And in this I myself am becoming a person.[23]

In Bonhoeffer's opinion, the acknowledgment of the other *as an I* is neither given through the union of species-consciousness with self-consciousness and the nature of human spirit nor is it found through that encounter with the other as a You.[24] The I of the other can be acknowledged only if the other reveals him/herself.[25] This means that it is not the species-consciousness which makes the encounter with another I possible but his or her self-revelation: "there is no encounter with another person except that the person wills to reveal him/herself."[26] Such a self-revelation does not happen always; it only takes place from time to time and when the I wants to. Bonhoeffer himself distinguishes three basic structures existing in the church: "Einzelperson" (the I), the "community of persons" (the I-You-relations), and the "collective person"[27] – or, put in pneumatological terms: "*plurality of spirit*," "*community of spirit*," and "*unity of spirit*."[28] Whenever Bonhoeffer argues that Schleiermacher somehow fails in understanding these ecclesiological structures the question of personhood turns

---

[21] *DBWE* 1, 49 (*DBW* 1, 29). It is important to note that for Bonhoeffer the You has this significance only because it is *God's* You that encounters me in the human You; cf. *DBWE* 1, 54–55 (*DBW* 1, 32–33).

[22] *DBWE* 1, 52 (*DBW* 1, 32).

[23] Cf. *DBWE* 1, 48 (*DBW* 1, 28): "The person exists always and only in ethical responsibility."

[24] Cf. The Christian Idea of God, *DBW* 10, 427: "For Christian thought, personality is the last limit of thinking and the ultimate reality. ... Personality is free and does not enter the general laws of my thinking."

[25] Cf. *DBWE* 1, 56 and 213 (*DBW* 1, 34 and 144). Cf. *DBW* 10, 428.

[26] *DBW* 12, 290; in the original: "Es gibt keinen anderen Zugang zum Menschen, als daß dieser sich von sich aus offenbart."

[27] Cf. *DBWE* 1, 193 and 30 (*DBW* 1, 129–130 and 16).

[28] *DBWE* 1, 193 (*DBW* 1, 129–130). Cf. "Sichtbare Kirche im Neuen Testament," in *DBW* 14, 440 note 93 (in the transcript of Erich Klapproth): "Einheit der Gemeinde – Gemeinschaft – einzelner. Fehlt einer dieser drei Begriffe, so ist etwas verkehrt!"

out to be decisive. Idealism (which includes Schleiermacher in this case[29]) fails to understand the structures of the church because it did not see the necessity of the described ethical concept of the person.[30]

Nonetheless, Bonhoeffer acknowledges that Schleiermacher's insight in the sociality of the community in the primal state is "an important doctrine without which the ideas of *original sin* and especially the *church* could not be fully understood."[31]

2. Original Sin as Destroyed Community

In Bonhoeffer's view, the main problem of the doctrine of *original sin* is how "the individual culpable act and the cupability of the human race" can "be connected conceptually."[32] Bonhoeffer stresses that Schleiermacher managed to connect both because he "rediscovered the significance of original sin as a problem of social philosophy."[33] From his theory of the social orientation of the individual in the primal state, Schleiermacher deduces the simultaneity of the individual character and the social character of original sin: He calls original sin "the individual's own guilt" because it is perpetuated "by the exercise due to the voluntary action of the individual."[34] But original sin is also "genuinely common to all."[35] On the one hand, it "operates in every individual through the sin and sinfulness of others," and, on the other hand, "it is transmitted by the voluntary actions of every individual to others and implanted within them."[36] In this respect, it is "in each the work of all, and in all the work of each" because "the sinfulness of each pointes to the sinfulness of all alike."[37] Thus the individual constitutes the "representative of the whole human race."[38] This expression is almost identical to Bonhoeffer's discussion of original sin. The individual "is representative of fallen humanity."[39] For Bonhoeffer this means that

---

[29] Sometimes Bonhoeffer counts Schleiermacher as an idealistic thinker (cf. *DBWE* 1, 196, note 68 (*DBW* 1, 131, note 68) and *DBW* 11, 149), sometimes he does not (cf. *DBWE* 9, 319 (*DBW* 9, 347)).

[30] Cf. *DBWE* 1, 193 (*DBW* 1, 130).

[31] *DBWE* 1, 64, note 1 (*DBW* 1, 38, note 1); my emphasis.

[32] *DBWE* 1, 110–111 (*DBW* 1, 71).

[33] *DBWE* 1, 113, note 11 (*DBW* 1, 245, note 9).

[34] *The Christian Faith*, 1, 286 and 287 (§ 71.1).

[35] *The Christian Faith*, 1, 288 (§ 71.2). Therefore, the doctrine of original sin is not an expression of the individual self-consciousness but of the consciousness of the species.

[36] *The Christian Faith*, 1, 287 (§ 71.2).

[37] *The Christian Faith*, 1, 288 (§ 71.2).

[38] *The Christian Faith*, 1, 288 (§ 71.2), discussed in *DBWE* 1, 113, note 11 (*DBW* 1, 245, note 9).

[39] *DBW* 10, 375. The individual "ist selbst Repräsentant der abgefallenen Menschheit."

when, "in the sinful act, the individual spirit rises up against God ... the deed committed is at the same time *the deed of the human race ... in the individual person*. One falls away not only from one's personal vocation but also from one's generic vocation as a member of the human race. Thus all humanity falls with each sin, and not one of us is in principle different from Adam; that is, every one is also the 'first' sinner."[40]

This train of thought includes the ethical assumption that there "is a will of God with a people just as with individuals."[41] Bonhoeffer follows from this the necessity of the concept of collective person which describes a community as an ethical person.[42] Especially the human race is a collective person: "humanity-in-Adam ... is 'Adam', a collective person."[43] Even if Schleiermacher did not develop such a concept of a collective *person,* he "was doubtless correct in one respect, namely seeing that the concept of sin implies fulfillment in a social, collective concept."[44] But Schleiermacher in Bonhoeffer's opinion is mistaken in his description of sin as "sensuality, inhibition of God-consciousness."[45] Again, Bonhoeffer is not very precise in saying that sin *is* sensuality. While in the first edition of *The Christian Faith* Schleiermacher seems to interpret sensuality as such as sin, in the second edition (which Bonhoeffer used) he argues differently.[46] Now sin is a question of the proper *relation* of God-consciousness and sensuality.[47] Sensuality can inhibit the God-consciousness,[48] but it can also adequately be related to it.[49]

However, Bonhoeffer stresses that in relating sin to sensuality Schleiermacher interprets sin as a "biological category instead of the ethical-social one."[50] Bonhoeffer himself tries to understand sin as an ethical phenomenon: "Whereas in the primal state the relation among human beings is one of giving, in the sinful state it is purely demanding." Sin means "ethical atomism."[51] Everybody lives for his or her own benefit. Community with

---

[40] *DBWE* 1, 115 (*DBW* 1, 72).

[41] *DBWE* 1, 119. (*DBW* 1, 74).

[42] Cf. *DBWE* 1, 121 (*DBW* 1, 76).

[43] *DBWE* 1, 121 (*DBW* 1, 76).

[44] *DBWE* 1, 114, note 11 (*DBW* 1, 245–246, note 9).

[45] *DBWE* 1, 114, note 11 (*DBW* 1, 245–246, note 9). Cf. *The Christian Faith*, 1, 271–273 (§ 66).

[46] Cf. M. Junker, *Das Urbild des Gottesbewußtseins. Zur Entwicklung der Religionstheorie und Christologie Schleiermachers von der ersten zur zweiten Auflage der Glaubenslehre* (Berlin/New York 1990), 114–115.

[47] Cf. M. Junker, *Das Urbild des Gottesbewußtseins*, 156–158.

[48] Cf. *The Christian Faith*, 1, 273 (§ 66.2): sin is "an arrestment of the determinative power of spirit, due to the independence of the sensuous functions."

[49] Cf. *The Christian Faith*, 1, 20–22 (§ 5.3).

[50] *DBWE* 1, 114, note 11 (*DBW* 1, 245–246, note 9).

[51] *DBWE* 1, 108 (*DBW* 1, 70). Jacqueline Mariña argues that Schleiermacher's comprehension of sin includes that the self understands itself as "independent of others and in

God and with other human beings is destroyed. No longer is humanity a biological category: "'Humanity' is not a biological category but constituted by means of revelation."[52] This means: humanity is either "humanity in Adam" or "humanity in Christ."[53] The latter is "God's new will and purpose for humanity"[54] or, in the most precise term, the church.

3. The Church – Realized by Christ

Schleiermacher proclaims the formation of the church as necessary because religion is necessarily social: "Once there is religion, it must necessarily also be social."[55] Religion is social out of two reasons: the nature of human beings, and the nature of religion itself. First, it is the human nature to share the things inside oneself with others: It is "highly unnatural for people to lock up in themselves what they have created and worked out."[56] Second, this impulse is even stronger in case of religion. The individual especially wants to share his/her *religious* feelings with others "to have witnesses for and participants in that which enters his senses and arouses his feelings."[57] And s/he wants to listen to other religious people to amplify her/his own religious experience.[58] Church originates from this impulse: Church is "an ever self-renewing circulation of the religious self-consciousness within certain definite limits, and a propagation of the religious emotions arranged and organized within the same limits."[59] There-

---

competition with them for finite resources" (cf. "Christology and Anthropology in Friedrich Schleiermacher," in *CCFS*, 151–170, 164). Schleiermacher himself claims his own concept of sin as consistent with the idea of sin as a "turning away from the Creator" (*The Christian Faith*, 1, 273 (§ 66.2)).

[52] *DBW* 11, 263: "'Menschheit' [ist] nicht [ein] biologischer Begriff, sondern an [der] Offenbarung gebildet."

[53] Cf. *DBW* 11, 263–265 and *DBWE* 2, 153 (*DBW* 2, 152).

[54] *DBWE* 1, 141 (*DBW* 1, 87).

[55] *On Religion*, 163, cited in *DBWE* 1, 159, note 18 (*DBW* 1, 102, note 18). Cf. *The Christian Faith*, 1, 26 (§ 6): "The religious self-consciousness, like every essential element in human nature, leads necessarily in its development to fellowship or communion."

[56] *On Religion*, 163, cited (translation altered) in *DBWE* 1, 159, note 18 (*DBW* 1, 102, note 18). Cf. *The Christian Faith*, 1, 27 (§ 6.2): "the *consciousness of kind* [Gattungsbewußtsein] which dwells in every man ... finds its satisfaction only when he steps forth beyond the limits of his own personality and takes up the facts of other personalities into his own."

[57] *On Religion*, 163. Cf. *DBW* 11, 278, where Bonhoeffer describes the psychological derivation of the church: "Psychologisch: Religiöse Gemeinschaft [entsteht] durch Mitteilungstrieb, Missionstrieb u. a. der Menschen."

[58] Cf. *On Religion*, 163.

[59] *The Christian Faith*, 1, 29 (§ 6.4). Cf. also § 115, cited in *DBWE* 1, 159, note 18 (*DBW* 1, 102, note 18): "The Christian Church is formed through regenerate individuals coming together for mutual interaction and cooperation in an orderly way."

fore, "piety forms the basis of all ecclesiastical communions."[60] Of course, Bonhoeffer acknowledges that Schleiermacher conceives community and church as necessary.[61] But he refuses Schleiermacher's theory of the genesis of the church on the basis of five interdependent reasons.

First, Bonhoeffer judges that Schleiermacher concentrates at last on the individual: "The reason for the formation of religious community lies in the need of the *individuals* to communicate. The church ... is constructed individualistically."[62] Even if Schleiermacher has a strong interest in the community he begins with the individual and argues from the perspective of the individual. He conceives "the individual's community with Christ ... as being independent of the church."[63]

Bonhoeffer recognizes also the opposite that Schleiermacher sometimes sees the church "as the entity that exists before any individual, outside of which there is no religious self-consciousness."[64] In fact, Schleiermacher repudiates "the idea that one can share in the redemption and be made blessed through Christ outside the corporate life which He instituted, as if a Christian could dispense with the latter and be with Christ, as it were, alone." Such a view implies "an activity of Christ which is not mediated in time and space."[65] Nevertheless, Bonhoeffer is convinced that in the end Schleiermacher is "ultimately giving priority to the individual dimension over the communal."[66] Vice versa, the significance of the community lies in the development of the individual.[67]

---

[60] *The Christian Faith*, 1, 5 (§ 3).

[61] Cf. *DBWE* 1, 195, note 68 (*DBW* 1, 131, note 68). Bonhoeffer implicitly appreciates the structure of Schleiermacher's *The Christian Faith* when he argues that "it would be good ... if a presentation of doctrinal theology were to start not with the doctrine of God but with the doctrine of the church" (*DBWE* 1, 134; *DBW* 1, 85) which in fact is what Schleiermacher does (cf. *The Christian Faith*, 1, 5–31 (§§ 3-6)).

[62] *DBWE* 1, 159, note 18 (*DBW* 1, 101, note 18); my emphasis. In Bonhoeffer's eyes, this can lead to an understanding of the church as "Privatsache." Bonhoeffer believes that "Schleiermacher schmiedet [die] Waffen dafür!" (*DBW* 11, 276).

[63] *DBWE* 1, 159, note 18 (*DBW* 1, 101, note 18).

[64] *DBWE* 1, 159, note 18 (*DBW* 1, 101, note 18). Cf. *The Christian Faith*, 2, 525–528 (§ 113). For Schleiermacher the existence of the church in which the believer finds him/herself means that there existed already "a collective need for redemption and expectation of it" (*The Christian Faith*, 2, 526 (§ 113.2)).

[65] *The Christian Faith*, 2, 360 (§ 87.3).

[66] *DBWE* 1, 159, note 18 (*DBW* 1, 101, note 18). Bonhoeffer takes this critique from Albrecht Ritschl, *Die christliche Lehre von der Rechtfertigung und Versöhnung*, vol. 1 (Bonn, second edition 1882). Ritschl notices that Schleiermacher's concept of redemption and reconciliation is individual in focussing on the change of the individual's will and feeling: "... und indem diese Wirkungen immer nur an den Einzelnen anschaulich gemacht werden, so wird der Begriff der Lebensgemeinschaft ... unter der Hand zum Ausdruck eines ganz individuellen Verhältnisses, und das neue Gesammtleben tritt aus der Stellung der Voraussetzung in die der einfachen Folge davon" (ibid., 519; cf. 520).

[67] Cf. *DBWE* 1, 159, note 18 (*DBW* 1, 101, note 18).

Second, Bonhoeffer complains about Schleiermacher's question for the desires which are fulfilled in the church. "The reason for the formation of religious community lies in the *need* of the individuals to communicate. The church is the satisfaction of a need."[68] In this Schleiermacher's concept of the church is "utilitarian."[69]

Third, Bonhoeffer criticizes that Schleiermacher "thought he could deduce the concept of the church from the general concept of religion."[70] Bonhoeffer judges Schleiermacher's argument as wrong that church is necessary because of the nature of religion itself. Of course, the community with God is integral for religion; but "an impulse toward religious community is not in principle entailed in religion, and this must be so; the value of the holy is not exclusively actualized in a social context as, for example, the value of justice, or love, or equality ... but also in solitary communion with God. The mystics too were religious."[71] The fact that religion mostly is social [*gesellig*] is rooted in "psychological causes that are more or less accidental."[72]

That the church emerges from the individual wills which come together[73] in Bonhoeffer's judgment is a psychological and historical understanding of the genesis of the church,[74] because it talks about the process of becoming a unity. Church, and this is Bonhoeffer's fourth point, is thus constituted by human beings.[75] The individual wills have to become

---

[68] *DBWE* 1, 159, note 18 (*DBW* 1, 101, note 18); emphasis added. Cf. *DBWE* 1, 160, note 18 (*DBW* 1, 102, note 18): Schleiermacher claims "the individual's need to communicate to be the basic sociological structure of the church."

[69] *DBWE* 1, 132, note 23 (*DBW* 1, 253, note 25). This judgment can also be seen in his university lecture on "The Nature of the Church" (*DBW* 11, 278–279, note 277) where Bonhoeffer discusses the difference between "Gesellschaft" und "Gemeinschaft" which F. Tönnies argued for: While the latter wills the "being-with-one-another" "as an end in itself" the former wills the "being-with-one-another" "as a means to an end" (*DBWE* 1, 88; (*DBW* 1, 56). In Schleiermacher's concept, community is needed for satisfying the "Mitteilungstrieb" and thus is only a means to an end (*DBW* 11, 278). Bonhoeffer himself sees the community in the church above all as "Gemeinschaft;" cf. *DBWE* 1, 266–267 (*DBW* 1, 185–186).

[70] *DBWE* 1, 133, note 23 (*DBW* 1, 254, note 25).

[71] *DBWE* 1, 131, note 23 (*DBW* 1, 252, note 25). Cf. "The Nature of the Church," *DBW* 11, 278: "Dies Mitteilungsbedürfnis ist Zeichen jeder Gemeinschaft. Frömmigkeit [ist] auch individualistisch möglich." Bonhoeffer is keen to emphasize against Schleiermacher that there is "in fact only *one* religion in which the idea of community is an integral element of its nature, and that is Christianity" (*DBWE* 1, 130–131; *DBW* 1, 84); this means that community is an essential element of Christianity but not of religion as such.

[72] *DBWE* 1, 133 (*DBW* 1, 84).

[73] Cf. *DBW* 11, 262.

[74] Cf. *DBW* 11, 276, note 259.

[75] Cf. *DBW* 11, 277. Cf. also *The Christian Faith*, 1, 3 (§ 2.2). Church "is a society which originates only through free human action and which can only through such continue to exist."

united.[76] Thus Bonhoeffer criticizes: "Schleiermacher's concept of unity is not theological, but psychological, and therefore profoundly mistaken. It is based on an *identification of 'religious community' and 'church'*."[77] This leads to a concentration on religious experience and to an "Ideal des Erlebens."[78] Bonhoeffer warns of this concentration on religious experience. He sees "the danger of confusing Christian community with some wishful image of pious community, the danger of blending the devout heart's natural desire for community with the spiritual reality of Christian community."[79]

By identifying religious community and church, and this is Bonhoeffer's fifth criticism, Schleiermacher makes the methodological mistake of viewing the church only from the outside. Of course, church also is a religious community: "when viewed from the outside, the church is a religious community [but] this is precisely an untheological perspective."[80] It is untheological because it excludes what God does for the reality of the church: Schleiermacher "points to the 'religious motives' that in fact lead to empirical community (the missionary impulse, the need to communicate, etc.);" in this he "overlooks the fact that the new basic-relations established by God actually are real."[81] This is with what Bonhoeffer starts his own ecclesiology: with the divine reality of the church. The reality of the church is not made by human beings. Christ's presence in the church is constitutive for it. What does this mean?

First of all, through Christ the broken community with God is reconciled: "In Christ humanity really is drawn into community with God"[82]. And Christ is present only in the church – a fact which leads to the insight that community with God is possible only in the church: "Community with

---

[76] Cf. *DBW* 11, 262.
[77] *DBWE* 1, 195–196, note 68 (*DBW* 1, 131, note 68).
[78] *DBW* 11, 277.
[79] *DBWE* 5, 34–35 (*DBW* 5, 22).
[80] *DBWE* 1, 196, note 68 (*DBW* 1, 131, note 68). Cf. *DBWE* 1, 126 (*DBW* 1, 79–80): "it is certainly possible to focus on the empirical phenomenon 'church' qua 'religious community' ... and *to develop a sociological morphology* of it [but] in that case all theological reflections would be superfluous." Similarly, Bonhoeffer summarizes in his lecture on "The Nature of the Church" that for Schleiermacher "'Kirche' ist freiwilliger Zusammenschluß der christlichen Frommen. Damit ist [die] Kirche auf die Frömmigkeit der Einzelnen *zurückgeführt*." In Bonhoeffer's eyes, this includes that the church is deduced but not presupposed: "Kirche ist nicht letzte Voraussetzung. Individuelle Religiosität setzt er [Schleiermacher] vor die Klammer" (*DBW* 11, 253; emphasis added). Cf. ibid., 277: "Kirche ist ... Abgeleitetes ... da, wo sie als religiöse Gemeinschaft gesehen wird." Cf. ibid.: "[Auch wenn der] Gemeinschaftsbegriff aus [dem] Religionsbegriff abgeleitet [wird], ist religiöse Gemeinschaft immer etwas Sekundäres; [denn] die Religion muß [zuerst] da sein."
[81] *DBWE* 1, 125 (*DBW* 1, 79).
[82] *DBWE* 1, 146 (*DBW* 1, 91).

God exists only through Christ, but Christ is present only in his church-community, and therefore *community with God exists only in the church.*"[83] This means that being a Christian is possible only *in* the church. Being in the church is not a consequence of Christian existence but a necessary element of it since *"there is no relation to Christ in which the relation to the church is not necessarily established as well."*[84] Thus, "every individualistic concept of the church breaks down because of this fact."[85]

Fundamental for understanding the character of the church is the insight that the church is a mode of being of Christ.[86] The church is "Christ existing as church-community."[87] This is why "Christian community is ... a divine reality,"[88] a reality realized in Christ. "God established the reality of the church ... in Jesus Christ – not religion, but revelation, *not religious community, but church.*"[89] Whereas the unity of a *religious community* in fact is psychological, the unity of the church "transcends psychological categories, it is divinely established."[90] It is the unity constituted by Christ in whom "the plurality of persons [is united] into a single collective person."[91]

Even in *Life Together* when Bonhoeffer describes the concrete daily life of a Christian community he emphasizes that it is Christ who constitutes the reality of the church and not the communication of "piety": "The fact that we are brothers and sisters only through Jesus Christ is of immeasurable significance. Therefore, the other who comes face to face with me earnestly and devoutly [*fromm*] seeking community is *not* the brother or sister with whom I am to relate in the community. My brother or sister is instead that other person who has been redeemed by Christ ... What persons are in themselves ... in their inwardness and piety, cannot constitute the basis of our community, which is determined by what those persons are in terms of Christ. Our community consists solely in what Christ has done to both of us."[92]

---

[83] *DBWE* 1, 158 (*DBW* 1, 101).

[84] *DBWE* 1, 127 (*DBW* 1, 81).

[85] *DBWE* 1, 158 (*DBW* 1, 101).

[86] Cf. for example *DBWE* 1, 189–190 (*DBW* 1, 126–127).

[87] *DBWE* 1, 199 (*DBW* 1, 133).

[88] *DBWE* 5, 35 (*DBW* 5, 22). Cf. *DBWE* 1, 127 (*DBW* 1, 80): "The concept of the church is conceivable only in the sphere of reality established by God."

[89] *DBWE* 1, 153 (*DBW* 1, 79). Cf. *DBWE* 1, 126 (*DBW* 1, 80): The fact that constitutes the church is "the fact of Christ, or the 'Word'." Cf. *DBW* 11, 276–277: "Kirche ist ... *die schon in Christus realiter gesetzte Kirche*! Durch [die] Tat Gottes ist Kirche da."

[90] *DBWE* 1, 196, note 68 (*DBW* 1, 131, note 68). Cf. *DBWE* 5, 35 (*DBW* 5, 22): "Christian community is a spiritual and not a psychic reality."

[91] *DBWE* 1, 193 (*DBW* 1, 129).

[92] *DBWE* 5, 34 (*DBW* 5, 21–22); emphasis added.

Bonhoeffer interprets Jesus Christ's presence in the church which is essential for the church's reality as his *personal* presence. And he argues convincingly that this kind of presence is possible only on the background of Christ's resurrection.[93] Bonhoeffer judges that Schleiermacher is not able to conceive Christ's presence in the church as personal because Schleiermacher understands Christ's resurrection only symbolically.[94] Schleiermacher himself argues: "The facts of the resurrection and the ascension of Christ ... cannot be laid down as properly constituent parts of the doctrine of his person."[95] Different from Bonhoeffer, Schleiermacher claims that "neither the spiritual presence which He promised nor all that He said about His enduring influence upon those who remained behind is mediated through either of these two facts."[96] This means: For his presence, no resurrection is necessary. Bonhoeffer recognizes that Schleiermacher interprets the presence of Christ as "die von ihm ausgehende Wirkung, die in die Gemeinde hineinreicht ... Christus ist ... dynamisch gedacht, er ist eine historische Energie, die nicht verlorengeht, sondern sich weiter mitteilt. Die Gegenwart Christi ist hier unter der Kategorie von Ursache und Wirkung gedacht."[97] At the same time, Schleiermacher interprets the presence of Christ as rooted in the human attempt "über die Geschichte hinweg sich das Bild Christi immer wieder zur Anschauung zu bringen."[98] Bonhoeffer thinks that in both cases Schleiermacher understands Christ as a power, but not as a person.[99]

In Bonhoeffer's opinion this neglecting of the personhood of Jesus Christ is repeated in Schleiermacher's determination of the relation of the person and the deeds of Jesus Christ. Bonhoeffer sees Schleiermacher interpreting the person of Christ out of his deeds and thus dissolving the christological question into the soteriological one.[100] Admittedly, Schleiermacher argues that talking about the deeds of Christ means *the same* as talking about the person of Christ.[101] But he describes both: the

---

[93] Cf. *DBW* 12, 293: "Allein wo der auferstandene Christus als der Grund und die Voraussetzung der Christologie verstanden wird, nur da ist es möglich, seine Gegenwart als Person zu fassen."

[94] Cf. *DBW* 12, 293–294. Cf. also Schleiermacher's sermon on Romans 6, 4–8 in Sämmtliche Werke II.2 (Berlin 1843), 176ff., where Schleiermacher describes Christ's resurrection as "*Bild des neuen Lebens*, in welchem wir alle durch ihn wandeln sollen" (ibid., 177).

[95] *The Christian Faith*, 2, 417 (§ 99).

[96] *The Christian Faith*, 2, 418 (§ 99.1).

[97] *DBW* 12, 292.

[98] *DBW* 12, 292.

[99] Cf. *DBW* 12, 292–293.

[100] Cf. *DBW* 12, 289.

[101] Cf. *The Christian Faith*, 2, 375–376 (§ 92.3). Both categories are implicated in each other.

person of Christ[102] and the duty of Christ[103] and connects both reciprocally.[104]

However, Bonhoeffer himself argues for an interpretation of the deeds of Christ through the person of Christ. For, the deeds of Christ are conceived differently, depending on how the person of Christ is understood: "Nur wenn ich weiß, wer dies Werk tut, verstehe ich dieses Werk. Es kommt alles darauf an zu wissen, ob Jesus Christus ein idealistischer Religionsstifter oder der Sohn Gottes selbst gewesen ist ... War er ein idealistischer Religionsstifter, so kann ich durch sein Werk ... zur Nacheiferung angetrieben werden, aber meine Sünde ist mir nicht vergeben ... Ist aber das Werk Christi das Werk Gottes selbst, dann bin ich ... in diesem Werk getroffen als einer, der das in keiner Weise selbst tun konnte. Aber zugleich habe ich... durch diesen Jesus Christus den gnädigen Gott gefunden."[105] This makes clear that the deed of Christ is ambiguous[106] which can be put down to the fact that for knowing Christ a *revelation* is necessary.[107]

From this follows that for understanding the essence of the church, which is Christ's personal presence, as well a revelation is necessary: "*Only the concept of revelation can lead to the Christian concept of the church.*"[108] This means: "*The reality of the church is a reality of revelation, a reality that essentially must be* either believed or denied."[109]

Bonhoeffer is of the opinion that Schleiermacher's misunderstanding of Christ's personhood is not even avoided when Schleiermacher talks about the "personality" of Christ: "we can represent the growth of His personality from earliest childhood on to the fullness of manhood as a continuous transition from the condition of the purest innocence to one of purely spiritual fullness of power."[110] Bonhoeffer judges: "*Personality* in this context

---

[102] *The Christian Faith*, 2, 377–424 (§§ 93–99).

[103] *The Christian Faith*, 2, 425–475 (§§ 100–105).

[104] Cf. G. Lämmlin, *Individualität und Verständigung. Das Kirchenverständnis nach Schleiermachers Glaubenslehre* (Aachen 1998), 142.

[105] *DBW* 12, 290.

[106] Cf. *DBW* 12, 290.

[107] Cf. *DBW* 12, 291: "Nur durch die Offenbarung Christi erschließt sich mir seine Person und auch sein Werk."

[108] *DBWE* 1, 134 (*DBW* 1, 84).

[109] *DBWE* 1, 127 (*DBW* 1, 80). Cf. *DBW* 11, 277: "*Kirche* [ist] nicht als religiöse Gemeinschaft [zu verstehen]! Kirche ist [eine] Wirklichkeit des Glaubens." It is interesting to note that Schleiermacher has a similar idea when he argues that it is a statement of our self-consciousness that the church is of divine origin: "With the first stirrings of preparatory grace in consciousness, there comes a presentiment of the divine origin of the Christian Church; and with a living faith in Christ awakens also a belief that the Kingdom of God is actually present in the fellowship of believers" (*The Christian Faith*, 2, 528 (§ 113.4)).

[110] *The Christian Faith*, 2, 383 (§ 93.4).

characterizes the opposite of that which we call the *person*."[111] Jesus Christ's personality is interpreted as the appearance of a value: the idea of a religious personality, "a personality with an unclouded, strong 'God-consciousness'."[112] Christ is "the representative, the one who incorporates [*der Verkörperer*] this idea in history."[113] Bonhoeffer sees this as "docetic:" "There is a certain prior religious idea that is applied to the historical Jesus."[114] That Jesus Christ was a real human being is ignored.[115] Whoever understands Christ as the appearance of a religious idea which is true independently of this appearance ignores the historical revelation of Christ.[116] The historical revelation of Christ "is always anew a challenge to man. He cannot overcome it by pulling it into the system which he already had before."[117]

4. The Church – Actualized by the Holy Spirit

In Bonhoeffer's view, Schleiermacher ignores the difference between psychological and theological categories and repeats this mistake in his pneumatology. Schleiermacher assumes that every community has a "common spirit" [*Gemeingeist*]. It is "the common bent found in all who constitute together a moral personality, to seek the advancement of this whole; and this is at the same time the characteristic love found in each for every other."[118] The Holy Spirit is nothing else but "common spirit" of the Christian community.[119] Through the Holy Spirit "a multitude of people" becomes "a true unity through which the multitude of Christians also become a unity and the many individual personalities become a true common life or moral personality."[120]

---

[111] *DBW* 12, 293.

[112] *DBW* 12, 320. Cf. *DBW* 12, 293: "Persönlichkeit ist die Fülle und Harmonie der Werte, die in dem Phänomen Jesus Christus zusammengefaßt werden."

[113] *DBW* 12, 320.

[114] *DBW* 12, 321. Cf. *On Religion*, 218: "But the truly divine is the splendid clarity with which the great idea he [Jesus Christ] had come to exhibit was formed in his soul, the idea that everything finite requires higher mediation in order to be connected with the divine."

[115] Cf. *DBW* 12, 320–321. Cf. Ernst Feil, *Die Theologie Dietrich Bonhoeffers. Hermeneutik – Christologie – Weltverständnis* (Münster, 5th edition, 2005), 217: "Für Bonhoeffer hat Schleiermacher letztlich mit der Menschwerdung Gottes nicht ernst gemacht."

[116] Cf. H.-J. Abromeit, *Das Geheimnis Christi. Dietrich Bonhoeffers erfahrungsbezogene Christologie* (Neukirchen-Vluyn 1991), 190.

[117] *DBW* 10, 429.

[118] *The Christian Faith*, 2, 562 (§ 121.2).

[119] Cf. *The Christian Faith*, 2, 535 (§ 116.3).

[120] *The Christian Faith*, 2, 563 (§ 121.2).

Bonhoeffer acknowledges Schleiermacher's orientation on the community character of the Holy Spirit.[121] And he appreciates Schleiermacher's idea of a "collective life" (*Gesamtleben*) of the church.[122] Bonhoeffer praises emphatically Schleiermacher's pneumatological foundation of that "Gesamtleben:" "Schleiermacher [hat in der Lehre von der Kirche] neue Bahnen gewiesen, indem er kühn Gemeingeist und Heiligen Geist identificierte ... Schleiermacher war ... gewiß nicht vorbildlich verfahren mit seiner kühnen Identification, aber ebenso gewiß hatte er doch etwas gesehen, was zu sehen die Dogmatik nicht wieder hätte verlernen dürfen. Hätte die Dogmatik früh genug das Verhältnis von Heiligem Geist und kirchlicher Gemeinschaft durchdacht, so wäre vielleicht in der Praxis manches anders geworden."[123]

Furthermore, Bonhoeffer acknowledges Schleiermacher's general concept of spirit in his own idea of "objective spirit": "... where wills unite, a 'structure' is created – that is, a third entity, previously unknown, independent of being willed or not willed by the persons who are uniting. This general recognition of the nature of objective spirit was a discovery of the qualitative thinking that became dominant in romanticism and idealism ... Two wills encountering one another form a structure. A third person joining them sees not just one person connected to the other; rather, the will of the structure, as a third factor, resists the newcomer with a resistance not identical with the wills of the two individuals. Sometimes this is even more forceful than that of either individual ... Precisely this structure is objective spirit ... the persons themselves experience their community as something real outside themselves."[124]

However, Bonhoeffer complains Schleiermacher's concept of the Holy Spirit itself. Again, Bonhoeffer sees an ignoring of personhood: Schleiermacher understands the Holy Spirit as "personal,"[125] as a neutral power, as effect.[126] Bonhoeffer judges Schleiermacher's idea of the Holy Spirit as solely anthropological-biological, being a "category of the psychology of

---

[121] Cf. *DBWE* 1, 195, note 68 (*DBW* 1, 131, note 68): "Schleiermacher correctly recognizes a life of an individual only for and within the community – that the work of Christ and the Holy Spirit is primarily aimed at the church, at the corporate life."

[122] Cf. *DBWE* 1, 153, note 79 (*DBW* 1, 97, note 79).

[123] "Der Geist und die Gnade bei Frank" (1926) in *DBW* 17, 47–48.

[124] *DBWE* 1, 98–99 (*DBW* 1, 62).

[125] *DBWE* 1, 194, note 68 (*DBW* 1, 131, note 68). Cf. *The Christian Faith*, 2, 569–574 (§ 123). That Schleiermacher calls the Holy Spirit a "moral person" (*The Christian Faith*, 2, 535 (§ 116.3), but referring to the unity of the Christian community, not to the Holy Spirit) "cannot salvage anything" (*DBWE* 1, 194, note 68; *DBW* 1, 131, note 68). Similarly Jürgen Moltmann, *Der Geist des Lebens. Eine ganzheitliche Pneumatologie* (Munich 1991), 236.

[126] Cf. Bonhoeffer's notes on "Heiliger Geist" (1935) in *DBW* 14, 468, note 20.

peoples and species."¹²⁷ Bonhoeffer finds the fault in that that "the *Holy Spirit is apparently nothing but the consciousness of the species.*"¹²⁸ So Schleiermacher again ignores the basic difference between a psychological and a theological understanding of the church. While the consciousness of the species "is part of any community as such," the Holy Spirit "is present in principle only in the church."¹²⁹

In his dogmatic thinking Schleiermacher does not identify the Holy Spirit and consciousness of the species in a clear manner. He argues that the consciousness of the species in its unity with the God-consciousness is "no mere natural principle that would have developed of itself out of human nature as human nature would have remained without Christ."¹³⁰ This shows that Schleiermacher assumes a christological reason for the case that the consciousness of the species is the Holy Spirit.¹³¹ Bonhoeffer himself interprets the Holy Spirit – like Schleiermacher – as "the Spirit of the church-community." But he emphasizes that this means "something quite different"¹³² than Schleiermacher's concept of "Gemeingeist." Bonhoeffer is of the opinion that in talking about the unity which the Christians have to *become* in the "Gesamtleben," Schleiermacher misunderstands the *unity* of spirit.¹³³ The unity of spirit of the church-community is already given; it lies in the collective person of Christ: "The unity of spirit of the church-community is a fundamental synthesis willed by God; it is not a relation that must be produced, but one that is already established."¹³⁴ The unity of the church is "its existence as a collective person," it is "*Christ existing as church-community.*"¹³⁵ From this follows that "this unity does not exist because the members of the body have the same intentions; rather, if they

---

[127] *DBWE* 1, 195, note 68 (*DBW* 1, 131, note 68).

[128] *DBWE* 1, 194, note 68 (*DBW* 1, 131, note 68). Cf. *DBWE* 1, 195–196, note 68 (*DBW* 1, 131, note 68).

[129] *DBWE* 1, 196, note 68 (*DBW* 1, 131, note 68).

[130] *The Christian Faith*, 2, 565 (§ 121.3).

[131] Cf. Diederich, *Schleiermachers Geistverständnis. Eine systematisch-theologische Untersuchung seiner philosophischen und theologischen Rede vom Geist* (Göttingen 1999), 227–228. Bonhoeffer judges the identity between the consciousness of the species and the Holy Spirit as rooted in an "underlying doctrine of apocatastasis." The human race has a final claim on God, "exactly because it is the species. It is the 'value' God wants, which is to be realized and to which the individual is sacrificed" (*DBWE* 1, 195, note 68; *DBW* 1, 131, note 68). Pneumatologically this means "that the entire human race belongs to this spirit. The difference between individuals is merely temporal, namely that some already have the pneuma hagion [Holy Spirit] while others do not yet have it" (Die Christliche Sitte nach den Grundsätzen der evangelischen Kirche im Zusammenhange dargestellt, SW I.12, 514, cited in *DBWE* 1, 171, note 29; *DBW* 1, 111, note 29).

[132] *DBWE* 1, 195, note 68 (*DBW* 1, 131, note 68).

[133] Cf. *DBWE* 1, 195, note 68 (*DBW* 1, 131, note 68).

[134] *DBWE* 1, 192 (*DBW* 1, 128).

[135] *DBWE* 1, 199 (*DBW* 1, 133).

have the same intentions at all, they have them only as members of the body of Christ."[136]

Over and above that christological unity, the church of course should become a community of love; but this human action is possible only on the basis of the unity already established by God in Christ.[137] That is why the "immanent unity of spirit is only the initial actualization of the transcendent unity of Spirit that is in reality established in Christ."[138]

In the church community, "the plurality of persons [is united] into a single collective person ... without obliterating either their singularity or the community of persons."[139] Schleiermacher also misunderstands the *community* of spirit. The community of spirit is possible only between *persons*.[140] But in Schleiermacher's concentration of the effect of the Holy Spirit on the consciousness of species "the individual must become a tool, which means ... that the individual must be extinguished as a person."[141]

---

[136] *DBWE* 1, 200 (*DBW* 1, 134). Bonhoeffer argues for a simultaneity of act and being regarding the acting of the Holy Spirit and the being in the church: "the Holy Spirit is at work only in the church as in the community of saints; thus every person who is really moved by the Spirit has to be within the church-community already; but, on the other hand, no one is in the church-community who has not already been moved by the Spirit" (*DBWE* 1, 158–159; *DBW* 1, 101). This aspect is developed further in his *Act and Being* (*DBWE* 2); cf. my book *Bonhoeffers Kritik der verkrümmten Vernunft. Eine erkenntnistheoretische Untersuchung* (Tübingen 1999). Schleiermacher himself sees an identity between the acting of the Holy Spirit and being a member of the church: "for only when this common spirit of the whole begins to show itself at work in a given person can it be known that he is a constituent part of the whole; just as if anyone joins himself to the whole, it can be taken as certain that he will receive a communication of the Holy Spirit" (*The Christian Faith*, 2, 563 (§ 121.2)).

[137] Cf. *DBWE* 1, 202 (*DBW* 1, 135).

[138] *DBWE* 1, 203 (*DBW* 1, 136). While Schleiermacher understands the unity as caused by the abolition of the difference between one's own human and that of others (cf. *Psychologie*, Sämmtliche Werke III.6 (Berlin 1862), 194), Bonhoeffer concentrates on an equality which is not "discernible as 'uniformity'," but an "equality before God" that "cannot be perceived or demonstrated in any way" (*DBWE* 1, 205; *DBW* 1, 138).

[139] *DBWE* 1, 193 (*DBW* 1, 129).

[140] Cf. *DBWE* 1, 195, note 68 (*DBW* 1, 131, note 68).

[141] *DBWE* 1, 195, note 68 (*DBW* 1, 131, note 68). Cf. "Sichtbare Kirche im Neuen Testament," *DBW* 14, 440 note 93 (in the transcript of Erich Klapproth): "Einheit der Gemeinde – Gemeinschaft – einzelner. Fehlt einer dieser drei Begriffe, so ist etwas verkehrt! ... Fehlen die einzelnen, kommt Schleiermacher." This means that Schleiermacher loses the individual. Cf. the concept of instrument in *DBWE* 1, 196, note 208 (*DBW* 1, 270, note 195). Cf. also *The Christian Faith*, 2, 536 (§ 116.3): "in every corporate life all that is personal must be subordinated to the common spirit." Martin Diederich argues, however, "daß Schleiermacher das Aufgehen des Individuums in der Gemeinschaft gerade als sein Sichverwirklichen als Individuum zu denken vornimmt" (M. Diederich, *Schleiermachers Geistverständnis*, 250); "die Aufhebung der Personalität in die Gemeinschaft [ist] ein dialektischer Prozeß, der diese erst wahrhaft herstellt" (ibid., 252f.). Bonhoeffer's own concept of community with its threefold structure (I, I-You-relation, collective person) rejects such a mixture of structures.

Because the individual spirit is swallowed by the community spirit, "dissolving the personality,"[142] Schleiermacher has no "social concept of community."[143] Bonhoeffer judges harshly: "In summary, we have to say that Schleiermacher not only fails to understand social community, and thus the essence of social 'unity', but that, in spite of his efforts to develop the concepts of the corporate life and the union of humanity, he does not reach the social sphere at all ... He is a metaphysician of the spirit, and as such founders on the concept of sociality."[144]

II. Religion

Without doubt, Schleiermacher's reflections on religion are the basic source of the modern significance of the term "religion". In his works, Schleiermacher argues for the peculiarity of religion to the other expressions of human existence (1) and for the necessity of religion (2); he also describes the religious self-consciousness as the main subject of theology (3).

1. The Peculiarity of Religion

The main achievement of Schleiermacher's famous *Speeches on Religion* from 1799 is that they bring out the originality of religion. Compared with metaphysics and morals, religion is "something integral [*etwas eigenes*]."[145] Religion has the same subject as metaphysics and morals, "namely the universe and the relationship of humanity to it."[146] But it deals with this subject differently: Religion "does not wish to determine and explain the universe according to its nature as does metaphysics; it does not desire to continue the universe's development and perfect it by the power of freedom and the divine free choice of a human being as does morals."[147] Religion is neither "thinking" (= metaphysics) nor "acting" (= morals), but

---

[142] *DBWE* 1, 195, note 68 (*DBW* 1, 131, note 68). Cf. *On Religion*, 138: "Strive here already to annihilate your individuality and to live in the one and all."

[143] *DBWE* 1, 195, note 68 (*DBW* 1, 131, note 68). Cf. E. Hirsch, *Die idealistische Philosophie und das Christentum* (Gütersloh 1926), 103–194.

[144] *DBWE* 1, 196, note 68 (*DBW* 1, 131, note 68).

[145] *On Religion*, 100.

[146] *On Religion*, 97.

[147] *On Religion*, 101–102. Oberdorfer argues that this does not tear apart religion, morals or metaphysics, but makes clear the significance of religion for both, morals and metaphysics (cf. B. Oberdorfer, *Geselligkeit und Realisierung von Sittlichkeit. Die Theorieentwicklung Friedrich Schleiermachers bis 1799* (Berlin/New York 1995), 544).

"intuition and feeling"[148] regarding the universe or, as Schleiermacher says in *The Christian Faith*, a "feeling of absolute dependence."[149] It has its own anthropological function and its mental place, "its own province in the mind."[150]

In an early writing, an exegesis on James 1:21–25, Bonhoeffer makes a sceptical comment on this concept of religion. In Bonhoeffer's judgment, Schleiermacher's definition of religion means an exclusion of "doing." "There can scarcely be a sharper contrast between the Schleiermacherian definition of religious terms (knowing and doing as mutually exclusive) and the conception of the letter of James,"[151] a letter which focuses precisely on "doing." Bonhoeffer himself argues for a strong connection between faith and action in form of obedience to Christ ("could there possibly be Christian concepts that are more tightly woven together than faith and obedience?"[152]) and, accordingly, against a sharp contrast between the theology of James and that of Paul[153] – a position which remains crucial in his whole life.[154]

Truly, Schleiermacher distinguishes faith and morality but he does not separate faith and morality: "All actual action should be moral, and it ca be too, but religious feelings should accompany every human deed like a holy music; we should do everything with religion, nothing because of religion."[155] Religion "grounds the desire to act."[156] "Christian piety is an *incentive* to action."[157] But of course, Bonhoeffer would stress that *only* the person who acts really believes.[158]

2. The Necessity of Religion

Because religion has its place in an own "province in the mind," having religion is essential for human existence. Religion "shows itself to you as

---

[148] *On Religion*, 102.
[149] *The Christian Faith*, 1, 16 (§ 4.3).
[150] *On Religion*, 95. Cf. Bonhoeffer's lecture on the "History of Systematic Theology" in *DBW* 11, 147: "Schleiermacher hat das Eigenrecht der Religion begründet durch die Lokalisierung der Religion in der religiösen Provinz der S[eele]."
[151] *DBWE* 9, 492, note 2 (*DWB* 9, 537, note 2); emphasis in original.
[152] *DBWE* 9, 491 (*DWB* 9, 536).
[153] Cf. *DBWE* 9, 493 (*DBW* 9, 538).
[154] Cf. *DBWE* 4, 43ff.
[155] *On Religion*, 110.
[156] E. Herms, "Schleiermacher's Christian Ethics," in *CCFS*, 209–228, 214.
[157] E. Herms, "Schleiermacher's Christian Ethics," 215.
[158] *DBWE* 4, 63 (*DBW* 4, 52). Cf. Christiane Tietz, "'Nur der Glaubende ist gehorsam, und nur der Gehorsame glaubt.' Beobachtungen zu einem existentiellen Zirkel in Dietrich Bonhoeffers 'Nachfolge'," in *Dietrich Bonhoeffer Jahrbuch/Yearbook* 2 (2005–2006), 170–181.

the necessary and indispensable third next to those two [metaphysics/speculation and morals/praxis], as their natural counterpart, not slighter in worth and splendour than what you wish of them."[159] Having religion is "not an accidental element, or a thing which varies from person to person, but is a universal element of life."[160] This assumption includes the idea of a religious *a priori*: "A person is born with the religious capacity as with every other, and if only his sense is not forcibly suppressed, if only that communion between a person and the universe ... is not blocked and barricaded, then religion would have to develop unerringly in each person according to his own individual manner."[161] Or, as Schleiermacher argues in the *Christian Faith*, the feeling of absolute dependence develops from "the absolutely general nature of humanity."[162]

Bonhoeffer criticizes the idea of a religious *a priori* in human self-consciousness, because he fears that thus religion is "only anthropology" and hence "incapable of overcoming the immanence of the spirit."[163] As Barth he believes that religion then remains "die letzte, feinste der Möglichkeiten des Menschen. Der Mensch [wird] als Gott verwandt entdeckt."[164] This leads to a "'grand confusion' of religion and grace."[165]

In accordance to his understanding of religion as an anthropological constant, Schleiermacher sees atheism inversely as a "sickness of the soul"[166] in which the religious *a priori* remains undeveloped. Because religion is essential for the human soul, Schleiermacher assumes that this atheism "may revive sporadically and from time to time," but it will never become "anything that is historically permanent."[167] For theological reasons Schleiermacher does not reckon with a time of religionlessness.

Quite differently, Bonhoeffer is of the opinion that the religious *a priori* is only a "historically conditioned and transient form of human self-expression."[168] And he substitutes the idea of a religious *a priori* by the assumption: "We are moving towards a completely religionless time; people as they are now simply cannot be religious any more."[169] As Schleier-

---

[159] *On Religion*, 102.

[160] *The Christian Faith*, 1, 133 (§ 33). Cf. (§ 33.2), where Schleiermacher claims "that the feeling of absolute dependence ... and the God-consciousness contained in it are a fundamental moment of human life."

[161] *On Religion*, 146.

[162] *The Christian Faith*, 1, 134 (§ 33.1); translation altered.

[163] *DBWE* 5, 130 (*DBW* 5, 156). Cf. *DBW* 11, 158.

[164] *DBW* 11, 145. Cf. Bethge, *Dietrich Bonhoeffer*, 100: Bonhoeffer "reagierte ... heftig gegen jeden ... Verweis auf eine wie immer geartete religiöse Potenz des Menschen, die wieder in die Selbsterforschung führte."

[165] *DBWE* 2, 154 (*DBW* 2, 153).

[166] *The Christian Faith*, 1, 135 (§ 33.2).

[167] *The Christian Faith*, 1, 136 (§ 33.2).

[168] *LPP*, 280 (*DBW* 8, 403).

[169] *LPP*, 279 (*DBW* 8, 403).

macher, Bonhoeffer has not only historical, but also theological arguments for his position: Religion is not adequate for Christian faith. For Jesus Christ is the "reversal of what the religious man expects from God."[170]

While this seems to be a fundamental refusal of religion as such, we have to keep in mind that Bonhoeffer's late concept of religion is different from Schleiermacher's. Schleiermacher describes a basic anthropological dimension while Bonhoeffer's late understanding of religion concentrates only on a few aspects of religion: metaphysics, inwardness, individuality, and partiality. But if we look carefully, we can see that Schleiermacher is at least in mind when Bonhoeffer argues against those elements of religion.[171] Of course, Schleiermacher's idea of religion is not metaphysics in that supernatural sense of a *deus ex machina* who breaks through the worldly order.[172] But the term inwardness seems to refer to Schleiermacher's concept of religion as self-consciousness. And Bonhoeffer's critique of religious individualism might refer to his early remarks on Schleiermacher's individualistic ecclesiology. Could it finally be that the aspect of partiality refers to Schleiermacher's concept of religion as a special "province in the mind?"[173] "The 'religious act' is always something partial; 'faith' is something whole, involving the whole of one's life. Jesus calls men, not to a new religion, but to life."[174]

Nevertheless, Bonhoeffer's criticism of religion is not arguing against every form of what Schleiermacher would call religion. When Bonhoeffer asks: "What is the place of worship and prayer in a religionless situation?,"[175] we see that religionlessness is no contradiction to cultus and prayer. Faith necessarily seeks expression in religious forms.

In this we can perceive the re-adoption of an early insight of Bonhoeffer. The young Bonhoeffer distinguishes religion and faith. Faith is "directed towards Christ," "pure intentionality,"[176] is "*actus directus*,"[177] non-reflexive. But faith necessarily becomes religion ("in the community of Christ faith takes form in religion"[178]), or, as Bonhoeffer says, credulity

---

[170] *LPP*, 361 (*DBW* 8, 535); cf. *DBW* 8, 534.

[171] Cf. Ernst Feil, *The Theology of Dietrich Bonhoeffer*, translated by Martin Rumscheidt (Philadelphia 1985), 102–103.

[172] Cf. for example *LPP*, 281 (*DBW* 8, 407). Cf. *Der christliche Glaube*, Kritische Gesamtausgabe I 13,1, edited by Rolf Schäfer (Berlin/New York, 2003), 276–277 (§ 47): "Aus dem Interesse der Frömmigkeit kann nie ein Bedürfniß entstehen, eine Thatsache so aufzufassen, daß durch ihre Abhängigkeit von Gott ihr Bedingtsein durch den Naturzusammenhang schlechthin aufgehoben werde."

[173] Feil, *The Theology of Dietrich Bonhoeffer*, 238, note 219.

[174] *LPP*, 362 (*DBW* 8, 537).

[175] *LPP*, 281 (*DBW* 8, 405).

[176] *DBWE* 2, 153 (*DBW* 2, 152–153).

[177] *DBWE* 2, 158, note 29 (*DBW* 2, 158, note 29).

[178] *DBWE* 2, 154 (*DBW* 2, 153–154).

[*Gläubigkeit*]. "Every act of faith is credulous insofar as it is an event embedded in the psyche ... and accessible to reflection."[179] "Christ is apprehended in believing [*gläubigem*] faith."[180] In this "Gläubigkeit" the Schleiermacherian terms like "experience, piety, feeling" have their right.[181] But "Gläubigkeit" and faith are not identical.

3. Religious Self-Consciousness as Subject of Theology

For Schleiermacher, the religious self-consciousness is the topic of theology.[182] Theology reflects the religious feelings or – as Schleiermacher says in his *The Christian Faith*: "Christian doctrines are accounts of the Christian religious affections set forth in speech."[183] For Schleiermacher, "we must declare the description of human states of mind to be the fundamental dogmatic form"[184] whereas sentences on the essence of God or the world are acceptable only if they can be developed from the sentences on religious self-consciousness. For example, God is the whence of the feeling of absolute dependence.[185]

Bonhoeffer conjectures that in concentrating on the religious self-consciousness the question of truth remains unasked.[186] Here we have no criterion of right or wrong.[187] Schleiermacher himself says that if we look at the consciousness everything is true: "it can rightly be said that in religion everything is immediately true, since nothing at all is expressed in its individual moments except the religious person's own state of mind."[188] In religion, "in the infinite everything finite stands undisturbed alongside one

---

[179] *DBWE* 2, 154 (*DBW* 2, 154). Cf. "Theologische Psychologie," in *DBW* 12, 187, where Bonhoeffer argues that faith [*Glaube*] is and stays veiled in credulity [*Gläubigkeit*].
[180] *DBWE* 2, 154 (*DBW* 2, 154).
[181] *DBWE* 2, 154 (*DBW* 2, 154). Cf. "Theologische Psychologie," in *DBW* 12, 187.
[182] Cf. *DBW* 11, 147.
[183] *The Christian Faith*, 1, 76 (§ 15).
[184] *The Christian Faith*, 1, 136 (§ 30.2).
[185] *The Christian Faith*, 1, 16 (§ 4.4).
[186] Cf. *DBW* 11, 147. It seems as if Bonhoeffer took this critique from Barth who argues in *Die christliche Dogmatik im Entwurf (1927)*, Gesamtausgabe II, 14 (Zurich 1982), 407, that Schleiermacher in defining "christliche Glaubenssätze" as "Auffassungen der christlich frommen Gemütszustände in der Rede dargestellt" does not refer to truth or even to the expression of truth in the human self-consciousness.
[187] Cf. *DBW* 11, 150.
[188] Friedrich Schleiermacher, *Über die Religion*. Edited by Günter Meckenstock, Kritische Gesamtausgabe I.12 (Berlin/New York 1995, (2.-) 4. edition), 136; translation R.M. Adams, "Faith and Religious Knowledge," in: J. Mariña (ed.), *CCFS*, 35–51, here 35.

another; all is one, and all is true."[189] In Bonhoeffer's eyes, this would mean: "If everything is true, then the concept of falseness is abolished; as a result, so too is the concept of truth."[190] For Bonhoeffer, this is unacceptable, because the question of truth is fundamental for Christianity.[191] In Bonhoeffer's view, Ludwig Feuerbach – who, like Schleiermacher, concentrates on a person's religious self-consciousness but comes to the conclusion that there is no God beyond the religious feelings – is worthy to be called "the most consequent student of Schleiermacher."[192] Indeed, this is a quite devastating judgment.

As we saw, Bonhoeffer acknowledges Schleiermacher's interest in sociality: his emphasis on the primal social community, his collective concept of sin, the interest in the church, and Schleiermacher's attempt to connect Holy Spirit and church-community. But Bonhoeffer criticizes Schleiermacher's carrying out of these ideas in numerous ways. They can be summarized as the critique that Schleiermacher has a mere psychological approach to sociality which has no understanding of the ethical-social relations between persons and ignores the theological characteristics of the church. Furthermore, Bonhoeffer sees Schleiermacher's concept of religion excluding action, passing by, and suspending the question of truth.

---

[189] *On Religion*, 108.

[190] *DBWE* 9, 215 (*DBW* 9, 219).

[191] Cf. *DBW* 11, 330. In the context of the Confessing Church and the ecumenical movement (1935), Bonhoeffer discusses the relation of unity and truth in regard to two different ecumenical concepts: "So wahr und so biblisch der Satz sein mag, daß nur in der Einheit Wahrheit sei, so wahr und biblisch ist auch der andere Satz, daß nur in der Wahrheit Einheit möglich sei" (*DBW* 14, 390). Supporters of the first position would describe the ecumenical movement as a tree with many different branches. Bonhoeffer refers to this picture also in a lecture on church order: "Konfessionen Äste am Baum – Harmonie der Ökumene. Darstellendes Handeln, – ästhetisch-romantisch ... 'Verschiedene Worte – dieselbe Sache'" (*DBW* 14, 307–308). In Eberhard Bethge's transcript follows: "(Schleiermacher) ... (Luther wollte das Konzil als die Wahrheit scheidend, hier aber Konzil als 'Darstellung' der Einheit. 'Auf gemeinsames hinarbeiten, nicht trennendes')" (*DBW* 14, 308 note 8). It seems reasonable to assume that Bonhoeffer saw Schleiermacher as someone who proposed the unity of the church at the expense of truth.

[192] *DBW* 11, 148.

Geffrey B. Kelly

Kierkegaard as "Antidote" and as Impact on Dietrich Bonhoeffer's Concept of Christian Discipleship

One of the more fascinating exchanges between Dietrich Bonhoeffer and his fiancée, Maria von Wedemeyer, took place in February, 1944. Maria was apparently eager to show Bonhoeffer that, because of her love for him, she was developing an interest in his theological career to the point that she had actually been reading theology. "The fact is I'm in the middle of a theological tome! What's more, I don't find it half as boring as I expected. You weren't supposed to know, really. I started it to be a little closer to you, not to become a 'Burckhardthaus' type, but now I'm reading it eagerly and greedily. It's '*Das Evangelium*,' by Paul Schütz. (If you don't like the book, that'll be the last straw)."[1] It wasn't the "last straw." Bonhoeffer wrote back that he was delighted that she had been reading Schütz, but that in an earlier, more theological, phase of his career he had criticized such a book. He then wrote that it would take too long to specify his objections. "However, I'd welcome it if you took a strong dose of Kierkegaard ('Fear and Trembling,' 'Practice in Christianity,' 'Sickness unto Death') as an antidote."[2]

Antidote, indeed! What was Bonhoeffer thinking? Was the authenticity and personal integrity of Kierkegaard that he admired the correct "antidote" to the kind of self-serving theologizing that Bonhoeffer had abhorred in tomes like that of Schütz? In any event, Maria took Bonhoeffer's advice to heart and stowed the book by Schütz in a trunk where "may it remain to all eternity!" To which she added in her letter of 2 March 1944: "You're putting me through the mill where books are concerned. I'll soon be timidly consulting you first every time, and end by reading nothing by Kierkegaard with 'fear and trembling,' 'sick unto death.'"[3] Kierkegaard's impact on Bonhoeffer lasted throughout his ministry, though with the reservations that eclectic Bonhoeffer had with any and all of his sources. It is

---

[1] *Love Letters from Cell 92: The Correspondence Between Dietrich Bonhoeffer and Maria von Wedemeyer* (Nashville: Abington Press, 1992), 176–177.

[2] *Love Letters from Cell 92*, 185–186.

[3] *Love Letters from Cell 92*, 193–94.

significant that Bonhoeffer evidently believed reading Kierkegaard was a wise path for his fiancée to begin reading theology.

Bonhoeffer's esteem for Søren Kierkegaard came through very clearly in papers written during his year at Union Theological Seminary when he twice listed him in the same line of "genuine Christian thinking" as Paul, Augustine, Luther and Barth.[4] At that time Bonhoeffer was convinced that Kierkegaard, alone among nineteenth-century theologians and philosophers, had correctly perceived the true dialectic of faith and obedience present in Luther's earlier interpretation of the biblical word on justification. Bonhoeffer complained that Luther's doctrine of *sola fide*, coupled with his teaching of the "two kingdoms," had been vitiated in the contemporary world dominated by the Nazi ideology and by widespread neglect of Jesus' demands on his disciples as these were recorded in the Gospels. His misgivings echoed Kierkegaard's own passionate appeal for a return to the authentic principles of the Reformation in several of his polemical writings against bourgeois complacency in Danish Lutheranism.

Wondering whether Luther himself would be able to recognize contemporary Christendom, Kierkegaard has written: "The misfortune of Christianity is clearly that it has become a hiding place for sheer paganism and Epicureanism. People forget entirely that Luther was urging the claims of faith against a fantastically exaggerated asceticism."[5] According to Kierkegaard, the softening of Jesus' heroic demands on his followers came about because later students of Luther had altered Luther's passion for faith alone in favor of a doctrine that diminished the vital role faith played in Christian deeds done in imitation of Jesus Christ in the process of sanctification. This had the unexpected consequence of downgrading the positive value of good works. In authentic Reformation teachings doing good emanated as emanating from the faith with which God gifted followers of Jesus Christ. The moral slope Kierkegaard found so annoying was nothing more than a misinterpretation of Luther who had never disparaged good works as such, except when drawn into conflict with claims that smacked of Pelagianism in high Roman places. In Kierkegaard's opinion, Roman Christianity had substituted doing good works for the faith that saves.

Bonhoeffer's classic text, *Discipleship*, was composed at the height of the German Church's having either embraced Nazism or timidly retreated from any meaningful opposition to the Nazi regime. Having read selections from Kierkegaard, Bonhoeffer was strongly influenced by his critical insights on the dangers of misusing Luther in order to make his teachings on Christian faith more accommodating to the popular mood and its comfort

---

[4] "Concerning the Christian Idea of God," in *DBW* 11, 423–433; "The Theology of Crisis and Its Attitude Toward Philosophy and Science," in *DBW* 11, 434–449.

[5] Kierkegaard, *The Journals of Kierkegaard, 1834–1854*, edited and translated by Alexander Dru (London 1967), 166.

zones. The problem in the church, as Bonhoeffer then understood it, was the seductive lure of a comfortable Christianity, gliding along with an all-powerful ideology that promised law and order, stability and security, state-bestowed benefits that appealed to clerical interests and the churches' passion for survival as an institution enjoying civil privileges. Bonhoeffer wanted to intrude on the ensuing church complacency which he blamed for the deterioration of Gospel values in Germany. "Cheap grace is the mortal enemy of our church," he wrote. "Our struggle today is for costly grace." He goes on in that opening chapter of *Discipleship* to specify that "cheap grace means justification of sin but not of the sinner. Because grace alone does everything, everything can stay in its old ways ... Thus, the Christian should live the same way the world does. In all things the Christian should go along with the world and not venture (like sixteenth century enthusiasts) to live a different life under grace from that under sin!"[6]

As a segue to his denunciation of cheap grace, Bonhoeffer then points out, in Kierkegaardian fashion, that Luther's leaving the monastery was actually a "frontal assault" on the world's subtle rejection of Christ's demands. "Following Jesus now had to be lived out in the midst of the world ... Complete obedience to Jesus' commandments had to be carried out in the daily world of work. This deepened the conflict between the life of Christians and the life of the world in an unforeseeable way. The Christian had closed in on the world. It was hand-to-hand combat."[7] By leaving the monastery Luther was not liberated from the challenges of following Jesus Christ. On the contrary, he found his liberation through the very risky task of actually following Christ in a world hostile to genuine Gospel values. Far from being relieved of the duty to obey Jesus' difficult demands, Luther was impelled to live out his faith in a much more conflicted world by answering the call to the "costly grace" of Christian discipleship.

At this stage in his exposé of "cheap grace," Bonhoeffer invokes Kierkegaard who had warned his church of the dangers of claiming to be justified by faith alone as a *presupposition* for an attitude of comfortable indolence toward one's sins and the implications of one's justification for genuine Christian living. He recalls Kierkegaard's allusion to Faust who, after bartering his soul for knowledge, could conclude at the end of his life that he could know nothing. That was the *result* of a lifelong experience. But, as a presupposition, it was dangerous if, for example, a student used such a statement to justify a reprehensible laziness.[8] Bonhoeffer draws this conclusion from Kierkegaard's assertion: "Only those who in following

---

[6] *DBWE* 4, 43–44 (*DBW* 4, 29–30).
[7] *DBWE*, 48–49 (*DBW* 4, 34–35).
[8] *DBWE* 4, 51 (*DBW* 4, 34–35). See Kierkegaard, *Søren Kierkegaard's Journals and Papers*, Volumes 1–4, edited and translated by Howard V. Hong and Edna H. Hong (Bloomington, 1967–1975), volume 3, 94.

Christ leave everything they have can stand and say that they are justified solely by grace. They recognize the call to discipleship itself as grace and grace as that call. But those who want to use this grace to excuse themselves from discipleship are deceiving themselves."[9] Bonhoeffer's insistence on obedience to the call of Jesus Christ to discipleship was not intended to be a blanket endorsement of good works apart from the saving grace of justification. On the contrary, Bonhoeffer saw himself engaged in a struggle for the very soul of the Reformation, namely, the affirmation of personal faith lived in obedience to the call of Jesus Christ in simultaneity with the demands of the Gospels. Obedience to Jesus Christ, inextricably bound to the gift of faith, is Bonhoeffer's salient theme throughout *Discipleship*.

Bonhoeffer was aroused by the root causes within the churches that had led to weakening of the demands of faith in a world apparently bereft of peace, compassion, integrity, and courage in working for justice, yet willing to "go along" to "get along" with an evil ideology. His denunciation of "cheap grace" was of a piece with his anger at the ways churches seemed to offer "grace as bargain-basement goods, cut-rate forgiveness, cut-rate comfort, cut-rate sacrament," where "everything can be had for free."[10] Such attitudes meant in practical terms a reduction of Christianity to a principle or system, faith becoming mere intellectual assent, and Christian living itself slimmed down to Sunday ritualism, mindless dogmatism, and soulless legalisms. Cheap grace was without discipleship, and without Jesus Christ and his cross. This was the mushy way of evading the sacrifices demanded in following Jesus Christ.

Although the phrase, "cheap grace," has become a slogan marker for his book on *Discipleship* and, together with the catch phrase, "costly grace," led to the book's original title in English, *The Cost of Discipleship*, the phrase was used by Bonhoeffer at least five years prior to the publication of *Discipleship*. In a 1932 lecture to a branch of the German Christian Students Movement, Bonhoeffer pointed out to the audience that "discipleship of Christ comes from and depends entirely on simple faith."[11] He went on to link this "simple faith" with obedience to the Gospel mandates and taking one's innate sinfulness with utter seriousness, given the ready forgiveness of a soft-hearted deity. He asks: "How are we to go on believing in God with pure hearts if we refuse to follow the path of obedience by our sinning in expectation of the grace of forgiveness and our not taking seriously that grace and especially our prayer to God? *We thus make grace cheap* and with the justification of the sinner through the cross of Christ,

---

[9] *DBWE* 4, 51 (*DBW* 4, 38).
[10] *DBWE* 4, 43 (*DBW* 4, 29).
[11] *TF*, 94.

we thereby forget the cry of the Lord who never justifies sin."[12] He then took two of Christ's single-minded commands: "You shall not kill" and "love your enemy" to illustrate what he meant by Christ's words given to Christians, not to quibble over, but only to obey. He applies those commands to their rampant violation in acts of war that contradict, even reject the teachings of Jesus Christ.[13]

As for the origin of the expression, "cheap grace," it is possible that Bonhoeffer borrowed the expression from either Luther or Kierkegaard or from both of them. As a Lutheran theologian, Bonhoeffer was undoubtedly familiar with Luther's *Rationis Latominae Confutatio* of 1521. Two specific passages of this work seem to be echoed in the opening themes of *Discipleship*. Luther had written against the "sophists": "It amounts to this ... it is within your power and on very easy terms to acquire grace from good works performed ... By doing so they both make Christ's grace cheap and God's mercy of little worth."[14]

But strong evidence exists that the phrase also came from Kierkegaard. During a consultation over the phrase in Bonhoeffer's *Nachfolge* – Bonhoeffer's own edition of the text had been destroyed in the bombardment of Berlin – Eberhard Bethge suggested the additional possibility that the expression had been influenced by Søren Kierkegaard whose book, *Der Einzelne und die Kirche. Über Luther und den Protestantismus* [The Individual and the Church: Concerning Luther and Protestantism] undoubtedly served as a direct source for several sections of *Discipleship*. I was able to examine Bonhoeffer's own copy of this book which is heavily underlined by Bonhoeffer in several places where the influence of Kierkegaard seems most obvious.[15]

In this book Kierkegaard had, in fact, described in rather ironic terms the reasons for Luther's becoming more popular than the Pope. This was because the Pope had become "too costly" (*zu teuer*) in demanding five marks for conferring full holiness. Luther, by contrast (as people mistook

---

[12] *TF*, 94–95; emphasis added.

[13] *TF*, 95.

[14] "...tamen in manu tua et prorsus facile [gar leicht] sit gratiam consequi, operibus secundum substantiam facti paratis ... per hoc et Christi gratiam vilem (die "Gnade Christi billig) et misericordiam dei levem." From the *Library of Christian Classics*, XVI (London 1962), 314, 356 (*WA*, 8, 54, 30; 8, 115, 36).

[15] Kierkegaard, *Der Einzelne und die Kirche. Über Luther und den Protestantismus*, Translated and with a Foreword by Wilhelm Kütemeyer (Berlin 1934). The connections between Kierkegaard and Bonhoeffer in this text were first brought to the attention of the theological world through an excursus in the doctoral dissertation of Traugott Vogel. See *Christus als Vorbild und Versöhner. Eine kritische Studie zum Problem des Verhältnisses von Gesetz und Evangelium im Werke Sören Kierkegaards* [Christ as Exemplar and Redeemer. A critical study on the problem jof the relationship of Law and Gospel in the works of Søren Kiergaard] Doctoral Dissertation, Berlin (Humboldt) University, 1968.

his preaching of faith) holiness was far cheaper (*nun nahm man Luther eitel, so dass man mit Hilfe der Wendung welche er der Sache gab die Seligkeit noch weit <u>billiger machte</u>*).[16] Later in the book, Kierkegaard complains that, in Luther's time and in his own, grace had become an object of priestly speculation like money (*die Priester spekulieren in Gnade*) and used to exact expensive "guilt obligations" (*sie sich von uns Menschen in teueren Schuldverschreibungen bezahlen lassen*).[17] That "costly grace" had become corrupted into "cheap grace" whenever the church took grace as a principle of precondition, instead of as a *result* of justification is an important point in Bonhoeffer's development of the concept of "costly grace."

Bonhoeffer's focus on the distinction between grace as "principle" and grace as "result" of justification can likewise be associated with Kierkegaard who had written that discipleship, correctly understood, can never mean a reduction of Jesus Christ to a mere idea or abstract principle. For Kierkegaard, as for Bonhoeffer, the grace of discipleship does not admit either to inflicting monastic styled discipline on one's body or to ascetical hypocrisy. The grace of discipleship to Jesus Christ is essentially the justifying presence of Christ who offers both example and commands drawn from the Gospels that Christians are to follow.[18] Kierkegaard's critique of monasticism is connected to the same distinction. He sees the incorporation of the so-called "evangelical counsels" into the structures of the church as an inverted way of separating a special elite under that structure and encouraging a more comfortable Christian praxis for all others who would then be at ease in conforming themselves with the values of a thoroughly secularized world.[19] Bonhoeffer recognized in Kierkegaard a kindred soul who could argue that the Reformation insights of Martin Luther had the potential to re-evangelize the secular where most people lived their lives and where the Gospel in all its "riskiness" needed once again to infiltrate.

However, in the world where resistance to the gospel challenges was rampant, whether of nineteenth century Danish Lutheranism or twentieth century ideologically polluted Germanism, both Kierkegaard and Bonhoeffer called for a shocking reversal of Luther's most dramatic act and verbal ambiguity against Roman Christianity's corrupt ways. Kierkegaard advocated a return to the monastery. He had even written that "Christianity's

---

[16] *Der Einzelne und die Kirche*, 170–171; emphasis added.

[17] *Der Einzelne und die Kirche*, 175–176.

[18] Kierkegaard writes that Christendom does not become poetry, mythology, or idea in an abstract sense which has recently happened in Protestantism, "but by doing away with discipleship and through a covert turning inward [Christendom] just about reaches the point where Christ is not the ideal or the example... but an idea;" cf. *Der Einzelne und die Kirche*, 163 (translation mine).

[19] *Der Einzelne und die Kirche*, 145–47.

first and foremost duty is to return to the monastery from which Luther broke away."[20] Bonhoeffer appears to echo this contention in a letter to his Swiss friend, Erwin Sutz, and in a letter from prison to his parents on Reformation Day, October 31, 1943. To Sutz, he wrote of his loss of faith in the university to achieve any progress in achieving social change. "The entire training of the budding theologians belongs today in church, monastery-like schools in which the pure doctrine, the Sermon on the mount, and worship can be taken seriously – which is really not the case with all three things at the university and, in present-day circumstances, is impossible." He added that the church ought to lose its fear and to speak up for the victims of state-sponsored oppression.[21] Would monastic-like schools give them that fearlessness? Bonhoeffer hoped so. Perhaps his experiment in Finkenwalde, as reported in *Life Together*, provided a partial answer.

In his letter to his parents, he declared that Reformation Day offered an occasion to reflect on how, even in his lifetime, Luther's insights had consequences never intended. Toward the end of his life, even Luther had doubts about the value of what he had accomplished. His dream of restoring Christian unity had given way to "disintegration of the church and of Europe." Likewise, his dreams of the freedom of Christians had as consequence only "indifference and licentiousness." Instead of a "genuine secular social order free from clerical privilege," he had witnessed war and the loss of societal orderliness. Hence Bonhoeffer's comment: "As long as a hundred years ago, Kierkegaard said that today Luther would say the opposite of what he said then. I think he was right – with some reservations."[22]

Bonhoeffer does not spell out just what Luther would have said differently. On the other hand, one could extrapolate from *Discipleship* Bonhoeffer's conviction that the Reformation ideals, especially Luther's practical steps to repristinate God's word in Jesus Christ, were never to be taken for granted, but were in need of continuing renewal in both church and society, in the sense of *ecclesia semper reformanda*, a church always in need of reform. In his *Ethics* Bonhoeffer saw the need to rescue Luther's insights from distortion by future generations. The problem was one of a church "separating itself from the reality in Christ."[23] In Bonhoeffer's view, Luther had protested against the tendency of Roman Christianity to condemn the secular in order to achieve a clericalized papal domination. Luther wanted, instead, to bring about a better secularity in a Christianity fully attuned to an integration of the spiritual with the secular. In the 1930s Bonhoeffer was witnessing a Christianity either deaf or indifferent to the

---

[20] *Journals*, 240.
[21] Letter of 11 September 1934 in *TF*, 412.
[22] *LPP*, 123 (*DBW* 8, 179).
[23] *DBWE* 6, 60 (*DBW* 6, 47).

truth of what was happening in a Nazified secular reality. The secular was in dire need of a faithful church and a reformed secularity within that church's mission. Kierkegaard, before Bonhoeffer, had also seen Christianity degenerate into dogmas, rituals, and legalisms with the consequence that the person of Jesus Christ was no longer the one to whom Christians were to commit themselves irrevocably. The loss of the genuine Reformation perspective of the *sola scriptura* led to Bonhoeffer's subsequent lamentation that the trouble in Germany was that Germans had taken Adolf Hitler for their conscience and not Jesus Christ.[24]

In illustrating how the call to discipleship can be heard by believers who are obedient, Bonhoeffer turns to the story of the disappointed, rich young man of the gospel stories. Kierkegaard's version, which Bonhoeffer marked in his copy of Kütemeyer's edition, focused on the rich young man's hesitancy to step into the deep waters, an allusion to the plight of Simon Peter, in order to attain the infinite of his potential as a follower of Christ. Bonhoeffer uses this story to explain how the rich young man avoided asking the real question of just how far would God lead him to attain perfection. Instead, he wanted only reassurance of his past and answers to his question about how to become perfect. Jesus gives him, what he did not expect, the challenge of God's own word, commanding obedience beyond the established orders. The "extra" demands on being a follower of Christ then seemed to many Christians like stepping into those 70,000 fathoms deep of the waters in Kierkegaard's example. It is intriguing to observe that, while Bonhoeffer acknowledged the story as commented on by Kierkegaard, he used the story to go beyond Kierkegaard in delineating three important lessons to ascertain in understanding the call: the need to recognize that it is Jesus commanding; the need for clarification so that the call be not misunderstood; and, finally, a need to recognize the additional demands in Jesus' call to perfection that transforms a follower into one willing to not rest on one's past but to do those more daring deeds in and because of one's personal relationship with Jesus Christ.[25]

Another important convergence with Kierkegaard with which Bonhoeffer was undoubtedly familiar was Kierkegaard's emphasis on simple obedience to the Gospel mandates. Kierkegaard had written in his journals, "if the gospel demands that we renounce this world ... then the simple thing to do is: do it."[26] In *Discipleship* Bonhoeffer insisted on the same attitude of simple obedience as a way to cut through all the subterfuges of rationalizations that had become a wedge between Jesus' word and obedience to that word. In his earlier talk on "Christ and Peace" to the German Student

---

[24] *DBWE* 278 (*DBW* 6, 278). See also, Geffrey Kelly and Burton Nelson, *The Cost of Moral Leadership: The Spirituality of Dietrich Bonhoeffer* (Grand Rapids 2002), 114.

[25] *DBWE* 4, 69–76 (*DBW* 4, 59–67).

[26] *Journals*, volume 3, 93–95. See also *DBWE* 4, 77 (*DBW* 4, 69).

Christian Movement, Fall 1932, for example, Bonhoeffer had, indeed, spoken in words not unlike Kierkegaard's own opinion to just "do it." Bonhoeffer had declared to those students: "The command, 'you shall not kill,' and the word, 'love your enemy,' are given to us simply to obey."[27] The same grounding of discipleship in such simple obedience, neither coerced nor surrounded by self-serving caveats, became a steady theme throughout *Discipleship*. Following Christ meant, put in its clearest, unambiguous terms, obeying the gospel with particular emphasis on the Sermon on the Mount.

There are additional traces of Kierkegaard either by himself or through Karl Barth in Bonhoeffer's chapter on "Discipleship and the Individual." There Bonhoeffer insists that "Christ makes everyone he calls into an individual. Each is called alone. Each must follow alone."[28] He concedes that the fear of being alone moves people to seek safety in numbers rather than face up to the demands of Jesus Christ to each individual. Bonhoeffer was familiar with the spectacle of Christians seeking the security that one found in the mass hysteria of Nazi rallies in which so many Germans thought they had found their sense of unity and purpose in quasi pagan liturgies under the banner of a mesmerizing leader. For Kierkegaard, the very accessibility of Christianity "occurs through and only through each one's becoming an individual, the single individual."[29] He adds that for Christianity not to degenerate into either mythology or theatrical preaching, authentic discipleship is required "and the sobriety involved in making men into single individuals, so that every single individual relates himself, is obliged to relate himself, to the ideal."[30]

Both Kierkegaard and Bonhoeffer recognized that belonging to a large pack or sizeable group, where sacrifices in order to follow Christ to the cross were unthinkable, could provide the best places to hide from Jesus' embarrassing demands on individual Christians. Bonhoeffer counters this by an emphasis on how discipleship enhances both individual integrity and the Christian community. That, he argues, is the stark reality, but the only way of becoming an authentic individual in line with Jesus' call can, ironically, provoke a break with the world and even with one's own family. This escalation of Jesus' challenges to Christians recalls that "leap of faith" into which, as Kierkegaard put it, one might have to venture in order to become a genuine believer with the only certitude coming from trust in the love of Christ.[31] Bonhoeffer contends, further, that the break with one's

---

[27] *TF*, 95.
[28] *DBWE* 4, 92 (*DBW* 4, 87).
[29] *Journals*, volume 2, 398.
[30] *Journals*, volume 2, 348.
[31] *Journals*, volume 2, 368.

"immediate relationships," caused by Jesus' unconditional call on obedience, "is inevitable."

In fact, the public impact of breaking with family, friends, or one's nation, in the manner of Abraham setting out into the unknown, could, he concedes, bring on the public reproach that one's conduct is "antihuman." In support of this contention, Bonhoeffer had marked that passage from Kierkegaard's journals where Kierkegaard had noted the early pagan objection to Christianity. They had labelled Christianity "antihuman." But in Kierkegaard's day, Christianity had avoided that criticism by becoming "humanity"; in essence, conforming to standards of social respectability and, in the process, abandoning Jesus Christ and genuine faith. That attitude, in part, was what troubled Bonhoeffer in dealing with the neglect of Jesus' words and commands in Nazi Germany. It was too easy to surrender faith in Jesus Christ to the attraction of loyalty to one's prideful belonging to the crowds who adulated their great political leader and blinded themselves with a noxious nationalism.

The segue into that aspect of discipleship is also related to passages from Kierkegaard that also impressed Bonhoeffer to the extent of his marking those passages from Kierkegaard's journals as significant.[32] In commenting on the need to love one's enemies, the very context of Jesus' mandate to love of neighbour in the Sermon on the Mount, for example, Bonhoeffer reminds his seminarians and readers that the followers of Christ knew well what it was like to be considered an enemy of the state. They were hated as lawbreakers; They were "insulted and scorned ... for their weakness and humility." They were persecuted as subversive revolutionaries. He went on to declare that even Jesus himself was considered a political enemy of imperial Rome.[33] On this very point Bonhoeffer drew from Kierkegaard's reference to the persecution that early Christians suffered. The pagan rationale was "that it was unpatriotic, a danger to the state, revolutionary."[34] This section of *Discipleship* goes in two directions, namely, to love one's enemies, but also to be aware that the integral following of Christ, so often rejected as "unpatriotic" will inevitably lead to persecution and the cross.

Toward the end of his analysis of that aspect of *Discipleship* Bonhoeffer retrieves Jesus' demand that his disciples' righteousness must outdo that of the Pharisees. Bonhoeffer links this to the extraordinary challenge to be faced by Christians which, if absent or neglected, diminishes what is essential to Christian praxis. At issue is the temptation to conform comfortably to the world as opposed to an unconditional, "extraordinary" embrace of Jesus' cross. The "extraordinary" was likewise a focus of Kierkegaard.

---

[32] *DBWE* 4, 137 (*DBW* 4, 140). See *Journals and Papers*, volume 4, 182.
[33] *DBWE* 4, 137–138 (*DBW* 4, 140–141).
[34] *Journals and Papers*, volume 4, 182.

He frequently used the expression o to argue against opinions that exalted aspects of Christianity, such as voluntary poverty, as "extraordinary" or highly laudatory above other actions. Instead, Kierkegaard sees the "extraordinary" as that made possible "through his immediate God-relationship. Only in this sense can Christianity admit to extraordinary Christians."[35] Although he is aware of Kierkegaard's slant on the "extraordinary" that Jesus declared as a mark of distinction for his followers, Bonhoeffer goes beyond Kierkegaard in relating the "extraordinary" to actual deeds that are highly visible, such as loving one's enemies, though the very visibility of such love can lead in all its simplicity, to the "*passio*," or communion in the cross of Christ, and even persecution at the hands of those to whom love has been extended.[36]

According to Bonhoeffer, in such visibility, Christians remain in the world as a visible sign that they are in conflict with the worldly values cherished by people who live in ignorance of or contradiction to the teachings of Jesus Christ. Here again, in Bonhoeffer's personal notes on discipleship, are found connections to Kierkegaard's comments on Luther's attempt to rescue the discipleship of Christ from the gross misunderstanding so prevalent at the time.[37] In those days leaving the world by entering a monastery had been elevated to the level of the "meritorious or extraordinary," thus cheapening Jesus' demands, that should permeate every believer's life, and diminishing the impact of those demands for ordinary people unable or unwilling to see through the deception. In Kierkegaard's words, "if the established order wants to have a direct attack, well, here it is ... Luther rescued 'discipleship, the imitation of Christ' from a fantastic misunderstanding."[38] The unfortunate result of that "misunderstanding," against which Bonhoeffer, following Kierkegaard, inveighed was that the error proclaiming justification without works was as corrupting as good works without the grace of justification. Christians are not called to slink into the shadows of the hiding places provided by the power brokers of this world for those who dare not live as Christ intended.

For Bonhoeffer the crux of the grace of justification that generates the courageous works of Jesus' followers lies in the example and image of none other than Jesus Christ. Bonhoeffer sets his thoughts on imitating the example of Jesus Christ in the final chapter of *Discipleship*.[39] Here, too, Bonhoeffer draws on Kierkegaard as is evident from his having underlined in his copy Kierkegaard's comment that, for Christ's followers, the master's "example (toward which single individuals are to orient themselves,

---

[35] *Journals and Papers*, volume 2, 356.
[36] *DBWE* 4, 144–145 (*DBW* 4, 148).
[37] See *DBWE* 4, 144 (*DBW* 4, 147).
[38] *Journals and Papers*, volume 3, 87; translation slightly altered.
[39] See *DBWE* 4, 281–282 (*DBW* 4, 297–298).

all the while admitting honestly where they really are),"[40] served as a pointer to the New Testament call that Christians are to be "like Jesus Christ." Kierkegaard's parenthetical aside is a reminder to Christians to be honest in their trying to be like Jesus; they must never lose sight of their being sinners. Bonhoeffer insists that, because we have been *a priori* formed by Jesus, it is divinely made possible to be like him.

All the biblical quotations, cited by Bonhoeffer in his call to model one's Christian behaviour after that of Jesus come down to how the mind of Jesus Christ achieves its presence in the spirit of those who declare to be his followers, given the disparate individuals and different contexts in which the Christian faith has taken root. Bonhoeffer extends this call to follow Jesus to martyrdom. "It is by Christians' being publicly disgraced, having to suffer and being put to death for the sake of Christ, that Christ himself attains visible form within his community. However, from baptism all the way to martyrdom, it is the same suffering and the same death. It is the new creation of the image of God through the crucified one."[41] These thoughts are very similar to what Kierkegaard had presented as the downside of following Christ in which there is no possibility of compromising God's will in Jesus Christ in favour of being at peace with the world's powers. Nor does Kierkegaard accept the idealized, exaggerated estimates of the value of human suffering. His words are as raw as the dreaded reality of the sufferings inflicted upon those who would imitate the example of Jesus dragged by his enemies to his death on the cross. In Kierkegaard's words, "to suffer in likeness with Christ does not mean to encounter the unavoidable with patience, but it means to suffer ill at the hands of men because as a Christian or by being a Christian one desires and strives after the good, so that one could avoid the suffering by ceasing to will the good."[42]

Kierkegaard's attitude towards the voluntary sufferings of Christ and of Christians also connects with Bonhoeffer's Christology lectures, as well as his *Discipleship* and the letters from prison. For both Kierkegaard and Bonhoeffer, Christ's fullness as a human being is appealing precisely because he did not shrink from all the pathos of a life lived with his special commitments and mission, including its dark moments and the shattering experience of being battered and made to suffer at the hands of brutish soldiers and heartless religious hierarchs. In a passage that Bonhoeffer will echo in his Christology lectures, Kierkegaard declares that the communion between God and humans was made possible by God's becoming "the equal of the human and by Christ's appearance in the likeness of the hum-

---

[40] *Journals and Papers*, volume 2, 350–351.

[41] *DBWE* 4, 286 (*DBW* 4, 302).

[42] Kierkegaard, *Training in Christianity*, translated by Walter Lowrie (New York and London 1941), 196.

blest of human beings ... But this servant-form is no mere outer garment, like the beggar-cloak of the king (dressed up in order to love a beggar girl) which therefore flutters loosely about him and betrays the king ... It is his true form and figure. For this is the unfashionable nature of love that it desires equality with the beloved, not in jest merely but in earnest and truth ... The servant form is no mere garment, and therefore God must suffer all things ... His entire life is a story of suffering."[43] In his Christology lectures, Bonhoeffer had in like manner stated that "Christ, of his own free will, enters the world of sin and death. He enters it in such a way as to hide himself in it in weakness and not to be recognized as God-man. He does not enter in kingly robes ... His claim ... must provoke contradiction and hostility. He goes incognito as a beggar among beggars, as dying among the dying. He also goes a sinner among sinners."[44] Like the "servant form" of Kierkegaard's Christ, Bonhoeffer's Christ is one who, as beggar and sinner, can be approached by the lowly even as he provokes the hostility of the powerful. To be like Christ for any serious follower of Jesus Christ becomes, then, a willingness to embrace suffering, whether voluntarily or inflicted by acts of persecution, as the lot of any serious follower of Jesus Christ.

Both Kierkegaard and Bonhoeffer had been turned off by the grandiosity of theological blather that so cavalierly bestows honorific titles on Jesus while ignoring the real meaning of Jesus for Christian living. At the outset of his lectures on Christology, Bonhoeffer does, in fact, cite Kierkegaard's advice that one should "be still, for that is the absolute" in his own claim that "teaching about Christ begins in silence." He adds that this "has nothing to do with the silence of the mystics, who in their dumbness chatter away secretly in their soul by themselves. The silence of the church is silence before the Word."[45] The church, he went on to say, needed to speak only out of a respectful silence for Christ to be properly proclaimed. For Bonhoeffer, that "silence" was, however, not the same as the silence of the churches that he lamented during the Nazi period when the churches did little to prevent the evil then being perpetrated on the innocent victims of Nazi Germany.

Kierkegaard's uneasiness about "mystical chatter" is of a piece with his running criticism of what he viewed as the excesses of idealism and its thought patterns. That feature of Kierkegaard's writings opened up segments of Bonhoeffer's two Berlin dissertations in which he himself could

---

[43] Kierkegaard, *Philosophical Fragments*, translated by David F. Swenson (Princeton 1936), 225–226.
[44] *CC*, 107.
[45] *CC*, 27. See also that section of *Life Together* where Bonhoeffer speaks of the necessity of silence in the "day alone" phase of one's life in the church community, in *DBWE* 5, 81–83 (*DBW* 5, 65–67).

express his diffidence toward idealist categories of religious thought in his theological exploration of both church and revelation. Bonhoeffer found Kierkegaard helpful for his own analysis of how the Christian concept of personhood could impact, even indirectly, on the manner in which communities are constituted. Like Kierkegaard, Bonhoeffer's understanding of community rests upon the personal integrity of those who become not just "with" one another but, what is more important "for" one another in creating a life together.[46] Kierkegaard had argued that becoming a person occurred through a process of establishing one's self in ethical decision making. Of necessity Kierkegaard views this ethical personhood as taking place and being reinforced only in concrete situations. He sees the precise moment of crossing the threshold as the time when one can invest one's whole life in crucial decisions to accept to do one's duty both to God and to oneself. He eschews any retreat into the more abstract "universal" which promises security and even requires a certain, admirable courage. But in a given moment, a more pressing duty can shatter the complacency engendered by attachment to universals despite all their attractiveness and security. The real passion of genuine existence, for Kierkegaard, is fired up only when duty overrides any powerful attachments to persons, however much loved, as in the case of Abraham sacrificing Isaac and Agamemnon giving up his daughter, Iphigenia. The ethical person's faith is then tried and confirmed in the pathos of personal conflict. In Kierkegaard's words, "the knight of faith has first and foremost the requisite passion to concentrate upon a single factor the whole of the ethical which he transgresses."[47]

The leading character in Kierkegaard's stories, Abraham, becomes a genuine person in sacrificing what is, in less trying circumstances, cherished, such as the love and life of his own son. Bonhoeffer contrasted Kierkegaard's attitude toward Abraham with the more rigid attitude of Calvin against what Abraham was about to do, saying that Abraham would certainly have been excommunicated by a Calvinist church."[48] On the other hand, Kierkegaard admires the steadfastness and obedience to the higher authority on the part of Abraham because his act illustrates the paradox of how the "murder" of Isaac could transform "a murder into a holy act well-pleasing to God, a paradox which gives Isaac back to Abraham, which no thought can master, because faith begins precisely there where thinking leaves off."[49]

---

[46] *DBWE* 1, 180–184 (*DBW* 1, 118–122).

[47] Kierkegaard, *Fear and Trembling*, translated by Walter Lowrie (Garden City, NY. 1954), 88. Here Kierkegaard dwells upon the paradox of obeying God while at the same time seemingly violating God's command not to kill.

[48] *DBWE* 1, 259, note 130 (*DBW* 1, 287, note 384).

[49] See Kierkegaard, *Fear and Trembling*, 64.

While Bonhoeffer would hardly agree that "thinking leaves off" in acting on faith under the lead of the Holy Spirit, he does concede that Kierkegaard's conclusions make sense in situating personhood in those concrete and challenging moments when it is imperative, without delay, to respond to the ethical demands set in the here and now and not consigned to the abstract postulates of idealistic norms that seem to transcend time and reality. In a later passage of his doctoral dissertation, in fact, he praises Kierkegaard for this emphasis on the concrete and the individuality of the believer. Bonhoeffer wrote that like Luther, "Kierkegaard ... spoke like no other about the individuality of human beings."[50] Nonetheless, he rejects Kierkegaard's overemphasis on the rugged individual. For Bonhoeffer, Kierkegaard's radical subjectivism lacks the give and take of relationships that impact directly and indirectly on the origins of personhood. Hence he writes that he departs from Kierkegaard who had insisted that "becoming a person is an act of the self-establishing I – to be sure in a state of ethical decision." He goes on to say that "Kierkegaaard's ethical person, too, exists only in the concrete situation, but his is not in any necessary relation to a concrete You. His person is self-established rather than being established by the You. In the last analysis, then, Kierkegaard remained bound to the idealist position."[51] According to Bonhoeffer, Kierkegaard's "foundations" of personhood conveys "an extreme sort of individualism in which the significance of the other for the individual is no longer absolute but only relative."[52]

While it may be a stretch to accuse Kierkegaard of being bound to the idealist position, Bonhoeffer does acknowledge that Kierkegaard is on the right track in focusing on the ethical and the concrete reality of one's decisions in determining what constitutes personhood. Bonhoeffer's complaint is that Kierkegaard's position is not amenable to fully understand the dynamics of how individuals with differing personalities can form one community in Jesus Christ, and become "Christ existing as the Church community."[53]

In the analyses of Christian community in *Sanctorum Communio* and *Life Together* Bonhoeffer appears to have again agreed with Kierkegaard, this time on the function of solitude both in the act of listening to God's word and in forming community. While Kierkegaard does concede that solitude can also be a burden, he is equally insistent that solitude is essential for persons in dealing with the shadowy side of their human existence and in efforts to awaken the human spirit to the senselessness of the hubris that drowns out their aspirations truly to know themselves in their particu-

---

[50] *DBWE* 1, 249 (*DBW* 1, 171).
[51] *DBWE* 1, 57, note 12 (*DBW* 1, 34, note 12).
[52] *DBWE* 1, 57, note 12 (*DBW* 1, 34, note 12); see also *DBWE* 1, 249 (*DBW* 1, 171).
[53] *DBWE* 1, 121 and 199 (*DBW* 1, 76 and 133).

lar reality. Christians confronting their sinfulness ("despair" is his word for sin in its torturous impact on human equilibrium) experience a need "for solitude which [for them] is a vital necessity – sometimes like breathing, at other times like sleeping." This, he says, is a sign of one's "deeper nature." He goes on to claim that "the need of solitude is a sign that there is spirit in a man after all, and it is a measure of what spirit there is."[54] Kierkegaard laments the fact that, while solitude was prized in ancient times, in his own day, it had become a form of punishment.

As with Kierkegaard, so with Bonhoeffer, solitude has a special function as God's gift in which God's word can be heard and the atmosphere conducive to individual strengthening in faith for the sake of a more loving community. In *Sanctorum Communio*, Bonhoeffer declares that solitude allows the divine law to be heard[55]; solitude makes possible a necessary sense of *"shared sinfulness"*[56] and of being separated from God and other believers.[57] Solitude is that experience to which the Holy Spirit leads each person willing to listen to God's word[58]; solitude is never abolished in the course of one's individual life.[59] Solitude is where alone one faces the judgment that could in the end of a life lived recklessly become the "solitude of God's wrath."[60] Despite the many connections between solitude and church in which Bonhoeffer supports the need for solitude, he seems surprised that Kierkegaard appears either unable or unwilling to connect solitude to its important function in the creation of a Christian community.[61]

This connection is explored more explicitly and with greater depth in Bonhoeffer's spiritual classic, *Life Together*, where he writes: "Whoever cannot be alone should beware of community" and its correlative, "whoever cannot stand being in community should beware of being alone."[62] To which he adds the stern warning: "Those who want community without solitude plunge into the void of words and feelings, and those who seek solitude without community perish in the bottomless pit of vanity, self-infatuation, and despair."[63] For Bonhoeffer, going several steps beyond Kierkegaard, the moments of solitude, interspersed in one's day together

---

[54] Kierkegaard, *The Sickness unto Death*, translated by Walter Lowrie (Garden City, NY. 1954), 197–198.
[55] *DBWE* 1, 108 (*DBW* 1, 70).
[56] *DBWE* 1, 109 (*DBW* 1, 70).
[57] *DBWE* 1, 149 (*DBW* 1, 93–94).
[58] *DBWE* 1, 161 (*DBW* 1, 102).
[59] *DBWE* 1, 182 and 191 (*DBW* 1, 120 and 128).
[60] *DBWE* 1, 284–285 (*DBW* 1, 194–195).
[61] *DBWE* 1, 162, note 20 (*DBW* 1, 104, note 20). See also Kierkegaard, *Fear and Trembling*, 84–85.
[62] *DBWE* 5, 82 (*DBW* 5, 65–66).
[63] *DBWE* 5, 83 (*DBW* 5, 66).

with one's brothers and sisters in community, allows the strength of God's word to be heard while alone and listening. Solitude thus enables the individual believer to bring the empowering of God's word to one's brothers and sisters and thus to preserve the community, "in the strength of solitude."[64] Bonhoeffer advocates periods of solitude in community as a way of conditioning the human spirit to be attentive to the inspiration of God's Holy Spirit.

Indeed, how the Holy Spirit actualizes the church community established in its essence by Jesus Christ, led Bonhoeffer to include a segment on the "Community of Spirit" in his doctoral dissertation. There he speaks of how the "Holy Spirit brings to human hearts God's love which has been revealed in the cross and resurrection of Christ."[65] At the same time Bonhoeffer isolates a problem: how what one understands by "love" can give any significance to one's sociality and still be integrated into both the Christian concept of agape and confer meaning on the Christian concept of community. At this juncture he also acknowledges the difficulty posed by the wide divergence of what is meant by "love" in the first place and whether there can ever be a consensus on love's relation to community life.

For Bonhoeffer, the true meaning of love can only be determined by sifting through references in the New Testament where one is encountered by the divine word. This approach, he believes, avoids the danger of beginning the search with the obvious humanitarian appeal of human love with its altruistic outreach that could end up "confusing eros and agape."[66] Here he draws on Karl Barth who, in turn, had applauded Kierkegaard's distinction between "natural love" and "spiritual love."[67] Kierkegaard had, indeed, argued that Christianity had displaced erotic love and friendship. He even ridiculed the notion that, though Christianity had taught a higher love (that of God), it had also praised erotic love and friendship as if they were of the same nature or on the same level. In his *Works of Love*, he declared, with all the conviction that Kierkegaard could muster, that Christianity had "thrust erotic love and friendship from the throne, the love based on drives and inclination, preferential love in order to place the spirit's love in its stead, love for the neighbor, a love that in earnestness and truth is more tender in inwardness than erotic love in the union and more faithful in sincerity than the most celebrated friendship in the alliance."[68] Bon-

---

[64] *DBWE* 5, 92 (*DBW* 5, 76).
[65] *DBWE* 1, 165 (*DBW* 1, 106).
[66] *DBWE* 1, 167 (*DBW* 1, 108).
[67] *DBWE* 1, 167, note 124 (*DBW* 1, 265, note 115).
[68] Kierkegaard, *Works of Love*, edited and translated by Howard V. Hong and Edna V. Hong (Princeton 1995), 44.

hoeffer accepted the Kierkegaardian distinction but not all the implications Kierkegaard and Barth would draw from it.

Bonhoeffer goes on to elaborate on the distinction, declaring that love, whether humanitarian action or eros or even sacrifices made in times of conflict, could have only self love as its point of reference. He refuses to set the starting point at either our love for God or at our love for others. Instead, he declares that "we know love solely from the love of God that manifests itself in the cross of Christ, in our justification, and in the founding of the church-community." He adds that we also know love "in our egotistical attitude toward ourselves."[69] In that latter setting he sees the function of love to reveal love's crude potential when directed only toward oneself.

At this juncture Bonhoeffer draws the line against the implications of the Barth-Kierkegaardian distinction for both genuine love of the other and the importance of love of others in the creation of Christian community. Bonhoeffer objects to the exaggerated relegation of the other in a relationship to mere instrumentality or as a stepping stone to the love of God or simply reduced to a way of hearing and honouring the commanding word of God. He challenges this assertion with a counter, more scripturally based view, namely, "being one with God" necessarily means being "one with my neighbour."[70] For Bonhoeffer, "love really does love the other."[71] Then in a strongly worded rebuke to the Barth-Kierkegaardian position, he adds his acerbic question: "Who gives Barth the right to say that the other is 'as such infinitely unimportant,' when God commands us to love precisely that person? God has made the 'neighbor as such' infinitely important ... The neighbor is not a sort of tool by means of which I practice the love of God."[72]

Bonhoeffer goes on to disagree with the way Barth, following on Kierkegaard's *Works of Love*, identifies human oneness with God and neighbour as being in community with them. No communion is possible, Bonhoeffer concludes, "where only the one is loved in the other."[73] On the contrary, Bonhoeffer insists that the divine command to love is unrestricted because directed by God "to surrender our self-centered will to our neighbor, which neither means to love the other instead of God, nor to love God in the other, but to put the other in our own place and to love the neighbor instead of ourselves."[74] This attitude, consonant with Christian faith and the nature of the Christian church-community is made possible

---

[69] *DBWE* 1, 167 (*DBW* 1, 108).
[70] *DBWE* 1, 169, note 28 (*DBW* 1, 110, note 28).
[71] *DBWE* 1, 170, note 28 (*DBW* 1, 110, note 28).
[72] *DBWE* 1, 170, note 28 (*DBW* 1, 110–111, note 28).
[73] *DBWE* 1, 170, note 28 (*DBW* 1, 111, note 28).
[74] *DBWE* 1, 171 (*DBW* 1, 111).

only by God's Spirit poured relentlessly into human hearts. That is the New Testament sanctioned dynamic whereby God's will creates the possibility for human beings, impelled by love for one another, to form Christian community, where genuine love is awakened and nourished.[75]

Bonhoeffer addresses more clearly and more at length the relationship of love to the formation of community in his classic treatment of Christian community in *Life Together*, written some nine years later. As in *Sanctorum Communio*, Bonhoeffer builds again on the Kierkegaardian distinction between earthly love and spiritual love. In this instance, however, Bonhoeffer's terminology has changed. Like Kierkegaard, he is still bent on contrasting love as agape with love as eros and agreeing with Barth and Kierkegaard that Christian love "is not eros, which always only desires something; it is agape, which never ceases to love."[76] But, in maintaining this distinction Bonhoeffer creates his own antithesis of *geistliche Liebe* (spiritual love) versus *seelische Liebe* – literally of the human soul or in Bonhoeffer's idiosyncratic use of the term, self-centered or emotional love. Bonhoeffer was attempting to contrast the love mediated by Jesus Christ in a truly Christian community with that self-serving love in a community that will prove to be only a hollow imitation of genuine love.[77]

In offering that distinction Bonhoeffer packs into his concept of *seelisch* all the negative aspects of the Pauline *sarx* (flesh) and *eros* (love in accord with one's emotional, sexual nature) that are the legacy of one's fallen nature. In this context Bonhoeffer uses *seelisch* to single out the negative aspects of one's emotional, self-centered, or even self-gratifying nature as opposed to the spiritual love or agapeic love, mediated by Jesus Christ in the gift of the faith community. Bonhoeffer's concern in *Life Together* is to present spiritual love as an essential dynamic of community in all its truth while, at the same time, cautioning the faith community against all the expressions of a false love that can destroy community life.

Here, too, he sees in the self-centered love (*seelisch*) the desire of "immediacy" that has its own insidious power to corrode community life. This "immediacy," is a word strongly reminiscent of Kierkegaard's own maxim in which he called "the direct relationship with God ... simply paganism."[78] Such immediacy, in Bonhoeffer's words, can be mere flesh "yearning for immediate union with other flesh" or the "desire of the human soul [for] the complete intimate fusion of I and You," or a self-gratifying relationship in which one dominates another.[79] Christian com-

---

[75] *DBWE* 1, 172–173 (*DBW* 1, 112–113).
[76] *DBWE* 5, 40, note 17 (*DBW* 5, 27, note 10).
[77] *DBWE* 5, 39 (*DBW* 5, 27).
[78] *DBWE* 5, 41 (*DBW* 5, 27); see also Kierkegaard, *Concluding Unscientific Postscript*, 243.
[79] *DBWE* 5, 41 (*DBW* 5, 28).

munity, Bonhoeffer concludes, cannot be built on merely emotional love of one's neighbour. Nor can it be permitted to deviate into domineering self-centeredness or self-satisfaction. According to Bonhoeffer, because spiritual love originates in Christ and his word, this results in the divine giftedness whereby Christian community makes possible "the freedom to be Christ's."[80] In *Life Together* Bonhoeffer does not deviate in any substantial way from the foundational insights of *Sanctorum Communio*. He does not repudiate the Kierkegaardian distinction between natural-erotic love and spiritual love, but he does bring that distinction to the next level. There he elaborates on why the Christian community must reflect the presence of Jesus Christ in the love of others, totally bound to one another in the truth of the self and of the other that is found in Christ alone. If self-centered love tends to dominate others and in the process erodes community, spiritual love, on the other hand, "recognizes the true image of the other person as seen from the perspective of Jesus Christ. It is the image Jesus Christ has formed and wants to form in all people."[81]

One can only wonder if the antidote that Bonhoeffer "prescribed" for his fiancée Maria was related to that distinction between natural-erotic love and spiritual love that Kierkegaard made so emphatically. Certainly, Bonhoeffer's caveat in *Sanctorum Communio* is important if we make that assertion, namely, that "love really does love the other"[82] and never in the sense of using the other only as a springboard to the love of God. Bonhoeffer's letters to Maria attest to the genuineness of their love for each other.[83] But the most enduring attraction of Bonhoeffer to Kierkegaard seems to lie in his having found in Kierkegaard a person of integrity who was able to see through and expose the religious, philosophical, and political hypocrisies of his day. For Kierkegaard, grace was not cheap. Kierkegaard, unlike so many of his contemporaries, could criticize the slavish, fundamentalist attitudes toward Luther that Bonhoeffer found so troublesome in writing *Discipleship*. It pleased Bonhoeffer that Kierkegaard was able to interpret Luther's dialectic approach to faith and obedience in a way that emphasized honesty and courage in assessing the contemporary meaning of Luther's original insights for a perennially troubled world. Even in the midst of their theological and ecclesiastical disagreements, Bonhoeffer could recognize in Kierkegaard a kindred soul who, like him, could lament the ways in which Christianity could be seduced so easily into patterns of comfort and pusillanimity that produced those anti-Christian attitudes that had cheapened faith and denied the gospel call to follow Christ to the

---

[80] *DBWE* 5, 44 (*DBW* 5, 31).

[81] *DBWE* 5, 44 (*DBW* 5, 31).

[82] *DBWE* 1, 170, note 28 (*DBW* 1, 110, note 28).

[83] See *Love Letters from Cell 92: TheCorrespondence Between Dietrich Bonhoefer and Maria von Wedemeyer, 1943–45.*

cross. A good dose of Kierkegaard, as recommended by Bonhoeffer to Maria, would perhaps be the best preparation for a beginner in theology. There Maria could learn to judge more sharply the large wasteland of theological, philosophical, religious, and political assertions that served only to reinforce dangerous attitudes and behaviours that were responsible for so much mediocrity in Christianity. And there she could better confront the many dangers in their world where dishonesty had prevailed and the teachings of Jesus Christ ignored or distorted. Appreciating Kierkegaard for any seeker after truth, and as prelude to reading Bonhoeffer, could very well be a kind of "unscientific postscript" to both their legacies.

Ralf K. Wüstenberg

The Influence of Wilhelm Dilthey on Bonhoeffer's *Letters and Papers from Prison*

From Tegel prison, Bonhoeffer asks the question of "what Christianity really is, or indeed who Christ really is, for us today."[1] The question regarding Christ links the Tegel theology with Bonhoeffer's *Ethics*, and what is new in the *Letters and Papers from Prison* is found in the various formulations from Tegel that expand Bonhoeffer's christological understanding by adding a critique of religion. Bonhoeffer goes further in his evaluation of maturity and autonomy. Whereas in the *Ethics*, especially in the fragment "Heritage and Decay,"[2] he negatively interprets the development of autonomy as leading ultimately to nihilism,[3] we find quite the opposite in the *Letters*. Here Bonhoeffer evaluates positively the autonomy of the world, of human beings and of life, and he affirms the coming-of-age process. Between the *Ethics* and these positive statements in the *Letters* he had read Wilhelm Dilthey.

Scholars have only marginally discussed the question of Dilthey's influence as a "philosopher of life." After Eberhard Bethge's[4] and then Ernst Feil's[5] initial and general references to the significance of the "philosophy of life" for Bonhoeffer, it was T. R. Peters[6] who first pointed out concretely that Bonhoeffer's appropriation of Dilthey's thought was not limited to the latter's historicism but included his philosophy of life as well. However, Peters did not thoroughly examine how Bonhoeffer appropriated elements of Dilthey's philosophy of life and dealt instead with the continuing significance of Nietzsche's philosophy of life on Bonhoeffer's work. It

---

[1] Letter of Dietrich Bonhoeffer to Eberhard Bethge (30 April 1944), in *LPP*, 279 (*DBW* 8, 402).
[2] *DBWE* 6, 103–133, esp. 122–123 (*DBW* 6, 93–124, esp. 113–114).
[3] The only positive aspect in this fragment addresses the liberation of *ratio*; cf. *DBWE* 6, 117–118 (*DBW* 6, 107–108).
[4] Cf. Eberhard Bethge, "The Challenge of Dietrich Bonhoeffer's Life and Theology," *Chicago Theological Seminary Register* 51 (1961), 1–38.
[5] Cf. Ernst Feil, *Die Theologie Dietrich Bonhoeffers* (Munich 1971), 132, note 20.
[6] Cf. T.R. Peters, *Die Präsenz des Politischen in der Theologie Dietrich Bonhoeffers* (Munich 1976), 133–135.

was only the study of Karl Bartl[7] and the book by Hans-Jürgen Abromeit[8] that took things further. Bartl demonstrates Dilthey's relevance to Bonhoeffer's "understanding of reality" as *one* reality, and shows that Bonhoeffer closely adheres not only to Dilthey's "presentation of history" but to his "basic concept of life."[9] But Bartl does not apply this insight to the view of religion in the *Letters* and instead stays with the theme of his study, namely "Theology and Secularity." Abromeit also demonstrates Dilthey's significance for Bonhoeffer as a philosopher of life, working this out for the *Ethics*. Yet in the *Ethics*, Dilthey is not yet providing any new impulses to Bonhoeffer. Only in the *Letters* does Bonhoeffer's appropriation of Dilthey emerge through his own systematic reading. Abromeit does not address the importance of Dilthey's philosophy of life for the *Letters*, though he does coin the term "life theology" for the later Bonhoeffer, thereby showing the close connection with the philosophy of life, one that he alleges consists in "the interdependence of understanding and experience undergirding the two."[10]

In short, these two initiatives fail to throw new light on the connection between the philosophy of life on the one hand and the critique of religion on the other. Commensurately, they also do not illuminate the importance of Dilthey's *concept of life* for the nonreligious interpretation. However, they certainly do raise the pertinent question of Dilthey's possible significance for Bonhoeffer as a philosopher of life.

The following discussion will concentrate exclusively on the writing by Dilthey on which Bonhoeffer worked beginning in March 1944 during his incarceration, namely *Weltanschauung und Analyse des Menschen seit Renaissance und Reformation.*[11] There Dilthey combines the concept of life with that of history into a particular interpretation of history, namely historicism.[12] To acknowledge the interdependence of *history* and *experience*, it is decisive to recognize Dilthey's conception of a *historical philosophy of life* ("historische Lebensphilosophie" or "Historismus").

In studying *Weltanschauung und Analyse*, Bonhoeffer probably proceeded chronologically. Several considerations suggest this, for example,

---

[7] Karl Bartl, *Theologie und Säkularität. Die theologischen Ansätze Friedrich Gogartens und Dietrich Bonhoeffers zur Analyse und Reflexion der säkularisierten Welt* (Frankfurt am Main et al. 1990).

[8] Hans-Jürgen Abromeit, *Das Geheimnis Christi. Dietrich Bonhoeffers erfahrungsbezogene Christologie* (Neukirchen, 1991).

[9] Bartl, *Theologie und Säkularität*, 204.

[10] Abromeit, *Dietrich Bonhoeffers erfahrungsbezogene Christologie*, 126.

[11] Cf. Wilhelm Dilthey, *Gesammelte Schriften*, volume 2 (Leipzig/Berlin 1921).

[12] See for more detail my study, *A Theology of Life. Dietrich Bonhoeffer's Religionless Christianity* (Grand Rapids, 1998) and "Dietrich Bonhoeffers theologische Rezeption der Lebensphilosophie Wilhelm Diltheys," in *Dilthey-Jahrbuch* (2000), 260–270.

the citations from Giordano Bruno on the friend and from Spinoza on the affections in Bonhoeffer's "Miscellaneous Thoughts"[13]; these references are found at the end of *Weltanschauung und Analyse* (341f). Bonhoeffer cites these sentences in July 1944 – at the end of his reading of Dilthey. We can assume that at this time the whole of Dilthey in view. In this context, mention of the philosopher and scientist G. Cardano in both the *Letters* and *Weltanschauung und Analyse* is also revealing. In a letter at the end of April 1944, Eberhard Bethge draws his friend's attention to Cardano's significance.[14] Bonhoeffer answers him at the beginning of May 1944 – when he begins to read Dilthey. "I don't know Cardano. Is he translated into German?"[15] In the middle of June, he then says to Bethge in an aside, "By the way, there's a good deal about Cardono in Dilthey."[16] Dilthey first mentions Cardano on page 284 of *Weltanschauung und Analyse*.[17] From this reference we can conclude that by mid-June Bonhoeffer had already read over half, if not more, of *Weltanschauung und Analyse*, while at the beginning of May he is quite obviously just beginning to read Dilthey. In any event, he has not yet come to Dilthey's discussion of the Renaissance philosopher.

Bonhoeffer's mention of Cardano exemplifies how carefully he is reading *Weltanschauung und Analyse*. Here I should mention other names that acquired meaning for him as he studied Dilthey: Herbert of Cherbury, Hugo Grotius, Jean Bodin, Michel de Montaigne, Giordano Bruno.[18] This selection is limited to the key letter of 16 July 1944. Bonhoeffer associates these names with specific themes and with those serving the "*one great development that leads to the world's autonomy.*"[19] These themes include "theology" (Herbert of Cherbury), "morality" (Montaigne, Bodin) and "politics" (Machiavelli); the name of Hugo Grotius is mentioned in connection with the theme of "autonomy" in human society.[20]

Quite obviously Bonhoeffer is systematically organizing *Weltanschauung und Analyse* according to certain thematic groups and groups of names from the perspective of autonomy and coming of age. In the 16 July letter he then brings together various historical reflections in the different sec-

---

[13] *LPP*, 375–376 (*DBW* 8, 550–552).

[14] *LPP*, 274–275 (*DBW* 8, 394–396).

[15] *LPP*, 288 (*DBW* 8, 420).

[16] *LPP*, 288 (*DBW* 8, 492).

[17] He then speaks more extensively about Cardano in *Weltanschauung und Analyse des Menschen seit der Renaissance und Reformation* (cf. 416–417 and 429–431). Since Bonhoeffer says he is reading *a great deal* about the philosopher, it is also conceivable that he is already referring to these later passages.

[18] Cf. Dilthey, *Weltanschauung und Analyse*, 248ff, 279f, 274f, 263f, 297f. Bonhoeffer mentions these names in *LPP*, 359 (*DBW* 8, 530).

[19] *LPP*, 359 (*DBW* 8, 529–530).

[20] Cf. *LPP*, 359 (*DBW* 8, 530).

tions of *Weltanschauung und Analyse*.[21] Yet nowhere in that volume does Dilthey himself actually examine "autonomy" or "coming of age" as concepts in and for themselves.[22] As an example, consider how Dilthey understands Grotius. He sees how in the first three decades of the seventeenth century Pierre Charron, Francis Bacon, and Herbert of Cherbury establish the line of thought that Grotius will then carry forward: The "natural system of the moral world"[23] is established. Dilthey examines the "task" (277), "method" (278), and "concepts" (279) of Grotius, and finds that the "universally valid concepts" are "life concepts" (278-79). These concepts are "coherent in the entirety of life and draw from life their persuasive power" (279). The "legal concepts" thus deduced (namely "life concepts," 280) following Grotius are concepts whose "validity does not depend on faith in their grounding within a teleological order resting in God. "Even if there were no God," the principles of natural law would maintain their independent and universal validity" (280).

The famous citation of Grotius, which Bonhoeffer renders in Latin,[24] thus appears in the immediate context of the philosophy of life. Dilthey adduces Grotius as a Renaissance legal thinker who takes the concepts of life as his point of departure, thereby renewing "the true intention of Roman jurisprudence."[25] The concept of justice is a life concept. This also explains why Bonhoeffer speaks about *life* without God[26] and why his historical excurses on striving for autonomy in various areas all end up basically talking about life.

From Dilthey, Bonhoeffer saw that Grotius' statement is an assertion about life and "that we must *live* in a world 'etsi deus non daretur'."[27] What we find in the case of Grotius applies as well to the other themes and

---

[21] Cf. also the parallel letter of 8 June 1944 in *LPP*, 324–329 (*DBW* 8, 474–483).

[22] Scholars have repeatedly noticed that Bonhoeffer, too (motivated by Dilthey), variously concluded his historical excurses by focusing on the thematic material of life. Cf. my discussion of the letters of 8 June and 16 July 1944 in Wüstenberg, *A Theology of Life*, 126–130.

[23] Dilthey, *Weltanschauung und Analyse*, 276.

[24] Scholars have not determined the source from which Bonhoeffer derives the Latin version "etsi deus non daretur." Dilthey, *Weltanschuung*, 280, cites this expression in German (English rendering: "as if there were no God"). The original version in H. Grotius, *De jure belli ac pacis libri tres. Prolegomena* 11,7 reads: *etiamsi daremus, quod sine summon scelere dari nequid, non esse deum* ("Even if we were to give – which cannot be done without great sacrilege – that there is no God"). Bonhoeffer uses a construction with Latin *datur*; Grotius also uses *datur* twice. I conclude that Bonhoeffer was familiar with the citation in its original, longer Latin version, and under the influence of the (shortened) German rendering in Dilthey constructed the Latin form that we now have from him.

[25] Dilthey, *Weltanschauung und Analyse*, 279.

[26] Cf. *LPP*, 360 (*DBW* 8, 533).

[27] *LPP*, 359–360 (*DBW* 8, 530); emphasis added.

names mentioned above.[28] A larger examination of Dilthey's work reveals that all the names enumerated there are associated with the philosophy of life.[29] Regardless of the sphere in which Dilthey observes the striving to come of age or to attain autonomy, he always begins with human life as it is actually lived in a given epoch. The maturity of the world derives from the maturity of life in the world. Life as a cognitive-theoretical maxim becomes the historical understanding of a given epoch. The autonomy of life becomes the autonomy of human beings and of the world. Bonhoeffer consciously goes along with this progression, beginning hypothetically with the conclusion: "it is one great development that leads to the autonomy of the world."[30] When he speaks elsewhere of the autonomy of human beings and of life, he lets us know that he is interpreting Dilthey's cognitive-theoretical position – namely, life – in a christological manner: the "claim of a world that has come of age by Jesus Christ."[31] In the preceding sentence of the letter just cited, Bonhoeffer demands that "the entirety of human life" must be claimed by Christ. The conceptual pairs "mature world" and "worldly life," as well as "world come of age" and "mature life," can thus be used alongside one another.

Bonhoeffer's formulation of the theme of his Tegel theology progresses from the general to the particular, from the initial christological question to the appropriation of earthly life. We can discern the following development in his christological understanding of life (emphasis added):

1. Initial question: "... who *Christ* really is *for us today*."[32]
2. Basic theme: "*Christ and the world come of age*."[33]
3. Ethical theme: The "*appropriation of the world come of age* through Jesus Christ."[34]
4. Theme of life: "*Jesus lays claim to the entirety of human life for himself.*"[35]
5. Theme: The biblical "blessing is the *appropriation of earthly life for God.*"[36]
6. Ecclesiological conclusion: The church "must tell people of all vocations what *life with Christ* is, what it means "to be for others."[37]

---

[28] One notices that the mention of names is important for both Dilthey and Bonhoeffer. Dilthey explicates his "historical philosophy of life" with the aid of such names (Bruno, Montaigne, Bodin), while Bonhoeffer similarly explicates his "nonreligious interpretation" with the aid of such names, whereby biblical names acquire significance alongside the philosophers taken from Dilthey such as Paul (306ff., 369), Cornelius, Jairus, Nathanael (396).

[29] See my study *A Theology of Life*, 68ff and 104ff.

[30] *LPP*, 359 (*DBW* 8, 529–530).

[31] *LPP*, 342 (*DBW* 8, 504).

[32] Letter, 30 April 1944 in *LPP*, 279 (*DBW* 8, 402).

[33] Letter, 8 June 1944 in *LPP*, 288 (*DBW* 8, 479).

[34] Letter, 30 June 1944 in *LPP*, 342 (*DBW* 8, 504).

[35] Letter, 30 June 1944 in *LPP*, 342 (*DBW* 8, 504).

[36] Letter 28 July 1944 in *LPP*, 374 (*DBW* 8, 548).

[37] "Outline for a Book" in *LPP*, 383 (*DBW* 8, 560).

From his initial christological question (1), Bonhoeffer formulates the basic theme of his Tegel theology (2), then applies it ethically (3), and also with respect to "life" (4); and finally gives it an exclusive concrete orientation toward life (5), including the ecclesiological conclusion of this Christology of life (6). The essence of these formulations is thus Christian life and life come of age.

When I said that Bonhoeffer applies Dilthey's philosophy of life christologically, I am speaking of the unique accent he gives to his reading of Dilthey. Our examination of *Weltanschauung und Analyse* repeatedly encountered Dilthey's concept of religion, one he obviously draws into his own philosophy of life. His intention is to show the relationship between life and religiosity in their various manifestations during the Renaissance and Reformation. For example, Ulrich Zwingli's "religiosity" is allegedly "true life."[38] Dilthey raises the question of "true religion" in regard to Jean Bodin (151) and also admires "the religious vivacity of Luther" (231). On the whole, Dilthey is inclined to engage in criticism whenever religion and life are isolated and opposed to one another (137). The *whole* of life is for him *religious* life: "God wants to be enjoyed" (160). Religion is to be asserted "in life" (237), and Dilthey thus demands a "livable" religion – a religion of the here and now. His *Weltanschauung und Analyse* contains no critique of religion, something already explicated with respect to his other writings; nor, according to him, can any sort of religion*lessness* come about.[39]

In substance, a critique of religion and the notion of religionlessness as two significant motifs in Bonhoeffer's conception of religion do *not* derive from Dilthey, although the critique of metaphysics – as a further basic motif of Dilthey's philosophy of life – exerts considerable influence on him. Bonhoeffer emphatically followed the critique of metaphysics as grounded in the philosophy of life. The critique of religion, however, is grounded for him by means of the critique of religion presented by Karl Barth.[40] Where Dilthey finds an antithesis between *life* and *metaphysics*, Bonhoeffer juxtaposes *life* and *religion*. Where Dilthey interprets *life and inwardness* from a mutually inclusive perspective, Bonhoeffer does the same with *life and Jesus Christ*.

Given Bonhoeffer's systematic reading of Dilthey, the concept of life becomes his basic cognitive-theoretical concept.[41] From the philosophy of

---

[38] Dilthey, *Weltanschauung und Analyse*, 226.

[39] Cf. Dilthey, *Einleitung in die Geisteswissenschaften*, 138, according to which the notion of a "religiousless condition" is historically incomprehensible.

[40] See my study *A Theology of Life*, 31–99.

[41] Here the Tegel theology differs from the fragments to the *Ethics*. Although both in and prior to his *Ethics*, Bonhoeffer appropriates elements of the philosophy of life, he does not yet understand these as motifs integral to cognition. The ethical theme is Christ and the good. It is

life, Bonhoeffer acquired an important impulse for his understanding of life, and the theological understanding of life remains determinative for his reading of Dilthey. Viewed philosophically, life is equivocal; it becomes unequivocal only in view of Christ. Thus we arrive at the question of *how* this life in *being for others* really looks like. This is the boundary question regarding an unequivocal understanding of the concept of *life*. Was Bonhoeffer able to define this concept unequivocally? Here we become more acutely aware of the fragmentary character of his late theology, and must answer the question with a *no*. He passes onto us the task of searching for the answer. Although various reflections in the *Ethics* might help us, they are too fragmentary. In his Tegel theology, Bonhoeffer equipped us with the guiding questions on the correct relationship between life come of age and Christian faith – that was his theme, and it was the essence of the question of nonreligious interpretation. Both the church and theology will have to struggle ever anew to find the appropriate answer.

---

only in the *Letters and Papers from Prison* that this becomes the theme of Christ and the world come of age. In this context, we encounter *discontinuity in continuity* in Bonhoeffer's understanding of religion. We discern continuity in his christological questions, and discontinuity with respect to his understanding of the world and of autonomy. In the *Ethics*, Bonhoeffer evaluates mature life and autonomy negatively as apostasy from God, while in the *Letters and Papers* he poses the question of Christ and a world come of age. In Tegel, the ethical alternative "Christ or an autonomous world" becomes the relation "Christ *and* the world come of age." Parallel to this discontinuity, the continuity in Bonhoeffer's initial christological question is maintained: *Christ and/or* life come of age.

Peter Frick

Friedrich Nietzsche's Aphorisms and Dietrich Bonhoeffer's Theology

I. Introduction

Dietrich Bonhoeffer's first encounter with both the philosophy of Ludwig Feuerbach and Friedrich Nietzsche was during his early teen years. According to Eberhard Bethge, when Karl-Friedrich, Bonhoeffer's oldest brother, returned from World War I at the age of nineteen he read Feuerbach and discussed his writings with the family."[1] At the end of the First World War in 1918, Dietrich Bonhoeffer was no more than twelve years old. During that age, Bonhoeffer also had his first encounter with the thought of Friedrich Nietzsche. This first encounter came by way of a teacher, Martin Havenstein, during the time when Dietrich Bonhoeffer attended Grunewald *Gymnasium*. Havenstein was a Nietzsche expert and wrote the work *Nietzsche als Erzieher*.[2] Whether the high school student Bonhoeffer read this work cannot be known for certain. It seems conceivable, however, to surmise that a teacher who is absorbed in the thought of Nietzsche to the extent that he wrote a work on the philosopher would share some of his insights with his students.[3] From Bonhoeffer's biographer, Eberhard Bethge, we know that in preparation for writing his book *Ethics*, Bonhoeffer's reading included Karl Jaspers' introduction on Nietzsche, a work entitled *Nietzsche*.[4] According to Bethge, Bonhoeffer owned eight of the sixteen volumes of the Nietzsche works edited by

---

[1] For bibliographical details, cf. *DBWE* 7, 7.
[2] Cf. *DBWE* 9, 569, note 49 (*DBW* 9, 622, note 49); cf. Martin Havenstein, *Nietzsche als Erzieher* (Berlin 1922).
[3] The editors of *DBWE* 9, 569, note 49 (*DBW* 9, 622, note 49) speak of the young Bonhoeffer as writing under "the influence of his philosophy professor," namely Havenstein, when he worked on his *Abitur* essay on the philosophy of Euripides.
[4] Eberhard Bethge, *Dietrich Bonhoeffer*, 715 and *DBWE* 6, 222, note 19 (*DBW* 6, 221, note 15). Cf. Karl Jaspers. *Nietzsche: Eine Einführung in das Verständnis seines Philosophierens* (Berlin and Leipzig 1936).

Nietzsche's sister.[5] We also know from a remark of Bethge's that the young Bonhoeffer "read all of Nietzsche very carefully."[6]

II. Friedrich Nietzsche (1844–1900)

A study of Nietzsche[7] and Bonhoeffer is telling in that the first came from the church and ended up entirely as the prodigal son who never returned from the world while the latter came from the world and discovered the church. As each of them began his intellectual quest at the opposite end from the other, somewhere along the trajectories of those two journeys, Bonhoeffer encountered Nietzsche long enough, as it were, to breath in the philosophical air of the wayward son of a Lutheran pastor. In several volumes of the *Dietrich Bonhoeffer Werke/Works*, we have explicit references to the philosophy of Nietzsche. In a first step, we will survey Bonhoeffer's engagement with the philosophy of Nietzsche in a chronological order; in other words, we will focus on specific passages or allusions to Nietzsche's aphorisms as they appear in Bonhoeffer's work and do so, deliberately, with a minimum of interpretive comments in order to let Bonhoeffer's use of Nietzsche emerge as objectively as possible. In a second step, we will then examine how Nietzsche's philosophy shaped Bonhoeffer's own theological formation.

1. Nietzsche's Aphorisms in Bonhoeffer's Works until 1939

In Berlin in 1926, the student Bonhoeffer presented a meditation for children entitled "Address on the Decalogue." He asks the children the rhetorical question whether "freedom or force" is better. If someone prefers force over freedom, Bonhoeffer answers himself, "that kind of person has the

---

[5] Nietzsche scholars are suspicious of this edition; cf. *DBWE* 6, 222, note 19 (*DBW* 6, 221, note 15).

[6] Eberhard Bethge, "The Challenge of Dietrich Bonhoeffer's Life and Theology," in *WCA*, 22–88, here 27. Later in the same essay Bethge repeats: "Bonhoeffer had been an ardent reader of Nietzsche in his youth" (76).

[7] For this essay I have used the collected works published by Giorgio Colli and Mazzino Montinari as *Kritische Studienausgabe*, dtv (Munich 1980) in 15 volumes. The first six volumes are Nietzsche's writings, usually understood as aphorisms rather than philosophical discourses. Volumes 7–13 are a collection of his fragments and letters and volumes 14 lnd 15 consist of introduction, commentary, index etc. Good recent studies of Nietzsche as a philosopher are Eugen Fink, *Nietzsche's Philosophy* (New York 2003); Lawrence J. Hatab, *Nietzsche's Life Sentence. Coming to Terms with Eternal Recurrence* (New York and London 2005) and Stephen Williams, *The Shadow of Antichrist. Nietzsche's Critique of Christianity* (Grand Rapids 2006).

soul of a slave."[8] About a year later, the student Bonhoeffer writes for a seminar a meditation on "Honour." He opens his meditation by questioning how "honor, Christianity, young people ... can be brought together?" Then he adds: "The Nietzsche complex about the slave morality of Christianity comes into play here."[9] In both instances Bonhoeffer sees the dangers of young people having the misconception that Christianity may be reduced to a restrictive morality, in Nietzsche's term, a slave morality. In a third instance of that same period, in one of Bonhoeffer's sermons (on James 1:21–25) prepared in the summer of 1926, Nietzsche is cited twice by name and referred to several times in allusions. Bonhoeffer proclaims the transformative power of God's word and then says: "We have arrogantly and conceitedly driven it [God's word] from us. We have uttered impressive words, mumbled something about philosophy and Nietzsche and about being bigger than our sins,[10] and have carried our wise heads exceedingly high."[11] A few paragraphs further into the sermon, Bonhoeffer comes to speak of obedience. "Obedience," he laments, "is a word that we don't like to hear very much today and whose meaning we don't want to understand. It is a word that, since the time of Nietzsche, we have contemptuously driven out from ethics and especially from religion."[12] Finally, Bonhoeffer proclaims: "Jesus Christ is the path from God to humanity," and hence all other paths are false, no matter where they may lead, including to the Übermensch.[13]

Nietzsche's thought plays only a minor role in Bonhoeffer's two academic dissertations. In the doctoral dissertation *Sanctorum Communio* there is only one brief citation of Nietzsche. In the context of arguing for the validity of prayer and intercession, Bonhoeffer cites the philosopher's statement "'waiting for God to draw near' (Nietzsche),"[14] but *de facto* reverses the statement's original meaning rather than taking it as the criticism of prayer that Nietzsche intended it to be.[15]

Bonhoeffer's year (1928–1929) as a vicar in Barcelona was the first substantiated period in which he seems to have read and reflected on Nietzsche's philosophy. In his congregational lecture on "Jesus Christ"

---

[8] *DBWE* 9, 456 (*DBW* 9, 491). Cf. Nietzsche, *On the Genealogy of Morals* (section I, 10).
[9] *DBWE* 9, 529 (*DBW* 9, 585).
[10] *On the Genealogy of Morals* (section III, 20).
[11] *DBWE* 9, 494-495 (*DBW* 9, 541).
[12] *DBWE* 9, 495 (*DBW* 9, 542).
[13] *DBWE* 9, 496 (*DBW* 9, 543).
[14] *Beyond Good and Evil*, aphorism 58. Nietzsche says (*KSA* 5, 75) that "Gebet [ist] eine beständige Bereitschaft für das 'Kommen Gottes'."
[15] In *Act and Being* there is no citation of Nietzsche's works, only the vague possibility that Bonhoeffer's critique of philosophical systems may have been inspired to a certain degree by Nietzsche's critique; cf. editor's reference to Kierkegaard and Nietzsche in *DBWE* 2, 67, note, 69.

Bonhoeffer makes the first explicit references to Nietzsche. There he notes that "everywhere there is a terrible refusal to obey the harsh demands of Jesus words. These are for heroes and those on the way to the overman [*Übermensch*]."[16] Further into the same lecture Bonhoeffer notes that being a Christian is essentially not something religious since religion remains "menschlich-allzumenschlich."[17] Finally, he also speaks of Jesus' life as one that revaluates all traditional values.[18] The theme of revaluation of traditional, Christian values is a major theme in Nietzsche and thus becomes, as we shall see, also crucial to Bonhoeffer, especially in his articulation of ethics. This is already evident in Bonhoeffer's second congregational lecture in Barcelona on the topic "What is a Christian Ethic?" There he says plainly: "Thus the discovery of what is beyond good and evil was not made by Friedrich Nietzsche, who from this standpoint utters polemics against the hypocrisy of Christianity; it belongs to the original material of the Christian message, concealed, of course, as it is."[19] A few pages further on Bonhoeffer returns to the same theme. "The Christian himself creates his standards of good and evil for himself. Only he can justify his own actions, just as only he can bear the responsibility. The Christian creates new tables, a new Decalogue, as Nietzsche said of the Superman. Nietzsche's Superman in not really, as he supposed, the opposite of the Christian; without knowing it, Nietzsche has here introduced many traits of the Christian made free, as Paul and Luther describe him."[20] At the end of his lecture, Bonhoeffer refers to the saga of the giant Antaeus who could not be defeated "until once in a fight someone lifted him from the ground; then the giant lost all the strength which had flowed into him through the contact with the earth." Bonhoeffer uses this saga in analogy to human life. "The man who would leave the earth, who would depart from the present distress, loses the power which holds him by eternal, mysterious forces."[21] In August 1928 Bonhoeffer preached in Barcelona on 1 John 2:17: "And the world and its desire are passing away, but those who do the will of God

---

[16] *DBW* 10, 311, note 18.

[17] *DBW* 10, 321. The reference to "menschlich-allzumenschlich" is of course an allusion to Nietzsche's work of the same title.

[18] Cf. *DBW* 10, 314, note 18. Bonhoeffer says: "Alle überkommenen Werte scheinen zu stürzen, umgewertet zu werden." Nietzsche spoke of the "Umwertung aller Werte" (*Ecce Homo*, KSK 6, 365). In the prologue (9) to *Thus Spoke Zarathustra*, Nietzsche speaks of "the one who breaks the tablets of values [der, der zerbricht ihre Tafeln der Werthe]" and the one "who will write new values on new tablets [die, welche neue Werthe auf neue Tafeln schreiben]."

[19] *NRS*, 41. Cf. *DBW* 10, 327: Die Entdeckung des Jenseits von Gut und Böse gehört also durchaus nicht dem Christentumsfeind Fr. Nietzsche, der von hier aus gegen das Moralin des Christentums polemisiert, sondern sie gehört zum freilich verschütteten Urgut der christlichen Botschaft."

[20] *NRS*, 44 (*DBW* 10, 331; cf. note 20).

[21] *NRS*, 47 (*DBW* 10, 344–345).

live forever." In the context of speaking of eternity Bonhoeffer cites Nietzsche: "All joy wants eternity – wants deep, wants deep eternity."[22]

After his return to Berlin from Barcelona, Bonhoeffer entered the academy once more in order to write his *Habilitation* and then as a lecturer in theology. In July 1930 Bonhoeffer submitted an essay on the topic of how to selection and determine the significance of a biblical text for a sermon. In passing he observed that some preachers use extra-biblical texts, such as Goethe or Nietzsche texts, to appeal to a more educated audience. For Bonhoeffer, however, this is a severe mistake [*Irrweg*]. "For only the Bible is the Word of God and not a religious poem by Nietzsche – this is the indissoluble and concealed mystery of the revelation of God."[23]

During the winter semester of 1931–1932 Bonhoeffer presented a lecture at the University of Berlin on the "History of Systematic Theology in the Twentieth Century." Nietzsche is mentioned six times in the course of those lectures. In his social analysis of German society at the turn of the century, Bonhoeffer refers, among many others, also to Nietzsche, whom he understands to attack the spirit of scepticism with his "eschatological anticipation of the overman [*Übermensch*]."[24] In a discussion of religion, Bonhoeffer refers to Nietzsche a second time. "Friedrich Nietzsche," explains Bonhoeffer, "took over Feuerbach's teaching of complete humanity [*Lehre vom ganzen Menschen*]. A human being is not a transcendent illusionary being [*Scheinwesen*], but the ens realissimum [the most real being]."[25] After several more sections Bonhoeffer treats the issue of culture and ethics. "Nietzsche," he declares, "rejected Christianity most completely since it embodies the most severe reticence toward autonomous culture. Mercy becomes the basic principle of human anti-nature [*Unnatur*] and serves him as the principle of Christian ethic."[26] A little further in the same lecture Nietzsche is mentioned as one who supported a culture of personhood [*Persönlichkeitskultur*].[27] In the section on "Proclamation," Nietzsche is mentioned once more. Bonhoeffer postulates that there is no such thing as a Christian way to God and not even faith is a religious path. That Christians have, nonetheless, lived as if faith is a religious possibility

---

[22] *DBW* 10, 500 citing *Thus Spoke Zarathustra*, "The Sleepwalker Song," section 12.
[23] *DBW* 10, 349–350
[24] *DBW* 11, 142.
[25] *DBW* 11, 148.
[26] *DBW* 11, 186. The editors refer to Nietzsche's work *The Antichrist*, aphorism 7, as a possible parallel to Bonhoeffer's discussion. There Nietzsche says: "Christianity is called the religion of *pity*. Pity stands opposed to the tonic emotions which heighten our vitality: it has a depressing effect. We are deprived of strength when we feel pity" (*The Portable Nietzsche*, selected and translated, with an Introduction, Preface, and Notes by Walter Kaufmann (New York 1968), 572–573).
[27] Cf. *DBW* 11, 191.

and thus become boastful has been clearly perceived by Nietzsche in his critique of "slave salvation" [*Knechtsseligkeit*].[28]

On the day of his birthday in 1932, the young Bonhoeffer gave a public lecture at the Technical University in Berlin on the topic of self-determination. In passing he mentions Nietzsche's Zarathustra who, similar to the prophet Jeremiah, curses the day of his birth.[29] There are also two[30] sermons of the year 1932 in which Bonhoeffer draws on Nietzsche without mentioning his name. In a sermon on Colossians 3:1–4, Bonhoeffer opens his deliberations by questioning whether those who "set their minds on things that are above, not on things that are on earth" (verse 2) would not do better by destroying old tablets and making new ones. Because Christians "set their minds on things that are above, not on things that are on earth" they are castigated as traitors of the earth.[31] As before in a lecture in Barcelona, here too, Bonhoeffer appeals to Nietzsche's dictum to be faithful to the earth.[32] In another sermon, Bonhoeffer preached on John 8:32: "The truth shall make you free." "The person who loves," he proclaims, "because s/he is set free by the truth of God is the most revolutionary person. Such a person is the revaluation of all values, dynamite of human societies, the most dangerous human being."[33] Here we have an allusion to Nietzsche in the words "revaluation of all values" even though Bonhoeffer employs the word *Umsturz* rather than the usual *Umwertung*.

In his lecture at the University of Berlin on "Creation and Sin" in 1932–1933, Nietzsche was an important – although incognito – partner in theological dialogue. There are several unambiguous allusions to Nietzsche's thought even though his name was never mentioned. The most unmistakable allusion is found in the context of Bonhoeffer's discussion of Genesis 2:8–17. Bonhoeffer interprets these verses to mean that "Adam knows neither what good nor what evil is and lives in the strictest sense *beyond good and evil*; that is, Adam lives out of the life that comes from God, before whom a life lived in good, just like a life lived in evil, would mean an unthinkable falling away."[34] The reference to "beyond good and evil" is, of

---

[28] Cf. *DBW* 11, 205. The editors point out (in note 281) that the term "Knechtsseligkeit" is not extant in Nietzsche's writings. The suggestion that Bonhoeffer may have been thinking of *The Antichrist*, aphorism 191, does not seem compelling.

[29] Cf. *DBW* 11, 222.

[30] The editors of *DBW* 11 point to two other sermons that may go back to Nietzsche's thought. The evidence is not, however, strong enough to establish Bonhoeffer's dependence on Nietzsche; cf. *DBW* 11, 387, note 9 and 431, note 16.

[31] Cf. *DBW* 11, 444.

[32] *Thus Spoke Zarathustra*, "Prologue," 3, in Del Caro and Pippin, 6.

[33] *DBW* 11, 461.

[34] *DBWE* 3, 87–88 (*DBW* 3, 82); italics in original.

course, the exact title of one of Nietzsche's works, *Beyond Good and Evil*, and was hinted at in the earlier work *Thus Spoke Zarathustra*.[35]

In his interpretation of the fall of humanity in Genesis 3:6, Bonhoeffer remarks that "the extent of the fall is such that it affects the whole of the crated world. From now on that world has been robbed of its creatureliness and drops blindly into infinite space, like a meteor that has torn itself away from the core to which it once belonged. It is of this fallen-falling world that we must now speak."[36] Many scholars find it quite likely that Bonhoeffer was drawing on parallel idea in Nietzsche's *The Gay Science*, where the latter asks: "are we not continually plunging downward? And backward, sideways, forward, in all directions? Is there still any up or down? Do we not wander as though through and endless nothing? Do we not feel empty space breathing upon us?"[37] Apparently, in Bonhoeffer's copy, this passage was marked.[38]

Other allusions to Nietzsche are less obvious. On his reflections on Genesis 1:1–2, Bonhoeffer says: "the thinking of fallen humankind, lacks a beginning because it is a circle. We think in a circle. But we also feel and will in a circle. We exist in a circle."[39] Commentators have seen a parallel with Nietzsche's aphorism in *Thus Spoke Zarathustra*. In "Concerning the Virtuous," he says: "The circle's thirst is within you; every circle curves and turns in order to catch itself up again."[40]

In his interpretation of Genesis 2:7 Bonhoeffer observes that "the human being whom God has created in God's image – that is, in freedom – is the human being who is taken from earth. Even Darwin and Feuerbach could not use stronger language than is used here."[41] As the editors of this volume rightly point out, Nietzsche, and in turn Bonhoeffer, employ Feuerbach's characterization of the human being as *ens realissimum* [the most real being] in their own philosophical reflections.[42]

In his discussion of good and evil Bonhoeffer explains that "the words tob and ra speak of an ultimate split [*Zwiespalt*] in the world of humankind in general that goes back behind even the moral split, so that tob means also something like 'pleasureable' [*lustvoll*] and ra 'painful' [*leidvoll*]."

---

[35] *KSA* 4, 208 ("Vor Sonnen-Aufgang"): "Denn alle Dinge sind getauft am Borne der Ewigkeit und jenseits von Gut und Böse; Gut und Böse selber aber sind nur Zwischenschatten und feuchte Trübsale und Zieh-Wolken."
[36] *DBWE* 3, 120 (*DBW* 3, 112).
[37] *DBWE* 3, 120, note 11 (*DBW* 3, 112, note 10), citation from *The Portable Nietzsche*, 95.
[38] *DBWE* 3, 120, note 11 (*DBW* 3, 112).
[39] *DBWE* 3, 26 (*DBW* 3, 26).
[40] *DBWE* 3, 26, note 7 (*DBW* 3, 26, note 6); cf. *KSA* 4, 121 ("Von den Tugendhaften"): Des Ringes Durst ist in euch: sich selber wieder zu erreichen, dazu ringt und dreht sich jeder Ring."
[41] *DBWE* 3, 76 (*DBW* 3, 71).
[42] *DBWE* 3, 76, note 7 (*DBW* 3, 71). Cf. above *DBW* 11, 148.

The editors refer to Nietzsche who also combines the pairs good and evil and pleasure and pain in his *Thus Spoke Zarathustra*.[43]

In his interpretation of Genesis 3:7 Bonhoeffer once more may have drawn on Nietzsche. He suggests that sexuality is a "passionate hatred of any limit" since sexuality seeks to possess the other person and thereby "destroy[s] the other person as a creature, robs the other person of his or her creaturliness, lays violent hand on the other person's limit, and hates grace."[44] Nietzsche's definition of love in *Ecce Homo* similarly portrays love as war and ultimately as "the deadly hatred of the sexes."[45]

Also during the winter semester 1932–1933 Bonhoeffer delivered a public lecture on the kingdom of God. He begins the very first sentence with these words: "We are hinterlanders [*Wir sind Hinterweltler*] or we are secularists; but this means that we no longer believe in the kingdom of God."[46] It may be the case that Bonhoeffer employed the term *Hinterweltler* in analogy to Nietzsche. In *Thus Spoke Zarathustra*, Nietzsche entitled one of the sections "On the Hinterlanders [*Von den Hinterweltlern*]."[47] The following two sentences refer several times to the earth, our mother, a motive that Bonhoeffer used before in one of his Barcelona lectures.[48] The topic of the earth plays also an important part in the section "On the Hinterlanders" in *Thus Spoke Zarathustra*.

In one of his London sermons, delivered in English, Bonhoeffer preached on 2 Corinthians 12:9: "my strength is made perfect in weakness." In exposition of this text he notes: "What is the meaning of weakness in this world? We know that Christianity has been blamed ever since its early days for its message to the weak. Christianity is a religion of slaves, of people with inferiority complexes; it owes its success only to the masses of miserable people."[49] Toward the end of the same sermon, Bonhoeffer uses a Nietzschean concept once more, but reverses it completely: "Not the powerful is right, but ultimately the weak is always right. So Christianity means a devaluation of all human values and the establishment

---

[43] *DBWE* 3, 88, note 25 (*DBW* 3, 71). Cf. *Thus Spoke Zarathustra*, the section "On the Afterworldly." Cf. also *DBWE* 3, 90, note 32 (*DBW* 3, 71).

[44] *DBWE* 3, 123 (*DBW* 3, 116).

[45] Cf. *DBWE* 3, 123, note 10 (*DBW* 3, 116, note 8).

[46] *DBW* 12, 264.

[47] Walter Kaufmann translates this section "On the Afterwordly" (*The Portable Nietzsche*, 142) and Del Caro and Pippin, 20 (in *Thus Spoke Zarathustra. A Book for All and None*, translated by Adrian del Caro, edited by Adrian del Caro and Robert B. Pippin, Cambridge Texts in the History of Philosophy (Cambridge 2006)), as "On the Hinterworldy." Both translations do not make it very clear that Nietzsche is speaking of people and not merely of an idea, although the idea of a *Hinterwelt* is implicated.

[48] Cf. *NRS*, 47 (*DBW* 10, 345).

[49] *DBWE* 13, 402 (*DBW* 13, 410).

of a new order of values in the sight of Christ."[50] Here Bonhoeffer turns Nietzsche upside-down. Whereas Nietzsche proclaimed the revaluation of all values as a feat of the overman,[51] Bonhoeffer assigns the creation of values exclusively to Christ. In another sermon, on the occasion of the wedding of Albrecht and Hilde Schönherr in April 1936, Bonhoeffer addresses the groom directly with these words: "Albrecht, be a joyous pastor! Whoever knows himself to be one with Jesus Christ knows that he is saved. And whoever looks like it will be a great help for his congregation."[52] Possibly Bonhoeffer was thinking of Nietzsche's reproach of priests: "Better songs they will have to sing for me before I learn to believe in their redeemer; more redeemed his disciples would have to look."[53]

It is telling that Bonhoeffer's two spiritual classics, *Discipleship* and *Life Together*, make no reference to Nietzsche. How can we explain this lacuna? The answer, it seems, is straightforward. As a philosopher, Nietzsche raised and debated philosophical issues which, to be sure, do impinge on the crucial issues of the Christian faith to some extent. But his intention as such was not to discuss matters of spiritual direction. Nietzsche's aphorisms were far from Bonhoeffer's interest in the spiritual life, discipleship and costly grace and thus had no value for Bonhoeffer with regard to the Christian life.

2. *Nietzsche's Aphorisms in Bonhoeffer's Writings after 1940*

After the closing of the underground seminary in Finkenwald, Bonhoeffer continued to teach the seminarians of the Confessing Church in the collective vicariates in Pomerania. In the winter of 1939–1940 Bonhoeffer presented his meditation on Psalm 119. In contrast to genuine thankfulness, "the thankfulness of the world is ultimately about itself; thankfulness has the purpose of affirming and sanctifying one's own good fortune."[54] In a similar vein, in another session in July 1940 the topic was also that of thankfulness. After looking at the biblical evidence, he cites the views of a few select thinkers: Thomas à Kempis, Larochefoucauld, Rousseau and then Nietzsche. He quotes two sentences, but in reversed order from Nietzsche, from an aphorism in *Human, All-too Human*. Bonhoeffer begins

---

[50] *DBWE* 13, 403 (*DBW* 13, 412).
[51] Cf. *Thus Spoke Zarathustra*, "Prologue 9."
[52] *DBW* 14, 928.
[53] *Thus Spoke Zarathustra*, "On Priests," (Del Caro and Pippin, 71).
[54] *DBW* 15, 413–414. Note 41 points to the fact that Bonhoeffer wrote the word "Nietzsche" in the margin of the manuscript and refers as a possible parallel to *Thus Spoke Zarathurstra*, the section on "Old and New Tablets." However, it is more likely that Bonhoeffer was thinking of another context, namely *Human, All-too Human*, *KSK* 2, 66; cf. the following note below.

with the statement: "Thankfulness is a milder from of revenge," and then proceeds to cite the answer to the question which Nietzsche actually posed, namely: "what is the reason for the thankfulness of the powerful?" The answer it this: "The benefactor abused through his good deed the realm of power and forced his way into it."[55]

In *Ethics* the philosophy of Nietzsche figures more prominently and deliberately than in his other writings. Most notable are Bonhoeffer's allusions to *Thus Spoke Zarathustra* and, to a lesser extent, allusions to *Ecce Homo* and *Beyond Good and Evil*. In the section "Christ, Reality and Good," Bonhoeffer speaks of ultimate reality: "That God alone is the ultimate reality," he proposes is "not an idea meant to sublimate the actual world, nor is it the religious perfecting of a profane worldview. It is rather a faithful Yes to God's self-witness, God's revelation. If God is merely a religious concept, there is no reason why there should not be, behind this apparent 'ultimate' reality, a still more ultimate reality: the twilight or the death of the gods."[56] The reference to "the twilight or the death of the gods" is, of course, unmistakably Nietzschean, except that Nietzsche combines the death of the gods and the coming of the overman [*Übermensch*].[57]

Pilate's acclamation – "look, what a person!" – when Jesus appeared before him during his trial (cf. John 19:5) has been used by Bonhoeffer – in the rendering of the Vulgate: *ecce homo* – on several contexts in the section "Ethics as Formation."[58] Since Nietzsche has entitled one of his works *Ecce Homo*, interpreters are quick to point out that Bonhoeffer may have deliberately used Nietzsche's title to set it in stark relief to his portrayal of Jesus Christ.[59] It is impossible to make a judgement with certainty and the question needs to remain open.[60] There is, however, solid evidence that a few pages further into his discussion in the same section, Bonhoeffer does deliberately invoke a concept of Nietzsche, only to rebut it "The human being should and may be human," Bonhoeffer affirms, but then continues: "All super-humanity [*Übermenschentum*], all efforts to outgrow one's nature as human, all struggle to be heroic or a demigod, all fall away from a person here, because they are untrue."[61]

---

[55] *DBW* 15, 365–366 and *Human, All-too Human*, KSK 2, 66.

[56] *DBWE* 6, 48, note 10 (*DBW* 6, 32, note 8).

[57] Cf. *Thus Spoke Zarathustra*, in the section "On the Bestwoing Virtue," (Del Caro and Pippin, 59) Zarathustra says: "Dead are all gods; now we want the overman to live."

[58] *DBWE* 6, 82, 83, 84, 88, 91 (*DBW* 6, 69, 70, 74, 78).

[59] Cf. *DBWE* 6, 82, note 22 (*DBW* 6, 69, note 21).

[60] I am also rather skeptical as to Bonhoeffer's reference to people as "failures [gescheiterte Existenzen]" and a possible parallel in Nietzsche's lament that "with the Jews the slave revolt in morality begins;" cf. *DBWE* 6, 90, note 58 (*DBW* 6, 77, note 53).

[61] *DBWE* 6, 94 (*DBW* 6, 81).

In Bonhoeffer's first draft of "History and Good [1]" Nietzsche is cited once by name. After he rejects the view that ethics can be reduced to a categorical knowledge of good and evil,[62] Bonhoeffer argues that freedom underlies all concrete ethical behaviour and hence "the action of the responsible person is most profoundly in accord with reality."[63] He continues to say that "this concept of 'accordance with reality' [*das Wirklichkeitsgemäße*] requires further clarification. A misunderstanding would lead to that 'servile attitude toward the facts' (Nietzsche) that always retreats wherever pressure is greater, that justifies success on principle, and that in any given situation chooses the expedient as being in accord with reality. Misunderstanding accordance with reality in this sense amounts to irresponsibility."[64] For Bonhoeffer, however, "the most fundamental reality is the reality of the God who became human."[65] Below we will return to a discussion of what these reflections on reality mean for Bonhoeffer vis-à-vis Nietzsche.[66]

In the section "History and Good [2]," Bonhoeffer refers to Nietzsche by name and then quotes a passage from *Thus Spoke Zarathustra*. "Unknowingly," Bonhoeffer comments, "Nietzsche speaks in the spirit of the New Testament when he chides the legalistic and narrow-minded misunderstanding of the commandment to love your neighbor with the following words: 'You crowd around your neighbor and have fine words for it. But I say unto you: your love of the neighbor is your bad love of yourselves. You flee to your neighbor from yourselves and would like to make a virtue out of that: but I see through your "selflessness." ... Do I advise love of those nearest to you [*Nächstenliebe*]? Sooner I should even advise you to flee from those nearest you and to love those farthest away [*Fernsten-*

---

[62] Bonhoeffer also wrote "A Theological Position Paper on State and Church," a piece that was originally published in the various editions of *Ethics*, but now appears in *DBWE* 16, 502–528 (*DBW* 16, 506–535). In the course of his discourse Bonhoeffer says: "Like everything that exists, government is also in a certain sense beyond good and evil" (*DBWE* 16, 513). The phrase "beyond good and evil" is of course Nietzschean, but Bonhoeffer's exposition does not contribute to a greater understanding how he employed Nietzsche in this context.

[63] *DBWE* 6, 222 (*DBW* 6, 221).

[64] *DBWE* 6, 222–223 (*DBW* 6, 221–222). On Bonhoeffer's appropriation of this Nietzschean aphorism, see *DBWE* 6, 222, note 19 (*DBW* 6, 221, note 16).

[65] *DBWE* 6, 223 (*DBW* 6, 222).

[66] In the second draft of the section "History and Good [2]" Bonhoeffer repeats, almost verbatim, what he has said about Nietzsche in the first draft of "History and Good [1]"; cf. *DBWE* 6, 261 (*DBW* 6, 260–261). The Editors of *DBW/E* 6 suggest in this section Bonhoeffer may also be drawing on Nietzsche when he notes that "love for human beings leads into the solidarity of human guilt." Though possible, it seems to me that the allusion to Nietzsche's notion of guilt is not strong enough to substantiate such a claim; cf. *DBWE* 6, 233, note 59 (*DBW* 6, 232–233, note 55).

liebe]."⁶⁷ To illustrate the concreteness of a person's love for the neighbour far away, Bonhoeffer recalls the following incident. "In a terrible miscarriage of justice in the United States in 1931, nine young black men accused of raping a white girl of dubious reputation were sentenced to death even though their guilt could not be proven. This triggered a storm of outrage that found expression in open letters from the most respected European public figures" except from Germans who hid behind their "'Lutheran' understanding of vocation."⁶⁸ Regarding this incident Bonhoeffer wonders whether Jesus' call to love the neighbour who is far away "lead[s] us here to understand Nietzsche's statement: 'My brothers, love of the neighbor I do not recommend to you: I recommend to you love of the farthest'?"⁶⁹

In the section "Heritage and Decay," Bonhoeffer refers to Nietzsche three times by name. "From Win[c]kelmann to Nietzsche," Bonhoeffer elucidates, "in Germany there is a deliberately anti-Christian appropriation of the Greek heritage. The reason for this particular relation to the heritage of antiquity, so different from that of the more western European peoples, lies doubtless in the form that the gospel assumed through the Reformation in Germany. Nietzsche could have arisen only from the soil of the German Reformation. Here, the contradiction between the natural and grace is starkly opposed to the reconciliation of nature with grace in the Roman heritage. From a Greek point of view, Nietzsche could receive a positive assessment from German Reformation theology – something incomprehensible for Western peoples."⁷⁰ Further on in the same section, Bonhoeffer discusses western godlessness as the result of the French Revolution. The tragedy, Bonhoeffer laments, is that "this godlessness is emphatically Christian. In every possible Christianity – nationalist, socialist, rationalist, or mystical – it turns against the living God of the Bible, against Christ. Its God is the new human being, whether the 'factory of new humanity' is Bolshevist or Christian."⁷¹ According to the editors notes of *Ethics*, Bonhoeffer wrote the word "Nietzsche" in the margin of his manuscript besides these lines.⁷² The association with Nietzsche in this context suggests that Bonhoeffer may have been thinking of Nietzsche's *Übermensch* or

---

⁶⁷ *DBWE* 6, 294 (*DBW* 6, 295). Bonhoeffer cites from (and slightly alters) the section "On Love of the Neighbour." Cf. *DBW* 10, 633.

⁶⁸ *DBWE* 6, 295 (*DBW* 6, 296).

⁶⁹ *DBWE* 6, 295 (*DBW* 6, 296) and Nietzsche, *Thus Spoke Zarathustra*, in the section "On Love of the Neighbour."

⁷⁰ *DBWE* 6, 106–107 (*DBW* 6, 97).

⁷¹ *DBWE* 6, 122–123 (*DBW* 6, 113). The reference to the "factory of new humanity" is the title of a book, published in 1935, by the Russian Alexandra Rachmanova.

⁷² Cf. *DBWE* 6, 123, note 93 (*DBW* 6, 113, note 87).

Übermenschentum; as we saw already, the latter term he employed earlier in *Ethics*.[73]

Bonhoeffer cites Nietzsche twice in the section "God's Love and the Disintegration of the World." In the first instance, Bonhoeffer discusses the meaning of shame following the fall. "Covering is necessary," notes Bonhoeffer, "because it keeps shame alive, reminding them [Adam and Eve, humanity] of their estrangement from the origin; it is also necessary because human beings must now just endure themselves and live a hidden life as the estranged and divided beings they are. Otherwise they would betray themselves. 'Every deep spirit needs a mask' (Nietzsche)."[74] In the second instance, Bonhoeffer is exegeting Jesus' saying in the Sermon on the Mount: "Do not judge, so that you may not be judged" (Matt. 7:1). Bonhoeffer rejects judging as reprehensible "not because it springs from dark motives, as Nietzsche thought, but because judging is itself the apostasy from God."[75]

Bonhoeffer opens the section entitled "Church and World [1]" with these words: "We begin this section by calling attention to one of the most astounding experiences we have had during the years of trial for all that was Christian. Whenever, in the face of deification of the irrational powers of blood, of instinct, of the predator within human beings, there was an appeal to human reason."[76] Köster correctly identified that Bonhoeffer's words "the predator within human beings [*das Raubtier im Menschen*]" is an allusion to Nietzsche's expression that the human being is the best of predators.[77]

Bonhoeffer's *Fiction from Tegel Prison* has no mentioning of Nietzsche and, following the editors of this volume, conceivably only a handful of allusions. These are as follows: In the Drama, scene 1, Grandmother reads to little brother, a ten year old boy. The story is that of a hunter who shoots a "wondrous beast."[78] The editors suggest that Bonhoeffer may have thought of Nietzsche's image of the hunter,[79] an image Bonhoeffer had incorporated into a sermon in London to describe the calling of the prophet Jeremiah.[80] In scene 2 of the Drama Bonhoeffer puts these words in the mouth of Ulrich: "Suddenly, there in the middle of hell, I met – God." The

---

[73] *DBWE* 6, 94 (*DBW* 6, 81).
[74] *DBWE* 6, 304 (*DBW* 6, 306).
[75] *DBWE* 6, 315 (*DBW* 6, 317).
[76] *DBWE* 6, 339–340 (*DBW* 6, 342).
[77] Cf. Peter Köster, "Nietzsche als verborgener Antipode in Bonhoeffers 'Ethik'," in *Nietzsche Studien* 19 (1990), 397, note 140. Cf. *Thus Spoke Zarathustra*, the section "On Old and New Tablets." Del Caro and Pippin (*Zarathustra*, 169) translate the expression as "the human being is, after all, the best beast of prey."
[78] *DBWE* 7, 26–27 (*DBW* 7, 21–22).
[79] Cf. *Thus Spoke Zarathustra*, the section "The Magician."
[80] Cf. *DBWE* 13, 3 (*DBW* 13, 347).

editors refer to Nietzsche's *Thus Spoke Zarathustra* as a possible source for this saying.[81] In scene 3 of the Drama, the Stranger says that "dying is interesting, not being dead. Dying takes a long time and is just as varied as life."[82] Here again the editors point to Nietzsche as a possible source, conceivably the section "On Free Death" in *Thus Spoke Zarathustra* where Nietzsche contrasts death and dying. In the section entitled "The Major's Story" in Bonoeffer's prison novel, Hans speaks of "all kinds of flying vermin [*Ungeziefer*] – bumblebees, mosquitoes, horseflies – stinging, biting, and tormenting me horribly."[83] Again, it is conceivable that Nietzsche's *Thus Spoke Zarathustra* may have been Bonhoeffer's inspiration behind these lines; for Nietzsche does, indeed, speak of vermin, although mostly of poisonous flies.[84] Further on in the same section, Franz reminisces about an old teacher who himself reflects on the theme of "historiography" and the fact that history reveals the viewpoint of those who succeeded. That, however, "is barbarism over and over again, because it systematically makes people savage and base."[85] Once more, the editors refer to Nietzsche who may have guided Bonhoeffer in his musings. It seems to me that all these possible allusions to Nietzsche cannot be established with any degree of certainty. To be sure, there are conceptual parallels between Bonhoeffer and Nietzsche on the points mentioned. However, the evidence is not conclusive to determine the degree of Bonhoeffer's dependence on Nietzsche as his source.[86]

It is a bewildering and curious fact that in *Letters and Papers from Prison* the thought of Nietzsche plays a very inconsequential, if any, role. Given Bonhoeffer's repeated attempts to conceptualize a "religionless Christianity" within the context of a "world come of age," one would think that Nietzsche's critique of the traditional forms of Christianity may have animated Bonhoeffer's thinking to a certain degree. Surprisingly, however, Bonhoeffer does not even hint at such Nietzschean ideas as the coming of the *Übermensch*, the revaluation of old values, faithfulness to the earth or a new ethical framework beyond good and evil. There are three allusions to Nietzsche in *Letters and Papers from Prison* that strike the reader to be more cursory than substantial. The first one in a letter to Eberhard Bethge, dated 12 February 1944. Bonhoeffer notes that he reminisces about his childhood and thinks of the many impressions of nature. Beside the *Harz*

---

[81] *DBWE* 7, 41 (*DBW* 7, 38). Cf. *Thus Spoke Zarathustra*, the section "On the Pitying," where Nietzsche says: "Thus the devil once spoke to me: 'Even God has his hell: it is his love for mankind" (Del Caro and Pippin, 69).

[82] *DBWE* 7, 57 (*DBW* 7, 57).

[83] *DBWE* 7, 150 (*DBW* 7, 157).

[84] Cf. *Thus Spoke Zarathustra*, the section "On the Flies of the Market Place."

[85] *DBWE* 7, 164 (*DBW* 7, 172–173).

[86] This caution also applies to another place in the novel; cf. *DBWE* 7, 172 (*DBW* 7, 181) where Bonhoeffer refers to "salves" and the editors suggest parallels with Nietzsche.

and *Wesergebirge* there is also "a fashionable and a Nietzschean Engadin."[87] In a letter to Eberhard Bethge of 9 March 1944 Nietzsche – together with Kierkegaard – is briefly mentioned, among many others, as having a different kind of *hilaritas* (*Heiterkeit*; serenity) than Michelangelo, Burckhardt, Mozart, Luther, Barth and others.[88] In a third instance, again in a letter to Eberhard Bethge, dated 25 March 1944, Nietzsche is mentioned in the context of Bonhoeffer and Bethge's discussion of landscape painting. "We are apt to acquiesce in Nietzsche's crude alternatives, as if the only concepts of beauty were on the one hand the 'Apolline' and on the other the 'Dionysian,' or, as we should now say, the demonic."[89]

There are, however, two instances in which Bonhoeffer employs an expression that, to my knowledge, have never been traced back to Nietzsche. In a letter to Eberhard Bethge of 29 May 1944, Bonhoeffer relates that he was in the process of reading Weizsäcker's book *The World-View of Physics*. This book, he says, "has again brought home to me quite clearly how wrong it is to use God as a stop-gap [*Gott als Lückenbüßer*] for the incompleteness of our knowledge ... God is not a stop-gap; he must be recognized at the centre of life, not when we are at the end of our resources."[90] The editors of *DBW* 8 quite correctly point out that the phrase "God as a stop-gap [*Gott als Lückenbüßer*]" was used by Paul Tillich in his book *Die religiöse Lage der Gegenwart*, a work Bonhoeffer consulted for his lecture on the "History of Theology in the Twentieth Century" in the winter semester of 1931–1932.[91] The fact that Tillich used the expression should not detract from the more important fact that he did not coin it. Its author is actually Nietzsche. In *Thus Spoke Zarathustra,* Nietzsche says "Aus Lücken bestand der Geist dieser Erlöser; aber in jede Lücke hatten sie ihren Wahn gestellt, ihren Lückenbüßer, den sie Gott nannten (The spirit of these redeemers consisted of gaps; but into every gap they had plugged a delusion, their stopgap, whom they named God)."[92] The same allusion to God as stop-gap is repeated once more. In his "Outline for a Book" of August 1944, Bonhoeffer wants to include the following in the first chapter: "The religionlessness of man who has come of age. 'God' as a working hypothesis, as a stop-gap for our embarrassments, has become superfluous (as already indicated)."[93]

---

[87] *LLP*, 211 (*DBW* 8, 322).
[88] *LLP*, 229 (*DBW* 8, 352).
[89] *LLP*, 239 (*DBW* 8, 366).
[90] *LLP*, 311–312 (*DBW* 8, 454–455).
[91] Cf. *DBW* 8, 454, note 5.
[92] *Thus Spoke Zarathustra,* section "On Priests."
[93] *LLP*, 381 (*DBW* 8, 557).

III. Nietzsche's Influence on Bonhoeffer's Theology

Above we saw that Bonhoeffer draws on Nietzsche in many different ways. Our task now is to discuss those salient features in Nietzsche that shaped Bonhoeffer's own theology in response to the challenges posed by the philosopher. Being mindful not to systematize unduly – either Nietzsche or Bonhoeffer – there are several interrelated themes that are decisive for both of them, albeit in their idiosyncratic contexts. We will briefly discuss each of them.

1. Critique of Christendom

If a person has any knowledge of the philosophy of Friedrich Nietzsche it is typically the impression that it is blatantly anti-Christian. This impression is of course the intentional creation of Nietzsche himself. He not only entitled one of his writings *The Antichrist*, but the numerable aphorisms throughout his oeuvre leave no doubt as to his unconcealed view, bitter critique and at times sacrilegious and grotesque attack on Christianity and on Jesus Christ.[94] Much could be speculated about Nietzsche's (mis)interpretation and (mis)understanding of Christianity, but for our purposes it suffices to articulate the *cantus firmus* of Nietzsche's disparaging of Christianity.

In Nietzsche's estimate "Christianity has sided with all that is weak and base, with all failures; it has made an ideal of whatever *contradicts* the instinct of the strong life to preserve itself; it has corrupted the reason even of those strongest in spirit by teaching men to consider the supreme values of the spirit as something sinful, as something that leads into error – as temptations."[95] The cynic Nietzsche continues: "Christianity is called the religion of *pity* [*Religion des Mitleidens*]. Pity stands opposed to the tonic emotions which heighten our vitality: it has a depressing effect. We are deprived of strength when we feel pity ... Under certain circumstances, it [pity] may engender a total loss of life and vitality out of all proportions to the magnitude of the cause (as in the case of the death of the Nazarene) ... Pity negates life and renders it *more deserving of negation*. Pity is the *practice* of nihilism."[96]

---

[94] For a recent study on Nietzsche and his relation to Christianity, see Williams, *The Shadow of Antichrist. Nietzsche's Critique of Christianity*. For an assessment of Nietzsche and the biblical tradition, see Hans Hübner, *Nietzsche und das Neue Testament* (Tübingen 2000).

[95] *The Antichrist*, aphorism 5 (in *The Portable Nietzsche*, 571–572).

[96] *The Antichrist*, aphorism 7 (in *The Portable Nietzsche*, 572–573). Bonhoeffer also interprets Feuerbach in this vein: "Der egoistische Urtrieb [ist] der Trieb zum Leben, [die] Urhemmung der Tod, alle Religion [stammt] aus dem Erlebnis der Hemmung des Todes,

These words leave no doubt as to Nietzsche's repugnance with Christianity: *it denies life*! The state of the Christian is the worst in the hierarchy of sentient beings. Out of fear, Nietzsche claims, humanity unfolded in this downward spiral: "the domestic animal, the herd animal, the sick human animal – the Christian."[97] Ultimately, the reason for such a low view of life has its momentum in the Christian conception of God. In Christianity, "God degenerated into the *contradiction* of life, instead of being its transfiguration and eternal Yes! God as the declaration of war against life, against nature, against the will to live! God – the formula for every slander against 'this world,' for every lie about the 'beyond'! – God the deification of nothingness, the will to nothingness pronounced holy!"[98] The great tragedy for Nietzsche is that "in Christianity neither morality nor religion has even a single point of contact with reality. Nothing but imaginary *causes* ('God,' 'soul,' 'ego,' 'spirit,' 'free will' – for that matter, 'unfree will'), nothing but imaginary *effects* ('sin,' 'redemption,' 'grace,' 'punishment,' 'forgiveness of sins")."[99] In sum, for Nietzsche, the religion that is based on the εὐαγγέλιον, the *good* news for humanity, has become the very epitome of the devaluation of life in general and the human being in particular. Bonhoeffer clearly perceives that Nietzsche "rejected Christianity most completely since it embodies the most severe reticence toward autonomous culture. Mercy becomes the basic principle of human anti-nature [*Unnatur*] and serves him as the principle of Christian ethic."[100] In other words, the correlation between Christianity and "human anti-nature" is so deeply entrenched in Nietzsche's thinking that the second cannot be rehabilitated apart from the first. And this is precisely the issue at which Bonhoeffer and Nietzsche part their ways. Whereas for Nietzsche the sequence is logically from the life-denial forces of Christianity to human anti-nature for Bon-

---

aus der Furcht vor dem Tode. Der Mensch betet in Gott das Wunschbild seines Lebenstriebes an. Darum gab es stets in der Christenheit nur Anthropologie. Feuerbach denkt hoch vom Menschen wegen dieser hohen Fähigkeit des Menschen ... Feuerbach der konsequenteste Schüler Schleiermachers; nur hat er als Illusion angesehen, was Schleiermacher als unbewiesene Voraussetzung gelten ließ" (*DBWE* 11, 147–148).

[97] *The Antichrist*, aphorism 3 (in *The Portable Nietzsche*, 570–571).

[98] *The Antichrist*, aphorism 18 (in *The Portable Nietzsche*, 585–586). Nietzsche has a particularly difficult time with the concept of sin. For him, sin "ist bisher das grösste Ereignis in der Geschichte der kranken Seele gewesen; in ihr haben wir das gefährlichste und verhängnisvollste Kunststück der religiösen Interpretation" (*Genealogy of Morality*, KSA 5, 389).

[99] *The Antichrist*, aphorism 15 (in *The Portable Nietzsche*, 581).

[100] *DBW* 11, 186. The editors of *DBW* 11 refer to Nietzsche's work *The Antichrist*, aphorism 7, as a possible parallel to Bonhoeffer's discussion. There Nietzsche says: "Christianity is called the religion of *pity*. Pity stands opposed to the tonic emotions which heighten our vitality: it has a depressing effect. We are deprived of strength when we feel pity" (*Portable Nietzsche*, 572–573).

hoeffer the power of the resurrected Christ leads to the fullness of human life. These two worlds are so far apart that they cannot be reconciled.

And yet, Bonhoeffer accepts to a certain degree Nietzsche's stinging criticism that Christians all too often forfeit their most basic humanity. This is most evident in his later writings, especially in *Letters and Papers from Prison*. On 18 July 1944, two days before the failed conspiracy on Hitler, Bonhoeffer writes in a letter to his friend Eberhard Bethge: "Jesus asked in Gethsemane, 'Could you not watch with me one hour?' That is a reversal of what the religious man [*der religiöse Mensch*] expects from God. Man [*der Mensch*] is summoned to share in God's sufferings at the hands of a godless world. He must therefore really live in a godless world, without attempting to gloss over or explain its ungodliness in some religious way or other. He must live a 'secular' life, and thereby share in God's suffering. He *may* live a 'secular' life (as one who has been freed from false religious obligations and inhibitions)."[101] Here Bonhoeffer insists that a Christian person must and *may* live in a secular, godless world without diminishing either the world's godliness or the person's humanity. The day after the failed conspiracy, on 21 July 1944, Bonhoeffer writes another letter to Bethge and comes back to the theme of how one should live. "I discovered later," he says, "and am still discovering right up to this moment, that it is only by living completely in this world that one learns to have faith. One must completely abandon any attempt to make something of oneself, whether it be a saint, or a converted sinner, or a churchman (a so-called priestly type!), a righteous man or an unrighteous one, a sick man or a healthy one. By this-worldliness [*Diesseitigkeit*] I mean living unreservedly in life's duties, problems, successes and failures, experiences and perplexities. In so doing, we throw ourselves completely into the arms of God, taking seriously, not our own sufferings, but those of God in the world – watching with Christ in Gethsemane. That, I think, is faith; that is μετάνοια; and that is how one becomes a human and a Christian."[102]

Precisely at this point it becomes clear that Bonhoeffer overcomes Nietzsche's charge that in "Christianity neither morality nor religion has even a single point of contact with reality." There is perhaps no theologian of the twentieth century who emphasized "this-worldly" living as much as did Bonhoeffer. Just as Nietzsche was ready to affirm all of life unconditionally without recourse to an "other-worldly" reality,[103] Bonhoeffer likewise calls the Christian to a life that is unconditionally rooted in all of this world's reality. Only then "one becomes a human [*ein Mensch*] and a Christian." In other words, Bonhoeffer stresses the symbiotic relation between

---

[101] *LPP* 361 (*DBW* 8, 535).
[102] *LPP* 369–370 (*DBW* 8, 542).
[103] Cf. Hatab, *Nietzsche's Life Sentence. Coming to Terms with Eternal Recurrence*, 20, 148–151.

becoming a human being and living fully entrenched in this world's reality and – at the same time and without contradiction – being a Christian. A passage from *Ethics* says it most eloquently: "As reality is *one* in Christ, so the person who belongs to this Christ-reality is also a whole. Worldliness does not separate on from Christ, and being Christian does not separate one from the world. Belonging completely to Christ, one stands at the same time completely in the world."[104]

What living unreservedly in the world means for Bonhoeffer is nicely expressed in his essays "After Ten Years." In the section on optimism he writes: "The essence of optimism is not its view of the present, but the fact that it is the inspiration of life and hope [*eine Lebenskraft, eine Kraft der Hoffnung*] when others give in; it enables a man to hold his head high when everything seems to be going wrong; it give him strength to sustain reverses and yet to claim the future for himself instead of abandoning it to his opponent ... The optimism that is will for the future should never be despised ... it is health and vitality."[105] In terminology reminiscent of Nietzsche himself Bonhoeffer points to the Christian's expression of life in strength, fullness and vitality. For him, being Christian and being fully human are not mutually exclusive,[106] as for Nietzsche, but indissolubly joint together in the reality of Christ.

2. Beyond Good and Evil; Revaluation of all Values

Nietzsche seems to have shaped Bonhoeffer's theology in an interesting way with respect to the notion of good and evil. As we noted above, Bonhoeffer addressed this question in a lecture in Barcelona on the topic "What is a Christian Ethic?" followed by his interpretation in *Creation and Fall*. To repeat, for Bonhoeffer, "the discovery of what is beyond good and evil was not made by Friedrich Nietzsche, who from this standpoint utters polemics against the hypocrisy of Christianity; it belongs to the original material of the Christian message, concealed, of course, as it is."[107]

Bonhoeffer agrees with Nietzsche – but for different reasons – that the distinction between good and evil is a fragile conception. Whereas Nietzsche's anthropology simply disregarded such a distinction as the in-

---

[104] *DBWE* 6, 62 (*DBW* 6, 48).

[105] *LPP* 15 (*DBW* 8, 36).

[106] Cf. Bonhoeffer's letter of 8 July 1944, in which he argues that from a biblical perspective, the human being is always understood as the "complete human being" and not separated into an "inner" and "outer" person. Bonhoeffer says that "we should frankly recognize that the world, and people [Menschen], have come of age, that we shouldn't run man down into worldliness, but confront him with God at his strongest point;" cf. *LPP* 346 (*DBW* 8, 511).

[107] *NRS*, 41. Cf. *DBW* 10, 327.

vention of human feebleness, Bonhoeffer employs it in the course of coming to terms with ethics. Audaciously he declares: "The knowledge of good and evil appears to be the goal of all ethical reflection. The first task of Christian ethics is to supersede that knowledge."[108] Why is Bonhoeffer so adamant about deconstructing traditional Christian approaches to ethics? His answer is lucid: "In knowing about good and evil, human beings understand themselves not within the reality of being defined by the origin, but from their own possibilities, namely, to be either good or evil. They now *know themselves beside and outside God*, which means they know nothing but themselves, and God not at all. For they can only know God by knowing God alone. The knowledge of good and evil is thus disunion with God. Human beings can know about good and evil only in opposition to God."[109] Elsewhere in *Ethics* Bonhoeffer asks the rhetorical question: "Does this mean negating the distinction between good and evil? No, but it means that human beings cannot justify themselves by doing good."[110]

It is crucial to understand that Bonhoeffer is not arguing that there is no reality or distinction between good and evil; given the historical context within which he wrote the *Ethics* manuscript, it would be absurd to think that he has given up the belief that good and evil are tangible realties. Here he is merely contending that the distinction between good and evil cannot be the foundation upon which a Christian ethic should be constructed. Christian ethics is beyond the distinction of good and evil. Everything hinges on the little word *beyond*. Christian ethics is beyond good and evil for two chief reasons.

First, the knowledge of good and evil is the result of the fall of humanity; only as a sinner is the human being preoccupied with this distinction. As Williams puts it: "The knowledge of good and evil, as the biblical narrative of the fall tells us, is a sign of disunity and not a knowledge on which humanity is originally perched in authentic creatureliness."[111] Hence, any human attempt to catalogue deeds into good and evil is thus the attempt to retract to a state before the fall or, as Bonhoeffer puts it, a refusal "of being defined by the origin." Accordingly, because of the fall into sin, there exists no possibility[112] of a person to know the difference between good and evil. The sinner, even the redeemed sinner, cannot place her/himself into the truth of knowing the difference between good and evil. Second, and very briefly, the reality of the redemptive act of God in Jesus Christ becomes tangible in the world not by recourse to deeds catalogued as either

---

[108] *DBWE* 6, 299 (*DBW* 6, 301).

[109] *DBWE* 6, 300 (*DBW* 6, 302); emphasis added.

[110] *DBWE* 6, 227 (*DBW* 6, 226). Cf. also Williams, *The Shadow of Antichrist*, 243.

[111] Williams, *The Shadow of Antichrist*, 242.

[112] See our discussion below on Bultmann and Tillich and the reasons why Bonhoeffer rejected that there is such a thing as "possibility" or "potentiality" in theology.

good or evil, but only in the obedient pursuit to do the will of God in responsible action – a point we will return to below.

Given Nietzsche's ultra-pessimistic analysis of Christianity as a whole and of its life-sapping morality in particular it comes of no surprize that Nietzsche calls for a radical revaluation [*Umwertung*] of all values. Since his culture and personal milieu were overwhelmingly Christian, Nietzsche is essentially calling for a revaluation of all *Christian* values. Moreover, since he fundamentally rejects a morality that is predicated on the basic categories of good and evil, it follows as a logical consequence that he postulates values that are beyond good and evil. Curiously employing biblical terminology, Zarathustra shouts: "Break, break me these old tablets of the pious, my brothers! Gainsay me the sayings of the world slanderers!"[113] And again he announces: "Look at the faithful of all faiths! Whom do they hate the most? The one who breaks their tablets of values, the breaker, the lawbreaker – but he is the creative one. Companions the creative one seeks and not corpses, nor herds and believers. Fellow creators the creative one seeks, who will write new values on new tablets."[114] But for the moment Zarathustra has to comfort himself: "Here I sit and wait, old broken tablets around me and also new tablets only partially written upon. When will my hour come?"[115]

At first glance it seems that Bonhoeffer largely agrees with Nietzsche's deconstruction of laws and values. In his lecture "What is a Christian Ethic?" delivered during the year in Barcelona, Bonhoeffer daringly declares: "There are no actions which are bad in themselves – even murder can be justified – there is only faithfulness to God's will or deviation from it; there is similarly no law in the sense of a law containing precepts, but only the law of freedom, i.e. of a man's bearing his responsibility alone before God and himself. But because the law remains superseded once and for all and because it follows from the Christian idea of God that there can be no more law, the ethical commandments, the apparent laws of the New Testament must also be understood from this standpoint."[116] It is decisive at this point to understand that Nietzsche's revaluation of all values is tied to the coming of the overman and hence, as Bonhoeffer clearly recognizes,[117] is a futuristic, eschatological event. But for Bonhoeffer, a Christian's new humanity, though in its full realization also an eschatological

---

[113] *Thus Spoke Zarathustra*, section "On Old and New Tablets," 15 (Del Caro and Pippin, 164).

[114] *Thus Spoke Zarathustra*, section "Zarathustra's Prologue," 9 (Del Caro and Pippin, 14).

[115] *Thus Spoke Zarathustra*, section "On Old and New Tablets," 1 (Del Caro and Pippin, 156).

[116] *NRS*, 44–45 (*DBW* 10, 332).

[117] Cf. *DBW* 11, 142.

event, is already reality in this fallen and broken world.[118] This new humanity begs the question of how one should live and what the criteria are for one's ethical framework and moral actions? And here Bonhoeffer parts ways with Nietzsche once again. For in Bonhoeffer's view, it is Jesus Christ himself who is the source and power for the revaluation of all traditional values.[119] In a sermon given in London, Bonhoeffer unequivocally affirmed that "Christianity means a devaluation of all human values and the establishment of a new order of values in the sight of Christ."[120] Moreover, in the Barcelona lecture Bonhoeffer elucidates: "The Christian himself creates his standards of good and evil for himself. Only he can justify his own actions, just as only he can bear the responsibility. The Christian creates new tables, a new Decalogue, as Nietzsche said of the Superman. Nietzsche's Superman is not really, as he supposed, the opposite of the Christian; without knowing it, Nietzsche has here introduced many traits of the Christian made free, as Paul and Luther describe him."[121]

What Bonhoeffer assumes here is the underlying principle of freedom which finds it tangible manifestation in the acts of love. As Bonhoeffer once commented in a sermon on John 8:32 ("The truth shall make you free"): "The person who loves because s/he is set free by the truth of God is the most revolutionary person. Such a person is the revaluation of all values, dynamite of human societies, a most dangerous human being."[122] Paradoxically, Christian freedom is always bound to the will of God. Put otherwise, Christian values are free in the sense that they are always a response to the search for the will of God. Bonhoeffer puts is this way: "Time-honoured morals – even if they are given out to be the consensus of Christian opinion – can never for the Christian become the standard of his actions. He acts, because the will of God seems to bid him to, without a glance at others, at what is usually called morals, and no one but himself and God can know whether he has acted well or badly. In ethical decision we are brought into the deepest solitude, the solitude in which a man stands before the living God. No one can stand beside us there, no one can take anything from us, because God lays on us a burden which we alone must bear."[123]

---

[118] Cf. Clifford Green, *Bonhoeffer. A Theology of Sociality*, 52–65.

[119] Cf. *DBW* 10, 314, note 18.

[120] *DBWE* 13, 403 (*DBW* 13, 412). Bonhoeffer's notion of freedom may well go back to Nietzsche. In *Creation and Fall*, Bonhoeffer says emphatically that "there is no 'being-free-from' without a 'being-free-for'" (*DBWE* 3, 67 (*DBW* 3, 63)). Nietzsche expresses very similar sentiments: "You call yourself free? Your dominant thought I want to hear, and not that you have escaped from a yoke ... Free *from* what? As if that mattered to Zarathustra! But your eyes should tell me brightly: free *for* what" (*Thus Spoke Zarathustra*, in *The Portable Nietzsche*, 175).

[121] *NRS*, 44 (*DBW* 10, 331; cf. note 20).

[122] *DBW* 11, 461.

[123] *NRS*, 44 (*DBW* 10, 331-332).

3. New Humanity and Faithfulness to the Earth

Given Nietzsche's unrelenting critique of Christianity and his desire for a revaluation of all values, it follows for him that *human beings as such* are inextricably intertwined in these two predicaments and hence constitute much of the cause of the problem. Since human beings alone are the bearers of both Christianity and all moral values, for Nietzsche it is in one way or another inexorable that current humanity is largely superfluous.[124] The answer Nietzsche proposes to overcome the life-sapping reality of Christianity and the dysfunction of moral values *vis-à-vis* the human being lies in the coming of a new human being. The "human being is something that must be overcome," he proclaims loudly, "overcome yourself even in your neighbour; and you should not let anyone give you a right that you can rob for yourself!"[125]

Superfluous humanity is the cosmos's predicament that must be overcome. Nietzsche announces the new being, most extensively in *Thus Spoke Zarathustra*, as the coming of the overman. In the *Prologue* Nietzsche sets out his ideas: "*I teach you the overman (Übermensch)*. Human being is something That Must be overcome. What have you done to overcome him? ... Behold, I teach the overman! The overman is the meaning of the earth. Let your will say: the overman *shall be* the meaning of the earth!"[126] And elsewhere Zarathustra says: "Uncanny is human existence and still without meaning: a jester can spell its doom. I want to teach humans the meaning of their being, which is the overman, the lightning from the dark cloud 'human being'."[127] "It was there too that I picked up the word 'overman' (*Übermensch*) along the way, and that the human is something that must be overcome, – that human being is a bridge and not an end; counting itself blessed for its noon and evening as the way to new dawns ... I taught them all *my* creating and striving: to carry together into one what is fragment in mankind and riddle and horrid accident – as poet, riddle guesser and redeemer of chance I taught them to work on the future, and to creatively redeem everything that *was*. To redeem what is past in mankind and to recreate all 'It was' until the will speaks: 'But I wanted it so! I shall want it

---

[124] Cf. *Thus Spoke Zarathustra*, inn "On the New Idol," (Del Caro and Pippin, 35): "Far too many are born; the state was invented for the superfluous! ... Just look at these superfluous! They steal for themselves the works of the inventors and the treasures of the wise: education they call their thievery – and everything turns to sickness and hardship for them! Just look at these superfluous! They are always sick, they vomit their gall and call it the newspaper. They devour one another and are not even able to digest themselves. Just look at these superfluous! They acquire riches and yet they become poorer. They want power and first of all the crowbar of power, much money – these impotent, impoverished ones!."

[125] *Thus Spoke Zarathustra*, in "On Old and New Tablets," 4 (Del Caro and Pippin, 159).

[126] *Thus Spoke Zarathustra*, in "Zarathustra's Prologue," 3 (Del Caro and Pippin, 5-6).

[127] *Thus Spoke Zarathustra*, in" Zarathustra's Prologue," 7 (Del Caro and Pippin, 12).

so.' This I told them was redemption, this alone I taught them to call redemption. – Now I wait for *my* redemption – so that I can go to them for the last time."[128]

In the face of Nietzsche's violent claim to dispense with superfluous humanity in favour of the coming *Übermensch* Bonhoeffer proclaims: "Jesus Christ is the path from God to humanity," and hence all other paths are false, no matter where they may lead, including the path that leads to the *Übermensch*.[129] It is decisive here to recognize, as Hatab argues, that Nietzsche's notion of the *Übermensch* is to be understood as "a structural model for a new way of *experiencing* the world, rather than a new type of person," namely a "structural concept that prepares the possibility of life-affirmation."[130] As a "structural model," "the overman is the meaning of the earth" and calls humanity "to remain faithful to the earth."[131] Nietzsche's passionate plea to affirm (by means of *überwinden*) unconditionally the purely immanent life of physical existence on this earth as the *meaning* of life comes in a sense close to Bonhoeffer's own affirmation that Nietzsche "took over Feuerbach's[132] teaching of complete humanity [*Lehre vom ganzen Menschen*]. A human being is not a transcendent illusionary being [*Scheinwesen*], but the ens realissimum [the most real being]."[133] Both agree that the essence of humanity lies not in its transcendent horizon, but in its immanent, earthly affirmation of life in all its manifestations. Only in the total affirmation of all of life is the affirmation of all of humanity, and vice-versa. For Nietzsche, this affirmation is the end in itself, the meaning of both the overman and earth; for Bonhoeffer, it is the hallmark of following Christ, whose reality brings about on this earth the very groundedness and life-affirmation that Zarathustra announces. As Green suggests, Nietzsche's critique of religion as dehumanizing "people by robbing them of their strength and creativity" finds its ally in Bonhoeffer in that "the constructive significance of Bonhoeffer's non-religious *theologia crucis* may be appreciated for its originality and its historical contribution."[134] For just like Nietzsche, Bonhoeffer craved so deeply for a

---

[128] *Thus Spoke Zarathustra*, in "On Old and New Tablets," 3 (Del Caro and Pippin, 158).
[129] *DBWE* 9, 496 (*DBW* 9, 543).
[130] Hatab, *Nietzsche's Life Sentence. Coming to Terms with Eternal Recurrence*, 55.
[131] *Thus Spoke Zarathustra*, "Prologue," 3, in Del Caro and Pippin, 6.
[132] Elsewhere Bonhoeffer credits Feuerbach for his insight that humanity and earth are inseparable entities. The chief significance of Genesis 2:7, says Bonhoeffer, is that "the human being whom God has created in God's image – that is, in freedom – is the human being who is taken from earth. Even Darwin and Feuerbach could not have used stronger language than is used here. Humankind is derived from a piece of earth. Its bond with the earth belongs to its essential being" (*DBWE* 3, 76). On Nietzsche's adaptation of Feuerbach, cf. Williams, *The Shadow of Antichrist*, 26–27.
[133] *DBW* 11, 148.
[134] Green, *Bonhoeffer. A Theology of Sociality*, 272.

life unflinchingly rooted in the reality of this earth. For Bonhoeffer, however, that life was possible in Christ's reality and power. And precisely at this point Bonhoeffer's *amor mundi* comes as close to the centre of his theology and life as that is possible. But this love for the world is not merely a component of or an addition to his faith or an anticipatory foreshadowing of what we call now a "theology of the earth." Quite to the contrary, as Sabine Dramm says so concisely: "love for the world springs from the midst of this faith. It is the basis for Christian existence in the here and now of the world. It embraces the person as a whole. From it come the understanding and practice of a worldly Christian existence, one that is fully in accordance with Bonhoeffer's own way. It is precisely the very core of his thought that love for the world is grounded in the Christ event – and even more – it only comes into being in Him. In Christ, assent to the worldliness of the world becomes definitive."[135] Because Bonhoeffer conceived of the love for the world in such a radical but christocentric manner was he able to stand so firmly rooted in his own life and take Nietzsche seriously.[136] For him the power of the reality of Christ is such that it can transform all worldly and human reality in precisely the terms that Nietzsche envisioned. In the words of Green, "the weak and suffering Christ, then, is the ultimate critic of religion. The transformation of human life brings people from the periphery of life to its center, from a fragmented existence to an integrated life, from otherworldliness to a historical life in the world, from episodic regression to a faith which informs their whole life, from subjective inwardness to responsibility in public life, from dishonest and humiliating apologetics to meaningful acceptance or reality, from individualistic self-preoccupation to 'existing for others'."[137] In Bonhoeffer's own words: "As reality is *one* in Christ, so the person who belongs to the Christ-reality is also a whole. Worldliness does not separate one from Christ, and being Christian does not separate one from the world. Belonging completely to Christ, one stands at the same time completely in the world."[138]

---

[135] Sabine Dramm, *Dietrich Bonhoeffer. An Introduction to His Thought* (Peabody 2007), 106.

[136] Bethge, "The Challenge of Dietrich Bonhoeffer's Life and Theology," 78, suggests that "Bonhoeffer liberates the Christians so that they can listen to Feuerbach and Nietzsche and give them their honest share for their contribution. These people now give us a bad conscience when we make the Christian faith a shop for religious needs or a skilful technique for avoiding this world."

[137] Green, *Bonhoeffer. A Theology of Sociality*, 271.

[138] *DBWE* 6, 62 (*DBW* 6, 48).

Martin Rumscheidt

The Significance of Adolf von Harnack and Reinhold Seeberg for Dietrich Bonhoeffer

I. Introduction

Volume 17 of the German edition of the *Dietrich Bonhoeffer Werke, Register und Ergänzungen,* comprising extensive and helpful indexes plus some 68 addenda to volumes 9 to 16, lists 168 references to Reinhold Seeberg and 134 to Adolf von Harnack.[1] If one correlates the frequency of reference – a quick survey shows that by far the greatest number of references to these two men are by Bonhoeffer himself – to the periods of Bonhoeffer's life, one notes that for the period of his studies up to the presentation of his *Habilitationsschrift Act and Being,* Seeberg is mentioned 134 times and Harnack 56 times. After that Seeberg almost disappears from Bonhoeffer's frame of reference;[2] he is mentioned eight times in the prison correspondence, the highest number in any of Bonhoeffer's subsequent writings. Harnack fares considerably better: the 78 references are spread out over all of Bonhoeffer's writings after the publication of the second dissertation. Harnack remains in his view; in fact Bonhoeffer cites him in places critical in his thoughts.

The point of these statistics is to propose a way of describing how the term "influence" is understood in this essay. When Bonhoeffer refers to these two teachers in his letters, seminar-presentations, essays, dissertations, etc. during the years covered by volumes 1, 2, 9, 10 and 17 of the *Dietrich Bonhoeffer Werke/Works,* he is demonstrating that he is capable of performing the requirements of the academy rather than indicating how

---

[1] Their distribution among the 17 volumes of the *Dietrich Bonhoeffer Werke* is revealing. Seeberg appears not at all in volumes 7 and 13; once in volumes 4, 5 and 15; twice in volumes 3, 14 and 16; 4 times in volume 6; 6 times in volume 11; 7 times in volume 12; 8 times in volume 8; 10 times in volume 2; 15 times in volume 17; 18 times in volume 10; 24 times in volume 9 and 67 times in volume 1. Harnack's references are these: once in volumes 5, 7, 13 and 17; twice in volume 2; 4 times in volumes 15 and 16; 5 times in volume 6; 7 times in volumes 12 and 14; 8 times in volumes 1 and 4; 10 times in volume 3; 14 times in volume 8; 16 times in volume 11; 21 times in volume 10 and 24 times in volume 9.

[2] Eberhard Bethge, *Dietrich Bonhoeffer,* 72, writes that after 1933 "the break with Seeberg became complete."

is own thought is being shaped by their work. What manifests itself is more what a footnote to an examination paper by Bonhoeffer names *Gelehrsamkeit*: scholarly acumen. That term was used by an examiner in 1927.[3] It is when one studies the thoughts that Bonhoeffer presents as his own, the positions he defends and his life, that one discerns who influenced him and how.

The point is to distinguish between genuine "influence" and drawing upon others' ideas or "intellectual resources" in the development and advancement of one's own position or one's "theology." In light of this understanding, it is my conclusion that, as far as I can determine, Seeberg's influence on Bonhoeffer can be demonstrated in relation to one aspect only, that of "voluntarism" or "sociality." The picture is quite different in relation to Harnack and his impact as a teacher and a human being.

II. Seeberg and Bonhoeffer

Even though Harnack entered the life of Dietrich Bonhoeffer much earlier than Seeberg, it is the latter we shall consider first. – A brief description of this teacher must suffice here.

Seeberg's dates are 1859–1935; his most influential and prestigious academic position was at the University of Berlin where he taught from 1898 –1927. He was renowned as an outstanding historian of dogma and of social ethics. Next to Adolf von Harnack, Seeberg was heralded as the most significant professor in the Faculty of Theology. He was known as a representative of the "conservative-positive" orientation of nineteenth century Protestant theology which Seeberg himself called "modern-positive" theology. It opposed the pronounced preoccupation with metaphysics and epistemology of earlier theologies of that century and focused more on the moral and hence social dimensions of theological reflection. That was the "modern" aspect Seeberg wanted to signal about his theology. The "positive" represents "an explicitly conservative orientation toward preserving and defending existing reality; ... the positive was identified with the organic, with what grew naturally out of existing reality, ... local customs and laws."[4] Seeberg's major work *Die Grundwahrheiten der christlichen Religion*, published in 1902, develops that theology. Christianity is depicted there as a life-process between the Absolute Spirit and the spirits created by the Spirit. Religious knowledge draws humans into that process

---

[3] *DBW* 17, 65, note 50.

[4] Russell Jacoby, *Social Amnesia. A Critique of Conformist Psychology from Adler to Laing* (Boston 1975), 60, cited in Wayne W. Floyd, Jr., *Theology and the Dialectics of Otherness. On Reading Bonhoeffer and Adorno* (Lanham, MD. 1988), 37. Floyd's discussion of the phenomenon of "positivism" is highly illuminating; cf. 32–46.

which originates with and from God. The form of our participation in it is the application of Christian morality to concrete social, political and national problems. Seeberg develops this in his book *Christliche Ethik* where he lays out his "voluntarism." Here, setting out to reach his "modern" fellow human beings, Seeberg appealed to the will of humans both qua individuals and qua members of corporate communal entities – churches, nations, *Volk* – and was heard to be "positive," that is, life-related and experience-focused rather than theory-bound. Sentences such as the following are classical examples of "positive" or "practical" theology. "Christianity is the community of mutuality between God and humans, established and made real by Jesus; the community exists in Christian faith which is the acceptance of God's saving rule, and in Christian love which is devotion to God and to the reign of God that is to be realized." [5]Others, such as Harnack, recognized features in that "positive" theology which they found abhorrent in that it appealed to values that nurtured nationalism and the "unrealistic acquisitiveness of most Germans; ... During the First World War, Seeberg favoured the furthest possible expansion of the German borders ... while Harnack regarded such claims as excessive and dangerous."[6] This would support Bethge's assertion that Bonhoeffer "broke" with Seeberg by 1933, the year when the National Socialists made the expansion of the German Reich official policy.

Bonhoeffer came into personal contact with Seeberg in the academic year 1924/25. He knew of him, of course, not only as the acclaimed teacher of systematic theology but also as his father's colleague in the university senate. It was after a meeting of the senate in 1925 that Seeberg expressed his pleasure with Dietrich Bonhoeffer's solid preparation in and wide knowledge of contemporary philosophy to Karl Bonhoeffer.[7]

Systematic theology was Bonhoeffer's favourite subject in Berlin; it meant that he enrolled in Seeberg's seminars every semester between 1925 and 1927. This led him to ask Seeberg to direct his doctoral thesis which he successfully completed in 1927. There is no doubt that he learned much from this teacher whose mastery of the history of dogma became the source of knowledge of early, medieval and Reformation theology Bonhoeffer worked with all his life. Thus, it was the rigor of the pursuit of knowledge demonstrated by Seeberg as well as Harnack that left its mark on Bonhoeffer as a scholar and, perhaps even more importantly, as a human being. A passage from his essay *Heritage and Decay*, part of his *Ethics*, describes what this meant. "Intellectual honesty in all things, including questions of faith, was the great good of liberated ratio. It has belonged ever since to the essential moral requirements of western humanity. Con-

---

[5] *Christliche Dogmatik*, volume 1 (Erlangen and Leipzig 1925), 161.
[6] Bethge, *Dietrich Bonhoeffer*, 29 and 70.
[7] Bethge, *Dietrich Bonhoeffer*, 56.

tempt for the age of rationalism is a suspicious sign of a deficient desire for truthfulness. Just because intellectual honesty does not have the last word on things and rational clarity often comes at the cost of the depth of reality, we are not absolved from our inner duty to make honest and clean use of ratio."[8] Still, it is one thing to learn and make good use of one's teachers' work, to embrace their way of pursuing their vocation and its aims and another to be influenced by them.

Seeberg's influence on Bonhoeffer can be seen in the aspect of "voluntarism" or, in the term that more sharply depicts this dimension: "sociality." "It struck [Dietrich Bonhoeffer] that Seeberg was not content to leave theological tenets in the epistemological field, but emphasized their volitional aspects. To him, 'being' also meant 'will,' and faith was the awareness of the will created by the primary will. This gave wings to Bonhoeffer's antispeculative inclinations ... Seeberg taught Bonhoeffer to take the social aspect of existence seriously. To Seeberg the essential mark of human existence, besides its historical nature, was that people exist in sociality. Bonhoeffer made this an essential part of all theological concepts."[9] It must be added here, though, that "the origins of Bonhoeffer's interest in sociality ... are much more complicated than the fact that he was Seeberg's student. The complex set of concepts he uses to explicate sociality was not simply taken over from Seeberg, but hammered out in debate with others."[10]

Bonhoeffer took some time pondering with whom to write his dissertation. It was clear that he had his own ideas and was not prepared simply to write on a subject entirely chosen by the *Doktorvater*. The letter he wrote to his parents on 21 September 1925 is telling. "I have been thinking things over: doing work for Holl or Harnack would be pointless, since with a dogmatic-historical subject I should meet with no resistance from Seeberg either, so it makes very little difference whether I go to one or the other, as I think that on the whole Seeberg is also well-disposed toward me. So I decided to remain with Seeberg, to whom I have now suggested a subject that is half historical and half systematic; and he is very pleased with it. It is connected to the theme of religious community."[11]

In one way, it is not surprising that the dissertation *Sanctorum Communio* should contain the largest number of references Bonhoeffer made to Seeberg; after all, he was the *Doktorvater*. But it was clearly the theme of

---

[8] *DBWE* 6, 115–116 (*DBW* 6, 106).
[9] Bethge, *Dietrich Bonhoeffer*, 70.
[10] Clifford J. Green, *Bonhoeffer. A Theology of Sociality* (Grand Rapids/Cambridge, revised edition, 1999), 24, note 8. The author of this essay is not aware of another work which has so thoroughly analyzed the depth of the concept of sociality in and its continuing significance for Bonhoeffer than this study of Green.
[11] Bethge, *Dietrich Bonhoeffer*, 81.

"sociality" that had Bonhoeffer's attention as a "lens" through which to consider and, to him more importantly, to re-consider theology. Seeberg had made use of that concept in his *Christliche Dogmatik* where it occupied a significant position. Hegel, who had influenced Seeberg, had "[socialized] all the concepts for dealing with human experience"[12] and Seeberg had taken this aspect into his interpretation of "voluntarism" and the dimension of the will's interconnection with other wills (the dialectics of otherness, to use Wayne Floyd's term here), that is, the social reality of existence. When Bonhoeffer declares in his thesis that he wants to set forth a "Christian philosophy of spirit [*Geist*] that will provide a direction for Christian *social* philosophy,"[13] he takes up this Hegel-Seebergian socializing orientation.

When the dissertation was published in 1930, Bonhoeffer wrote in the preface: "The goal of the following ecclesiological study is a dogmatic-theological reflection on the church in light of insights from social philosophy and sociology. Creating a real conceptual connection between theology and both social philosophy and sociology is the basic task and also the difficulty of this essay, whose concrete subject matter is the idea of the church as *sanctorum communio*. The dogmatic character of the work prevails; both disciplines of social science are to be made fruitful for theology.

Thus the basic problem can be defined as the problem of a specifically Christian social philosophy and sociology. My intention is to discuss neither a general sociology of religion, nor genetic-sociological questions; rather, I intend to show that an inherently Christian social philosophy and sociology, arising essentially out of fundamental concepts of Christian theology, is most fully articulated in the concept of the church.

The more I have focused on this problem, the more clearly I have recognized the social intention of all fundamental Christian concepts. 'Person', 'primal state', 'sin', and 'revelation' appeared fully understandable only in relation to sociality ... I hope this study will be seen as a modest contribution to a "philosophy of the church" as was recently called for by Reinhold Seeberg in his *Christliche Dogmatik* [cf. Seeberg, *Dogmatik*, 2, 385], namely one which not only clarifies the nature of the church and of religious community, but which "would result in new understanding of the cohesion of the spirit of humanity, new ideas about the nature of objective spirit [*objektiver Geist*] and the manner in which absolute spirit is revealed in the spirit of humanity ... My ... wish in presenting this study is to contribute something to the understanding that our church, profoundly impoverished and helpless though it appears today, is nevertheless the *sanctorum*

---

[12] John Hermann Randall, *The Career of Philosophy*, volume 2 (New York 1965), 315, cited in Green, *Theology of Sociality*, 24.

[13] *DBWE* 1, 44, note, 30 (*DBW* 1, 215, note 29); emphasis added.

communio, the holy body of Christ, even Christ's very presence in the world."[14]

Two things need specifying here in relation to Bonhoeffer's intention. He seeks to develop an understanding of *Gesamtperson*, a term he derived from Max Scheler,[15] in relation to Christ, that is, seeing Christ as one in relation, incorporating in himself all humanity, on the one hand, and his community, the *Gemeinde*, on the other, embodying *realiter* his concrete existence in the world. Secondly, when he uses the term "person," he uses it as a completely relational term. This perception "makes ethical *will* fundamental in its anthropological and theological presuppositions. [He] insists equally on the irreducible, independent integrity of the individual person, and on the fact that this person exists *essentially* in relation to others and in corporate human structures. His paradigm is not "cogito, ergo sum," but "I relate to others, ergo sum."[16] This is where Seeberg's voluntarism is apparent. The way Bonhoeffer puts it in the dissertation is like this: *"for the individual to exist, 'others' must necessarily be there,"*[17] hence, "from an ethical perspective, human beings do not exist 'unmediated' qua spirit in and of themselves, but only in responsibility vis-à-vis an 'other'."[18]

"At the moment [*Augenblick*] of being addressed, the person enters a state of *responsibility* or, in other words, of decision ... The person exists always and only in ethical responsibility ... In the last analysis the reason why idealist philosophy fails to understand the concept of person is that it has no *voluntaristic* concept of God."[19] Here, perhaps, the influence of Seeberg on Bonhoeffer's later explorations of what it is to be human in the concrete historical contingencies of life is quite visible. When he develops his perception of what existence before God in the worlds means and places it in the domain of responsibility and decision, he draws on what Seeberg had (perhaps?) intended to communicate in his concept of "voluntarism" or "sociality."

The "perhaps" in the previous sentence is caused by the following. When Bonhoeffer wrote in the thesis, "What has become of... the question of the significance of Christianity for the solution of the social problem of the present day? This social problem is vast and complicated. It includes the problem of the capitalistic economic period and of the industrial proletariat created by it; and of the growth of militaristic and industrial giant states; of the enormous increase in population, which affects colonial and world policy; of the mechanical technique ... that produces enormous

---

[14] *DBWE* 1, 22-23 (*DBW* 1, 200–201).
[15] Green, *Bonhoeffer. A Theology of Sociality*, 24.
[16] Green, *Bonhoeffer. A Theology of Sociality*, 30.
[17] *DBWE* 1, 51 (*DBW* 1, 30); emphasis in original.
[18] *DBWE* 1, 50 (*DBW* 1, 30).
[19] *DBWE* 1, 48 (*DBW* 1, 28).

masses of material and links up and mobilizes the whole world for purposes of trade, but also treats people and labor like machines,"[20] Seeberg wrote in the margin, "Does this really belong in the framework of this study? If so, only brief or rewrite."[21] As I see it, it took Bonhoeffer very little time to become convinced that the day to day experience and the view of life that marked people of the "proletariat" – he came to call it later "the view from below" – is an essential element in the understanding of the gospel Jesus gave to humanity. Here, Seeberg "failed" in Bonhoeffer's eyes.

Seeberg urged Bonhoeffer, after the successful completion of the first dissertation and the awarding of the Doctor of Theology in 1927, to proceed in his *Habilitation* with an historical topic, something in the area of ethics in Scholasticism, or else in a topic of the method of interpretation of Scripture. Bonhoeffer ignored the advice.[22] Instead, he addressed the epistemological problem related to God's revelation in light of the subject-object paradigm of transcendental philosophical philosophy.[23] The study, entitled *Act and Being. Transcendental Philosophy and Ontology in Systematic Theology*, was not directed by Seeberg but by his successor Wilhelm Lütgert; it was submitted in early 1930 and the *Habilitation* took place in July that year and published in 1931.

What Helmut Gollwitzer referred to as "the theological style in Berlin, namely the constant engagement with philosophy and even sociology,"[24] had spoken directly to Bonhoeffer's own interest in philosophy. Seeberg, whose "great models [were] Schleiermacher, Hegel and Ritschl,"[25] recognized that interest and furthered it. It is safe to surmise that Bonhoeffer's term "Christ existing as church-community," or its functional equivalent: the church, the holy body of Christ, even Christ's very presence in the

---

[20] *DBWE* 1, 271, note 430 (*DBW* 1, 290, note 411).

[21] *DBWE* 1, 271, note 430 (*DBW* 1, 290, note 411).

[22] Bethge, *Dietrich Bonhoeffer*, 132.

[23] The work of Wayne W. Floyd (see note 4 above) is addressed entirely to the presentation of what Bonhoeffer had set his mind to in this work. Floyd attends to the sharp epistemological clash that Bonhoeffer witnessed at the time of his studies in theology. One may describe it simply by referring to the public controversy in 1923 between Adolf von Harnack and Karl Barth. Their issue was, among others, how we know what we claim to know in our theological statements. Is method in theology really the essential problem for contemporary theology and its tasks? More broadly speaking, what interested Bonhoeffer was the troubled relationship between the transcendental philosophical tradition, embraced in both the ontology and epistemology of Continental "liberal" theology – which Harnack represented magnificently – and "modern" theology with its radical questioning of theology's very capacity for critical reflection – of which Barth was a significant representative. This is what Floyd examines in detail in his book.

[24] Raymond Mengus, *Wirkungen. Gespräche über Dietrich Bonhoeffer mit E. Bethge, G. Ebeling. H. Gollwitzer und W. A. Visser 't Hooft* (Munich 1978), 9.

[25] Bethge, *Dietrich Bonhoeffer*, 70.

world[26] was formulated under the impact of Seeberg's teaching. What was initially most likely a term of Hegelian dialectics became an essential concept for Bonhoeffer's growing understanding of sociality.

But I see it as an example of "negative" influence. Bonhoeffer who had deeply experienced the collapse and crisis that followed Germany's defeat in World War I, the growth of an impoverished proletariat in Berlin, could not accept the optimism of the theology and anthropology represented by Seeberg and others. He saw clearly that such realities were not factors for the theological reflection of those teachers. For an understanding of what he could not accept, it may be permissible to turn to his thoughts expressed later in his prison correspondence. What had troubled him about the philosophy of idealism and the liberal theologies that built on it was the confinement to the self. In his late reflections on "religion," he identifies that confinement by calling it "interpreting in a religious sense," that is, "to speak individualistically." The era of religion was an era of inwardness, with its "temporally conditioned presuppositions of inwardness." What is attempted there is to keep God's place for us "secure at least in the sphere of the 'personal', the 'inner' and the 'private'."[27] The very notion of "keeping a place for God secure among us" was for Bonhoeffer a dangerous invitation to establish spheres in life where God would not be present or would be forced out. His own political experience even as early as the mid-nineteen-twenties, nurtured by his growing understanding of the sociality of Christ and his community in the world, alerted him to what such a restriction to more or less respectable spheres can lead to. Seeberg's comment in the foreword to volume 1 of his *Christliche Dogmatik* (1925) that "I might just as well have written a philosophy of religion. Interested philosophers and historians would have understood me without sharing my presuppositions,"[28] must have caused Bonhoeffer apprehension. As he

---

[26] *DBWE* 1, 23, note 5 (*DBW* 1, 201, note 1). "Christ existing as church-community" occurs 14 times in *DBW/E* 1, twice in *DBW/E* 2 and 4, once in *DBW/E* 5, 9, 13, and three times in *DBW/E* 10, 11 and 14; cf. *DBW* 17, 483.

[27] *LPP*, 285–286, 280, 344 (*DBW* 8, 414, 403, 509).

[28] Cited in Karl Barth, *Kirchliche Dogmatik*, volume I/2 (Zurich 1934), 317. Barth comments that in such a statement it is apparent that theology no longer takes itself seriously as theology. But as *Sanctorum Communio* testifies, Bonhoeffer was wholeheartedly committed to the task of *theology qua theology*. Eberhard Bethge, *Dietrich Bonhoeffer*, 84, cites Karl Barth's comment from *Kirchliche Dogmatik*, volume IV/2: "If there can be any possible vindication of Reinhold Seeberg, it is to be sought in the fact that his school could give rise to this man and his dissertation which not only awakens respect for the breadth and depth of its insight as we look back to the existing situation, but makes far more instructive and stimulating and edifying reading today than many of the more famous works which have since been written on the problem of the church ... I openly confess that I have misgivings whether I can even maintain the high level reached by Bonhoeffer, saying no less in my own words and context, and saying it no less forcefully, than did this young man so many years ago."

moved on his journey from theology as an intellectual challenge to theology as an exploration of the praxis of Christian sociality, influenced to whatever degree by the voluntarism of Seeberg's system, the distance between him and his teacher grew more decisive. Bethge sums it up as follows: "In Berlin, his choice of Seeberg as a mentor reflected [a] spirit of independence, since Seeberg imposed the fewest restrictions and obligations on him. In addition, his own upbringing and his father's example gave Bonhoeffer a broader perspective, enabling him to respect and to learn from those who taught something different from what he believed. Only with the church struggle in 1933 did Bonhoeffer's oppositional stance move from ideas to actively participating in conflict and selecting his own personal contacts carefully. At that point, the break with Seeberg became complete."[29] Observations such as these are the ground for my assessment of "negative" influence.

III. Harnack and Bonhoeffer

Any examination of the influence of Adolf von Harnack on Dietrich Bonhoeffer has to take most seriously the personal and familial relations between the families and homes of the Harnacks and Bonhoeffers. Those relations cannot be overestimated, for here the very dimensions of concrete sociality evoke and shape what we now call the "contextual" theology exemplified and practiced by Dietrich Bonhoeffer.

In 1912, when Dietrich Bonhoeffer was six years old, his family moved from Breslau to Berlin; in 1916 they moved into a house in the Grunewald district. It was a neighbourhood of academics, among whom were friends and colleagues of his father, including the quantum physicist Max Planck. In the home of historian Hans Delbück, just a few doors away, "every Wednesday evening a distinguished company gathered... including Adolf von Harnack, Troeltsch, Meinecke ... During the war, these circles turned against the too-broad peace goals and unrealistic acquisitiveness of most Germans. They attacked the nationalist colleagues [including] Reinhold Seeberg. The Bonhoeffer children were not part of these Wednesday gatherings, but its atmosphere and direction had an effect."[30] Biographer Josef Ackermann depicts another but no less important aspect of the "sociality" of this unique neighbourhood. In Grunewald "the parents find good neighbours and the children like-minded friends. In the Bonhoeffer house there is great delight in music; all Bonhoeffer children learn to play an instrument and music brings them together also with the neighbours' chil-

---

[29] Bethge, *Dietrich Bonhoeffer*, 72.
[30] Bethge, *Dietrich Bonhoeffer*, 29.

dren. Four of Dietrich's siblings later marry a partner who lived in the quarter of the city. Emmi Bonhoeffer, née Delbrück, the wife of Klaus Bonhoeffer, describes this neighbourly life. 'We Delbrücks were seven sisters and brothers and soon there developed friendships through hiking, ice skating and making music. Klaus with his cello, his five years younger brother Dietrich at the piano and I with my violin - we made our way into classical chamber music. Soon the circle grew: the new brother-in-law Rüdiger Schleicher with his violin and my cousin Ernst von Harnack with his flute enlarged it'."[31] Her brother Justus, her cousin Ernst, her husband Klaus and brothers-in-law Dietrich and Rüdiger, as well as Hans von Dohnanyi, husband of Christine Bonhoeffer but not member of this little chamber orchestra, were later murdered by the National Socialists for their resistance against Hitler.

Who is Adolf von Harnack, neighbour, mentor and significant public persona of whom, in the judgment of some, Bonhoeffer was his "most genuine pupil,"[32] and who read stories to the younger children of the Grunewald neighbourhood?[33]

Von Harnack (1851–1930) was himself the son of a professor of church-history and homiletics at the University of Dorpat (now Tartu in Estonia,) a man deeply rooted in a personal faith and Lutheran orthodoxy. Adolf von Harnack found his life in the university, especially in scholarly methodology. An academic from age twenty-four until his retirement at seventy, he taught at four universities in Germany: Giessen, Leipzig, Marburg and Berlin, at the last-named from 1888 until 1921. He twice declined invitations from Harvard University to join its faculty. He was co-founder and for almost thirty years editor of the prestigious *Theologische Literaturzeitung*. His students founded and edited the weekly *Christliche Welt*, "An Evangelical-Lutheran congregational paper for the educated members of the Protestant churches," as it described itself on the paper's masthead. Next to his teaching duties as church-historian at the Faculty of Theology of the University of Berlin – for a period he was also rector of the university – he was the executive director of the Royal Library in Berlin for sixteen years, president of the Academy of Sciences, the first president of the Kaiser Wilhelm Society for the Advancement of the Sciences from 1911 until his death, and president of the Evangelisch-Sozialer Kongress, a society for the promotion of Christian values in society. In 1891, Harnack founded the Commission on the Church-Fathers whose purpose was to

---

[31] Josef Ackermann, *Freiheit hat offene Augen. Dietrich Bonhoeffer. Eine Biographie* (Gütersloh 2005), 23.

[32] Carl-Jügen Kaltenborn, "Adolf von Harnack and Bonhoeffer," in A. J. Klassen (ed.), *A Bonhoeffer Legacy* (Grand Rapids, MI., 1981), 48.

[33] Conversation with Dr. Margarete von Zahn, the granddaughter of Adolf von Harnack, Berlin, June 1982.

publish a critical edition of the Greco-Christian literature up to the year 325 CE. By 1924, forty-five of the planned fifty volumes had appeared, most of them edited by him. His bibliography, compiled and published by Friedrich Smend in 1931, contains 1611 titles. On his seventieth birthday Harnack was awarded a citation of honour by President Hindenburg: "To the Bearer of German Culture."

Dietrich Bonhoeffer belonged to the circle of students whom Harnack chose personally to work with him in his seminars on church-history after his retirement. Often the two walked together to the train station on their way to the university. Bonhoeffer participated in three of those "special seminars" in addition other seminars in a span of six semesters. At the close of them, he wrote to Harnack, "What I have learned and come to understand in your seminar is too closely associated with my whole personality for me to be able ever to forget it."[34] There is a communication from one of Bonhoeffer's fellow-participants, Helmut Goes, who describes an aspect Harnack recognized, valued and promoted in Bonhoeffer. "What really drew me to Bonhoeffer was that there was someone who did not merely study and absorb the words and writings of some master, but who thought for himself and already knew what he wanted and also wanted what he knew. I actually had the experience ... of seeing the young blond student contradict the revered polyhistorian His Excellency von Harnack politely, but on objective theological grounds. Harnack replied, but the student contradicted him again and again ... I recall the secret enthusiasm that I felt for this free, critical and independent theological thought."[35] Another such fellow-participant, Bertha Schulze, reports the following, "For Harnack Bonhoeffer was a highly-valued pupil; one noticed this in the way he treated him. It was not customary in Harnack's seminars to receive praise ... Bonhoeffer's participation was regular and very active."[36]

What Goes calls "free, critical and independent theological thought" is precisely the hallmark of Harnack's scholarly character. It is what I call "liberal theology at its height."[37] The term "liberal" is used here in the literal sense of liberal: free. We speak here of a theology that is under the imperative of freedom: freedom of thought in the pursuit of truth on every path taken, freedom from interference by those into whom authority has been invested, freedom from structures such as dogmas and ideologies and freedom from the institutions built on them. "It was the imperative that

---

[34] Bethge, *Dietrich Bonhoeffer*, 68.
[35] Bethge, *Dietrich Bonhoeffer*, 67.
[36] Reinhart Staats, "Adolf von Harnack im Leben Dietrich Bonhoeffers," in *Theologische Zeitschrift* 37 (1981), 105.
[37] Martin Rumscheidt (ed), *Adolf von Harnack. Liberal Theology at its Height*, The Making of Modern Theology, volume 6. John de Gruchy, General Editor (San Francisco 1988).

conscience develop itself as freely and fully as possible while attaining to and maintaining full responsibility. The 'liberal' position exhibited confidence in the human spirit, reverence for the dignity, competence and authority of the power of thinking, and trust in the ability of human beings to transcend their subjectivity in the endeavour to reach true objectivity ... The imperative of freedom establishes its own commandments, which constrain the knower to methodological objectivity and ethical responsibility and to placing everything before the judgement of reason, the final arbiter."[38]

The biographies of both Harnack and Bonhoeffer testify to Harnack's appreciation of Bonhoeffer's respect for and personal appropriation of that freedom and its imperatives. As we shall see later more fully, an inseparable component of that freedom for both men was a clear grasp of social and political responsibility. It was with foreboding that Harnack uttered these words in 1924, "One ought not to imagine that the ravages of our time can be healed with parades, swastikas and steel-helmets."[39] It is unambiguous that Harnack had Hitler and his emerging movement in mind. When the National Socialists took power nine years later, Rüdiger Schleicher, the husband of Ursula Bonhoeffer, summed up what was clear to the whole Bonhoeffer family: this means war![40] There is much evidence that Dietrich Bonhoeffer never wavered in his adherence to those high imperatives of freedom and responsibility shared with his teacher Harnack.

Yet he was critical of something at the core of liberal theology. It held that the dignity of human beings resides also in their ability to lay hold of reality, in the sense of the literal meaning of *com-prendre*, to *grasp* reality. With solid faith in "methods," Christian faith, in the mind of liberal theologians like Harnack, is a faith that *knows*: it knows not only God and the reality God created, it also knows *how* it knows them. What Descartes and the Enlightenment had bequeathed to liberal Protestantism was that the noetic ratio of the mind's comprehension, its *comprendre*, is univocally expressive of the ontic ratio of what is being comprehended. "In theological terminology, liberal theology assumes the existence of a perfectly symmetrical relation between faith and what faith claims to be its subject or object. [Here] the distance between the knower and the known – it was axiomatic that faith was a matter of knowledge – is reduced to the extent that what is known cannot be a limit on the knower. Thus, the knower or believer is radically free from *and* for reality."[41]

Already in his *Sanctorum Communio*, and then more fully in *Act and Being*, Bonhoeffer submits this aspect to critique. As he develops his no-

---

[38] Martin Rumscheidt, "The Formation of Bonhoeffer's Theology," in *CCDB*, 54.
[39] Cited without reference in Staats, "Adolf von Harnack," 94.
[40] Bethge, *Dietrich Bonhoeffer*, 257.
[41] Martin Rumscheidt, "The Formation of Bonhoeffer's Theology," 54.

tion of sociality, he insists on what Wayne Floyd calls "a dialectics of otherness," that is, on how the other – in terms of faith: God – imposes *Grenzen*, limits that are insurmountable methodologically and, in the final analysis, also ethically. Transgression of those limits means epistemologically that one does not know the "other" subject or object at all; one knows only oneself.

However Bonhoeffer assessed and critiqued the epistemological dimension of Harnack's work, the aspect he fully recognized and embraced in his mentor's liberal position was the rigor with which it sought to address itself to the "modern" human being. Harnack's assignment of a very positive character to "the world" left a permanent mark on Bonhoeffer.[42] That appreciation found a perhaps curious expression in that Bonhoeffer introduced a rather "monkish custom" into the community at Finkenwalde that met with opposition: the reading aloud of chosen works of literature. One of them was the biography by Agnes von Zahn-Harnack of her father.[43]

Karl Barth became a more and more prominent reference point for Bonhoeffer from the later years of the nineteen-twenties onward. When the German Church-Struggle broke out in 1933, Harnack receded for a time in Bonhoeffer's ongoing work.[44] Bonhoeffer's former student Albrecht Schönherr notes that "in the phase of my life when I had much to do personally with Bonhoeffer (1932–1940) Harnack played a very minor role, at least in my conversations with him."[45] Bethge's observations here help understand what led to that diminution of Harnack's impact at that time.

In the Bonhoeffer's immediate circle the deaths of two men who sacrificed old allegiances for the sake of the Weimar Republic epitomized the demise of a great liberal and humanitarian tradition. "The historian Hans Delbrück, who was Klaus Bonhoeffer's father-in-law, died in the house next door in the summer of 1929; one year later, Adolf von Harnack died too ... during the 1920's they watched the political course taken by the Protestant church with concern, for royalism and anti-Semitism had not died with the disappearance of the monarch ... the values for which Harnack and Delbrück had stood began to succumb rapidly to the defamation and ridicule of the growing forces of irrational nationalism; these values were viewed as the decadent morality of the 'state system,' which was now ripe for the final assault. The Christian bourgeoisie did not find much in it to defend; ... True, [it] did not have much use for the raucous Nazis, but they listened with pleasure to speeches about the 'Western decadence' that democracy had introduced to Germany, and liked to think that a 'rebirth of

---

[42] In order to assess Bonhoeffer's perception of this positive view of the world, it is instructive to read the text of his address at Harnack's funeral. Cf. *DBW* 10, 346–349.
[43] Bethge, *Dietrich Bonhoeffer*, 429.
[44] Cf. the chapter on Bonhoffer and Barth by Andreas Pangritz in this volume.
[45] Staats, "Adolf von Harnack," 109.

the national spirit in a German national community' might yet transform the defeat of 1918 into victory."[46]

But when Bonhoeffer's work in the illegal seminaries was brought to a violent end by the Gestapo and he had become involved in the conspiracy against Hitler in the group around Admiral Walter-Wilhelm Canaris and Major General Hans Oster, he refers once again to Harnack more unambiguously and deliberately. Writing to is parents on Reformation Day 1943, after his arrest and imprisonment, he says, "I remember from my student days a discussion between Holl and Harnack as to whether the great intellectual and historical movements made headway through their primary or secondary motives. At the time I thought Holl was right in maintaining the former; now I think he was wrong."[47] He refers again to Harnack 18 days later. Speaking about Bach's Mass in B-minor, he says, "I well remember the evening when I first heard it. I was eighteen, and had just come from Harnack's seminar, in which he had discussed my first seminar essay very kindly, and had expressed the hope that some day I should specialize in church history. I was full of this when I arrived at the Philharmonic Hall; the great *Kyrie Eleison* was just beginning, and as it did so, I forgot everything else – the effect was indescribable."[48]

Whence this turn to *Geistesgeschichte* and something spiritual-cultural? Writing about what Bonhoeffer was reading in his prison cell, Bethge says: "He wanted to become better acquainted with particular aspects of nineteenth-century literature and *rehabilitate* the tradition of the forefathers, from Keller to Harnack, from Pestalozzi to Dilthey, over against more modern existentialist tendencies. ... These writers opened his cell to that familiar world from which he had been shut out. ... It was one of Bonhoeffer's great moments in Tegel when, after his family at home had hunted for it for a long time without success, he unexpectedly came upon Stifter's *Witiko* in the prison library. ... It was ... not only the literary quality of the book that fascinated him, but its theme, which placed his own life within the most universal context of the wide sweep of history. ... He discovered for himself what Hermann Bahr had already noted in *Witiko* in 1922: 'This old book seems to have waited just for us, to have been written especially for us ... only now do we comprehend ... the aim, of depicting the terrible majesty of the moral law, which destroys ... the great criminals and bends their violent schemes like straws, in such a powerful and brilliant way that people, seeing the terror of it ... submit in trembling and wonder to the power that forbids evil. ... then Witiko starts doing injustice for the sake of good and helps to bring out of this new justice. ... Where there has been a lasting victory for revolution it has always been the victory of legitimacy,

---

[46] Bethge, *Dietrich Bonhoeffer*, 126.
[47] *LPP*, 123 (*DBW* 8, 179).
[48] *LPP*, 126–127 (*DBW* 8, 184).

the victory of illegal justice over the law that has become unjust. ... New justice must always first expiate its defects through profound suffering; ... with the wrongdoing burned away. Only then, through penance, will justice finally emerge from good injustice'."[49]

What members of Harnack's wider family had inherited from him and then took into their conspiratorial activities in the Third Reich, paying for it with their lives, is described in Bahr's words. It is to the world of such values that Bonhoeffer turns, fighting with good injustice against laws that are unjust, to the world that his most influential teacher had represented to him.

He then asked specifically, among other works, for Harnack's *History of the Prussian Academy*, the four-volume work, written over a period of four years and presented to the Academy on the occasion of its bicentenary in 1900. Bonhoeffer's focus was "the past," as his own literary works and some poems from Tegel prison show. And his interest was to "rehabilitate" it, to discern more deeply its spirit, its theological themes. The purpose of embracing the past was to help overcome the present reality that had abandoned all values, a time that was so empty and wasted.[50] It is really no surprise that Harnack re-enters Bonhoeffer's thinking.

Beginning in August 1943, imprisoned for nearly four months, Bonhoeffer began to write a novel. He calls it a history of a contemporary bourgeois family. This is how he describes his "bold enterprise" to Eberhard Bethge. "The background for this consisted of all our innumerable conversations we had on this subject and what we ourselves experienced; in short, a rehabilitation of the bourgeoisie that we came to know from our own families and particularly through Christianity. The children of two families, bonded in friendship, grow up gradually entering into the responsibility of a small town's official tastes and positions and together try themselves, as mayor, teacher, priest, doctor and engineer, for the good of the community. You would recognize many familiar features, and you come into it too."[51] It is not difficult to identify some persons of his own life, as Bonhoeffer had signalled in that letter.

The "poet-novelist" Bonhoeffer introduces a character called Franz who reminisces about his "old history teacher." This teacher was "the only teacher for whom he had great love and admiration ... He made an effort to do justice to anyone who was at all serious about something. Only when someone churned out borrowed platitudes ... did he sometimes become furious ... I'll never forget how he presented the great historical movements to us ... But then, when the teacher finished lecturing on these topics, he always followed up with several classes in which conclusions could be

---

[49] Bethge, *Dietrich Bonhoeffer*, 844–846; emphasis added.
[50] *LPP*, 129 (*DBW* 8, 188).
[51] *LPP*, 129–130 (*DBW* 8, 189).

drawn from the material. In these classes it was as if our history teacher became a different person. While he lectured with fire and passion before, now there was a certain melancholy about him. He said history shows that all these great movements and ideas have brought disaster to humanity in the end. The French Revolution ended in terror and was the beginning of the rule of the masses in Europe, he told us; the Reformation destroyed the unity of the West forever and rendered it defenseless against materialism; Christianity tore apart the inner life of nations and individuals and, because of that, hardly anyone was able to find inner unity again. But then at the last possible moment, he explained, to prevent catastrophe, there was always a mediocre compromise between the world and the new ideas, and these compromises were exactly what buried the actual idea and the original impulse. You were never allowed to say that the original idea was getting lost without being branded a heretic and a misanthrope by society. But he thought perhaps this was basically right. In any case the outcome and the lesson of history and of life – and we should listen well – was that one can only live by compromise ... I asked our teacher if people were created for the purpose of being happy. And he looked at me with an indescribably kind and sad look, behind which was a little smile, and said, almost like a child, that he really didn't know. And he even said he didn't know if anybody did, but that he would talk with me about it again in twenty years; maybe then we'd both know more. Well, soon after that he died. Perhaps he knows more now."[52]

Professor Reinhart Staats, to whom I owe this reference to that section from the prison fiction, suggests that "it is quite possible that memories even of Harnack in his late years were woven into the story by [Bonhoeffer.] He would have erected a beautiful memorial to him if we note the congruencies of the image of Harnack in Bonhoeffer's student years with the Harnack-Holl controversy referred to earlier that had a lasting effect on Bonhoeffer."[53] The final sentences in the quotation from the novel are remarkably close to what Agnes von Zahn-Harnack tells of her father's last birthday. "That evening the family gathered for prayer and meditation; Harnack led it and reflected on the words of Isaiah 40:27–29, 'God, give strength to the tired and to the powerless new energy.' These words gave great solace to all present until they discovered, after his death, that on the same day he had written in the margin of his Bible, next to that very text, 'my sadness is so great that I do not know where to turn'." 34 days later Harnack died.[54]

In the course of writing the novel, Bonhoeffer wrote to his parents how he felt about possibly still being in prison over Christmas. In his letter of

---

[52] *DBWE* 7, 162–163, 166 (*DBW* 7, 170–171, 174–175).
[53] Staats, "Adolf von Harnack," 110–111.
[54] Agnes von Zahn-Harnack, *Adolf von Harnack* (Berlin, second edition 1951), 440–441.

December 17, 1943, he says that the memory of past Christmases at home will overcome a bleak one. "It's not till such times as these that we realize what it means to possess a past and a spiritual inheritance independent of changes of time and circumstance. The consciousness of being borne up by a spiritual tradition that goes back for centuries gives one a feeling of confidence and security in face of all passing strains and distresses." And he speaks of "the memory of a good and rich past" and that those "who hold fast to the values [cannot have them taken] away from them."[55]

Bonhoeffer had asked that Harnack's history of the Prussian Academy be sent to him; he wanted to read it because, among other reasons, Harnack had called it his best work.[56] He wanted to be in touch with the best of his teacher. When he had finished it he wrote to Eberhard Bethge, "The longer we are uprooted from our proper professional activities and our personal lives, the more we feel how fragmentary our lives are, compared with those of our parents. The portraits of the great savants in Harnack's *History of the Academy* make me acutely aware of that, and almost sadden me for awhile. Where is there an intellectual *magnum opus* today? Where are the collecting, assimilating, and sorting of material necessary for producing such a work? Where is there still that beautiful purposelessness and yet the extensive planning that is part of such a life?"[57] A few days later he writes to his parents, "Harnack's *History of the Academy* has made a deep impression on me; it made me feel partly happy, partly regretful. There are so few people today who still want to have an inner and spiritual connection with the 19th and 18th centuries ... who still have an idea of what our grandfathers labored on and achieved and how much of what they knew is already lost to us! I believe that people will one day not cease to be amazed about how fruitful that time was which is now so disdained and so little known."[58] This lengthy exploration of the impact Harnack's *person* had on Bonhoeffer is not in itself a demonstration of influence as such but provides the context for the development of what Eberhard Bethge calls Bonhoeffer's "new theology."[59]

Shortly before he died, Harnack wrote a brief, testament-like essay entitled *Stufen wissenschaftlicher Erkenntnis* (Stages of Scientific Knowledge). It is a concise statement of how he interpreted his own life's work. The opening sentence reads, "Science is knowledge of reality for purposeful

---

[55] *LPP*, 165 (*DBW* 8, 240). Note 3 in *DBW* 8, 240 refers to *Fiction from Tegel Prison* (*DBWE* 7, 64–66 (*DBW* 7, 65–66) and to *LPP*, 295–296 (*DBW* 8, 430) "Thoughts on the Day of the Baptism of Dietrich Wilhelm Rüdiger Bethge" (May 1944). In both instances, Bonhoeffer speaks of such "values."
[56] *LPP*, 200 (*DBW* 8, 304).
[57] *LPP*, 219; translation slightly altered (*DBW* 8, 335).
[58] *LPP*, 227; translation slightly altered (*DBW* 8, 349).
[59] Bethge, *Dietrich Bonhoeffer*, 853–891.

action."⁶⁰ In an earlier essay, he had specified that everything which advances the birth and growth of true humanity is of value, is the norm, the good; everything that hinders it is evil.⁶¹ Given the respect for the man whose life and, one must add, that of his whole family, was in a manner of speaking mid-wifery for a true, decent humanity, Bonhoeffer would have understood that "purposeful action" was embedded in values "that cannot be taken away" Those values, partly derived from the knowledge that science provides, nurture responsible action in the world.

In his study of Harnack as Bonhoeffer's teacher, Carl-Jürgen Kaltenborn shows that Bonhoeffer derived the significance of "arcane discipline" from Harnack's theology even though he then developed that concept very much on his own. Similarly, Kaltenborn identifies Bonhoeffer's ethics and its "orientation towards action" as derived from Harnack.⁶² "Arcane discipline" is closely associated with Bonhoeffer's understanding of "responsible action" and "prayer." Both are essential components of a Christianity – or of Christian faith as such – that is open to the world.

In July 1942 Bonhoeffer wrote to a former Finkenwalde seminarian; in that communication he refers to Rudolf Bultmann's *Neues Testament und Mythologie* and to his own response to it. He writes, "I belong to those who welcomed that writing – ... [he] let the cat out of the bag ... He has dared to say what many repress in themselves." In the midst of his reflection, he says, "In this regard perhaps I have remained Harnack's student to this day."⁶³ One may safely surmise, I believe, that he meant the same in

---

⁶⁰ The full text can be found in Rumscheidt (ed), *Adolf von Harnack. Liberal Theology at its Height*, 43–45.

⁶¹ Cited in Staats, "Adolf von Harnack," 103.

⁶² Carl-Jürgen Kaltenborn, *Adolf von Harnack als Lehrer Dietrich Bonhoeffers* (Berlin, 1973), 125–128. It was my choice not to present, or repeat, Kaltenborn's exploration of Harnack's "influence" on Bonhoeffer, since the work cited is readily available from any reputable theological library. His argument is that, in searching out the "spiritual ancestry" of Bonhoeffer, "Harnack's impetus and the way he formulated problems shaped Bonhoeffer's thinking and acting far more than has hitherto been shown" (p. 5). Kaltenborn's work and my presentation overlap in the assessment of the importance of the familiar relationship between the Harnacks and the Bonhoeffers, their disdain for and resistance against German fascism and the renewed appropriation of the German high bourgeois tradition. We similarly discern Harnack's influence on how Bonhoeffer perceived "arcane discipline" and its concomitant orientation on purposeful action within the "penultimate." What Kaltenborn examines in greater detail is the idea of "Jesus Christ – the *one* reality." Here I see Harnack's view of Jesus, his "Jesuanism," fundamentally differently than Kaltenborn. For Harnack, Jesus – as he describes him most explicitly in his *What Is Christianity* – is no more than the best expression of a particular form of religion, a notion Bonhoeffer simply could not have shared, particularly after he came under the influence of Karl Barth. – But I do want to commend Kaltenborn's work as an important contribution to the study of Bonhoeffer's "spiritual ancestry."

⁶³ *DBWE* 16, 347 (*DBW* 16, 344).

his letter of August 3, 1944 to Eberhard Bethge. "The church must come out of its stagnation. We must move out again into the open air of intellectual discussion with the world, and risk saying controversial things, if we are to get down to serious problems of life. I feel obliged to tackle these questions as one who, although a 'modern' theologian, is still aware of the debt that he owes to liberal theology. There will not be many of the younger generation who combine both of these aspects in themselves."[64]

Here Bonhoeffer develops the now well-known concepts of "world come-of-age," "non-religious interpretation of Christian concepts" and "arcane discipline" in which he seeks, as he put it in his letter to Bethge of June 8, 1944, to overcome liberal theology but at the same time genuinely take up its questions and answer them.[65] That had to take place, as he put it, in the "fresh air" of open, unreserved and presupposition-less intellectual dialogue. But not at the expense of the Gospel, as he feared Bultmann's demythologization was doing. The human being in and of the world come-of-age is to hear the Gospel but not in terms of conceptualities that are at home in a world other than that. The human being to be addressed today needs to have the Gospel interpreted "non-religiously."

Reinhart Staats carefully outlines how Bonhoeffer's understanding of "arcane discipline" is influenced by Harnack. – In two essays, published in anthologies of addresses and essays, Harnack says, "What matters is not the form but the reverence with which one lays hold of the *mystery* of the person of Christ and then submits one's own life to the spirit of Christ." And then, "In light of my historical understanding and my feeling, the formulae 'human and divine' (*Mensch und Gott*) and 'humanity of God' (*Gottmenschlichkeit*) are not above any and all dispute because they touch upon a *mystery* into which we are not allowed to enter. Yet the formulae may be kept because they basically do not seek to explain something but only protect the extraordinary against profanation, somewhat like the expression 'Son of God'."[66] On May 5, 1944 Bonhoeffer writes, "There are degrees of knowledge and degrees of significance; that means that a secret discipline must be restored whereby the *mysteries* of the Christian faith are protected against profanation."[67] The parallelism in the wording is surely not coincidental. But it is beyond doubt that "profanation" was perceived differently by him. Staats refers to a communication he received from Bertha Schulze; she had been the senior of Harnack's late seminars, a position in which Bonhoeffer succeeded her. Subsequently, she worked for Bon-

---

[64] *LPP*, 378; translation slightly altered (*DBW* 8, 555).
[65] Cf. *LPP*, 328 (*DBW* 8, 482).
[66] Adolf von Harnack, *Reden und Aufsätze*, 2 volumes (Giessen 1906), vol. 1, 296 and vol. 2, 15; emphasis added.
[67] *LPP*, 286 (*DBW* 8, 415)

hoeffer as what we today would describe as a research associate.[68] In her letter to Staats, she says that she has no recollection that "arcane discipline" was discussed in those seminars. But she adds, "Harnack used to stress that not every Christian can claim to have genuine religious experience, but one may confidently put one's trust in the few Christians with mature experience."[69] Harnack's sense of profanation arose in relation to those segments of the church that clung to a seemingly untouchable orthodoxy, or what he described as "the bonds of burdensome and conscience-breaking tradition."[70] When he became involved in the so-called *Apostolikumstreit* in 1892 – a public controversy over the continued use of the Apostles' Creed in the regular liturgy of the Lutheran Church – he wrote, "In my view, there is no more serious and burning issue for the general synods of the evangelical churches than to discuss the question of the Creed freely and openly."[71] The response he received to that view is described by his biographer: there was "a horde of small, yelping dogs, pious twisters of truth, people of an unholy simplemindedness" that went on the attack against Harnack, calling him "a forger in the pit of heathenism."[72] To borrow Bonhoeffer's phrase related to Bultmann: Harnack had let the cat out of the bag. And clearly Bonhoeffer saw here a *form* of the "fresh air of intellectual discussion with the world" that he himself took to be a necessity in the "world come-of-age." But for him what Christian faith needed to be protected against was not orthodoxy, on the one hand, and liberal theology, on the other, but the "theological" assertions of the German Christians and, equally so, the shrill asseverations of Hitler and, by extension, of any other leaders, that they are doing the will of God, that God is with them and "with us." The arcane discipline that protects Christianity in face of that profanation is "prayer and righteous action [*Beten und das Tun des Gerechten unter den Menschen*]."[73] "It is not up to us to foretell the day – but the day will surely come – when men and women will once again be called so to utter the word of God that the world will be changed and made new. It will be a new language, perhaps quite non-religious, but liberating and redeeming, like Jesus' language; it will terrify people yet overcome them by its force, a language of new justice and truth, a language that heralds God's peace with humankind and the coming of God's reign."[74] This is not an observation by and on intellectual history, a comment made in the course of doing *Geisteswissenschaft*; rather, it is an

---

[68] Bethge, *Dietrich Bonhoeffer*, 68 and 137.
[69] Staats, "Adolf von Harnack," 117.
[70] Agnes von Zahn-Harnack, *Adolf von Harnack*, 131.
[71] Staats, "Adolf von Harnack," 118.
[72] Agnes von Zahn-Harnack, *Adolf von Harnack*, 151.
[73] *LPP*, 300 (*DBW* 8, 435).
[74] *LPP*, 300; translation slightly altered (*DBW* 8, 436).

expression of an assured hope in what by God's grace is to come after Hitler and the defeat of Germany that draws upon that value-tradition that Bonhoeffer knows himself to be borne by. It was that very hope and sense of inheritance that had also moved Harnack's son Ernst whom like Bonhoeffer the Nazis murdered for resisting the one whom another upright man, a co-conspirator of the 20 July 1944 assassination plot, called during his trial: *"der Vollstrecker des Bösen in der Geschichte* [the executor of evil in history]."[75] This was said by Hans-Bernd von Haeften, a friend who had been confirmed with Bonhoeffer and similarly brutally murdered by Hitler's henchmen.

IV. Conclusion

This exploration proposed and maintained the distinction between "influence" and "the use of intellectual resources." On the basis of that differentiation, it can be said, in conclusion, that the influence Reinhold Seeberg had on Dietrich Bonhoeffer was small and limited to Bonhoeffer's theology, essentially, albeit not exclusively, to its first phase. In contrast, Adolf von Harnack influenced not only Bonhoeffer's theological thinking in its final phase;[76] he influenced Bonhoeffer the human being and the citizen in rich ways. Seeberg appears not to have been someone who made a formative impact on Bonhoeffer's life in the manner Harnack did.

Bonhoeffer's interest in philosophy, evident already in his final years of high school, was certainly nurtured by Seeberg's extensive acquaintance with the history of philosophy, particularly of modern German philosophy. Since the Enlightenment, Protestant theology in Germany had entered into a symbiotic relationship with philosophy; by the mid-nineteenth century, this philosophical theology had shifted from epistemological concerns to those of ethics. Seeberg's theological thought was steeped in that tradition and Bonhoeffer was engulfed in it while a student in Berlin. When he read philosophical works in Tegel prison – Kant, Heidegger, Ortega y Gasset, Dilthey and Natorp among them – he complained that he needed to know more philosophy and achieve a fuller grasp of its diversity. His reflections, for example in the long letter to Eberhard Bethge of 9 March, 1944,[77] show his desire to comprehend more profoundly and thus understand more deeply what French historian Paul Hazard has most insightfully called *la*

---

[75] Cited in Staats, "Adolf von Harnack," 101.
[76] The use of the word "phase" is not meant to signal the existence of distinct phases such as an "early," a "middle" and a "late" one, with each representing a new start in which what had been there before is somehow superseded. I use "phase" as a way of dating Bonhoeffer's theology biographically.
[77] Cf. *LPP*, 228–233 (*DBW* 8, 351–358).

conscience européenne. Here Seeberg's advocacy of the ethical and, therefore, the communal or *polis* aspect, but also Harnack's insistence on the imperative of "purposeful action," emerge in Bonhoeffer's thinking.

From both men Bonhoeffer had learned the rigorous demands as well as the necessity and promise of *Wissenschaftlichkeit* or *Redlichkeit*, scholarly procedure with integrity, in the labor of theology, the priority of *Sachlichkeit*, objectivity over *Unredlichkeit*, subjectivity, if the latter means the elaboration of personal, emotional or irrational positions. That legacy remained with Bonhoeffer even though he brought into it more and more contextual reality as a necessary, essential dimension of theology. The ideal of theology, or science as such, to be free of aspects of its actual context and to apply its academy-created methods to its subject matter, disappears from Bonhoeffer's reflection, as I see it, from the early years of the thirties.

As I understand the meaning of "influence," it is Harnack to whom Bonhoeffer looked as a scholar *and* as a human being in seeking his own way of being human in his context. As Seeberg waned in and, by 1933, disappeared from Bonhoeffer's personal and intellectual horizon, Harnack actually deepened there as the brutalization of the Nazis misshaped the image of what it means to be a human being, a German, a Christian, someone of culture and civilization. When Bonhoeffer focused on writing his *Ethics* it is, in my judgment, not because he had learned from Seeberg the essential necessity of the active, voluntaristic dimension of what comprises viable philosophy-theology but because he had experienced concretely that genuine life, genuine humanness is lost without sociality. The very essence of sociality was under attack in the Third Reich. "The church is the church only when it exists for others," he wrote in Tegel prison.[78] And the "others" had by then a specific reference: it was "the excluded, the suspects, the maltreated, the powerless, the oppressed, the despised, in short ... those who suffer," as he wrote in his *After Ten Years* early in 1943.[79] Each of those terms brought to his mind names and addresses of real human beings, alive or by then killed by the Nazis. It is questionable whether Harnack would have put the issue like that in his liberal-Protestant mind; what in my view is not questionable is that he affirmed and lived a tradition of values that would have put the matter just like that had he been in the context in which Bonhoeffer was when he wrote that. Here is the echo of the values, of the legacy to which Bonhoeffer makes reference in his letters to his parents.

Bonhoeffer's *Fiction from Tegel Prison* illustrates that the legacy he depicts there, and then seeks to formulate in his explorations of what "doing

---

[78] *LPP*, 382 (*DBW* 8, 560).
[79] *LPP*, 17; translation slightly altered (*DBW* 8, 38).

justice" means, is the value-tradition of the bourgeoisie to which he belonged. It has been described by some as "national-conservative;"[80] Bonhoeffer himself uses the terms "Prussian" and "Protestant."[81] "The question is not whether Bonhoeffer was conservative but how conservative he was."[82] This is a helpful insight. I see Bonhoeffer's participation in the resistance against Hitler nurtured also by something readily ascribable to Harnack, namely that he was a decent human being. He was "Prussian-Protestant" and in his ethical-political life a national-conservative. And he was an elitist.[83] But it was in the context of his personal, political and intellectual elitist position that he manifested the values that mark "the decent human being."

I draw on Hans von Dohnanyi for the meaning of "decent human being." In a letter to his wife shortly before he too was murdered by the Nazis, he wrote, "Dietrich and I did not do what we did [in the resistance] as political beings [*Politiker*]. It was quite simply what a decent human being would inevitably do."[84] That describes precisely also the impulse for Harnack's son Ernst to oppose the horrid dehumanization that was the Nazis' pervasive praxis.

When Bonhoeffer writes to Bethge that he wants to take up the questions of liberal theology, including those Harnack raised and sought to answer, his intent is clearly to meet a central concern of liberal theology but also to go beyond it. Here we see the *Harnackschüler*, the person influenced by his teacher and how he drew on that very influence to respond to a contextual reality that liberal theology, embedded in a national-conservatism, could not adequately address. I draw here on the insightful assessment offered by Sabine Dramm in the book already mentioned. "On the broad scale between elitist and egalitarian thought, Bonhoeffer would have to be located in relation to his politics more appropriately at the elitist and in relation to his theology more at the egalitarian end of the scale. In many respects he was then already more 'progressive' in the best sense of the word in theological and church-policy questions than in those of politics. In other words: his theological being was ahead of his political con-

---

[80] In her recent book *V-Mann Gottes und der Abwehr? Dietrich Bonhoeffer und der Widerstand* (Gütersloh 2005), 237–238, note 12, Sabine Dramm cites Ekkehard Klausa, *Politischer Konservatismus und Widerstand*, Peter Steinbach and Johannes Tuchel (eds.), *Widerstand gegen den Nationalismus* (Bonn 1994) and Klemens von Klemperer, *Die verlassenen Verschwörer. Der deutsche Widerstand auf der Suche nach Verbündeten 1938–1945* (Berlin 1994), as sources for that assessment.

[81] *LPP*, 193 (*DBW* 8, 291).

[82] Dramm, *V-Mann Gottes und der Abwehr?*, 238.

[83] Cf. "Introduction. Harnack's Liberalism in Theology: A Struggle for the Freedom of Theology," in Rumscheidt (ed), *Adolf von Harnack. Liberal Theology at its Height*, 9–41.

[84] Cited in Dramm, *V-Mann Gottes und der Abwehr?*, 241.

sciousness."[85] When I concur in this assessment, I mean to affirm that precisely this "national-conservative, Prussian-Protestant" position allowed a theological-ethical consciousness to emerge within the context of the Nazi era that embraced the inherited value-tradition Bonhoeffer treasured and enabled it to move into a sociality that went beyond the theology Harnack and Seeberg presented each in their own distinct way.

Sabine Dramm puts this point as follows, showing how a Christian faith attentive to liberal Protestantism but moving with it beyond it looked, at least in Bonhoeffer's understanding and existence. "Bonhoeffer was a pioneer of hope. To live with hope – and with guilt is what could be learned from [him]. His understanding of Christian faith could lead to an ethical liberation that enabled action. It was patently his concern to free peoples' conscience for that. The uniqueness of Bonhoeffer's liberating acceptance and admission of guilt lay in its readiness to live with the dilemma that non-action meant guilt and that action meant guilt, that acting in a certain way meant *consciously* taking guilt upon oneself and yet being able to live before God in the knowledge of that guilt. He knew whereof he spoke. Knowing of the assassination plans and participating himself in the conspiracy he consciously accepted guilt. We make ourselves guilty but we must do so and we can live with that guilt before God. ... In this liberation for guilt lies the *proprium* of Bonhoeffer,"[86] his unique contribution to living in a world come-of-age beyond the limitations of the theology of Harnack's liberal Protestantism.

The questions every theology raises are contextual as are the answers given by it. In the final analysis there really are no perennially valid truths. Yet it is precisely those questions and answers that portray values to be held on to, to advance or to reject that enrich the legacy given to every new generation. And that is the locus where one discerns how forebears, teachers and mentors are "influences" or "intellectual resources" like Adolf von Harnack and Reinhold Seeberg for Bonhoeffer or, for that matter, for us.

---

[85] Dramm, *V-Mann Gottes und der Abwehr?*, 238.
[86] Dramm, *V-Mann Gottes und der Abwehr?*, 242–243.

Peter Frick

Rudolf Bultmann, Paul Tillich and Dietrich Bonhoeffer[*]

I. Introduction

The year 1924 at the University of Marburg was historically unique in that three thinkers who shaped Bonhoeffer's theology in substantial ways all taught in the same university for that short period: Rudolf Bultmann (1884–1976) came to Marburg to the faculty of theology in 1921 and stayed there for the rest of his life, Paul Tillich (1886–1965) was appointed to teach systematic theology and philosophy in 1924 and Martin Heidegger (1889–1976) was appointed to the faculty of philosophy between 1923 and 1928. In this study we will focus on the first two thinkers.[1] The main questions we will examine are the extent to which Bonhoeffer's thought betrays the theological contours of Bultmann and Tillich as found in his written legacy and why Bonhoeffer engaged these two theologians in his own theological construction. In other words, our objective is to ascertain the theological significance of Bultmann and Tillich in Bonhoeffer's theology.

II. Rudolf Bultmann

1. Bultmann's Thought in Bonhoeffer's Writings

In order to be in a position to assess Bultmann's influence on Bonhoeffer we will present a succinct review of how the latter incorporates and interprets the work of the former in his writings. In his doctoral dissertation,

---

[*] I wish to acknowledge the financial support for this research from the Social Sciences and Humanities Research Council of Canada.

[1] For Heidegger's influence on Bonhoeffer's thought, see below Stephen Plant's study in this volume. On Heidegger's influence on Bultmann, see the illuminating study by Hans-Georg Gadamer, "Martin Heidegger und die Marburger Theologie" in Erich Dinkler (ed.), *Zeit und Geschichte. Dankesgabe an Rudolf Bultmann zum 80. Geburtstag* (Tübingen 1964), 479–490. On Heidegger's relation to theology, see John Caputo, "Heidegger and Theology," in *CCH*, 326–344.

Sanctorum Communio, the young Bonhoeffer argued that Christian love "loves the real neighbor."[2] In a discussion that was later deleted from the published version of the dissertation but included as a footnote in the recent volume of the *Dietrich Bonhoeffer Works*, Bonhoeffer argues against Karl Barth's interpretation of the love commandment. He protests: "Who gives Barth the right to say that the other is 'as such infinitely unimportant' when God command us to love precisely that person? God has made the 'neighbor as such' infinitely important, and there isn't any other 'neighbor as such' for us."[3] Then Bonhoeffer draws on Bultmann'a recent book, simply entitled *Jesus* (published in 1926).[4] Bonhoeffer cites Bultmann to refute Barth and to strengthen his own understanding of Jesus' commandment to love one's neighbour. To this end, he approvingly cites Bultmann: "Whatever of kindness, pity, mercy I show my neighbor is not something that I do for God ...; the neighbor is not a sort of tool, by means of which I practice the love of God ... As I can love my neighbor only when I surrender my will completely to God's will, so I can love God only while I will what [God] wills, while I really love my neighbor."[5]

In his *Habilitation*, entitled *Act and Being*, completed in 1930 and published in 1931, Bonhoeffer refers among many others to Bultmann[6] as one of those thinkers who in "the most recent developments in theology ... attempt to come to an agreement about the problem of act and being,"[7] the very problem Bonhoeffer himself made the focus of his study. It is therefore not surprising that Bultmann's writings become a critical point of ref-

---

[2] *DBWE* 1, 169 (*DBW* 1, 109).

[3] *DBWE* 1, 170 note 28 (*DBW* 1, 110 note 28).

[4] For a concise introduction to the life and work of Bultmann see Walter Schmithals, "Rudolf Bultmann," in *TRE* 7, 387–396.

[5] *DBWE* 1, 170, note 28 (*DBW* 1, 111 note 28). The young Bonhoeffer also lists Bultmann's *Jesus* in the list of works he consulted in preparation for the sermon he submitted as part of his first theological examination in 1927; cf. *DBWE* 9, 180 (*DBW* 9, 180). During the same period, Bonhoeffer also refers to Bultmann's essay "Die Bedeutung der neuerschlossenen mandäischen und manichäischen Quellen für das Verständnis des Johannesevangeliums," in: *Zeitschrift für die neutestamentliche Wissenschaft* 24 (1925), 100–146. In a study of John and Paul, Bonhoeffer rejects the Mandean parallel (regarding the question of the meaning of the vine in John 15) Bultmann had suggested in his exegesis of that passage (cf. *DBWE* 9, 395 (*DBW* 9, 441–442)).

[6] Bonhoeffer employed the following studies of Bultmann in his *Act and Being*: "What does it Mean to Speak of God" (1925), in Rudolf Bultmann, *Faith and Understanding*, volume 1, edited by Robert W. Funk (London 1969), 53–65; "The Question of Dialectic Theology: A Discussion with Peterson" (1926), in James M. Robinson (ed.), *The Beginnings of Dialectic Theology* (Richmond 1968), 257–274; "On the Question of Christology" (1927), in *Faith and Understanding*, 116–144; " "The Significance of 'Dialectical Theology' for the Scientific Study of the New Testament" (1928), in *Faith and Understanding*, 145–164 and "The Historicity of Man and Faith" (1930), in: Rudolf Bultmann, *Existence and Faith*, edited by Schubert M. Odgen (Cleveland/New York 1960), 92–110.

[7] *DBWE* 2, 25 (*DBW* 2, 21).

erence for the development of Bonhoeffer's own positions in *Act and Being*.

Bonhoeffer's first major debate with Bultmann's theology centers on the question of the relation, on the one hand, between philosophy and theology, and, on the other hand, between philosophy/theology and revelation. In a long note,[8] Bonhoeffer briefly describes Bultmanns's understanding of that relation in these terms: According to Bultmann "the task of philosophy [is] to examine phenomenologically those structures of Dasein which represent the existential-ontological possibilities (as distinct from ontic ones, of course) for believing and unbelieving Dasein ... The theme of philosophy is existentiality [*Existenzialität*], whereas the theme of theology is concrete (believing) existence [*Existenz*]."[9] Bonhoeffer continues by saying that Bultmann's line of thinking is also evident in his understanding of revelation when he asserts that "believers can state no more accurately or completely than unbelievers what revelation is."[10] Believers only know that revelation touched them, that they found grace and that they are forgiven. Hence, for Bultmann, notes Bonhoeffer, "the event-character [*Ereignischarakter*] of revelation and the event-character of faith can be thought of within the existential-ontological possibilities of Dasein."[11] Bonhoeffer sees the assumptions for Bultmann's thought rooted in the latter's unexplained assertion that "believing Dasein is still Dasein, in every instance."[12]

Precisely here, however, Bonhoeffer detects "the roots of the unbounded claim of philosophy ... [for] it must be asked whether one can assert this [unity of Dasein], even only of its existential-ontological possibilities, apart from revelation without making revelation impossible. If the answer is 'yes,' then believers do in fact know nothing 'more' about revelation than unbelievers."[13] Not surprisingly, Bonhoeffer rejects this position. For him, "the letting go of the ontic by retreat into the ontological [unity of Dasein] is considered futile by revelation. In the *existentiell* event of revelation, the *existential* structure of Dasein is touched and changed. There is no second mediator, not even the existential structure of Dasein. For reve-

---

[8] The editor of *DBW* 2 correctly surmises that Bonhoeffer may have added the note after he had the manuscript of *Act and Being* already finished. On the one hand, the note is excessively long and of such an importance that it belongs in the main body of the text, and on the other hand, some of the literature Bonhoeffer refers to appeared most likely after he had completed the manuscript.

[9] *DBWE* 2, 77, note 89 (*DBW* 2, 71, note 89). Bonhoeffer refers to Bultmann's "The Historicity of Man and Faith."

[10] *DBWE* 2, 77, note 89 (*DBW* 2, 72, note 89).

[11] *DBWE* 2, 77, note 89 (*DBW* 2, 72, note 89).

[12] *DBWE* 2, 78, note 89 (*DBW* 2, 72, note 89). Cf. Bultmann, "The Historicity of Man and Faith," 94.

[13] *DBWE* 2, 78, note 89 (*DBW* 2, 72, note 89).

lation, the ontic-existentiell and ontological-existential structures coincide."[14]

In the following chapter in *Act and Being*, in the section entitled *Knowledge of Revelation*, Bonhoeffer refers to Bultmann's view that "talk of God is possible 'only as talk of ourselves,' since 'to apprehend our existence' would mean 'to apprehend God'."[15] This view sits uneasy with Bonhoeffer for whom talking of God enables a person to talk of oneself. Put otherwise, Bultmann's statement seems to ignore "the fact that faith can be directed solely and exclusively to God."[16] A few pages further in Bonhoeffer's study, we find what may well be one of the most important theological engagements between Bonhoeffer and Bultmann. About half through his work, Bonhoeffer draws a grand conclusion: He explains: "For human beings, to exist means to stand, act, and decide under God's claim. Existence is in pure actuality. Consequently, self-understanding is given only in the act itself. There are no concepts of existence prior to existence. The existence of human beings is either in sin or in grace. Through revelation there is only sinful or pardoned existence, without potentiality."[17] The crux of Bonhoeffer's argument is that he wants to safeguard any attempt – theological or philosophical – to arrive at an understanding of human existence apart from revelation. In this regard, he sees Bultmann's attempt to explain human existence along Heideggerian lines leaning in just that false direction. In Bonhoeffer's own words, "the danger of a concept of existence derived apart from revelation lurks in Bultmann's attempt to interpret the insecurities of Dasein in the sense of 'always-being-already-guilty', on the basis of its historicity."[18] Why Bonhoeffer is so insistent in linking revelation and human existence, we will discuss below.

While Bonhoeffer worked on *Act and Being*, he also produced several other studies. In his essay, "Die Frage nach dem Menschen," Bonhoeffer remarks that a person's self-understanding is always dependent on the word of God that comes from the outside – namely by revelation – and constitutes an absolute limit. Bultmann, Bonhoeffer claims, uses Heideg-

---

[14] *DBWE* 2, 78, note 89 (*DBW* 2, 72, note 89); emphasis added. A little further into his study, Bonhoeffer refers once more to Bultmann. In a note he compares the understanding of Barth and Bultmann respectively and seems to agree with the latter, which he defines in these terms: "'Dialectical' does not mean so much 'determined by the opposite' as determined by historical reality, by the concrete question of the context and by God's answer;" cf. *DBWE* 2, 85, note 9 (*DBW* 2, 79, note 9) and Bonhoeffer's reference to Bultmann's study "The Significance of 'Dialectical Theology' for the Scientific Study of the New Testament," 163–164. See also Christiane Tietz-Steiding, *Bonhoeffers Kritik der verkrümmten Vernunft*, Beiträge zur historischen Theologie 112 (Tübingen 1999), 181–183.
[15] *DBWE* 2, 95 (*DBW* 2, 90).
[16] *DBWE* 2, 95 (*DBW* 2, 90).
[17] *DBWE* 2, 97 (*DBW* 2, 92).
[18] *DBWE* 2, 97 (*DBW* 2, 92).

ger's philosophy to show that a person has "the possibility of being" [*sein Sein ist Sein-können*], either in sin or in God. But since for Bonhoeffer revelation is the limit of human self-knowledge it is only a logical consequence for him to ban the concept of possibility from theology. In his own words: "The concept of potentiality has no right in theology and hence in theological anthropology."[19] In a seminar on theological psychology that Bonhoeffer held during the winter semester 1931–1933 at the University of Berlin, he makes a brief mention of Bultmann. He explains that in Barth' theology the I breaks apart into an old and a new I at the expense of a unified I [*Gesamt-Ich*]. The same split is the case in Bultmann's thought, but the continuity of the new I comes at the expense of the new I even though Bultmann is concerned with the *Gesamt-Ich*.[20]

Bultmann's theology has no discernible influence in Bonhoeffer's classic works *Discipleship* and *Life Together*, except that he apparently consulted Bultmann's study "Das christliche Gebot der Nächstenliebe" while he was preparing the manuscript for *Life Together*.[21]

In his *Ethics*, Bonhoeffer refers to Bultmann on several occasions. In Bonhoeffer's second version of the section entitled *History and the Good*, he discusses what it means to say that Christ is life and cites Bultmann's commentary on John. Bonhoeffer quotes Bultmann's translation of John 1:4a "What has come into being – in it he was life."[22] In the next paragraph, Bonhoffer says in typical fashion that "Christ is the life that we cannot give ourselves, but which comes to us completely from the outside, completely from beyond ourselves ... This new life is not present other than hidden under the mark of death." The expression that life is under "the mark of death" is taken straight from Bultmann's commentary on John 11:26[23] which, in turn, is probably an allusion to Heidegger's philosophy.

During the years of Bonhoeffer's involvement in the conspiracy, there are several important letters in which Bonhoeffer defends Bultmann. In a letter of March 1942 to Ernst Wolf, the editor of the journals *Evangelische Theologie* and *Verkündigung und Forschung*, Bonhoeffer relates the fol-

---

[19] *DBW* 10, 373. In Bonhoeffer's words: "*Der Begriff der Möglichkeit hat in der Theologie und damit in der theologischen Anthropologie kein Recht*" (emphasis in original).

[20] *DBW* 12, 186. Also in the early 1930s Bonhoeffer encouraged his American friend Paul Lehman, who planned a study tour to Europe, to study either with Barth or Bultmann; cf. *DBW* 17, 107, 112 and 136.

[21] Cf. *DBWE* 5, 186 (*DBW* 5, 177).

[22] *DBWE* 6, 250, note 13 (*DBW* 6, 249, note 12); cf. Rudolf Bultmann, *The Gospel of John. A Commentary* (Philadelphia 1971), 39. Bonhoeffer's citation is not entirely accurate as Bultmann's original translation ("Was da geworden ist, – in dem war er (der Logos) das Leben") is more precise in specifying the role of the Logos.

[23] Cf. *DBWE* 6, 251 (*DBW* 6, 250) and Bultmann, *The Gospel of John*, 404.

lowing: "I take great pleasure in the new Bultmann volume.[24] The intellectual honesty of his work never ceases to impress me. Apparently Dilschneider recently disparaged you and Bultmann quite stupidly here at a Berlin pastors' meeting; and, as I was told, the meeting came within a hair's breadth of sending you a protest against Bultmann's theology! And from Berliners, of all people! I would like to know if any of them has actually worked through the commentary on John. This arrogance, which flourishes here – under the influence of several blowhards, I think – is a real scandal for the Confessing Church."[25] What impressed Bonhoeffer so much about Bultmann' work is made explicit in a letter he wrote in July 1942 to his Marburg friend Winfried Krause (who died in Marburg in 1943). "Now as to Bultmann," explains Bonhoeffer, "I belong to those who welcomed his writing – not because I agree with it. I regret the twofold approach it takes (the argument deriving from John 1:14 and from the radio should not be mixed together; I do consider even the latter to be a valid argument, but the distinction should be clearer) – in this regard perhaps I have remained Harnack's student to this day. To put it bluntly: Bultmann has let the cat out of the bag, not only for himself but for a great many people (the liberal cat out of the confessional bag), and in this I rejoice. He has dared to say what many repress in themselves (here I include myself) without having overcome it. He thereby has rendered a service to intellectual integrity and honesty. Many brothers oppose him with a hypocritical faith and that I find deadly.[26] Now an account must be given. I would like to speak with Bultmann about this and open myself to the fresh air that comes from him. But then the window has to be shut again. Otherwise the susceptible will too easily catch a cold. If you see Bultmann, please give

---

[24] Bonhoeffer refers to Bultmann's monograph *New Testament and Mythology*. In a letter to Karl Bart of May 1942, Bonhoeffer notes: "The most recent theological happening for us was the Bultmann volume, which gave rise to a fiery dispute between Asmussen and Wolf and beyond. Despite it all, I took great joy in the essays" (*DBWE* 16, 277 (*DBW* 16, 267)).

[25] *DBWE* 16, 260–261 (*DBW* 16, 248). Karl Barth, in a letter to Otto Solomon of May 1942, remarks that he has heard "of the repercussions of the most recent Bultmann furor." Then he laments: "Oh, if only our dear friends in the Confessing Church would leave all that and would finally begin to rack their brains, five minutes before midnight, whether there is anything, anything, they could do to deal with the inexorable coming disaster! The demythologized New Testament is truly only the dotting of an I, that is, in comparison with all that the Germans have done and daily continue to do in the occupied regions, stirring up a cloud of wrath. But I am afraid that all their eyes are still closed and behind them they are only dreaming, dreaming" (*DBWE* 16, 275 (*DBW* 16, 265)).

[26] In another letter to Ernst Wolf in September 1942 Bonhoeffer protests: "As I hear from Marburg, the Council of Brethren there is presently in the midst of deciding about the expulsion of Bultmann from the Confessing Church! These theological hypocrites, so works-righteous! Were it actually to come to expulsion ... I think I would have to have myself expelled as well, not because I agree with Bultmann, but because I consider the others' attitude by far more dangerous than Bultmann's" (*DBWE* 16, 359 (*DBW* 16, 358)).

him my greetings ... Tell him that I would like to see him, and how I see these things."[27]

As is well-known, during his imprisonment in Berlin, Bonhoffer wrote several letters to his friend and biographer Eberhard Bethge in which he dared to share some of the fresh thoughts he had gained in his theological reflections. In a letter dated 5 May 1944, Bonhoeffer returns to a topic he had written about in earlier letters: "A few more words about 'religionlessness.' I expect you remember Bultmann's essay on the 'demythologizing' of the New Testament? My view of it today would be, not that he went 'too far,' as most people thought, but that he didn't go far enough. It's not only the 'mythological' concepts, such as miracle, ascension, and so on (which are not in principle separable from the concepts of God, faith, etc.), but 'religious' concepts generally, which are problematic. You can't, as Bultmann supposes, separate God and miracle, but you must be able to interpret and proclaim *both* in a 'nonreligious' sense. Bultmann's approach is fundamentally still a liberal one (i.e., abridging the gospel), whereas I'm trying to think theologically."[28] Bonhoeffer was exceedingly anxious to hear Bethge's reaction to his thoughts expressed on Bultmann. In a subsequent letter he wonders whether Bethge did indeed receive, as he himself called it, his "Bultmann letter" of 5 May. But Bethge did not, not even a month later; he eventually received it on 26 June 1944.[29] In the meantime, however, on 8 June 1944, Bonhoeffer wrote another long letter in the course of which he discusses Barth, Tillich and Bultmann as some length. About Bultmann he says this: "Bultmann seems to have somehow felt Barth's limitations, but he misconstrues them in the sense of liberal theology, and so goes off into the typical liberal process of reduction – the 'mythological' elements of Christianity are dropped, and Christianity is reduced to its 'essence'. – My view is that full content, including the 'mythological' concepts, must be kept – the New Testament is not a mythological clothing of a universal truth; this mythology (resurrection etc.) is the thing itself – but concepts must be interpreted in such a way as not to make religion a precondition of faith ... Only in this way, I think, will liberal theology be overcome ... and at the same time its question be genuinely taken up and answered ... Thus the world's coming of age is no longer an occasion for polemics and apologetics, but is now really better understood

---

[27] *DBWE* 16, 347 (*DBW* 16, 344–345).

[28] *LPP*, 285 (*DBW* 8, 414). The reference is to Rudolf Bultmann, "Neues Testament und Mythologie. Das Problem der Entmythologisierung der neutestamentlichen Verkündigung," in idem., *Offenbarung und Heilsgeschichte* (Munich 1941), 27–69.

[29] On Bonhoeffer's eagerness to know about the fate of the letter, cf. *LPP*, 315, 316, 324, 329, 339 (*DBW* 8, 460, 461, 474, 483, 497).

than it understands itself, namely on the basis of the gospel and in light of Jesus Christ."[30]

2. Bultmann's Influence on Bonhoeffer's Theology

As we noted above, Bonhoeffer was extremely impressed with Bultmann's courage and intellectual honesty in articulating crucial issues for contemporary German theology. Indeed, Bonhoeffer saw a good deal of intellectual sincerity and personal integrity in Bultmann's attempt to work out a theology that attempted to do full justice to both human existence and the divine answer to the dilemmas of that existence. At the risk of oversimplifying a complex matter, I propose that Bonhoeffer's dialogue with Bultmann's theology focussed on primarily two broad issues. On the one hand, it is the question to what extent Bultmann's program of demythologizing the Bible may have shaped Bonhoeffer's own theses regarding "religionless Christianity," and on the other hand, it is the issue of how a person may attain a theologically adequate and proper self-understanding.[31] We shall briefly sketch out both of these complex issues.

Clifford Green notes quite correctly that "in some quarters Bonhoeffer's project [of a religionless Christianity in a world come of age as articulated in the letters from prison] was seen as parallel to Rudolf Bultmann's demythologizing proposal"[32] while Hans-Richard Reuter, the editor of *DBW* 2, maintains that "the systematic affinity of Bonhoeffer to Rudolf Bultmann's theological thought – which in *Act and Being* is hard to deny – has not as a rule had much exposure."[33] In other words, the question before us is whether Bultmann's notion of demythologizing the biblical narratives is the backbone for Bonhoeffer's conceptualization of a "religionless Christianity?" This question, to be sure, defies an easy answer. No doubt, there are "paral-

---

[30] *LPP* 328–329 (*DBW* 8, 482).

[31] Cf. Tietz-Steiding, *Bonhoeffers Kritik der verkrümmten Vernunft*, 191: "Was Bonhoeffer mit seiner Kritik an Bultmann abwehren will, dürfte klar sein. Philosophie ist nicht in der Lage, dem Menschen ein theologisch angemessenes Selbstverständnis zu ermöglichen."

[32] *DBWE* 6, 2; cf. also *DBWE* 6, 435 (*DBW* 6, 441). One of the first scholars to articulate the parallel between Bultmann and Bonhoeffer was Gerhard Ebeling, "Die 'nicht-religiöse Interpretation biblischer Begriffe'," in idem., *Wort und Glaube* (Tübingen, third edition, 1967), 90-160. It is, moreover, interesting to note that Bonhoeffer's cousin, Hans-Christoph von Hase, in a letter to addressed to Bonhoeffer when he was at Union Theological Seminary, says that he himself was thinking of the recent developments in theology and was tempting to place *Bonhoeffer together with Bultmann* behind Ritschl (cf. *DBW* 11, 208; emphasis added). At any rate, his cousin clearly understood the affinities between Bonhoeffer and Bultmann. For an excellent recent discussion of Bonhoeffer's notion of "religionless Christianity," see Clifford J. Green, *Bonhoeffer. A Theology of Sociality* (Grand Rapids/Cambridge, second edition, 1999), 269–282.

[33] *DBWE* 2, 170 (*DBW* 2, 172).

lels" and "affinities" between Bultmann and Bonhoeffer; nonetheless, I am inclined to think that the differences between their theological conceptions warrant the conclusion that their proposals are sufficiently nuanced, unique and independent.[34]

Bonhoeffer agreed with Bultmann that the unscientific worldview of the Bible presents a problem for a modern, enlightened, technologically oriented person. In short, the biblical worldview is a problem in that it requires of the modern person a *sacrificius intellectus*. Bonhoeffer similarly understood that the *mündige* person can no longer simply believe as if science and biblical scholarship did not exist. For example, in his interpretation of creation in Genesis 1:6–10, Bonhoeffer boldly asserts: "Here the ancient image of the world confronts us in all its scientific naïvité. To us today its ideas appear altogether absurd."[35] Both Bonhoeffer and Bultmann agree that to a person who is wholly and completely entrenched in all of life, with body and mind, the current scientific worldview has made religion problematic.

In spite of this agreement in terms of the unscientific, mythological worldview of the biblical texts, their respective proposals are distinct, at least methodologically and in terms of their ultimate objectives. Bultmann's program of demythologizing is essentially a hermeneutical and existential attempt to remove the unscientific stumbling block of the kerygma so that the modern person can hear it anew and accept it by means of a clear decision and with faith. For Bonhoeffer, however, Bultmann's proposal remained essentially a liberal one.[36] Bonhoeffer's musings on "religionless Christianity," while not entirely void of hermeneutical elements, have as the main objective precisely the overcoming of the kind of liberal "reductionism"[37] espoused by Bultmann. There is really no term that fittingly expresses the type of theology Bonhoeffer was envisioning; the kind of theology he began to construct, at least in its fragmentary conception in his letters from prison,[38] had not yet been articulated, not even by himself. To some extent Bonhoeffer's theological vision was liberal, existential,

---

[34] Contra Gerhard Krause, "Dietrich Bonhoeffer und Rudolf Bultmann," in Erich Dinkler (ed.), *Zeit und Geschichte*., 439–460, who seems to press the evidence of the sources too much in terms of possible affinities and agreements between Bultmann and Bonhoeffer.

[35] *DBWE* 3, 50 (*DBW* 3, 47).

[36] Cf. *LPP*, 285 (*DBW* 8, 414).

[37] Cf. Gerhard Ebeling, "Die 'nicht-religiöse Interpretation biblischer Begriffe'," 135, who argues that Bonhoeffer is mistaken in characterizing Bultmann's program of demythologizing as a liberal reductionism. Bultmann himself was interested, as Bonhoeffer, in *interpreting* mythological concepts in the biblical narratives rather than merely eliminating them.

[38] I agree with the critique of Karl Barth when he cautions against taking the isolated sayings on "religionless Christianity" in the prison correspondence as the cornerstone for much of Bonhoeffer's theology. For the details of the discussion, cf. Gerhard Krause, "Dietrich Bonhoeffer und Rudolf Bultmann," 447.

ontological, biblical, systematic etc. and yet, paradoxically, it was neither eclectic nor uncritical.[39] Only one thing was sure: it was a theology that had a Christocentric focus and aimed at nothing less than life in its fullness. Bonhoeffer's construction of theology – in distinction to Bultmann, Tillich and Barth – was fundamentally rooted in the desire to articulate a theology of life that was unshakably anchored in the perennial question "Who is Christ for us today?" In that sense, as Bethge comments, "Bonhoeffer's Christological 'reality' stands against Bultmann's anthropological 'potentiality'."[40] Bonhoeffer's was a theology that took seriously human existence and literally the "mythological" account of Christ's resurrection. Bonhoeffer is clear on that point: "My view is that full content, including the 'mythological' concepts, must be kept – the New Testament is not a mythological clothing of a universal truth; this mythology (resurrection etc.) is the thing itself – but concepts must be interpreted in such a way as not to make religion a precondition of faith."[41]

The issue at stake between a religionless interpretation of Christianity and the program of demythologizing the biblical world view is still most aptly illuminated by Bethge. His comments are worth to be cited it at length. Bethge assumes that Bonhoeffer's "non-religious interpretation speaks of a dimension different from Bultmann's existential interpretation" and then explains: "Bultmann, the professor in the lecture-room, gives an account of the process of interpretation ... and builds up a systematic epistemology of it. Bonhoeffer thinks about the God-forsaken world. Bultmann's problem is that of faith and understanding. This problem is not to be found in Bonhoeffer's letters ... The hindrance with Bonhoeffer is not just misunderstanding, but God's absence and hiddenness."[42]

Put differently, Bonhoeffer's religionless interpretation aims at a theological reconception that claims a person's entire life[43] in the very encoun-

---

[39] Cf. Götz Harbsmeier, "Die 'nicht-religiöse Interpretation biblischer Begriffe' bei Bonhoeffer und die Entmythologisierung." in Ernst Wolf, Charlotte von Kirschbaum, Rudolf Frey (eds.), *Antwort*. Karl Barth zum Siebzigsten Geburtstag am 10. Mai 1956 (Zurich 1956), 544–561. Harbsmeier notes that "weder im positiven noch im negativen Sinne darf der Bonhoefferische Gedankengang als Beitrag zu einer existentialen-theologischen Hermeneutik genommen werden ... Bonhoeffer steht ganz außerhalb einer derartigen Grundkonzeption der Hermeneutik. Er macht jedenfalls die für Bultmann so grundlegende Unterscheidung von existential und existentiell, ontologisch und ontisch nicht zum Fundament aller weiteren Erwägungen" (546).

[40] Eberhard Bethge, "The Challenge of Dietrich Bonhoeffer's Life and Theology," in *WCA*, 22–88, here 84.

[41] *LPP* 329 (*DBW* 8, 482).

[42] Eberhard Bethge, "The Challenge of Dietrich Bonhoeffer's Life and Theology," 84.

[43] Cf. Green, *Bonhoeffer. A Theology of Sociality*, who notes that in his interpretation of biblical concepts Bonhoeffer "is clearly after something more than conceptual alteration; he is, as stated before, trying to describe a new *psychic posture* which affects a person's whole life" (269).

ter with Jesus Christ. "Religionless Christianity," then, seems to suggest that there is no religious, cultural, intellectual or any other precondition that makes a person *a priori* open to matters of the Christian faith in a modern context. The transforming and life-changing encounter with Christ himself is the "thing as such," but its character is not religious, experiential but personal-Christological.[44] But how is such an encounter possible, how can it be explicated in theological stringent terms? For an answer, let us turn to our second question, namely how a person can attain a theologically proper self-understanding.

As we saw, Bonhoeffer discusses Bultmann very substantially in *Act and Being*. One of the most pressing questions for Bonhoeffer was the issue of how a person can come to have proper self-knowledge and knowledge of God. In a nutshell, Bonhoeffer rejects what he understands to be Bultmann's position, namely, that a person has the ontological-existential possibility to arrive at a proper understanding of self based on a (Heideggerian) analysis of self and (almost) apart from revelation.[45] Decisive for this complex discourse are the concepts of "possibility"[46] or "potentiality" and "revelation." In Bonhoeffer's own words: "The concept of possibility ... is clearly suggested to Bultmann by Heidegger's existential-ontological analysis of Dasein as the possibility of ontic existence.[47] Consequently, it includes the possibility of an ontological[48] understanding of Dasein unaffected by revelation. But, seen from the position of revelation, 'to be possible' in relation to sin or grace (whether *existential* or *existentiell*) always means to be already really in one or the other."[49]

Why Bonhoeffer rejects the notion of "possibility" so radically is most evident in his view of the ontological status of a person's being either in Adam or in Christ. "Were it really a human possibility for persons themselves to know

---

[44] Cf. the comments of the editors of *DBW* 8, 652–653.

[45] Cf. *DBWE* 2, 97 (*DBW* 2, 92): "the danger of a concept of existence derived apart from revelation lurks in Bultmann's attempt to interpret the insecurities of Dasein."

[46] For a detailed discussion of Bultmann's concept of possibility, see Tietz-Steiding, *Bonhoeffers Kritik der verkrümmten Vernunft*, 184–193.

[47] See, for example, Martin Heidegger, *Being and Time*, translated by John Macquarrie and Edward Robinson (New York 1962), 183: "The kind of Being which Dasein has, as potent-iality-for-Being, lies existentially in understanding. Dasein is not something present-at-hand which possesses its competence for something by way of an extra; it is primarily Being-possible. Dasein is in every case what it can be, and in the way in which it is its possibility." For a discussion of potentiality in Heidegger and Bonhoeffer, cf. Charles Marsh, *Reclaiming Dietrich Bonhoeffer. The Promise of his Theology* (New York 1994), 120–125.

[48] On Bonhoeffer's attempt to construct a "theological ontology" in *Act and Being*, see the penetrating study by Robert P. Scharlemann, "Authenticity and Encounter: Bonhoeffer's Appropriation of Ontology," in *Theology and the Practice of Responsibility. Essays on Dietrich Bonhoeffer*, edited by Wayne W. Floyd and Charles Marsh (Valley Forge, PA. 1994), 253–265.

[49] *DBWE* 2, 96, note 24 (*DBW* 2, 92, note 24).

that they are sinners apart from revelation, neither 'being in Adam' nor 'being in Christ' would be existential designations of their being. For it would mean that human beings could place themselves into the truth, that they could somehow withdraw to a deeper being of their won, apart from their being sinners, to be regarded as a potentiality of a more profound 'possibility of being in the truth'. It would rest on being untouched by sin."[50] In other words, for Bonhoeffer there is no such thing as an ontological-existential possibility of a person's coming to understand her/himself as a sinner by means of Dasein's structural analysis. Knowledge of sin can only come by means of revelation. Here Bonhoeffer flatly rejects what he thinks Bultmann has taken from Heidegger's dictum that "Dasein is not something present-at-hand which possesses its competence for something by way of an extra; it is primarily Being-possible."[51] Heidegger's expression "the way of an extra" Bonhoeffer conceptualizes concretely as revelation. Bonhoeffer repeatedly stressed that "it is the genuine 'from outside' that gives us an understanding of Dasein, that makes it intelligible that this 'from outside' is what places us into truth."[52] Concretely – since "revelation is essentially an event of God's free activity [and] supersedes and challenges also the existential-ontological possibilities of Dasein"[53] – knowledge of sin, and consequently the forgiveness of sins and faith, is not a mere matter of philosophy but becomes a moment in the transformation of one's life. "In the existentiell event of revelation," says Bonhoeffer, "the existential structure of Dasein is *touched* and *changed*."[54]

In all fairness to Bultmann, it may have been the case that Bonhoeffer saw the gap between them as too wide. Bultmann himself seems to suggest this much in an essay written in 1963, entitled "The Idea of God and Modern Man."[55] In this study Bultmann affirms that "Christian faith speaks of a *revelation*, by which it understands God's act as an event ... which does not communicate doctrines, but concerns the existence of man and teaches him, or better, enables him to understand himself as sustained by the transcendent power of God."[56] Bultmann goes on to say that theologians like Tillich,

---

[50] *DBWE* 2, 136 (*DBW* 2, 135). Already in *Sanctorum Communio*, Bonhoeffer had rejected the Heideggerian category of "possibility" as belonging to theological discourse. Cf. *DBWE* 1, 143 (*DBW* 1, 89): If "one regarded revelation only as beginning (potentiality), and not at the same time also as completion (reality), this would take away what is decisive about the revelation of God, namely that God's word became history;" cf. also note 40, where Bultmann is mentioned. Cf. Ernst Feil, *The Theology of Dietrich Bonhoeffer*, translated by Martin Rumscheidt (Philadelphia 1985), 29–32, 37–39.
[51] Martin Heidegger, *Being and Time*, 183.
[52] *DBWE* 2, 110 (*DBW* 2, 106). In the next sentence Bonhoeffer remarks that a philosophy of the possibility of Dasein has no room for "the occurrence of revelation in the cross and resurrection in the Christian church."
[53] *DBWE* 2, 78, note 89 (*DBW* 2, 72, note 89).
[54] *DBWE* 2, 78, note 89 (*DBW* 2, 72, note 89).
[55] First published in *ZThK* 60 (1963); English translation in *WCA*, 256–273.
[56] *WCA*, 265.

Ebeling and others agree that the transcendent must be sought not beyond but in the midst of the world. Then he cites a letter from Bonhoeffer *expressis verbis*: "The 'beyond' of God is not the beyond of our cognitive faculties. The transcendence of epistemological theory has nothing to do with the transcendence of God. God is transcendent in the midst of our life."[57] Bonhoeffer himself wanted to pursue these ideas further in the book he planned in prison. Chapter Two was to examine how "the transcendental is not infinite and unattainable tasks, but the neighbour who is within reach in any given situation."[58]

II. Paul Tillich

1. Tillich's Early Theology in Bonhoeffer's Writings

Compared to Bultmann, there are not as many references to Tillich in Bonhoeffer's writngs.[59] One of the first substantive discussions of Tillich is in *Sanctorum Communio*, where Bonhoeffer discusses Tillich's work *Masse und Geist*.[60] Bonhoeffer asks himself whether there is "such a thing as a Protestant community constituted as a mass [*Massengemeinde*]"[61] similar to the Roman Catholic understanding of Christian community or church. His answer includes a reference to Tillich. "Prompted by the well-founded sense that the 'spirit' withdraws from the masses," he comments, "Tillich has attempted to uncover a direct relation between the two; he sees the holiness of the formless mass in the fact that it can be given form by the revelation of the forming absolute. But this no longer has anything to do with Christian theology. We know only that holiness of God's church-community that is bound to and formed by the word in Christ. The word is received only by personal appropriation, which is why God's church-community is impelled away from the mass. But Tillich has nevertheless pointed out something important. The church-community must be engaged with the mass; it must hear when the masses are calling for community, such as in the Youth Movement or in sports, and must not fail to proclaim its word about the *sanctorum communio* within their very midst. The basic rule, however, remains unchanged: the Christian concept of the church-

---

[57] *WCA*, 265–266 citing *LPP*, 282 (*DBW* 8, 408). In the next paragraph, Bultmann cites Bonhoeffer once more approvingly, once again an excerpt from a letter he wrote from Tegel prison: "And we cannot be honest without recognizing that we must live in the world – *etsi deus non daretur*. And this is just what we do recognize – before God! God himself drives us to that recognition;" cf. *LPP*, 360 (*DBW* 8, 533).

[58] *LPP*, 381 (*DBW* 8, 558).

[59] On the relation between Tillich and Bonhoeffer, cf. the remarks by Bethge, "The Challenge of Dietrich Bonhoeffer's Life and Theology," in *WCA*, 83.

[60] *Masse und Geist. Studien zur Philosophie der Masse* (Berlin 1922).

[61] *DBWE* 1, 239 (*DBW* 1, 163–164).

community is the criterion for evaluating the notion of the mass, and not the other way around."[62]

In *Act and Being*, Bonhoeffer discusses Tillich in the following manner: "If Paul Tillich believes that there is no possibility of distinguishing between philosophical and theological anthropology (*Religiöse Verwirklichung*, Berlin 1930, 300), one need only refer to the concept of revelation. If, from the viewpoint of revelation, theological anthropology sees human existence as essentially determined by guilt or by grace – and not merely as 'under threat in an unconditional sense' – then philosophical anthropology is able to adopt such concepts from theology only at the expense of bursting its own framework. For in doing so, philosophical anthropology turns its analysis of human existence, too, into an analysis of humanity's attempt to lay hold of itself; that is to say, it can do so only at the expense of becoming theological anthropology. This leaves the question of truth untouched. It is to be tested only in conjunction with the concept of contingency inherent in revelation."[63]

Moreover, during his inaugural lecture at the University of Berlin in July 1930, on the topic "Humanity in Contemporary Philosophy and Theology," Bonhoeffer comments again on Tillich's anthropology. The human being, Bonhoeffer asserts, is a self-questioning being by virtue of his or her essence, but in such a way that a person cannot simply discover answers to these questions in the deeper strata of the soul. A person is bound to the questionability of his or her existence. The answers to human existence, according to Bonhoeffer's review of Tillich may be conceptualized in this manner: "Paul Tillich, whose thought starts from this point, sees man characterized as a finite being by the fact that he does not come to his nature by himself, because for him there is simply no assured, unitive point from which self-understanding might be possible. Man cannot rise to be lord over the world, because everything human is on principle put in question by the ground of all being, everything finite is put in question by the infinite. Man therefore first comes at his nature where standing at his limit he experiences the incursion of the infinite ... The absolute *limit* is the incursion of the absolute itself, the absolute 'No' *is* the absolute 'Yes'. Man understands himself from his limitation."[64] Similar ideas are also discussed in Bonhoeffer's lecture on the "History of Systematic Theology."[65] Once again he mentions Tillich. "But here is the decisive difference with Tillich:

---

[62] *DBWE* 1, 239–240 (*DBW* 1, 164).
[63] *DBWE* 2, 77 (*DBW* 2, 71).
[64] *NRS*, 58 (*DBW* 10, 366).
[65] Bonhoeffer presented this lecture during the winter semester 1931–1932 at the University of Berlin. Cf. *DBW* 11, 139–213. In addition to the instance discussed above, Tillich is mentioned several times more in the same lecture within contexts that are not crucial for the development of Bonhoeffer's arguments; cf. 140, 141, 143, 187, 194, 203.

a person experiences the radical 'No' at the limit of one's existence; but the person who accepts this borderline situation [*Grenzsituation*] experiences the 'Yes.' A person has the knowledge of sin essentially also in the knowledge of grace.[66] This identity (Holl) must be blown apart as it anticipates God's gracious act as a self-empowered one. For God is also sovereign regarding a person's knowledge of sin."[67] Further in the same lecture Bonhoeffer remarks that it is possible to speak differently than Tillich of the "human being" [*Mensch*] and "transcendence."[68] Regarding the human being, Bonhoeffer characterizes Tillich's view briefly as including the newness of created life, community and a new discovery of transcendence. Transcendence, says Bonhoeffer, means for Tillich a widening of perspectives.

Other, more sporadic references in Bonhoeffer's writings to Tillich's theology occur in the following contexts. In his lecture on "The Nature of the Church" during the summer semester 1932 Bonhoeffer approvingly refers to Tillich's critique of the civilizing process [*Verbürgerlichung*] of the German church.[69] Elsewhere, in one of the letters written during his imprisonment, Bonhoeffer makes reference to the expression "Gott als Lückenbüßer." Tillich employed this essentially Nietzschean[70] expression in his work *Die religiöse Lage der Gegenwart*, a book Bonhoeffer had probably read as early as 1928 during his year in Barcelona.[71] If so, the citation of the expression gives testimony both to Bonhoeffer's good memory and the significance he attached the phrase.

More substantial is Bonhoeffer's discussion of Tillich in a long letter written from Tegel prison on 8 June 1944 and addressed to his friend Eberhard Bethge. In the course of his theological reflections, he also mentions Tillich. In Bonhoeffer's view, "Tillich set out to interpret the evolution of the world (against its will) in a religious sense – to give it its shape through religion. That was very brave of him, but the world unseated him and went on by itself; he, too, sought to understand the world better than it understood itself; but it felt that it was completely misunderstood, and re-

---

[66] According to the editors of *DBW* 11, 206, note 284, this sentence ("der Mensch hat in seiner Sündenerkenntnis wesenhaft schon die Gnadenerkenntnis") cannot be located in Tillich's works.

[67] *DBW* 11, 206 (my translation).

[68] Cf. *DBW* 11, 196.

[69] *DBW* 11, 246–247.

[70] Cf. my study on Bonhoeffer and Nietzsche in this volume, 189.

[71] Cf. *DBW* 8, 454, note 4. Fuller (*LPP*, 311) translates the words "Gott als Lückenbüßer" with the phrase "God as stop-gap." Bonhoeffer knew Tillich's work *Die religiöse Lage der Gegenwart* (Berlin 1926), reprinted in Paul Tillich, *Main Works/Hauptwerke*, vol. 5, edited by Robert P. Scharlemann (Berlin/NewYork 1988), 91. In preparation for a lecture he planned to give for his congregation in Barceleona in 1928, Bonhoeffer had requested a copy of this book from Walter Dress; cf. *DBW* 17, 88.

jected the imputation. (Of course, the world *must* be understood better than it understands itself, but not 'religiously' as the religious socialists wanted)."[72]

2. Tillich's Influence on Bonhoeffer's Theology

It is noteworthy that in retrospect Tillich remarks of Bonhoeffer's *Letters and Papers from Prison*: "In these letters Bonhoeffer dealt with the same problem that I have dealt with in all my books, namely, the problem of seeking a solution to the conflicts between the religious tradition and the modern mind."[73] Even though, any attempt to determine Paul Tillich's theological influence in Bonhoeffer's thought must reckon with the crucial datum, as Bethge reminds us, that "all Bonhoeffer knew of Tillich was what had been published before the Nazi period. It was this he had in mind when he argued for or against Tillich."[74] In other words, modern interpreters must be mindful to resist the temptation to judge that influence in terms of Tillich's post-war works, such as his *Systematic Theology*[75] and other writings.

Tillich's theology prompted for Bonhoeffer questions that were similar to those raised by Bultmann's work. In a broad sense, these were the two issues of the meaning of religion in the world and a precise conception of theological anthropology.

In one sense, Bonhoeffer applauds Tillich's objective to work out a proper relation between the Christian world as a mass [*Massengemeinde*] and the role and need of religion; but in another – and more decisive – sense, he critiques Tillich for precisely his theological attempt to do so. For in Bonhoeffer's theological reasoning, the significance of the masses

---

[72] *LPP*, 327–328 (*DBW* 8, 480).

[73] *A History of Christian Thought* (New York 1968), 359.

[74] Eberhard Bethge, *Dietrich Bonhoeffer*, 857–858. One of the puzzling questions for Bonhoeffer scholars is whether the two men ever met face to face either in Germany or at Union Theological Seminary in New York. There is evidence for a face to face meeting between the two men. In a letter (dated 7 May 1936) Bonhoeffer says that he was trying to recruit Tillich as a speaker for one of the ecumenical conferences and mentions explicitly: "Ich habe auch mit ihm in London vor zwei Wochen gesprochen" (Cf. *DBW* 14, 154). In a different letter (dated 5 December 1938) Bonhoeffer answers to Gerhard Leibholz's question, whether he knew Tillich, in these words: "Du fragst nach Tillich. Ich kenne ihn, d. h. ich lernte ihn 2 Tage bei seiner Arbeit hier kennen ... sage ihm, daß ich mich des Kirchentages bei seinen Freunden in Wannsee sehr gern erinnere" (*DBW* 15, 86). It seems that Bonhoeffer is referring to a visit of Tillich in Berlin. The term "Kirchentag" does not refer to the annual Evangelischer Kirchentag since this conference was started in 1949. Regarding Tillich's view of Bonhoeffer, we know that he thought very highly of him and wished to bring him to the United States in 1939; cf. *DBW* 15, 178.

[75] *Systematic Theology*, 3 volumes (Chicago 1951, 1957, 1963).

of people gains its shape not by "the revelation of the forming absolute" but only in the encounter of "the word of Christ."[76] Tillich's reference to "revelation" and the "forming absolute" are far too vague for Bonhoeffer and are a far cry from Christian theology. For him, the masses of people are not so much formed or shaped by a "forming absolute" but only as a church–community that is in turn constituted by the word of Christ. Here Bonhoeffer's christocentric focus to sociality is abundantly evident. It is not the case that the masses need more religion. In a strict sense, the masses do not need Christianity or even a "non-religious" form of Christianity. It is not the mass that determines what it needs *vis-à-vis* religion. Quite to the contrary, "the Christian concept of the church-community is the criterion for evaluating the notion of the mass, and not the other way around."[77] By criticizing Tillich on this point he is in a sense foreshadowing what he later penned in *Ethics* under the rubric of "Ethics as Formation." There he says plainly: "The church's concern in not religion, but the form of Christ and its taking form among a band of people."[78] In the next sentence, Bonhoeffer makes a pronouncement that seems to be tailor-made as a critique for the kind of program Tillich had in mind. "If we let ourselves stray even the least bit from this perspective," warns Bonhoeffer, "we fall unavoidably into those programs of ethical or religious world-formation from which we departed above."[79] In one of the letters from prison he says of Tillich: "Of course, the world *must* be understood better than it understands itself, but not 'religiously' as the religious socialists wanted."[80] Hence, for Bonhoeffer, it is not a religious or socialist form that the world needs, but exclusively the form of Christ.

When Bonhoeffer claims that the world needs the form of Christ there seems to be some affinity with Tillich's idea that for modern humanity God is often merely a "gap stop" or "gap-filler." In one of his early works, *Die Religiöse Lage der Gegenwart* (1926) [*The Religious Situation*], Tillich broadly analyzes the contemporary German context of science, art, politics and religion. He asserts that the church lost the battle between the claims of faith and knowledge and that science is now autonomous. On the one hand, the triumph of science brings "an end to all attempts to deduce proofs of the eternal from the finite and its forms. It made impossible the use of gaps in scientific knowledge for the sake of introducing God as gap-

---

[76] *DBWE* 1, 239–240 (*DBW* 1, 164).

[77] *DBWE* 1, 240 (*DBW* 1, 164).

[78] *DBWE* 6, 97 (*DBW* 6, 84). In the same context Bonhoeffer remarks: "The church is nothing but that piece of humanity where Christ really has taken form. It is solely the form of Christ that matters, not any form besides Christ's own... Therefore [the church's] first concern is not with the so-called religious function of human beings, but with the existence in the world of whole human beings in all their relationships."

[79] *DBWE* 6, 97 (*DBW* 6, 84).

[80] *LPP*, 327–328 (*DBW* 8, 480).

filler in the scientific description of the world. It forced the recognition that the eternal appears at a deeper level than the level of rational thought."[81] But on the other hand, the understanding of the non-scientific realm as "feeling ... led to the separation of the whole sphere of truth from religion. Religion left it alone to work out its finite realization. And religion itself was dealt with as a matter of subjective moods which could make no claims to understand or reform the world."[82] According to Tillich's theological analysis, German Protestantism thus failed in articulating a proper relation between science and faith. God was consequently reduced to a mere "gap-filler," a second rate recourse to cheap explanations of scientific phenomena. God was thus pushed to the periphery. Although Bonhoeffer does not disagree with Tillich's view of God as a "gap-filler," precisely at this point he goes beyond Tillich. If Tillich pointed to the question, Bonhoeffer attempts to give an answer. In Bonhoeffer's conception of reality there is an unshakable *cantus firmus*: "Christ is the center and power of the Bible, of the church, of theology, but also of humanity, reason, justice and culture."[83] Elsewhere he avows: "The whole reality of the world has already been drawn into and is held together in Christ. History moves only from this center and toward this center."[84] In other words, a "gap-filler" God cannot give any form to the world, neither can religion. The form of the world is Christ alone; he is the center of all reality, including science, culture and faith. The separation of science and faith surely produced a second rate concept of God and yet "the reality of Christ embraces the reality of the world in itself. The world has no reality of its own independent of God's revelation in Christ."[85] Expressed differently, a proper conception of the one reality of the world places God, in Christ, at the centre and not at the periphery of all of life.

Regarding Bonhoeffer's critique of Tillich's anthropology, he treated it in a manner that was not unlike his criticism of Bultmann's theological anthropology. The main issue is once more the question of revelation. Bonhoeffer agrees with Tillich's basic analysis of human existence in that a finite person cannot come to one's own self-understanding because "there is simply no assured, unitive point from which self-understanding might be possible."[86] But Bonhoeffer rejects Tillich's view that human self-understanding might somehow come into sharper relief when a person stands at one's limit and "experiences the incursion of the infinite ... The

---

[81] Paul Tillich, *Main Works/Hauptwerke*, vol. 5, 91. Translation is from *The Religious Situation*, translated by H. Richard Niebuhr (New York 1956), 204.
[82] *The Religious Situation*, 204–205.
[83] *DBWE* 6, 341 (*DBW* 6, 344).
[84] *DBWE* 6, 58 (*DBW* 6, 44).
[85] *DBWE* 6, 58 (*DBW* 6, 43).
[86] *NRS*, 58 (*DBW* 10, 366).

absolute *limit* is the incursion of the absolute itself, the absolute 'No' *is* the absolute 'Yes'. Man understands himself from his limitation."[87] Although Bonhoeffer may grant what Tillich views as the incursion of the absolute into human finiteness, he himself expressed these matters in a non-abstract manner. For Bonhoeffer, arguably, Tillich's language is too ambiguous in saying exactly what is meant by the incursion of the absolute. Bonhoeffer perceives Tillich's notion of "incursion" as the event of revelation and "the absolute" as God. In other words, Tillich's "incursion of the absolute" is expressed more sharply – and traditionally – by Bonhoeffer as "the revelation of God." Moreover, what Tillich terms "the absolute limit" corresponds to Bonhoeffer's notion of sin and the claim that "being in Adam" is an ontological category. Here, too, Bonhoeffer holds against Tillich what he already critiqued in Bultmann: "Were it really a human possibility for persons themselves to know that they are sinners apart from revelation, neither 'being in Adam' nor 'being in Christ' would be existential designations of their being. For it would mean that human beings could place themselves into the truth, that they could somehow withdraw to a deeper being of their own, apart from their being sinners, to be regarded as a potentiality of a more profound 'possibility of being in the truth'. It would rest on being untouched by sin."[88] Whereas in Bultmann the notion of "possibility" was the issue for Bonhoeffer, in view of Tillich's concept of the incursion of the absolute into a person's limit, Bonhoeffer sees the danger of somehow leaving a small window open that would make knowledge of one's own sinfulness possible, no matter how deficient that knowledge may be. Against these notions Bonhoeffer never wavers in postulating that human self-knowledge cannot in any way mean that a person could come to have an autonomous understanding as a sinner.[89] No existential analysis of Dasein and no incursion of the absolute into a person's limits can accomplish this. Only God himself in the revelation[90] of Jesus as the Christ can break into that reality and bring about self-knowledge that is adequate.

---

[87] *NRS*, 58 (*DBW* 10, 366).

[88] *DBWE* 2, 136 (*DBW* 2, 135).

[89] Regarding a person's knowledge of sin, Bonhoeffer invoked Luther's dictum: *sola fide credendum est nos esse peccatores* [we know by faith alone that we are sinners]; cf. *DBWE* 2, 135 (*DBW* 2, 135). Hence, even the knowledge that we are sinners cannot come to us apart from revelation.

[90] Bonhoeffer's understanding of Tillich's view of revelation begs at least the question of whether the first understood the latter correctly. For by 1930 Tillich had written two articles on the subject of revelation, namely "Die Idee der Offenbarung" (1927) in Paul Tillich, *Main Works/Hauptwerke*, volume 6, edited by Gert Hummel (Berlin/NewYork 1992), 99–106 and "Offenbarung: Religionsphilosophisch" (1930) in Paul Tillich, *Main Works/Hauptwerke*, volume 4, edited by John Clayton (Berlin/NewYork 1987), 237–242. It cannot be discerned from Bonhoeffer's writings whether he knew of these essays.

III. Conclusion

The lives of Bultmann, Tillich and Bonhoeffer were characterized by two essential common denominators. One was the historical context of a native country that was overrun – ideologically, politically, culturally, socially and religiously – by Nazi propaganda and the ensuing destruction of human lives; the other was the fact that all three were theologians deeply concerned with the contemporary situation *vis-à-vis* the question of how the biblical kerygma can become a transforming reality in lives of godless and religionless people who are either explicitly or implicitly participating in one of the twentieth century's most atrocious tyrannies. The theological and personal answers these three thinkers provided in that context took on different form, radicality and cost.

To recall Tillich's words once more, both he and Bonhoeffer were dealing with "the problem of seeking a solution to the conflicts between the religious tradition and the modern mind."[91] Even though Bonhoeffer took both Bultmann and Tillich very seriously as theological and philosophical thinkers, in the end he judged their theological programs as not entirely convincing, or at least as not going far enough. As we saw, the crux of the difference between himself and their theologies lies in the estimation of the role of revelation in a person's self-understanding. Bonhoeffer believed that his own theological attempt to work out a "genuine ontology"[92] went beyond both Bultmann and Tillich. A true ontology, Bonhoeffer argued extensively in *Act and Being*, cannot be conceived of apart from revelation. For revelation alone is the guarantor of the continuity between the old and new "I," the old "I" trapped in the ontological category of "being in Adam" and the new "I" transformed into the new ontological category of "being in Christ."

---

[91] Tillich, *A History of Christian Thought*, 359.
[92] Cf. *DBWE* 2, 109–109 (*DBW* 2, 105).

Andreas Pangritz

Dietrich Bonhoeffer:
"Within, not Outside, the Barthian Movement"

There can be no doubt that among Dietrich Bonhoeffer's contemporaries Karl Barth was the theologian of highest importance for him, although Bonhoeffer never had studied with Barth. Trained in the tradition of liberal theology Bonhoeffer experienced the encounter with the new approach of Barth's dialectical theology as a "liberation."[1] During his stay at Union Theological Seminary in New York in 1930–31 he was perceived as a "disciple" of Barth, although at that time he had a reading knowledge of Barth's theology only. According to Eberhard Bethge the first face-to-face meeting with Barth in July 1931 in Bonn had the result that "subsequent relations between the two were characterized by complete frankness and, occasionally, completely frank disagreement."[2]

Bonhoeffer's charge in his *Letters and Papers from Prison* against Barth of having mislead theology into what he calls "positivism of revelation" has become famous. The perception is wide-spread that Bonhoeffer was in search of an alternative to Barth's approach in his quest for a "non-religious Christianity." However, this is a misjudgement motivated by anti-Barthian prejudice rather than by a thorough reading of Bonhoeffer's writings. The critical remarks on "positivism of revelation" are always introduced by eulogies on Barth's approach. Bonhoeffer's intention was not to overcome Barth's theology but to develop some aspects within Barth's approach in a way, which had not yet been carried out by Barth himself.

I. Bonhoeffer's Early Reception and Discussion of Barth's Theology

Bonhoeffer's first encounter with the theology of Karl Barth took place in the winter of 1924–1925. During a period of "several attacks of influenza"

---

[1] Eberhard Bethge, *Dietrich Bonhoeffer*, 74.
[2] Bethge, *Dietrich Bonhoeffer*, 176.

he found time enough to "read more than ever," among others the first volume of Barth's essays *The Word of God and the Word of Man* (1924) and probably also Barth's commentary on Paul's *Epistle to the Romans* (second revised edition, 1922). The "liberation" experienced in the encounter with Barth's writings led Bonhoeffer to a critical attitude regarding the liberal theology of his teachers.[3] In his seminar essay entitled "Can One Distinguish Between a Historical and a Pneumatological Interpretation of Scripture, and How Does Dogmatics Relate to This Question?" (summer 1925) his reading experiences of Barth's theology are reflected for the first time. According to Bonhoeffer every exposition has to start from the premise that revelation is contained in Scripture, "because this is where God speaks."[4] Bonhoeffer adopts Barth's programmatic epistemological principle: "Like can be understood only by like. God can be understood only by God."[5] Bonhoeffer's elaboration was marked by Reinhold Seeberg as being "satisfactory." In his eyes the essay seems to have expressed "irritating ... Barthianism" only.[6]

The debate between Barth and Adolf von Harnack, the head of liberal theology, which was published in the journal "Die christliche Welt" (The Christian World) in 1923, must have been of special interest to Bonhoeffer, since he studied with Harnack since 1924.[7] In Harnack's seminar on Augustin's "De Civitate Dei" in winter 1925-26 Bonhoeffer seems to have quarrelled with the teacher about Barth's exposition of 1 Corinthians – *The Resurrection of the Death* (1924).[8] Among Bonhoeffer's papers are the dictated notes (transcripts) of Barth's Göttingen dogmatics lectures ("Instruction in Christian Religion," summer 1924 and winter 1924-1925), which were circulated at that time among students of theology. It seems that

---

[3] Bethge, *Dietrich Bonhoeffer*, 73f. Cf. Karl Barth, *Das Wort Gottes und die Theologie* (Munich 1924; English translation, *The Word of God and the Word of Man*, Essays 1916-1923, translated by Douglas Horton (New York 1957)); *Der Römerbrief* (Munich, second revised edition, 1922; English translation *The Epistle to the Romans*, translated by Edwyn C. Hoskyns (London 1933)).

[4] "Can One Distinguish Between a Historical and a Pneumatological Interpretation of Scripture, and How Does Dogmatics Relate to This Question?," in *DBWE* 9, 289 (*DBW* 9, 311).

[5] *DBWE* 9, 290-291 (*DBW* 9, 313). In his seminar paper on „Frank's Understandings of the Spirit and of Grace" (19 November 1926, not contained in *DBW/E* 9!) Bonhoeffer again quotes Barth's principle: "But finitum incapax infiniti, like is known only through like, God only through God's spirit;" cf. A. Pangritz, *Karl Barth in the Theology of Dietrich Bonhoeffer* (Grand Rapids/Cambridge 2000), 16, note 3.

[6] Bethge, *Dietrich Bonhoeffer*, 79; translation altered.

[7] Bethge, *Dietrich Bonhoeffer*, 73f.

[8] Cf. Helmut Goes, "Der Sichere und der Suchende," in *Begegnungen mit Dietrich Bonhoeffer*, edited by W.-D. Zimmermann (Munich, fourth extended edition, 1969), 34. Cf. Bethge, *Dietrich Bonhoeffer*, 67.

Bonhoeffer "deplored Barth's relapse into servitude" and feared a "reactionary gesture" in connection with his turn towards dogmatics.[9]

In his dissertation *Sanctorum Communio* and particularly in his second dissertation *Act and Being* Bonhoeffer discussed Karl Barth at length.[10] *Sanctorum Communio* can be read as Bonhoeffer's attempt at completing Barth's "theology of revelation" with respect to sociality.[11] Therefore he chooses the subtitle: "A dogmatic inquiry into the sociology of the church" and coins the definition of the church as "Christ," that is the revelation of God's Word, "existing as church-community", that is the social concretion of revelation.[12]

In *Sanctorum Communio* Bonhoeffer emphasized his basic agreement with the theological insight that "the Christian church is the church of the Word, that is, of faith," an insight that had "been brought home to us by modern Luther research," that is, by Karl Holl and the so-called Luther renaissance, as well as "by the most recent change of direction in theology," that is, by Karl Barth and dialectical theology.[13] However, Bonhoeffer expresses a certain hesitation with respect to Barth stressing that the concept of the church cannot be "understood theologically 'in itself', but only within a real historical dialectic – not a dialectic of concepts."[14]

Typically, Bonhoeffer holds it to be necessary to stress a point of difference with Barth in the understanding of the "other." In the context of the exposition of the church as "spiritual community," where Bonhoeffer reflects on the nature of Christian love as "real love of the neighbour" in the I-You relationship,[15] we find a footnote, where he discusses the ecclesiology and ethics of Barth's commentary on the *Epistle to the Romans* (second edition). Bonhoeffer "cannot concur with the exegesis of the command to love presented here, nor with the concept of communication it entails." One may well say with Barth that "the neighbour visibly poses the question of God that must be visibly answered." But one must then also concede "that love really does love the other, not the One," namely God

---

[9] R. Widmann, Letter to D. Bonhoeffer (25 February 1926), in *DBWE* 9, 154 (*DBW* 9, 160). Cf. E. Bethge, *Dietrich Bonhoeffer*, 76.

[10] Cf. Bethge, *Dietrich Bonhoeffer*, 178: "As he eagerly and gratefully absorbed Barth's message during 1927 and 1929, Bonhoeffer directed a number of theological-epistemological questions toward Barth, under the principle of *finitum capax infiniti*."

[11] Cf. Clifford J. Green, *Bonhoeffer. A Theology of Sociality* (Grand Rapids/ Cambridge, revised edition, 1999).

[12] *DBWE* 1, 121, 141, 189 (*DBW* 1, 76, 87, 126).

[13] *DBWE* 1, 212–213 (*DBW* 1, 143).

[14] *DBWE* 1, 62 (*DBW* 1, 36). Cf. the ninth of his theses for the doctoral examinations (17 December 1927): "The dialectic of the so-called dialectical theology bears logical, not real character and is in danger of neglecting the historicity of Jesus" (*DBWE* 9, 441 (*DBW* 1, 478)).

[15] *DBWE* 1, 169 (*DBW* 1, 109).

"in the other," as Barth maintains.[16] Christian love, according to Bonhoeffer, is aimed at *"the real neighbour,"* it does not do so, because the possibility of integration into the Christian community lies dormant in the other or because it "would derive pleasure from that person's individuality." Christian love loves the neighbour, because "God's claim" is experienced in the You.[17]

This yields the critical question: "Who gives Barth the right to say that the other is 'as such infinitely unimportant' ... when God commands us to love precisely that person? God has made the 'neighbour as such' infinitely important, and there isn't any other 'neighbour as such' for us ... rather, the other is infinitely important as such, precisely because God takes the other person seriously. Should I after all ultimately be alone with God in the world?" Bonhoeffer perceives another difference with Barth in the understanding of Christian community: "'To be one' with God and with the neighbour is something entirely different from being in community with them. Barth, however, uses both expressions synonymously." In the final analysis, Barth's understanding of oneness, "where only the one is loved in the other," ends up, according to Bonhoeffer, in "romanticism."[18]

In the published version of *Sanctorum Communio* (1930) we find a new chapter on "Authority and Freedom in the Empirical Church," which refers to Barth's *Christian Dogmatics in Outline* (published in late summer 1927).[19] It seems that during his stay as an assistant pastor in Barcelona (1928–1929) Bonhoeffer had read Barth's *Outline* with great interest.[20] Among Bonhoeffer's papers are notes reflecting his critical reading, referring particularly to chapter 3: "The Sacred Scripture."[21] Already the headline of the new chapter of *Sanctorum Communio*, which was to replace the chapter on "Church and Proletariat" of the original typescript, can be read as contraction of two headlines in Barth's *Outline*: § 21 ("The Authority of the Church") and § 22 ("The Freedom of Conscience"). Bonhoeffer refers to these two chapters in a footnote to the first sentence of his new chapter: "The church rests upon the word."[22] Obviously the reading of Barth's

---

[16] *DBWE* 1, 169–170, note 28 (*DBW* 1, 109–110, note 28).

[17] *DBWE* 1, 169 (*DBW* 1, 109).

[18] *DBWE* 1, 170, note 28 (*DBW* 1, 110–111, note 28).

[19] K. Barth, *Die christliche Dogmatik im Entwurf*, volume 1: *Die Lehre vom Worte Gottes. Prolegomena zur christlichen Dogmatik (1927)* (Zurich, new edition 1982).

[20] Cf. Letter to Walter Dress, 13 March 1928, in *DBW* 17, 71. Bonhoeffer's sermons and speeches in Barcelona show that he tried to explain Barth and dialectical theology, as he understood it, to members of the German community there (cf. *DBW* 10, 318–319 and 323).

[21] Cf. *DBWE* 9, 436–438 (*DBW* 9, 473–475).

[22] *DBWE* 1, 250 (*DBW* 1, 172). Cf. K. Barth, *Die christliche Dogmatik im Entwurf*, 473 and 506. The same combination of authority and freedom can be found already in §§ 9 and 10 of Barth's Göttingen dogmatics, which Bonhoeffer knew from the students'

Christian Dogmatics in Outline induced Bonhoeffer to qualify the nearly complete identification of Christ and church, as it had been suggested by the formula "Christ existing as community," which could have provoked misunderstandings with respect to the demand of obedience to the church. The fact that "the church rests upon the word" should not be interpreted in a fundamentalist way; rather, it implies the freedom of a Christian. In contrast to the absolute authority of the Word, upon which the church rests, the church itself can claim only "relative authority." Therefore it can demand "relative obedience" only, which allows at the same time "relative freedom" for the individual.[23]

After *Sanctorum Communio* had been published in second edition (1954) Barth praised Bonhoeffer's dissertation in the context of his *Doctrine of Reconciliation*, where he speaks about "The Growth of the Community" in the Holy Spirit.[24]

More clearly and decisively than in *Sanctorum Communio* Bonhoeffer tried to intervene into the contemporary theological debates in his *Habilitation* dissertation *Act and Being*. He "criticized Bultmann for his dependence on Heidegger" and he "criticized Barth for his formalistic understanding of the freedom of God." Now Bonhoeffer "wanted to persuade him of his own belief in the *finitum capax infiniti* – that, despite everything, God *was* accessible."[25] On the one hand Bonhoeffer admits that "the proviso made by dialectical theology is not a logical one that might be cancelled by the opposite but, in view of predestination, a real one in each case."[26] On the other hand he senses in Barth's "attempt of unsystematic thought"[27] the danger that "the contingent positivity" of "the occurrence of salvation" be formalized[28] in that God is "understood as pure act."[29] Bonhoeffer insists: "In revelation it is not so much a question of the freedom of God – eternally remaining within the divine self, aseity – on the other side of revelation, as it is of God's coming out of God's own self in revelation. It is a matter of God's *given* Word, the covenant in which God is bound by God's own action. ... God is free not from human beings but for them. Christ is the word of God's freedom. God *is* present, that is, not in eternal nonobjectivity but – to put it quite provisionally for now – 'haveable,' graspable in

---

transcripts (cf. K. Barth *Unterricht in der christlichen Religion*, volume I: *Prolegomena* (*1924*), edited by Hannelotte Reiffen (Zurich 1985), 276 and 305.

[23] *DBWE* 1, 250 (*DBW* 1, 172).
[24] K. Barth, *KD* IV/2 (*Die Lehre von der Versöhnung*), 1955, 725.
[25] Bethge, *Dietrich Bonhoeffer*, 133.
[26] *DBWE* 2, 86 (*DBW* 2, 80).
[27] *DBWE* 2, 87 (*DBW* 2, 81).
[28] *DBWE* 2, 124 (*DBW* 2, 122).
[29] *DBWE* 2, 83 (*DBW* 2, 77).

the Word within the church. Here the formal understanding of God's freedom is countered by a substantial one."[30]

Interestingly, in this passage Bonhoeffer protests as a Lutheran theologian against the Reformed "*non capax.*" Yet, Bonhoeffer's purpose is similar to Barth's, namely, to shake up the theological system. In Bonhoeffer's view the disturbance is to arise from Christ, whom he thinks as "existing as community."[31] It is in the congregation where "God's freedom" manifests itself precisely in that "God binds God's self to human beings," and that "the revelation is somehow held fast here."[32] If this is true, the question of the "continuity of revelation" raises itself unavoidably. It is obviously not sufficient for Bonhoeffer to say with Barth that God's revelation "impinges on the existence" of the listening human being "in each instance." Rather, everything depends on revelation being "always present (in the sense of 'what is in the future')."[33] For "it is only in the community of faith itself that revelation can be understood in its real, existence-affecting being." In this context Bonhoeffer even goes so far as to assert that in the congregation "every member of the church may ... 'become a Christ' to the others."[34]

It is not at all Bonhoeffer's intention in his insistence on „the continuity of revelation" to nullify Barth's repudiation of the ideas of continuity found in liberal theology. In his debate with Harnack, Barth had made clear: "You empty revelation by saying that there is a continuity between history and revelation... I do repudiate every continuity between hither and yon... Parable, parable only can be all 'becoming' in view of the birth from death to life."[35] Bonhoeffer, too, is not concerned with the continuity between hither and yon, but with an endured, an imposed continuity in the opposite direction: from the there to the here, that is to say, from above to below. He could well endorse Barth's statement from the Tambach address, "always from above to below, and never the reverse, if we want to

---

[30] *DBWE* 2, 90–91 (*DBW* 2, 85). Interestingly, in his essay on *The Humanity of God* (1956) Barth himself later allowed that, properly understood, "the *deity* of the *living* God" finds "its meaning and its power only in the context of His history and of His dialogue with *humans*, and thus in the *togetherness* with humans. ... It is precisely God's *deity* which, rightly understood, includes His *humanity*" (K. Barth, *The Humanity of God*, translated by Thomas Wieser and John Newton Thomas (Richmond 1960), 44–45).

[31] *DBWE* 2, 112 (*DBW* 2, 108).

[32] *DBWE* 2, 112 (*DBW* 2, 109); translation altered.

[33] *DBWE* 2, 113 (*DBW* 2, 110).

[34] *DBWE* 2, 113 (*DBW* 2, 109).

[35] K. Barth, Letter to Adolf von Harnack, in: H. Martin Rumscheidt, *Revelation and Theology: An Analysis of the Barth-Harnack Correspondence of 1923* (Cambridge 1972), 49.

understand ourselves rightly."³⁶ But the Word really became flesh and, in Christ, "exists as community"; therefore, Bonhoeffer immediately ascribes a social and historical dimension to this vertically-from-above. "Thus revelation happens in the community of faith; it requires primarily a specific Christian sociology."³⁷ For that reason, "how existentiality and continuity come together in the concept of *pati*" must be examined in relation to "the concept of the church."³⁸

Consequently, Bonhoeffer could not adopt for his purposes Barth's statement in the Tambach address: "*We* live more deeply in the No than in the Yes, more deeply in criticism and protest than in naïveté, more deeply in longing for the future than in participation in the present."³⁹ In relation to the church, Bonhoeffer would stress the exact opposite. In the community of faith, the naïveté of the child is quite possible; "Home is the community ... of Christ, always 'future,' present 'in faith' because we are children of the future."⁴⁰ Here what is yet to come is already present and – albeit in a preliminary way – at our disposal "in faith."⁴¹

According to Bonhoeffer, Barth's "fateful mistake ... to have substituted for the concept of creator and lord that of the subject" was symptomatic of his formalization of God's freedom. For that ultimately means that God is not understood "as person."⁴² Bonhoeffer insists that "the Protestant idea of the church is conceived in personal terms – that is, God reveals the divine self in the church as person... Hence, the gospel is somehow held fast here. God's freedom has woven itself into this personlike community of faith, and it is precisely this which manifests what God's freedom is: that God binds God's self to human beings."⁴³

The acuity of the critique of Barth present in *Act and Being* should not deceive one into ranking Bonhoeffer with the colleagues at the Berlin faculty in their opposition to Barth. The converse is more likely: Precisely because he feels close to Barth – the many approvingly cited quotations

---

[36] K. Barth, "The Christian's Place in Society," in: K. Barth, *The Word of God and the Word of Man* (New York 1957), 324 (translation altered). In his lectures on "Recent Publications in Systematic Theology" (1932–1933) Bonhoeffer comments approvingly: "Human speech" concerning God "must take note of this from above to the below" (*DBW* 12, 154).

[37] *DBWE* 2, 113 (*DBW* 2, 109).

[38] *DBWE* 2, 116 (*DBW* 2, 113).

[39] K. Barth, *The Word of God and the Word of Man*, 311–312.

[40] *DBWE* 2, 161 (*DBW* 2, 161).

[41] *DBWE* 2, 112 (*DBW* 2, 109).

[42] *DBWE* 2, 125 (*DBW* 2, 122). Cf. K. Barth, *Die christliche Dogmatik im Entwurf*, New Edition, 166: "It is quite simply the logical question about the subject, predicate and object of the little sentence: 'God speaks,' Deus dixit." Note Barth's comments (in *KD* I/1, 340) on these "then in fact ... unguardedly and ambiguously" used words.

[43] *DBWE* 2, 112 (*DBW* 2, 109).

affirm this perception – Bonhoeffer endeavours to work out as clearly as possible the differences which nevertheless exist between them. In fact, he rather tries to keep in conversation with each other the controversial positions of Barth, on the one side, and those of the Berlin faculty, on the other. Thus, *Act and Being* can be regarded as "a masterpiece of mediating theology."[44]

Accordingly, in his inauguration lecture "The Question of Man in Contemporary Philosophy and Theology" (31 July 1930) Bonhoeffer on the one hand agrees with Barth's interpretation of the "incapax infiniti:" "the person to whom God reveals himself is the person to whom God cannot become manifest."[45] On the other hand, he criticizes Barth's dialectic in agreement with the personalistic concept of the I-You relationship as "speculative" and "individualistic."[46]

II. A "Barthian" in New York

During his stay at Union Theological Seminary in New York in 1930–1931 Bonhoeffer presented himself so decidedly as an advocate of Barth's theology that he was seen by John Baillie as "the most convinced disciple of Dr. Barth that had appeared among us up to that time."[47] Bonhoeffer's "Barthianism" becomes apparent in his seminar papers for Union Theological Seminary. In "Concerning the Christian Idea of God" Bonhoeffer explicitly refers to Barth, who had maintained that "theological thinking is not a construction a priori, but a posteriori ... Therefore it has to be conscious of its limitations."[48]

Even more evident becomes Bonhoeffer's "Barthianism" in his article "The Theology of Crisis and its Attitude toward Philosophy and Science." Right in the beginning he declares "that I do not see any other possible way for you to get into real contact with his [Barth's] thinking than by forgetting at least for this hour everything you have learned before concerning

---

[44] Hanfried Müller, *Von der Kirche zur Welt. Ein Beitrag zu der Beziehung des Wortes Gottes auf die societas in Dietrich Bonhoeffers theologischer Entwicklung* (Leipzig 1961), 152.

[45] "Die Frage nach dem Menschen in der gegenwärtigen Philosophie und Theologie," in *DBW* 10, 370–371. Cf. K. Barth, *Die christliche Dogmatik im Entwurf*, 383.

[46] *NRS*, 63 (*DBW* 10, 372).

[47] Cf. Bethge, *Dietrich Bonhoeffer*, 158.

[48] "Concerning the Christian Idea of God," in *DBW* 10, 426. An allusion to Barth's concept of the "word of God" can be seen in the characterization of the "word of God" as "God in his revelation as the Holy Spirit... God remains always and entirely subject" (431).

this problem."[49] In contrast to the philosophy of religion prevailing in the United States, Barth stands, according to Bonhoeffer, "in the tradition of genuine Christian thinking," that is in the theological ancestry of Paul, Augustine, Luther, and Kierkegaard.[50] Therefore Barth tries to let "the world of biblical thinking" come alive again and he "finds the Bible full of the testimony of the awkwardness and foolishness of God's revelation."[51]

When Bonhoeffer emphasizes that "the revelation of God is executed not in the area of ideas, but in the area of reality,"[52] this statement is corresponding Barth's intentions, which was to place the reality of revelation into priority over its possibility.[53] Contrary to those scholars, who suggest that Bonhoeffer here is "not in line with Barth's intentions,"[54] the differences should not be exaggerated. Even in "Fate and Idea in Theology" (1929), usually referred to in order to prove that Bonhoeffer is not in accordance with Barth, the latter seeks to understand "God as reality" and as "real in the eminent sense."[55] Both, Barth and Bonhoeffer, though using different formulations, seek to secure the concept of God's reality against being misunderstood as flat "reality" in the sense of the merely factual, and to keep it open for changes.[56]

Bonhoeffer knows well that however much he depends on Barth, he is very much on his own in addressing the problem of the "relation between

---

[49] The meaning of this statement should not be generalized; rather, it refers to the immediate context of the seminar on the attitude of theology towards philosophy and science only (cf. Reinhard Staats, "Nachwort," in *DBW* 10, 627).

[50] "The Theology of Crisis and its Attitude Toward Philosophy and Science," in *DBW* 10, 435.

[51] *DBW* 10, 437–438; cf. "The logic of the Bible" is "God's coming which destroys all human attempts to come" (438).

[52] *DBW* 10, 436.

[53] Cf. K. Barth, *Die christliche Dogmatik im Entwurf* (The Christian Dogmatics in Outline [1927]), section 14 ("The Objective Possibility of Revelation"), 306f.: "We did not construct and shall wisely avoid constructing ... The Word, God's Son, Jesus Christ himself, the reality of revelation, without which we would be in no position to give an account to ourselves about its possibilities."

[54] Hans Pfeifer, *Das Kirchenverständnis Dietrich Bonhoeffers*. Unpublished dissertation, Heidelberg 1963, 79. Cf. R. Staats, Afterword in *DBW* 10, 626; cf. *DBW* 10, 436, editorial note 9. Bethge, *Dietrich Bonhoeffer*, 158–159, maintains that Bonhoeffer "suppressed" his critical questions to Barth "so completely that ... his proselyting zeal led him to mingle his own propositions with those of Barth and actually attribute them to him, no doubt without realizing it."

[55] K. Barth, *Schicksal und Idee in der Theologie* (1929); ("Fate and Idea in Theology," in *The Way of Theology in Karl Barth: Essays and Comments*, edited by H. M. Rumscheidt, translated by G. Hunsinger (Allison Park, PA. 1986), 37: The thought of God, "to be taken seriously ... must be an expression of reality, indeed of the great reality which includes and surpasses all other reality in itself."

[56] In *DBWE* 2, 115 (*DBW* 2, 112). Bonhoeffer had put it as follows: "There is no God who 'is there'."

theology and philosophy with regard to the use of forms of general philosophical thinking in theology,"[57] "since Barth never has published any comprehensive treatment of our problem."[58] However, the result is that – as Bonhoeffer approvingly cites Barth – "there is no Christian philosophy or philosophical terminology at all." Thus, Bonhoeffer seems to agree with Barth that "it does not make very much difference what philosophy a theologian has, but everything depends upon how strongly he keeps his eyes on the category of the word of God, on the fact of revelation, of justification by faith."[59]

III. First Face-to-Face Encounter with Barth in Bonn

In July 1931 the first face-to-face meeting of Dietrich Bonhoeffer with Karl Barth took place in Bonn.[60] The fact that Bonhoeffer had been regarded as a "Barthian" in New York, although he never had studied with Barth, must have enforced his interest to get to know the head of "dialectical theology" in a way that now a journey to Bonn seemed to become unavoidable. The Swiss theologian Erwin Sutz, with whom he had become friends at Union Theological Seminary, had announced his visit to Barth.[61]

Only a few days after his arrival in Bonn Bonhoeffer wrote to his American friend Paul Lehmann on 10 July 1931, after having visited Barth's dogmatics lectures for the first time: "this morning at 7 I heard K. Barth for the first time. I could not help thinking all the time very much of you. How much would you have enjoyed this lecture! ... It would be wonderful if you could be here! I am totally alone."[62] The same evening a discussion "with people from Maria Laach,"[63] namely Benedictines from the famous monastery, took place in Barth's home. On a postcard Bonhoeffer gave a report to his parents: "I have now met Barth and got to know him quite well at a discussion evening at his house. I like him very much in-

---

[57] *DBW* 10, 440.

[58] *DBW* 10, 435.

[59] *DBW* 10, 447. The assumption that in this article Bonhoeffer in contrast to Barth meant to highlight the task of a "general philosophical thinking" in the field of theology (Gerhard Krause, "Dietrich Bonhoeffer," in *TRE* 7, 58) is erroneous.

[60] Cf. Bethge, *Dietrich Bonhoeffer*, 175ff.

[61] Cf. Bethge, *Dietrich Bonhoeffer*, 153.

[62] Letter to Paul Lehmann, 10 July 1931, in *DBW* 17, 90. Cf. also Bonhoeffer's postcard to E. Sutz (15 July 1931) in *DBW* 11, 16 (*NRS*, 119): "Here I am sitting in the park in front of the University. Barth lectured this morning at seven. I had a short talk with him ... Despite your thorough preparation, there was a great deal in the lecture which surprised me ... I am all alone here and waste the rest of the day quite uselessly."

[63] *DBW* 11, 16–17.

deed, and am also very much impressed by his lectures. Everything is so well worked out and has not yet become mechanical to him. I think I shall gain a great deal from the time spent here."[64]

In his lectures of summer 1931 Barth was occupied with the "Prolegomena to Dogmatics," which would be published as the first part-volume of his *Church Dogmatics* in autumn 1932. In addition to his dogmatics lectures Barth taught a seminar on Schleiermacher's „Doctrine of Faith," and in another seminar for advanced students (*Sozietät*) he treated Schleiermacher's "Short Explanation of Theological Studies."[65] Bonhoeffer participated also in these seminars. According to a student's recollection he quoted in one session Luther's statement "that the curses of the godless sometimes sound better to God's ear than the hallelujahs of the pious."[66] This phrase seems to have delighted Barth, so that his interest in the young colleague from Berlin increased.

On 23 July 1931 Bonhoeffer was invited by Barth for lunch and a conversation that lasted several hours. The next day he wrote to Erwin Sutz in order to give him a report. He starts by expressing a certain feeling of uneasiness in the inner circle of Barth's disciples: "You will well be able to imagine that I have often wished that you were here, particularly so that you could have had a good laugh on a number of occasions with the pundits. I don't dare do that so much here, only hesitantly ..., but with my bastard theological derivation I have less occasion, as I notice again quite clearly. They have a sharp scent for thoroughbreds here. No Negro passes 'for white'; they even examine his fingernails and the soles of his feet. Up till now they have shown me hospitality as unknown stranger."[67]

Obviously, already at that time, a kind of "school" had formed around Barth, a closed circle of disciples which had a deterring effect on outsiders. One of them, Helmut Gollwitzer, hosted an evening meeting of Barth's initiates with Bonhoeffer.[68] It seems that Bonhoeffer made a great impres-

---

[64] Postcard to the parents (14 July 1931) in *DBW* 11, 15 (cf. Bethge, *Dietrich Bonhoeffer*, 176).

[65] Cf. E. Busch, *Karl Barths Lebenslauf. Nach seinen Briefen und autobiographischen Texten* (Munich 1978), 227.

[66] Cf. Bethge, *Dietrich Bonhoeffer*, 176 (recollection by Winfried Maechler). Bonhoeffer quoted this phrase repeatedly in his writings and lectures; cf. *DBWE* 2, 160 note 31 (*DBW* 2, 160, notes 31 and 67); cf. "Das Wesen der Kirche," in *DBW* 11, 293, note 377; cf. Ethics *DBWE* 6, 124 (*DBW* 6, 115).

[67] Letter to E. Sutz (24 July 1931) in *NRS*, 120 (*DBW* 11, 18–19); cf. Bethge, *Dietrich Bonhoeffer*, 176; translation altered.

[68] Letter to E. Sutz (24 July 1931) in *DBW* 11, 21. Cf. Helmut Gollwitzer, "Weg des Gehorsams," in *Begegnungen mit Dietrich Bonhoeffer*, edited by W.-D. Zimmermann (Munich, fourth extended edition, 1969), 130. Gollwitzer's recollection confirms Bonhoeffer's impression that the "Barthians" looked upon outsiders with a certain arrogance. However, it seems incorrect with respect to Bonhoeffer, who in the days of his visit in

sion on some of these students; at least one of them, Winfried Maechler, decided to continue his studies with Bonhoeffer in Berlin.

In his letter to Sutz Bonhoeffer continues: "Now with Karl Barth himself, of course, everything is completely different. One breathes in an orderly way, one is no longer afraid of dying of suffocation in the thin air. I don't think that I have ever regretted anything that I have failed to do in my theological past as much as the fact that I did not come here earlier. Now there are only three weeks for me to be here, lectures ..., seminars, meetings, an open evening and now yesterday a couple of hours at lunch with Barth. One hears and sees something there ... But it is important and surprising in the best way to see how Barth stands over and beyond his books. There is with him an openness, a readiness for any objection which should hit the mark, and along with this such concentration and impetuous insistence on the point, whether it is made arrogantly or modestly, dogmatically or completely uncertainly, and not only when it serves his own theology. I am coming to understand more and more why Barth's writings are so tremendously difficult to understand. I have been impressed even more by discussions with him than by his writings and his lectures. For he is really there. I have never seen anything like it before and wouldn't have believed it possible."[69]

Bonhoeffer's enthusiasm regarding Barth is well recognizable in these lines. His admiration does not diminish the fact that he had some critical questions to ask and that Barth's answers for the time being did not completely satisfy him. Bonhoeffer was mainly interested in "the ethical problem."[70] Barth, as Bonhoeffer reports to Sutz, "would not make concessions to me where I expected that he would have to. Beside the one great light in the night, he said, there were also many little lights, so-called 'relative ethical criteria;' he could not, however, make their significance and application and nature comprehensible to me – we didn't get beyond a simple reference to the Bible." When Barth finally remarked that his guest "turned grace into a principle and thereby killed everything else," Bonhoeffer rejects the suspicion of going-on about principles; on the other hand he cannot understand "why everything else should *not* be killed."[71] It is remark-

---

Bonn certainly was not yet regarded as a "new theological light" by his students, because he started his theological teaching at the university of Berlin only after his return from Bonn in October 1931 with the lecture on "The History of Systematic Theology in the Twentieth Century."

[69] Letter to E. Sutz (24 July 1931), in *NRS*, 120–121 (*DBW* 11, 19). Cf. Bethge, *Dietrich Bonhoeffer*, 176.

[70] Bonhoeffer was well prepared for the conversation, because he had already studied the transcripts of Barth's Münster "Ethics" lectures (winter 1928/29), which were circulated by the World Student Christian Federation (cf. D. Braun, "Vorwort," in: K. Barth, *Ethik II*, edited by Dietrich Braun (Zurich, 1978), IX.

[71] *NRS*, 121 (*DBW* 11, 20).

able in this report that it is just Bonhoeffer, who in a christomonistic way rejects "relative ethical criteria," whereas Barth cultivates a perspective more flexible, an early version of his "doctrine of lights."[72]

Bonhoeffer sums up his impression from the personal meeting with Barth: "There is really someone from whom one take away much; yet I sit in the impoverished Berlin and complain because no one is there who can teach theology and in addition other useful things."[73] Some weeks later Bonhoeffer recalls those days in Bonn in a letter to Paul Lehmann: "The time at Bonn was marvellous not only from the theological point of view but also or perhaps even more by the fact that I got to know Barth personally. He is really a theologian at home as well as in the classroom. ... When you see Barth you know at once – even if [you] come entirely from outside – that there is something worthwhile to risk your life for."[74] And at Christmas 1931, in another letter to Sutz, Bonhoeffer contrasts his feeling of theological isolation in Berlin with his recollection of the meeting with Barth in Bonn: "Since my return from Bonn, things here seem to be worse than ever."[75]

IV. Lectures at the University of Berlin

It is not by chance that the first course taught by Bonhoeffer in the winter semester of 1931–1932 on "The History of Systematic Theology in the Twentieth Century" culminates in a section entitled "The Word of God and Theology," containing a detailed presentation of the theological "revolution" brought about by Barth. Bonhoeffer describes Barth's position underlining that "the subject of theology" is "solely the *logos theou*," the Word of God. "Human beings can no longer go behind this beginning."[76] Barth's theology is, according to Bonhoeffer, "a theology which once again wants to understand wholly the sola fide, and for that reason speaks on the grounds of predestination and, hence, dialectically ... There is nothing in all of recent literature that seriously poses a challenge to Barth."[77]

---

[72] Concerning Barth's doctrine of "true words" outside the church – often referred to in the simplified term "doctrine of lights," cf. *KD* IV/3, First Part (Zurich 1959), 3ff.

[73] *DBW* 11, 20–21.

[74] Letter to P. Lehmann (23 August 1931) in *DBW* 17, 92–93. Cf. also Bonhoeffer's recollection in his letter to E. Sutz (8 October 1931) that he "would immediately return to Bonn. Those days were truly an extraordinary time" (*DBW* 11, 28).

[75] Letter to E. Sutz (25 December 1931) in *NRS*, 140 (*DBW* 11, 50–51).

[76] "Die Geschichte der systematischen Theologie des 20. Jahrhunderts," in *DBW* 11, 199.

[77] *DBW* 11, 211.

But Bonhoeffer does want to challenge Barth. Once again he repeats his critique of Barth's understanding of God's freedom. "The understanding of the sola fide calls for the radical concept of God's freedom. Barth's term 'in each instance.' ... In contrast the Lutheran: (it is) God's freedom and honor to have bound Godself wholly to the Word. Not freedom from but freedom for ... The community lives of this in freely given continuity which is Christ himself present."[78] In this context Bonhoeffer again mentions "the ethical problem." Barth's understanding of ethics as "demonstration" excludes "an ethics of principles," and Bonhoeffer agrees; however, the same conception prevents "every concrete" ethics. How then is it possible to develop a Christian ethics "as a scholarly discipline"?[79] Bonhoeffer is concerned with God's visible coming and with a corresponding preaching of the Law as "concrete commandment." He tries to resolve his critical questions in a recollection of the unresolved issues of the religious-socialist first edition of Barth's commentary on *The Epistle to the Romans* (1919) which the famous revised second edition had not settled. At the center of the first edition was "God's visible approach to the world," while the "second edition" emphasized the God who comes ever anew to the world "in each distinct instance."[80] In those months of 1931–1932 Bonhoeffer aligned himself with Barth in the "Günter Dehn case," defending the defamed "religious socialist" against attacks by Nazi students.

In his lectures on "The Nature of the Church" in the summer of 1932 Bonhoeffer referred to some recently published essays by Barth on ecclesiology.[81] In his seminar entitled "Is There a Christian Ethics?" Bonhoeffer sought further clarification of the ethical issue. He is interested in the "connection" between the "self-acting and working" will of God and the "action of human beings."[82] Following the approach of "dialectical theo-

---

[78] *DBW* 11, 211.

[79] *DBW* 11, 212–213.

[80] Cf. *DBW* 11, 209. The editors of *DBW* 11 assume (cf. note 300) that the reference here is to the difference between Barth's *Die Kirchliche Dogmatik* (1932) and his earlier *Die Christliche Dogmatik im Entwurf* (1927). However, this is impossible, because Bonhoeffer finished his lecture on 2 February 1932, whereas the foreword to *Die Kirchliche Dogmatik*, volume I/1 dates from August 1932. Bonhoeffer could not have used this volume for his lecture.

[81] "Das Wesen der Kirche," in *DBW* 11, 245. Cf. K. Barth, "Der Begriff der Kirche," in *Zwischen den Zeiten* 5 (1927), 365–378; "Quousque tandem ...?," in *Zwischen den Zeiten* 8 (1930), 1–6; "Die Not der evangelischen Kirche," in *Zwischen den Zeiten* 9 (1931), 89–122.

[82] "Gibt es eine christliche Ethik?," in *DBW* 11, 305. Here Bonhoeffer refers to Barth's exposition of Romans 13 and 14 in *The Epistle to the Romans* (second edition, 1922); "Das Problem der Ethik in der Gegewart," in *Zwischen den Zeiten* 1 (1923), 30–57; "Der heilige Geist und das christliche Leben," in Beiheft 1, *Zwischen den Zeiten* (Munich 1930), 39–105.

logy" he asks if there is something like an "ethics of revelation."[83] Bonhoeffer searches for an answer in "the concept of sacrament" which he wants to "draw into" the discussion of ethics.[84] "The gospel becomes concrete through the sacrament, the commandment through reality."[85] An "ethics of revelation," in contrast to the conservative Lutheran concept of "orders of creation," can speak of *orders of preservation* only as these are oriented "toward Christ."[86] In his lectures on "Recent Publications in Systematic Theology," delivered in the winter of 1932–1933, Bonhoeffer treated among others Barth's book on Anselm, *Fides Quaerens Intellectum* (1931).[87] Bonhoeffer had already praised that book in his Christmas Letter of 1931 to Sutz.[88] Now Bonhoeffer agrees with Barth that "theology is a thinking that is bound to the church as the place of revelation. ... Its object is the creed, spoken and affirmed beforehand. That is why theology is possible only within the domain of the church."[89]

Only one of Bonhoeffer's lectures at the university of Berlin was prepared by himself for publication, "Creation and Sin. Theological Exposition of Gen 1–3" (winter semester of 1932–1933), published as *Creation and Fall* (1933). Much later this publication became relevant within the first part-volume of Barth's *Doctrine of Creation* (1945), where he explicitly refers to Bonhoeffer's concept of *analogia relationis* (analogy in relationship) and makes it his own.[90] Bonhoeffer's exposition of Gen 1,26f.,

---

[83] "Gibt es eine christliche Ethik?," in *DBW* 11, 308, note 20.

[84] Letter to E. Sutz (17 May 1932) in *DBW* 11, 89. After a meeting with Barth in Berlin on occasion of Barth's lecture on "Theology and Mission in the Present" (11 April 1932) Bonhoeffer was convinced that in the matter of ethics as God's concrete commandment Barth did not side with him. However, Barth had admitted that "this point was still uncannily troublesome for him."

[85] "Gibt es eine christliche Ethik?," in *DBW* 11, 311, note 42.

[86] *DBW* 11, 312.

[87] Cf. K. Barth, *Fides Quaerens Intellectum. Anselm's Proof of the Existence of God in the Context of His Theological Scheme*, translated by Ian W. Robertson (Allison Park, PA. 1931).

[88] Letter to E. Sutz (25 December 1931) in *NRS*, 140–141 (*DBW* 11, 50–51): "Barth's book on Anselm is a great delight to me; you must read it when you have time. He shows the countless academic cripples, once and for all, that he really does know how better to interpret and still remain sovereign." However, Bonhoeffer continues: "Nothing of course has in fact become less questionable" (translation slightly altered).

[89] "Besprechung und Diskussion systematisch-theologischer Neuerscheinungen," in *DBW* 12, 160–161.

[90] K. Barth, *KD* III/1 ("Die Lehre von der Schöpfung"), (Zurich 1945), 218–219, here *CD* III/1, 194–195: "Dietrich Bonhoeffer ... offers us important help in this respect ... As God is free for man, so man is free for man; but only inasmuch as God is for him, so that the *analogia relationis* as the meaning of the divine likeness cannot be equated with an *analogia entis*." Cf. *DBWE* 3, 65 (*DBW* 3, 61): "The likeness, the analogia, of humankind to God is not *analogia entis* but *analogia relationis*."

according to which the analogy of humanity's life "in the image of God" is concretized in the duality of and in the "relationship" between "male and female,"[91] is extensively worked out by Barth in his "anthropology" in the second part-volume of his *Doctrine of Creation* (1948).[92]

Bethge remarks that in the years at the eve of the rise of National Socialism Bonhoeffer did not receive, "in the form he had desired," "Barth's support in his concern for the concrete ethical commandments."[93] However, after having visited Barth on the 'Bergli' (a cottage in Switzerland, where Barth spent many of his holidays), Bonhoeffer wrote Barth on Christmas Eve 1932 that he had "a peculiarly sure feeling that the way you see things is somehow right ... that somehow the point of it all is being touched on."[94] In February 1933 Barth thanked Bonhoeffer for the Christmas letter and also for his review on Karl Heim's book *Glauben und Denken*, where Heim had attacked Barth.[95] In his review Bonhoeffer had written that Heim's charge against Barth – that he lacks concreteness – turns "directly back on himself." For if Barth is in danger of "making God an object of thought," then Bonhoeffer is convinced that this is the crux of every theology. "The idiosyncratic feature" of Barth's theology is his belief "that he cannot secure himself against this danger while constantly keeping an eye on this danger."[96] In his letter of thanks Barth describes his feeling of theological isolation. "Over the past months I have begun to feel more and more strongly that a great many of the theological alliances claimed to have been seen in Germany in recent years have been deceptive." It seemed to Barth as if he had been "thrown back into the same solitude" from which he "rode into this peculiar arena twelve years ago." And he thanks Bonhoeffer that he had made a stance for him at the faculty of theology in Berlin.[97]

---

[91] Cf. *DBWE* 3, 64 (*DBW* 3, 60): "How is the creature free? The creature is free in that one creature exists in relation to another creature, in that one human being is free for another human being. God created them man and woman. The human being is not alone. Human beings exist in duality, and it is in this *dependence on the other that their creatureliness consists*" (emphasis in original).

[92] Cf. K. Barth, *KD* III/2 (Zurich 1948), 262f., 390f.

[93] Bethge, *Dietrich Bonhoeffer*, 178. This does not prevent Bonhoeffer from recommending Paul Lehmann to go to Bonn for a year of study in order to get to know Barth's approach to the "discussion of ethical problems" (cf. Bonhoeffer's letter to P. Lehmann (30 May 1932) in *DBW* 17, 107).

[94] Letter to K. Barth (24 December 1932) in *DBW* 12, 37.

[95] K. Barth, Letter to Bonhoeffer (4 February 1933) in *NRS*, 201–202 (*DBW* 12, 48).

[96] "Zu Karl Heims Glaube und Denken," in *DBW* 12, 228.

[97] K. Barth, Letter to Bonhoeffer (4 February 1933) in *NRS*, 201 (*DBW* 12, 48–49). Bonhoeffer had openly sided with Barth in the winter of 1932–1933 and campaigned – in vain – that he be called to the university of Berlin.

V. The "Aryan Clause" as Status Confessionis

After the Nazi rise to power, when the Protestant Church of Prussia aligned itself with the new legislation and the anti-Semitic policies of the Nazi state, Bonhoeffer tried to settle every theological difference between himself and Barth seeking at the same time the support of the latter. In his "Christology" lectures (summer 1933) he qualified his earlier criticism of Barth. Whereas according to *Act and Being* (1930) "the old *extra calvinisticum*" had been "in error,"[98] Bonhoeffer now speaks of the Lutheran "capax" in terms of what sounds like a Reformed proviso: "Finitum capax infiniti, non per se, sed per infinitum" [The finite can hold the infinite, not by itself, but it can by the aid of the infinite]."[99] Barth could have put the matter that way.[100]

Bonhoeffer believed himself to be following entirely the directions Barth had signalled in his pamphlet *Theological Existence Today!* (25 June 1933), when he wrote Barth in September 1933, after the "brown" synod of the Prussian Church had adopted the "Aryan Clause" excluding church members of Jewish descent from ministry and other official positions: "In your booklet you said that where a Christian church adopted the Aryan Clause it would cease to be a Christian church ... Now the expected has happened." According to Bonhoeffer "there can be no doubt at all that the *status confessionis* has arrived." Therefore the question that concerns him above all is what this ecclesiological perception will mean concretely in terms of church politics. "What we are by no means clear about," he writes, "is how the confession is most appropriately expressed today." Bonhoeffer mentions that "several of us are now very drawn to the idea of the Free Church," and he adds: "I know that many people now wait on your judgment; I also know that most of them are of the opinion that you will counsel us to wait until we are thrown out."[101]

Barth promptly replied form the "Bergli." He agrees: "Naturally the decision of the General Synod has at least partly realised the possibility which I considered. They do not, or apparently do not yet, want to go as far as excluding non-Aryans from church-membership. But even the decree about officials and pastors is intolerable." And he concurs: "I too am of the

---

[98] Bethge, *Dietrich Bonhoeffer*, 134.
[99] "Christologie," in *DBW* 12, 332.
[100] Cf. K. Barth, Church Dogmatics I/1 (Edinburgh 1975), 406– 407.
[101] Letter to K. Barth (9 September 1933) in *NRS*, 226–227 (*DBW* 12, 124); translation altered. Against the majority of the pastors of the oppositional "Young Reformers Movement" in Berlin, Bonhoeffer and his friend Franz Hildebrandt, who himself was a victim of the Aryan clause, insisted "that to effect an immediate exodus would not only be more theologically consistent but more strategically successful than a delay" (Bethge, *Dietrich Bonhoeffer*, 308).

opinion that there is a *status confessionis*." Regarding the question when there is a possibility of leaving the church, however, Barth's answer was as "most of them" had expected: "Otherwise I am for waiting. When the schism comes, it must come from the other side ... It could then well be that the collision might take place at a still more central point ... Perhaps in that case it may not be absolutely necessary to be willing to wait until one is expelled or dismissed. Perhaps one will then really have to 'walk out.' But that should only be a last resort for us ... We will in no way need to regret at a later date an extremely active, polemical waiting."[102]

Bethge suggests that Bonhoeffer's "going off to England"[103] in fall 1933 was at least in part a reaction to his disappointment with Barth's answer.[104] In his letter to Barth from London (24 October 1933) Bonhoeffer writes that, after the adoption of the "Aryan Clause" in the Prussian Church, he knew that he "could not accept the pastorate for which I had been longing, particularly in that part of the city, if I was unwilling to give up my unconditional opposition to *this* church ... It would have meant abandoning my solidarity with the Jewish Christian pastors." Then he confesses to Barth: "I even feel as though, by going away, I have been personally disloyal to you"[105] by having made the decision to accept the call to two German congregations in London without obtaining Barth's advice in advance.

Bonhoeffer's feelings of uneasiness were not without reason, as is demonstrated by Barth's response: "You were quite right not to seek any wisdom from me before doing it. I would have advised against it, unconditionally and certainly bringing up the heaviest artillery ... No, to all the reasons and apologies that you may still have to offer, I can only and shall always have the same answer: And what of the German church? And what of the German church? – until you are back in Berlin, manning your abandoned machine gun like a loyal soldier. Haven't you seen yet that we have entered a time of altogether *un*dialectical theology?" He urged Bonhoeffer to return to his post "by the next ship! Well, let's say, with the one after that."[106] And Bonhoeffer did return, but only in April 1935, nearly one year after the Confessing Church had been founded in Barmen (May 1934).

---

[102] K. Barth, Letter to Bonhoeffer (11 September 1933) in *NRS*, 232–233 (*DBW* 12, 126–127).

[103] K. Barth, Letter to Bonhoeffer (20 November 1933) in *DBWE* 13, 39 (*DBW* 13, 31).

[104] Bethge, *Dietrich Bonhoeffer*, 309.

[105] Letter to K. Barth, London (24 October 1933) in *DBWE* 13, 23–24 (*DBW* 13, 12–14).

[106] K. Barth, Letter to Bonhoeffer (20 November 1933) in *DBWE* 13, 39–40 (*DBW* 13, 32–33).

VI. An "Ongoing, Silent Discussion"

Bonhoeffer's return to Germany in April 1935, in order to serve as director of a new Preachers' Seminary of the Confessing Church, must not blind us to the fact that his theological position differed from the understanding of many other protagonists in the German "church struggle." Regarding the relationship with Barth it can be said that "to some extent, the church struggle strengthened [their] alliance ... against secessionists and renegades. Nonetheless, during this ... period of their relationship it was not only the geographical distance between them that increased."[107] Shortly after Bonhoeffer's return Barth himself was driven out of Nazi Germany, after he had been forced to retire from his leading position in the Confessing Church and from his teaching position in Bonn.[108] Moreover "the Sermon on the Mount had moved into the foreground" of Bonhoeffer's thought, and in this respect "he did not yet find anything helpful in Barth."[109]

Bonhoeffer's turn to the Sermon on the Mount had already taken place in London. Writing to Sutz in April 1934 he says: "While I am working with the church opposition with all my might, it's perfectly clear to me that *this* opposition is only a temporary transitional phase on the way to an opposition of a very different kind ... You know, it is my belief – perhaps it will amaze you – that it is the *Sermon on the Mount* that has the deciding word on this whole affair. I think Barth's theology ... [has] delayed recognition of this a little while, but [has] certainly also made it possible."[110] Then he concludes: "*Following* Christ – what that really is, I'd like to know – it is not exhausted by our concept of faith." In this context Bonhoeffer mentions that he is "doing some writing that I think of as a 'spiritual exercise' – only as a first step."[111]

The rediscovery of the Sermon on the Mount constitutes the point of departure for Bonhoeffer's church struggle; it is from here that he decides to return to Germany. At the time when the Confessing Church declined more and more, Bonhoeffer tried to bring together in the "house of broth-

---

[107] Bethge, *Dietrich Bonhoeffer*, 185.

[108] Cf. Hans Prolingheuer, *Der Fall Karl Barth 1934–1935. Chronographie einer Vertreibung* (Neukirchen-Vluyn, second edition, 1984).

[109] Bethge, *Dietrich Bonhoeffer*, 185.

[110] Letter to E. Sutz, London (28 April 1934) in *DBWE* 13, 135 (*DBW* 13, 128–129). Bonhoeffer wants to know how Sutz preaches on the Sermon on the Mount. "I am currently trying to preach on it, very simply, without pretension. And I speak always for keeping the commandment and against evading it" (translation altered).

[111] *DBWE* 13, 136 (*DBW* 13, 129). The reference to "exercises" is Bonhoeffer's first reference to what he was later to present to the seminarians at Finkenwalde under the title *Discipleship*.

ers" Finkenwalde seminarians who would be prepared to try out "a life of uncompromising discipleship, following Christ according to the Sermon on the Mount."[112] Bethge comments that "for Bonhoeffer, Barth's answers to his questions at this stage did not take him far enough. He provided his own answer in *Discipleship*, but only after his death did Barth express the agreement and approval that Bonhoeffer had longed for."[113]

And so it was that, while working on his book *Discipleship*, Bonhoeffer was looking for other theological teachers; Søren Kierkegaard's discovery of the "individual" in particular seemed to be of help to him. In an undated letter from 1934 concerning the development of the church struggle, he expresses his belief that there will be a second, real battle, when "we shall rediscover ourselves as individuals, and through individual witness – and only so – shall we rediscover what discipleship means."[114] In *Discipleship* Bonhoeffer devotes a whole chapter to "the individual," and in the section on the discipleship faith of Abraham he makes use of the interpretation of Kierkegaard that he had criticized in *Sanctorum Communio*,[115] where he had shown his critical assessment of the use Barth had made of Kierkegaard's "individualism" in his commentary of *The Epistle to the Romans* (second, revised edition of 1922).[116] It seems that Bonhoeffer discovered Kierkegaard's "individual" for himself at the time Barth was turning his back on the Danish prophet of "existentialism."[117]

It was not until September 1936, when the work for the book *Discipleship* was nearly completed, that Bonhoeffer again wrote Barth: "The whole period was basically an ongoing, silent discussion with you, and so I had to keep silent for a while. The chief questions are those of the exposition of the Sermon on the Mount and the Pauline doctrine of justification and

---

[112] Letter to Karl-Friedrich Bonhoeffer, London (14 January 1935) in *DBWE* 13, 285 (*DBW* 13, 273).

[113] Bethge, *Dietrich Bonhoeffer*, 186.

[114] *DBWE* 13, 190 (*DBW* 13, 177). Concerning Bonhoeffer's engagement with Kierkegaard cf. A. Pangritz, *Karl Barth in the Theology of Dietrich Bonhoeffer*, 53–56 and Geffrey Kelly's essay above.

[115] *DBWE* 4, 94–95 (*DBW* 4, 89–90); cf. the references to Kierkegaard's *Fear and Trembling* in *DBWE* 1, 162 (*DBW* 1, 104).

[116] Cf. *DBWE* 1, 170, note 28 (*DBW* 1, 111, note 28).

[117] Cf. K. Barth, "A Thank-You and a Bow: Kierkegaard's Reveille," in *K. Barth, Fragments Grave and Gay*, edited by H. Martin Rumscheidt (London 1971), 98: "The second edition of my *Epistle to the Romans* is the very telling document of my participation in what has been called 'the Kierkegaard Renaissance' ... It is true, however ... that in my later books, writings, and sermons, express references to Kierkegaard have become fewer and fewer." Cf. also Barth's foreword to his *Church Dogmatics* (Munich 1932), where he writes that compared with his earlier *Christian Dogmatics in Outline* he has cancelled everything which could be perceived as a foundation of theology in existentialism (*KD* I/1, VIII).

sanctification. I am engaged in a work on the subject and would have asked and learnt a very, very great deal from you." Even if Bonhoeffer is clearly aware that in relation to Barth and Reformation theology he is moving on new paths with his interpretation of the Sermon on the Mount, he wants to make explicit that his independent thinking not be misunderstood as a separation from Barth. Even though he is "not counted as one of the theologians associated with you,"[118] he himself knows well "that it is not true." And usually, "most of us who feel that they had to keep away from you for a while ... seem to find that afterwards, in a personal conversation with you, they learn that once again they have seen the whole question in far too crude terms." Concerning the "communal life" in the Preacher's Seminary with its combination of "theological work" and "spiritual community," rooted in "morning and evening gathering around the word" and in "fixed times for prayer," Bonhoeffer mentions explicitly that he perceives it to be "only the consequence of what you have made very clear in 'Anselm.' The charge of legalism does not seem to me to fit at all."[119]

Obviously, Bonhoeffer knew of the mistrust on the side of Barth regarding the attempt at realizing a kind of "evangelical monastery" in Finkenwalde.[120] Even though Barth's book on Anselm encouraged Bonhoeffer's experiment it could not reduce Barth's suspicions concerning the "theoretical-practical system" he saw taking shape in Finkenwalde. Barth does tell Bonhoeffer, however, that he has "much sympathy with that" and does not think it to be an "impossible" undertaking in principle. But what troubles him about an "Introduction to Daily Meditation" from Finkenwalde, composed by Eberhard Bethge,[121] is the "odour of monastic eros and pathos" for which "at the moment I still have neither a positive feeling nor a use for it." In addition, he preferred not to "go with the distinction in principle between theological work and devotional edification." He "looked forward openly, but not without concern," to the attempt in the new book to raise in a new way "the inexhaustible theme of justification and sanctification." He considered it a mistake to resign „in the face of the original Christological-eschatological beginning in favour of some kind of realisa-

---

[118] To his disappointment Bonhoeffer had not been invited to contribute to the Festschrift for Barth's fiftieth birthday in 1936.

[119] Letter to Karl Barth (19 September 1936) in *DBW* 14, 235–237.

[120] There had been an indirect contact between Barth and Bonhoeffer in August 1935, when Bonhoeffer's assistant Wilhelm Rott, "a Barthian influenced by the Reformed tradition of the Rhineland" (Bethge, *Dietrich Bonhoeffer*, 424) had visited Barth in Switzerland. On 21 August 1935 Barth's assistant Charlotte von Kirschbaum noted on this occasion about Rott's report from Finkenwalde: "In the afternoon Mr. Wilh. Rott – former student – here, reports about attempts at reform with monastic tendency in Finkenwalde under Bonhoeffer. Karl *warns*. It seems to be an escape movement. The real question there is the issue of objection to military service" (in: *DBW* 14, 250, note 3).

[121] "Anleitung zur täglichen Meditation," in *DBW* 14, 945–950.

tion (in fact becoming more and more abstract) in a specifically human sphere." Nevertheless, Barth did not wish his questions to be understood "as a criticism of your efforts, simply because the basis of my knowledge and understanding of them is still far too scanty."[122]

We may leave open the question as to what extent Bonhoeffer's book *Discipleship* and especially the project of the "Brothers' House" contained features of resignation.[123] In a letter to Sutz Bonhoeffer complains that his real concern is being misunderstood when Barth detects in it an extension of the contemporary "groups movement." That movement was indeed taking on "an extremely serious appearance" in Germany so that suspicion was quite appropriate. But Bonhoeffer insists that his Finkenwalde experiment ought not be aligned with such an "apolitical, living phenomenon" and its sanctimonious retreat to the backwoods of religion.[124] What he wants to accomplish is not at all a softening of the confrontation by means of withdrawal into the pious group but, on the contrary, a strengthening of the Confessing Church's intransigent position on the basis of the decisions reached at the Synods of Barmen and Dahlem. He made that clear in his essay on "The Boundaries of the Church and Church Union" (April 1936).[125] Reporting to Barth about the conflicts around the publication, he writes: "Unfortunately I am at the moment involved in a big battle over my article on church union. People are getting frightfully excited about it. And I thought that I was writing something obvious. I would be very glad to have a word from you on the matter."[126] Helmut Gollwitzer's "Comments and Concerns" may to some extent be taken as Barth's "word" on the matter.[127] He called attention to Bonhoeffer's hotly disputed sentence, "Those who knowingly cut themselves off from the Confessing Church in Germany cut themselves off from salvation."[128] Gollwitzer asserted that this sentence could indeed not be interpreted as something "legalistic," but that it was an actualization of what the church had declared from the beginning:

---

[122] K. Barth, Letter to D. Bonhoeffer (14 October 1936) in *DBW* 14, 250–253. When in the second part-volume of the "Doctrine of Reconciliation" Barth reached the chapter on "Sanctification" he expressed his unconcealed admiration for Bonhoeffer's book as "by far the best that has been written" on the topic. He even felt "tempted" to insert the first chapters of *Discipleship* as "an extended quotation" into the chapter entitled "The Sanctification of the Human Being;" cf. K. Barth, CD IV/2, 533–534 (KD IV/2, 604).

[123] On the fraternal community of the "Brothers' House" in Finkenwalde, cf. *Life Together* (*DBW/E* 5).

[124] Letter to Erwin Sutz (24 October 1936) in: *DBW* 14, 256.

[125] "Zur Frage nach der Kirchengemeinschaft," in *DBW* 14, 655–680.

[126] Letter to Karl Barth (19 September 1936) in *DBW* 14, 238.

[127] Gollwitzer was at that time writing his dissertation on the early Lutheran doctrine of the Holy Supper in its controversy with Calvinism under the supervision of Karl Barth.

[128] "The Question of the Boundaries of the Church and Church Union," in *WF* 93–94; translation altered.

extra ecclesiam nulla salus [outside the church, there is no salvation]."[129] On the other hand, there are formulations in Bonhoeffer's essay about which doubts may be raised.[130] This goes especially for the assertion that „we can no longer go back behind Barmen and Dahlem ... because we can no longer go back behind the Word of God."[131] Gollwitzer counters that "the Confession of the church is not the Word of God but the church's testimony of the Word of God. It is not God, but the church which has spoken at Barmen and at Dahlem, however great the part played by God may be thought to have been."

No matter, Bonhoeffer believes himself to be wholly with Barth, the author of the Barmen Declaration, when he writes that "since Barmen, Lutherans and Reformed have been speaking with one voice in Synodal declarations. Schismatic differences of confession no longer make it impossible to form a Confessing Synod."[132] And that is why Bonhoeffer can turn to Barth and ask precisely of him to bring out into the open and to discuss "some of the questions of substance which divide Lutherans and Reformed."[133]

VII. Renewed Proximity:
Ethics and Bonhoeffer's Journeys to Switzerland

Since 1938 Barth in his publications repeatedly called for political resistance against Hitler, including "tyrannicide" and military activities.[134] That call earned him disavowal in the ranks of the Confessing Church, but Bonhoeffer took no part in the widespread abandonment of Barth at this time; rather, by his entry into the activities of the political underground, he gave practical expression to Barth's call. In a letter to his brother-in-law, lawyer Gerhard Leibholz, who had emigrated from Germany and was living in Oxford, Bonhoeffer appears to comment on Barth's essay on *Rechtfertigung und Recht* (1938): "Karl has now made the attempt, based on the rig-

---

[129] H. Gollwitzer, "Comments and Concerns," in *WF*, 97–98.
[130] H. Gollwitzer, *WF*, 99.
[131] "The Question of the Boundaries," in *WF*, 87.
[132] "The Question of the Boundaries," in *WF*, 89.
[133] Letter to Karl Barth (19 September 1936) in *DBW* 14, 238 (cf. *WF*, 118).
[134] Cf. K. Barth, *The Knowledge of God and the Service of God, according to the Teaching of the Reformation: Recalling the Scottish Confession of 1560*, translated by J. L. M. Haire and Ian Henderson (London 1938). Cf. also K. Barth, "Rechtfertigung und Recht" (1938); English translation: "Church and State" (1939), in K. Barth, *Community, State and Church. Three Essays* (Gloucester, MA. 1968); cf. also K. Barth, "Open Letter to Josef L. Hromádka" [on occasion of the Munich treaty of September 1938], 19 September 1938, in *Eine Schweizer Stimme 1938-1945* (Zurich, second edition, 1948), 58–59.

orously Reformed thesis, nevertheless to avoid relativizing the historical. That is very tempting. (In good biblical fashion) he relates every order of the created world strictly to Christ and says that they can be properly understood only in relation to him and that they need to find their orientation from him. One simply must read this. Once these problems have been dealt with, the question of the relationship of law, justice and love (in the sense of the Sermon on the Mount) has to be raised, in my judgment ... Law that is oriented toward justice and becomes a historical reality through the use of force (rather than remaining an abstract idea!) is 'a tutor to conduct us to Christ,' as Gal 3:24 puts it."[135] While affirming Barth's "rigorously Reformed" attempt, Bonhoeffer apparently pushes forward independently, his specific concern being the integration of the Sermon on the Mount into Barth's approach.[136]

One may interpret Bonhoeffer's drafts for an *Ethics* as attempts to concretize Barth precisely in relation to the "political worship of God"[137] with the necessary completeness.[138] Obviously, the chapter entitled "The Ultimate and the Penultimate Things" in Bonhoeffer's *Ethics*, on which he was working during the winter of 1940–1941 in Ettal, was influenced by Barth's essay on *Rechtfertigung* ("justification," as the ultimate) and *Recht* ("justice" or "law," as the penultimate thing).[139] This would be especially true in relation to the coordination of the ultimate and the penultimate depicted in the section of that chapter on "preparing the way for the word."[140]

---

[135] Letter to Gerhard Leibholz (7 March 1940) in *DBW*, 15, 298–299. Cf. K. Barth, "Church and State," 101: "Is there a connection between justification of the sinner through faith alone, completed once and for all by God through Jesus Christ, and the problem of justice, the problem of human law?"

[136] Reinhold Niebuhr recalled some years later that, during a conversation in London in 1939, Bonhoeffer asserted "that Barth was right in becoming more political." However, he held that "a little pamphlet" was, in this respect, too little in comparison to the size of Barth's dogmatics (cf. E. Bethge, *Dietrich Bonhoeffer*, 621).

[137] Cf. K. Barth, "Church and State," 101: "Is there something like a political service of God?" (translation altered).

[138] Later Bonhoeffer regarded his *Ethics* as "his actual life work" (cf. Letter to E. Bethge (15 December 1943) in *LPP*, 163 (*DBW* 8, 237).

[139] Bonhoeffer's distinction of "ultimate" and "penultimate" and particularly the understanding of the "ultimate" as "a complete break with everything penultimate, with all that has gone before" (*DBWE* 6, 149) may well go back to the early Barth, who in his Tambach address (1919) had firmly maintained that "the ultimate, the eschaton, the synthesis, is not at all the continuation, the result, the consequence, the next step after the penultimate, but, on the contrary, is the radical break with everything penultimate" (K. Barth, "The Christian's Place in Society," in: K. Barth, *The Word of God and the Word of Man*, 324; translation altered).

[140] *DBWE* 6, 161 (*DBW* 6,153). Cf. K. Barth, "Church and State," 119, according to which the task of the state, in Christological perspective, is to "administer justice and

On the one hand, Bonhoeffer speaks of "the ultimate" as "a complete break with the penultimate."[141] On the other hand, his chief concern is the "relation" of the "penultimate things ... to the ultimate," the "preparation" of the way for the ultimate in the penultimate.[142]

It was in the years of the war only that Bonhoeffer met again with Karl Barth face-to-face. In the course of three journeys to Switzerland in charge of the group of conspirators under the cover of the military's intelligence section he had the opportunity to visit Barth. In his letters Bonhoeffer repeatedly thanks Barth for the "conversations," but only little of these discussions has been recorded, because they had to confine themselves to oral exchanges. However, it seems possible to reconstruct the main topics with some clarity.

During his first Swiss journey (24 February–24 March 1941) Bonhoeffer was able to obtain the latest volume of Barth's *Church Dogmatics* II/1 ("The Doctrine of God"), published in 1940.[143] Before having the volume sent to Berlin, he removed the binding and title page as a matter of precaution. In a letter, written after his return to Germany, Bonhoeffer tells Barth what great joy it was for him to take possession of that volume: "I am well into it by now and am pleased every day to be reading real theology again." At that time Bonhoeffer himself was working on his *Ethics* every free day available to him. However, as he reported to Barth in his letter: "Along with several others I have now also received a ban on doing any writing for publication." Then he announces a further journey to Switzerland, for the late summer of 1941, hoping to read and write during that visit: "Much encouraged by my trip, I have recently been making excellent progress in my work. Yet it is often difficult to concentrate, and soon I would very much like to be able to discuss with you, at some length, certain questions concerning my work."[144]

It seems that during the second journey to Switzerland (29 August to 26 September 1941) it was primarily ethical questions that Bonhoeffer raised in the "conversations" with Barth. At the same time, Barth was also occupied with problems of ethics; in the summer of 1941 he was composing along with the doctrine of "Israel and the Church" the ethical chapter of his "Doctrine of God".[145] On the basis of a communication by Charlotte von Kirschbaum, Bethge concludes that "Bonhoeffer was now concerned ...

---

protect law" and, "in so doing," grant "the gospel of justification a free and assured course."

[141] *DBWE* 6, 151 (*DBW* 6, 142).

[142] *DBWE* 6, 151 and 161 (*DBW* 6, 142 and 153).

[143] Cf. Letter to Charlotte von Kirschbaum (19 March 1941) in *DBWE* 16, 174 (*DBW* 16, 164).

[144] Letter to K. Barth (30 May 1941) in *DBWE* 16, 190–191 (*DBW* 16, 182).

[145] Cf. K. Barth, *CD* II/2 (*KD* II/2), chapter 8: "God's Commandment."

with the way Christians are drawn into contemporary history. In addition it was questions of an ethics of responsibility and, thirdly, how the church handles the guilt it had incurred through its complicity that interested him, as did the question of how he himself and his associates in the conspiracy had to bear guilt."[146]

According to the editors of *Ethics* Bonhoeffer was primarily occupied with the chapter "Guilt, Justification and Renewal" in 1941, a chapter that contains a concrete "Confession of Guilt" on the part of the church.[147] This chapter was preceded by the chapter "Inheritance and Decay," which in a broad *geistesgeschichtliche* tour d'horizon introduces into the problems of the Christians' participation in history. In this chapter Bonhoeffer had written that "it is the fact of the appearance of Jesus Christ" that "evokes the question of our historical heritage." More precisely, "the line of our forefathers reaches back" even "before the appearance of Jesus Christ into the people of Israel," because "Jesus Christ was the promised Messiah of the Israelite-Jewish people." Therefore, "Western history is by God's will inextricably bound up with the people of Israel." Later, probably after his return from the second journey to Switzerland in 1941, Bonhoeffer added in the margin of the page that this inextricable link between Western history and Israel is to be understood "not just genetically but in an honest, unceasing encounter. The Jews keep open the question of Christ; they are the sign of God's free, gracious election [*freie Gnadenwahl*] and of God's rejecting wrath." Here Bonhoeffer refers to Rom 11,22: "See the kindness and the severity of God." Finally he notes his conviction most relevant to the contemporary situation: "An expulsion/rejection [*Verstoßung*] of the Jew(s) from the West must result in the rejection of Christ. For Jesus Christ was a Jew."[148]

The editors of *Ethics* mention in a footnote that in the night of 16 to 17 October 1941 the mass deportations of Jews from Berlin residences had started, suggesting that Bonhoeffer's insertion should be read as a reaction onto the contemporary history. There is no reason to draw this contextualization into doubt. However, Bonhoeffer's specific choice of words – "Verstoßung" can be translated by "rejection" or "repudiation" as well as by

---

[146] E. Bethge, "Bemerkungen," in: *Dietrich Bonhoeffer, Schweizer Korrespondenz 1941/42*, Theologische Existenz heute, Neue Folge, 214 (Munich 1932), 26. Cf. Charlotte von Kirschbaum, Letter to Paul Vogt (22 September 1941) in *DBWE* 16, 218–219 (*DBW* 16, 207).

[147] Cf. *DBWE* 6, 138–141 (*DBW* 6, 129–132). This confession ends with a reference to the connection between God's justification and human justice resembling Barth's essay "Rechtfertigung und Recht" (Church and State): The church "has not so proclaimed the justice of God that all human law must see there it's own source and essence" (141; translation altered).

[148] *DBWE* 6, 105 (*DBW* 6, 95); translation altered.

"expulsion" or "driving out" – signals an allusion to the doctrine of "Israel and the Church," which Barth was developing at the begin of the forties in the context of the "Doctrine of God" of his *Church Dogmatics* in a great paraphrase of *Romans* 9 to 11.[149] When Bonhoeffer uses the term "free gracious election" he uses a recognizable Barthian term: In Barth's "Doctrine of God" the term "gracious election" [*Gnadenwahl*] serves at dismissing a misunderstanding in the traditional doctrine of predestination as something threatening. Describing God's predestination as "gracious election" Barth wants to emphasize the "triumph of grace" over the repudiation.[150] Because God in Jesus Christ chooses the rejection for himself, there can be no rejected humans any more. In Barth's exposition of Rom. 11, 17–22 we find the following phrasing: "He, who has Jesus in faith, cannot want *not* to have the Jews, he must have them together with Jesus as his ancestors and relatives. Otherwise he also cannot have the Jew Jesus. Otherwise he rejects with the Jews *Jesus* himself."[151] The formulation resembles very much Bonhoeffer's phrasing in *Ethics*.

When Bonhoeffer speaks of a polarity of "election-grace" and "repudiation" he makes clear that he, too, reflects on the doctrine of predestination. And it is not by chance that in his reflection on the relationship between the Christian West and the Jews he uses "Barthian" terminology. However, the volume of Barth's *Church Dogmatics* referred to was published only after Bonhoeffer had inserted the passage into his *Ethics*. Thus we must assume that the topic was part of the "conversations" with Barth in March and September 1941. In addition, it is likely that during his Swiss journeys Bonhoeffer had got knowledge of Barth's address "Our Church and Switzerland Today" (November 1940), which in summer 1941 had earned him a ban on speaking in Switzerland. In his address Barth had described "the rough and fine maltreatment of the Jews" in Germany as the real core of "the foreign rule and tyranny imminent today." And he had concluded that "the inner center of the empire rising today" consisted "in hate against and rejection [*Verstoßung*] of the Jews. ... But the Son of Man, who was God's Son, was a Jew ... We cannot bow to this empire, because we cannot reject the salvation, which has come to the Jews and has come to us from the Jews."[152] With this statement and Bonhoeffer's similar insertion into his

---

[149] *CD* (*KD* II/2, 1942), § 34. "Die Erwählung der Gemeinde," especially section 1. Israel und die Kirche, 215–226.
[150] *KD* II/2, 214.
[151] *KD* II/2, 318f.
[152] K. Barth, "Unsere Kirche und die Schweiz in der heutigen Zeit," in K. Barth, *Eine Schweizer Stimme 1938-1945*, 161 and 175.

Ethics the tendency of proselytism regarding the Jews, which was widespread in the Confessing Church, is called into question for the first time.[153]

From 11-26 May 1942, the third of Bonhoeffer's journeys to Switzerland during his conspiratorial activities took place. He immediately procured the page proofs of the as yet unpublished volume of Barth's *Church Dogmatics* (CD II/2).[154] Still in Switzerland, and even before the visit to Barth, Bonhoeffer initially studied the second chapter of that volume, the one dealing with ethics.[155] The influence of Bonhoeffer's reading of this volume of Barth's *Church Dogmatics* can be demonstrated in the shift of accent in the understanding of "responsibility" in the two versions of the chapter "History and Good," conceived earlier and later in 1942. Whereas the first version explains "responsibility" more or less in the line of Max Weber,[156] the second version adopts Barth's explanation of "responsibility" in the light of "Christ as our life"[157] as "answerability," that is: answering to God's word in Christ. Now Bonhoeffer writes: "This life, lived in answer to the life of Jesus Christ (as the Yes and No to our life), we call 'responsibility.' ... Reponsibility thus means to risk one's life in its wholeness, aware that one's activity is a matter of life and death.[158] Accordingly the precision of "reality" in Bonhoeffer's description of responsibility in the section on "The Structure of Responsible Life" as "being in accord with reality," where reality means "*the Real One [der Wirkliche]*, namely the God who became human," can be regarded as an allusion to Barth's *Church Dogmatics* II/2.[159]

---

[153] For more details cf. A. Pangritz, "Marginalie zu Bonhoeffers Ethik," in: *Momente der Begegnung. Impulse für das christlich-jüdische Gespräch*, edited by M. Haarmann et al. (Wuppertal/Neukirchen-Vluyn 2004), 206–212; cf. also in: *Dietrich Bonhoeffer Yearbook/Jahrbuch* 2 (2005), 210–217.

[154] *KD* II/2: "Die Lehre von Gott [The Doctrine of God]," chapters 7: "God's Gracious Election," and 8: "God's Commandment."

[155] Cf. Letter to K. Barth (13 May 1942) in *DBWE* 16, 276–277 (*DBW* 16, 266–267). Cf. E. Bethge, "Bemerkungen," 28: "Since Bonhoeffer was working on his own 'Ethics' and was grappling with new approaches, and because earlier he had critically questioned Barth precisely in relation to ethics, he particularly wanted to know how the master approached this complex of issues." After his imprisonment Bonhoeffer managed to have Barth's "doctrine of predestination (unbound)" smuggled even into prison (cf. *LPP*, 171).

[156] Cf. *DBWE* 6, 220 (*DBW* 6, 219). The manuscript breaks off where "political action" is defined as "taking on responsibility. This cannot happen without power. Power is to serve responsibility" (245).

[157] *DBWE* 6, 248–251 (*DBW* 6, 246–249).

[158] *DBWE* 6, 254–255 (*DBW* 6, 254). Cf. K. Barth, *KD* II/2, 713–714: "Wir leben verantwortlich, d.h. unser Sein, Wollen, Tun und Lassen ist ... ein fortwährendes Antworten auf das uns als Gebot gesagte Wort Gottes."

[159] *DBWE* 6, 261 (*DBW* 6, 260). Cf. also *DBWE* 6, 325 (*DBW* 6, 328), the section "The Love of God and the Desintegration of the World," where Bonhoeffer emphasizes

Again, in the chapter "God's Love and the Disintegration of the World", written toward the end of 1942, we find allusions to Barth. When Bonhoeffer starts describing "Christian ethics" as an "attack on the presuppositions of all other ethics" and therefore as a "critique of all ethics,"[160] he clearly refers once more to the second edition of Barth's commentary on *The Epistle to the Romans*, where Barth in the chapter "The Problem of Ethics" commenting on Rom 12,1 had written. When "a Church embarks upon moral exhortation, its exhortation can be naught else but a criticism of all human behaviour."[161]

Still, the last chapters Bonhoeffer wrote for his *Ethics*, before his work was halted by his arrest, were influenced by his reading of Barth's *Church Dogmatics*. At issue is "The 'Ethical' and the 'Christian' as a Topic" as well as "The Concrete Commandment and the Divine Mandates," drafted early in 1943. Here Bonhoeffer tries to find a new solution for his quest for a concrete commandment. Following closely Barth's ethical argumentation in *Church Dogmatics* II/2, he wants to understand "the commandment of God" as "permission," namely, the "permission to live before God as a human being." And he characterizes the commandment of God: "It is distinguished from all human laws in that it *commands freedom*."[162] In the chapter "The Concrete Commandment and the Divine Mandates" Bonhoeffer tries to concretize the social dimension of the divine commandment in the four "mandates" which occur "in the church, in marriage and family, in culture, and in government."[163]

When, in 1949, Bethge published Bonhoeffer's manuscripts for the *Ethics*, Barth made use of it in the fourth part-volume of his *Doctrine of Creation*, containing the ethical chapter on "The Commandment of God, the Creator," praising Bonhoeffer's "brilliant 'Ethics'" for its orientation towards the dogmatical context.[164] However, Bonhoeffer's "doctrine of the mandates", this concededly "constructive" attempt, did not find Barth's approval. He wondered whether an enumeration of precisely those four

---

that Christ is "not some kind of neutral entity, but the historical person of Jesus himself." Cf. Karl Barth, *KD* II/2, 565: "kein Neutrum, sondern eine Person."

[160] *DBWE* 6, 299–300 (*DBW* 6, 301–302).

[161] K. Barth, *Der Römerbrief* (second edition), 413. The original reads: "Es ist, wenn es zu *Ethik* kommen soll, nichts anderes möglich, als Kritik alles *Ethos*."

[162] *DBWE* 6, 382 (*DBW* 6, 386). Cf. K. Barth, *KD* II/2, 650 (*CD* II/2, 585): "The form by which the command of God is distinguished from all other commands ... consists in the fact that it is permission – the granting of a very definitive freedom [*Gewährung einer ganz bestimmten Freiheit*]."

[163] *DBWE* 6, 388 (*DBW* 6, 392). The notion of "the four mandates of God" appears first in an insertion, made in 1941, into the first manuscript for the Ethics, entitled "Christ, Reality and Good. Christ, the Church and the World," of 1940; cf. *DBWE* 6, 68 (*DBW* 6, 54–55).

[164] *KD* III/4, 2.

mandates with an appeal to Scripture "does not still contain some arbitrary elements" and whether those mandates had to be about relations of authority rather than relations of freedom.[165]

While on his second journey to Switzerland, Bonhoeffer apparently also had an open exchange with Barth about his secret activity. Subsequently he believed that everything was "now clear" between him and Barth in relation to this matter. He refers to this when, at the beginning of the third journey, he learns of the rumour that his newest visit to Switzerland was "uncanny" for Barth "because of my commission." In the interest of "the admittedly difficult effort to continue our solidarity," he tells Barth "that at least in the eastern part of Germany there are only few who have remained as loyal to you in countless conversations over these years as I have attempted to do."[166] Thereupon Barth's assistant Charlotte von Kirschbaum informs Bonhoeffer that there was indeed, in Barth's circle of friends, the question "how it is that you have such freedom" but "in conversation with you the question was answered for him clearly." However, she admits that "there actually is something 'uncanny' for Karl Barth," not in relation to Bonhoeffer's person but in relation to "all the attempts to save Germany from the evident misery into which it has now been plunged by still more 'national' undertakings. This includes those that the generals might venture. He has told you so himself and is ready to talk to you about it."[167]

Here one may indeed detect a difference between Barth and Bonhoeffer in relation to the concrete forms that the "political worship" would need to take in the resistance against National Socialism.[168] However, as the so-called Operation Seven was being prepared – an attempt in 1942 to rescue a group of persecuted men and women of Jewish descent from the imminent deportation – Barth and Bonhoeffer cooperated in a very practical manner. With their support Charlotte Friedenthal, a coworker in the Con-

---

[165] *KD* III/4, 21–22: "In Bonhoeffer's doctrine of the mandates, one cannot entirely shake that little taste of North German patriarchalism ... Would it not be advisable ... [not to be] rushing on to the rigid assertion of human relationships arranged in a definite order, and the hasty assertion of their imperative character?" Interestingly, in his prison correspondence, Bonhoeffer himself relativized his "doctrine of the mandates" in a way that to a great extent anticipates Barth's critique: "Our 'Protestant' (not Lutheran!) Prussian world has been so dominated by the four mandates that the sphere of freedom has receded into the background" (Letter to Renate and Eberhard Bethge (23 January 1944) in *LPP*, 193 (*DBW* 8, 291).

[166] Letter to K. Barth (17 May 1942) in *DBWE* 16, 277–279 (*DBW* 16, 267–269).

[167] C. v. Kirschbaum, Letter to Dietrich Bonhoeffer (17 May 1942) in *DBWE* 16, 279–280 (*DBW* 16, 270–271); cf. *More Bonhoeffer-Barth Correspondence*, edited by John D. Godsey, 7–8.

[168] In a letter to Jørgen Glenthøj (7 September 1956) Barth recalls that the "main topic" of his "conversation with Bonhoeffer at the time" had been the "question whether the planned new German government would be conservative or authoritarian, or have a democratic form;" cf. *DBWE* 16, 281, note 8 (*DBW* 16, 271, note 7).

fessing Church, was brought safely across the Swiss border on 5 September 1942, in the "disguise" of a spy of the "intelligence."[169]

VIII. Barth's Theology in Bonhoeffer's Prison Correspondence

We now turn to Bonhoeffer's renewed discussion of Barth's theology in the prison correspondence containing the famous or infamous reproach of "positivism of revelation" against Barth. It should be noted from the outset that every critical remark of Barth to be found in *Letters and Papers from Prison* is preceded by a praise of the Basilean theologian. Praise and blame of Barth should therefore carefully be weighed up against each other.

After Bethge, together with Bonhoeffer's parents and Maria von Wedemeyer, had found the opportunity to visit the prisoner on 26 November 1943, more than half a year after his incarceration, Bonhoeffer thanks for "Karl's cigar ... something really indescribable," the gift he had received via Bethge, who in summer 1943 had visited Barth in Switzerland.[170] On Advent IV, 1943, he asks Bethge: "if you can get without difficulty Barth's *Doctrine of Predestination* (unbound), or his *Doctrine of God*, please have them sent to me."[171] It seems that Bonhoeffer hoped to continue his theological work in prison with the help of these books. Perhaps the recent reading of Barth's *Church Dogmatics* is reflected in Bonhoeffer's mention in March 1944 of Barth as one example among other representatives of "*hilaritas*," which he describes as "a steadfast certainty that in their own work they are showing the world something good (even if the world doesn't like it), and a high-spirited self-confidence."[172]

In the first "theological" letter from prison to Bethge (30 April 1944) Bonhoeffer starts his new "theological thoughts" on "the question what Christianity really is, or indeed who Christ really is, for us today." He suggests that the "religious *a priori*" that had been the basis of "our whole nineteen-hundred-year-old Christian preaching and theology," did "not exist at all."[173] This contestation of the basic assumption of liberal theology can be read as an implicit approval of Barth's criticism of religion. However, Bonhoeffer's description of the "religious *a priori*" as a thinking, in

---

[169] Cf. Winfried Meyer, *Unternehmen Sieben. Eine Rettungsaktion für vom Holocaust Bedrohte aus dem Amt Ausland/Abwehr im Oberkommando der Wehrmacht* (Frankfurt a. M., 1993), 70–82 and 290–306.

[170] Letter to E. Bethge (26 November 1943) in *LPP*, 145 (*DBW* 8, 209).

[171] Letter to E. Bethge, Fourth Advent (19 December 1943) in *LPP*, 171 (*DBW* 8, 249); translation altered. Reference to K. Barth, *CD*, volumes II/1 and II/2, which Bonhoeffer had received during his journeys to Switzerland in 1941 and 1942.

[172] Letter to E. Bethge (9 March 1944) in *LPP*, 229 (*DBW* 8, 352).

[173] Letter to E. Bethge (30 April 1944) in *LPP*, 279–280 (*DBW* 8, 402–403).

which "'Christianity' has always been a form – perhaps the true form – of 'religion'," seems to include Barth, who in his *Church Dogmatics* had developed the "problem of religion" in a dialectic of "religion as unbelief" and "true religion," where the church is the "place of true religion."[174] It can be left open here, if Bonhoeffer's description of this "a priori" as "a historically conditioned and transient form of human self-expression" is in complete accordance with Barth or not.[175] In any case Bonhoeffer continues his reflections praising Barth, who was "the only one to have started along this line of thought," that is along the line of "religionless Christianity." However, he "did not carry it to completion, but arrived at a positivism of revelation, which in the last analysis is essentially a restoration. For the religionless worker or human being in general nothing decisive is gained here." Bonhoeffer's concern is a "Christian life in a religionless world," in which Christ "is no longer an object of religion but ... really the Lord of the world."[176]

In the next letter (5 May 1944) we read again that "Barth was the first theologian to begin the criticism of religion," which "remains his really great merit." However, he put in the place of religion "a positivist doctrine of revelation which says, in effect, 'Take it or leave it': virgin birth, Trinity, or anything else; each is an equally significant and necessary part of the whole, which must simply be swallowed as a whole or not at all." But that is "unbiblical," for there are "degrees of knowledge and degrees of significance. ... The positivism of revelation makes it too easy for itself, by setting up, as it does in the last analysis, a law of faith, and so mutilates what is – by Christ's incarnation! – a gift for us. In the place of religion there now stands the church – that is in itself biblical – but the world is in some degree made to depend on itself and left to its own devices, and that's the mistake."[177]

There is a third letter (8 June 1944), in which Bonhoeffer praises Barth's merits before uttering his criticism. Now he writes that "Barth was the first to realize the mistake" that all the apologetic attempts of Heim, Althaus and Tillich "(which were all, in fact, still sailing, though unintentionally, in the channel of liberal theology) were making in leaving clear a space for religion in the world or against the world. He brought in against

---

[174] Cf. K. Barth, *KD* I/2, 304ff. Cf. already K. Barth, *The Epistle to the Romans*, second, revised edition, 211ff. (chapter "Freedom" with the sections "The boundaries of religion," "The meaning of religion" and "The reality of religion").

[175] Ernst Feil, *The Theology of Dietrich Bonhoeffer*, 173, maintains that Bonhoeffer's reflections on "non-religious Christianity" are conceived mainly in the way of "Geistesgeschichte," whereas Barth's criticism of religion is to be understood primarily as a "systematic concept."

[176] *LPP*, 280–281 (*DBW* 8, 405); translation altered.

[177] *LPP*, 286 (*DBW* 8, 415); translation altered.

religion the God of Jesus Christ, '*pneuma* against *sarx*.' That remains his greatest merit (his *Epistle to the Romans*, second edition, in spite of all the neo-Kantian egg-shells). Through his later dogmatics, he enabled the church to effect this distinction, in principle, all along the line." And then Bonhoeffer, in contrast to his own earlier criticism, continues: "It was not in ethics, as is often said, that he subsequently failed – his ethical observations, as far as they exist" – Bonhoeffer would have had the ethical section of *Church Dogmatics* II/2 in mind – "are just as important as his dogmatic ones." Now Bonhoeffer's criticism refers to another point: "it was that in the non-religious interpretation of theological concepts he gave no concrete guidance, either in dogmatics or in ethics. There lies his limitation, and because of it his theology of revelation has become positivist, a 'positivism of revelation', as I put it."[178]

Even more serious is the charge against the Confessing Church, which according to Bonhoeffer "has now largely forgotten all about the Barthian approach, and has lapsed from positivism of revelation into conservative restoration."[179] Bonhoeffer's concern is to "overcome" liberal theology, which, albeit still negatively, determines even Barth, by genuinely taking up and answering "its question," something that "is *not* the case in the Confessing Church's positivism of revelation!"[180] It is therefore not by chance that the last reported note by Bonhoeffer on Barth – without employing the term of "positivism of revelation" any longer – is directed against a certain conservative "Barthianism" within the Confessing Church rather than against Barth himself. In his "Outline for a Book" (August 1944) Bonhoeffer writes: "Barth and the Confessing Church bring about that one entrenches oneself persistently behind the 'faith of the church' and never asks and declares what one really believes. That is why there blows no fresh breeze in the Confessing Church either."[181]

Unfortunately, research to date has had to find its way in heavy fog in relation to the precise meaning of the term "positivism of revelation" in Bonhoeffer's prison correspondence.[182] Worse than that is the claim that everybody pretends to know what Bonhoeffer meant to chide Barth for,

---

[178] Letter to E. Bethge (8 June 1944) in *LPP*, 328 (*DBW* 8, 480–481).

[179] *LPP*, 328 (*DBW* 8, 481). Bonhoeffer continues: "The important thing about that church is that it carries on the great concepts of Christian theology; but it seems as if doing this is gradually just about exhausting it."

[180] *LPP*, 329 (*DBW* 8, 482). It should be noted that in this last mention of "positivism of revelation" the charge is directed not against Barth, but against the Confessing Church.

[181] "Outline for a Book," in *LPP*, 382 (*DBW* 8, 559–560); translation altered.

[182] Cf. A. Pangritz, *Karl Barth in the Theology of Dietrich Bonhoeffer*, 82ff. and Ralf K. Wüstenberg, *A Theology of Life: Dietrich Bonhoeffer's Religionless Christianity*, (Grand Rapids/Cambridge 1999).

namely, the "Old Testament, prophetic,"[183] the authoritarian gesture "vertically from above" that does not sit well with the interpreters. "When one was tired of Karl Barth one could go to Bonhoeffer's 'positivism of revelation' for ammunition," Bethge said.[184] But such false certainty in relation to the point of Bonhoeffer's polemics does not match well the admiration Bonhoeffer still held for Barth's "really great merit."

Besides, it should be noted that the term "positivism of revelation" originally was used in the faculty of theology at the University of Berlin as an approving characterization of the "irrationality" or even "anti-rationality" of Luther's theology, in which faith asserts the divine revelation as the "positively" given reality against all "natural" reason.[185] In *Act and Being* Bonhoeffer had – with similar terminology – criticized Barth for his tendency to emphasize God's freedom beyond the "contingent positivity" of revelation and thereby to "rationalize" it.[186] In contrast to this language, "positivism of revelation" is used as a charge against Barth and even more seriously against the Confessing Church in Bonhoeffer's prison correspondence. It is therefore difficult to describe a simple continuity between Bonhoeffer's early criticism of Barth and his later reproach.

When, in 1951, Eberhard Bethge published for the first time Bonhoeffer's *Letters and Papers from Prison*, Barth reacted confused with respect to Bonhoeffer's rebuke of "positivism of revelation." He wrote: "Now he has left us alone with the enigmatic utterances of his letters – at more than one point clearly showing that he sensed, without really knowing, how the story should continue – for example, what exactly he meant by the 'positivism of revelation' he found in me, and especially how the programme of an unreligious speech was to be realized." And Barth added the advice to rest content in "remaining behind, somewhat confused," in order "to take the best" of Bonhoeffer.[187] It seems that Barth, like Bonhoeffer, is not aware of the fact that he himself first had spoken about a biblically qualified non-religious "worldliness" in his Aarau address on "Biblical Questions, Insights and Vistas" (1920), an address that had provoked Harnack's

---

[183] Bethge, Letter to Bonhoeffer (3 June 1944) in *LPP*, 317 (*DBW* 8, 463).
[184] Bethge, *Dietrich Bonhoeffer*, 890.
[185] The church historian Erich Seeberg, son of Bonhoeffer's supervisor Reinhold Seeberg, used the term in this way in his book *Luthers Theologie. Motive und Ideen*, volume 1 (Göttingen 1929), 185 and 218. Cf. G. Krause, "Dietrich Bonhoeffer," *TRE* 7, 58.
[186] Cf. *DBWE* 2, 124 (*DBW* 2, 122).
[187] K. Barth, Letter to P. W. Herrenbrück (21 December 1952), in *World Come of Age*, 90–91.

protest.[188] Anyhow, Barth preferred to listen to Bonhoeffer's earlier writings rather than to the prison correspondence.[189]

In his posthumously published fragment on *The Christian Life*, Barth later came to a more cautious assessment of Bonhoeffer's non-religious "worldliness": "Because a Christian knows that the world out there in not just all darkness without light, one has the freedom ... to show solidarity with those out there in the world, in a serious manner, by standing unconditionally by their side. Something like this may have been on Dietrich Bonhoeffer's mind in his last years of life."[190]

IX. Conclusion and Evaluation

Since his first encounter with Barth's theology Bonhoeffer had developed his own theology in an ongoing debate with Barth, a debate that sometimes contained sharp criticisms as for instance in the charge of "postivism of revelation," that on the other hand never could suppress the fact that Barth remained the most important theological authority for Bonhoeffer among his contemporaries.

A number of models have been offered with respect to the "basic difference" between Barth and Bonhoeffer, which allegedly characterized their relationship right from the beginning, until Bonhoeffer's reproach of "positivism of revelation" got to the heart of it. Regin Prenter thought that he could demonstrate that from Bonhoeffer's early questions about Barth's doctrine of revelation there is "a straight line ... to the criticism of Barth's positivism of revelation." With Barth "everything points to eternity," while Bonhoeffer's road led "into temporality."[191] Another suggestion was presented by Heinrich Ott, who maintained that "the controversy between Barth and Bonhoeffer" did not refer to "a difference in *substance*"; the

---

[188] Cf. K. Barth, "Biblical Questions, Insights and Vistas," in *The Word of God and the Word of Man*, 66: "Biblical piety is not really pious; one must rather characterize it as well-considered, qualified worldliness."

[189] K. Barth, Letter to P. W. Herrenbrück, (21 December 1952), in in *World Come of Age*, 90–91. Cf. also Barth's letter to Hanfried Müller (7 April 1961), on occasion of the publication of Müller's dissertation on Bonhoeffer's theology (in *Weißenseer Blätter* (2006), 4): "It seems to me that in a really responsible representation of Bonhoeffer's theology Letters and Papers from Prison should be treated in an appendix only."

[190] K. Barth, "Das christliche Leben" in *KD* IV/4, Fragmente aus dem Nachlaß, Vorlesungen 1959–1961, edited by Hans-Anton Drewes and Eberhard Jüngel (Zurich 1976), 339.

[191] Regin Prenter, "Dietrich Bonhoeffer and Karl Barth's Positivism of Revelation," in *World Come of Age*, 125–126 and 128.

difference was to locate "in *method*" or "theological language" instead.[192] James H. Burtness expressed the suspicion that "the two do divide on the capax/non capax question along classical Lutheran/Reformed lines."[193] Although each of these suggestions has something to be said for it, they miss the decisive point: the basic agreement between Bonhoeffer and Barth.

More balanced are statements by Eberhard Bethge, Heinz Eduard Tödt, Paul Lehmann and John D. Godsey. In his biography of Dietrich Bonhoeffer Bethge writes: "While the early Barth, desiring to proclaim God's majesty, began by removing him to a remote distance, Bonhoeffer's starting point, inspired by the same desire to proclaim his majesty, brought him into close proximity."[194] Tödt suspected that "the most important basis" for Bonhoeffer's critique of Barth in the prison correspondence was Barth's treatment of "predestination and God's commandment." He asks: "Could Barth ... depict God's pre-eminent sovereignty in such a way that human beings did not become puppets but emerged with spontaneity, as self-acting agents being of age in the condition of the world that God had made possible?" However, Tödt emphasizes that in their basic understanding of revelation and world the assumptions of Barth and Bonhoeffer are not controversial, but they "converge."[195] Lehmann, too, relates the difference to a mutually shared concern, namely, their search for the concreteness of revelation. "For Barth, the *incapax* protected the concreteness of *God* in his revelation, as it were, on the giving end of the stick. For Bonhoeffer, the *capax* protected the concreteness of the *revelation* of God, as it were, on the receiving end of the stick, that is, in the reality of faith. For both, the major question of theology was the question of concreteness."[196]

Godsey appears to be right: "Although the confessional differences are important, they are not decisive."[197] He asks: "Can it be that the basic difference between Bonhoeffer and Barth has to do with their assessment of liberal theology and how it was to be overcome?"[198] And he suggests "that their deepest theological differences come at the point where they are most

---

[192] Heinrich Ott, *Reality and Faith: The Theological Legacy of Dietrich Bonhoeffer*, (Philadelphia, Pa., 1971), 129 and 136.

[193] James H. Burtness, "As though God Were Not Given: Barth, Bonhoeffer and the Finitum Capax Infiniti," in *Dialog* 19 (1980), 250.

[194] Bethge, *Dietrich Bonhoeffer*, 134.

[195] Heinz Eduard Tödt, "Glauben in einer religionslosen Welt. Muß man zwischen Barth und Bonhoeffer wählen?," in *Genf '76. Ein Bonhoeffer-Symposion*, ed. by Hans Pfeifer (Munich 1976), 100–101 and 104.

[196] Paul Lehmann, "The Concreteness of Theology: Reflections on the Conversation between Barth and Bonhoeffer," in *Footnotes to a Theology: The Karl Barth Colloquium of 1972*, edited by Martin Rumscheidt (Waterloo 1974); cited by James H. Burtness, "As though God Were Not Given," 251.

[197] John D. Godsey, "Barth and Bonhoeffer," in *Quarterly Review* 7 (1987), 18.

[198] Godsey, "Barth and Bonhoeffer," 23.

closely bound together. Both accepted the general guidelines of Chalcedon that in Jesus Christ there is united both true divinity and true humanity. But Barth tended to emphasize the divinity ... Bonhoeffer, on the other hand, stressed the hiddenness of divinity in the humiliated One." Finally, "Barth's theology tends toward a *theologia gloriae* in order to assure the *graceousness* of God's action in Christ ... In contrast, Bonhoeffer's theology is a *theologia crucis* in order to assure the *costliness* of God's grace in Christ." Yet, all these differences notwithstanding, Godsey does not want to play off Barth and Bonhoeffer against each other. "Barth and Bonhoeffer, Bonhoeffer and Barth. They make quite a team!"[199]

In this context it seems important to note a comment by Bethge in which he speaks of "*A Shift of Interest*" in Barth and Bonhoeffer that occurred at different times. "For all their mutual liking ..., each was at a different phase of his development. One had just arrived at the point of departure of the other – that is, the other was leaving the point that his companion was trying to reach."[200] This observation seems to be true not only for the moment of the first face-to-face encounter in Bonn in 1931, where Bethge refers to, but also for the other phases of their encounter. Throughout the different phases of this change-filled relationship Bethge's observation is valid: "Whatever the implications of Bonhoeffer's criticisms of Barth ... Bonhoeffer viewed these criticisms as coming from within, not outside, the Barthian movement."[201]

Summing up, it seems to be necessary in the first place to emphasize the fact that there is a great continuity of approval and even enthusiasm in Bonhoeffer with respect to Barth's theological approach. On the other hand Bonhoeffer continuously has his critical questions to ask. However, these criticisms do not form a straight line; rather, they resemble a winding path. The unclear charge of "positivism of revelation" in *Letters and Papers from Prison* should not be regarded as the key, by which the relationship as a whole can be interpreted. Sharper than this later reproach is Bonhoeffer's earlier criticism in *Act and Being*. And in the phase, when Bonhoeffer conceived his book *Discipleship* and organized the experiment of *Life Together* in Finkenwalde, there seems to have prevailed a certain distance, which was explained by Bonhoeffer as a time of "ongoing, silent discussion" with Barth. In the prison letters, on the other hand, where Bonhoeffer utters the reproach of "positivism of revelation," he praises Barth at the

---

[199] Godsey, "Barth and Bonhoeffer," 26–27. Mention should also be made of the fact that one of the first comprehensive studies about Bonhoeffer's theology, John D. Godsey's *The Theology of Dietrich Bonhoeffer* (Philadelphia, Pa., 1960), was written under Barth's supervision in Basle.
[200] Bethge, *Dietrich Bonhoeffer*, 179.
[201] Bethge, *Dietrich Bonhoeffer*, 178; translation altered.

same time as "the first one" and even "the only one" to have started directing theology towards a new perspective which Bonhoeffer shares.

Barth's latest statement regarding Bonhoeffer handed down to us is his letter to Bethge on occasion of his reading of Bethge's recently published biography of Dietrich Bonhoeffer. Concerning Bonhoeffer's attitude towards "the question of the Jews" Barth writes that "for a long time now I have considered myself guilty of not having raised it with equal emphasis during the church struggle." Barth is thinking particularly of "the two Barmen Declarations I composed in 1934." In his view, a different text would not have been accepted then, "but this does not excuse the fact that I (my interests lay elsewhere) did not offer at least formal resistance in this matter at that time."[202] Barth is surprised reading that he himself had become and remained so "impressive" to Bonhoeffer, in spite of the reproach of "positivism of revelation." What Barth thinks is most important in Bonhoeffer's life is the "journey from Christian faith to *political* action," a journey which Barth maintains had been his own, too. The fact that his own theology had been perceived in Germany as something apolitical, is due, at least in part, to his exercise of political restraint during the Weimar period of the twenties, as Barth concedes. He regards Bonhoeffer's strong insistence on ethical clarification as an "overdue completion," of what Barth himself had had in mind. "Germany, burdened with the problem of her Lutheran tradition, was very much in need of a 'refresher course' in just the outlook which I presupposed without so many words and emphasized merely in passing, namely ethics, brother/sisterliness, a servant church, discipleship, Socialism, movements for peace – and throughout all these in politics. Obviously, Bonhoeffer sensed this void and the need to fill it with increasing urgency right from the start and gave expression to it on a very broad front."[203]

---

[202] K. Barth, Letter to Eberhard Bethge (22 May 1967) in *Fragments Grave and Gay*, 119.

[203] K. Barth, in *Fragments Grave and Gay*, 120–121; translation altered.

Josiah U. Young

Dietrich Bonhoeffer and Reinhold Niebuhr: Their Ethics, Views on Karl Barth and Perspectives on African-Americans

I. Introduction

Dietrich Bonhoeffer was a conservative, classically-trained, introspective and very gifted Christian theologian. Reinhold Niebuhr (1892–1971) was a mercurial, intensely public Christian intellectual and activist. During a period from September 1930 to June 1931, Dietrich Bonhoeffer lived in New York City where he studied at Union Theological Seminary. Reinhold Niebuhr was a popular professor there and Bonhoeffer took several of his classes: "Ethical Interpretations," "Ethical Viewpoints in Modern Literature" and "Religion and Ethics."[1] Bonhoeffer was a German national and Niebuhr, a German-American whose father emigrated from Germany to the United States in 1881. While a young pastor of the Bethel Evangelical Church, a German church in Detroit, Michigan, Niebuhr spearheaded efforts to conduct services in English and professed loyalty to the United States during World War I.[2] He was an Anglophile – far more enamored of the British than the people from whom he was descended.[3] Bonhoeffer found the Americans (and the Anglo-Saxon nominalism he claimed they retained over generations) very different from the Germans (and their Idealism).[4]

---

[1] Eberhard Bethge, *Dietrich Bonhoeffer*, 159.

[2] According to Richard Fox, *Reinhold Niebuhr: A Biography* (New York 1985), 43: "raw feelings of loyalty to the Fatherland were re-emerging after decades of submersion. For Niebuhr the problem of Americanization – for himself, his congregation, and his church – took on grave new meaning. It was no longer a matter of replacing one language with another, but of rooting out one preconscious emotion in favor of another. It was a question of politics and ideology as well as culture. It was a matter of casting his lot with the English, and ultimately the American, war effort."

[3] Fox, *Reinhold Niebuhr*, 43.

[4] See Bonhoeffer's "Protestantism without Reformation," in *NRS*, 93 (cf. *DBW* 15, 431–460). Bonhoeffer writes that the American Protestant denominations were fragmented – lacked unity from the very beginning because they as a whole subscribed to the

Despite their cultural differences, the two men respected one another. Bonhoeffer thought Niebuhr was "one of the most significant and most creative of contemporary American theologians." He thought that Niebuhr's *Moral Man and Immoral Society, Interpretation of Christian Ethics* and *Beyond Tragedy* had established him as an indispensable barometer of the American "theological situation." He was, moreover, "the sharpest critic of contemporary American Protestantism and the present social order" and had done much to lift up the cross as both the center and dénouement of history while embodying "a strongly active political theology." He saw "the right way between neo-orthodoxy, for which Jesus Christ becomes the ground of human despair, and a true liberalism, for which Christ is the Lord, the norm, the ideal and the revelation of our essential being."[5] In 1939 when Bonhoeffer feared he would be drafted into Hitler's army, he asked Niebuhr to help him find a position in the United States. Niebuhr did, though Bonhoeffer did not stay long. He preferred to return to Germany to take action against the Nazi regime. As Niebuhr saw it, Bonhoeffer "finally convinced himself that it was his duty to participate in the plot on Hitler's life ... He reasoned that Germany could only be saved by Hitler's destruction."[6]

In this study, I will deepen my examination of Dietrich Bonhoeffer's relationship to Reinhold Niebuhr in discussing their ethics, views on Karl Barth and perspectives on African-Americans. Their ethics reveal their different christologies and shed light on their opinions of Barth, who influenced their theologies. Their perspectives on African-Americans provide insight into their "politics," which were closely aligned with their understandings of the church.

---

republic's cardinal value: the freedom of the individual. From the nation's founding, then, American Protestants had not understood that the Reformation was about "the one holy universal church of Jesus Christ on earth." As a result, American Protestants thought mistakenly that "the unity of the church of Jesus Christ" is be strived for and is not "originally given by God:" "It is less origin than goal." For the Americans, then, church unity belonged to the realm of sanctification rather than justification. Their failure to see that justification and sanctification are *homoousios* – go together consistent with the confession of Constantinople, 381 – was a ramification of Anglo-Saxon nominalism, the legacy of Occam *qua* individualism. "For nominalism the individual precedes the whole, in that the individual and empirically given thing is what is real, while totality is only a concept a *nomen*. The individual stands at the beginning, unity at the end. On the other hand, the German-continental philosophical tradition is governed by *realism* and *idealism*, for which the whole is the original reality and the individual entity only a derivative." For Bonhoeffer, *the whole* is no doubt the Trinity, the one God to whom the Three Articles refer.

[5] Bonhoeffer, "Protestantism without Reformation," *NRS*, 112.

[6] Niebuhr, "Dietrich Bonhoeffer," in *Union Seminary Quarterly Review* 1 (1946), 3.

II. Their Ethics

On the surface, the two men appeared to be similar ethically, but their christologies differed, and that difference affected their ethics. In fact, Bonhoeffer asserted that Niebuhr lacked "a doctrine of the person and redemptive work of Jesus Christ."[7] Niebuhr surely upheld a doctrine of justification,[8] but Bonhoeffer thought that Niebuhr did not adequately stress that *God's* grace is preeminently a pneumatological gift en route to being made perfect in the eschaton. For Bonhoeffer, Christian ethicists worth their salt looked forward to such perfection – namely the resurrection of the body and the life everlasting. But Niebuhr was agnostic about the resurrection. Edified by his Union colleague Tillich, Niebuhr held that the resurrection is only "true" insofar as it affirms "historical reality (which is a unity of body-soul, freedom-necessity, time-eternity)."[9] Christ's glorified body symbolizes "the completion of this unity."[10] Niebuhr did not forego the *possibility* of personal immortality (Kant), but did not set much stock in it either since a life lived "beyond history [was] beyond logical conception."[11] Still, the resurrection was truer than the "doctrines which seek to comprehend and to effect the completion of life by some power or capacity inherent in man and history." As a symbol, then, the resurrection was for Niebuhr "an integral part of the total Biblical conception of the meaning of life." There is a "center and source beyond ourselves" who we must not appropriate "as our secure possession."[12] For Bonhoeffer, however, any biblically-informed ethic that did not look forward to "life everlasting" was itself dead and so could not in any sense be said to be *in* Christ.

---

[7] Bonhoeffer, "Protestantism without Reformation," *NRS*, 112.

[8] Niebuhr, *The Nature and Destiny of Man* (New York 1964), vol 1, 148. Niebuhr writes that "the doctrine of Atonement and justification ... is an absolutely essential presupposition for the understanding of human nature and human history. It is a doctrine which ... was subordinated to the 'time-eternity' implications of the doctrine of the Incarnation in patristic Christianity. It was qualified by that same doctrine in medieval Catholicism, so that Catholicism failed to understand the full seriousness of human sin or the full tragedy of human history. It emerged with elemental force in the Protestant Reformation, to become the central truth of the Christian religion. But it quickly lost its central position, so that modern liberal Protestantism knows less of its meaning or significance than the Middle Ages did."

[9] See Fox, *Reinhold Niebuhr*, 215. According to Fox, Niebuhr's *magnum opus*, the prestigious Gifford Lectures published as *The Nature and Destiny of Man*, was not well received in the churches largely because it undermined what many thought the faith was all about. Niebuhr made much of the risen and crucified one, but "offered only a very abstract Incarnation and scant assurance of the eternal life most believers yearned for." Niebuhr, Fox writes, "did not want to give comfort to literalists," especially since he, to quote Niebuhr, had "not the slightest interest in the empty tomb or physical resurrection."

[10] Fox, *Reinhold Niebuhr*, 215.

[11] Niebuhr, *The Nature and Destiny of Man*, vol. 2, 295.

[12] Niebuhr, *The Nature and Destiny of Man*, vol. 2, 298.

Although Niebuhr and Bonhoeffer were not on the same page ethically, Bonhoeffer no doubt came to appreciate one of Niebuhr's emphases in his book *Moral Man and Immoral Society* (1932). In times of dire crisis, Christians may decide to violate the "thou–shall–not–kill" ethic to bring about societal change. As Niebuhr put it, "A reflective morality is constantly under the necessity of reanalyzing moral values which are regarded as intrinsically good and of judging them in instrumental terms."[13] Bonhoeffer agreed as he became embroiled in a struggle against the Nazis and along with certain family members participated in a plan to plant a bomb in an airplane transporting Hitler.[14] The bomb, however, failed to ignite. Bonhoeffer believed that the assassination would have enabled Germany to take a giant step toward peace. Bonhoeffer, though, did not adopt those measures for reasons that square with Niebuhr's ethics.

In his very brief reference to Niebuhr's *Moral Man and Immoral Society*, Bonhoeffer asserted in his book *Ethics* that Niebuhr's distinction between *moral* man and *immoral* society failed to emphasize adequately that both were immoral without Christ.[15] Truth be told, ethics in the first instance stemmed from God's self-revelation in Christ rather than an individual's awareness of the relative merits of violence. According to Bonhoeffer, the "*subject matter of a Christian ethic is God's reality revealed in Christ becoming real among God's creatures,* just as the subject matter of doctrinal theology is the truth of God's *reality* revealed in Christ. The place that in all other ethics is marked by the antithesis between ought and is, idea and realization, motive and work, is occupied in Christian ethics by the relation between reality and becoming real, between past and present, between history and event (faith) or, to replace the many concepts with the simple name of the thing itself, the relation between Christ and the Holy Spirit. The question of the good becomes the question of participating in God's reality revealed in Christ."[16]

To participate in God's reality – to grow in grace as a result of the Spirit of Christ – was to live for the sake of the new creation. This old world had begun to pass away on Good Friday and Easter; ethics devoid of such apocalyptic eschatology were still born. Again: the fact that Niebuhr was an agnostic in regard to the Resurrection – or surely set no great stock in *his own* – went, I think, a long way toward accounting for Bonhoeffer's disagreement with him. Bonhoeffer thought Niebuhr's ethics personified the

---

[13] Reinhold Niebuhr, *Moral Man and Immoral Society* (New York 1960), 174.

[14] R. Wind, *Dietrich Bonhoeffer: A Spoke in the Wheel* (Grand Rapids 1991), 148.

[15] Cf. *DBWE* 6, 51–52 (*DBW* 6, 36–37). According to Bonhoeffer Niebuhr's distinction "between individual and society" is a fiction: "What is inseparable is here torn apart, and each part, which by itself is dead, is examined separately. The result is the complete ethical aporia that today goes by the name 'social ethics'."

[16] *DBWE* 6, 49–50 (*DBW* 6, 34–35).

"craziest Don Quixotry."[17] An ethicist with a rusty blade stood in place of Christ with his double-edged sword; and all because he failed to see that without God's grace both the person and his or her works are bad, no matter how good the person *appears* to be. After all, "'good intentions' can grow out of very dark backgrounds in human consciousness and sub consciousness," which is to say that "the worst things can happen as a result of 'good intentions'."[18]

Bonhoeffer's critique notwithstanding, Niebuhr made a similar point in *The Nature and Destiny of Man* (1941): Sin is hardly a "violation of the good within freedom [qua spirit] itself."[19] The human spirit itself is thoroughly deficient because it is *mortal* rather than divine. According to Niebuhr, humans' failure to accept that deficiency has produced anxiety and resulted in hubris: the very fact that men and women are bound to time and to nature but transcend them, and so anticipate "their caprices and perils," provokes the anxiety that leads them to sin: They "transmute ... finiteness into infinity ... weakness into strength ... dependence into independence." The only remedy for such pride is "obedient subjection to the will of God," as "expressed in the words of Jesus: 'He that loseth his life for my sake shall find it'."[20] Unlike Bonhoeffer's, however, Niebuhr's Christ was not the incarnate Word, the One who ascended into heaven. He was, rather, "the norm of human history," the moral man who defined "the final perfection of man in history" on account of his "sacrificial love."[21] For Niebuhr, the doctrine of the incarnation was the mythic expression of the faith that "the final mystery of the divine power which bears history is clarified [in Christ]; and with that clarification, life and history are given their true meaning."[22]

Bonhoeffer, however, insisted that Christ was pre-existent, begotten of the Father before all worlds, and was therefore much more than a moral man. Christ, the Second Person of the Trinity, transcended morality, or ethics, and thus the knowledge of good and evil. Christ revealed "the single way of God to" humankind, for he was "the merciful love of God for unrighteous ... sinners."[23] In emphasizing the incarnation, Bonhoeffer held that the "Christian message speaks of grace" while "ethics speaks of righteousness." Ethics signified humans' attempt to do right by God; and if such ethics had anything going for them, they signified "the encounter of the holy God with unholy" men and women. For Bonhoeffer, that distinc-

---

[17] *DBWE* 6, 51 (*DBW* 6, 35).
[18] *DBWE* 6, 52 (*DBW* 6, 37).
[19] Niebuhr, *The Nature and Destiny of Man*, vol. 1, 120.
[20] Niebuhr, *The Nature and Destiny of Man*, vol. 1, 251.
[21] Niebuhr, *The Nature and Destiny of Man*, vol. 2, 68.
[22] Niebuhr, *The Nature and Destiny of Man*, vol. 2, 55.
[23] *NRS*, 37.

tion between grace and ethics helped one realize that "the grace of God" is not "dependent upon the extent of man's good or evil ... but God's will to be gracious or not."[24] Niebuhr, however, found Bonhoeffer's sublation of ethics to grace too otherworldly – which is why he evaluated one of the papers Bonhoeffer wrote for him as follows. "In making grace as transcendent as you do, I don't see how you can ascribe any ethical significance to it. Obedience to God's will may be a religious experience, but it is not an ethical one until it issues in actions which can be socially valued. Any other interpretation of 'ethical' than one which measures an action in terms of consequences and judges actions purely in terms of notions empties the ethical of content and makes it purely formal."[25]

Niebuhr's "low" Christology goes along way toward accounting for his ethical disagreements with Bonhoeffer, and critiques of Karl Barth.

III. Views on Karl Barth

While Niebuhr appreciated "Barth's rejection of 'immanent theologies' that minimized God's transcendence," Niebuhr eschewed Barth's christological absolutism (i.e., his "absolute Christ-idea") as "a new kind of fundamentalism," "a new and terrifying subjectivism" – a "sanctified futilitarianism."[26] In his *The Nature and Destiny of Man*, moreover, Niebuhr argues that Barth's focus on "the ultimate religious fact of the sinfulness of all men" threatened "to destroy all relative moral judgments." With so much focus on individuals' moral deficiencies, the "relative moral achievements of history" were obscured. Niebuhr traced Barth's anthropology to the "Augustinian-Lutheran theological inheritance," which, as Niebuhr saw it, went a long way toward accounting for why Germany, reeling from the Nazi horror, "had greater difficulty achieving a measure of political sanity and justice than the more Pelagian, more self-righteous and religiously less profound Anglo-Saxon world."[27] Presumably, the Augustinian focus on humans' total depravity and the acquiescence to the state it engendered became a cultural cornerstone to such an extent that it evolved into a self-fulfilling prophecy in Germany. At least the English, for Niebuhr, had a pragmatic edge, a realism based on respect for practical reason. Implicitly acknowledging his debt to Kant (as well as to the English), Niebuhr asserted "we can escape relativity and uncertainty only by piling experience upon experience, checking hypothesis against hypothesis, correcting errors by considering new perspectives, not by the mere as-

---

[24] *NRS*, 37.
[25] Fox, *Reinhold Niebuhr*, 125.
[26] Fox, *Reinhold Niebuhr*, 117, 123.
[27] Niebuhr, *Nature and Destiny of Man*, vol. 1, 220.

sertion of an absolute idea that is beyond experience."[28] Although Niebuhr was critical of the liberals, "he jumped to defend [the] bedrock assumptions against Barth"[29] that the liberals held because of Barth's assent to ancient dogmas that liberals thought were "primitive" – the triune God's essential oneness, humankind's sickness unto death as a consequence of the Fall, and Christ's salvific natures.

Those themes struck a responsive chord in Bonhoeffer, though he understood the liberal worldview Barth had once upheld, but abandoned, as is borne out by the esteem in which he held his professor and neighbour, Adolf von Harnack (a favourite of Niebuhr's too). Still, Bonhoeffer agreed with Barth that the terrors of World War I were the damning consequences of liberalism and the tragic means through which the Lord moved theologians to reconsider both the Bible and the ancient Christology.[30] For them, the triune God in the Personhood of the Logos had become incarnate in Jesus Christ to save humankind from sin and death.[31] For Bonhoeffer and Barth, the *Logos*'s human nature – *qua* the new, or second, Adam (to make an allusion to Paul) – was so all-encompassing as to give humankind, eschatologically and in faith here and now, a new lease on life despite the noxiousness of sin.[32]

Niebuhr thought the ancient soteriology – *the Logos became human so that humans can become like God* – was analogous to Plato's sense that the soul alone was godlike. No wonder many liberals found the thought that Christ is simultaneously human and divine "rationally absurd" – "the re-

---

[28] Fox, *Reinhold Niebuhr*, 117.

[29] Fox, *Reinhold Niebuhr*, 117.

[30] *NRS*, 75. Bonhoeffer writes: "Before the war we lived too far from God; we believed too much in our own power, in our almightiness and righteousness. *We attempted to be a strong and good people, but were too proud of our endeavor, we felt too much satisfaction with our scientific, economic and social progress, and we identified this progress with the coming of the kingdom of God.* We felt too happy and complacent in this world. Then the great disillusionment came. We saw the impotence and weakness of humanity, we were suddenly awakened from our dream, we recognized our guiltiness before God and we humbled ourselves under the mighty hand of God" [emphasis added].

[31] *DBWE* 4, 214 (*DBW* 4, 227–228): "The Son of God becomes a human being ... When contemplating this miracle, the early church fathers insisted passionately that while it was necessary to say that God had taken on human nature, it was wrong to say that God has chosen a single, perfect human being with whom God would then unite. God became human. This means God took on the whole of our sick and sinful human nature, the whole of humanity which had fallen away from God. It does not mean, however, that God took on the individual human being Jesus. *The entire gospel message can be understood properly only in light of this crucial distinction. The body of Jesus Christ, in which we together with all of humanity are accepted by God, has become the foundation of our salvation*" [emphasis added].

[32] Bonhoeffer put it this way in *CC*, 105: [In the resurrection] the humanity [i.e., God's human nature] is taken up into the Trinity ... the Trinitarian God is seen as the incarnate one. The glorification of God in the flesh is now at the same time, the glorification of man, who shall have life through eternity with the Trinitarian God."

levance between time and eternity was stated in terms of Greek philosophy in which it is not possible to state it, since this philosophy assumes an absolute gulf between the 'passible' and the 'impassible'."[33] To its credit, two–natures Christology, which Niebuhr also calls "Hellenistic Christianity," realized that true humanity "stands in the dimension of eternity as well as time." Idioms such as hypostatic union and the *communicatio idiomatum* therefore made the point that nature and Spirit ought not be separated or confused. The insistence on the resurrection of the God–man's *body and mind,* moreover, modified Hellenism considerably in refusing to separate the body from the soul where salvation is concerned.[34] Even so, *Hellenistic* Christianity was a contradiction in terms for Niebuhr. The biblical worldview was one thing and Greek thought another. Why not uphold the former and embrace its claim that the problem is not *death* per se – i.e., "involvement in the flux of nature" – but sin, "abortive efforts to escape that flux"? According to Niebuhr, "The issue of Biblical religion is not primarily the problem of how finite man can know God but how sinful man is to be reconciled to God and how history is to overcome the tragic consequences of its 'false eternals,' its proud and premature efforts to escape finiteness."[35]

Niebuhr's concern was how "*man*" should think about himself in relation to God and the world while Bonhoeffer's and Barth's concern was how *God* thinks about humankind in relation to Godself and the world. As pretentious as the latter sounds – who knows what God thinks? – it makes the point that Bonhoeffer thought that Niebuhr's perspective was anthropological (religious and ethical) rather than theological (christocentric and pnematological). On his side, Niebuhr thought Bonhoeffer's perspective was quasi-Gnostic (Barthian and incredible) rather than biblical (earthly and historical).

Clearly, the two men differed in their views on Barth; but Niebuhr, at least, thought Bonhoeffer demonstrated an affinity with him as things heated up in Germany.[36] Niebuhr writes of a conversation he had with

---

[33] Niebuhr, *The Nature and Destiny of Man,* vol. 1, 145.

[34] Niebuhr, *The Nature and Destiny of Man,* vol. 1,147: "The doctrine of the Incarnation, the belief that God has become man and the hope that man can become divine, is asserted against the dualism of non-Christian and Platonic Hellenism, according to which a great gulf is fixed between the flux of nature and history and the perfection and calm of eternal order."

[35] Niebuhr, *The Nature and Destiny of Man,* vol. 1, 147.

[36] Cf. Niebuhr's "Dietrich Bonhoeffer." Niebuhr writes that Bonhoeffer "had been strongly influenced by Barthian theology in the form and emphasis which it then had. He felt that political questions in which our students were so interested were on the whole irrelevant to the life of a Christian. Shortly after his return to Germany he became very much interested in ethical and political issues and for a time considered going to India to study Gandhi's movement. The rise of Hitlerism brought this interest to the fore in his

Bonhoeffer in London in 1939. "He assured me that Barth was right in becoming more political; but he criticized Barth for defining his position in a little pamphlet. 'If ... one states an original position in many big volumes, one ought to define the change in one's position in an equally impressive volume and not in a little pamphlet'."[37] Nonetheless, Bonhoeffer's theological difference from Niebuhr remained even when, near the very end of his life, Bonhoeffer criticized Barth for his "positivism of revelation."[38] What is more, Bonhoeffer had been critical of Barth even before his association with Niebuhr. As early as *Act and Being*, Bonhoeffer argued that Barth's Christology was Kantian to the extent that it missed the "fact" that God gets his hands dirty, so to speak, as a result of the incarnation.[39] Eternity really *touches* time for Bonhoeffer, and his political activities stemmed from that conviction. If, as he suggests in *Discipleship*, God the Son takes on a true, albeit non-personal, humanity, and if this incarnation is one of the presuppositions for his death on the cross – so that humankind might be heirs to eternal life – the disciple should be prepared to suffer unto death too. For death is but a station on the road to *freedom*.[40]

In *Discipleship*, Bonhoeffer argued that following Christ was so costly as to cause the faithful to throw every security to the wind – for Christ's

---

thought and life, and he became one of the most courageous and uncompromising foes of Hitlerism in the Confessional Church, particularly as a leader of its 'underground' theological seminary" (30). See also Niebuhr's "The Death of a Martyr," in *Christianity and Crisis* 5 (1945), 6–7.

[37] Niebuhr, "The Death of a Martyr," 6.

[38] *LPP*, 286 (*DBW* 8, 415–416). Bonhoeffer appreciates Barth's critique of religion but argues that he sought refuge in "a positivist doctrine of revelation which says, in effect, 'Like it or lump it': virgin birth, Trinity, or anything else; each is an equally significant and necessary part of the whole, which must simply be swallowed as a whole or not at all." Bonhoeffer did not think such positivism was biblical. "There are degrees of knowledge and degrees of significance" in the Bible. The most important things for Bonhoeffer were "the concepts of repentance, faith, justification, rebirth, and sanctification," and primarily because they conveyed the imperative to be disciples in times of dire crisis. In making a certain "orthodoxy" the benchmark of obedience, Barth's positivism of revelation, his church dogmatics, functioned so legalistically that they "mutilate[d] what is – by Christ's incarnation! – a gift for us. In the place of religion there now stands the church – that is in itself biblical – but the world is left to its own devices, and that's the mistake."

[39] Cf. *DBWE* 2, 83, 85 (*DBW* 2, 77, 79). Bonhoeffer suggests that Barth's sense of God's freedom in revelation ("understood as pure act") is too agnostic. Revelation "is an event that happens to someone who listens, free to suspend the relation at any moment." But does not this "freedom" therefore become for us "just that: possibility." Bonhoeffer suspects "that transcendentalism is lurking here" (83). "God recedes into the nonobjective, into what is beyond our disposition. That is the necessary consequence of the formal conception of God's freedom ... God remains always the Lord, always subject, so that whoever claims to have God as an object no longer has *God;* God is always the God who 'comes' and never 'the God who is there' (Barth)" (85).

[40] *LPP*, 371 (*DBW* 8, 570).

sake – though ultimately the disciple would live and not perish. Reportedly, some of the last words he uttered before the Nazis hanged him involved his assertion that his death would be more of a beginning than an end. He thought he was going the way of his Lord who called him to remain faithful despite the apostasy of so many church-goers content to compromise and make concessions. The very doctrine of justification Bonhoeffer thought Niebuhr neglected moved him to hazard the conspiratorial politics he undertook during the war.

IV. Perspectives on African-Americans[41]

Bonhoeffer's political activity during the war – his opposition to White supremacists – bears a strong affinity to his friendship with African-Americans. Bonhoeffer spent much of his time in Harlem while he studied at Union. Frank Fisher, an African-American Union student and one of Bonhoeffer's closest friends during his stay in New York City, introduced Bonhoeffer to Harlem and to the Abyssinian Baptist Church. Bonhoeffer attended the church most Sundays during the time he studied at Union. He taught Sunday school there in fact. The Black saints edified *him* regarding the ecclesiology he explored in his book *Sanctorum Communio*, which argues that the church is "Christ existing as church-community," has an eschatological goal and should never be co-opted by its society.[42] The society can be whatever individuals will it to be in accordance with their "objective spirit," which serves utilitarian, and often demonic, ends.[43] As a Christ-centered community, however, a church "*is sustained* by the Spirit" and so cannot be derived from "individual wills" or serve vulgar pragmatic goals.[44] The church, rather, is a communion of love that looks forward to "life everlasting," for Christ's sake. Abyssinian fit the bill but the White churches Bonhoeffer attended were for him religious extensions of American society.[45] He found Christ existing as church-community at the Abys-

---

[41] I use the terms "African-American" and "Black" interchangeably as both terms connote the same reality – a mostly non-white people, a Black people, who are indigenous to the Americas but bear, until today, the likenesses of their (our) African ancestors, physically and spiritually.

[42] *DBWE* 1, 141 (*DBW* 1, 87).

[43] Cf. *DBWE* 1, 100 (*DBW* 1, 63–64).

[44] *DBWE* 1, 160 (*DBW* 1, 102).

[45] Bonhoeffer, "Protestantism without Reformation," 113. During his time in New York, Bonhoeffer concluded – all too generally, perhaps – that the white churches were in the dark about faith in the Word of God, preferring instead the blindness of civil religion and one of its corollaries, anti-Black ethics. He argues in "Protestantism" that such religion and ethics push Christ's "person and work into the background" and so ignore them as "the sole ground of radical judgment and radical forgiveness."

sinian Baptist Church: "Nowhere is revival preaching still so vigorous and so widespread as among the Negroes." Bonhoeffer writes, "the Gospel of Jesus Christ, the savior of the sinner, is really preached and accepted with great welcome and visible emotion."[46] His experience within the church moved him to look into the history and culture of its people.[47] "He spent nearly every Sunday and many evenings" in Harlem. "He participated in guided visits to the area, including a 'trip to Negro Centers of Life and Culture in Harlem,' which began with a flight over the district in which 170,000 African Americans lived per square mile."[48] He collected the *Crisis*, the official journal of the National Association for the Advancement of Colored People (NAACP), and recordings of the Spirituals. He also "read a great deal of African-American literature."[49]

Paul Lehman, one of Bonhoeffer's close friends at Union Theological Seminary, reinforces that point in his observation that Bonhoeffer considered the so-called "Negro question" "in its minutest detail through books and countless visits to Harlem, through participation in Negro youth work, but even more through a *remarkable kind of identity with the Negro community*" – so much so "that he was received there as though he had never been an outsider at all."[50] According to a letter that Bonhoeffer's brother, Karl-Friedrich, wrote him, he studied the so-called "Negro problem" indeed. Karl-Friedrich writes, "I am delighted you have the opportunity of studying the Negro question so thoroughly. I had the impression when I was over there that it really is the problem, at any rate for people with a conscience and, when I was offered an appointment at Harvard, it was quite a basic reason for my disinclination to go to America for good, because I did not want either to enter upon that heritage myself or to hand it on to my hypothetical children. It seems impossible to see the right way to handle the problem."[51] Bonhoeffer read African-Americans' perspectives on the problem. W.E.B. Du Bois' stinging Postscripts during the time he edited the *Crisis*; African-American novelists, such as James Weldon Johnson; and poets, such as Countee Cullen. He was therefore aware of what Blacks thought about their predicament: The problem has been the Whites.[52]

Bonhoeffer said as much in his essay "Protestantism without Reformation." The problem has had to do with the legacy of the White Protestants

---

[46] Bonhoeffer, "Protestantism without Reformation," *NRS*, 109.
[47] I make this argument in my book *No Difference in the Fare: Dietrich Bonhoeffer and the Problem of Racism* (Grand Rapids 1998).
[48] Bethge, *Dietrich Bonhoeffer*, 150.
[49] Bethge, *Dietrich Bonhoeffer*, 150.
[50] Bethge, *Dietrich Bonhoeffer*, 155; emphasis added.
[51] Bethge, *Dietrich Bonhoeffer*, 110.
[52] See my *No Difference in the Fare: Dietrich Bonhoeffer and the Problem of Racism*.

descended from the English colonists, who had confused the demands of the slaveholding state with the mission of the church.[53] African-Americans had, in the main, been treated with the utmost contempt by Anglo-Saxon Protestants, even within the churches. Held disdainfully at a distance, the Blacks felt they had no choice but to found their own churches. This was undoubtedly to the relief of the Whites, for whom the Blacks had been a nuisance.[54] For Bonhoeffer, segregated churches indicated "a deep cleft in the church of Jesus Christ." As a lover of the Spirituals, the sacred music of the African-American church, Bonhoeffer didn't understand how White Americans could be so disobedient to the Lord Jesus as to eschew worship with Blacks. African-Americans' "sorrow songs" (Du Bois) were biblical and theologically sound.[55] Why wouldn't many White American Christians worship with people who had produced such "gospel" music?

Bonhoeffer appreciated the humanity of the Blacks he encountered. Consider a letter he wrote to his grandmother, Frau Julie Bonhoeffer: "I have again just finished a quite outstanding novel by a quite young Negro. In contrast to other American writing, which is either cynical or sentimental, I find here a very productive strength and warmth, which continually

---

[53] See Bonhoeffer's "Protestantism without Reformation." Bonhoeffer concludes his section entitled "The Negro Church," with the assertion that the "solution to the Negro problem is one of the decisive future tasks of the white churches."

[54] Bonhoeffer, "Protestantism without Reformation," 108-109. Bonhoeffer points out the colonists' initial unwillingness to Christianize the Africans they enslaved. The masters justified slavery by arguing that the Africans were subhuman – heathen. To baptize them would be to acknowledge their humanity, endanger their status as chattel and so undermine both the economic viability of the colonies and the master's equation of Whiteness with God's sovereignty. The Africans later became outcast Christians as well as chattel on account of what Bonhoeffer calls a "dreadful letter of reassurance from the bishop of London [which] promised the white masters that the external conditions of the Negro need not be altered in the least by Baptism, that Baptism was a liberation from sin and evil desire and not from slavery or from any other external fetters." "So it came about," writes Bonhoeffer, "that the Negroes became Christians and were admitted to the gallery at white services and as the last guests to the communion table. Any further participation in the life of the congregation was excluded; holding offices in the congregation and ordination remained preserved for whites." Bonhoeffer continues: "Under these circumstances worship together became more and more of a farce for the Negro, and after the complete failure of all attempts to be recognized as equal members in the community of Jesus Christ, the Negroes began to ... organize themselves into their own Negro congregations. It was a voluntary decision which led the Negro to this, but one which circumstances made inevitable ... Since then the great denominations have been divided, a significant example of the make-up of a denomination in the United States."

[55] Bonhoeffer, "Protestantism without Reformation," NRS, 109. He cites "Go Down Moses," "Nobody Knows the Trouble I've Seen," and "Swing Low Sweet Chariot" as especially compelling. "Go Down Moses" signifies "the distress and delivery of... Israel; "Nobody Knows the Trouble I've Seen," the "misery and consolation of the human heart"; and "Swing Low Sweet Chariot," the "love of the Redeemer and longing for the kingdom of heaven."

arouses in one a desire to meet the man himself."[56] To satisfy the requirements for a seminar he took with Reinhold Niebuhr entitled "Ethical Viewpoints in Modern Literature," Bonhoeffer wrote a paper on James Weldon Johnson's novel, *Autobiography of an Ex-Colored Man.*[57] Niebuhr had included Johnson's novel in his bibliography – a sign, perhaps, of Niebuhr's personal history with African–Americans?

During the time Niebuhr served as pastor of the Bethel Evangelical Church in Detroit, Michigan, he spoke "repeatedly to secular and religious groups ... about the race problem." "His four Bethel forums on race in January, 1927, were advertised in oversized print in the Saturday press." He not only preached "about race prejudice in general, but about the much more ticklish question of 'Where shall the Negro live?' – as he titled his ... talk."[58] Niebuhr's broaching of this sensitive topic was courageous: Most of his Bethel parishioners did not want Blacks living next door. Niebuhr also discussed the problem as a columnist for the *Christian Century,* but warily: According to Richard Fox, author of *Reinhold Niebuhr: a Biography,* Niebuhr's anonymous editorial "Race Prejudice in the North" was "the only article he wrote in the twenties on the racial conflict, when the question was most urgent in Detroit and other northern cities." Niebuhr "itemized the problems black Detroiters faced: overcrowded housing, usurious rents, refusal of White neighborhoods or the banks to countenance moves beyond the Negro district, police 'severity, not to say brutality,' exclusion of black women from factory work and of all blacks from certain professions such as high school teaching, failure of White churches to assist black congregations even of their own denominations." The writing was "tame, methodical, and detached ... clinical." For Fox, Niebuhr's column lacked his characteristic passion, his prophetic zeal. He acknowledged that "increasing the number of black policemen, teachers, and girls certified 'in the household arts'" would be good for Blacks; but the matter of where Blacks should live – the "housing dilemma, 'the crux of the race problem in every city'" – was for Niebuhr an unanswerable problem.[59]

As Niebuhr saw it, an *African* people who had been slaves for centuries could hardly be integrated into an *Anglo-Saxon* nation built upon the pre-

---

[56] Bethge, *Dietrich Bonhoeffer,* 150.

[57] The novel is about a "Negro" who passes for White after he witnesses a lynching. The mob poured gasoline on the chained victim and burned him alive. The victim's desperate attempts to free himself and his death cries so traumatized the ex-colored man (we never learn his name) that he crosses over into anonymity to protect himself from the Negro question. He often feels like a coward and a defector who craves contact with his mother's kinfolk. The noble thing would have been to join the struggle for civil and, moreover, *human* rights. The ex-colored man surmises at the novel's end that he has given himself over to moral mediocrity and spiritual atrophy.

[58] Fox, *Reinhold Niebuhr,* 93.

[59] Fox, *Reinhold Niebuhr,* 93–94.

mise that Blacks were little more than beasts of burden. Then, too, Blacks' migration to the urban north had so crushed their hopes and aspirations that they were just about useless "as allies in the rebuilding of American society." According to Niebuhr, Blacks were too "unadjusted to our [sic] industrial civilization." Their "inadequacies [sic!] and the hostility of a White world" had crippled them. African-Americans had to fight too hard just "to keep body and soul together, to say nothing of developing those amenities which raise life above the brute level [sic!]."[60] So long as Blacks were so very far behind the eight-ball, they "could be objects of Christian charity, but not participants in the reform of ... civilization." In the hope "that the American worker could join with enlightened professional people to form a Labor Party on the British model," Niebuhr found it far more pragmatic to focus on "the industrial conflict between skilled workers and their employers."[61] Let another prophet – and for Niebuhr that prophet turned out to be Martin Luther King, Jr. – take on the problem. In the meantime, he "put his own prophetic energies elsewhere – where he could have visible impact, where problems were not structurally resistant to practical reform."[62]

In 1929, while Niebuhr's star was rising at Union, he learned that the Bethel Evangelical Church, his former Detroit parish, was up in arms about the prospect of admitting two African-Americans into church membership. Both those in favor of admitting the Blacks and those against it wanted Niebuhr to intervene on their behalf. Niebuhr monitored the situation as he did not want to impugn his reputation by being aligned with the action opposed to admitting the Blacks. He did not come out too strongly in favor of the pro African-American group either as he understood all too well the congregation's ambivalence toward Blacks. Niebuhr's successor at Bethel, Reverend Adelbert Helm, was so vociferously in support of the Blacks as to turn off many who wanted to admit them to membership. The crisis moved Niebuhr to come to Detroit and argue "at the Sunday evening forum – for Helm's edification – that 'racial prejudice never can be wiped out by preaching against it'."[63] Helm, however, remained as resolute as ever, bringing to mind Bonhoeffer's refusal to let the Aryan clause slide. With Niebuhr's implicit blessing, the church got rid off Helm. Niebuhr followed through with an unsigned *Christian Century* editorial disparaging "self-deluded 'martyrs' who resigned from church posts with lofty declarations of their superior Christian insight."[64] Niebuhr, however, did not side with those who wanted to bar the two Blacks from membership. The fact that

---

[60] Fox, *Reinhold Niebuhr*, 94.
[61] Fox, *Reinhold Niebuhr*, 94.
[62] Fox, *Reinhold Niebuhr*, 94.
[63] Fox, *Reinhold Niebuhr*, 119.
[64] Fox, *Reinhold Niebuhr*, 119.

the church as a whole voted to exclude them bothered Niebuhr, in fact. He did "not see how any church [could] be so completely disloyal to the Gospel of love as to put up bars against members of another racial group." Few Blacks would have sought membership in the church anyway, so the church would have been hardly swamped with African-Americans. The Bethel congregation would thus "never have been forced to meet the ultimate test," which Niebuhr acknowledged would have been difficult for most White churches to handle at any rate. Niebuhr thought that Bethel's refusal to tolerate two Blacks was "apostasy," his own ambivalence toward Blacks notwithstanding.[65]

His *Moral Man and Immoral Society* provides another example of Niebuhr's perspective on African-Americans. He writes that every "effort to transfer a pure morality of disinterestedness to group relations has resulted in failure." African-Americans have shown that to be case ever since the Civil War. According to Niebuhr, Blacks "did not rise against their masters during the war and remained remarkably loyal to them." For Niebuhr, Blacks' benign temperament stemmed from their "genuine religious virtues of forgiveness and forbearance and *a certain social inertia which was derived not from religious virtue but from racial weakness.*"[66] Yet neither their piety nor their feebleness softened their oppressors' hearts.

Would Niebuhr have taken this point of view if he had consulted W.E.B. Du Bois, Niebuhr's intellectual equal and one who lived and worked in Harlem around the time Niebuhr penned his book? In his *Black Reconstruction*, published about three years after *Moral Man and Immoral Society*, Du Bois argues that African people made a massive contribution to the Union's victory: Slaves who had once worked behind confederate lines joined the Union forces to serve the Union as farmers, servants, spies and soldiers. They helped turn the tide of the war.[67] It is problematic for me that Niebuhr did not seek Du Bois' counsel, particularly given their socialist politics and the fact that Du Bois was one of African-Americans' great intellectuals.

---

[65] Fox, *Reinhold Niebuhr*, 119.
[66] Niebuhr, *Moral Man and Immoral Society*, 268; emphasis added.
[67] W. E. B. Du Bois, *Black Reconstruction in America 1860-1880: An Essay Toward a History of the Part Which Black Folk Played in the Attempt to Reconstruct Democracy in America* (New York 1962), 121: "Freedom for the slave was the logical result of a crazy attempt to wage war in the mist of four million black slaves, and trying sublimely to ignore the interests of those slaves in the outcome of the fighting. Yet, these slaves had enormous power in their hands. Simply by stopping work, they could threaten the Confederacy with starvation. By walking into the Federal camps, they showed to doubting Northerners the easy possibility of using them as workers and as servants, as farmers, and as spies, and finally, as fighting soldiers. And not only using them thus, but by the same gesture, depriving their enemies of their use in just these fields. It was the fugitive slave who made the slaveholders face the alternative of surrendering to the North, or to the Negroes."

Du Bois and Niebuhr were in fact on the same page regarding the shortcomings of White philanthropy and the paternalistic ways in which "race commissions" stop short of agitating for genuine societal transformation. As Niebuhr put it, Black schools underwritten by White philanthropists have inspired individual Blacks to strive for excellence but have not made "a frontal attack upon the social injustices from which the Negro suffers." The "race commissions" in their turn have sought a modicum of societal reform, but "without arousing the antagonism of the whites." The race commissions have sought to "secure minimum rights for the Negro such as better sanitation, police protection and more adequate schools." But they have been allergic to Blacks "political disfranchisement or ... economic disinheritance." What the well-meaning Whites and the well-meaning Blacks controlled by them have not been able to see, argues Niebuhr, is that White Americans "will not admit the Negro to equal rights" unless "forced to do so."[68]

In the paper he wrote for Niebuhr on James Weldon Johnson's novel, Bonhoeffer indicates that the tide was surely turning in that regard: "According to the whole mood in present Negro literature, it seems to me that that the race question is arriving at a turning point. The attempt to overcome the conflict religiously or ethically will turn in a violent political objection."[69] Niebuhr thought that non-violent coercion as represented by Mohandas Gandhi would move Whites to treat African-Americans fairly. Niebuhr writes: "One waits for such a campaign with all the more reason and hope because the peculiar [sic] spiritual gifts of the Negro endow him with the capacity to conduct it successfully." Given Niebuhr's sense that Blacks possessed an uncanny ability to take it on the chin, he asserted that all they needed to do to pull off this campaign was to "fuse the aggressiveness of the new and young Negro with the patience and forbearance of the old Negro, to rob the former of its vindictiveness and the latter of its lethargy."[70]

While in the United States, Bonhoeffer also observed a tension between the generations. He attributed this rift to the younger generation's impatience with the "strong eschatological orientation" of their elders. The young generation's sense that Christianity was in effect the White man's religion and hindered Blacks' quest for civil and human rights was "one of the *ominous* signs of a failing of the church in past centuries and a hard problem for the future."[71]

Bonhoeffer had been dead nearly a decade when Niebuhr finally began to see what Bonhoeffer saw: Blacks were not racially weak (as Niebuhr put

---

[68] Niebuhr, *Moral Man and Immoral Society*, 253.
[69] Bethge, *Dietrich Bonhoeffer*, 150.
[70] Niebuhr, Moral *Man and Immoral Society*, 254.
[71] Bonhoeffer, "Protestantism without Reformation," 108; emphasis added.

it). To quote Richard Fox, Niebuhr "had lived on the border of the black ghetto for thirty-five years" before he began to "understand the character of racism in New York."[72] Only long after Bonhoeffer had been executed did Niebuhr see the ominous character of young Black militants' rage, their willingness to embrace the rifle as a sign of resistance, *and* realize why: there was in the United States no such thing as – to quote him – "an open society [which] prevents revolutions by allowing all economic, racial, and cultural groups to state their claims and adjust their interests."[73] He was a strong supporter of Martin Luther King Jr., and took his side against Black Power advocates such as Stokely Carmichael, but he realized that nonviolent resistance would do little to break down segregation in places such as New York City.

Niebuhr's concern with ethics, his labor-oriented politics and prodigious output as a writer made him one of the greatest theological figures in American history. His great emphasis on human sinfulness led him to accent humans' limitations. I have been particularly interested in the implications of that with regard to race. As I see it, there was thus a pragmatic edge to Niebuhr's race politics – why devote one's energy to a people who are not ready to step up to the plate? – but there was also a good bit of chauvinism in Niebuhr's pragmatism too. Consider his paternalism toward African-Americans – his claim that Blacks were hobbled by "a certain social inertia ... derived not from religious virtue but from racial weakness." He did not appear to find anything ethically wrong with such chauvinism as it seemed to square with empirical evidence. Niebuhr's blindness in that regard goes a long way toward making Bonhoeffer's critique of Niebuhr's ethics compelling to me. Even so, Niebuhr is credited with being more influential on the Christian activism of Martin Luther King Jr. than Gandhi. Allegedly, King thought his non-violent tactics to be "a Niebuhrian stratagem of power."[74]

Bonhoeffer's ecclesiology had a lot to do with both his identification with the Black community and the fact that the Abyssinian Baptist Church embraced him. If one takes Bonhoeffer's distinction between ethics and Christology to heart, his relationship to the Blacks was not an ethical one, but had to do with his understanding of grace. The ambivalence that Niebuhr displayed toward African-Americans was for Bonhoeffer, then, the failure to acknowledge without qualification a point Bonhoeffer made in *Sanctorum Communio*: "Before God there is no longer Jew or Gentile, with their mutual claims upon each other. Nobody has any claim. Each must live by grace. Is it then possible, after all, to assert that God's church community is built upon ultimately equal human beings? As far as every-

---

[72] Fox, *Reinhold Niebuhr*, 282.
[73] Fox, *Reinhold Niebuhr*, 283.
[74] See Fox, *Reinhold Niebuhr*, 283.

one's relation to God is concerned, this is certainly true."[75] His life story witnesses to how costly this grace turned out to be; but none should be surprised that he stood up to the Nazis.

Although I am impressed with Bonhoeffer's witness in Harlem, I do not find that his openness to Blacks was a consequence of his Barthian-like position. I do not hold, either, that Niebuhr's more problematic attitudes towards Blacks stemmed from his low Christology and ethics. It is surely the case that their ethical differences and views on Karl Barth have much to do with their perspectives on African-Americans; but that is only because those values and attitudes are integral to their gestalts and should not be abstracted from them. The deeper reasons for their differences rest in the mystery of their persons and the spiritual gifts that have made them giants in the history of Christian thought.

---

[75] *DBWE* 1, 204–205 (*DBW* 1, 137–138).

Stephen Plant

"In the Sphere of the Familiar:" Heidegger and Bonhoeffer

I. Context and Text

In an unusually expansive moment towards the end of his *Letter on "Humanism,"* Martin Heidegger retails an anecdote concerning Heraclitus, the pre-Socratic philosopher he regarded with affectionate esteem. In a story reported by Aristotle, a group of foreigners make a surprise visit to Heraclitus's house and find him warming himself at a stove. Expecting to find the philosopher deep in thought, the visitors are put out to discover him in an everyday activity they could have observed at home without the rigours of their long journey. Observing their discomfort Heraclitus welcomed them with the words: "εἶναι γὰρ καί ἐνταῦθα θεούς. 'here too the gods are present'."[1] This phrase, Heidegger interprets, "places the abode (ἦθος) of the thinker and his deed in another light ... 'even here,' at the stove, in that ordinary place where every thing and every circumstance, each deed and thought is intimate and commonplace, that is, familiar [*geheuer*], 'even there' in the sphere of the familiar, εἶναι θεούς, it is the case that 'the gods come to presence.' Heraclitus himself says, ἦθος ἀνθρώπῳ δαίμων, 'The (familiar) abode for humans is the open region for the presencing of god (the unfamiliar one)'."[2]

The anecdote is vintage Heidegger. It encapsulates one of his main contributions to philosophical thought – the insight that the human condition is embedded (or "thrown" in his distinctive vocabulary) in the everyday world of simple things. In Heidegger's "hands" everyday objects – a pair of worn shoes, a hammer, a lectern, a stove – become occasions of philosophical revelation. "Vintage" Heidegger too, in that with the anecdote Heidegger sums up the counter-intuitive view articulated in the *Letter* that the world needs *less* philosophy, and more thinking that "gathers language

---

[1] Martin Heidegger, *Pathmarks*, edited by William McNeill (Cambridge 1998), 269–270.
[2] Heidegger, *Pathmarks*, 270–271.

into simple saying."³ Yet unwittingly the anecdote also puts before us one of the most immediate questions to arise from Heidegger's legacy: what is the relationship between the everyday life of the philosopher and the philosophy that arises from it? If thinking is an everyday activity, what are we to make of the way a thinker's life interprets – or obfuscates – the meaning of his thought? How, if at all, are readers to make connections between context and text, life and thought; between a philosopher's bio*graphy* and the *graffiti* he leaves scratched upon the history of ideas?

Few writers in the twentieth century raise these questions more vexingly than Martin Heidegger. Yet he is hard pressed by the presence of similar questions arising from reflection on the life and writings of Dietrich Bonhoeffer. Heidegger was a Nazi; Bonhoeffer expended his life opposing Nazism: how do these biographical data help or hinder our apprehension of their writings? Is it possible, or even desirable, to insulate a comparison between their writings from the sphere of these familiar facts? In an essay that sets out to examine the influence of one man on the other, how can we handle their respective attitudes to Nazism in ways that are not prejudicial to the outcome? "What needs careful sifting" in George Steiner's wise words "is the distinction to be drawn – if it can be drawn - between the singularity of the person, with all its pathological markers, and the autonomous weight of the work." And if Steiner is right to judge that "generations will pass before any confident delineation can be proposed in our sense of Martin Heidegger"[4] may not the same be said of Bonhoeffer? These questions never quite drop below the horizon in what follows, but my aim in the body of this essay is to place "the autonomous weight" of their work in the scales and see which way the balance tilts.

Comparing Heidegger's thought with Bonhoeffer's is a formidable task for any individual, and is certainly impossible within the compass of a single essay. Bonhoeffer's writings extend through 17 volumes; the publication of Heidegger's *Gesamtausgabe* is ongoing, but is scheduled for publication in 102 volumes.[5] The question therefore is not whether to be selective, but how to be selective. An obvious means by which to limit the scope of the present essay is to concentrate attention upon those passages in Bonhoeffer's writings in which Heidegger is explicitly discussed; and

---

[3] Heidegger, *Pathmarks*, 276.

[4] George Steiner, *No Passion Spent: Essays 1978–1996* (London 1996), 178. The *Letter on "Humanism"* provides a striking example of the difficulty of bracketing knowledge of Heidegger's life off from what he writes. The *Letter* was Heidegger's first published essay after the end of the war, and it is hard to read statements such as the following and forget he was undergoing denazification: "Because we are speaking against 'humanism' people fear a defense of the inhuman and a glorification of barbaric brutality" (Heidegger, *Pathmarks*, 263).

[5] For details and updates of the publication of the various volumes see the publisher's web-site: http://www.klostermann.de.

this is indeed where I propose to begin. But I want to suggest that the most lasting and most significant impact that Heidegger's thinking had on Bonhoeffer's is not to be found in the most obvious place – namely the influence of Heidegger's *Being and Time* on Bonhoeffer's *Act and Being* – but lies tucked away in the methodology of a text which does not once mention Heidegger's name: Bonhoeffer's formative lecture series on *Christology*. In what follows I trace the origins of Heidegger's *Being and Time*, before turning to its central themes and arguments; next I turn to Bonhoeffer's reading of Heidegger, and thence, to the reasons for believing that it is in his theological method, displayed in the *Christology* lectures, that Heidegger's thinking may be most influential on Bonhoeffer's.

II. The Origins of Heidegger's Being and Time

Being and Time made Heidegger's name, but his journey towards philosophical fame and fortune had been far from easy.[6] Born in 1889 in Messkirch, a small town between the Swabian Alps and Lake Constance in South West Germany, Heidegger grew up in the house that came with his father's job as sexton of the town's Roman Catholic Church. In his maturity Heidegger often dwelt on his small-town upbringing, comparing himself to a plant with roots in the earth, and at the end of his life he naturally chose to reunite his body with the soil of the Messkirch graveyard for which his father had been responsible. Though not especially poor, the family lacked the funds for the best education money could buy and Heidegger learned the Latin he needed to enter the *Gymnasium* (high school) from the parish priest, who also helped obtain a Church grant to pay his fees, beginning a period of thirteen years during which Heidegger was financially dependent on the Catholic Church.[7] He lodged in Constance in a Catholic boarding house, and in 1906 entered the archiepiscopal seminary in Freiburg where he began training for the priesthood. Essays written by Heidegger in his early years in Freiburg are models of Catholic anti-modernism, and in 1909 he entered the Society of Jesus as a novice. After two weeks, however, the Jesuits let him go on account of heart pains. Yet even in what would prove to be the final years of his training, Heidegger's attention was turning increasingly to formal and mathematical logic that became "a kind of worship" to him.[8] Though at this stage he considered the objectivity of strict logic as a complement to the authority of faith, on

---

[6] Far the fullest intellectual biography of Heidegger is Rüdiger Safranski's *Ein Meister aus Deutschland: Heidegger und seine Zeit* (Munich 1994). English Translation, *Martin Heidegger: Between Good and Evil* (Cambridge, MA. 1998).

[7] Safranski, *Martin Heidegger: Between Good and Evil*, 9–19.

[8] Safranski, *Martin Heidegger: Between Good and Evil*, 24.

the recurrence of heart trouble two years later he discontinued his training for the priesthood (he abandoned Catholicism altogether in 1919). It was in these years, in 1911–1912, that a decisive intellectual discovery directed Heidegger finally on the path that would lead him to *Being and Time:* he began reading the writings of Edmund Husserl, and in particular Husserl's *Logical Investigations*. Fifty years later the smell of that book was still in his nostrils: "I remained so fascinated by Husserl's work" remarked Heidegger looking back, "that I read in it again and again in the years to follow ... The spell emanating from the work extended to the outer appearance of the sentence structure and the title-page."[9]

Husserl's "spell" on Heidegger lay in a distinctive philosophical method which Husserl deployed with such verve that he re-branded it as his own: the phenomenological method. Husserl had started out academic life as a scientist, and came to philosophy via psychological investigation of how subjects arrive at concepts such as number. Initially, he tried to reduce logic and arithmetic to psychological functions. But in the two volumes of the *Logical Investigations* (1900–1901) he argued that a distinction is to be drawn, key to phenomenology, between the *objects* of consciousness and our *consciousness* of such objects. Because Heidegger at once adopts, adapts, and ultimately remoulds the phenomenological method in *Being and Time* it is important to get to grips with what is at stake in it.

"Phenomenology" is etymologically derived from two Greek words. τὸ φαινόμενον is derived from the Greek verb φαίνεσθαι, meaning "to make appear" or "to show." τὸ φαινόμενον thus suggests "that which shows itself" or the "self-showing" of things, and "phenomenology" describes giving an account of the self-showing of things.[10] In *Being and Time* Heidegger describes phenomenology as a going "back to the things themselves" (*Zu den Sachen selbst!*). Husserl thought that most philosophers before him had failed adequately to consider the role that the act of cognition made by a perceiving subject plays in her encounter with things. Even before I *sense* the world, Husserl thought, my experience of it is already organising itself in my mind. I don't hear a series of noises made by catgut echoing over a chamber of wood, and then, as a next step think "aha ... that's music!" When I hear the sounds my mind presents them to me instantly as a Bach cello sonata. Husserl called this process in the mind the structure of *intentionality*. The world is to be thought of as a network of meaning (intentionality) that is the horizon in which we come across phenomena. It was not Husserl's intention to oppose appearance and essence –

---

[9] Safranski, *Martin Heidegger: Between Good and Evil*, 25.

[10] For the etymology of the notion of "phenomenology," Heidegger's own account is illuminating; cf. Heidegger, *Being and Time*, translated by J. Macquarrie and Edward Robinson (Oxford 1962), 49–63.

as if all the mind encounters along this horizon is the *appearance* of things, but never their *essence*. Rather, Husserl asserted that *essences appear*. His own illustration was to picture himself seeing a table while walking around it: though his perspective on the table changes with each step, his consciousness of the table existing "in person" remains unchanged: what the mind perceives is always a table, which it "organises" in the mind into a single continuous impression. In a subsequent book Husserl developed the phenomenological approach by means of another methodological innovation that would be employed and reshaped by Heidegger with startling effect: the coining of a new philosophical vocabulary in order to draw the eye to the newness of the insights and ideas that the philosopher is attempting to convey. In *Ideas Pertaining to a Pure Phenomenology and to a Phenomenological Philosophy*,[11] Husserl ceases to speak of intentional conscious acts and their contents – appearances and essences – and speaks of *noesis* and *noema* to help take philosophy beyond the old distinction between subject and object in which he thought it had stagnated. The point of all this was to say that what should really matter to philosophy is not the perceiving subject or the object perceived: rather the object as meant (*noema*) and the intentional act (*noesis*) that presents the object as meant are inextricably bound up in one another. One simple consequence is that a phenomenologist, according to Husserl, must suspend judgement about the actual existence of things and pay exclusive attention to the way those things present themselves within the structures of consciousness (an insight we shall return to in relation to Bonhoeffer's christology).

To begin with, Heidegger was a good and loyal servant of Husserl's phenomenological method. In his doctoral dissertation *The Doctrine of the Judgement in Psychologism* (1914), Heidegger expressly echoed Husserl's argument that logic is not reducible to psychology, and he is again phenomenological in the approach taken in his *Habilitation* thesis[12] and "inaugural" lecture (1916) exploring the way time "shapes up" in the human consciousness. But then Heidegger fell into a long reflective silence. From 1916–1927 (years "interrupted" by war service, marriage and children) Heidegger busied himself reading – Paul, Augustine and Luther from the Christian tradition; classical Greek thought, and in particular the pre-Socratic philosophers in whose fragmentary writings ontology (the "science" of being) is an important emphasis. But he published nothing and in consequence, though his teaching began to earn him a reputation as an in-

---

[11] Translated by F. Kersten (Dordrecht 1982).
[12] The thesis was written to qualify him as a University Lecturer. It was titled: *Duns Scotus's Doctrine of Categories and Meaning* and is a study of a treatise subsequently re-attributed to Thomas of Erfurt. The terms of Heidegger's funding determined that he should concern himself with Catholic metaphysics, but he may already be seen finding his own "voice" by means of the phenomenological method.

dependent thinker, he struggled to win the professorial chair that would guarantee him status and financial security. He served as Husserl's assistant in Freiburg from 1918–1923 when he took a post as an *extraordinarius* professor – not yet a full and secure Chair – in Marburg, which he disdained rather as an academic backwater. As Husserl drew closer to retirement, he attempted to engineer a smooth succession for Heidegger to a philosophical Chair. Heidegger was nominated to the Chair of philosophy at Marburg but the Minister of Culture in Berlin who was responsible for ratifying appointments to full professorial rank, while recognising Heidegger's success as a teacher, wrote that "it does not seem appropriate to me to entrust him with an established full professorship ... until major literary achievements have earned that special recognition from his colleagues in the field which such an appointment calls for."[13] It was in order, therefore, to make Heidegger eligible for a full professorship that, meanwhile, Husserl encouraged the publication of *Being and Time* in a relatively obscure volume of phenomenological research. As he published it, Heidegger intended the volume to be most of the first part of a two-part book. In part II he planned to stand on the foundations of the ontology of part I and from this vantage point to lob grenades into the representative ontologies of philosophers such as Aristotle, Descartes and Kant.[14] Though, in the event, the project was never completed, it continued to be published for some time as if the rest of Division Two would soon appear.

From Husserl's point of view as Heidegger's mentor, it seemed natural to ensure that his phenomenological legacy would be left in the hands of his supposed *protégé*. Husserl had it in mind that his erstwhile assistant would follow faithfully in his footsteps, and as he turned to the dedication page of Heidegger's book (two years after it had been published![15]) he would have felt his hopes had been fulfilled.[16] But as he read on it dawned on Husserl that his pupil had not only moved beyond phenomenology as Husserl envisaged it, he had blown it apart; in George Steiner's words, "dedicated to Edmund Husserl, *Sein und Zeit* is that rarest of paradoxes: a monument which would destroy."[17] From theologian to Catholic philosopher, from Catholic philosopher to phenomenologist, from phenomenologist to ... what? What was the innovation that would lead Hannah Arendt

---

[13] Since Professors were employed essentially as senior civil servants, see Safranski, *Martin Heidegger: Between Good and Evil*, 143.

[14] Safranski, *Martin Heidegger: Between Good and Evil*, 171.

[15] Thomas Sheehan, "Reading a Life: Heidegger and Hard Times," in *CCH*, 84.

[16] Heidegger dedicated the volume to "Edmund Husserl in friendship and admiration," a dedication removed from editions during the Nazi period – on Heidegger's account of events – because his publisher advised him that censors would not countenance the reissue of a book dedicated to a Jew.

[17] George Steiner, *No Passion Spent: Essays 1978–1996*, 182.

to say that Heidegger had regained for philosophy "a thinking that expresses gratitude that the 'naked That' had been given at all?"[18]

III. Being and Time

Like many pupils who go beyond the premises of their teachers, Heidegger *seems*[19] to have thought that Husserl had not gone far enough to make the break with traditional philosophy. The argument that explains why, according to Heidegger, all modern philosophy – Husserl included – had been travelling up a blind alley when it came to epistemology, extends through the whole 500 pages (including notes) of *Being and Time* in the English translation. But to aid navigation through this complex text we may say at this point that the gist of Heidegger's argument may be glimpsed in the image of Heraclitus warming his back-side at a stove. For Heidegger, traditional philosophers were like Heraclitus' visitors: they expected philosophical insights to arise from deep reflection on the world they live in when, in the event, the "gods" are revealed in the everyday and the familiar. Heidegger's basic idea is that, in fact, the philosopher is not one who *reflects on* the world but one who *is in* the world. The world is not a thing that I understand by thinking about it because the world is not something separate from myself at all. Philosophy had taken epistemology to be the *primary* problem; that is, the question of how we may know anything so it may be trusted is the question that philosophy has to get right before it can ask any other question. From Heidegger's point of view, this was also true of Husserl who, for all that he was concerned with appearance of essences, was nonetheless concerned with recasting the subject/object relation. Husserl's sort of phenomenology showed too much of its origins in psychologism; it was constantly treading over the eggshells of its origins in science. Heidegger's departure was to say that epistemology is in fact a secondary problem, one *derived* from the problem of ontology – the question of the meaning of being. The real starting point for philosophical enquiry is to learn to ask the right questions, and the right questions are not "how" questions, such as "*how* may I know a thing in the world?"; the right question is the "is" question: "*the question of the meaning of Being.*"[20] All other forms of human enquiry, all sciences, natural or human,

---

[18] Hannah Arendt, *The Life of the Mind: Thinking – Willing – Judging* (San Diego 1981) volume 1, 185 (cited in Safranski, *Martin Heidegger: Between Good and Evil*, 427).
[19] Readers are left to draw their own conclusions about Heidegger's view of Husserl's legacy since he hardly mentions him in *Being and Time*.
[20] Citations are from Heidegger, *Being and Time*, translated by J. Macquarrie and Edward Robinson (Oxford 1962). For an alternative translation see *Being and Time*, trans-

interesting as they are, beg the truly fundamental question, of what being means. Heidegger wants in *Being and Time* to push back to this fundamental question, and it is here where the slogan, already cited above, bears reiteration: Heidegger urges enquirers after knowledge to go: "*zu den Sachen selbst!*" – "back to the things themselves."[21]

It is useful to recall that the immediate historical context for *Being and Time* – as for Karl Barth's similarly iconoclastic *Römerbrief* – was the aftermath of the Great War of 1914–1918, which devastated that fundament of the Enlightenment: belief in human progress. Enlightenment philosophy had typically been characterised by a quest for a transcendent truth that would steer humanity towards its fulfilment. After the trenches, humankind seemed more to be at the whim of history than at its helm, and "the philosophical issue of the day was the relation between truth and history."[22] In reflecting upon "being" and "time" Heidegger's intention was to show that the apparent conflict between truth and history disappears where human beings are located where they truly are: "thrown" in the everyday.

Heidegger opens *Being and Time* with a gnomic citation from Plato's *The Sophist*: "For manifestly you have long been aware of what you mean when you use the expression '*being*.' We, however, who used to think we understood it, have now become perplexed."[23] For Heidegger, in his "perplexity" concerning the meaning of being Socrates was at least one stage in advance of modern people, for at least he recognised that the question mattered. "This question has" however, "today been forgotten" and a dogma has developed that sanctions the complete neglect of the question.[24] Heidegger gives three apparently contradictory reasons to explain this state of affairs: "being" has been regarded as the most universal concept; it has been maintained that "being" is indefinable; and it has been claimed that the meaning of "being" is obvious. Yet Heidegger does not despair. He finds in the word "being" an important clue pointing to a way forward in his investigation: the language of being is in everyday use. People use phrases like "I am", "we are" and "she is" and do so in ways that suggest that they have a basic understanding of what the verb "to be" means. Heidegger believes – and here he displays his indebtedness to the phenomenological method of Husserl – that investigations such as the one he is embarking upon have a familiar structure. Every investigation is, in the first

---

lated by J. Stambaugh (New York 1996). For a German edition see *Sein und Zeit* in the Martin Heidegger *Gesamtausgabe Band 2* (Frankfurt am Main 1977). See *Being and Time*, 19, where Heidegger makes this question the starting point of his investigation.

[21] *Being and Time*, 50.
[22] Jonathan Rée, "Heidegger: History and Truth in Being and Time," in R. Monk and F. Raphael (eds.) *The Great Philosophers* (London 2000), 293–330.
[23] Plato, *Sophistes*, 244a; *Being and Time*, 19.
[24] *Being and Time*, 21.

place, a seeking (*Suchen*). It involves something that is asked about (*sein Gefragtes*) and – which is subtly different – something that is interrogated (*ein Befragtes*). Finally, an investigation also seeks something that is found out by asking (*das Erfragte*). Already in the first pages of his long book – Heidegger may be seen using language in a distinctive way, a way that is unfortunately not always obvious when his terms are translated into English. On the one hand he uses words that are familiar in everyday speech and reshapes them into a special philosophically serviceable language. And on the other hand, he uses etymological relationships between the words he is using beguilingly to draw the eye of his reader to the intimate philosophical relationships between the words he uses.

Armed with this description of philosophical enquiry, Heidegger turns to the question of the meaning of Being. The "seeking" in this particular investigation is the question of Being; the "that which is asked about" is "Being" as it is given to us in the distinction between "Being" and the "beings" that exist; the "that which is interrogated" is beings and the "that which is to be found out by asking" is the meaning of Being. In suggesting that in this enquiry beings are "that which is interrogated" Heidegger does not intend to "reduce" his enquiry to the scientific investigation of things that exist in the world (for example through anthropology, through astrophysics or through biology); in fact he distinguishes enquiry into human beings, the planets and the stars, and the beings in the animal kingdom from his more fundamental investigation calling the former sorts of enquiry *ontic* questions, and only the latter sort of enquiry *ontological* questions. Particle physics is an ontic science; philosophy is ontological. Of course, even for philosophy, one sort of being – human being – takes ontical priority, since human beings are distinguishable from other sorts of being precisely because they – and they alone – ask ontological questions. To denote this unique characteristic Heidegger uses a special term to describe human being, *Dasein:* "Dasein is an entity which does not just occur among other entities. Rather it is ontically distinguished by the fact that, in its very Being, that Being is an *issue* for it."[25] Dasein alone, that is, grasps at the question of the meaning of existence, which is not merely a question of Da-sein (literally "being there") – but as a self-understanding of human possibilities. Once more, to nuance what he means, Heidegger makes a subtle distinction between *existentiell* questions – questions concerned with the meaning of existence that we either face up to, or ignore; and *existential* questions that are concerned with the structure of existence. "Being" is thus not an epistemological question, because what is at stake is not the knowledge of objects that arises from the study of them by investigating subjects: *we* are the "ontological analytic of Dasein" i.e., the descrip-

---

[25] *Being and Time*, 32.

tion of Dasein's existence. It is this that brings Heidegger to *time*, for time, he asserts, is the horizon in which both the meaning of "our" Dasein will be laid bare, and also that on which the meaning of "Being" appears. He calls this laying bear of the meaning of time "historicity" to distinguish it from the mere sequence of events and historical facts.

Dasein's existence for Heidegger may not be understood as the mere presence of a thing in the world, but is to be understood in terms of its possibility. This does not mean, however, that all beings understand themselves in this way: many, perhaps most, do not, and this fact means that there are in practice two ways in which Dasein is in the world: inauthentic and authentic. This is a tempting distinction for theology, and indeed Rudolf Bultmann, Heidegger's colleague in Marburg, seized on it in order to describe the life of Christian faith as authentic life and the life of sin as inauthentic life. Heidegger, however, does not make value judgements about authenticity and inauthenticity, but sees them as ways of being – the former way, a way in which I can see that who I am is a choice, the latter as a way in which I am unreflective about who I am. We may return at this point to the question of how, if at all, Heidegger distinguishes his own philosophy from that of Husserl. Husserl, Heidegger believed, thought that the primary problem was the problem of how subjects may truthfully know the world in which they dwell. But in fact, Heidegger continued, such knowing is "founded" on another question, because before it can know anything, Dasein has to exist! In this sense the question of the world is an ontological question, and not an ontic one; the sciences, therefore, because they are concerned with ontic questions, can tell us nothing truly interesting about the world. The really riveting question is what Heidegger terms the "worldhood" – *die Weltheit* – of the world.

It is to get at the *worldhood* of the world that Heidegger takes up the relation of Dasein to the world as it is instructively displayed in beings' use of tools. Think for a moment about how the world appears to us: you have in your hands a book, but, until I draw your attention to the fact that you are holding a book, you are not really conscious of it. You are not holding a book for the fun of it but in order for this piece of equipment, this tool, to function as it was made to function – in the case of a book to convey to you what I am trying to say. Heidegger's own example is a hammer: when I pick up a hammer to bang in a nail it is something present-at-hand; I'm not conscious of it as it is made up of a metal head and a wooden handle; I'm not conscious of it at all ... unless it breaks, I use it in order to do something, and in this everyday function, it is transparent. Just so, in the everyday, lots of things remain invisible to my perception as I just get on with life. But it only *makes sense* as it has this function along the horizon of Dasein.

So far, Heidegger has been speaking chiefly about being-in the world – Da sein. In Chapter Four of *Being and Time*[26] he turns his attention to questions of being in the world as a being-with (others) in the world, and to the question of how to be-oneself. As with authentic and inauthentic existence, it is not Heidegger's aim to make moral judgements, but to *describe* Dasein's being. Dasein has two means by which to concern itself with others, with the "they:" it may dominate and control, or, it may liberate itself by means of liberating the other. What it may not do, and still be authentic, is to remain indifferent. Unfortunately, this is what Heidegger thinks most people are, most of the time. The majority are swept along by social forces and fashions they barely understand. The "they" (*das Man*) rules existence: "We take pleasure and enjoy ourselves as *they* (*man*) take pleasure; we read, see, and judge about literature and art as *they* see and judge; likewise we shrink back from the "great mass" as *they* shrink back; we find 'shocking' what *they* find shocking. The "they," which is nothing definite, and which all are, though not as the sum, prescribes the kind of Being of everydayness."[27]

This "public" life is the common form Dasein's existence takes, but Heidegger thinks he sees a way to be free of it, and that way is the possibility afforded by existential analysis. Before existential analysis can get to work, however, Dasein has to come to a sense that something is awry, it has to become *anxious*.

Heidegger was not the first philosopher to notice that anxiety was a part of the human condition – Søren Kierkegaard (or more precisely his "persona," Anti-Climacus) had anatomised despair in *The Sickness unto Death*. Kierkegaard thought that *"before God,"* it was a sin *"in despair not wanting to be oneself, or wanting in despair to be oneself."*[28] Now, as we have seen, Heidegger was not interested in making moral judgments in *Being and Time*; his interest is the meaning of being. And anxiety, he thinks, has an important role in alerting Dasein to its place in the world. He is not, of course, talking here of the location of Dasein on planet earth (the fact I live in Cambridge does not illuminate the meaning of being). Moods perform an important role in waking us from our indifference to our Da-sein – our being-there in the world. I can bumble along for weeks without really being conscious of myself; but if I receive a knock – a job interview goes the wrong way, a friend dies, or my back develops an agonising pain – I may become anxious and begin to reflect on the "there" of Dasein. "The basic state-of-mind of anxiety" as Heidegger puts it, is therefore "a distinctive

---

[26] *Being and Time*, 149 ff.
[27] *Being and Time*, 164.
[28] Søren Kierkegaard, *The Sickness unto Death* (Harmondsworth 1849), Penguin Classics, 1989, p. 109; italics in original.

way in which Dasein is disclosed."[29] Not that anxiety discloses anxiety as a matter of course: "when something threatening brings itself close, anxiety does not "see" any definite "here" or "yonder" from which it comes. That in the face of which one has anxiety is characterised by the fact that what threatens is *nowhere*. Anxiety "does not know" what that in the face of which it is anxious is."[30] What in fact anxiety directs us to is the "nowhere," and Heidegger draws the dramatic conclusion that this "nowhere" turns out to be Dasein's being: "this means that *Being-in-the-world itself is that in the face of which anxiety is anxious*."[31] We are afraid of (the disclosure of) our own shadow. As in a nightmare, life feels like "falling;" the task of Heidegger's project is to make Dasein turn back towards that it instinctively flees from in its anxiety, which is the "nothing" (*das Nichts*) of the world. He wants Dasein to stop filling the world with shallow pleasures, with the din of TV's and MP3 players, of ceaseless "business" and traffic, and come face to face with the being of Dasein: "in anxiety there lies the possibility of a disclosure which is quite distinctive; for anxiety individualizes. This individualization brings Dasein back from its falling, and makes manifest to it that authenticity and inauthenticity are possibilities of its *Being*."[32] Anxiety, in short, can put life into perspective.

Thus far, everything we have discussed falls in Division One of *Being and Time*. Heidegger now shifts gear, and we move into the incomplete Division Two of his argument, and to that which is signalled in the title of the book, as he begins to explore the theme of "Dasein and Temporality."[33] Yet though this is a new phase of his argument, Heidegger at pains to reiterate that the basic question he is investigating remains the same: the meaning of being.[34] The preceding phase of the argument has clarified what the question is, but what it has succeeded in revealing is that "in Dasein's very state of Being, there are important reasons which seem to speak against the possibility of having it presented (*Vorgabe*) in the manner required" for it to be accessible in its being-a-Whole.[35] To sort out these and other questions posed in Division One, in Division Two Heidegger has "the task of characterizing ontologically Dasein's Being-at-an-end and of achieving an existential conception of death."[36] At first glance, it may seem odd to look for the meaning of being in death – in which my being would appear to be extinguished. But Heidegger thinks that, though we

---

[29] *Being and Time*, 228.
[30] *Being and Time*, 231.
[31] *Being and Time*, 232.
[32] *Being and Time*, 235.
[33] *Being and Time*, 274ff.
[34] *Being and Time*, 274.
[35] *Being and Time*, 279.
[36] *Being and Time*, 280–281.

cannot *per definitionem* experience our own ceasing to be, we may see what is involved in our death through a meaningful encounter with the death of others: "When Dasein reaches its wholeness in death, it simultaneously loses the Being of its 'there.' By its transition to no-longer-Dasein [*Nichtmehrdasein*], it gets lifted right out of the possibility of experiencing this transition and of understanding it as something experienced. Surely this sort of thing is denied to any particular Dasein in relation to itself. But this makes the death of Others more impressive. In this way a termination [*Beendigung*] of Dasein becomes 'Objectively' accessible. Dasein can thus gain an experience of death, all the more so because Dasein is essentially Being with Others."[37]

It is not, for Heidegger, the case that I can experience my *own* death through the death of others; what the death of others *does* do, however, is to awaken me to the *possibility* of my own death, to bring me to an existential realization that I am going to die. This Being-towards-death becomes a way of relating to my own mortality. "Death is a way to be,"[38] and what this Being-towards-death reveals is not only that the human condition is indelibly uncertain, but that the proper way to orient oneself to Dasein is to embrace uncertainty, accept the possibility of death, and thereby turn back from flight and discover the meaning of Dasein in the sphere of the familiar. So what did Bonhoeffer make of it all?

IV. Direct Evidence of Bonhoeffer's Reading of Heidegger

In spite of the relatively obscure location of its publication, *Being and Time* fell with a great splash into the waters of German intellectual life, an assertion we find substantiated in Bonhoeffer's own flurry of interest in Heidegger. In the first place, the book had its desired effect: published in April 1927, by the autumn of that year Heidegger could finally settle his behind into the Chair in philosophy at Marburg University; a year later he was appointed to the position he most coveted when he succeeded Husserl in the Chair of philosophy at the University of Freiburg. Heidegger was not the only German academic to write a foundational text in 1927. In Berlin a scarce-bearded Bonhoeffer submitted his doctoral dissertation to the University authorities, eventually published in 1930 as *Sanctorum Communio*.[39] Unsurprisingly, since *Being and Time* was Heidegger's first significant publication and his first of any kind for several years, Bonhoeffer does not mention him in this, or indeed in any of his student writings. Yet it was probably in 1927 that Bonhoeffer first became aware of Heidegger's

---

[37] *Being and Time*, 281.
[38] *Being and Time*, 289.
[39] *DBW/E* 1.

growing reputation, since Hans-Christoph von Hase, a theologian and Bonhoeffer's cousin, was a student in Marburg and the two were regular correspondents.[40] Though there is no direct evidence, Hans-Richard Reuter is most likely right to suggest that "presumably Bonhoeffer first familiarised himself with *Sein und Zeit* while he was in Barcelona, at the insistence of his cousin"[41] sometime between February 1928 and February 1929, though Bonhoeffer gave no indication of having done so when he outlined the likely subject of his thesis to Reinhold Seeberg in July, 1928.[42] If Bonhoeffer owned a copy of Heidegger's book, it does not survive and we are therefore deprived of any possible insights to be gleaned from his marginal notes. And if Bonhoeffer was blown away by his first impressions, he kept quiet about it and does not rave about Heidegger in his letters as he did, for example, on "discovering" Karl Barth.[43] So the first impression we have of Bonhoeffer's reading of Heidegger is in the published text of *Akt und Sein*, Bonhoeffer's *Habilitation* thesis, which he completed in February 1930, and which he successfully defended in an oral examination at Berlin University later in the same year. Even before the outcome of his defence was known, Bonhoeffer must have been working on his inaugural lecture on "Humanity in Contemporary Philosophy and Theology," which deepened his discussion of Heidegger, and which he delivered on 31 July 1930. Whatever Bonhoeffer's views of the matter, Professor Wilhelm Lütgert, to whom Bonhoeffer acted as a teaching assistant in 1929 and 1930, thought of Bonhoeffer as a follower of Heidegger, a fact still lodged in his mind when in 1933 he felt it important enough to mention in a reference for Bonhoeffer.[44] Lütgert was suspicious of Heidegger's philosophy for what he took to be its neo-Thomism, and told Hans-Christoph von Hase, who succeeded Bonhoeffer as his assistant, that he had only taken Bonhoeffer on as a favour to Seeberg, his predecessor and Bonhoeffer's *Doktorvater*. No amount of protest from Hase could persuade Lütgert that Bonhoeffer may not have been a Heideggerian.[45] In fact, after his inaugural lecture, Bonhoeffer became largely silent on the subject of Heidegger's philosophy. He mentioned Heidegger in a seminar presentation at Union Seminary

---

[40] According to Eberhard Bethge, *Dietrich Bonhoeffer*, 82–83, "Hans-Christoph von Hase, who was a student in Marburg" kept Bonhoeffer "supplied with news of Heidegger and Bultmann who were working there." Bonhoeffer sometimes shared lecture notes with students in other universities, and it is possible he had access to notes of some of Heidegger's Marburg lectures.

[41] Editor's Afterword *DBWE* 2, 167 (*DBW* 2, 168).

[42] Cf. *DBW* 10, 81–85.

[43] The closest we get to such discussion is hinted at in a memoir of Hans-Christoph von Hase, who recalls after dinner conversation with Bonhoeffer revolving around several thinkers including Heidegger (*DBW* 10, 593).

[44] Cf. *DBW* 12, 113.

[45] Cf. Bethge, *Dietrich Bonhoeffer*, 129–130.

in 1930–1931 as part of the background to "The Theology of Crisis."[46] "Phenomenology/Heidegger' are mentioned in lectures given during the winter semester 1932–1933 on recent publications in systematic theology as one of three important streams of philosophical thought shaping theology (the others are Grisebach and the *völkische* movement).[47] Bonhoeffer again referred to Heidegger in 1932 in an essay on Karl Heim;[48] and in the same semester he may have tied Heidegger into a discussion of "*das Nichts*" (i.e., nothingness/nonbeing) in lectures on Genesis 1–3.[49] Certainly, Bonhoeffer's vocabulary in the lectures echoed Heideggerian themes,[50] and there may be at least one similar echo in *Discipleship*[51] (1937). In 1938 Bonhoeffer contrasted the Christian experience of temptation with an existentialist ethic, since "the saying that every moment of life is a time of decision is for him [i.e., the Christian] a meaningless abstraction," a view that Bonhoeffer may have thought was exemplified by Heidegger's existentialism.[52]

Strangely – given the different paths their political views had taken them in – it was during the war years that Bonhoeffer's interest in Heidegger appears modestly to have revived. In his essay on "Natural Life," intended as part of the *Ethics*, Bonhoeffer describes the distinctively human capacity for suicide with a phrase lifted from Heidegger when he writes that "human beings have freedom toward death."[53] Similarly, in the first draft of "History and Good" Bonhoeffer recalls Heidegger in describing the inevitable failure of human ethics that follows from the "historicity" (*Geschichtlichkeit*) of human existence.[54] A reference to Heidegger is unmistakeable in the second draft of "History and Good" in a discussion of conscience as the call of (authentic) human existence.[55] Heidegger may also lie behind Bonhoeffer's thoughts about the essence of truth in the essay "What does it mean to tell the truth?"[56] However, the editor's footnote on this essay misleadingly reports that "from a letter from his father, Karl

---

[46] *DBW* 10, 445.
[47] *DBW* 12, 155.
[48] *DBW* 12, 213.
[49] Some students taking notes during the lectures record such a link, but it is not explicit in the published version of the lectures, see *DBWE* 3, 33, note 28 (*DBW* 3, 32, note 22).
[50] *DBWE* 3, 65, note 24 (*DBW* 3, 61, note 21).
[51] *DBWE* 4, 58, note 3 (*DBW* 4, 46, note 3).
[52] Dietrich Bonhoeffer, *Temptation* (London 1955), 11; the link is made by the editors of *DBW* 15, 373, note15.
[53] *DBWE* 6, 197, note 93 (*DBW* 6, 192, note 87).
[54] See *DBWE* 6, 220, note 6 (*DBW* 6, 219, note 7) in which the editors draw a parallel with paragraph 75 of *Being and Time*, 439–444) on "Dasein's Historicality."
[55] *DBWE* 6, 276, note 112 (*DBW* 6, 277, note 96); see paragraphs 56 and 57 of *Being and Time*, 317–325.
[56] *DBWE* 16, 604 (*DBW* 16, 623).

Bonhoeffer, dated 11 July 1943 ... we know that Bonhoeffer had wrestled with Heidegger while in Tegel prison."[57] In fact, as a closer reading of Karl Bonhoeffer's letter, and as Eberhard Bethge's list of books Bonhoeffer read in prison make clear,[58] the book that Bonhoeffer read in his cell in June 1943 was *Phänomenologie des Zeitbewusstseins* which was written by Husserl, in a volume "merely" edited by Heidegger.

In the face of this summary of the evidence concerning Bonhoeffer's reading of Heidegger, it is clear that after Bonhoeffer engaged the philosopher in *Act and Being* and in his inaugural lecture – that is between 1928 and 1930 – Heidegger's *Being and Time* dropped off the theologian's radar screen. In order to find references to Heidegger in Bonhoeffer's writings from 1930, editors of the critical editions of Bonhoeffer's writings are, in the absence of similarly substantive discussions of Heidegger, left reading the runes of Bonhoeffer's books, essays and papers, in order to speculate in footnotes about possible echoes of Heideggerian themes. We may say with more certainty that after *Being and Time* Bonhoeffer did not bother to read any of Heidegger's subsequent writings – which one might have expected if he had thought Heidegger was genuinely significant. Yet it would be a mistake to conclude from the virtual absence of direct references to Heidegger in Bonhoeffer's writings after 1930 that Bonhoeffer was not either consciously or unconsciously bearing him in mind. Following Bonhoeffer's two academic dissertations in 1927 and 1930, the style of Bonhoeffer's theological writings changes dramatically, and he abandons many of the conventions of academic writing, such as extensive footnotes and discussion of primary and secondary sources. From this point, Bonhoeffer very rarely discusses the thinking of other theologians and philosophers, even where there is compelling evidence that they influenced him. There are two sorts of evidence for this assertion: textual evidence, and the evidence of content. Two examples suffice to make this point. In notes written during the drafting of the *Ethics* Bonhoeffer frequently named sources that he had read – including scriptural sources – that are *not* mentioned explicitly in the essays arising from his notes.[59] The second example is related to content: in Switzerland in May 1942 Bonhoeffer got hold of proofs of volume II/2 of Karl Barth's *Church Dogmatics* in which, especially in paragraphs 36–39, Barth discusses ethics in terms of "the command of God". Immediately thereafter, Bonhoeffer began work on "The "ethical" and the "Christian" as a Topic" and on "The concrete commandment and the Divine Mandates.[60] In both texts ethics is characterised – for the first time in

---

[57] *DBWE* 16, 604, note 9 (*DBW* 16, 623, note 9).
[58] Bethge, *Dietrich Bonhoeffer*, 944.
[59] See Dietrich Bonhoeffer, *Zettelnotizen für eine "Ethik,"* edited by Ilse Tödt (Gütersloh 1993) and compare notes with parallel sections in *DBW/E* 6.
[60] *DBWE* 6, 363–408 (*DBW* 6, 365–412).

the *Ethics* – in terms of divine command and commandment. The influence of Barth is unmistakeable; yet one searches in vain for a direct reference to Barth within the text. This is not a case of plagiarism; Bonhoeffer simply chose, by and large, not to discuss the work of others directly unless he was engaged explicitly in biblical exegesis or in decidedly historical theology (as when he discusses Luther's understanding of law and gospel in the 1943 essay on the "*Primus Usus Legis*"). I have laboured this point because it is important for the purposes of what follows in my argument to keep an open mind about the possibility that the writings of an important source may lie behind a text or texts written by Bonhoeffer that he does not explicitly cite or discuss. We shall return to this possibility when we take up Bonhoeffer's *Christology* lectures, but for now, we turn to the two texts in which Heidegger *is* discussed at length.

V. A Monument That Would Destroy?
Bonhoeffer's Theological Reading of Heidegger's Philosophy

If commentators must speculate about Heidegger's significance in Bonhoeffer's later writings, the evidence for Heidegger's importance in *Act and Being* is plain. Most immediately there is what *must* be Bonhoeffer's admiring nod in the direction of *Sein und Zeit* in his choice of title for *Akt und Sein*. More concretely, as Eberhard Bethge for example has pointed out, there are more references in *Act and Being* to Heidegger than to any other thinker, bar Luther, "even before Barth."[61] To get at quite *how* Heidegger's thinking functions in Bonhoeffer's *Act and Being* we shall need now to read that text with bi-focal lenses that allow us to keep one eye on Bonhoeffer's discussion of *Being and Time* and the other focussed on how that discussion fits into the argument of the book as a whole.

In reading *Act and Being* there is a seductive possibility that – taking its lead from the dialectic implicit in the title – we may come to think that Bonhoeffer is saying something like this: "some philosophies/theologies (e.g., Kant) approach the problem of revelation primarily through the *act* of reason; other philosophies/theologies approach the problem of revelation primarily through *being* (e.g., Heidegger). But the proper method is one that approaches the problem of revelation through the categories of act *and* being (i.e., Bonhoeffer)." It is important, if we are to make sense of Heidegger's role in Bonhoeffer's argument, straightway to disabuse ourselves of thinking that this is in fact what Bonhoeffer is doing. To be sure, Bonhoeffer's theological "answer" to the problem he takes on in the book will result in him concluding that Heidegger has not got matters quite

---

[61] Bethge, *Dietrich Bonhoeffer*, 133.

right; Bonhoeffer is in this sense offering a critique of Heidegger. But he is decidedly *not* saying that Heidegger has got it all wrong. And this takes us immediately into one of *Act and Being*'s most significant features: Dietrich Bonhoeffer believed that theology, without slavishly taking its lead from philosophy, can nonetheless learn from it.

Like *Being and Time*, *Act and Being* begins by outlining the problem that it sets out to resolve. "The most recent developments in theology," Bonhoeffer writes, "appear to me to be an attempt to come to an agreement about the problem of act and being."[62] At stake is "the issue of determining the relationship between 'the being of God' and the mental act which grasps that being. In other words, the meaning of 'the being of God in revelation' must be interpreted theologically, including how it is known, how faith as act, and revelation as being, are related to one another and, correspondingly, *how human beings stand in light of revelation*."[63]

At the outset, Bonhoeffer is clear that "the concept of revelation must, therefore, yield an epistemology of its own" and he undertakes to show, building on his doctoral dissertation on the Church, that "the dialectic of act and being is understood theologically as the dialectic of faith and the congregation of Christ."[64]

It is perhaps striking, given what he had read in *Being and Time* about the erroneousness of making epistemology the *primary* question of philosophy, that Bonhoeffer concedes that the act/being problem arises from "the question that Kant and idealism have posed for theology"[65] which is "the attempt of the I to understand itself."[66] Having outlined the problem, Bonhoeffer turns to a more detailed analysis of how act and being have been treated in recent philosophy. First, he outlines the approaches of Kant, of neo-Kantians, and of Hegelian Idealism, each of which he sees as caught in the snare of the "I" turned in on itself, of, in Luther's words, the "*ratio in se ipsam incurvato*" [reason turned in upon itself]. Here, Bonhoeffer turns to "the ontological attempt." Summarizing these "failed attempts" Bonhoeffer writes: "Transcendental philosophy regards thinking to be 'in reference to' transcendence; idealism takes transcendent being into thinking; and finally, ontology leaves being fully independent of thinking and accords being priority over thinking,"[67] that is, being over the *act* of thinking.

It is important to note here that Bonhoeffer lumps "the ontology of the Husserlian school" in with idealism, and equally important (for the pur-

---

[62] *DBWE* 2, 25 (*DBW* 2, 21).
[63] *DBWE* 2, 27–28 (*DBW* 2, 22–23) Bonhoeffer's italics.
[64] *DBWE* 2, 31 (*DBW* 2, 26).
[65] *DBWE* 2, 27 (*DBW* 2, 22).
[66] *DBWE* 2, 33 (*DBW* 2, 27).
[67] *DBWE* 2, 60 (*DBW* 2, 54).

poses of this essay) to ask what is the substance of his suspicion of Husserl. Bonhoeffer's worry is that in Husserl "the 'noetic-noematic parallel structure' remains immanent in consciousness,"[68] the consequence of which is that "the a priori belongs not on the side of the object but on that of consciousness."[69] Two things are at stake here, and for both of them Bonhoeffer may be indebted to Heidegger. Let us recall what it was that was at issue in Heidegger's departure from Husserlian thinking. In so far as we can tell, Heidegger believed, that in spite of identifying problems in traditional epistemologies, in the end Husserl had been incapable of leaving behind a world-view based on the subject/object divide. Bonhoeffer simply takes over this view in asserting that "phenomenology poses no questions of being, only of essence."[70] Husserl's is *not*, for either Heidegger or Bonhoeffer, a genuinely ontological attempt; indeed it "passes over" being altogether.[71] The second problem with Husserl is what becomes of Dasein's relation to the "Other", i.e., to the possibility of transcendence. Heidegger identified that being-with-others was a condition for the existential analysis of Dasein. In *Sanctorum Communio* Bonhoeffer had similarly established sociality as an essential aspect of being human. If "the question of existence is 'bracketed out' from the outset,"[72] as Husserl has it, others become simply pieces of furniture within consciousness, blunting a sense of obligation towards them.

Now, with the drama of the arrival of the Commendatore at Don Giovanni's dinner table, Heidegger comes centre stage in Bonhoeffer's discussion: "precisely where Husserl 'brackets,' Heidegger discloses being itself."[73] This introduces a summary of the key points in *Being and Time* which Bonhoeffer offers without critical comment. He concludes that, for Heidegger: "being understands itself in Dasein, in spirit. But Dasein is the existence of human beings in their historicity, in the momentariness of the decisions that they, in every instance, have already taken."[74] This leads Bonhoeffer to the apparently affirmative provisional conclusion that: "From the perspective of the problem of act and being, it would seem that here a genuine coordination of the two has been reached."[75] Unlike Hegel, continues Bonhoeffer, Heidegger successfully makes being temporal; and unlike Husserl, he does not allow consciousness to dominate. Moreover, Heidegger, unlike earlier transcendentalist, idealist and phenomenological philosophies, is

---

[68] *DBWE* 2, 62 (*DBW* 2, 56).
[69] *DBWE* 2, 63 (*DBW* 2, 57).
[70] *DBWE* 2, 64 (*DBW* 2, 58).
[71] *DBWE* 2, 67 (*DBW* 2, 61); the use of the wording "has done violence to" for "*vergangen*" in the English translation here is misleading.
[72] *DBWE* 2, 62 (*DBW* 2, 56).
[73] *DBWE* 2, 67 (*DBW* 2, 62).
[74] *DBWE* 2, 71 (*DBW* 2, 65).
[75] *DBWE* 2, 71 (*DBW* 2, 65).

awake to the limitations of Dasein: being is limited not only by the "other" but by its being-towards-death, i.e., the realization of the finitude of Dasein.

But there is a problem: "no room has been left for the concept of revelation."[76] For a start, Heidegger has not, thinks Bonhoeffer, allowed scope for the being of God, who in Heidegger's account would have to exist in time since all beings, *per definitionem*, exist temporally. Revelation teaches that God is eternal. Now, Bonhoeffer continues, there might be a way to open up ontology to the question of revelation, through the Thomist idea of an *analogia entis* between God's "Dasein" and human Dasein – a way sign-posted in the ontology of the Catholic Thomistic philosopher Erich Przywara.[77] In the event, however, for Bonhoeffer even this Christianly oriented philosophy remains "merely" philosophy, and *"per se*, a philosophy can concede no room for revelation unless it knows revelation and confesses itself to be a Christian philosophy in full recognition that the place it wanted to usurp *is* already occupied by another – namely, by Christ."[78]

The offence of philosophy – Heidegger's included – turns out to be the attempt to achieve self-understanding autonomously, since such thinking is "as little able as good works to deliver the *cor corvum in se* [the heart turned in upon itself] from itself,"[79] an insight that concludes the first part of *Act and Being*, and with it the discussion of philosophical contributions to the problem under investigation.

We may discuss Part B of *Act and Being* much more briefly. From the point of view of revelation "only those who have been placed into the truth can understand themselves in truth."[80] But what are the consequences for knowledge of this theological claim? Just what sort of thinking does God permit human beings to undertake if philosophy is so peremptorily swept aside? This question leads Bonhoeffer to what are among the most penetrating and precise sentences of the book: "In revelation it is not so much a question of the freedom of God – eternally remaining within the divine self, aseity – on the other side of revelation, as it is of God's coming out of God's own self in revelation. It is a matter of God's *given* Word, the covenant in which God is bound by God's own action ... God is free not from human beings but for them. Christ is the word of God's freedom. God *is* present [and here is a lasting imprint of Bonhoeffer's dialogue with Heidegger's ontological enquiry], that is, not in eternal nonobjectivity but – to

---

[76] *DBWE* 2, 72–73 (*DBW* 2, 67).
[77] *DBWE* 2, 74 (*DBW* 2, 68).
[78] *DBWE* 2, 76–78 (*DBW* 2, 71–72).
[79] *DBWE* 2, 80 (*DBW* 2, 74).
[80] *DBWE* 2, 81 (*DBW* 2, 75).

put it quite provisionally for now – 'haveable', graspable in the Word within the church."[81]

What room does this leave for Heidegger? The answer is "none", and Bonhoeffer spells this out in dialogue with the Heideggerian existential theology of Rudolf Bultmann, who portrays the Christian as "the person of decision."[82] Being in Christ calls for a certain kind of continuity. Heidegger's Dasein calls for continuity, too, but it is a continuity of perpetual crises in which decisions are called for, a continuity of "always-being-already-in-guilt", which means – in Bonhoeffer's devastating judgement – that "Heidegger's concept of existence is of no use for the elucidation of being in faith."[83]

Part C of *Act and Being* – the shortest of the three parts that make up the book – elucidates the difference between always-being-already-in-guilt (being in Adam) and being in faith (being in Christ). Here too, though Heidegger is not discussed as he has been earlier in the book, he plays an important cameo role in a contrast Bonhoeffer draws between being-towards-death and being in Christ as a being towards the future. Being-towards-death is still to exist in sin. Being in Christ alone opens up the future since "the human being 'is' in the future of Christ – that is, never in being without act, and never in act without being."[84]

Bonhoeffer's inaugural lecture on "The problem of the human in contemporary philosophy and theology"[85] recasts the problem of *Act and Being* – the question of revelation – as the question "what does it mean to be human?" Once more, Bonhoeffer uses Heidegger as a key dialogue partner. But both his approach and his conclusions are substantively the same as they had been in *Act and Being*. Heidegger's analysis of Dasein takes thinking beyond previous philosophies to the heart of the question: but "once again, in the last resort, it is man himself who is answering the question of man."[86] Heidegger helps sharpen the question, but revelation alone can answer it.

VI. Secondary Discussion of Heidegger's Influence on Bonhoeffer

For reasons that are perhaps plain in the light of our earlier remarks concerning a lack of explicit discussion of Heidegger in Bonhoeffer's writings after 1930, the standard compendia of Bonhoeffer's theology which

---

[81] *DBWE* 2, 90–91 (*DBW* 2, 85).
[82] *DBWE* 2, 96–103 (*DBW* 2, 91–99).
[83] *DBWE* 2, 98 (*DBW* 2, 93).
[84] *DBWE* 2, 159 (*DBW* 2, 159).
[85] *DBW* 10, 357–378.
[86] *NRS*, 53.

mapped out the first stages of Bonhoeffer interpretation, are by and large silent on the question of if and how Heidegger influenced Bonhoeffer's thought.[87] In one leading text on Bonhoeffer's theology – Ernst Feil's *Die Theologie Dietrich Bonhoeffers*[88] – Heidegger is generally conspicuous by his absence: Feil mentions Heidegger only seven times, mostly in footnotes, and mostly in connection with Rudolf Bultmann rather than Bonhoeffer. This may reflect the tendency in the early stages in the reception and interpretation of Bonhoeffer's writings, to read his theology backwards, i.e. beginning with the drama of the prison correspondence, interpreting earlier material in the light of the later. The academic dissertations *Sanctorum Communio* and *Act and Being* did not sit easily with attempts to harness Bonhoeffer to radical or liberal theological agendas.[89] More recently, however, several commentators have begun to show interest in Heidegger's influence on Bonhoeffer, leading to a number of very fruitful discussions. Charles Marsh seeks to bring "theological clarity" to Bonhoeffer's reading of Heidegger particularly with respect to the influence of the latter's "notions of potentiality-for-being, authenticity, and being with others" on Bonhoeffer's thinking about "human selfhood and sociality."[90] Robert P. Scharlemann considers Bonhoeffer to be the only one among Heidegger's theological interpreters to have taken the significance of "time" seriously.[91] Craig J. Slane uses Heidegger's notion that the structure of *Dasein* is disclosed as *Sein zum Tode* (being towards death) to take him "towards a hermeneutic of Martyrdom"[92] "I want", Slane writes, "to illuminate the *passageway* between belief and behaviour with the use of martyrdom."[93] Joel Lawrence, asks, however, whether Slane's treatment neglects Bon-

---

[87] For example, John Godsey simply mentions Heidegger as one of several dialogue partners in *Act and Being* (*The Theology of Dietrich Bonhoeffer* (London 1960)); André Dumas briefly discusses Heidegger, again in relation to *Act and Being* (in *Dietrich Bonhoeffer: Theologian of Reality*, (London 1971), 101–103) and in passing as an influence on Bultmann's existentialist theology.

[88] Ernst Feil, *Die Theologie Dietrich Bonhoeffers: Hermeneutik, Christologie, Weltverständnis*, (München/Mainz, 1971); *The Theology of Dietrich Bonhoeffer*, translated by Martin Rumscheidt (Philadelphia 1985), is a slightly abridged version of the German original.

[89] For discussion of the reception of Bonhoeffer, see Stephen R. Haynes *The Bonhoeffer Phenomenon* (Minneapolis 2004) and Ralf K Wüstenberg (ed.) *Dietrich Bonhoeffer lesen im Internationalen Kontext* (Frankfurt 2007).

[90] Charles Marsh, *Reclaiming Dietrich Bonhoeffer* (New York 1994), 111–134, citation from 112.

[91] Robert P. Scharlemann, "Authenticity and Encounter: Bonhoeffer's Appropriation of Ontology," in Wayne W. Floyd and Charles Marsh (eds), *Theology and the Practice of Responsibility* (Valley Forge, PA. 1994), 353–365.

[92] *Bonhoeffer as Martyr* (Grand Rapids 2004), 119–136.

[93] *Bonhoeffer as Martyr*, 119.

hoeffer's sharp critique of Heidegger concerning Being-towards-death.[94] Brian Gregor contrasts Heidegger and Bonhoeffer's respective conceptions of the proper relation between philosophy and theology.[95] Collectively, these studies are suggestive of a much deeper relationship between Heidegger and Bonhoeffer than was previously thought.

VII. Bonhoeffer's Christology Lectures as "Phenomenological Theology"?

I turn now to the *denouement* of the present study: my suggestion that Heidegger's most lasting legacy in the writings of Bonhoeffer may lie in the methodology of the *Christology* lectures. In making this suggestion it is important explicitly and openly to acknowledge that I am engaged in conjecture. Earlier in this essay I laboured the point that tracing the origins of Bonhoeffer's thinking to sources is by no means a simple matter of reckoning on the basis of explicit references: Bonhoeffer was not – at least after 1930 – the sort of writer to disclose each and every occasion when he had a source in mind. The most that my speculation can hope for is to enumerate a number of points of *resemblance* between Heidegger's reworking of Husserl's phenomenological philosophy and what Bonhoeffer may be seen to be doing in the *Christology* lectures. And as if this were not already to rely uncomfortably on guess-work, we must also reckon with the fact that in *Christology* we are working, since Bonhoeffer's manuscript is lost, with a text assembled from student notes, with the added textual problems that brings.[96]

The first resemblance that I want to point out is a relatively cosmetic one: Bonhoeffer, like Heidegger, draws his reader's eye by coining a distinctive vocabulary around which he structures his argument. In Heidegger, we see this most plainly in the deployment of a group of words – some in common use and others neologisms created by him for the purpose – concerned with "Being." Some of these words take on different meanings in different contexts, and pose considerable problems for his translators (which is why key terms are often followed in translation by their German

---

[94] "Bonhoeffer's freedom is freedom that is grounded not in his future death but in his past death... the freedom that Bonhoeffer has towards death exists because he knows he has already died in Christ," Joel D. Lawrence, unpublished Cambridge University dissertation, *Death Together: Thanatology and Sanctification in the Theology of Dietrich Bonhoeffer*, 2007.

[95] Brian Gregor, "Formal Indication, Philosophy and Theology: Bonhoeffer's Critique of Heidegger," forthcoming in *Faith and Philosophy* (2007).

[96] The textual status of *Christologie* is detailed in *DBW* 12, 279, note 1; an English translation, based on an earlier compilation of student notes, may be found in *Christology*, translated by E. Robertson (London 1978).

original). The group includes: *Dasein* (which Macquarrie and Robinson leave untranslated); *Da-sein* (being there); *daseinsmässig* (of the character of *Dasein*, etc.,); *seiend* (being); *Seiendes* (entity); *sein* (be); *Sein* (Being); *Sein-bei* (being alongside); *Sein zu* (being towards) and so on.[97] For Bonhoeffer's part, the primary term in the lectures with which he engages in "word-play" (pun intended) is "Logos", taken ultimately, of course, from the Prologue to John's Gospel. There is *Christologie* (Christology); *Logologie* (logo-logy – the study of the Logos); *Gott-Logos* (Logos of God); *menschlicher Logos* (human logos) and *Gegen-Logos* (counter-logos). As with Heidegger, Bonhoeffer finds some of these terms in use already; others are his own neologisms. And as with Heidegger, Bonhoeffer claims to begin his investigation by attending to clues in everyday conversation: "The question, 'Who are you?', is common in daily life," writes Bonhoeffer. "But it is often loosely phrased to amount to the same question as the question of classification, the question, 'How?' Tell me how you are, tell me how you think, and I will tell you who you are."[98]

Beyond these superficial stylistic resemblances is anything more *methodological* going on? To begin to explore this it may be helpful to recall Heidegger's summary, sketched above, of the phenomenological method, which he describes as an attempt to go *Zu den Sachen selbst!* – back to the things themselves. Partly, this is perhaps simply to express the desire to do what all philosophers think they are doing, namely to ask fundamental questions. But Heidegger thought that modern philosophy, in its preoccupation with epistemology, had in fact been pursuing *secondary questions* derived, on close inspection, from the true primary question, which is the meaning of being. In *Being and Time* Heidegger presses *zu den Sachen selbst* in at least three ways that, I want to suggest, are paralleled in three key ideas in Bonhoeffer's *Christology* lectures.

The first is Heidegger's appropriation of Husserl's "discovery" that the object as meant (*noema*) and the intentional act (*noesis*) that presents the object as meant are inextricably bound up in one another. Subjects do not, as traditional epistemologies had conceived, observe things and think about them: Dasein is thrown in the world. For a phenomenologist, we may recall, the stuff philosophy has to work on is already being organised in the mind before we reflect upon it. A phenomenologist, therefore, cannot press beyond appearances to essences. The significance of this for Bonhoeffer's christological method occurs in his discussion of the Chalcedonian definition. At Chalcedon the Fathers had attempted, Bonhoeffer thought, to preserve the mystery of the incarnation. In doing so, they recognised that human beings simply *cannot* press beyond the God-Man, Jesus Christ. The-

---

[97] See *Being and Time*, "Glossary of German expressions," 505–523.
[98] *Christology*, 31 (*DBW* 12, 283).

ology cannot get behind the formulation of Chalcedon to work out *how* divine stuff and human stuff are able to cohere in the one God-Man, Jesus Christ: all that we may say is that they do. One must – and here is the phenomenological echo – suspend judgement about the nature/s and will/s of the incarnate Son of God and pay exclusive attention to the way those things present themselves within the structures of faith. All the Church has to go on is the appearance of his essence in its appearing.

From this, there follows a second methodological similarity between Heidegger's philosophical method and Bonhoeffer's christological method; this concerns Heidegger's distinction between *ontic* questions and *ontological* questions. Ontic questions, we may recall, are for Heidegger questions about beings (about planets and stars, about biology, about geology etc.). These are interesting questions, to be sure, but they are not basic questions; investigating beings does not take us to the meaning of Being. Now look at what Bonhoeffer says about "how" questions and about "who" questions. "All scientific questions" Bonhoeffer teaches (and by "*wissenschaftliche Fragen*" he means, of course, not only questions in natural science but in the human sciences): "can be reduced to two: What is the cause of X? and, What is the meaning of X? The first question embraces the realm of the exact sciences and the second that of the study of the arts; both belong together." These questions are basically questions of classification. But "what happens", Bonhoeffer continues, "if a counter-logos appears which denies the classification? Another logos which destroys the first? ... what happens if the counter-logos makes its claim in a totally different form? If it is not only an idea, but 'Word' which challenges the dominion of the logos? If this 'Word' appears somewhere and somehow in history as 'Person'? If he declares himself as judgement upon the human logos and says of himself: 'I am the way, the truth, the life', 'I am the death of the human logos, I am the life of the Logos of God'."[99]

Of course there is an insight here that is *not* present in Heidegger – the theological claim that attempts by the human logos to classify the world by means of how questions are radically called themselves into question by the logos of God. Nonetheless, the distinction with which Bonhoeffer is working here between questions about classification and *the* basic question addressed by the Logos to the human logos, resembles closely Heidegger's distinction between ontic and ontological questions.

The conclusion to this phase of his lectures brings Bonhoeffer's text to what, I want to suggest, is a third resemblance with Heidegger: the question of the meaning of Being. Let us try a thought-experiment: imagine for a moment that what Bonhoeffer does in his lectures is essentially to re-

---

[99] *Christology*, 28–30 (*DBW* 12, 281–282). It is unclear whether Bonhoeffer would have determined that Heidegger's *suchen* into the meaning of being belongs or does not belong to the second sort of question.

place ontology with christology as *the* fundamental human question. What would Bonhoeffer's enquiry look like? If we return to the description of his investigation that Heidegger outlines in the opening pages of *Being and Time* we may recall that what Heidegger seeks is the meaning of Being, whereas Bonhoeffer seeks the meaning of Christ. Heidegger's "that which is asked about" is "Being" as it is given to us in the distinction between "Being" and the "beings" that exist; Bonhoeffer's "that which is asked about" is "Christ" as he is given in his self-revelation. Heidegger's "that which is interrogated" is beings; Bonhoeffer's "that which is investigated" is the human logos, which is "interrogated" by the counter-logos. And finally, Heidegger's "that which is to be found out by asking" is the meaning of Being; while Bonhoeffer's "that which is to be found out by asking" is the answer to the question "who is Jesus Christ?" The "authenticity" that would follow would then be being-towards-death, but a being-towards-death to sin and birth to new life in Jesus Christ. True life would be found in conformation to the form of Jesus Christ, who alone can teach us what it means to be truly human. The connections click home so sweetly that it is difficult for me to imagine that Bonhoeffer was *not* influenced – wittingly or unwittingly – by Heidegger in the formation of his christology, such that it may not be entirely fanciful to characterise Bonhoeffer's christology as a *phenomenological christology*.

VIII. Towards-a-Conclusion

I began this essay by making explicit the difficulty of delineating the distinction between Heidegger's life and his writings; I conclude it in the place where I began. Does it matter to our interpretation of his philosophy that he was a Nazi? Heidegger himself gives mixed signals about that question. On the one hand, his philosophical method is *par excellence* one that asserts the significance of Dasein's "throwness" in the world. On the other hand, he also suggests in *Being and Time* that it is possible to achieve, through existential analysis that moves beyond the anxiety typical of Dasein to an authentic, "disinterested" answer to the question of the meaning of Being. Several of Heidegger's interpreters have attempted to say that his was a short-lived flirtation with Nazism, later corrected, that left little mark on his thought. John Macquarrie, for example – the theologian who co-translated the English edition of *Being and Time* I have been using – writes that although Heidegger "was a firm supporter of the party, he did not share in its fanatical excesses. In any case, he very soon became disillusioned," which leads Macquarrie to deride as "quite unscrupulous" attempts to "discredit" Heidegger on account of his Nazi connections.[100] To my mind this is wholly inadequate; it neglects both the *extent* and the *duration* of Heidegger's Nazism.[101] More troublingly, it fails adequately to grasp the historical contingency of ideas and the consequent blurriness of the edges between life and thought. Of course it matters that Heidegger was a Nazi because Heidegger's life was the "sphere of the familiar" in which his ideas came to presence. But that is no reason to dismiss him, and in this Macquarrie is right: one must weigh the texts.

In this study I have attempted to weigh Heidegger's and Bonhoeffer's work in the scales and found both differences and resemblances – perhaps more of the latter than previous readings may have led us to expect. In my view, Bonhoeffer is right to think it axiomatic that theology does not take its lead from any philosophy. But that is no reason for theologians not to read philosophy with interest and with profit, especially where, as is the case with Heidegger, so much of his thinking is in dialogue with theology: as Fergus Kerr observes, "... almost every philosophical innovation in *Sein und Zeit* may easily be traced to a theological source".[102] I have suggested that in the end, Heidegger's legacy in Bonhoeffer's theology may not lie so much in his "close reading" of *Being and Time* in the early 1930's, but in certain stylistic and methodological features of the *Christology* lectures. It is difficult to demonstrate conclusively whether this suggestion arises from exegesis or eisegesis. Yet the possibility alone conjures the thought that in May 1933, the month that Martin Heidegger was installed as Rector of Freiburg University and, amidst swastikas and a loud chorus of "Sieg Heil," was delivering the infamous Rectorial address that lent intellectual credence to the Nazi revolution, a junior *Privatdozent* in Berlin University may have been sublimating the great professor's phenomenological method in order, against the *Verführer*, to proclaim "Jesus is Lord."

---

[100] John Macquarrie, *Martin Heidegger* (London 1968). See also Walter Biemel, *Martin Heidegger: An Illustrated Study* (London 1973), 150: "the political error was of short duration ... it is superficial to pounce on it in order to discredit Heidegger." For a lucid short study, see Jeff Collins, *Heidegger and the Nazis* (Cambridge, UK., 2000).

[101] This is painfully clear in the interview Heidegger gave to *Der Spiegel* on 23 September 1966 and which was published on 31 May 1976. During the interview Heidegger is unedifyingly defensive, evasive and dissimulating with regard to his earlier support for Nazism.

[102] Fergus Kerr, *Immortal Longings* (London 1997), 47.

Contributors

Barry Harvey
A native of Denver, Colorado, Barry Harvey is Professor of Theology in the Honors College at Baylor University. He has earned degrees from the University of Colorado at Boulder and the Southern Baptist Theological Seminary, and was awarded the Ph.D. degree in Theology and Ethics by Duke University. He is the author of three books, *Politics of the Theological: Beyond the Piety and Power of A World Come of Age*, published by Peter Lang, *Another City: An Ecclesiological Primer for a Post-Christian World*, published by Trinity Press International, and *Can These Bones Live? A Catholic Baptist Engagement with Ecclesiology, Hermeneutics, and Social Theory*, to be published in 2008 by Brazos Press. He is also a co-author of a fourth, *StormFront: The Good News of God*, with James V. Brownson, Inagrace T. Dietterich and Charles C. West, published by Eerdmans. Harvey has also written numerous articles in collections and scholarly journals such as *Modern Theology, Pro Ecclesia, Scottish Journal of Theology, Christian Scholar's Review, First Things* and *Perspectives in Religious Studies*. He is a member of the Board of the International Bonhoeffer Society, English Language Section, and of the Editorial Board of the Dietrich Bonhoeffer Works (*DBWE*).

Wayne Floyd
Dr. Wayne Whitson Floyd develops and oversees the educational programs of The Alban Institute in Herndon, VA. Previously he served as director of the Center for Christian Formation in the Cathedral College of Washington National Cathedral, and as a special consultant to the Bishop of the Episcopal Diocese of Washington. Before moving to Washington, DC, Dr. Floyd served as Canon Theologian for the Episcopal Diocese of Southern Virginia and as director of their Anglican Center for Theology and Spirituality. Prior to that he served as Dean of the School of Christian Studies in the Diocese of Central Pennsylvania, where he also held the position of Canon Theologian for the Cathedral Church of St. Stephen in Harrisburg. Dr. Floyd holds an M. Div. and Ph.D. in systematic theology from Emory University. He was an Assistant Professor of systematic theology at the Episcopal seminary at Sewanee, TN, and later was for eight years a Visiting Professor of Anglican Studies at the Lutheran Theological Seminary at Philadelphia. He also has taught biblical studies, Judaic studies, and reli-

gion and modern culture at Dickinson College. Dr. Floyd is a well-known scholar of the theology of Dietrich Bonhoeffer, and served from 1993 to 2004 as the General Editor of the new 16-volume English critical edition, *Dietrich Bonhoeffer Works*. He has written two books, edited two others, and has written numerous articles for book compilations and for journals such as *The Christian Century, Religious Studies Review, Dialog, Journal of the American Academy of Religion*, and *Modern Theology*.

Peter Frick
Dr. Frick studied theology and religious studies at the universities of Waterloo, Tübingen and McMaster. Currently Associate Professor of Religious Studies and Academic Dean at St. Paul's United College, University of Waterloo, Canada, Frick teaches in the fields of New Testaments, Greek, Theology, and Western Religions. He published *Divine Providence in Philo of Alexandria* (Tübingen 1999) and *A Handbook of New Testament Greek* (Montreal 2007). He is currently working on a book entitled *An Introduction to the Writings of Dietrich Bonhoeffer*. Frick is a member of the Board of the International Bonhoeffer-Society, English Language Section and a member and translator of the Editorial Board for the *Dietrich Bonhoeffer Works*.

Geffrey Kelly
Dr. Geffrey B. Kelly is Professor of Systematic Theology and Chairperson of the Department of Religion at La Salle University. He is the author or editor of eleven books and over 80 articles in the various fields of his expertise. His writings include studies on the theology and spirituality of Dietrich Bonhoeffer, the systematic theology of Karl Rahner, biomedical ethics and health care, Christian Spirituality, Pneumatology, Catholicism in the Modern World, biblical exegesis, the religious history of Ireland, and the hermeneutics of religious education. He served as Secretary of the English Language Section of the International Bonhoeffer Society for 19 years before being elected to two terms as society president from 1992 to 2000. He is an Emeritus member of the Board of Directors of the Society.

Wolf Krötke
From 1957–1965 Dr. Krötke studied theology in Leipzig, Naumburg und Berlin. During this time (1958–1959) he was also incarcerated in the former German Democratic Republic as a political prisoner. He received his doctor in theology in 1971 with a dissertation on Barth, published in English as *Sin and Nothingness in the Theology of Karl Barth* (2005). From 1973 until his retirement in 2004 Dr. Krötke was professor of systematic theology, first at the Kirchliche Hochschule and then at the Humboldt University in Berlin. He was also a member of the editorial board of the

Dietrich Bonhoeffer Werke. Dr. Krötke has published over a dozen monographs and countless articles. His most recent books are *Gottes Klarheiten. Eine Neuinterpretation der Lehre von den 'Eigenschaften Gottes'* (Tübingen 2001) and *Erschaffen und Erforscht. Mensch und Universum in Theologie und Naturwissenschaft* (Berlin 2002).

Andreas Pangritz
Andreas Pangritz is professor of systematic theology and director of the Ecumenical Institute at the University of Bonn, Germany. From 1999 to 2004 he taught systematic theology at the University of Aachen. He holds a PhD and post-doctoral degree (*Habilitation*) in systematic theology of the Free University of Berlin, where he was assistant professor from 1984 to 1995. He studied theology and political sciences at the universities of Tübingen, Amsterdam and Berlin. Among his fields of research are the theology of Dietrich Bonhoeffer, the "hidden theology" of Walter Benjamin, the theology of the Jewish-Christian relationship "after Auschwitz." His major publications include *Polyphonie des Lebens* (On Bonhoeffer's "Theology of Music;" 1994, 2nd edition 2000), *Vom Kleiner- und Unsichtbarwerden der Theologie* (1996), and *Karl Barth in the Theology of Dietrich Bonhoeffer* (2000), and numerous essays on the theology of Bonhoeffer, Helmut Gollwitzer and Friedrich-Wilhelm Marquardt.

Stephen Plant
Dr. Plant, a Methodist minister, is a graduate of Birmingham University and of Cambridge University, where he wrote a doctoral study of Bonhoeffer's uses of the Bible in ethics. From 1995 to 2001 he was Europe Secretary of the British Methodist Church. He is Senior Tutor and Director of Studies at Wesley House, the Methodist Theological College within the Cambridge Theological Federation, a partnership between 11 institutions representing Anglican, Methodist, Orthodox, Reformed, Roman Catholic traditions and incorporating centers for the study of Jewish, Muslim and Christian relations. He teaches theology and ethics in the Cambridge theological Federation and is an affiliated lecturer in the University of Cambridge Faculty of Divinity. He is a senior member of St. Edmund's College, Cambridge. Dr Plant is co-editor of the series *International Bonhoeffer Interpretations* (published by Peter Lang), is the author of several books (including *Bonhoeffer,* Continuum, 2004) and is a regular contributor to *The Times* newspaper.

Martin Rumscheidt
Martin Rumscheidt, a native of Germany, was educated in Germany, Switzerland, Canada, with post-doctoral studies in Canada, the United States and the Czech Republic. An ordained minister in the United Church of

Canada, he served three congregations in Quebec and Ontario and, as of 1970, was professor of Historical Theology in Windsor, Ontario and Halifax, Nova Scotia. He retired in 2002. His areas of research and publication are the work of Karl Barth, Dietrich Bonhoeffer, Helmut Gollwitzer and Friedrich-Wilhelm Marquardt, as well as the Holocaust, Christian-Jewish relations, and the Protestant Church's witness in the former German Democratic Republic from 1945 to 1989. He has translated numerous articles and books from German into English, including works by Dietrich Bonhoeffer, Luise Schottroff, Dorothee Sölle and Andreas Pangritz.

Christiane Tietz
Former Visiting Teaching Scholar at Union Theological Seminary in New York, Dr. theol. habil Christiane Tietz (born 1967), is currently Heisenberg Scholarship Holder of the Deutsche Forschungsgemeinschaft and Privatdozentin for Systematic Theology at the Faculty for Protestant Theology of the University of Tübingen. Her work on Bonhoeffer includes the book *Bonhoeffers Kritik der verkrümmten Vernunft. Eine erkenntnistheoretische Untersuchung* (Tübingen 1999); she also published her *Habilitation* dissertation, *Freiheit zu sich selbst. Entfaltung eines christlichen Begriffs von Selbstannahme* (Göttingen 2005). Tietz is member of the Board of the International Bonhoeffer-Society, German Section, and of the Editorial Board of the *Dietrich Bonhoeffer Yearbook*.

Ralf Wüstenberg
Dr. Wüstenberg studied theology in Berlin, Cambridge und Heidelberg. He is currently visiting professor in theology and the director of the Institute of Protestant Theology at the Free University in Berlin. In 1995 he received his doctoral degree, published as *A Theology of Life. Dietrich Bonhoeffer's Religionless Christianity* (1998). In 1999 Dr. Wüstenberg was Research fellow University of Cape Town, in 2002 he was the Visiting Dietrich Bonhoeffer Scholar Union Theological Seminary. In 2003 he completed his *Habilitation* on the Political Dimension of Reconciliation (currently in print). From 2003 until 2005 Dr. Wüstenberg also worked as one of the pastors at the Berlin Dom. Other publications include *Theology in Dialogue. The Impact of Arts, Humanities and Science on Contemporary Theological Discourse* (edited with Lyn Holness in 2002).

Josiah Young
Josiah Young is Professor of Systematic Theology at Wesley Theological Seminary. His published writings include *No Difference in the Fare: Dietrich Bonhoeffer and the Problem of Racism*; *Dogged Strength within the Veil: Africana Spirituality and the Mysterious Love of God*; and "An African-American Perspective on an Experience of Incomparable Value."

Index of Names

Note: references to Dietrich Bonhoeffer are not listed in this index. When the name of an author is mentioned in the main body of the essays the referenced page number below is printed in regular font; a name mentioned in the notes only is printed in italics. When an author is mentioned in the main text and in a corresponding footnote the referenced page number is only printed in regular font.

Abromeit, Hans-Jürgen *134*, 168
Ackermann, Josef *209*
Adams, R. M. *142*
Adorno, Theodor 85, 92, *112*, 113, 115, *202*
Ahlers, Rolf *90*
Althaus, Paul 276
Anselm of Canterbury 259, 265
Aquinas, Thomas 6, 11–29
Arendt, Hannah 307
Aristotle 24, 301, 306
Arnold, Hardy *48*
Athanasius 28
Augustine 6, 11–29, 107, 146, 253, 305

Bach, Johann Sebastian *38*
Bacon, Francis 170
Bahr, Hermann 214, 215
Balthasar, Hans Urs von 24
Barth, Karl 3, 6, 11, 24, 27, 53, 54, 57, 90, 94, *100*, 104–107, 111, 113, 121, 140, *142*, 146, 153, 61–163, 172, 189, *207*, 213, *218*, 26, *228*, 229–231, *233*, 234, 245–82, 283, 284, 288–292, 300, 308, 14, 316, 317
Bartl, Karl 168
Baumgärtel, Friedrich *59*
Beck, Lewis W. *88*
Bell, George *32*
Bell, Henrietta *32*
Benjamin, Walter *90*
Bethge, Eberhard 4, *5*, 11, *12*, 29, *32*, 33, 36, 38–40, *46*, 48, 49, *53*, *55*, *59*, 81, 91, *102*, *114*, *121*, *140*, *143*,
149, 167, 169, 175, 176, 89, 192, 199, *201*, 203, *204*, *207*, *08*, 209, *211*, *212*, 213–215, 217, 19, 221, 223, 231, 234, *237*, 239, 40, 245–247, *249*, 250, *252*, *253–56*, *258*, 260–265, 265, *268*, 269, *270*, *272*, 273–275, 277, 278, 280, 281, *282*, *283*, *293*, *295*, *298*, *314*, 316, 317
Bodin, Jean 169, *171*
Bonhoeffer, Julie 32, *56*, 294
Bonhoeffer, Karl 203, 316
Bonhoeffer, Karl-Friedrich 117, 175, *264*, 293
Bonhoeffer, Emmi 210
Bonhoeffer, Klaus 210, 213
Bonhoeffer, Christine 210
Bonhoeffer, Ursula 212
Bozzetti, Mauro *90*
Braun, D. *256*
Brunner, Emil 27
Bruno, Giordano 169, *171*
Buber, Martin 90, 94, 103
Bultmann, Rudolf 3, 6, 90, *194*, 218–220, 225–244, 249, 310, *314*, 321, 322
Burtness, James H. 279, *280*
Busch, Eberhard 255
Burrell, David 18, 22
Calvin, John 11, 27, 54, 57, 158, 266
Canaris, Walter-Wilhelm 214
Caputo, John *225*
Cardano, G. 169
Carmichael, Stokely 299
Cassirer, Ernst 88
Charron, Pierre 170
Cherbury, Herbert of 169, 170

Clayton, John *243*
Cohen, Hermann 88
Copernicus 84
Coxe, A. Cleveland *14*
Cullen, Countee 293

Darwin, Charles 181
Dehn, Günter 258
Delbrück, Hans 210
Delbrück, Emmi 213
Del Caro, Adrian *180, 182–184, 187,188, 195, 197, 198*
Derrida, Jacques 113, 114, *119,*
Descartes, René 95, 212, 306
Diederich, M *136, 137*
Dilthey, Wilhelm 5, 88, *95, 114,* 167–173, 214, 221
Dinkler, Erich *225, 233*
Dohnanyi, Hans von 223
Dramm, Sabine 199, 223, 224
Dress, Walter *67, 239, 248*
Dru, Alexander *146*
Du Bois, W.E.B. 293, 294, 297, 298
Dumas, André *322*
Dyson, R. W. *12, 28*

Ebeling, Gerhard 66, *207, 232,* 237
Ebner, Ferdinand 94
Elert, Werner *72*
Englund, Elizabeth *14*
Ehrenberg, Hans 94

Feil, Ernst *1,* 31, 91, *114, 134, 141, 167, 236, 276,* 322
Feuerbach, Ludwig 87, 143, 179, 181 198, *199*
Fichte, Gottlieb *8,* 90, 101, 102, 108
Fink, Barbara *1,* 31
Fink, Eugen 176
Fisher, Frank 292
Floyd, Wayne 4, *19, 52, 83,* 85, 88, 90, *102, 115, 202,* 205, *207,*213, *235, 322*
Fox, Richard. *283, 285, 288, 289, 295, 296,* 297, 299,
Frank, F.H.R. *135*
Frick, Peter *53*
Friedenthal, Charlotte 274
Frey, Rudolf *234*
Funk, Robert W. 228
Fuller, Ilse *94, 239*

Gadamer, Hans-Georg *225*
Gandhi, Mohandas *291,* 298, 299
Gerhardt, Paul 29, 38, 46
Gilkey, Langdon 115
Glenthøj, Jørgen *274*
Godsey, John *274,* 280, *281, 322*
Goerdeler *5*
Goes, Helmut 211, *246*
Goethe 179
Gogarten, Friedrich 94, 100, *168*
Gollwitzer, Helmut 207, 255, 266, 267
Green, Clifford 2, 3, 75, 91, 92, *114, 123, 195,* 198, 199, *204, 205, 206, 232, 234, 247*
Gregor, Brian 323
Grisebach, Eberhard *8,* 94, 97, 100, 103, 108, 315
Groos, Karl 4, 89
Grotius, Hugo 169, 170

Haarmann 274
Haeften, Hans-Bernd von 221
Hale Brandt, Lori 90, *91, 93,* 108
Hall, John 52
Harbsmeier, Götz *234*
Harnack, Adolf von 3, 12, 35, 88, 90, 201–204, *207,* 209–224, 230, 246, 250, 278, 289
Hart, Bentley 22
Hart, David 23
Hartmann, Nicolai 5, 88
Hase, Hans-Christoph von 232, 314
Hatab, Lawrence *192,* 198
Havenstein, Martin 175
Haynes, Stephen R. *1, 322*
Hazard, Paul 221
Herbert of Cherbury 169, 170
Hegel G.W.F. 3, 4, *6,* 7, 23, *63,* 83, 86–96, 98–102, 104, 105, 108, 111–120, 205, 20, 208, 318, 319
Heidegger, Martin 3, 5, 6, 7, 101, 108, 221, 225, 228, 249, 301–327
Heim, Karl 260, 276,315
Helm, Adelbert 296
Herms, E. *139*
Heraclitus 01, 307
Herrenbrück, P.W. *278*
Hindenburg, Paul von 211
Hitler, Adolf 33, 46, *68,* 78, 89, 152, 192, 210, 212, 214, 220, 221, 223, 267, 284, 286, *291*

Index of Names

Hildebrandt, Franz 53, 55, 56, *261*
Hirsch, Emmanuel 94, 95, *138*
Hodgson, Peter 85, 99
Holl, Karl 13, *14*, 54, *74*, 80, 90, 204, 214, 216, 239, 247
Hong, Edna *161*
Hong, Howard V. *147, 161*
Hoskyns, Edwyn C. *246*
Hromádka, Josef L. *267*
Hunsinger, George *253*
Husserl, Edmund 101, 304–307, 309, 310, 313, 316, 318, 319, 323, 324

Ignatius of Loyola *31*
Ibn-Sina *18*
Irenaeus 30

Jacoby, Russell *202*
Jairus, Nathanael *171*
Jay, Martin 89
Johnson, James Weldon, 293, 295, 298
Junker, M. *126*
Kaltenborn, Carl-Jürgen 3, *210*, 218
Kant, Immanuel 4, 5, 6, 83–91, 93–97, 99–105, 107–115, 117–121, 291, 306, 317, 318
Kaufmann, Walter *179, 182*
Keller *214*
Kelly, Geffrey B., *47, 152, 264*
Kelsey, David H., 84, *85*
Kempis, Thomas á 7, 31, 32–40, 42–45, 47–49, *50, 51,* 52, 184
Kerr, Fergus 327
Kersten, F *305*
Kierkegaard, Søren 3, 6, 7, 31, 47, 56, 73, 107, 145–147, 149–165, 189, 253, 264, 311
King, Robert 85, *114*
King Jr., Martin Luther 296, 299
Kirschbaum, Charlotte von *234,* 265,269, *270,* 274
Klapproth, Erich 33, *124, 137*
Klassen, A.J. *210*
Klausa, Ekkehard *223*
Knittermeyer, Hinrich *102*
Köpf, Ulrich *31*
Köster, Peter 187
Kohl, Margaret *23*
Krause, Gerhard 33, 47, *233, 254,* 278
Krause, Winfried 230

Krauth, Lothar *26*
Krötke, Wolf 53, *61*
Kütemeyer, Wilhelm *149*

Lämmlin, G. *133*
Lange, Stella *26*
Larochefoucauld, François 184
Lasson, Georg *63, 102*
Lawrence, Joel D. 322, *323*
Lehman, Paul *229, 254,* 293
Leibholz, Gerhard *57, 267, 268*
Livingstone, James C. *84,* 85, 110
Lotze, Herman 88
Lowe, Walter J. *93, 100*
Lowrie, Walter *156, 158, 160*
Lubac, Henri de *14*
Lütgert, Wilhelm 90, *98, 207,* 314
Luther, Martin 3, 7, 11, 13, 14, *31,* 53–82, 90, 93, 107, 143, 146, 147, 149–151, 155, 159, 164, 172, 189, 196, 247, 253, 305, 317
Mackintosh, H.R. *122*
Macquarrie, John *235, 304, 307,* 324, *326,* 327
Maechler, Winfried *255,* 256
Maier, Heinrich 4, 90
Maimonides *18*
Mannheim, Karl 88
Marcuse, Herbert *89*
Mariña, Jacqueline *126, 143*
Marsh, Charles 4, *52,* 90–97, *100, 101,* 108, 113, 114, 118, *119, 235,* 322
Marx, Karl 87, 90
McCabe, Herbert *19, 23*
McNeill, William *301*
Meckenstock, Günter *143*
Meinecke 209
Melanchthon, Philip 67, 72
Mengus, Raymond *207*
Meyendorff, John 29
Meyer, Winfried *274*
Michelangelo 189
Milbank, John *22*
Miller, A.V., *86*
Mokrosch, Reinhold *66, 67*
Moltmann, Jürgen *23, 94, 116, 135*
Monk, R. *308*
Montaigne, Michel de 169, *171*
Morino, Zen-emon *31*
Mozart, Wolfgang Amadeus 189

Müller, Hanfried 110, *255, 281*

Natorp, Paul 5, 88, 221
Nelson, Burton *152*
Niebuhr, Reinhold 7, *34,* 268, 283–293, 295–299
Niebuhr, Richard 242
Niemöller, Martin 55
Nietzsche, Friedrich 3, 6, 7, 87, 94, 179–199

Oakes, Edward T. *24*
Obayashi, Hiroshi *90*
Oberdorfer, B. *138*
Odgen, M., *226*
Ortega y Gasset, José 5, 221
Oster, Hans 214
Ott, Heinrich 279
Otto, Rudolf 88

Pangritz, Andreas *213, 246, 264, 271, 277*
Peck, William J. *90*
Pegis, Anton C. *26*
Pestalozzi, R. 214
Peters, T.R. *167*
Pfeifer, Hans *253, 280*
Picken, Stuart *90*
Pieper, Josef 26
Pilate 64, 185
Pippin, Robert B. *180, 182–184, 187, 188, 195, 197, 198*
Plato 23, *308*
Planck, Max 209
Plutarch 5,
Pohl, M.J. *32*
Prenter, Regin 279
Prolingheuer, Hans 263
Pyzywara, Erich *8,* 18, 19, 22, 320

Rachmanova, Alexandra 187
Rades, Jörg 3, 93, 108
Randall, Herman *205*
Raphael, F. *313*
Rasmussen, Larry 33
Rée, Jonathan *308*
Reuter, Hans-Richard *101,* 232, 314
Rickert, Heinrich 88
Rieffert, Johann 4, 90
Ringer, Fritz K. *89,* 115
Ritschl, Albrecht 88, *128,* 207
Robertson, Ian W. *259*

Robertson, E. *323*
Robinson, Edward *235, 304, 307,* 324
Robinson, M., *226*
Rößler, Helmut 72
Rose, Gillian *111*
Rosenstock-Huessy, Eugen 94
Rosenzweig, Franz *94,* 114
Rott, Wilhelm *265*
Rousseau, Jean-Jacques 184
Rumscheidt, Martin *141, 211, 212, 218, 223, 236, 250, 253, 264, 280, 322*

Safranski, Rüdiger *303, 304, 306, 307*
Scheler, Max 94, *95,* 108, 206
Scharlemann, Robert P. *93, 235, 239,* 322
Schlatter, Adolf *8*
Schleicher, Rüdiger 210, 212
Schlenke, D. *123*
Schleiermacher, Friedrich 7, 90, 121–130, 132–143, 207
Schmithals, Walter *226*
Schmitt, Carl 89
Scholem, Gerschom 90
Schönherr, Albrecht *63,* 183
Schönherr, Hilde 183
Schütz, Paul 145
Schulze, Bertha 211, 219
Scotus, Duns 21
Seeberg, Reinhold 12, 15, *20,* 54, 90, *98,* 210, 209, 221, 222, 224, 246, *278,* 314
Seeberg, Eric 278
Sheehan, Thomas *306*
Sheppard, Lancelot C. *14*
Simmel, Georg 88
Slane, Craig J. 322
Smith, Norman Kemp *101*
Socrates 308
Soosten, Joachim von 94
Spinoza, Baruch 169
Spranger, Eduard 88
Staats, Reinhart *211, 212, 213,* 216, *218,* 219, 220, *221,* 253
Stambaugh, J., *308*
Steiner, George 302, 306
Stern, Fritz *87*
Stewart, J.S., *122*
Stroup, George 85, *86*

Sutz, Erwin 34, 35, 41, *55, 60,* 151, 254–257, 259, 263, 266
Swenson David F. *157*

Taylor, Mark C. *112*
Thomas, John Newton *250*
Thomas of Erfurt *305*
Tietz(-Steiding), Christiane *139, 228, 232, 235*
Tillich, Paul 3, 6, 189, *194,* 225, 231, 234, 236–244, 276, 285
Tödt, Heinz Eduard. 3, 280
Tödt, Ilse *4, 316*
Tönnies, F. *129*
Troeltsch, Ernst *8,* 92, 209
Tuchel, Johannes *223*
Turner, Denys *19, 22, 23*

Visser't Hooft, W. A. *207*
Voegelin, Eric *113*

Weber, Max 88, 272

Wedemeyer, Maria von 145, *164,* 275
Weissbach, Jürgen *94*
Weizsäcker 189
Widmann, R. *247*
Wilcox, David 3,
Williams, Raymond *12, 190,* 194
Williams, Robert C. *99*
Willey, Thomas *88*
Wind, Renate *286*
Windelband, Wilhelm 88
Wolf, Ernst 229, *230, 234*
Wüstenberg, Ralf K. *170, 277, 322*

Vogt, Paul *270*
Vogel, Traugott *149*

Zahn, Margrarete von *210*
Zahn-Harnack Agnes von 217
Zinn, Elizabeth 75
Zwingli, Ulrich 54, 172
Zimmermann, W.D. *246, 255*

Index of Subjects

Abel 109
Abraham 154, 158, 264
Acedia 79, *80*
Act and Being 3, 4, 5, 16, 18, *19*, 24, 71,88, 91–93, 95, 96, 100–108, 110, 111, 116, *137*, *177*, 201, 207, 212, 226–228, 232, 235, 238, 244, 247, 249, 251, 252, 261, 278, 281, 291, 303, 316–318, 320–322
Actus directus 91, 106, 142
Actus reflexus 106
Adam 5, 14–16, 20, 24, 66, 69, 110, 126, 127, 180, 187, 235, 236, 243, 244, 289, 321
Analogia entis 18–23, 108, *259*, 320
Analogia relationis 24, 108, 259
Antaeus 178

Being 5–7, 15, 18–28, 41, 43, 46, 62, 64, *71*, 86, 98, 99, 102–104, 107, 108, 115, 122, *129*, 131, 156, 160, 162, 173, 179, 181, 191, 193, 194, 197–199, 204, 222, 223, 228, 229, 235, 236, 238, 243, 244, 250, 272, 284, 305, 307–313, 317–326
Berlin 3, 4, 31–33, 35, 36, *45*, 47, 53–55, 88–90, 92, 97, 104, 108, 111, *121*, 149, 157, 176, 179, 180, 202, 203, 207–210, 221, 229–231, 238, *240*, 251, 252, 255–257, 259–262, 269, 270, 278, 306, 314, 327
Book of Concord 54, *59*, *67*, *72*, *74*, *78*,
Breakthrough 50, 51
Bruderhof 48
Cain 17, 109
Christianity/Christendom 43, 56, 60, 62, 68, 74, 76, *90*, *129*, 143, 145–148, 150, 151, 153–155, 161, 164, 165, 167, 177–179, 182, 186, 188, 193–197, 202, 206, 215, 216, 218, 231– 235, 241, 245, 275, *276*, *285*, 290, 298,
Christology 1, 60–64, 78, 109, 156, 157, 261, 288–291, 299, 300, 303, 305, 317, 323–327
Church 1, 6, 11–14, 16, 17, 28, 29, 33, 34, 40, 52, 53–56, 59–61, 64, 67, 71–79, 89, 91, 97–100, 109, 110, 112, 116–119, 121, 122, 124, 125, 127–137, 143, 146–152, 157–162, 171, 173, 176, 183, 187, 203, 205, 207, 209–211, 213, 214, 219, 220, 222, 223, 230, 237, 239, 241, 242, 247–251, 258, 259, 261–264, 266– 278, 281, 282–285, 292–297, 299, 300, 303, 318, 321, 325
Commandments 34, 40, 41, 59, 72– 74, 77, 79, 147, 185, 195, 212, 226, 258–260, 263, 273, 280, 316, 317
Community 12–14, 33, 35, 36, 46–51, 61, 64, 67, 74, 93–100, 109, 110, 112, 118, 121–132, 134–138, 142, 143, 153, 156–164, 203–208, 213–215, 237–239, 241, 247–251, 258, 292, 299, 300
Confessing Church 53–55, *143*, 183, 230, 262, 263, 266, 267, 271, 277, 278
Confession 37, 38, 43, 50, 51, 53–55, 67, *99*, 261, 262, 267, 270
Conscience 54, 57, 65–67, 71, 152, 212, 220, 222, 224, 248, 293, 315
Cor curvum in se 5, 70, 105,
Cornelius *171*
Creation 17, 23, 24, 26, 27, 33, 35. 69, 77, 92, 108, 109, 116, 156, 160, 162, 180, 233, 259, 260, 286
Creation and Fall 12, 16, 17, *20*, 24, *33*, *35*, 58, *63*, 69, 77, 108, 109, 193, *196*, 259

Index of Subjects

Critique of Pure Reason 4, 89, *101*, 110, 111, 119
Critique of Practical Reason 117
Cross 42–44, 51, 52, 61, 62, *64*, 68, 73, 80, 81, 148, 153–156, 161, 162, 165, *236*, 284, 291

Dasein 18, 19, 103, 227, 228, 235, 236, 243, 309–313, 319–322, 324, 326
Death 1–3, 15, 43, 56, 62, 63, 81, 92, 93, 107, 116, 118, 145, 156, 157, *160*, 184, 186, 188, 190, 210, 213, 216, 229, 246, 250, 264, 272, 289–292, 295, 311–313, 315, 320–323, 325, 326
Decalogue 55, 74, 77, 176, 178, 196
Ding-an-sich 85, 95, 104, 116
Discipleship 1, 32–36, 40, 41, 51, 58, 59, 63, 67, *71*, 73–76, 110, 118, 146–149, 151–156, 164, 183, 229, *263*, 264, 266, 281, 291, 292, 315
Dietrich Bonhoeffer Werke/Works 3, 176, 201
Dissertation 2, 3, 5, 12, 15, 60, 63, 92–94, 97, 111, *149*, 157, 159, 161, 177, 201, 204–208, 225, 226, 247, 249, *266*, *278*, 305, 313, 316, 318, 322

Ecclesia crucis 52
Ecce homo 62, *178,*
Ecclesiology 7, 12, 121–138, 141, 292, 299
Epicureanism 146
Epistemology/epistemological 5, 6, 7, 88, 90, *92*, 94–96, 100, 101, 103, 106, 107, 109, 115, 116, 118, 119, 202, 204, *207*, 213, 221, 234, 237, 246, *247*, 307, 309, 318, 319, 324
Eros 161–163, 265
Esse 18, 21, 23, *45*, 69, *243,*
Essentia 18, 21, 23
Ethics/ethical 1, 15–18, 28, 55, 60, 62, 63, 75. 79, 91, 92, 94–97, 99, 100, 106, 108, 109, 117, 119, 123–126, 143, 158, 159, 171–173, 177–179, 185, 188, 191, 193–196, 202, 206, 207, 212, 213, 218, 221–224, 241, 247, 256–260, 267–274, 276, 277, 282, 283–288, 290–293, 295, 298–300, 315, 316
Ethics 17, 18, 24–26, 28, *29*, 53, 64, *69*, 70, 76, 77, *98*, 110, 119, 151, 167, 168, *172*, 173, 175, 184–186, 193, 94, 222, 229, 241, *255*, *256*, 267–274, 286, 315–317
Eve 187
Exercises *31*, 33–36, 39, *45*, 47–50, 52, 61, 125, 263, 282
Existence/existential 6, 16, 18, 21, 23, 25, 28, 41, 43, *59*, 61, 65, 69, 71, 79, 81, 82, 87, 92, 94, 97, 102, 103, 107, 109, 110, 118, 122, 131, 136, 138, 140, 158, 159, 197–199, 204–206, 212, 214, 224, 227, 282, 232–236, 238, 239, 242, 243, 250, 251, 264, 287, 305, 309–313, 315, 319, 321, *322*, 326
Ezra *59*

Faith 1, 13, 25, 27, 33, 34, 40–42, 46, 54–57, 62–64, 67, 70–74, 76, 77, 80–82, 91, 99, 116, 117, 121, *133*, 139, 141, 142, 146–148, 150, 151, 153, 154, 156, 158–160, 162–164, 170, 173, 179, 183, 192, 199, 203, 204, 210, 212, 213, 218–220, 224, 227, 228, 230, 231, 233–236, 241, 242, 247, 250, 251, 254, 255, 263, 264, 271, 276–278, 280, 282, *285*, 286, 287, 289, *291*, 303, 310, 318, 321, 325
Faust 147
Finkenwalde 32, 33, 35, 36, 38, 40, 41, 48, 49, 51, 53, 55, *62*, 66, *80*, *99*, 117, 151, 213, 218, 263, 265, 266, 281
Forgiveness 40, 51, 64, 65, 67, 148, 191, 236, *293*, 297,
Formation 2, 3, 5, 7, 36, 47, 48, 50, 62, 78, 79, 127–129, 163, 176, 184, *212*, 241, 326
Freedom 19, 43, 55–57, 63, 65, 72, 75, 77, *81*, 87, 99, 104, 108, 109, 117, 138, 151, 164, 176, 181, 185, 195, 196, 211, 212, 248–251, 257, 258, 273, 274, 278, 279, 285, 287, 291, *297*, 315, 320, *323*
Friendship *33*, 47, 73, 99, 161, 210, 215, 292, *306*

God-consciousness 126, 134, 136, *140*
God-is-dead theology 1
Good and evil 16, *20*, 81, *177*, 178, 180–182, 184, 185, 188, 193–196, 287, *303, 304, 306, 307*
Grace 6, 7, 13, 16, 19, 20, 21, 23, 25,

27, 40, 41, 43, 44, 57, 67, 68, 70–73, 76, 79, 99, *133*, 140, 147–150, 155, 156, 164, 182, 183, 186, 191, 221, 227, 228, 235, 238, 239, 246, 256, 271, 280, 285–288, 299, 300

Habilitation 4, 5, 66, 100, 104, 111, 179, 201, 207, 226, 314
Hermeneutics/hermeneutical 2, 60, 233, 322
Hirschluch *90*
Holy Spirit 55, 65, 134–138, 143, 159, 160, 161, 249, *252*, 286

Idealism 83, 86–98, 100–102, 105, 107, 108, 110, 112–119, *121*, 124, 135, 157, 208, 283, *284*, 318
Imago dei 20, 108, 109,
Imitatio Christi 31–52
Imprisonment 5, 31, *32*, 38, 51, 53, 70, 81, 214, 231, *272*,
Incarnation 24, *28*, 62, *64*, 97, 99, 112, *114*, 276, *285*, 287, 291, 324
Intellect/intellectual 2, 3, 5–9, 57, 83, 84, 88, 89, 91–93, 95, 96, 105, 115, 121, 148, 176, 202–204, 209, 217, 219–222, 224, 232, 233, 235, 259, 283, 297, 298, *303*, 304, 313, 327
Intercession 177

James 139, 177
Jesus Christ 17, 24, 28, 34, 40, 43, 46, 55–57, 59, 60–64, 66, 73, 76, 79, 131–134, 141, 146–157, 159, 161, 163–165, 171, 172, 177, 183, 184, 190, 194, 196, *218*, 232, 235, *253*, *268*, 270–272, 276, 280, 284, 285, 289, 293, 294, 324–326
Jeremiah 180, 187
John (biblical) *12*, 13, 62, *63*, 180, 184, 196, *226*, 229, 230, 324
Justification 25, 26, 47, 57, 65, 66, 70, 71–76, 146–148, 150, 155, 162, 254, 264, 265, 268, 270, *284*, *285*, *291*, 292

Kristallnacht 97

Letters and Papers from Prison 1, 28, 38, *114*, 167–173, 188, 192, 240, 245, 275, 278, 281,
Life Together 1, 32, 36–38, 44, 46, 50,
51, 59, *97*, *98*, 117, 131, 151, *157*, 159, 160, 163, 164, 183, 229, *266*
London 32–34, *48*, 92, 117, 182, 188, 196, *240*, 262–*264*, *267*, *268*, 291, *294*
Lord's Supper 50–51,
Love 12, 13, 20, 23, 37, 39, 46–47, 55, 63, 64, *69*, 70, 74, 99, 100, 109, 110, 118, 129, 134, 137, 145, 153, 155, 157, 161–164, 182, 185–188, 196, 199, 203, 215, 226, 247, 248, 268, 272, 287, 292, *294*, 297,

Mandates 17, 62, 76–79, 148, 152, 154, 273, *274*, 316
Maximus the Confessor 14
Meditation 37, 39, 47–50, 52, 59, 176, 177, 183, 216, 265,
Mensch, *Menschsein* 25, *40*, *47*, 71, 80, 104, *124*, *125*, *127*, 140, 150, 168, 179, 187, *191*, 192, 198, 219, 220, 228, 239, *252*,
Metanoia 28, 192
Method, methodological 2, 5, 7, 8, 18, 58, 59, 86–89, 94, 102, 111, 130, 170, 207, 210, 212, 213, 222, 233, 279, 295, 303–305, 308, 317, 323–327

Nathanael *171*
National Socialism 1, 87, 119, 274
Nazi(sm) 2, 83, 89, 111, *113*, 146, 152–154, 157, 213, 221–224, 240, 244, 258, 261, 263, 284, 286, 288, 292, 300, 302, *306*, 326, 327
Nehemiah 59
Neighbo(u)r 64, 96, 116, 117, 119, 154, 161, 162, 164, 185, 186, 197, 209, 210, 226, 237, 247, 248, 289,
New Testament 40, 42, 156, 161, 163, 185, 195, *226*, 231, 234
New York 3, 245, 252, 254, 283, 292, 299
Non posse non peccare 16

Ontology/ontological 5, 7, 18–21, 24, 43, 86–88, 93, 96, 102, 103, 107, 207, 227, 228, 234–236, 243, 244, 305–307, 309, 310, 312, 318–320, 325, 326
Ontotheology 23
Original sin 14–17, *69*, 91, 125–127

Paul (Apostle) 11, 15, *40*, 73, 107,

Index of Subjects

139, 146, *163*, *171*, 178, 196, *226*, 246, 253, 264, 289, 293, 305
Pen/ultimate 25, 47, 50, *70*, 76, 184, *218*, 268, 269
Person 5, 7, 8, 13–16, 25, 35, 37, 40, 41, 44, 45, 47, 56, 57, 61, 64–73, 79, 95–100, 105, 109, 110, 117, 118, 123–126, 131–140, 143, 142, 158–160, 162, 164, 176, 180, 182, 184–186, 190, 192–196, 198, 199, 205, 206, 208, 210, 215–217, 219, 223, 226, 228, 229, 232–236, 238, 239, 242–244, 248, 251, 252, 272, 274, 285, 287, *293*, 300, 302, 305, 321, 325
Philosophy/philosophical 2–8, 15, 18, 70, 83, 86–97, 100–110, 116, 119, 125, 164, 165, 167, 168, 170–173, 175–177, 181, 183, 184, 190, 203, 205–208, 221, 222, 225, 227–229, 236, 238, 244, 252–254, *284*, 290, 301–309, 313–321, 323–327
Potential/potentiality 5, *194*, 228, 229, 234–236, 243, 322
Postmodern/ism 83, 116
Preach(er)/preaching 34, 49, 50, 66, 67, *78*, 150, 153, 178–180, 182, 258, 263, 265, 275, 293, 295, 296
Prayer 49, 53, 59, 64, *73*, *80*, 81, 98, 141, 148, 177, 216, 218, 220, 265,
Prayerbook of the Bible 58, 59
Psychology/psychological 16, 33, 45–47, *66*, *70*, 75, 80, *92*, *127*, 129–131, 136, *142*, 143, 229, 304, 305

Reality 12, 18, 22, 26, 28, 33, 46, 57, *64*, 70, 71, 77, 78, 84, 85, 89, 91, 94, 96, 100, 102–107, 116, *124*, 130–133, 137, 151–153, 159, 160, 168, 184, 185, 191–194, 196–199, 202, 204, 205, 212, 215, 217, 222, 223, 234, 242–244, 253, 259, 268, 272, 278, 280, 285, 286, *292*, *322*
Reformation 25, 54–56, 71, 78, 146, 148, 150, 151, 168, 172, 186, 203, 214, 216, 265, *283–285*, *292–294*, 299,
Religion 1, 4, 18, 54, *63*, *74*, 81, 86, 90, 108, 121, 127, 129, 133, 138–143, 167, 168, 172, 177–179, 182, 190–192, 198, 199, 202, 205, 208, 234, 239–242, 246, 253, 266, 275, 276, 283, *285*, 290, *291*, *293*, 298,

Religionless/ness 1, 56, 60, 62, 68, 69, 81, *90*, 140, 141, 172, 188, 189, 231–235, 244, 276,
Revelation 5–7, 16, 20, 22–24, 27, 45, 54, 57, 59, 65, 66, 68, *85*, *91*, 99, 100, 102–104, 106–108, 110, 112, 115, 117, 119, 124, 127, 131, 133, 134, 158, 179, 184, 205, 207, 227–229, 235, 236, 238, 241–247, 249, 250, 252–254, 258, 259, 275–282, 284, 291, 301, 317, 318, 320, 321,
Roman Catholic/ism 11, *14*, 15, 18, 24, 27, *56*, 237, *285*, 303, 304, 306, 320

Salvation 5, 24, 26, 56, *100*, 122, 180, 249, 266, 271, *289*, 290,
Sanctification 37, 44, 71–75, 264, *266*, *284*, *291*, *323*
Sanctorum Communio 3, 12–17, 51, 64, *71*, 93–102, 106, 109, 111, 159, 160, 164, 177, 205, 212, 226, 237, 247–249, 264, 292, 300, 319, 322
Scripture 49, 50, 54, 57–60, 63, *73*, *79*, 207, 246, 248, 273
Secular/ization 1, *22*, 24, 28, 72, 74, 76, 92, 150–152, 168, 182, 192, 295
Self-consciousness 122–124, 127, 128, *133*, 138, 140, 142, 143
Self-denial 45, 52
Self-disclosure 5
Self-forgiveness 51
Self-knowledge 80, 229, 235, 243
Self-revelation 124, 286, 326
Self-understanding 6, 44, 45, 87, 228, 232, 235, 238, 242, 244, 309, 320
Sexuality 16, 17, 182
Sicut deus 16, 17, *20*, 69, 109
Silence 36, 37, 47–50, 42, 157, 305
Sin/sins/sinfulness 5, 7, 13–17, 20, 21, 24, 25, 27–29, 35, 37, 40, 45, 47, 50, 51, 56, 61–72, 74, 76, 79, 81, 91, 105, 107, 109, 122, 125–127, 143, 147–149, 156, 157, 160, 177, 190–192, 194, 205, 228, 229, 235, 236, 239, 243, *268*, *285*, 287–290, 293, 299, 310, 311, 321, 326
Solus Christus 56
Sola fide 45, 146, *243*, 257
Sola scriptura 152
Soul 14, 43, 45, 46, *64*, *134*, 140, 147,

148, 150, 157, 163, 164, 177, 191,
238, 285, 290, 296,
Stellvertretung 98
Suffering 28, 39, 40, 42–44, 51, 56,
61, 156, 157, 192, 199, 215,

Tegel prison 2, 31, 32, 38, *45*, 48,
114, 117, 167, 171–173, 187, 214,
215, 221, 222, *237*, 239, 316
Teleological 2, 170
Temptation *69*, 79–82, 106, 107, 110,
154, 190, 240, *315*
Theologia crucis 52
Transcendence/transcendental 5, 18–
20, 22–24, 28, 62, 83–89, 93, 95–97,
100–105, 107–111, 116, 188, 119,
137, 179, 198, 207, 236, 237, 239,
288, *291*, 308, 318, 319
Thomism 21, 314
Truth 5, 26, 54, 79, 102, 112, 117,

142, 143, 152, 157, 161, 163–165,
180, 194, 196, 211, 220, 224, 231,
234, 236, 238, 242, 243, *285*, 286,
308, 315, 320, 325
Tübingen 2, 4, 89,

Übermensch 177–179, 184, 186, 188,
197, 198
Union Theological Seminary 3, 34,
90, 104, 105, 146, *232*, *240*, 245, 252,
254, 283, 293
Usus legis 65, 72, 317

Vicarious representation 12, 62–64, 78

Word (of God) 37, 48, 49, 54, 57–60, 66,
71, 162, 179, 220, 228, 246, 249, 254,
257, 267, *292*, 320